# Recreation Economic Decisions:

## Comparing Benefits and Costs

# Recreation Economic Decisions:

## Comparing Benefits and Costs

Second Edition

**John B. Loomis**

**Richard G. Walsh**

Department of Agricultural and Resource Economics
Colorado State University
Fort Collins, Colorado

Venture Publishing, Inc.
State College, Pennsylvania

Venture Publishing, Inc.
1999 Cato Avenue
State College, PA 16801
(814) 234-4561; Fax (814) 234-1651



Production Manager: Richard Yocum
Design, Layout, and Graphics: Diane K. Bierly
Manuscript Editing: Diane K. Bierly
Additional Editing: Michele Barbin and Matthew S. Weaver
Cover Design: Sandra Sikorski, Sikorski Design

Library of Congress Catalogue Card Number 97-60788
ISBN 0-910251-89-4

# Contents

# Figures

# Tables

# Acknowledgments

We would like to thank professors Rebecca Johnson, Oregon State University, and Robert Leonard, University of Connecticut, for their suggestions improving this revision. Dirk Draper and Pete Fix assisted with the regional impact example. Mary Lou Jones and Denise Davis provided valuable secretarial support in preparing much of the text and tables. Mandy Storeim's careful proofreading of the entire manuscript and references caught numerous inconsistencies. We would especially like to thank Diane Bierly for her careful editing of this second edition. Her eagle eye and calculator caught several inconsistencies that would have bedeviled students for years to come. Research by members of Western Regional Research project W-133 have provided a great many of the examples used in this book. Both of us greatly appreciate the guidance and assistance provided by all of these people. Nonetheless, the authors are responsible for what follows. We continue to welcome all comments and suggestions from readers of the book.

## *Chapter 1*

# Introduction

This chapter defines important applications of economics to management of existing recreation areas, and evaluating issues in natural resource allocation affecting existing and proposed recreation areas. This chapter also introduces the basic approach to decision making used throughout this book.

What does economics have to do with recreation management? Planning and managing recreation areas is a series of choices. Not a day goes by that a manager doesn't face a question, which at its roots, is often economic. Managers faced with long lines of visitors often ask themselves whether they should raise entrance fees to reduce crowding, expand the facility or both. If they choose to expand the number of campsites or parking spaces, the next choice is just how many to add. As soon as that has been decided, a supervisor will ask for justification of the ranger's proposal to spend several hundred thousand dollars to expand the recreation area's capacity. "Is it worth it?" is a question parks and recreation managers frequently must respond to with hard facts to be able to compete with other state or federal agency demands for more schools, prisons and highways.

And just when the ranger thought it was safe to go back into the forest, the supervisor hears of plans to introduce mining in the area where the ranger was planning to expand recreation. As they prepare to respond to such plans at the weekly staff meeting, they are told that the mine will "generate" $50,000 in revenues and support 25 jobs. The ranger is asked, "What would the recreation area contribute to the local economy?"

This book will help recreation managers in answering these types of questions. While economics is not, nor should it be, the sole criteria by which we make any public decisions, economics often has a significant influence on many recreation management decisions and resource allocation decisions that are made.

Economics also plays a role in decisions made by people about which recreation activities they want to participate in, which sites to visit, how frequently, and whether to pay the new higher entrance fee or just stay home. Understanding and predicting visitors' reactions to improvements in site quality, new fees, new facilities and site closures often involves understanding how people combine preferences with limited time and money budgets in making these recreation choices. While the motto "build it and they will come" makes for a great movie plot, it is an unwise public management strategy and one unlikely to convince budget officers in most agencies.

How important is recreation and tourism industry in the economy? Recreation is one of the largest sectors of the U.S. economy. Private expenditures on recreation goods and services account for more than 14% of personal consumption expenditures and 8% of total gross domestic product, according to estimates prepared for a Nationwide Outdoor Recreation Plan. This is based on U.S. Department of Commerce figures, which show that consumer recreation expenditures exceed expenditures on national defense and home construction. In addition the federal, state and local governments spend more than $20 billion annually on recreation land, facilities and programs. With less than 0.3% of the nation's tax revenue, government provides nearly one-half of total outdoor recreation opportunities. In National Forests, for example, outdoor recreation is 85% of the total value produced (U.S. Forest Service, 1995).

Most states rank tourism as one of their major industries, in particular such states as Florida, Hawaii, and Colorado. Worldwide tourism is also an important sector in many developing nations. In Costa Rica, tourism is the second largest industry in the country. Ninety percent of private recreation companies are classified as small businesses, according to Owen (1969), and they provide nearly 7% of total employment in the United States. A relatively high proportion of these jobs are seasonal part-time and less-skilled jobs suitable for the underemployed and hard-to-employ workers. Recreation provides nearly double the number of jobs per dollar of Gross Domestic Product (GDP) as most other sectors in the U.S. economy (Douglas and Harpman, 1995). The recreation industry is relatively labor intensive compared to agriculture and other sectors of the U.S. economy.

What is the role of recreation in the quality of life? Recreation is more than just a means to employ people, it is a way to enrich our lives. Long regarded as a luxury, recreation is what many people live for and thrive on. The recreation valuation techniques presented in this book demonstrate there is a real economic value to the benefits recreation provides in our lives. People allocate significant portions of their income and time to pursuing recreation opportunities because of the enjoyment it provides. For some, recreation involves choosing a stimulating activity (e.g., downhill skiing, rock climbing, kayaking) while others choose relaxing activities (e.g., camping, sunbathing, picnicking). In either case the well-being of the participant is increased and this can be translated into dollar benefits which can be compared to the costs to designate and manage recreation sites.

Every society is vitally concerned with the role of recreation and play in its culture. However, the forces of economic development have radically shifted the demand and supply of recreation resources. On the demand side, the growth in population and per capita income, the shorter workweek, and improved transportation facilities have dramatically increased participation in recreation activities. From 1900 to 2000, population increased more than three times and individual income over one and a half times. Leisure time increased as the average workweek declined from nearly 60 hours in the 1900s to less than 40 hours today. Improved auto transportation (including four-wheel-drive vehicles) and air travel have made even remote recreation sites accessible to more and more consumers. The twentieth century has been characterized by some as the "age of leisure" with reduced workweeks, expanded holidays and vacations, earlier retirement age, greater longevity, and increases in the number of affluent who withdraw from ordinary society to vacation havens during much of the year. In general, observers believe that today a larger number of people have much more leisure than any population in history has ever had prior to this century.

On the supply side, private companies have responded to increased demand by providing more recreation goods and services at prices which reflect the conditions of demand and supply. However, increasing residential development and industrial exploitation of the natural environment have eliminated a large amount of land formerly available for recreation use. Environmental pollution also has contributed to the reduction in the quantity and quality of natural environment for recreation. For example, some waterways that were once major water recreation areas, are no longer available for certain water sports because of pollution. In some states, strip mining eliminates entire mountains, and mine tailings fill in the valleys. The dwindling availability of land and water suitable for recreation use presents a challenge to the public interest in providing access to natural environments for outdoor recreation.

Historically, governments (and many private landowners) have provided outdoor recreation resources free, with little or no formal consideration of benefits and costs. When demand was low, the cost of granting access for outdoor recreation was also low. However, as increased demand began to exceed supply, free access led to increased costs, including congestion and deterioration in the quality of the natural environment. Initially the response was to meet the need by developing more access roads and recreation facilities, such as campgrounds and boat-launching facilities at new reservoirs and parks. More recently, managers of both public and private recreation resources have become aware of the complexity of growth in recreation demand and, with the renewed emphasis on accountability in government, a concern with the benefits of expenditures on outdoor recreation programs. Increased attention has focused in recent years on comparing the benefits of proposed recreation programs to their costs in order to decide which alternative expenditure is most beneficial given a limited budget for parks and recreation programs.

## Purpose of Recreation Economics

The purpose of economics is to increase the well-being of the individuals in society, and each individual is the best judge of how well-off he or she is in a given situation. Both of these propositions follow the predominant Western moral tradition of recent centuries, which regards the individual as the ultimate objective of public policy. To economists, outdoor recreation is a part of the overall economic problem of how to manage our activities so as to meet our needs and wants with scarce resources.

The purpose of this book is to demonstrate to recreation resource planners and managers how to apply the benefit-cost approach to recreation economic decisions, in particular, how to make outdoor recreation as beneficial as possible at the lowest possible cost.

The subject matter includes:

1. consumer choice of outdoor recreation activities, site choice, trip frequency for a wide range of outdoor recreation activities such as boating, swimming, hiking, camping, hunting, fishing, skiing, traveling and sightseeing;
2. managerial decisions by private businesses to provide recreation goods and services (services include lodging, guides, ski areas, campgrounds and recreational equipment); and
3. public agency planning to develop parks, beaches, access roads, and trails; manage fish and wildlife; protect Wilderness Areas; and preserve a nation's cultural heritage of historic, natural and scenic resources.

## Recurring Recreation Management Issues Relevant to Economics

Nearly all of the concepts, techniques and applications discussed in this book are useful to address two central and recurring issues in outdoor recreation:

1. improved management of existing areas (the "management" issue, for short), and
2. defense against competing uses of existing natural resources allocated to recreation and evaluating allocation of additional natural and human resources to recreation (the "allocation" issue).

Nearly all tasks that recreation planners and managers face fall into these two categories that are often linked, as the following discussion will illustrate.

## *Optimum Management of Existing Recreation Areas*

The desirable level of use of existing areas is influenced by:

a. physical capacity,
b. environmental/ecological carrying capacity, and
c. socioeconomic carrying capacity.

Most developed recreation sites have well-defined physical capacities that cannot be exceeded. Tennis cannot be enjoyably played with more than four people per court. While 25 people could stand shoulder-to-shoulder on the court, it would not allow for an enjoyable (or safe for that matter) game of tennis. The same is true for ski areas that have well-defined lift and slope capacities. Increased lift line wait and skier collisions result when a facility is used beyond its design standard. Parking at a trailhead and the number of campsites or picnic tables are examples of visitor use limited by facilities regardless of how many people want to use the recreation area.

Some recreation sites are located in such fragile environments that more than a few visitors can harm irreparably the very features that attract them to the site. The number of hikers on trails which pass through alpine tundra (with a very short growing season) without damaging it may often be much less than trails on sandstone or in temperate forests. Too many recreation users camping along a small stream can often degrade water quality. In such cases, use may need to be limited to what the ecosystem can absorb on a sustainable basis.

Finally, there may be resilient ecosystems such as the Slickrock of Utah that can withstand thousands of hikers but the resulting visitor experience is simply intolerable. Visitors to Arches National Park in Utah do little damage to the sandstone as they hike to view the large free standing Delicate Arch. But their experience is similar to viewing an exhibit in a shopping mall rather than a National Park. Dozens of people all trying to get a picture and noise from over a hundred people running from one side of the arch to the other hardly makes for an inspirational experience. Wilderness Areas near large cities provide little of the Wilderness Act's promise of solitude and primitive, unconfined recreation. On the American River in California, rafts frequently bump one another going through the rapids, making the scene more similar to a ride at an amusement park than a scenic river. Clearly, there is a socioeconomic carrying capacity if visitor enjoyment is to be maximized.

During the current or upcoming recreation season, managers have little choice but to limit use to the lessor of these three types of carrying capacities. One of these will be the most limiting and visitation must be restricted to that level so as to not destroy the very features (e.g., solitude, the natural environment) that visitors sought out. But how might the manager limit use to the area's capacity? This is an economic question of scarcity that both public and private resource managers face all the time. For example, airlines and hotels face this problem every holiday season. There are several **rationing systems** that could be employed to limit visitor use (e.g., quantity demanded) to the available capacity. These include (a) first-come first-served; (b) advanced reservation; and (c) pricing. Economic principles can delineate the advantages and disadvantages of each of these rationing systems as demand management tools, something we discuss in Chapter 18 of this book.

Optimum management of existing recreation sites also involves rationing use between competing recreation user groups. Often hikers and mountain bikers or rafters and anglers desire to use the same resource at the same time. Motorized boating on the Snake and Colorado Rivers disrupts the solitude of rafters. Snowmobile use conflicts with cross-country skiers. Who gets to use what trails and when is a decision that economic valuation techniques and benefit-cost analysis can help managers answer in an objective way. The objective is to avoid allegations of favoritism or prejudice toward one group or another.

While agencies often see such demand-limiting strategies as involving minimal costs, they are only half right. While turning away visitors (or one type of incompatible user) may minimize the direct costs to the agency, the **opportunity cost** to society can be quite high and exceed agency costs. By opportunity costs we mean the foregone benefits that visitors who are turned away must give up since they cannot recreate at the site. Opportunity costs are a concept we return to in Chapter 15.

But is demand reduction the only management option available to the agency in the long run? Certainly not. Managers can increase the physical capacity or facilities at the site to meet increased demand. More parking areas can be provided, and separate trails added to accommodate incompatible users such as hikers, mountain bikers and horseback riders. Also additional campsites can be built. Unfortunately, these have direct costs to the agency and society. Competition for tax funds or raising campground fees to cover these costs must be justified. The method of benefit-cost analysis provides a systematic approach to evaluating whether the benefits of expanding the facilities justify the added costs.

Finally, we return to the resource allocation issue. If there is excess demand to hike in Wilderness Areas and to float rivers, it is a signal that more land and rivers need to be protected to provide these recreation experiences. But commodity users such as loggers and dam builders are often interested in using the same natural resources in a way that is incompatible with recreation. Inadequate river flows due to irrigation diversions often result in a short river recreation season. Production of peaking power at dams often disrupts downstream recreation. Once again, the method of benefit-cost analysis can be used to evaluate which natural environments should be allocated to recreational uses and which developed. Using the techniques discussed in Chapters 9, 10 and 14, one can estimate the dollar benefits of recreation as well as the jobs supported.

It is worth noting that an economic approach is also useful in dealing with conflicting uses that degrade environmental quality and sometimes cause managers to erroneously limit visitors rather than the conflicting use. Livestock such as cattle and sheep in many backcountry areas degrade meadows and riparian areas. Because livestock grazing has been a traditional use and pays fees (although they are less than the fair market value), managers sometimes incorrectly conclude they must limit recreation. This is where the management and allocation issues intertwine. Using the valuation techniques and benefit-cost analysis presented in this book, it can often be shown that benefits to society would be increased by reducing the conflicting use such as livestock grazing and increasing recreation use. But it is incumbent on recreation managers to be able to demonstrate their case, since it is often extraordinarily difficult to reduce well-entrenched traditional users of the resource. Reallocation of resources from previously high-valued, but currently lower valued uses in favor of new, high-valued uses is what makes resource use efficient. It is noteworthy that this flexibility in the private sector insures that metal is used today to make microwave ovens rather than potbelly stoves.

## The Role of Economics for Funding Recreation

Management of recreation areas takes money for maintenance and replacement of parking areas. Designing and building new trails, boat ramps, interpretative facilities and viewing platforms costs even more money. While many recreation areas could be self-sufficient using entrance fees (e.g., the State of Vermont Park System), public preferences to provide recreational access to all segments of society often result in such low entrance fees that only $0.20 to $0.50 of every $1.00 of cost is covered by fees. Thus, in addition to use of pricing as a demand management tool, pricing can also be used to raise revenue to pay for site management.

## A Systematic Approach to Decision Making

In developing the decision-making framework, we will rely on the techniques developed in economics as the basic approach. In this regard, we follow the lead of Becker (1976) whose book, *The Economic Approach to Human Behavior,* demonstrates that economics provides an effective way to organize the contribution of other subject matters to decision making. Benefit-cost studies draw on a variety of disciplines, including the other social sciences of psychology, sociology, and political science, on the one hand, and the physical and biological sciences of forestry, hydrology, and engineering, on the other. Indeed, this book is written for college students who are preparing to become managers of parks and recreation areas, forests, wildlife, and related natural resources. While specialization in recreation resources and programs is important, managers will need to comprehend the economic principles of decision making. Thus, the emphasis in this book is on how decisions ought to be made to maximize benefits, rather than on the details of information that should serve as inputs to the decisions. We will have little to say about the complementary disciplines, although you should recognize their relevance to the decisions of individual consumers and managers of recreation resources. Our concern here is with how decision makers should structure their thinking about a recreation choice and with the economic concepts that will aid understanding and prediction.

The approach to decision making throughout this book is that of the decision maker who considers the benefits and costs of alternative recreation activities and programs, then chooses the most beneficial one possible at the lowest possible cost. This approach has been described by Stokey and Zeckhauser (1978) in their excellent book, *A Primer for Policy Analysis*. The authors begin by showing that the individual consumer or manager may perform the analysis or commission others to do parts or all of it. The decision maker may be an individual or a group, such as a division of a private company or public agency that acts essentially as a unit. Also, we will consider the situation in which several decision makers with conflicting objectives participate in a decision. The approach presented here should prove helpful to an individual who takes part in such a process of shared decision making, whether as a legislator deciding how to vote, or as a manager trying to line up support for a proposal.

What do you do when a complicated recreation policy issue lands on your desk? Suppose it's your first day on the job as a policy analyst in a state park and recreation agency. You are directed to investigate the benefits and costs of alternative forest management programs in state recreation areas. The problem has so many ramifications you wonder how you will ever sort them out—and even where to begin. You can always muddle through, hoping eventually to develop a feel for the situation, but such a hit-or-miss approach rather goes against the grain. You would prefer to have a standard procedure that will at least help you make a start on digging into a complex resource management issue.

Planners have experimented with several ways to structure problems like this one. Stokey and Zeckhauser (1978) suggest the following five-part framework as a starting point. However, as you gain experience in thinking about the benefits and costs of recreation activities and programs, you may wish to revise it to suit your own needs. Their framework for decision making is as follows:

1. define the problem and objectives;
2. identify the alternative courses of action;
3. estimate the effects of each alternative;
4. value the effects as benefits and costs; and
5. choose the most beneficial alternative relative to costs.

You will find this outline useful as a background for the rest of this book, to help tie together the wide array of methods and concepts that are considered. The concepts described in the following chapters should enable you to provide better answers to one or another of the questions that come up as you follow the five-step decision-making approach. At every point as you work your way through the following chapters, ask yourself, "How does this concept fit into the overall picture?"

*Recreation Economic Decisions* is meant to be an essentially practical work, emphasizing all aspects of benefits and costs in recreation resource analysis. We want to get you thinking right away in terms of the benefit-cost framework, especially if this is a mode of thought you find a bit unfamiliar. Practice on all kinds of problems, large and small, public and private. Practice on your own outdoor recreation problems and decisions, using benefits and costs to get your thinking straight or to illuminate commonplace events. For example, when a friend proposes a weekend trip to a resort area, think about the travel costs that will be shared and about the opportunity costs of foregone alternative leisure activities. Will your benefits offset your costs? When you find yourself waiting in line to enter an outdoor concert, ask yourself what it would cost to provide additional service capacity, and what the benefits of such a move would be.

Stokey and Zeckhauser (1978) suggest that students look regularly at the local newspaper and think hard about one of the resource conflicts featured. Perhaps a proposed plan to build a dam on a local river is under discussion. See if you can define the immediate objectives of the plan and their relationship to the underlying problem. Who would benefit and who would pay the costs, including the costs of foregone river recreation? What further information would you want? What benefits and costs would you include in an evaluation of the proposed policy? On what basis should the decision be made? Or perhaps the city council advocates an inexpensive building with high maintenance costs for storage of equipment in a local park. Think about the trade-off between present and future spending that is implied. Make up your mind that at least once every day you will deliberately apply the benefit-cost framework to a problem you face. You'll be amazed at what it will do for your reputation for perceptiveness and good judgment.

There is an important relationship between outdoor recreation and natural environments. It is useful to classify outdoor recreation economics as a subpart of environmental and natural resource economics. The natural environment is a resource that yields a variety of valuable services to individuals in their roles as consumers and producers, as outlined by Freeman (1993). The environment can be used for outdoor recreation. It is the source of the basic means of life support—clean air and clean water—and provides the means for growing food. It is a source of energy, minerals and other raw materials such as timber. It is the source of visual amenities, the habitat for fish and wildlife, and it can be used as a place to deposit wastes from production and consumption activities.

The economic problem of the environment is that it is a scarce resource. It cannot provide all of the desired quantities of all of the services at the same time. Greater use of one type of environmental service usually means less of some others. Thus the use of the environment involves trade-offs, and it should be managed as an economically valuable resource.

This book consists of three major sections. In the first, we establish an appropriate framework for consumer decision making and present the unique definitions of quantity and price appropriate to outdoor recreation. These subjects are presented in Chapters 2, 3 and 4. A distinguishing characteristic of outdoor recreation presented in Chapter 2 is that the consumer is the producer, providing inputs of time and effort as well as dollars. The general problem is to combine these resources along with the natural environment in proportions that result in the most benefits. Chapter 2 also presents another unique feature of outdoor recreation—that it is a human activity. Thus, the quantity consumed is measured in terms of the number of occasions or amount of time that individuals choose to participate. In Chapter 4, a realistic proxy for the price of outdoor recreation is defined as direct travel and time costs.

The second, and longer section focuses on the demand for outdoor recreation. Chapter 5 describes in simple and direct terms the nature of a demand curve. One of the most important applications of demand curves is to estimate economic benefits. Learning how to calculate benefits from a demand curve will enable you to provide useful information for recreation economic decisions. Chapter 6 illustrates how to derive a demand curve from a demand function, and demonstrates how statistical demand functions provide estimates of the shifts in demand curves with changes in nonprice variables. Chapter 7 includes a discussion of the determinants of demand: characteristics of users, attractiveness of sites, availability of substitutes, travel time, and congestion. Chapter 8 addresses the issue of elasticity of demand for recreation. Chapters 9, 10 and 11 describe the three methods used by agencies throughout the world to estimate the economic benefits of recreation activities and recreation resources. These are the travel cost, contingent valuation, and unit day value methods. While any one of these may provide a satisfactory measure of the benefits of a recreation project, it is important to understand when each method should be used and how to improve the accuracy of results.

Chapter 13 presents techniques for forecasting future recreation use. Chapter 14 describes methods for quantifying the regional economic impacts on income and employment from tourism. Several examples of correct and incorrect use of input-output models and multipliers are presented. Much of the political motivation for the development of public parks represents an attempt to capture regional gains, which in many cases result in large increases in property values, jobs or county income. These changes in the distribution of economic activity represent transfers of income and not social benefits, i.e., not real gains to the nation unless the region has long-run unemployment, which is sometimes the case in economically depressed recreation areas.

The third section introduces benefit-cost analysis of public recreation projects and programs. We begin with resource supply and costs of recreation development in Chapter 15. There we define several different types of costs relevant for management of recreation areas. The chapter also describes three methods used to estimate costs: engineering-economic, cross-sectional, and time-series. Chapter 16 reviews several case studies that provide empirical estimates of the cost of providing recreation. These include marinas, campgrounds and ski areas. A technique used to compare revenue and costs, called break-even analysis, is introduced and applied to analysis of different size ski areas.

Chapter 17 examines the fee structure and pricing policies of public agencies and private firms. In particular, this chapter provides a detailed review of existing fee policies for state parks, state fish and game agencies as well as several federal agencies such as the U.S. Forest Service and National Park Service. Cost recovery using entrance fees is presented for state parks and federal land management agencies. Chapter 18 describes the principles of pricing such as average cost, marginal cost, peak load and price discrimination. Pricing practices related to different market structures such as monopoly are contrasted with that of competition. Chapter 18 also investigates the potential to use pricing as a management tool to redistribute use from congested sites or time periods to off-peak periods. An example is provided of such an experiment at campsites in Vermont State Parks.

Chapter 19 formalizes the basic approach of this book: benefit-cost analysis. In benefit-cost analysis the comparison is between the cost to the private sector of what it gives up to support a government recreation program (represented by taxes, user fees and opportunity costs) and the benefits of the output which the government provides with the resources (represented by the willingness of citizens to pay for the government-produced opportunities). A public recreation program can increase the well-being of society if the resources given up by the private sector are used to produce greater benefits than are foregone by the private sector. Benefit-cost analysis helps public officials choose among alternative recreation programs and projects which vary in size, design and purpose.

An important economic problem of governments throughout the world is how large should the public recreation program be? How much should government tax and spend for outdoor recreation? The techniques presented in this book can be applied to answer these questions. We also introduce the concepts of discounting and net present value which enable us to make systematic comparisons between benefits and costs occurring at different times in the future. Chapter 20 discusses some of the challenges in applying benefit-cost analysis to a nonmarketed resource such as recreation, as well as problems common to all benefit-cost analyses. These include choice of the interest or discount rate for making present and future benefits or costs comparable.

*Chapter 2*

# Recreation Production Process

This chapter describes household production in which recreation is produced by consumers with purchased goods and services, leisure time and other inputs that are publicly provided such as park facilities and natural environments.

Recreation experiences are produced by visitors combining the natural resources and facilities provided by managers and the visitors' own time, skill and equipment. The extreme left side of Figure 2-1 illustrates the production inputs to a recreation experience that managers must provide the visitor. These include the land resource, which may involve some biophysical features such as canyons, forests, and fish, labor in the form of maintenance and ranger-led walks, and capital in the form of investment in facilities, trails and signage. Some or all of these can be provided by the private sector or government agencies or some combination. For example, in some areas all of the campgrounds are provided by private firms (e.g., KOAs) whereas in many National Parks, campgrounds are solely provided by the National Park Service. However, commercial rafting trips are an example where labor and equipment are provided by the private sector while the natural resource is provided by the public sector.

The combination of land, labor and capital produces a supply of recreation opportunities or capacity. For the opportunities to be demanded or used, visitors must engage in their own "household" production process. This is illustrated in the upper middle box of Figure 2-1. Individuals, families or groups must combine their knowledge of the site (e.g., weather, type of equipment needed for the activity at that site) with purchases of both durable and nondurable supplies (e.g., bait for fishing, film for wildlife photography) with their time and income (e.g., in the form of travel expenses, lodging, entrance fees). The amount of time and money potential visitors have will influence whether they visit this site or not. The

**Figure 2-1. Recreation Production Process**

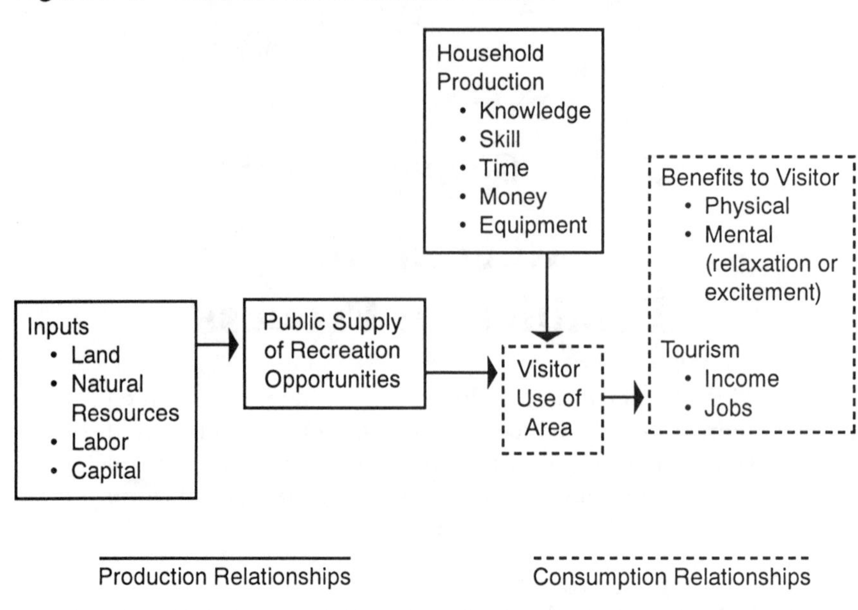


level of skill in this recreation activity will influence the beneficial effect of consuming this recreation activity. High-skilled participants may obtain more enjoyment than novices.

If individuals decide to commit their time and money to visiting the site, then visitor use will be observed, resulting in consumption of recreation. This consumption will lead to certain effects. From the standpoint of the visitor, these effects will likely be considered benefits. Recreational benefits are multidimensional. For some these benefits will be exercise, for others relaxation. For some the benefits will include stimulation or challenge, for others mental and physical relaxation. Whatever the motivations, if individuals realize these desired outcomes, they are made better off by some measure. The challenge of this and later chapters is to calculate the dollar equivalent of the improvement in the physical and mental well-being of individuals from consuming the recreation opportunity. However, the benefits may not stop with the recreationists. The community that provides the lodging, guides, restaurants and other support services also gains from the presence of recreation sites and visitors. These tourism effects are of a different kind than the benefits the visitor receives. It is often easier to see how one can translate visitor spending into community income and employment. Chapter 14 provides the techniques for doing just that. We now take a look in more detail at the household production process and how economists might measure the benefits that recreation provides to visitors.

# Details of Household Production

Two questions are basic to the recreation economic decisions of individual consumers: What do they want and what can they get? It is part of human nature to seek the maximum enjoyment of all life's activities, including outdoor recreation. How much they enjoy an activity determines how much they would be willing to pay rather than forego it. Many economists believe that willingness to pay provides a straightforward measure of the economic value of individual recreation benefits. What consumers want is based on their assessment of the relative benefits of alternative activities available to them. What they get depends on their ability to pay the costs. Economists believe that consumers do not measure costs in the same way that accountants do—as simply the price of goods and services purchased from others—for a distinguishing characteristic of outdoor recreation is that the consumer is one of the producers, providing inputs of time and effort as well as dollars. Choices are constrained by how much of these three types of resources are available and their opportunity costs. The economic decision rule is: Consumers should choose to participate in those activities that provide the most benefits.

## *Money Income*

The quantity of outdoor recreation consumed is determined, in part, by income, as it affects how much individual consumers are willing and able to pay. Money income is defined as the dollar amount of wages and salaries, interest and dividends on investments, and miscellaneous receipts such as transfer payments and payments in kind. Income is the most clearly understood individual resource available for allocation to participation in outdoor recreation. Personal income levels determine ability to pay. Income provides the dollars necessary to purchase recreation goods and services which are produced by others. These expenditures may include entrance fees, transportation costs, lodging, added food, consumable supplies, and recreation equipment such as special clothing, tents, fishing tackle, and recreation vehicles.

## *Income and Participation*

Income is positively related to participation in outdoor recreation. Overall, more higher income households participate more days per year. In this chapter, "household" and "family" are used interchangeably. Table 2-1 (page 16) illustrates the effect of income on the probability of participating and average number of days per year. An average of 95% of the U.S. population 16 years of age and older participated in outdoor recreation in 1994–95. Note that there is considerable variation among recreation activities with regard to income. For expensive activities like golf and downhill skiing, participation rates go up in almost direct proportion to income.

**Table 2-1. Effect of Family Income on Annual Participation in Outdoor Recreation 1994–95 (Percent Participating)**

| Activity | Less Than $25,000 | $25,000 –50,000 | $50,000 –75,000 | $75,000 –100,000 | Over $100,000 | Refused/ Don't Know |
|---|---|---|---|---|---|---|
| Golf | 8.0% | 14.6% | 22.6% | 24.6% | 30.0% | 10.7% |
| Tennis | 6.7 | 10.0 | 13.8 | 15.3 | 19.2 | 9.9 |
| Team Sports | 19.8 | 27.8 | 27.7 | 27.3 | 24.5 | 22.9 |
| Baseball | 5.1 | 7.3 | 7.3 | 7.5 | 6.4 | 7.3 |
| Softball | 10.0 | 15.3 | 16.7 | 14.4 | 10.4 | 10.9 |
| Football | 5.0 | 6.9 | 7.1 | 6.1 | 6.6 | 8.6 |
| Basketball | 10.5 | 13.3 | 14.3 | 15.1 | 11.8 | 13.0 |
| Soccer | 3.6 | 4.4 | 5.8 | 5.5 | 6.6 | 4.9 |
| Volleyball | 11.6 | 16.8 | 16.1 | 16.5 | 12.2 | 12.5 |
| Handball | 5.6 | 5.0 | 5.6 | 7.0 | 6.4 | 6.1 |
| Bicycling | 20.2 | 31.2 | 35.9 | 37.0 | 39.1 | 24.1 |
| Rock Climbing | 2.9 | 3.6 | 5.7 | 2.8 | 5.1 | 3.3 |
| Mountain Climbing | 3.4 | 4.6 | 5.9 | 6.1 | 6.7 | 3.4 |
| Caving | 3.7 | 5.1 | 5.5 | 5.2 | 5.1 | 4.3 |
| Running/Jogging | 19.9 | 26.5 | 29.6 | 30.9 | 38.1 | 25.9 |
| Walking | 57.1 | 71.9 | 74.9 | 77.1 | 74.8 | 59.0 |
| Downhill Skiing | 4.3 | 7.8 | 11.8 | 14.8 | 20.7 | 6.5 |
| Cross-Country Skiing | 1.8 | 3.2 | 5.3 | 5.9 | 6.2 | 2.0 |
| Hiking | 17.3 | 26.3 | 30.7 | 30.5 | 32.8 | 18.6 |
| Backpacking | 5.9 | 7.8 | 9.9 | 8.8 | 10.1 | 6.3 |
| Canoeing | 3.8 | 6.9 | 10.4 | 9.7 | 8.6 | 5.2 |
| Kayaking | 0.3 | 0.6 | 1.0 | 1.3 | 1.4 | 0.5 |

Source: U.S. Forest Service, 1996a.

For other activities like baseball, visitation is fairly constant. Some differences in participation are more related to tastes associated with higher income than expenses. For example, participation in hiking nearly doubles from the lowest income category to the highest, yet hiking is a very inexpensive activity.

While higher income may enable more households to participate in particular types of outdoor recreation, past surveys show their days per year may not be affected. Once the decision to participate in an activity is made, income is not uniformly related to number of days per year engaged in walking for pleasure, attending outdoor sports events, theater, concerts and fairs, fishing, bicycling, camping, nature walks, hunting, birdwatching, and wildlife photography. However, income is positively related to the number of days per year of swimming, boating, horseback riding, and playing outdoor games and sports. Middle-income households are more likely to participate in picnicking, camping, fishing and hunting than either higher or lower income groups.

Income is also positively related to level of expenditures on outdoor recreation. While information on the total expenditures on outdoor recreation is not available for income groups, it is indicative that higher income households spend more for recreation travel. Recreation expenditures are equal to about 10% of personal income in the United States, although official estimates have varied with incomplete coverage. Bureau of Labor Statistics data shows that only 35% of low-income families allocated income for overnight recreation trips. By comparison, 70% to 80% of middle-income families and 90% of high-income families choose to allocate discretionary income to overnight recreation trips. The proportion of households reporting overnight lodging expenses is particularly revealing. Of those families taking overnight trips only 11% of low-income families reported expenditures on overnight lodging compared with nearly 25% to 50% of middle-income families and two-thirds of high-income families. With higher income, an individual can afford to travel by air, sleep in a condominium or first-class motel adjacent to the recreation site, eat in restaurants, rent equipment, and pay for the services of a guide. Less than 5% of low-income families participate in all-expense-paid tours compared with nearly 10% of the middle-income families and 20% of those with high income.

According to U.S. Bureau of Labor Statistics (1977) about one-fourth as many households report expenditures on recreation equipment as on overnight recreation trips. The probability of household spending on recreation equipment was positively related to income, as expected.

This cross-sectional data shows a positive total relationship with income; that is, higher participation and expenditure on outdoor recreation are associated with higher income where no other variables are held constant. In Chapter 7 we will show several studies of the partial effect of income, which is the short-run effect of a change in income holding other features constant. The cross-sectional data presented here shows the total effect of being in particular income categories which includes a number of related variables such as education, patterns of preference, and position in society.

Spending out of income also depends on the phase of the consumer's life cycle of earnings and of expenditure needs. Young persons—with an expectation of rising income, with dependent children, and with the need to equip a household with standard durables—have a high preference for current consumption expenditures. Older persons, expecting a falling income and retirement, save to increase their consumption later on. Individual attitudes toward satisfaction enjoyed at different points of times vary substantially. Those with a very short time horizon will have strong preferences for present consumption, while misers will have the reverse. Of course, individual needs and desires for providing for financial emergencies will determine these preferences in part, as will many other factors.

## Tax Payments and Income

The information on income distribution presented in Table 2-1 is based on annual family income before the payment of taxes, which is the usual form in which income statistics are available from the U.S. census and most visitor surveys. Income before taxes is considered a reasonable proxy of ability to pay for outdoor recreation. Still, it should be noted that the actual dollars of income available for expenditure on goods and services are after taxes have been paid. It is simply that this statistic is not as readily available because people are not generally aware of their total tax bill.

It is possible to estimate total taxes paid from Internal Revenue Service summaries. Low-income households pay an average of 25% of their income as taxes compared with 30% for middle-income and 38% for high-income households. This indicates that total tax rates are not as progressive as is often assumed. The term *progressive* refers to a tax rate schedule in which higher income households pay a disproportionately higher percentage of their income in taxes than do lower income households. Federal income tax rates are considerably more progressive than these total tax rates. However, federal payroll, excise, and highway user taxes are regressive. Distribution of the state and local tax burden among income groups tends to be practically the same as the distribution of income. State income taxes are usually somewhat progressive, although not nearly so progressive as the federal income tax. Other state and local taxes tend to be regressive, with lower income households paying a disproportionately higher percentage of their income in taxes.

The policy of using tax revenues to provide free or nominal cost public outdoor recreation resources has been attacked by a number of critics. They have suggested that this policy constitutes a subsidy to upper middle-income and high-income households at the expense of lower income households. It is possible to provide a tentative test of the validity of this proposition. If the distribution of recreation use among income groups is substantially different from the distribution of tax payments, this would suggest that there is a subsidy. It becomes an empirical question as to which income groups receive an outdoor recreation subsidy if any.

The proposition that lower income households subsidize the public outdoor recreation opportunities of those with higher incomes is not supported by the information presented in Table 2-2. The tentative evidence suggests that high-income households subsidize those with low incomes and, in particular, middle incomes. Those less able to pay are subsidized by those most able to pay because of their higher absolute income and the progressive aspects of the tax system. Low-income and lower middle-income households have fewer days of outdoor recreation per year than upper middle-income and high-income households. However, the share of tax payments by low-income and lower middle-income households is even less than their share of participation in outdoor recreation.

On the basis of this information, it is concluded that lower income households receive a subsidy in kind from the use of public outdoor recreation resources, albeit a small one. Apparently, middle-income households receive the largest subsidy, as measured by how much their share of

**Table 2-2. Distribution of Households, Outdoor Recreation, Income and Tax Payments by Income Groups, United States**

| Category | Income Group | | | | | |
|---|---|---|---|---|---|---|
| | Low | Lower Middle | Middle | Upper Middle | High | Total |
| | Percent Distribution | | | | | |
| Proportion of Households | 27.4 | 30.3 | 23.2 | 15.1 | 4.0 | 100.0 |
| Income | 10.7 | 26.0 | 27.1 | 21.6 | 14.6 | 100.0 |
| Tax Payment[a] | 8.8 | 22.8 | 26.4 | 23.9 | 18.1 | 100.0 |
| Outdoor Recreation Days | 11.3 | 23.5 | 31.0 | 25.9 | 8.3 | 100.0 |
| Gain or Loss[b] | 2.5 | 0.7 | 4.6 | 2.0 | -9.8 | |

[a]Taxes as a percent of income for income groups: low, 25.3%; lower middle, 27.0%; middle, 30.1%; upper middle, 34.0%; high, 38.2%; and total, 31.4%. Taxes include federal income payroll, highway use, and other excise; state and local income, property, sales, highway use, and excise.

[b]The percent of outdoor recreation days of a group minus the percent of tax payment by the same income group.

Source: Bureau of Outdoor Recreation, 1973a; Bureau of the Census, 1980.

participation in outdoor recreation exceeds their share of tax payments. Upper middle-income households also receive a small subsidy. The proportion of tax payments by high-income households substantially exceeds their participation in outdoor recreation, even though their participation per household is the highest of any income group, as shown in Table 2-1 (page 16).

Payment of taxes for outdoor recreation programs varies with level of household income. Low-income households with $10,000 annual income paid $32 per year in taxes for recreation programs, which equaled $0.36 per day for the 91 recreation days per year by the average household of two persons. Upper middle-income households with $50,000 annual income paid $220 per year in taxes for recreation programs, equivalent to $2.12 per day for 104 recreation days per year by a typical middle-income person. High-income households with $100,000 annual income paid about $500 per year in taxes for recreation programs, which equaled $4.24 per day for 118 recreation days per year by the average high-income person.

Direct federal expenditures from tax revenues were estimated as $2 billion per year from 1990 to 1995, which was equivalent to only $20 per household in the United States. These federal expenditures included 46.7% for operation, maintenance, and management; 24.4% for construction and development; 15.6% for land acquisition; and 13.3% for other costs of recreation programs. Agencies include the National Park Service, Forest Service, Fish and Wildlife Service, Bureau of Reclamation, Army Corps of Engineers, and Tennessee Valley Authority. Transportation Department expenditures are for road construction in public recreation areas.

Most tax payments for outdoor recreation programs are made directly to state and local units of government and to the federal government for grants to state and local government. Nearly $2.4 billion of tax revenues for recreation programs are paid directly to state and local government and an additional $1.4 billion was paid to the federal government for grants to state and local government. Combined, the $3.8 billion recreation expenditures from tax revenues averaged nearly $52 per household or 86% of total public spending on outdoor recreation programs from tax revenues.

Expenditures by city government, nearly $13 billion in 1992, were larger than direct expenditures by either state or federal government, although a substantial portion represented grant monies from the federal government and some user fee revenues are included in total expenditures. Local park and recreation expenditures represented 4.7% of the total budget of city governments in the United States.

# Leisure Time

Time is one resource that every person has in equal amounts—24 hours a day, 365 days a year. This is related to the fact that time, unlike other economic resources, cannot be accumulated. Individuals and households cannot build up a stock of time as they would a stock of capital. Each person has around 16 waking hours a day to use in working, routine living, and enjoying life. For most persons, leisure time is the residual that is left after necessary obligations are met to work, sleep, eat, and maintain personal hygiene. Leisure is defined as discretionary time to be used as one chooses. As such, it is analogous to the concept of discretionary income which is available for spending on recreation goods and services after the necessary costs of living have been paid.

## *Measures of Time*

Availability of leisure time varies with relatively more for some individuals than others and at different times for the same individual. Clawson and Knetsch (1966) observe that leisure time for most persons ages 6–65 comes in three forms: (1) weekdays, for approximately 180 school days or 240 workdays, in amounts of three to six hours each day, not necessarily continuous, after demands for school or work, sleep, and personal chores have been met; (2) on weekends, for about 114 days per year, including 10 three-day holiday weekends when work is typically absent and leisure time may run as much as 12 hours per day; and (3) on vacations extending over a period of 75–90 days for school children and 7–30 days for employed persons. Preschool and retired persons have different patterns, less regular and less geared to weekly, seasonal, and annual cycles; to a lesser extent, so do housewives or househusbands who do not work outside the home. The use of leisure time by all households is affected by the schedules of the members in school and working.

Table 2-3 illustrates the distribution of leisure time per week for income groups of working adults and for college students in the United States. The table shows that all individuals, regardless of income, have roughly 108 waking hours per week. College students have the most average weekly leisure time, particularly summer vacation expressed on a weekly basis. For employed adults, the lowest income group has the most leisure time. Total leisure time per week declines as income increases, despite the fact that annual vacation time expressed on a weekly basis rises with added income. Some nonwork time of the low-income group is the result of inability to obtain full-time jobs. Forced idleness is not considered leisure time in the usual sense.

Higher income groups tend to work more hours per week and have less leisure time on weekdays than lower income groups. Individual business proprietors in the United States work 55 hours per week compared with 40 hours by their employees. There is a similar pattern in West Germany where managers of overnight lodging accommodations and restaurants work 67 hours weekly compared with 45 hours by their employees. Medical doctors and college professors typically work about 60 hours per week. Finally, it is interesting to note that leisure time during weekends and holidays tends to be the same for all income groups.

Outdoor recreation activities are a substantial part of leisure time in the United States. The proportion of leisure time used for outdoor recreation is positively related to income. For middle-income groups, approximately 21% of average weekly leisure time is used for outdoor recreation,

**Table 2-3. Estimated Distribution of Weekly Time by Income Groups, United States**

| Category | College Student | Low Income | Lower Middle Income | Middle Income | Upper Middle Income | High Income |
|---|---|---|---|---|---|---|
| Households U.S. | 4% | 24% | 30% | 23% | 15% | 4% |
| | | | **Hours per Week** | | | |
| Total Nonsleep Time | 108 | 108 | 108 | 108 | 108 | 108 |
| Leisure Time (total) | 55 | 53 | 51 | 48 | 47 | 45 |
| Weekday | 13 | 27 | 24 | 20 | 18 | 15 |
| Weekend | 25 | 25 | 25 | 25 | 25 | 25 |
| Vacation | 17 | 1 | 2 | 3 | 4 | 5 |
| Work Time | 27 | 30 | 35 | 40 | 48 | 55 |
| Other Time[a] | 26 | 25 | 22 | 20 | 13 | 8 |
| Outdoor Recreation Time | 16 | 7 | 8 | 10 | 11 | 12 |
| Outdoor Recreation as a | | | **Percent of Leisure Time** | | | |
| Percent of Leisure Time | 29% | 13% | 16% | 21% | 23% | 27% |

[a]Includes personal care, idle time and nonmarket work time averaging 18 hours per week according to Owen, 1971.

Source: Bureau of the Census, 1980; Bureau of Outdoor Recreation, 1973a.

compared with 13% for low-income and 27% for high-income households. College students use a larger proportion of their leisure time for outdoor recreation than employed persons, in particular, bicycling and playing organized games and sports.

The proportion of leisure time used for indoor recreation activities, such as watching television and videos, playing video games and reading is presumably the balance of leisure time after outdoor recreation has been subtracted from the total. Based on this measure, middle-income groups used approximately 79% of their leisure time indoors. Low-income groups tend to do physical labor at work and prefer indoor leisure pursuits. High-income groups are less likely to be physically active at work and favor more outdoor recreation activities.

## Leisure Versus Work

Economic analysis of leisure versus work is based on the following observations. Given the fixed amount of 108 waking hours in a week, an individual's decision to spend 60 of those hours working is simultaneously a decision to demand 48 of them for other purposes, including approximately 30 hours of leisure time. Another person's decision to spend 40 hours working is simultaneously a decision to demand 68 of them for other purposes, with 50 hours of leisure time, as 18 hours of personal care and other daily chores remains unchanged.

Wage rates have two effects on the demand for leisure time activities, including outdoor recreation. An increase in the wage rate raises the opportunity cost of earnings lost by taking leisure time. Thus, there is a substitution effect of an increase in wages which encourages individuals to demand less leisure time. Also, the wage increase raises income making people more able to afford to buy more goods and services, including outdoor recreation and other leisure activities. Thus, the income effect of an increase in wages is to encourage individuals to demand more leisure time. A rise in income also increases ability to pay for timesaving household appliances and services which increase leisure time by reducing the hours of personal care and other daily household chores. The actual change in an individual's demand for leisure is the net balance of the opposing influences.

Throughout the twentieth century, the income effect of increased wages apparently has prevailed, causing the demand for leisure to increase and the length of the workweek to decline. Owen (1971) found that about 75% of the increased demand for leisure since 1900 is explained by increases in the real hourly wage rate. About 25% is explained by declines in the relative price of recreation goods and services. Real wage rates (measured in dollars of 1967 purchasing power in the United States) had been rising until recently. At the beginning of the 1900s, the real wage rate averaged $0.70 per hour. By 1970, it averaged $3.00, and then declined to about $2.70 in 1980. Over the 80-year period, the real wage rate increased by nearly three times in terms of the quantity of goods and services those dollars could buy.

During the same time period, hours of work have generally declined and leisure time has increased. Organized labor has asked for and received reductions in the length of the workday and workweek. At the beginning of the century, a workweek of five to six days and a workday of 10 or more hours was standard, making a workweek of 50–60 hours. Since then, hours of work have generally declined, until today the standard workweek is down to 35–40 hours. This means that demand for other time, including leisure, increased by one-third, from an average of 53 hours per week at the beginning of the 1900s to 70 hours today. The trend has been much the same in most other developed countries. Recent trends of two income families and longer work commutes may have slowed (and Schor [1991] would say reversed) the trend toward more leisure time.

## Opportunity Cost of Leisure

Several approaches have been used to estimate the opportunity cost of leisure time including (1) theoretical, assumed equal to the average wage rate, and (2) empirical measurement of the value of work actually foregone.

According to the first approach, individual time used in leisure activities is valued at its opportunity cost, which theoretically is the price at which the individual can sell additional work on the labor market. Otherwise individuals would work more and take less leisure. This is usually interpreted to be the current hourly wage rate for their level of ability and occupation. For example, the cost of a college education includes the income foregone from work that could have been performed while attending college. Until recently, no empirical studies were available on the opportunity cost of leisure time in total or that portion used for outdoor recreation. The lack of evidence did not deter a theoretical approach to the subject by a number of economists, most notably Becker (1965), but also Owen (1971), McConnell and Strand (1981), Wilman (1980), and others.

Indiscriminate application of the opportunity cost principle has resulted in large estimates of the value of leisure time, ranging from 60% to 140% of income. The usual procedure has been simply to multiply hours of leisure time by the average wage rate. On this basis, Nordhaus and Tobin (1973) calculated the total value of leisure time as 140% of the value of national income in the United States. Using this procedure, the value of leisure time is equivalent to 120% of money income of middle-income households.

Application of the opportunity cost principle can result in very large estimates of the value of leisure time devoted to outdoor recreation activities. With on-site recreation time equal to the national average of five hours per day and average wage of $12 per hour (equal to $24,000 per year), then the opportunity cost of time is $60 per recreation day.

McConnell and Strand (1981) estimate that sport fishermen on the Chesapeake Bay value travel time as about 60% of their hourly household income.

These estimates are subject to a number of important qualifications. Not all leisure time has the same opportunity cost. For a typical individual who is already working an eight-to-five, 40-hour week, employment opportunities during weekday evenings, weekends, and vacations may be at a much lower rate of pay than regular employment on the first job. Moreover, if employment opportunities are unavailable during the hours when leisure time occurs, opportunity cost of wages foregone becomes zero.

An interagency committee of the U.S. government (Water Resources Council) recommends that recreation time costs for individuals whose work time is variable should be measured as the income foregone. Work time is variable for most professionals, such as doctors and lawyers, and other individuals who operate their own business. Their income is a direct function of the number of patients, clients, and customers served which varies with work time.

Alternatively, the opportunity cost approach assigns the wage rates to leisure time that have been explicitly rejected by the household as a true measure. Those individuals who could have offered more work time to the labor market preferred not to do so, either because they found the wages too low or job satisfaction less than desired.

Review of psychological studies led Scitovsky (1976) to the conclusion that apparently, there is some optimum proportion of work and leisure time for each individual. The principle of diminishing marginal returns would apply in both cases. Thus, the physical and mental abuse of working overtime or at a second job rather than enjoying recreation during usual leisure time may reduce individual productivity.

According to the second approach, only the value of work time actually foregone would be considered a cost of leisure time activities. The direct interview approach would enable the observer to question those household members who report they would have worked if they had not been engaged in the leisure time activity. Questions could be asked about the amount of time and the amount of wages foregone. Those who report no work time foregone would be assigned a zero opportunity cost and questioned about possible benefits foregone from alternative leisure time activities.

It seems likely that the direct interview approach would yield results significantly different from those obtained using a constant opportunity cost of time equal to (or a proportion of) the average wage rate. Studies of the opportunity cost of recreation time in the Rocky Mountains of the United States indicate that less than 30% of user households report any members would have worked during on-site recreation time spent fishing, hiking, backpacking, camping and picnicking. For households reporting opportunity cost, foregone wages were substantial. However, averaged over the entire sample, the opportunity cost of wages foregone was less than 10% of the reported wage rates. This suggests that the opportunity cost of recreation time may be an insignificant part of the total direct cost of outdoor recreation in the United States.

In between these two extremes, the opportunity cost of alternative leisure activity may be estimated by comparing willingness to pay for the two activities. For example, assume that in order to go fishing, an individual forgoes an alternative leisure activity such as tennis for which he or she would be willing to pay $10 per day. For individuals willing to pay $30 per day for fishing, the opportunity cost of fishing time is $10 per day. This $10 represents the individual's leisure time benefits foregone in order to go fishing and would be added to other direct costs to determine that individual's price of fishing. However, few consumers would knowingly choose the lesser valued leisure activity, so the direct leisure time cost of outdoor recreation usually will be zero.

There is another important application of the opportunity cost principle in recreation economic decisions by individual consumers. The benefits from work or alternative leisure activities actually foregone provide a minimum estimate of the benefits from outdoor recreation. If outdoor recreation benefits do not at least equal the benefits from work or the most valuable alternative leisure time activity, whichever is higher, the consumer should probably reexamine the decision to participate in the outdoor recreation. Benefits of the activity chosen should exceed the benefits of the activity foregone.

*Chapter 3*

# Measuring Consumption of Recreation

This chapter defines several alternative measures of the quantity of recreation; shows how to convert the results of each of these measures to be comparable with other measures; presents the results of recent surveys regarding participation in a variety of activities; and explores the effect of unique consumption patterns on recreation economic decisions regarding resource development and management.

The development and management of recreation resources provides an opportunity for people to take part in outdoor recreation. However, the production process always involves the participation of consumers, for a distinguishing characteristic of outdoor recreation is that it is a human activity (i.e., sightseeing, hiking, camping, skiing, swimming, fishing, hunting, and the like). Thus, the quantity of outdoor recreation consumed is measured in terms of the number of occasions or the amount of time that individuals choose to participate. The output of a recreation site is, therefore, the sum of the quantity of outdoor recreation activity demanded by individual consumers at the site.

## Alternative Measures of Visitor Use

Several approaches have been used to measure the quantity of outdoor recreation consumed. These include (1) recreation days or activity days; (2) recreation visitor days, user days or hours; (3) trips, visits or visitors; and (4) entrance permits, licenses, and tickets issued or units occupied. While each approach has provided a satisfactory measure of a particular type of recreation activity, a problem of comparability arises when two or more measures are combined. No standard unit of recreation use has been developed that is suitable for all purposes of measurement. Thus, it is important to understand when each measure should be used and how to convert the results of each approach to compare it with other measures. Accuracy of the alternative estimating procedures (e.g., car counters, campground and trail registration, licenses sold, and spot checks) is a continuing problem.

## *Recreation Day*

A recreation day is defined by the U.S. Water Resources Council (1983) as a visit by one individual to a recreation area for recreation purposes during any reasonable portion or all of a 24-hour period of time. This is virtually identical to an earlier definition by the Bureau of Outdoor Recreation of an activity day as one person participating in an activity for any part of one calendar day. Either definition provides a satisfactory measure of the quantity of single or similar recreation activities demanded by individual consumers at recreation sites, where length of stay measured in hours per day does not vary appreciably among individual participants. Moreover, the approach is consistent with the perception of individual consumers as to the meaning of a recreation day as an occasion or event with little or no regard for the amount of time involved.

Problems arise when the approach is used to measure individual participation in more than one recreation activity during a single recreation day. Application of the method results in double counting of recreation days where one individual camping, swimming, boating, and fishing during a single 24-hour day may be counted as four recreation days, i.e., one in each of the four categories. Also, problems occur when this approach is used to compare the number of recreation days of one to four hours in length (i.e., picnicking and hiking) with days of 6–12 hours in length (i.e., backpacking and camping), where the effects on recreation resources vary according to the amount of time they are used.

Some observers have suggested that problems may arise when the approach is used to measure the quantity of recreation in applications of the travel cost approach to recreation demand analysis to be discussed in Chapter 9, for travel costs are more directly related to number of trips than to recreation days at the site. Nevertheless, recreation days have been used in a number of successful travel cost demand studies. Perhaps consumers find it more convenient to make decisions concerning how much outdoor recreation to consume in terms of recreation days rather than trips with varying lengths of stay.

## *Recreation Visitor Day*

A recreation visitor day is defined by the U.S. Forest Service as 12 person-hours, which may be one person for 12 hours, 12 persons for one hour each, or any equivalent combination of individual or group use, either continuous or intermittently. An earlier term, recreation user day, had the same definition. A recreation visitor hour has been defined as one or more users for continuous or intermittent periods of time aggregating 60 minutes. The approach has provided a satisfactory measure of the total quantity of recreation at sites where individuals participate in more than one recreation activity during a single recreation day. The method avoids double counting of recreation days at recreation sites administered by the U.S. Forest Service where an individual who hiked for six hours, picnicked two hours, and fished four hours would be counted as a single 12-hour visitor day. The approach also has provided satisfactory measures of total recreation resource use in a National Forest where recreation activities of varying lengths of time are combined into standard 12-hour visitor days.

Problems arise when studies of the quantity of outdoor recreation activity demanded by individual consumers is aggregated into visitor day statistics. Individual consumers perceive outdoor recreation activity as an occasion or event rather than as a standard 12-hour visitor day. Activities such as hiking, horseback riding, fishing, hunting, boating, and skiing are typically four to six hours per day rather than 12 hours. Exceptions are overnight stays in campgrounds, backcountry campsites, lodges, and seasonal homes.

The result is that it takes three four-hour days of fishing to equal one 12-hour visitor day of camping. Moreover, the camper who stays an entire 24-hour day would be counted as two 12-hour visitor days, equal to six times the quantity of outdoor recreation attributed to a single four-hour day of fishing. It is obvious that this approach vastly understates the quantity of most outdoor recreation activities as perceived by individual consumers. Thus, it is important to adjust the recreation visitor day statistics when considering individual consumer's perception of outdoor recreation activity as an occasion of varying length.

## *Recreation Visit or Visitor*

A recreation visit or visitor is defined by the National Park Service as the use by one individual of a recreation area for recreation purposes for any length of time. This is identical to the definition of a recreation trip when the sole purpose is visiting a particular recreation site. The approach has provided satisfactory measures of the quantity of recreation demanded by individual consumers on single-day outings and/or overnight weekend trips to recreation sites within 150 miles of their place of residence. In this case, a recreation visit or trip is equivalent to one or, at most, two recreation days. When the length of stay by visitors to a recreation site is reasonably similar, the number of trips per person has provided the most suitable measure of the quantity of recreation in applications of the travel cost approach to recreation demand analysis, for travel costs obviously are more directly related to trips than to either recreation days or recreation visitor days.

Problems arise when the approach is used to measure the quantity of recreation demanded by individuals on vacation trips with varying length of stay at a recreation site and/or with visits to more than one recreation site during a single trip. The annual summary of visits to recreation sites administered by the National Park Service includes a combination of users on single-day outings, overnight weekend trips, and vacations with varying lengths of stay. As a result, comparisons of the quantity of recreation demanded at alternative recreation sites may be distorted unless adjusted for length of stay. Individuals usually visit more than one recreation site while on vacation trips and, to a lesser extent, on overnight weekend trips. In this event it is important to develop some reasonable basis for allocating total time on the trip among recreation sites visited. A number of approaches have been tried. Dividing total time on the trip by the total number of sites visited on the trip assumes an equal quantity of recreation at each site. Allocation on the basis of the proportion of recreation days at each site seems more reasonable, although it assumes that each day is of equal length.

## *Entrance Permits*

The quantity of recreation activity also has been defined as the number of entrance permits or licenses issued and the number of recreation units occupied. Examples include the number of fishing and hunting licenses sold by state agencies, lift tickets issued by ski areas, overnight stays at resort lodges, and number of campsites occupied. When these sources are adjusted for known deficiencies, they provide the most accurate measures available of the quantity of recreation activity. For example, the number of fishing and hunting licenses sold provides the best available estimate of total anglers and hunters in a state when adjusted for those over 65 and under 16, those who purchase a combination license, and estimated poaching. Wildlife management agencies supplement this information with that from game check stations or sample surveys to estimate number of days per hunter, amount of game bagged, and quantity of hunting in management units or resource areas.

Entrance permits to parks and historical monuments provide an accurate measure of the number of visits or visitors when adjusted for use of annual passes, size of parties, and periods of time when the entrance booth may not be occupied, such as at night and on special occasions when entrance is free. When individual recreation use is for less than one calendar day, as is frequently the case, a visit or trip is equivalent to a recreation day.

Problems arise when individuals enter a park for multiple-day visits and/or engage in more than one recreation activity while there. Entrance permits may provide little or no information about the quantity of sightseeing, hiking, picnicking, group games, fishing, and other recreation activities that occur in a particular park. Such information is essential to effective resource management. Thus, the statistical services branch of the National Park Service is making a concerted effort to overcome this deficiency in its park visitor statistics by using sample surveys to supplement the existing information on number of camping permits issued and number of concessionaire lodging units occupied.

The following example illustrates the problem of measuring the quantity of recreation activity by this method. It shows that the number of lift tickets issued probably is not as accurate as the perception of individual consumers. If you ask a friend about a recent winter vacation, he may reply that he went skiing at Aspen for a week. If you persist in your questioning, your friend will provide you with a day-to-day account of his trip. In fact he took an eight-day trip and purchased a six-day ski permit which entitled him to ski from 9:00 A.M. to 4:30 P.M. daily. However, on Sunday he skied for three hours in the afternoon. Monday, a blizzard kept him in the ski lodge. Tuesday, Wednesday and Thursday were sunny, and he skied six hours each day. Moreover, if your friend is a typical skier, he spent one-third of the time actually skiing, one-third in lift lines and riding ski lifts, and one-third in the base area. Friday he was sick and Saturday he departed. Thus, skiing for a "week" really meant the opportunity to ski six days with only four days of actual skiing. Thus, to improve the accuracy of lift tickets issued as a measure of number of skiers, it is necessary to adjust multiple-day permits for actual days of use.

## Methods of Conversion

The previous section defined the alternative measures of the quantity of outdoor recreation consumed which are currently applied by recreation resource managers. It should be clear to the reader that no standard unit of recreation consumption has been developed thus far that is suitable for all purposes of measurement. Thus, it is important to understand the methods of conversion from one approach to another.

To convert the number of recreation visitor days to recreation days, multiply by 12 and divide by the average number of hours per recreation day. Table 3-1 (page 32) shows the standard number of hours per recreation day for National Forests in the Rocky Mountain Region and the range for all National Forests. For example, with four hours of fishing per recreation day, each 12-hour visitor day is equal to three recreation days. To convert recreation days to recreation visitor days, multiply the average number of hours per day by the number of recreation days and divide the result by 12.

To convert the number of recreation visits or trips to recreation days, multiply the former by the average number of recreation days per trip. For example, with 2.5 camping days per trip, 100 trips equal 250 recreation days of camping. To convert recreation days to trips, divide number of days by the average number of recreation days per trip.

To convert the number of visits or trips to recreation visitor days, multiply the former by the average number of recreation days per trip times the average number of hours per recreation day, then divide the result by 12 hours. For example, with 2.5 camping days per one trip multiplied by 10 hours per camping day divided by 12 hours equals 2.08 visitor days of camping. To convert recreation visitor days to number of trips, multiply the number of visitor days by 12 and divide the result by average number of hours per recreation day. Then divide by the number of days per trip.

**Table 3-1. Standard Hours per Day of Outdoor Recreation, United States**

| Hours per Day in National Forests<br>Activity | Rocky Mountain Region | Range, United States |
|---|---|---|
| Bicycling | 3.0 | 0.9 – 3.0 |
| Horseback Riding | 4.0 | 1.0 – 4.6 |
| Playing Outdoor Sports | 3.0 | 0.9 – 6.0 |
| Fishing | 3.5 | 1.9 – 4.5 |
| Canoeing | 2.0 | 2.0 – 4.1 |
| Sailing | 2.5 | 2.4 – 4.5 |
| Other Boating | 4.0 | 2.5 – 4.1 |
| Swimming | 1.5 | 0.8 – 2.9 |
| Water-Skiing | 2.0 | 0.7 – 2.6 |
| Camping | 10.5 | 9.6 – 12.0 |
| Mountain Climbing | 6.0 | 3.5 – 7.4 |
| Hiking | 4.0 | 3.2 – 4.0 |
| Walking for Pleasure | 4.0 | 3.2 – 4.0 |
| Bird-Watching | 4.0 | 1.8 – 4.0 |
| Wildlife and Bird Photography | 3.0 | 1.8 – 4.0 |
| Nature Walks | 3.0 | 0.3 – 4.7 |
| Picnicking | 2.0 | 2.0 – 4.0 |
| Driving for Pleasure | 2.5 | 1.5 – 3.2 |
| Sightseeing | 1.5 | 0.9 – 2.0 |
| Attending Outdoor Sports Events | 1.5 | 0.5 – 2.0 |
| Hunting | 4.0 | 2.3 – 7.8 |

Source: U.S. Forest Service, 1983.

Entrance permits can be treated as equivalent to number of visits or trips when adjusted for number of persons per vehicle and for the estimated number of persons who enter without a permit. The number of fishing and hunting licenses sold can be treated as the number of participants when adjusted for the number of persons who are exempt from purchase of a license. To convert number of participants to other measures, it is necessary to conduct periodic sample surveys of the number of trips per participant, days per trip, and hours per day.

The number of ski-lift tickets issued and the number of overnight stays at resort lodges can be treated as recreation days when adjusted for the estimated number of users who do not pay and those who pay but do not use the service. The number of camping permits issued can be treated as the equivalent of recreation days when adjusted for number of persons per party and the number of users who do not pay.

Since the early 1980s, the President's Office of Management and Budget required all federal recreation agencies to report total visitor hours as well as their historic measures of recreation participation. This greatly facilitates the comparison of recreation output by the federal agencies. If a central clearinghouse would collect visitor hours for state, county, and city recreation facilities, recreation economic decision makers would have available information on total public output. Similar information on private facilities would allow the decision maker to estimate the trends in total outdoor recreation and compare the public and private sectors. Preliminary estimates are that all levels of government provided nearly one-half of total outdoor recreation activities.

## Consumption Patterns

An understanding of the participation patterns of individual consumers is essential to effective recreation resource development and management decisions. Recent national surveys have established a number of distinguishing characteristics of outdoor recreation consumption. These include:

1. the proportion of the population participating in each recreation activity;
2. the number of recreation activities per participant;
3. the seasonal pattern of participation in outdoor activities;
4. the frequency of partial-day or single-day outings, two- to three-day overnight stays, and vacation trips;
5. the proportion of outdoor recreation on weekends; and
6. the hours per day of outdoor recreation.

Recent studies have shown that approximately 95% of the people 16 years of age and over participate in outdoor recreation activities in the United States. Individual consumers exhibit considerable variation in preferences. Table 3-2 (page 34) shows the proportion of the U.S. population that participates in each of several outdoor recreation activities. Over half of the population engage in walking and visiting a beach or waterside. More than 25% picnic, fish, swim, attend outdoor sports events, visit nature centers, go bird-watching or bicycling.

There is a pronounced seasonal pattern of participation in most outdoor recreation activities. As a result, the use of outdoor recreation sites is concentrated into a peak season which seldom extends beyond 120 days in length. Table 3-3 (page 36) shows the seasonal variation in the proportion of the people who participate in selected outdoor recreation activities in the United States. The summer season and, to a lesser extent, the spring and fall are preferred over winter. This is particularly true for the northern half of the United States. Areas with a temperate climate year-round such as Florida, Texas, Arizona, and Southern California, experience much less seasonal variation in participation than the rest of the nation.

Numerous studies have pointed out that a unique characteristic of the consumption of outdoor recreation is that travel is necessary to participate. It is obvious that travel time is crucial in consumer decisions to

**Table 3-2. Percent and Number of Persons 16 Years and Older Participating in Outdoor Recreation by Activity, United States, 1994–95.**

| Activity | Percent (Millions) | Number |
|---|---|---|
| **Overall Participation** | **94.5** | **189.0** |
| Running/Jogging | 26.2 | 52.5 |
| Golf | 14.8 | 29.6 |
| Tennis | 10.6 | 21.2 |
| **Outdoor Team Sports** | **23.3** | **46.7** |
| Baseball | 6.8 | 13.6 |
| Softball | 13.1 | 26.2 |
| Football | 6.8 | 13.6 |
| Basketball | 12.8 | 25.6 |
| Soccer | 4.7 | 9.4 |
| Volleyball | 14.4 | 28.8 |
| Handball | 5.6 | 11.2 |
| Yard Games | 36.9 | 73.9 |
| Visiting a Nature Center | 46.4 | 93.0 |
| Visiting a Visitor Center | 34.6 | 69.4 |
| Attending an Outdoor Concert | 20.7 | 41.5 |
| Attending an Outdoor Sports Event | 47.5 | 95.2 |
| Picnicking | 49.1 | 98.4 |
| Gathering With Family | 61.8 | 123.8 |
| **Snow and Ice Activities** | **19.4** | **38.9** |
| Ice-Skating | 5.2 | 10.4 |
| Snowboarding | 0.8 | 1.6 |
| Sledding | 10.2 | 20.4 |
| Downhill Skiing | 8.4 | 16.8 |
| Cross-Country Skiing | 3.3 | 6.6 |
| Snowmobiling | 3.5 | 7.0 |
| **Hunting** | **9.4** | **18.8** |
| Big Game | 7.1 | 14.2 |
| Small Game | 6.5 | 13.0 |
| Migratory Bird | 2.1 | 4.2 |
| **Camping (Overall)** | **26.8** | **53.7** |
| Developed Area | 20.7 | 41.5 |
| Primitive Area | 14.0 | 28.0 |
| **Fishing** | **29.1** | **58.3** |
| Freshwater | 24.4 | 48.9 |
| Warm-Water | 20.4 | 40.9 |
| Cold-Water | 10.4 | 20.8 |
| Saltwater | 9.5 | 19.0 |
| Anadromous | 4.5 | 9.0 |
| Catch and Release | 7.7 | 15.4 |
| **Boating** | **30.0** | **60.1** |
| Sailing | 4.8 | 9.6 |
| Canoeing | 6.6 | 13.2 |
| Kayaking | 0.7 | 1.4 |

**Table 3-2. Continued**

| Activity | Percent (Millions) | Number |
|---|---|---|
| Rowing | 4.2 | 8.4 |
| Floating, Rafting | 7.6 | 15.2 |
| Motorboating | 23.4 | 46.9 |
| Water-Skiing | 8.9 | 17.8 |
| Jet-Skiing | 4.7 | 9.4 |
| Sailboarding/Windsurfing | 1.1 | 2.2 |
| Surfing | 1.3 | 2.6 |
| Swimming/Pool | 44.2 | 88.5 |
| Swimming/Nonpool | 39.0 | 78.1 |
| Snorkeling | 7.2 | 14.4 |
| Visit a Prehistoric Site | 17.4 | 34.9 |
| Visit a Historic Site | 44.1 | 88.3 |
| Walking | 66.7 | 133.6 |
| Hiking | 23.8 | 47.7 |
| Orienteering | 2.4 | 4.8 |
| Backpacking | 7.6 | 15.2 |
| Mountain Climbing | 4.5 | 9.0 |
| Rock Climbing | 3.7 | 7.4 |
| Caving | 4.7 | 9.4 |
| Bird-Watching | 27.0 | 54.1 |
| Wildlife Viewing | 31.2 | 62.5 |
| Fish Viewing | 13.7 | 27.4 |
| Off-Road Driving | 13.9 | 27.8 |
| Visiting a Beach or Waterside | 62.1 | 124.4 |
| Studying Nature Near Water | 27.6 | 55.3 |
| Bicycling | 28.6 | 27.3 |
| Horseback Riding | 7.1 | 14.2 |

Source: U.S. Forest Service, 1996a.

participate in outdoor recreation. Table 3-4 (page 37) shows that most outdoor recreation activities (75%) of individual consumers occurs during a few available hours of a day within one to five miles from home, and on single-day outings within 50 miles. A much smaller proportion (25%) of outdoor recreation occurs on two- to three-day overnight trips within 100–200 miles and on vacation trips 500–1,000 miles or more from home.

This reflects the fact that most people are constrained by a fixed workday and workweek. They lack the leisure time to travel very far to engage in outdoor recreation activities during the few available evening hours of the workday. Moreover, the limited leisure time during the typical two- to three-day weekend limits travel to one to three hours one way, whether it be for single-day outings or overnight weekend trips.

Most outdoor recreation activities of individual consumers take place on weekends. Table 3-5 (page 38) shows that in the case of every activity, more than one-half of total participation occurs on weekends. For some activities, weekend participation is 75% or more—tennis, bird-watching,

**Table 3-3. Seasonal Participation in Outdoor Recreation, United States**

| Activity | Spring | Summer | Fall | Winter |
|---|---|---|---|---|
| Bicycling | 29.0% | 34.1% | 21.0% | 15.9% |
| Horseback Riding | 26.6% | 40.6% | 25.0% | 7.8% |
| Golfing | 29.7% | 40.6% | 18.7% | 10.9% |
| Tennis Outdoors | 32.2% | 32.2% | 18.6% | 16.9% |
| Outdoor Team Sports | 31.3% | 30.6% | 19.4% | 18.7% |
| Canoeing or Kayaking | 17.6% | 58.8% | 17.6% | 5.9% |
| Sailing | 28.6% | 50.0% | 14.3% | 7.1% |
| Motorboating | 25.7% | 54.3% | 14.3% | 5.7% |
| Swimming in an Outdoor | 26.4% | 58.3% | 11.1% | 4.2% |
| Other Outdoor Swimming | 20.8% | 62.5% | 6.3% | 10.4% |
| Fishing | 38.0% | 36.0% | 14.0% | 12.0% |
| Hunting | 13.6% | 11.4% | 50.0% | 25.0% |
| Backpacking | 29.6% | 44.4% | 18.5% | 7.4% |
| Camping in Developed Campground | 19.4% | 48.4% | 19.4% | 12.9% |
| Camping in Primitive Campground | 21.4% | 50.0% | 17.9% | 10.7% |
| Other Camping | 21.7% | 47.8% | 17.4% | 13.0% |
| Day Hiking | 26.4% | 34.0% | 22.6% | 17.0% |
| Bird-Watching/Nature Study | 32.7% | 25.2% | 22.2% | 19.9% |
| Driving Off-Road Vehicles | 27.8% | 35.4% | 17.7% | 19.0% |
| Downhill Skiing | 10.0% | 5.0% | 15.0% | 70.0% |
| Cross-Country Skiing | 7.1% | 0.0% | 14.3% | 78.6% |
| Snowmobiling | 16.7% | 0.0% | 5.6% | 77.8% |

Source: National Park Service, 1983.

and sailing. Weekends also account for 70% of the nature walks and 80% of the camping in remote or wilderness areas. This means that average daily use of recreation resources on Saturday or Sunday exceeds average daily use on Monday through Friday by more than 2.5 times.

Weekend recreation behavior reflects the fact that most people are constrained by a fixed workweek and receive paid vacations of one to four weeks per year. Most outdoor recreation occurs during periods when no working time is lost. The resulting peak-day demand on weekends and holidays requires that much more recreation resource capacity be developed than would be necessary if the consumption of outdoor recreation activities were more constant through time. As a result of existing consumption patterns, there is usually a large amount of excess capacity of recreation resources on weekdays.

With the exception of camping, no outdoor recreation activity averages more than five hours per recreation day. For example, Table 3-5 (page 38) shows that picnicking averages 2.7 hours per recreation day.

**Table 3-4. Type of Occasion for Outdoor Recreation, United States**

| | Percent of Annual Participation | | | |
|---|---|---|---|---|
| | Vacations | 2- to 3-Day Overnight Trips | Single-Day Outings | Few Available Hours |
| **Total** | **13%** | **12%** | **52%** | **23%** |
| Bicycling | 10 | 6 | 14 | 70 |
| Horseback Riding | 15 | 9 | 28 | 48 |
| Playing Sports | 9 | 8 | 49 | 34 |
| Golf | 13 | 9 | 31 | 47 |
| Tennis | 8 | 9 | 32 | 51 |
| Fishing | 12 | 20 | 49 | 19 |
| Canoeing | 19 | 35 | 27 | 19 |
| Sailing | 19 | 19 | 46 | 16 |
| Swimming | 10 | 11 | 64 | 15 |
| Ocean | 11 | 8 | 72 | 9 |
| Freshwater | 10 | 15 | 62 | 13 |
| Pool | 13 | 5 | 48 | 34 |
| Water-Skiing | 10 | 20 | 59 | 11 |
| Camping | 35 | 65 | n.a. | n.a. |
| Mountain Climbing | 24 | 13 | 46 | 17 |
| Hiking | 20 | 18 | 42 | 20 |
| Walking for Pleasure | 16 | 12 | 46 | 26 |
| Bird-Watching | 14 | 15 | 43 | 28 |
| Wildlife and Bird Photography | 32 | 6 | 43 | 19 |
| Nature Walks | 18 | 15 | 48 | 19 |
| Picnicking | 7 | 6 | 73 | 14 |
| Driving for Pleasure | 16 | 8 | 41 | 35 |
| Sightseeing | 25 | 10 | 47 | 18 |
| Attending Outdoor Sports Events | 10 | 6 | 28 | 56 |
| Hunting | 10 | 22 | 20 | 48 |

n.a. = not applicable.

Source: Bureau of Outdoor Recreation, 1973b.

For the most part, picnicking trips would be combined with other activities such as sightseeing (3.1 hours per day), playing outdoor games or sports (2.6 hours), and outdoor swimming (2.6 hours). Thus, an individual consumer typically combines several activities while on a single trip. In the above example, the four activities total 11.0 hours which is nearly the equivalent of one recreation visitor day.

The measures of the quantity of recreation consumption introduced in this chapter are also used in empirical demand estimation. We shall refer to this material when we look at demand studies in Chapter 5.

**Table 3-5. Hours per Day and Weekend Participation in Outdoor Recreation, United States**

| | Percent of Total Activity Occurring on Weekends | Average Number of Hours of Participation per Activity Day |
|---|---|---|
| Picnicking | 71 | 2.7 |
| Sightseeing | 62 | 3.1 |
| Walking for Pleasure | 64 | 1.9 |
| Visiting Zoos, Fairs, Amusement Parks | 55 | 4.5 |
| Fishing | 68 | 4.4 |
| Playing Other Outdoor Games or Sports | 65 | 2.6 |
| Outdoor Pool Swimming | 52 | 2.8 |
| Nature Walks | 70 | 2.0 |
| Other Boating | 74 | 2.8 |
| Going to Outdoor Sports Events | 57 | 4.2 |
| Camping in Campgrounds | 62 | 12.0 |
| Bicycling | 69 | 2.0 |
| Going to Outdoor Concerts, Plays | 66 | 3.6 |
| Horseback Riding | 51 | 2.7 |
| Hiking With a Pack and Rock Climbing | 62 | 3.0 |
| Tennis | 79 | 2.1 |
| Water-Skiing | 69 | 2.6 |
| Golf | 51 | 4.9 |
| Camping in Remote or Wilderness Areas | 80 | 12.0 |
| Riding Motorcycles Off-Road | 62 | 4.0 |
| Bird-Watching | 75 | 2.1 |
| Canoeing | 72 | 2.3 |
| Sailing | 75 | 4.4 |
| Hunting | 64 | 4.4 |
| Wildlife and Bird Photography | 56 | 1.6 |
| Driving Four-Wheel-Drive Vehicles Off-Road | 56 | 3.1 |

Source: Bureau of Outdoor Recreation, 1973b.

## Psychology of Recreation Benefits

Outdoor recreation activities are valued because they provide pleasure to individual participants. Lancaster (1966) believes that demand is related to the characteristics of what is consumed. Activities with different characteristics vary in their capacity to satisfy our basic psychological needs and desires. The psychology of recreation benefits has been studied by a number of social scientists, most notably Driver and Brown (1975) as well as Hendee, Gale and Catton (1971). Such investigations provide evidence for the classification of outdoor recreation activities according to differences in the psychological motivation of individual participants. These include active, passive, extractive, appreciative, social, and learning motives. Each of these motivations is probably shared by all participants, but some are relatively more important for particular activities than are others.

Active outdoor recreation involves physically strenuous exercise, which heightens psychological stimulation, excitement, and benefits, according to studies reviewed by Scitovsky (1976). Active outdoor recreation includes jogging, bicycling, playing outdoor games, tennis, golf, driving off-road vehicles, snow skiing, swimming, water-skiing, boat racing, and snowmobiling. Number of users is limited by the capacity of facilities.

Passive outdoor recreation requires relatively little physical effort, and the emphasis is on individual comfort. Relaxation after overstimulation from work is an important part of balanced living. Thus, willingness to pay for the opportunity to relax outdoors may be substantial. Passive activities include attending outdoor sports events, concerts, and plays; relaxing and reading outdoors; sunbathing; trailer and motor-home camping; sightseeing by car or tour bus; and quiet boating and canoeing. Participants also are likely to attend interpretive programs. Managers providing opportunities for these types of outdoor recreation should develop convenient facilities to assure the comfort of participants. A natural environment may contribute, but it is usually not required. Daily use of facilities can be high, as participants expect to be part of a crowd.

Extractive outdoor recreation involves harvesting the bounty of nature. Psychological satisfaction from consumptive activities is related to the number and size or uniqueness of the trophy, which is symbolic of the skill of the individual participant. Extractive activities include fishing; hunting; and collecting rocks, shells, edible plants, driftwood and firewood. Individuals may pay for hunting and fishing licenses and for travel costs, and purchase equipment such as fishing tackle, guns, chain saws, guidebooks, and special clothing. A sizable state fish and game management program is required, as is an extensive natural or seminatural habitat. The development of recreation facilities can be minimal. Even with stocking programs, biological carrying capacity is limited, requiring that the number of users be limited.

Appreciative outdoor recreation involves viewing the natural beauty of the environment. Psychological satisfaction from nonconsumptive activities is related to individual knowledge and sensitivity to wildlife, geology, plants, color and natural form. Appreciative activities include hiking, backpacking, horseback riding in natural areas, mountain climbing, bird-watching, nature study, and photography. Some of these activities also involve physically strenuous exercise. Development of recreation facilities should be limited to trails and toilets, as appreciative users prefer to experience nature on foot or horseback rather than through the window of a restaurant, lodge, car, bus or train. Resource managers may provide interpretive programs. The manager's primary role should be preserving the natural environment by protecting air and water quality, controlling forest fires, restricting hunting, and maintaining relatively low user density.

Social interaction and learning includes visiting with family and friends; learning about nature and history; and acquiring special recreation skills by attending lectures, demonstrations and exhibits. Social interaction is a part of virtually all outdoor recreation activity in some degree. A stimulating conversation is the principal source of pleasure for some individuals. Social interaction includes visiting with family and friends while engaged in picnicking, camping, nature walks, and playing outdoor games such as volleyball, shuffleboard and horseshoes. A natural environment is not required.

Like beauty, what is a benefit of recreation to one person, may not be to another. Whatever the form of recreation benefits, whether stimulation or relaxation, trade-offs in natural resource management and competition for limited agency funds require that these benefits be put in dollar terms. This is a topic we turn to in Chapter 5.

# *Chapter 4*

# Direct Cost or Price

This chapter defines several alternative concepts of the price of outdoor recreation; describes when alternative measures of price can be used; discusses recent pricing patterns for outdoor recreation goods and services and their implications for recreation economic decisions.

Outdoor recreation poses a unique problem of defining a realistic proxy for price. Visits to most outdoor recreation sites are not priced in any market. Most public outdoor recreation is a nonmarket service provided free of any appreciable entrance fee or price in the usual sense. However, this does not mean that outdoor recreation activities do not have a price or exchange value. Individual consumers incur expenses such as travel and time costs. The sum of direct monetary and nonmonetary costs is a reasonable proxy for the price of outdoor recreation. The fact that these expenses are not uniform and are paid to a number of different businesses should not distract from the fact that, together, they constitute the necessary costs or price of outdoor recreation. The price of any good or service has two parts, a transaction cost and purchase price. Travel cost is considered a part of transaction costs, thus the unique feature of outdoor recreation is that transaction costs represent a larger part of direct cost or price.

## Alternative Measures of Price

Several approaches have been used in an attempt to develop a reasonably accurate proxy for the price of outdoor recreation. These include:

1. entrance fees and permits;
2. transportation costs, including fuel, tires, and repairs;
3. travel time costs, the dissatisfaction of driving;

4. opportunity cost of recreation time at the site;
5. on-site costs including lodging, added food and other consumable supplies; and
6. fixed costs of annual licenses and recreation equipment amortized over the expected period of use.

While any one of these approaches or a combination of approaches may provide a satisfactory measure of the price of a particular outdoor recreation activity, a problem arises when the results of two or more approaches are compared. Thus far, no standard proxy for the price of outdoor recreation has been developed that is suitable for all purposes of measurement. So, it is important to understand when each measure should be used and how to convert the results of each approach to compare it with other measures. Accuracy in defining price is particularly important for estimating the demand curve for outdoor recreation.

## *Entrance Fees*

An entrance fee is defined as the price of admission to a recreation site or event, entitling the purchaser to participate in a recreation activity for a specified length of time on a particular date. This is the most clearly understood aspect of the price of outdoor recreation. For example, an individual consumer who contemplates attending an outdoor concert, play, or sports event asks about the availability of tickets and the price of admission. The same is true, to a somewhat lesser extent, for going swimming or golfing, camping in developed campgrounds, downhill skiing, or visiting a zoo, amusement park, state or National Park, and the like. Usually there are no entrance fees involved in individual decisions to go sightseeing, riding a bicycle, camping in the backcountry or at undeveloped sites, walking for pleasure, picnicking or playing games in a city park, and bird-watching. If these recreation activities take place at a private recreation site, an entrance fee may be charged by the landowner or operator.

Entrance fees have provided a satisfactory measure of the price of outdoor recreation where participation requires little or no travel and other out-of-pocket costs. Examples are the recreation activities and events that take place in the neighborhood where individuals live. Other examples are recreation activities and events more distant from home where the entrance fee constitutes payment for a package of services which includes the provision of travel by bus to and from the site plus other on-site costs such as for food and incidental expenses.

By itself, the entrance fee approach has not provided a satisfactory measure of the price of most outdoor recreation, because it does not include other expenditures required to participate in most outdoor recreation activities. Travel is nearly always necessary, as are other on-site expenditures. As a result, the out-of-pocket cost of outdoor recreation usually exceeds the entrance fee, in most cases substantially as will be shown in the following section.

Problems arise when a basic entrance fee is uniformly assigned to all individual participants. Basic camping fees may vary with the quality of service such as hookups, location of the campsite (e.g., near a river or lake), number of persons, and number of nights. Individual consumers of outdoor recreation are willing to pay higher entrance fees for an 18-hole golf course rather than for a nine-hole course, all day ski-lift tickets rather than a half-day ticket and so forth. Tickets to outdoor athletic contests vary in price with nearness to the playing area and quality of the view. Entrance fees are often discounted during off-seasons and on weekdays. In addition, persons over 65 and under 12 years of age may be admitted free or at reduced rates.

## *Transportation Costs*

Travel costs are defined by the U.S. Water Resources Council as a proxy for the money price of outdoor recreation. Direct travel costs are the variable or out-of-pocket costs of operating an automobile. These include the average cost per mile of maintenance, parts, tires, gasoline, oil, and gas taxes. These are proposed as the costs that potential users would be most aware of when making a decision about whether to visit a recreation site. Such fixed costs as depreciation, insurance, and registration are not included, as these would generally not affect the individual consumer's decision to travel additional miles to recreation sites. Because most individual consumers already own an automobile and intend to continue to own and operate it, the relevant question is "what do additional miles of recreation travel cost?" Although the individual consumer may consider gasoline the only short-run out-of-pocket expense for a particular recreation trip, it may well be true that increasing the number of miles driven will also increase expenditures for maintenance such as lubrication, oil changes, tune-ups, general repairs, and tires.

Distance traveled is converted to dollar values by multiplying round-trip miles to and from the recreation site by average direct cost per mile and dividing by the number of users per vehicle to determine per capita travel cost. Any user charges or entrance fees are added to the cost.

Problems in defining cost can arise when trips to urban and National Parks include travel by cycle, bus, train or plane, in addition to private auto. Epperson estimates that roughly 20% of outdoor recreation travel is by means other than the private auto, with varying mileage costs. Moreover, auto travel costs tend to vary among individual users, depending on driving habits, the type and condition of the vehicle, and whether a trailer is being towed. Such information can be collected by directly interviewing visitors or sending them a questionnaire. This allows for individual variations in travel cost. Sample survey information also could enable travel costs to be allocated among recreation activities, such as sightseeing, fishing, and camping, by an individual on a single trip.

## *Travel Time Costs*

Travel and recreation time costs have been defined by the U.S. Water Resources Council (1983) as the opportunity cost of work or leisure activities that are foregone for travel to and recreation at the site. For individuals whose work time is variable, the opportunity cost should be measured as income foregone. Most people, however, are constrained by a fixed workweek and receive paid vacation days. Individuals who travel and recreate during weekends and vacations when no working time is lost incur only leisure time costs. This value may range between zero and the individual's wage rate. Leisure time costs are zero if individuals would not have engaged in any other leisure activity had they not taken the trip. Leisure time costs would equal the individual's wage rate if the alternative leisure activity were valuable enough to forego earnings, given the opportunity. Both travel and on-site time costs can be added to direct travel costs to determine the total or full price of a recreation visit. However, the preferable approach is to include them as separate independent variables in the demand function.

Including time costs has improved estimates of the price of outdoor recreation. Before 1970, the use of direct travel costs (and entrance fees) alone as a proxy for price ignored the effects of time on recreation decisions. Demand schedules were constructed under the hypothesis that increasing distance decreased use only because of higher monetary cost of travel. Exclusion of the opportunity cost of time introduced a bias resulting in the underestimation of the price and value of outdoor recreation. The nonmonetary cost of additional time required to travel increased distances to recreation sites would seem to be, for some individuals, a deterrent equal to or greater than out-of-pocket money costs.

Until recently, direct survey data on travel and recreation time costs have not been available. Thus, the U.S. Water Resources Council (1983) relied on commuter studies in its recommendation that travel time may be valued as one-third of the wage rate for adults and one-fourth of the adult value for children. For example, the average wage rate would be roughly $12 per hour for individuals receiving $24,000 for 240 eight-hour workdays per year. With two adults and one child in a typical party, recreation travel time cost would be estimated as $4 per hour for each adult and $1 for the child, or an average individual travel time cost of $3 per hour. On this basis, a round trip of 90 miles at 45 miles per hour would have average travel time costs of $6 (= 2 hours x $3) per person. It should be noted that this procedure is not applicable to the problem of estimating the opportunity cost of on-site time. It is designed to estimate average travel time costs for users grouped by distance zones or counties in applications of the zonal travel cost method where limited information is available on individual users.

Problems may arise in valuing travel time in terms of a constant foregone earning per hour traveled. The procedure approved by the Water Resources Council was derived from work by Cesario (1976) who reviewed several studies of the value of travel time to commuters on journeys to work in urban areas. Recreation travel usually involves distinctly different circumstances from work travel. With work travel commuters are required to travel to a destination not of their own choosing, often during peak, rush-hour traffic. Recreation travel, on the other hand, is a discretionary leisure time activity. The route, time of departure and destination may be chosen to provide a positive value of travel time.

For example, results of some household recreation surveys in the northwestern United States and Colorado suggest a majority of recreationists enjoyed the travel time on their last trip and were not willing to pay to reduce it. To them, travel time was not a cost and perhaps even had a positive value over the primarily short trips, averaging 30–50 miles from the point of origin to water-based recreation sites for fishing, boating, and swimming; camping trips averaging about 100 miles one way in the scenic Northwest or Colorado. However, it is likely that travel time costs per hour may increase with travel distance.

Wilman (1980) supported the Council's guidelines with respect to valuing on-site recreation time in terms of the opportunity cost of time in its best alternative use. However, she proposed that travel time be valued as the difference between the beneficial value of time and its opportunity cost. This would be equivalent to valuing travel time on the basis of individual willingness to pay to reduce it. Direct surveys could determine what portion of individual travel time is in fact, beneficial sightseeing activity and what part represents a cost. That portion of travel time that is enjoyable in itself because of roadside scenery would be attributed to sightseeing activity as would an identical portion of travel costs. The sightseeing portion of travel and time costs would be deducted from total travel and time cost of the trip to determine the price of on-site recreation activity at the destination.

Studies of outdoor recreation in the Rocky Mountains of the United States indicate that sightseeing is the primary purpose of nearly 40% of recreation travel, and a secondary purpose of 25% of travel to recreation sites for fishing, boating, hiking, backpacking, camping, and picnicking. Most households consider travel time either as a benefit or of zero value. Forty-two percent reported they were willing to pay for additional travel time on trips to rivers. Fifty percent were not willing to pay either to gain or to avoid an increment in travel time. Only 8% indicated that travel time was a cost, reporting that they were willing to pay to avoid it. However, a substantial amount of recreation travel tends to be destination-oriented, with travel time primarily a disutility. Many studies have found the vast majority of the travel by anglers and hunters is for the single purpose of fishing or hunting. The remaining hunters reported other purposes such as sightseeing, visits with relatives and friends, and business activities. Horvath (1973) reported that southeastern United States resident anglers rated travel time as the most important factor in their choice of where to fish, followed by the abundance of fish, and low angler population densities at the site.

## On-Site Costs

On-site costs are the added expenditures that the consumer must incur to allow them to stay at the recreation site. For those staying in lodges or hotels at or near the site, on-site costs are often a large part of the overall trip costs. Some of these may have been paid prior to the trip, such as prepaid hotel reservations, purchase of bait, film, and ice. These costs would not have been incurred had the trip to the site not been undertaken. Any food costs over and above what would have been consumed at home had the trip not been undertaken would usually be considered on-site costs as well. While these purchases may be from different types of stores, in different locations (i.e., at home, en route, at the site), that should not detract from the essential nature of the monetary price paid to visit the site.

The approach facilitates the separation of travel costs from on-site costs. Once the travel costs have been incurred for getting to a site, some individual users may consider them as sunk, and their decision about how long to stay may depend solely upon the on-site costs of an additional day. However, most recreation trips are preplanned, and the length of stay is constrained by available leisure time. Generally the relevant concept of price includes all out-of-pocket costs of the trip combined into a single variable.

## Perceived Versus Objective Measures of Costs

A problem may arise when the direct cost or price perceived by individual consumers differs from the economic definition of price. For example, some consumers may understate their cost of transportation on a recreation trip by considering their only out-of-pocket automobile cost to be for gasoline. However, increasing the number of miles driven on a recreation trip will also increase expenditures for lubrication, oil changes, tune-ups, repairs, and tires. Thus, the economic definition of direct cost or price includes these other auto costs. However, consumers have difficulty allocating such costs to short-run trips. The same is true for the allocation of the costs of fishing and hunting licenses that entitle the individual to multiple trips and/or days of use per year.

Along the same lines, some consumers of outdoor recreation may consider all out-of-pocket costs of food and beverage, in particular restaurant meals, as part of the direct cost or price of a trip to a recreation site. The economic definition of the price of a recreation trip would exclude that portion of food and beverage expenditures equivalent to what would have been spent for these items at home.

The U.S. Bureau of Labor Statistics (1996) reports that food and beverage expenditures equal 12% of annual household income. For example, for a household of 2.6 persons reporting annual income of $50,000, approximately $5 per person would be subtracted from daily expenditures of

$20 for food and beverage on the recreation trip. Thus, only $15 of additional expenditure for groceries and restaurant meals should be included as part of the direct cost or price of outdoor recreation.

Difficulties arise when the approach is used to measure the price of a single recreation activity at a site when the trip is multipurpose or multidestination. A similar problem would occur in applying the travel cost method (Chapter 9) where transportation costs must be allocated to each site visited on the trip. It is necessary to allocate the costs of lodging, added food and beverage, entrance fees, and consumable supplies among the recreation sites visited. When sample survey information is available, all trip costs can be assigned to sites based on the reported perception of individual consumers.

## *Fixed Costs*

Fixed costs are defined as the costs of consumer investment in durable recreation equipment and annual costs such as licenses over the period of use. Fixed costs include (1) cost of investments in durable recreation equipment such as boats, fishing gear, skis, special clothing, tents, camping gear, sporting equipment, binoculars, cameras, and seasonal homes; and (2) annual costs of fishing, hunting, and other licenses, insurance, and taxes that are the same regardless of the number of recreation trips.

The concept of fixed cost applies to consumer decisions to purchase durable recreation equipment. Thus, it is applicable to consumer decisions to begin participating in a recreation activity, where the purchase of durable equipment is often necessary in order to participate at all. It is also applicable to consumer decisions to continue participating in a recreation activity on those infrequent occasions when equipment owned wears out or becomes obsolete and the decision becomes whether to replace it with new or used equipment in order to continue participating. However, it is important to remember that the concept of fixed cost is not applicable to consumer decisions to take an additional trip to a recreation site. Thus, it would be unrealistic to consider fixed costs as part of the direct costs or price of outdoor recreation.

## *Short-Run and Long-Run Costs*

The price of outdoor recreation in the short run is defined as the direct or variable costs associated with taking an additional trip within a single year. These include travel costs to and from the recreation site, expenditures on consumable services and supplies while at the site, the opportunity cost of recreation time, and the disutility of travel time. Decisions to take an additional recreation trip are based on those direct costs that change as the number of trips is varied (and other variables such as income, age, quality of the site, price and availability of substitutes). In the short run, individual consumers will continue to visit a recreation site until their added benefits equal the additional short-run costs.

The price of outdoor recreation in the long run is defined as the total costs associated with the decision to participate one or more additional years. Decision making is distinguished by the fact that all costs become variable in the long run. In addition to the direct costs associated with recreation trips, the long-run concept of price includes fixed costs of (1) the vehicle and other recreation equipment annualized as depreciation and the opportunity costs of the investment, and (2) the annual expenditures such as for licenses, insurance, and taxes, that must be paid regardless of the number of trips.

The concept of long-run price applies to consumer decisions on whether to begin participating in a recreation activity and whether to continue participating from year to year. In the long run, consumers of outdoor recreation must decide whether to replace recreation equipment as it wears out or becomes obsolete. They must also decide at the beginning of each year whether to continue to incur the cost of licenses, insurance and taxes that must be paid if they are to use their equipment and continue to engage in particular outdoor recreation activities. Individual consumers will participate in outdoor recreation if their anticipated benefits equal or exceed total costs in the long run. Otherwise, consumers would not replace durable equipment when it wears out or becomes obsolete, and they would decide to discontinue the recreation activity. As would be expected, long-run price is considerably higher than short-run price. A number of studies show that the long-run price of these activities is more than double the short-run price.

## Price Patterns

An understanding of the variation in prices actually paid by individual consumers is essential to making accurate recreation use forecasts and estimating recreation demand. What to include in price depends on the analysis to be performed. The general rule is to include all expenses that increase as a result of a decision to take a recreation trip.

When a family goes to the beach for a weekend, it spends money on gasoline and maintenance of the car, on additional food at restaurants and grocery stores, on entrance fees, on entertainment at the boardwalk, on suntan lotion, souvenirs, and the like. It also may pay for one to two nights lodging in a motel, hotel, resort lodge, or campground.

The fact that these expenditures are paid to many different businesses should not detract from the conclusion that together they constitute the necessary direct costs or price of outdoor recreation. Combined, these expenditures are no less the price than expenditures paid in a lump sum to a travel agent for a package plan which may include transportation, lodging, food, and entrance fees. In addition, a nonmonetary cost may be incurred related to the dissatisfaction of driving, and there may be an opportunity cost of wages foregone to participate in outdoor recreation. Any individual time cost would be added to the monetary costs of the trip.

The price per day of outdoor recreation is often more dependent on choice of lodging than most other variables in automobile trips. Overnight lodging is the largest single expense for nearly one-third of individual consumers who stay in commercial lodging accommodations. Wilman suggests that the decision to stay overnight in commercial accommodations at a resort area is based on the relative costs of the overnight lodging compared to the monetary and time costs of traveling home and back again in the morning. Nearly 20% stay overnight in campgrounds, hiking shelters, recreation vehicles, water craft, or personal vacation homes and condominiums. Approximately 47% of participants stay at home or with friends and relatives at little or no expense other than food which also may be provided by friends and relatives.

As shown in Table 4-1, lodging and added food expenditures together account for half of the price of outdoor recreation, although this is highly variable among individuals. Transportation costs and entrance fees together account for only about one-fifth of the price of outdoor recreation. Expenditures for a variety of consumable retail products and services constitute an important part of the price of outdoor recreation. In fact, these items together account for a larger share of the direct costs of outdoor recreation than do transportation costs and entrance fees.

## *Seasonal Price Variation*

Seasonal price variation is common in resort communities which supply recreation lodging services. As a general rule, whenever there is a large variation in seasonal demand for services, businesses will charge higher prices when demand is greatest. In effect, businesses surcharge customers during the peak season a premium price sufficient to cover fixed overhead costs and profits. They will continue to supply services during the rest of the year at a price sufficient to cover direct operating costs. If not, they will shut down during part of the year.

**Table 4-1. Distribution of Expenditures on Recreation Travel, United States**

| Category | Percent |
|---|---|
| Lodging | 23 |
| Food and Beverage | 27 |
| Recreation Entrance Fees | 12 |
| Transportation | 9 |
| Clothing and Footwear | 11 |
| Jewelry and Souvenirs | 7 |
| Drugs, Cosmetics and Tobacco | 7 |
| Miscellaneous | 4 |
| Total | 100 |

Source: Adapted from Epperson, 1977.

Individual consumers are willing to pay higher prices during peak seasons because their benefits are higher when conditions for outdoor recreation are most favorable. For most winter resorts, the high-price season is from December 15 to April 16, which coincides with favorable ski conditions. For example, a four-star lodge at Vail charges more than twice as much per night during the ski season than during the balance of the year. For summer resorts, the high-price season is from May 1 to September 15. For example, the five-star Broadmoor at Colorado Springs charges nearly twice as much per night during the summer than during the winter.

## *Entrance Fees*

In the past, entrance to most public parks and recreation facilities was free. For example, the National Park Service charged no entrance fees at nearly 300 national monuments and historic sites and typically $4 to $5 per vehicle or party at major National Parks and recreation areas such as Rocky Mountain National Park, Mount Rainier, Arches, and Natural Bridges. It may be efficient to allow free admission to parks where fees generate less than $25,000 per year, as costs of collection are likely to exceed the revenue collected. One study showed that of 49 National Parks that charged an entrance fee, 45% that charged $1 per vehicle had fee receipts of less than $25,000 per year. Free admission to these parks would reduce revenues by only 3.6% of total entrance fee revenues of the agency.

Most individuals have used recreation resources administered by the U.S. government without payment of entrance fees. The U.S. Forest Service, U.S. Bureau of Reclamation and U.S. Fish and Wildlife Service charge no entrance fees for admission to the National Forests, Wilderness Areas, recreation areas, wildlife refuges, and reservoirs which these agencies administer. Fees were charged per campsite with other charges for services such as boat-docking facilities.

While entrance to city parks has remained free for the most part, the charge for use of recreation facilities such as swimming pools, zoos, tennis courts and golf courses within city parks has increased in recent years. Although such fees are generally small, they may deter the participation of low-income people and the costs of collection represent a significant proportion of the revenue collected. Huszar and Seckler (1974) have reported on problems after an entrance fee was first charged at the California Academy of Sciences in Golden Gate State Park, San Francisco. The installation of a $0.50 entrance fee for adults and $0.25 for children over 12 raised net revenue of $0.3 million in the first year, and eliminated an operating deficit. However, the estimated loss in visitor benefits of those who were not admitted because they were unwilling or unable to pay the fees was estimated as $0.4 million, or one-third more than the fee revenues generated. Thus, social welfare declined when a fee was charged for admission. They concluded that charging a fee for admission to museums is undesirable and not economically efficient, although it may be a better alternative than closing museums when general tax revenues and donations are insufficient to cover operation costs, in this case $1.7 million per year.

Nearly all state and local units of government have now initiated or increased entrance fees to recreational areas. Most states and counties charge entrance fees of $3–5 per vehicle or party at public parks and reservoirs which they administer.

States own the wildlife in the United States and collect license fees for hunting and fishing, whether on public or private land. Price discrimination between residents and nonresidents of states has been a controversial issue which remains unresolved. Public access to private land for purposes of outdoor recreation is a problem which is partially resolved by the payment of entrance fees and/or compensation for damages.

It is common for city park and recreation departments to offer tennis, golf, swimming, and ice-skating at a nominal or low fee compared with commercial facilities offering these same opportunities in resort areas. It should be noted that many of the popular outdoor recreation activities are not shown in Table 4-2. These include, among others, picnicking, sightseeing, driving for pleasure, walking for pleasure, and playing outdoor sports, all of which are available without payment of an entrance fee.

The charge per day of skiing, golf, river raft trips, jeep tours and other privately supplied recreation is shown in Table 4-2. These charges are minimal for swimming pools and ice rinks and substantial for rafting and golf. However, given that the hours of participation in the activity are also variable, there is slightly more uniformity in the cost per hour.

**Table 4-2. Prices and Fees for Selected Recreation Activities**

| Activity | Entrance Fee (Dollars) | Hours per Day | Dollars per Hour |
|---|---|---|---|
| Tennis | 0.00 – 16.00 | 2 | 0.00 – 8.00 |
| Golf | 12.00 –180.00 | 4 | 3.00 – 45.00 |
| Downhill Skiing | 30.00 – 54.00 | 6 | 5.00 – 9.00 |
| Ice-Skating | 0.00 – 5.00 | 2 | 0.00 – 2.50 |
| Swimming | 0.00 – 5.00 | 2 | 0.00 – 2.50 |
| 1 Day River Rafting | 45.00 – 95.00 | 6 | 7.50 – 15.83 |
| 2+ Days River Rafting | 123.00 –180.00 | 12 | 10.00 – 15.00 |
| Jeep Tours | 45.00 – 60.00 | 5 | 9.00 – 12.00 |
| Guided Mountain Biking | 40.00 – 75.00 | 4 | 10.00 – 18.75 |
| Attend Professional Baseball | 10.00 – 25.00 | 3 | 3.33 – 8.33 |
| Attend Professional Football | 25.00 – 35.00 | 3 | 8.33 – 11.66 |
| Attend College Football | 16.00 – 18.00 | 3 | 5.33 – 6.00 |
| Amusement Parks | 20.00 – 31.00 | 6 | 3.33 – 5.16 |

**Table 4-3. Average Variable Costs per Mile to Operate an Automobile in the United States, 1995**

| Type of Automobile | Variable Costs, Cents per Mile: Accessories, Repairs | Maintenance, Gasoline and Oil | Tires | Total |
|---|---|---|---|---|
| Standard | 2.8 | 6.6 | 1.4 | 10.8 |
| Compact | 2.6 | 6.0 | 1.4 | 10.0 |
| Subcompact | 2.4 | 4.8 | 0.9 | 8.1 |
| Average | 2.6 | 5.8 | 1.2 | 9.6 |

Source: Adapted from American Automobile Association, 1995.

## *Transportation Costs*

Table 4-3 (page 52) illustrates the costs of operating standard (e.g., large), compact (e.g., medium) and subcompact (e.g., small) automobiles in the United States. Average direct costs were estimated as $0.096 per mile in 1995 according to the American Automobile Association. Included are the variable costs of gasoline, oil, maintenance, repairs, tires, and taxes on these items. Over time, both gasoline prices and the fuel efficiency of the vehicle influence the cost per mile of operation. In addition, one needs to consider the effect of inflation on the posted price of gasoline. For example, if gas sells for $1 in 1990 and $2 in the year 2000, have the real or relative gasoline prices doubled? Not really, if the cost of all other goods (i.e., the overall price level or inflation) has also doubled, the real price of gasoline relative to other goods has stayed at $1. This is an important concept to remember when comparing the effect of gasoline prices on recreation visitation over time. To account for inflation, economists often "deflate" the posted price of gasoline by dividing it by the Consumer Price Index (CPI). Not included are the fixed costs of auto ownership, such as depreciation, insurance, and registration, which were an additional $0.41 per mile in 1995 according to the American Automobile Association.

Problems arise in application of these average variable costs of suburban-based auto travel to outdoor recreation travel. Gasoline prices and repair costs vary among regions and are typically higher on the Interstate Highway System and in parks and resort areas.

In addition, the variable costs of operating four-wheel-drive sport utility vehicles (e.g., Jeep, Chevy Blazer, Toyota 4-Runner) and minivans are omitted from the average variable costs calculated above. Most four-wheel-drive vehicle and van costs are much higher than the costs of passenger cars. Further, many vehicles used for recreation also include camper-pickups, recreation vehicles, and standard autos pulling a camper trailer. Thus even using the cost of a standard size vehicle may underestimate the costs per mile for many cars used by recreationists. To overcome this problem it is often advisable to survey visitors about their transportation costs.

Table 4-4 illustrates the round-trip miles traveled to participate in outdoor recreation activities in the central eastern region of the United States. The average out-of-pocket cost of transportation can be estimated using the figures in Table 4-3 or more recent figures available from the American Automobile Association. To calculate a cost per person, it is important to divide by the typical number of people per vehicle.

Table 4-5 (page 54) illustrates the range in round-trip miles traveled to participate in outdoor recreation in the United States. Nearly two-thirds of single-day trips are 50 miles or less. Twenty-two percent of single-day trips are 51–100 miles and 15% are over 100 miles.

**Table 4-4. Round-Trip Miles Traveled to Participate in Outdoor Recreation Activities, Maryland**

| Activity | Miles per Trip |
|---|---|
| Camping | 239 |
| Canoeing, Kayaking, River Running | 85 |
| Sailing | 59 |
| Water-Skiing | 93 |
| Other Boating | 93 |
| Fishing | 98 |
| Nature Walks, Bird-Watching, Photography | 26 |
| Outdoor Pool Swimming | 22 |
| Other Outdoor Swimming | 218 |
| Hiking or Backpacking | 60 |
| Other Walking for Pleasure | 5 |
| Jogging, Running | 3 |
| Bicycling | 11 |
| Horseback Riding | 62 |
| Driving Off-Road Vehicles | 61 |
| Hunting | 88 |
| Picnicking | 39 |
| Golfing | 48 |
| Tennis Outdoors | 9 |
| Skiing, Downhill and Cross-Country | 156 |
| Ice-Skating, Lake or Pond | 9 |
| Sledding, Tobogganing | 22 |
| Playing Softball, Baseball | 14 |
| Skateboarding | 9 |
| Archery | 24 |
| Sightseeing | 152 |
| Driving for Pleasure | 89 |
| Attend Outdoor Sports Events | 28 |
| Attend Outdoor Concerts, Plays | 39 |

Source: Heritage Conservation and Recreation Service, 1980.

**Table 4-5. Distribution of Round-Trip Miles per Trip to Participate in Outdoor Recreation, United States**

| Miles | Vacations | Overnights | Day Outings |
|---|---|---|---|
| 50 or less | 2% | 14% | 63% |
| 51–100 | 3 | 21 | 22 |
| 101–250 | 13 | 30 | 15[a] |
| 251–500 | 22 | 24 | n.a. |
| 501–1,000 | 25 | 9 | n.a. |
| Over 1,000 | 35 | 2 | n.a. |
| **Miles** | | | |
| Average Miles | 1,285 | 253 | 62 |
| Median Miles | 705 | 174 | 37 |

[a]Over 100 miles.
n.a. = not applicable.

Source: Bureau of Outdoor Recreation, 1973a.

*Chapter 5*

# Demand Curve

This chapter defines a demand curve as the relationship between price and quantity. It demonstrates how to calculate the economic value of recreation from a demand curve and illustrates the application of information obtained from demand curves to recreation economic decisions.

This chapter combines the discussion of the previous chapters on quantity of use (e.g., trips, visitor days) and the concept of price to establish a formal relationship called the demand curve or demand function. We will see that the aggregate demand curve for a recreation site is the sum of the demand curves of individual consumers. Demand is also affected by other variables, such as consumer income, quality of the site, prices of substitute sites, and other socioeconomic factors. We will consider these influences in Chapter 6 on the demand function.

Demand curves help us answer a number of key questions in recreation management. First, by using a demand curve, we can measure in dollar terms the recreation benefits received by a visitor. Second, the demand function is useful for predicting future recreation use. Third, the demand curve provides estimates of the effect of alternative entrance fee levels on visitation. Thus, recreation planners or economists are frequently assigned the task of studying consumer demand for a particular recreation site such as a park or other recreation area.

## Use-Estimating View of a Demand Curve

Of the three listed uses of the demand curve, it is easiest to illustrate the concept of a recreation demand curve by first taking the use-estimating view. Table 5-1 (page 56) and Figure 5-1 (page 57) illustrate an individual's demand curve for recreation activity at a particular area. The price variable is the sum of transportation cost, travel time and entrance fee. This

**Table 5-1. Demand Schedule for Trips to a Recreation Area**

| Price per Trip | Number of Trips per Year |
|---|---|
| $90 | 0 |
| $80 | 1 |
| $70 | 2 |
| $60 | 3 |
| $50 | 4 |
| $40 | 5 |
| $30 | 6 |
| $20 | 7 |
| $10 | 8 |
| 0 | 9 |

is plotted in Figure 5-1 against the number of trips per season to the area (the measure of quantity). The demand curve is nothing more than a pairing of the number of trips per season the individual would take to a particular site when faced with alternative prices.

If we start with a high price, say $80, due to high gasoline prices or high entrance fees, then, given the individual's limited income and enjoyment derived from the recreation activity he or she might only take one trip per season. If the price were $70 per trip, then the individual might decide it is "worth" taking two trips per year. If the recreation area lowered entrance fees to attract more visitors, the total price of the trip might be $60 per trip. Given this price, the individual might decide to take three trips per year. When the price falls to $50 per trip, he or she may decide to take four trips per year. Finally, if gasoline prices were low and entrance fees minimal, the total price per trip might be just $20 and the individual might take seven trips per year. Given this number of trips, the individual begins to get bored with this activity at this site. Even if trips had zero transportation cost and entrance fees, he or she would not want to take more than nine trips a year to this area since he or she is simply tired of it and would prefer to go somewhere else or participate in some other activity.

Plotting the information in Table 5-1, yields the demand curve in Figure 5-1. A demand curve shows how the quantity demanded of some recreation activity during a specified period of time will change as the price of that activity changes, all other things held constant. Figure 5-1 depicts our representative individual's demand curve for trips to a recreation area. The diagram shows the trip price or direct cost of trips on the vertical ($P$) axis and the quantity of trips that the individual wants to take on the horizontal ($Q$) axis, starting from the origin point labeled zero. It shows the quantity of trips that will be demanded in a year at each possible price ranging from $10 to $80 per trip.

Economic diagrams are generally read as one reads latitudes and longitudes on a map. On the demand curve in Figure 5-1, the point marked

**Figure 5-1. Relationship Between Price Per Trip and Number of Trips**

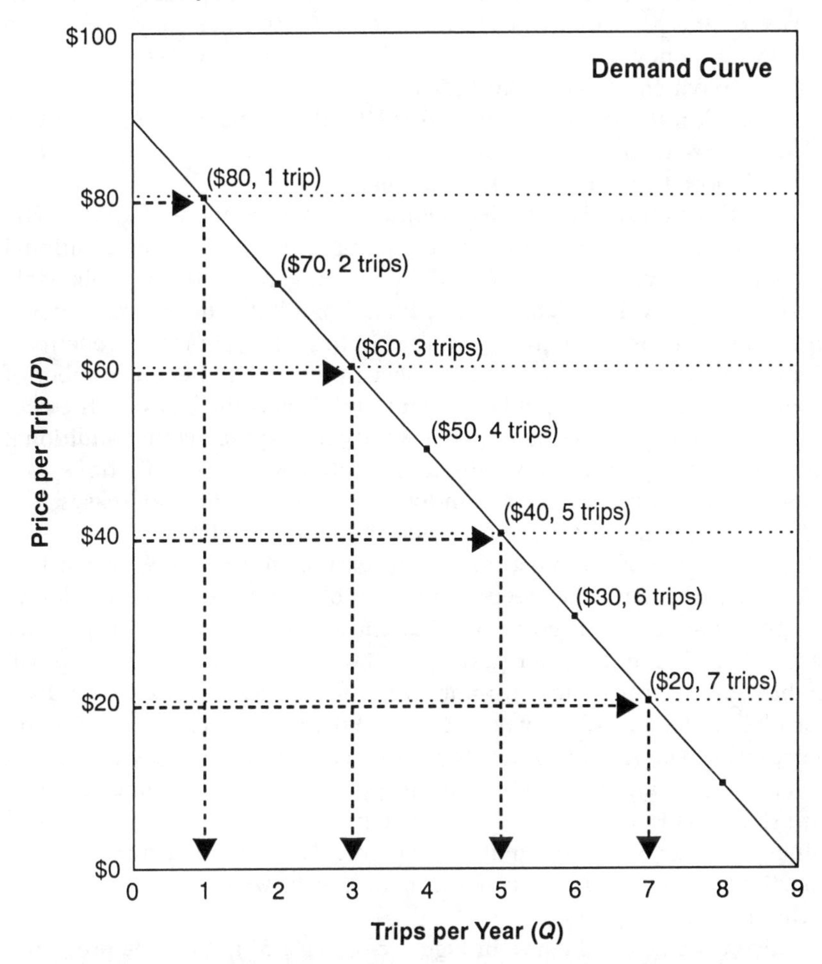


*($80, 1 trip)* represents a combination of price and quantity demanded by our individual consumer. By drawing a horizontal line leftward from that point to the vertical axis, we see that the average price of visiting the area is $80 per trip. By dropping a line straight down to the horizontal axis, we find that one trip is desired by our consumer at this price. The other points on the graph give similar information. The linear (straight line) form is used in order to make the illustration simple, but the same qualitative results would hold with nonlinear functions.

Notice the demand curve is downward sloping to the right. In such instances we say that the curve has a negative slope, because one variable falls as the other one rises. The negative slope to the demand curve results from three key properties. First is the fact that the demand curve is constrained by income. With a given income and hence amount of money to spend on recreation, when the price is $80 a trip, a person cannot afford to buy seven trips like he or she could when the price is $20. With a price of $80 per trip, five trips would cost $400 which may exceed the amount of money the person has for all recreation activities after paying rent, car payment, food, and utilities.

Second, if it costs $80 to visit this site, it may be cheaper to go to a substitute area more often. Thus, the individual will take few trips to this site and more trips to the substitute area.

The third reason is diminishing incremental or marginal utility. The more trips a person takes, other things being equal, the less the additional (marginal) enjoyment each trip will bring. In general, this is a plausible proposition. Psychological studies, including photos of eye movements and measurement of electrical impulses in the brain, show that repetition of an event renders it less and less pleasurable. A sufficient number of repetitions can extinguish all reaction to it. This is the basis for the economic "law" of diminishing marginal utility, which means that additional units of a good or service yield successively smaller contributions to a consumer's well-being. As the individual's consumption increases, the marginal utility or benefits of each additional unit declines.

Slope is one of the most important features of the diagrams used by economists, because the steeper the slope of a demand curve, the larger the price change required to bring about any given change in quantity demanded. Learning how to calculate the slope of a demand curve will enable you to provide useful information for recreation economic decisions. The slope of a linear (straight line) demand curve is the same, no matter where on that line you choose to measure it. That is why you can pick any horizontal distance and corresponding vertical distance to measure slope. This is not true of lines that are curved, where the numerical value of the slope is different at every point. The slope of a curved line at a particular point is the slope of a straight line drawn tangent to the curve at that point.

Given the demand curve in Figure 5-1 (page 57), it can be predicted that if the price of a trip (e.g., transportation, travel time and entrance fee) is $20 per trip, the individual would choose to make seven trips during a given season to this site. Thus, Figure 5-1 is a use-estimating view of the demand curve. If the trip price is higher, say $60, we see that only three trips would be demanded. This relationship between price and quantity allows recreation managers to predict the effect of higher gasoline prices or higher entrance fees on recreation visitation at their sites.

To better understand why a person would take the number of trips shown on the graph at these alternative prices one can look at an alternative view of the demand curve—the benefit estimation view.

# Using the Demand Curve to Measure Recreation Benefits

Recreation managers must first define the meaning of benefits and then consider how they are related to the individual's recreation economic decisions. The benefits to a consumer of some recreation activity, say trips to a park, are an economic measure meant to indicate how much pleasure, usefulness, or utility the consumer obtains from the experience. The trouble is that no one has yet invented a reliable sensory detector to tell how much pleasure or utility a recreation trip provides.

Figure 5-2 (page 60) illustrates a simple hypothesis about consumer behavior: The more trips to a given area a consumer has taken, other things being equal, the less a person would pay for an additional trip. As the individual's consumption increases, the additional utility or benefit of another trip declines. Economists call this effect diminishing marginal utility. It means that the increase in benefits gets smaller and smaller with each additional trip. Marginal benefit is the change in total benefit divided by the change in quantity.

If, for now, we hold constant variations in the quality of the recreation area (e.g., weather, crowding) and other conditions on individual trips, each successive trip adds less and less pleasure or satisfaction. Participants would be willing to pay the most for the first trip of the year when aesthetic satisfaction is at peak levels. The second trip provides substantial benefits but less than the first. With the third through the sixth trips, benefits diminish further; and, by the ninth trip, the experience provides no additional benefits. This is the same relationship that holds for cups of coffee in the morning (usually three is enough, even when the coffee is free).

The recreation economic rule is that consumers should continue to take trips if the added or marginal benefits exceed its price or direct costs. As long as the benefits of taking another trip exceed the price, the visitor is made better off by taking another trip. When possible, consumers should continue to participate until price and marginal benefits are exactly equal, because only this quantity will maximize the total benefits gained from the activity.

To see why this rule works, refer to Figure 5-2 (page 60). Suppose that the cost of a trip is $40 per person, and our consumer considers taking only two trips. We see that this is not a wise decision, because the added benefits of a third trip ($60) are greater than its $40 price. If the consumer were to increase the number of trips to three, the additional trip would cost $40 but yield $60 in marginal benefits; thus the additional trip would bring a clear net gain of the difference, or $20. Obviously, at a price of $40 per trip, the individual is better off with five trips than with two. Similarly, at this price, six trips is not an optimal decision, because the $30 marginal benefit of the sixth trip is less than its $40 price. Our consumer would be better off with only five trips, since that would save $40 in

**Figure 5-2. Benefit Estimating View of Demand Curve**

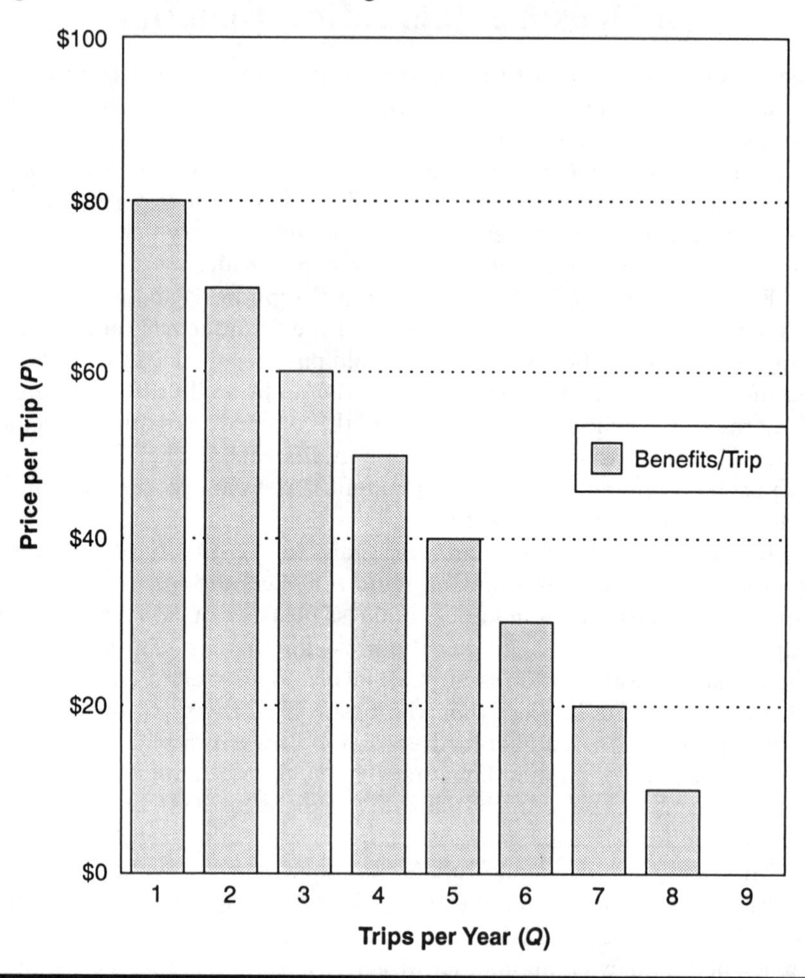


expenses with only a $30 loss in benefits, a net gain of $10 from the decision to reduce trips from six to five. The recreation economic decision rule tells us that our consumer should take five trips per year, as more than five trips yields a marginal benefit that is less than price, and less than five trips leaves marginal benefit greater than price.

## *Using the Demand Curve to Calculate Net Willingness to Pay*

Figure 5-2 also provides a benefit estimation view of the demand curve. The gross benefits or total willingness to pay for each trip is shown in this figure. The individual would pay up to $80 for the benefits received on the first trip, $70 for the second, $60 for the third and so on until the ninth trip for which he or she would be indifferent between going and not going even if the cost was zero.

To know how many trips will be taken we need to know the cost per trip. Assume the travel costs ($30) plus entrance fee ($10) is $40. The individual would make five trips.

The gross benefits (i.e., benefits without subtracting costs) is the sum of the benefits received on each of the five trips. In Figure 5-2, adding up the benefits of the first five trips, yields a total of $300 worth of benefits (= $80 + $70 + $60 + $50 + $40) for these five trips.

Of course, we need to subtract the costs to find the real or net benefits of being able to make five trips each season. The travel and entrance fees are costs or a payout from income. Clearly, the amount of benefits individuals actually retain is only the difference between their gross willingness to pay and the amount they actually had to spend. Put differently, if the recreation area had to be closed for the entire season, what would this user lose? It is not the $300 worth of benefits. The amount that would be lost is the difference between the $300 of lost benefits and the travel expenditures that are no longer made. The reduction in travel costs is a savings that partially offsets the foregone recreation benefits of $300.

With a cost of $40 per trip for each of five trips (see Figure 5.3, page 62), total expenditures or costs would be $200. Subtracting $200 in costs from the $300 in benefits this leaves a net benefit of $100. This is the net benefit retained by the individual from the opportunity to visit this site five times. If the user was asked what he or she would bid each year to have the opportunity to drive to the park and pay the entrance fee (say $10), the most this user would bid is $100. This is the amount of residual benefit or what economists call **consumer surplus.** It is the surplus benefit over and above the cost. The individual could bid up to $100, but certainly not $300. If the consumer bids his or her gross benefits of $300, he or she would have nothing left over to pay for the travel cost or the entrance fees.

The $100 of consumer surplus is illustrated in Figure 5-3 (page 62). Consumer surplus is the upper triangle. It is the area under the demand curve but above (i.e., in excess of) the price paid (i.e., in Figure 5-3 it is $40 + $30 + $20 + $10 + 0). Economists use the term consumer surplus synonymously with **net willingness to pay,** since consumer surplus represents willingness to pay, net of actual costs. The rectangle labeled *COST* is the actual expenditures made by the visitor. These expenditures are a useful starting point for analysis of the economic impacts of visitor expenditure on the local economy, but are a cost to the visitor, not a benefit.

To see that the expenditures are not a valid measure of the benefits to the visitor, consider Figure 5-3 (page 62). At present the individual takes five trips at a cost of $40 a trip for total expenditures of $200. What if instead, trips to the site cost $50. According to the demand curve, the individual would reduce the number of trips to four. What is total expenditure? It is $200 (= 4 trips x $50), the same as before. If we take the actual expenditure as a measure of visitor benefit we would state the

**Figure 5-3. Relationship of Consumer Surplus and Expenditure to the Demand Curve**

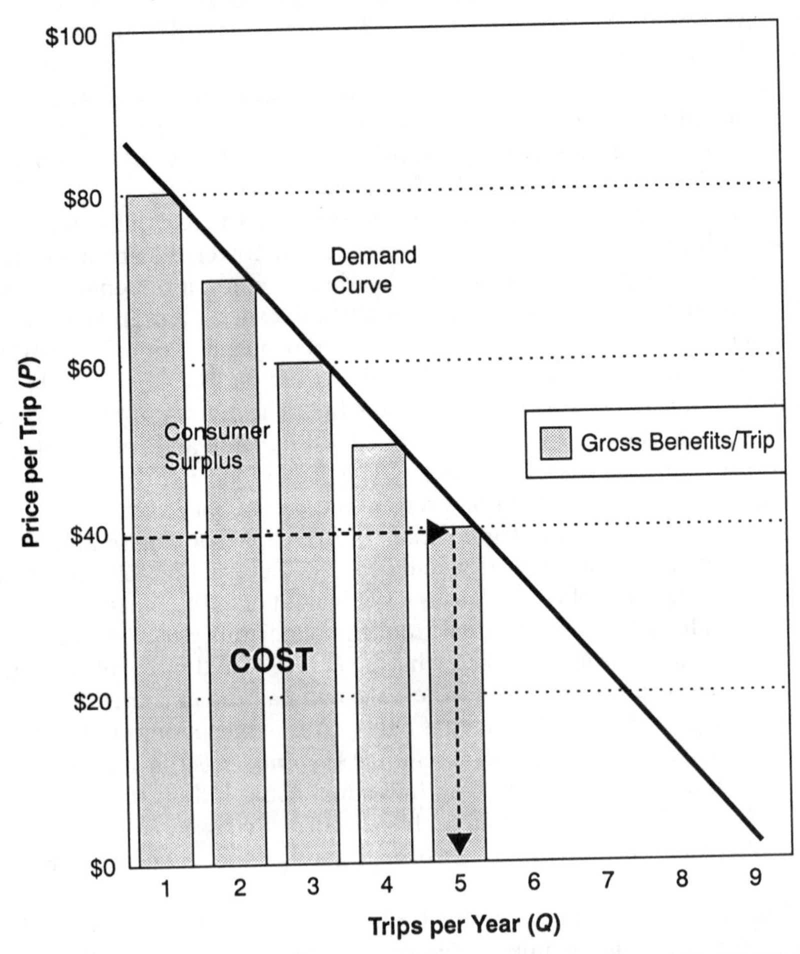


individual should receive just as much benefit with four trips at $50 a trip as with five trips at $40 since both yield expenditures of $200. But this is clearly wrong. Certainly most people would prefer to spend $200 and get five trips rather than just four trips. Since the expenditures are the same it suggests the individual would be indifferent. However, if one calculates the consumer surplus associated with four trips at $50 per trip it is only $60 (= $30 + $20 + $10 + 0). Recall that the consumer surplus with five trips costing $40 per trip is $100. Thus consumer surplus correctly indicates that five trips is preferred to four trips. While this seems like an incredible amount of intellectual effort to prove what should be obvious, many managers often fall into the trap of believing that recreation expenditures are an indicator of recreation benefits. We hope you will be able to avoid this trap and point out to others the fallacy of such a view.

Sometimes public recreation managers have trouble visualizing how consumer surplus is a real economic benefit to the visitor. The expenditures are cash that changes hands. Where is the consumer surplus, they wonder. The consumer surplus represents real income retained by the visitor in his or her wallet or purse. It is the money he or she would have spent rather than not visit the site, but did not have to spend because entrance fees or travel costs were less than his or her maximum willingness to pay. For example, assume that I am prepared to pay $40 to go hiking for one day in a nearby park. If I drive it will cost me $30, so I have a consumer surplus of $10. Now suppose a friend calls me at the last minute and offers to join me and split the travel cost. So now, it only costs me $15. Thus I get a total of $25 of consumer surplus. Where is this additional consumer surplus? It is in my wallet as $15 that I would have paid but now do not need to pay for this visit. My real income has increased by $15 because my friend pays half the trip costs.

Net willingness to pay or consumer surplus has been recommended as the preferred measure of the economic benefits of outdoor recreation programs by an interagency committee of the U.S. government (U.S. Water Resources Council, 1980; U.S. Department of the Interior, 1986). For public outdoor recreation programs, the benefit-cost ratio is defined as the consumer surplus (net benefits) of individual users divided by the sum of the agency's operating and opportunity costs. This means that if the average consumer surplus of outdoor recreation to our representative individual equals $20 per trip, the numerator in the benefit-cost ratio is this amount times the total annual trips to the area by all recreation users. For 100,000 trips per year, benefits would be estimated as $2 million annually. If the opportunity costs of foregone development, the costs of environmental damages, and the agency's costs of managing the recreation area sum to $1 million annually, the benefit-cost ratio to society would be 2 (= $2 million ÷ $1 million).

In Chapters 9 through 11 we will examine alternative methods to estimate this consumer surplus or net willingness to pay for outdoor recreation.

## Demand Equations

While graphical depiction of demand curves is useful for visualizing a demand relationship, actual application requires that the demand curve be represented mathematically as a demand equation or function. This also has the advantage of being able to include many other determinants of the number of trips taken in the demand function. As will be discussed in Chapter 6, variables such as income, age, and skill level can help explain the variation in number of trips taken by individuals living at similar distances from the recreation site with identical costs.

The equation for an ordinary demand curve is written:

$$Q = a - bP \qquad \text{(Equation 5-1)}$$

where $Q$ is the dependent variable number of trips, $P$ is the independent variable price or direct cost, $a$ is a constant representing the quantity demanded at zero price, and $b$ is the rate of change in quantity with a one-unit change in price, which is the slope of the line.

Notice that the dependent variable, quantity demanded, is plotted on the horizontal axis of Figure 5-1 (page 57) and the independent variable, price, is on the vertical axis. Mathematically, we would expect to see the reverse—the dependent variable on the vertical scale and the independent variable on the horizontal scale. However, the traditional practice in economics of plotting quantity on the horizontal axis and price on the vertical axis originated many years ago with the theory of competitive markets. In the case of competition, firms have no control over price but they can control output, and output of all producers determines market price. Hence, in the original model, price was the dependent variable and quantity (supplied, not demanded) was the independent variable. This is the reason price-quantity graphs appear as they do.

In the case of an inverse demand curve, price or marginal willingness-to-pay is the dependent variable. The equation is written:

$$P = a - bQ \qquad \text{(Equation 5-2)}$$

where $Q$ is the independent variable number of trips, $a$ is a constant term; and $b$ is the rate of change in price with a one unit change in quantity, which is the slope of the line.

The slope of an ordinary demand curve is the ratio of the horizontal change to the corresponding vertical change as we move to the left along the line, or the ratio of the *run* over the *rise*. Slope indicates how much the line falls or rises as we move right to left. Thus, in Figure 5-1 (page 57), as we go from the horizontal intercept to the vertical intercept, we go from zero trips to nine trips. But in that interval, the line rises from zero to a height of $90. Consequently, the slope of this ordinary demand curve is 9 ÷ $90 = 0.1. Equation 5-1 for this ordinary demand curve becomes:

$$Q = 9 - 0.1P \qquad \text{(Equation 5-3)}$$

This means that the individual demands nine trips when the price is zero and that the quantity demanded decreases by 0.1 trip with each one dollar increase in price.

The slope of an inverse demand curve is the familiar ratio of the vertical change to the corresponding horizontal change, or as is often said, the ratio of the *rise* over the *run*. Slope indicates how much the line falls as we move from left to right. Consequently, the slope of this inverse demand curve is 90 ÷ 9 = 10. Equation 5-2 for an inverse demand curve becomes:

$$P = 90 - 10Q \qquad \text{(Equation 5-4)}$$

This means that willingness to pay decreases by $10 with each additional trip per year.

The task remains to derive the site demand curve for a particular recreation area from individual demand curves. The procedure is straightforward if individual demand curves are additive as is the case when each individual pays no attention to other people's trip decisions when making his or her own. We simply add the individual demand curves horizontally (i.e., add up all of the individual quantities demanded at a given price). A shortcut approach is to multiply the number of visits by the representative (average) individual user at any given price by the total number of users of a particular site per year. This process is repeated for all alternative prices to obtain other points on the site demand curve.

Notice that information about price and quantity is all we can learn from the diagram. The demand curve will not tell us what kind of people visit, how long they stay or why. It tells us the price and quantity demanded at that price—no more, no less. A diagram abstracts from many details, some of which may be quite interesting, in order to focus on the two variables of primary interest—in this case, the price of recreation visits to this site and the number of trips demanded at each price. All of the diagrams used in this book share this basic feature. They cannot tell you the "whole story" any more than a map's latitude and longitude figures for a particular recreation area can make someone an authority on that area.

## *Chapter 6*

# Demand Function

This chapter introduces the concept of a statistical demand function; shows how to derive a demand curve from a demand function; demonstrates how to estimate shifts in a demand curve with changes in each of the nonprice variables, and discusses a number of important statistical tests of the results.

An important application of demand studies is to predict the effects of changes in circumstances. Because of these changes, demand curves often do not sit still; they shift around. As you will see in this chapter, any event that causes the demand curve to shift will also cause the consumer surplus estimate of benefits to change. Such events constitute the "other things" that we held constant in our definition of demand curves. We are now ready to consider how these nonprice forces affect demand.

Returning to our example of recreation trips, we might expect that in addition to price, demand will depend on such things as consumer income, quality of the resource, the price of trips to alternative areas, as well as other socioeconomic variables. Should any of these circumstances change, the number of trips demanded will also change, even if their direct cost or price remains constant. Graphically, this means that the entire demand curve will shift.

Previously, we saw that a change in the direct cost or price of a recreation trip produced a movement along a fixed demand curve. By contrast, a change in any other variable that influences quantity demanded will produce a shift of the demand curve. If consumers want to buy more at any given price than they wanted previously, the demand curve shifts to the right (or outward). If they desire less at any given price, the demand curve shifts to the left (or inward).

In Chapter 5, we dealt with the relationship between two variables—price and quantity—as if the trade-off could be decided separately from other determinants of demand. This is an oversimplification, for our choice of how many recreation trips to take depends on additional variables. The effect of direct cost or price is interdependent with other determinants of demand. When more than two variables are involved in the decision process, economists use multiple regression procedures to develop demand functions. Individual consumers rely upon a similar computation within the human brain, according to psychological studies reviewed by Scitovsky (1976) and Maslow (1965). The quality of a consumer's judgment depends upon how accurate he or she is in estimating the simultaneous effects of each of his or her determinants of demand.

Learning how to calculate the effects of changes in the nonprice variables in the demand function will enable you to provide useful information for recreation economic decisions. For example, you can estimate how much demand rises with increases in income, knowledge, or skill of the participant, direct cost or price of substitutes, quality of the recreation site, and population. At the same time, demand may fall with increases in age of participants and family size. Some of these variables can be controlled by recreation resource managers—the location of recreation sites and the quality of services offered, for example—and it is important to know the effects of altering these variables if effective managerial decisions are to be made. The benefits of a change in the quality of a site can be estimated as the area between demand curves with and without the improvement project.

Although many of these other variables are outside the control of recreation managers, they can be influenced by effective promotional programs. For example, information can be directed to particular groups of consumers: teenagers and young adults. Training programs can be provided for those who lack the necessary skills to participate in particular recreation activities. In addition, estimates of the sensitivity of demand to long-run trends in consumer income, population, and family size can enhance a recreation manager's ability to predict future growth potential and to establish effective long-run programs. We will refer to the information in this chapter when we discuss projections of future demand in Chapter 13.

## Shifts in Demand and Contour Maps

In Chapter 5, we presented a graphic illustration of a two-dimensional relationship between direct cost or price and the number of recreation trips demanded. Sometimes, when economic problems involve more than two variables, a two-dimensional graphic illustration is not enough, which is unfortunate as paper is only two dimensional. When we study the decision-making process of consumers of recreation, for example, we may want to keep track simultaneously of three variables: how much income is received, how much direct cost or price is paid, and how much recreation is consumed. Baumol and Blinder (1982) suggest that we think of the shifts in demand resulting from the introduction of a third variable as analogous to the information presented on detailed maps of mountain areas in the United States.

The U.S. Geological Survey has developed a well-known device for collapsing three dimensions into two, namely a contour map. Figure 6-1 is a contour map of Long's Peak, one of the highest mountains in the state of Colorado and a popular destination for hikers in Rocky Mountain National Park. On several of the irregularly shaped contour lines or "rings," we find a number indicating the height above sea level at that particular spot on the mountain. All points on any particular contour line represent geographic locations that are at the same height above sea level. Thus, unlike the more usual sort of map, which gives only latitudes and longitudes, this contour map exhibits three pieces of information about each point: latitude, longitude and altitude.

Figure 6-2 (page 70) looks more like the contour maps you will find in recreation economics. It shows how some third variable, $Y$ (think of it as consumer income, for example), affects the relationship between variable $P$ (think of it as direct cost or price paid per trip) and variable $Q$ (think of it as how much recreation is consumed). Just like the map of Long's Peak, any point on the diagram conveys three pieces of data. In this contour map, all points on a given contour line represent the different combinations of direct costs or price paid and recreation consumed by representative individuals receiving a given level of income. For example, all points

**Figure 6-1. U.S. Geological Survey Map of Long's Peak in Rocky Mountain National Park, Colorado**

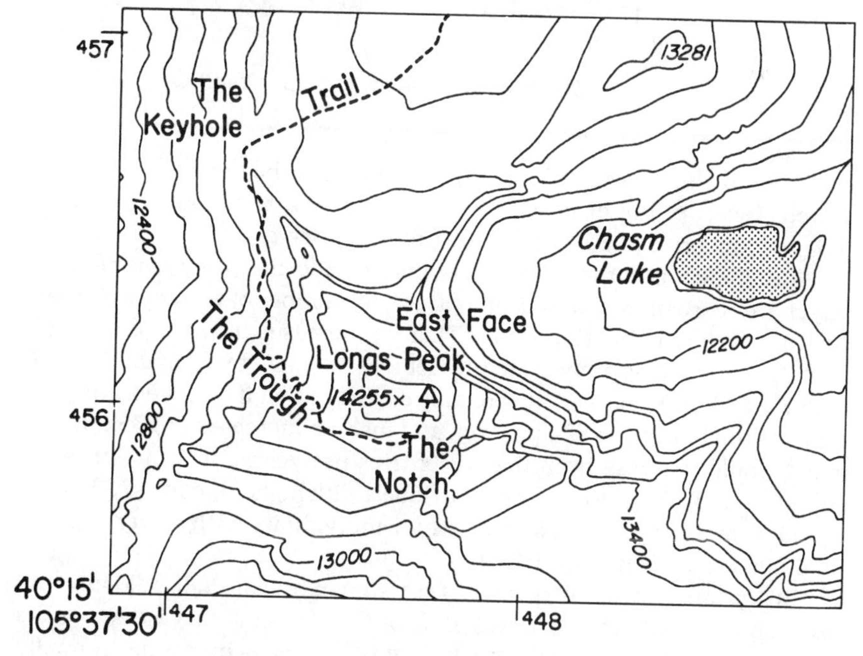

Figure 6-2. Income Shifts the Demand Curve for Recreation Trips by a Representative Individual

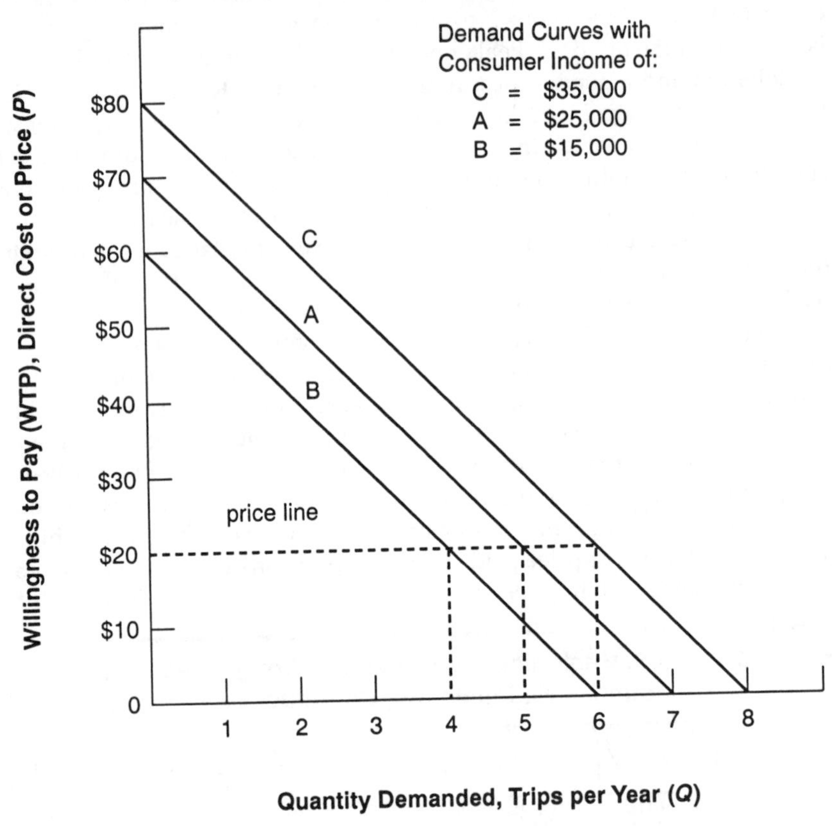


on Demand Curve A with $Y$ = \$25,000 represent the demand for trips at various levels of direct cost or price. Thus, five trips per year are demanded at a price of \$20, and four trips at a price of \$30.

If incomes increase, consumers may decide that they can afford to buy more recreation and thus increase their number of trips even if travel cost or price remains the same. That is, increases in income normally shift demand curves outward to the right, as depicted by Demand Curve C with $Y$ = \$35,000 per year. It is readily apparent that if direct cost or price remains unchanged at \$20 per trip, and income increases to \$35,000, demand would increase from five to six trips per year. Or, if the price increases from \$20 to \$30 per trip, individuals with higher incomes (\$35,000) would demand more trips (five) than individuals with lower income (\$25,000 income and four trips).

Everything works in reverse if consumer income falls. Figure 6-2 also depicts a leftward (inward) shift of the demand curve that results from a decline in consumer income. That is, decreases in income normally shift demand curves inward to the left, as depicted by Demand Curve B with $Y = \$15{,}000$ per year. It is clear that if the direct cost or price remains unchanged at $20 per trip and income decreases to $15,000, demand would decrease from five to four trips per year. Or, if the price of recreation trips increased from $20 to $30 per trip, individuals with lower income ($15,000) would demand fewer trips (three) than individuals with higher income (four trips for $25,000 and five trips for $35,000). Economists define such effects as resulting from shifts in the demand curve.

While most of the information presented in this book will be based on the simpler two-variable diagrams, contour maps also find their applications in this chapter on the demand function.

# Statistical Demand Functions

Demand functions for recreation sites can be estimated using the standard statistical procedures for multiple regression. This approach has been used because it fits an equation to a set of observed data providing statistical estimates of the effect of each variable, holding other variables in the demand function constant. There are limitations to the technique, but regressions frequently provide a reasonably good estimate of a demand function at a relatively small cost. The list of readings at the end of this book contain numerous examples of the application of regression analysis to estimate the demand functions for recreation sites.

## *Specify the Variables*

The first step in regression analysis is to specify the variables that are expected to influence demand. In an ordinary demand function for a recreation site, the dependent variable to be explained is always the quantity demanded ($Q$), although it may be measured in different physical units: recreation trips, days, hours, and visitor days per person or per capita. The list of independent variables that influence demand always includes a proxy for direct cost or price ($P$) and generally includes such factors as consumer income ($Y$), travel time ($T$), the price and availability of substitutes ($S$), other socioeconomic variables such as age ($G$), quality or attractiveness of the site ($A$), population of the consuming group ($K$), measures of individual taste or preference ($D$), expectations with respect to crowding or congestion ($C$), and other variables. If important determinants of demand are inadvertently omitted from the demand function, the equation will not predict demand accurately.

The individual demand function for a recreation site ($x$) is a statement of the relationship between the quantity demanded and all of these factors that affect this demand. Written in general form, the ordinary demand function may be expressed as:

$$Q_x = f(P_x, Y, T, S, G, A, K, D, C, \ldots) \qquad \text{(Equation 6-1)}$$

The inverse demand function specifies willingness to pay (WTP) the direct cost or price of outdoor recreation as the dependent variable to be explained; and it includes the quantity demanded as one of the independent variables. Otherwise, the variables specified in the ordinary and inverse demand functions for a recreation site can remain approximately the same. Written in general form, the inverse demand function may be expressed as:

$$WTP_x = f(Q_x, Y, T, S, G, A, K, D, C, \ldots) \quad \text{(Equation 6-2)}$$

## Collect the Data

The second step in regression analysis is to obtain information on the variables: measures of direct cost or price, travel time, consumer income and the like. The important determinants of demand must be measured correctly if the equation is to predict demand accurately. Obtaining accurate estimates of these variables is not always easy, especially if some key variables, such as consumer preferences and attitudes toward quality of the site (which are quite important in demand functions for many recreation sites) may have to be obtained by survey techniques as discussed in Chapters 7, 9 and 10.

## Functional Form: Linear or Nonlinear?

Once the variables have been chosen and the data gathered, the next step is to specify the form of the equation, or the manner in which the independent variables are assumed to interact to determine the level of demand. The generalized demand function expressed in Equation 6-1 is really just a listing of the variables that influence demand. For use in recreation economic decisions, the demand function must be made explicit. That is, the nature of the relationship between the quantity demanded and each of the independent variables must be specified. To illustrate, let us assume that we are analyzing the demand for trips to a recreation area, and the demand function has been specified as a linear relationship:

$$Q = a + bP + cY + dT + eS + fG + gA + hK + iD + jC \quad \text{(Equation 6-3)}$$

Linear demand functions, such as this, have great appeal in empirical work for two reasons. First, the slope or regression coefficients ($b$ through $j$), provide a direct measure of the marginal relationships in the demand function. That is, they indicate the change in quantity demanded caused by a one-unit change in each of the related variables. For example, if $b = -0.1$, demand will decline by 0.1 with each \$1 increase in the direct cost or price per trip. Second, experience has shown that many demand relationships are in fact approximately linear over the range in which decisions are made. The demand curve derived from a demand function such as this, is a straight line as shown in Figure 6-3.

There are numerous other functional forms that can be used as the basis for regression analysis of demand for recreation. These include the nonlinear forms such as the quadratic, semilogarithmic and double-logarithmic forms, all of which are consistent with the underlying theory of demand, in which the larger the price variable, the smaller the marginal effect of price on number of trips demanded. Figure 6-3 illustrates the most common functional forms used in regressions of the demand for recreation.

The quadratic equation includes, in addition to the linear variables, squared terms for one or more of the independent variables:

$$Q = a + bP + bP^2 + cY + cY^2 + \ldots \qquad \text{(Equation 6-4)}$$

**Figure 6-3. Functional Forms Used for Regression Analysis of Demand for Recreation**

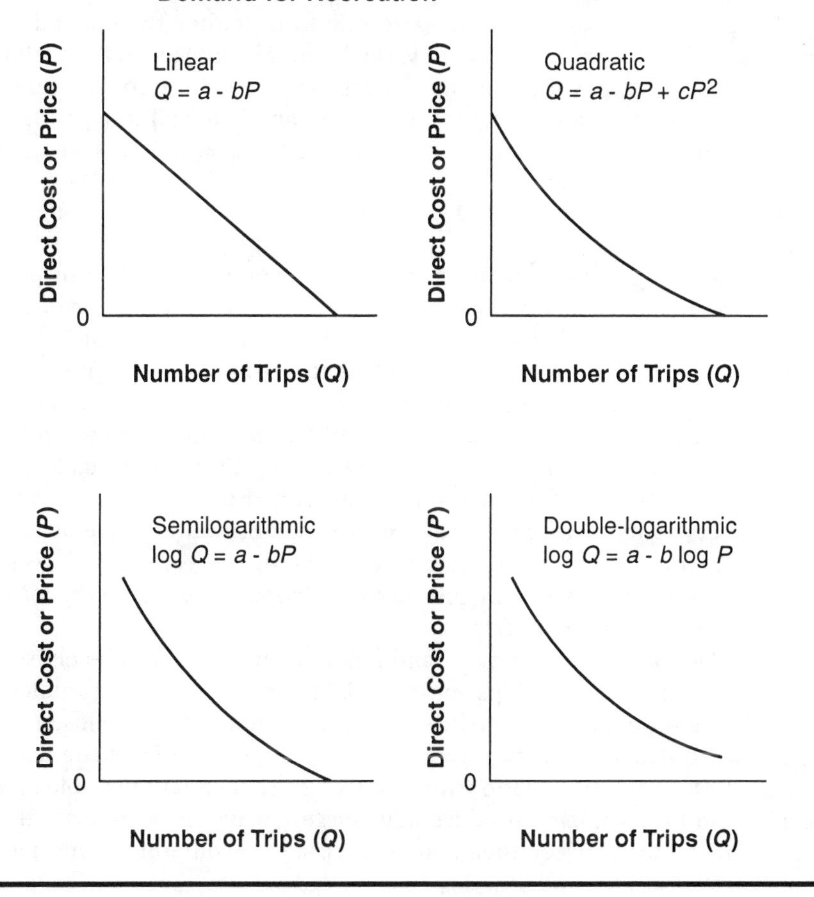

The quadratic form has been preferred for prediction because it provides the true arithmetic averages of the variables rather than the median values when using a semilog form. However, the quadratic curve may not reflect the true relationships among the variables in some cases.

The double-logarithmic equation takes the natural (i.e., to the base *e*) logarithmic form on both sides of the equation:

$$\log Q = a + b(\log P) + c(\log Y) + \ldots \qquad \text{(Equation 6-5)}$$

The double-logarithmic form is also frequently used in regression analysis of the demand and supply of outdoor recreation. Its unique advantage is the ease with which the regression coefficients can be compared. It is the only functional form in which the regression coefficients are the elasticities. In Chapter 8, elasticities are defined as the percent change in the dependent variable associated with a 1% change in each of the independent variables. The double-log form is somewhat faulty because it fails to account for either the upper limit or lower limit of the demand curve (i.e., the double-log demand curve approaches but does not touch either the price or quantity axis).

In specification of the semilogarithmic form, either the dependent variable or one or more independent variables may be logged. In recreation demand studies, applications of the semilog form frequently convert number of trips per capita to a natural logarithm and leave all independent variables in their linear form. This semilogarithmic equation is written:

$$\log Q = a + bP + cY + \ldots \qquad \text{(Equation 6-6)}$$

This has a unique advantage in estimating the average consumer surplus per trip; it is simply one divided by the regression coefficient for direct cost or price. Ziemer, Musser and Hill (1980) compare the semilog form to the linear and quadratic, and conclude that the semilog is the preferred form for warm-water fishing demand in the southeastern United States. They report household consumer surplus of $26 per trip or occasion for the semilog, compared to $29 for the linear and $20 for the quadratic. Cheshire and Stabler (1976) report, however, that the semilog form overpredicts visits to a recreation site in Great Britain at extreme distances (or prices) and underpredicts at middle distances. They suggest that a constant be added to the distance or price variable before the logarithmic transformation is performed.

The algebraic form of the demand function should always be chosen to reflect the true relationships among variables in the case being studied. That is, care should be taken to insure that the structural form chosen for an empirical demand function provides the best possible fit of the data. Scatter diagrams of the relationship between the dependent variable and each of the independent variables may suggest which form reflects the true relationships between them. In practice, several different forms may be tested, and the one that best fits the data should be selected as being most likely to reflect the true relationship. A more advanced technique called the Box-Cox transformation empirically determines the best functional form and allows the degree of nonlinearity to vary. Most advanced books on multiple regression will have a discussion of the Box-Cox procedure, and computer statistics packages such as LIMDEP contain routines for performing the Box-Cox procedure.

## Ordinary Least Squares Regression

Regression equations are statistically calculated, that is, the coefficients $a$ through $j$ of Equation 6-3 (page 72) are estimated—by the method of least squares. The method estimates the intercept ($a$) and the slope of a line which minimizes the sum of the squares of the difference between each of the actual data points and the estimated line. The deviation of each data point from the fitted line, or error term, is squared because the deviations are both positive and negative. By squaring the deviations we are summing a set of positive numbers. The line that minimizes this sum most accurately depicts the relationship between the dependent variable and each independent variable, holding constant the values of other independent variables in the demand function. The procedure is presented graphically in Figure 6-4 (page 76). Here each point represents the direct cost or price and number of trips by an individual in our sample. It shows the vertical deviation of each data point from the fitted line.

Most computer spreadsheet programs and nearly all statistics packages have regression programs. All you need to know is how to put the data into the computer program and, most importantly, how to interpret the output. Accordingly, we shall concentrate on setting up multiple regression problems for computer solution and interpreting the output, rather than dwelling on the mathematical process itself.

## Regression Coefficients

Multiple regression techniques provide useful statistical estimates of demand functions for outdoor recreation. Learning how to interpret the many regression statistics which are typically provided by computer-based regressions can enable you to provide useful information for recreation economic decisions. The important thing is how to interpret the values of the regression coefficients.

The most valuable information provided by statistical demand functions is the regression coefficient for each of the determinants of demand, $b$ through $j$, in Equation 6-3 (page 72). Each coefficient indicates the marginal relationship between the variable and the quantity demanded, holding constant the effects of all other variables included in the demand function. For example, assume that the computer printout of a statistical demand function for trips to a recreation site provides us with the following information:

**Figure 6-4. Vertical Deviation of Each Data Point from the Fitted Line**

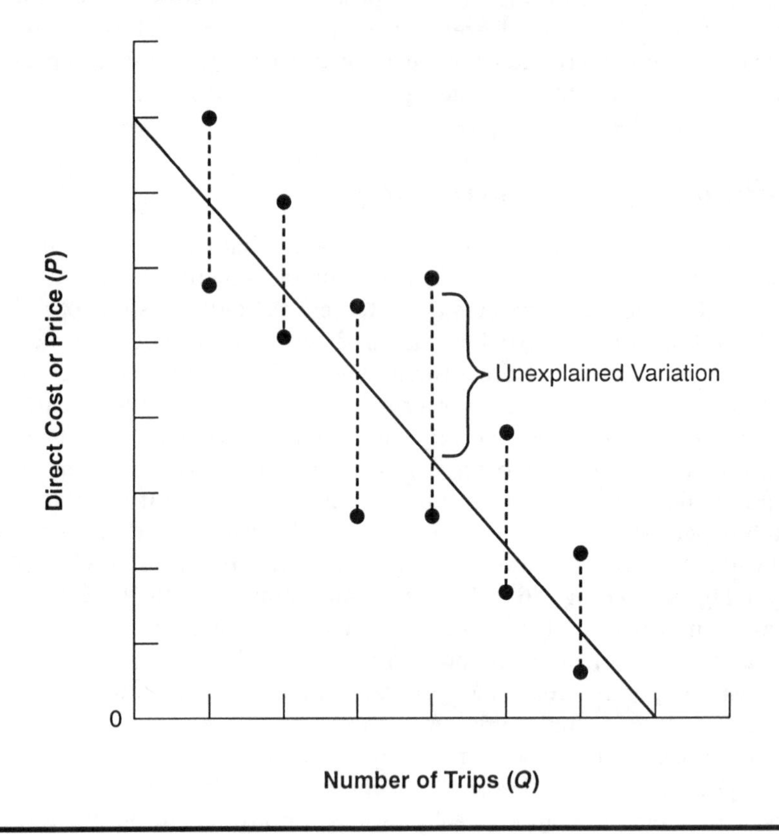


| $Q =$ | $0.5$ | $-\ 0.1P$ | $+\ 0.1Y$ | $-\ 0.4T$ | $+\ 0.054S$ | (Equation 6-7) |
|---|---|---|---|---|---|---|
| (t-statistics) | (3.06) | (−5.03) | (6.16) | (−3.04) | (1.03) | |
| $N = 200$ | $R^2 = 0.82$ | | $F = 126.4$ | | | |

Standard error of the estimate = 0.25

The values of the regression coefficients provide us with an estimate of the change in number of trips to the recreation site associated with a one-unit change in each of these independent variables, holding constant the effect of all other variables. For example, Equation 6-7 indicates that individual demand for trips to a recreation site falls by 0.1 with each $1 increase in average direct cost or price ($P$). The coefficient for income ($Y$, measured in thousands)indicates that when we hold constant the effect of all other demand variables, a $1,000 increase in income will cause the quantity demanded to increase by 0.1 of a trip per year.

Similarly, the regression coefficient for travel time ($T$) indicates that demand will decrease by 0.4 of a trip with each one-hour increase in travel time. The coefficient for the price of substitute sites ($S$) shows that demand for trips to a recreation site increases by 0.054 of a trip with each $1 increase in the average direct cost or price of substitute sites.

The constant or intercept term, $a$, from Equation 6-3 (page 72) has a value of 0.5 in Equation 6-7. This can be interpreted as the expected number of trips demanded with zero values for all of the independent variables. This would represent the demand for trips to the site that is not explained by the independent variables included in the equation. Alternately, it may have no economic meaning if the data points of observed values do not approach zero for each of the independent variables included. It is hazardous to generalize about the relationship beyond the range of observed values.

## *Tests of Regression Results*

The coefficient of determination, identified by the symbol $R^2$, indicates that the regression explains 82% of the variation in the dependent variable in Equation 6-7. It is defined as the proportion (or percent) of the variation in the dependent variable that is explained by the full set of independent variables included in the equation. Accordingly, $R^2$ can have a value ranging from 0, indicating the equation explains none of the variation in the dependent variable, to 1, indicating that all of the variation has been explained by the independent variables. In demand functions for recreation $R^2$ will seldom be equal to either 0 or 1. In empirical demand estimation $R^2$ values of 0.50, indicating that 50% of the variation in demand is explained, are quite acceptable. For some zonal travel cost equations $R^2$s as high as 0.80 are obtainable; for others, based on individual observations of consumer behavior, we must be satisfied with considerably less explanation of variation in demand. When the coefficient of determination is very low—say, in the range of 0.05 to 0.15—it is an indication that the equation is inadequate for explaining the demand for recreation. The most general cause of this problem is the omission of an important variable or variables from the equation.

Two additional points should be made with respect to the coefficient of determination, $R^2$. First, most computer programs print out two coefficients of determination; one is adjusted for degrees of freedom (roughly the number of observations less one) and the other is not. The unadjusted $R^2$ is usually higher and the temptation should be avoided to rely on it rather than the adjusted $R^2$, which is the appropriate measure. Second, some computer programs show the proportion of the variation in the dependent variable that is explained by each of the independent variables included in the equation, the sum of which equals the adjusted $R^2$. For example, direct cost or price may explain 20% of the variation, income 10%, and so on.

The numbers in parentheses below the regression coefficients in Equation 6-7 are the t-statistics which indicate whether the slope coefficients are statistically (i.e., meaningfully) different from zero. The **t-statistic** is calculated by dividing the coefficient by the "standard error of the coefficient." The standard error of the coefficient is like the standard deviation, it provides a measure of the variability of the coefficient. If the standard error is quite small relative to the coefficient then we can place more confidence in our conclusion that this particular variable has a systematic (i.e., nonrandom) effect on the number of trips taken. A frequent test of whether the variable is significant is whether each regression coefficient is at least twice its standard error. This is equivalent, in most cases, to observing a **t-value** of approximately two for a regression coefficient, since the **t-ratio** is merely the regression coefficient divided by its standard error, adjusted for the degrees of freedom. If this is the case, we can reject at the 95% confidence level the hypothesis that the independent variable is not significantly related to the dependent variable, because zero is outside this range.

The **F-test** or **F-ratio** is used to estimate whether there is a significant relationship between the dependent variable and all the independent variables taken together. Tables are available in any statistical textbook, showing the values of $F$ that are exceeded with certain probabilities, such as 0.05 and 0.01, for various degrees of freedom of the dependent and independent variables. The F-ratio of 126.4 in Equation 6-7 (page 76) indicates the overall equation is highly significant.

Another useful statistic calculated by the computer is the **standard error of the estimate,** which provides a measure of the precision of the estimates from the regression model as a whole. It is included as part of Equation 6-7 (page 76). Greater predictive accuracy is associated with smaller standard errors of the estimate. Assuming the errors are normally distributed about the regression equation, there is a 95% probability that observations of the dependent variable will lie within the range of $Q \pm$ two standard errors of the estimate at the mean of the data. The confidence band concept is illustrated in Figure 6-5. Here we see the least squares regression line (D) and the upper and lower 95% confidence limits. Thus, there is only a 5% chance that the true estimate of trips (at any given cost) lies outside this confidence interval. Note however, the confidence interval or confidence band is tightest around the center (e.g., the mean of price and trips) and wider the further one moves from the mean of the observed data. This suggests that predictions of trips at prices that are substantially above or below the mean of the data carry with it less confidence about their accuracy and the prediction errors are much greater than just two standard errors of the estimate. The interested reader should consult a regression or econometrics book for the details of calculating confidence intervals around regression predictions.

Figure 6-5. **Use of the Standard Error of the Estimate to Define 95% Confidence Intervals**

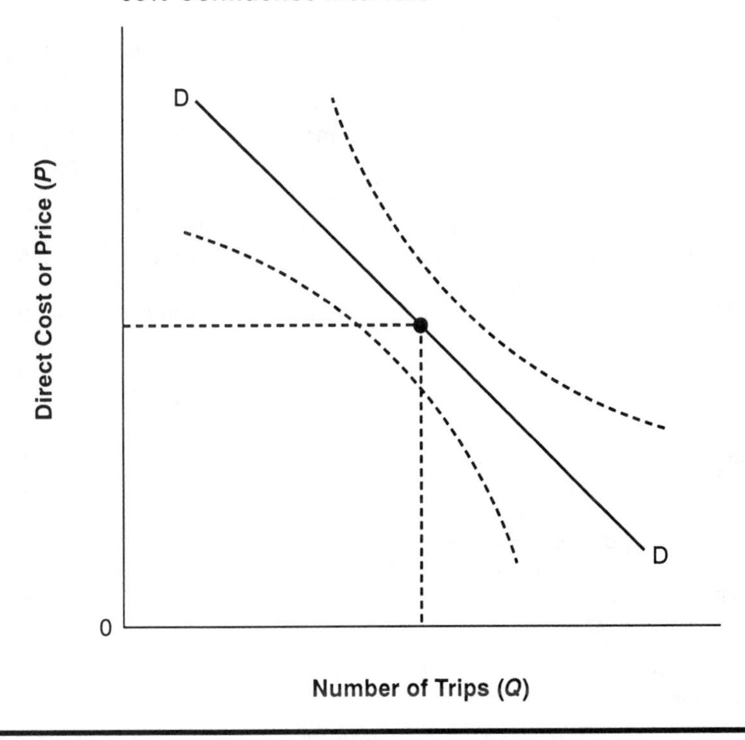


# Applications: Estimating Demand Curves and Shifts in Demand

Table 6-1 (page 80) shows how to estimate individual demand for trips to a recreation site using an estimated demand equation. If we multiply each regression coefficient by the mean value of the variable and sum these products (plus the constant), we have the estimated individual demand for trips per year to the site. From Table 6-1 we see that the estimated individual demand for the site will be five trips per year, given the average values of the independent variables. It would be a relatively simple matter to aggregate individual demand to estimate the total demand for the site, multiplying five trips per individual user by the total number of users per year.

## *Deriving a Demand Curve From a Demand Function*

A demand curve is defined as that part of the demand function showing the relation between the direct cost or price of a trip and number of trips demanded, holding constant the effects of all other independent variables.

**Table 6-1. Estimating Individual Demand for Trips to a Recreation Site Using a Demand Function**

| Independent Variables | Units | Estimated Mean Values of the Independent Variables (1) | Regression Coefficients for the Independent Variables (2) | (1 x 2) Estimated Total Demand, Trips per Year (3) |
|---|---|---|---|---|
| Direct Cost or Price (*P*) | Dollars/Trip | 20.0 | –0.100 | –2.0 |
| Consumer Income (*Y*) | Thousand Dollars | 25.0 | 0.100 | 2.5 |
| Travel Time (*T*) | Hours Round Trip | 3.0 | –0.400 | –1.2 |
| Price of Substitute Sites (*S*) | Dollars, Direct Cost/Trip | 24.0 | 0.054 | 1.3 |
| Age (*G*) | Years | 25.0 | –0.088 | –2.2 |
| Quality of the Site (*A*) | 5-Point Scale | 4.0 | 0.625 | 2.5 |
| County Population (*K*) | Thousand Persons | 200.0 | 0.025 | 5.0 |
| Taste or Preference (*D*) | 1 = Active; 0 = Passive | 0.8 | 1.250 | 1.0 |
| Daily Utilization/ Capacity Ratio (*C*) | 1 = Optimal | 0.9 | –2.667 | –2.4 |
| Constant (*a*) | | | | 0.5 |
| Total Demand (*Q*) | | | | 5.0 |

If we multiply each regression coefficient (except direct cost or price) by the mean value of the variable, sum these products, and add them to the value of the constant term $a$ the result equals the number of trips intercept of the demand curve. To illustrate the process, consider the relationship depicted in Table 6-1. Assuming that income, travel time, price of substitutes, etc., are all held constant at their average values, we can express the relationship between changes in direct cost or price and changes in number of trips demanded as:

$$Q = -0.1(P) + 0.1(25.0) - 0.4(3.0) + 0.054(24.0) - 0.088(25.0) + 0.625(4.0) + 0.025(200.0) + 1.25(0.8) - 2.667(0.9) + 0.5$$

$$= -0.1P + 2.5 - 1.2 + 1.3 - 2.2 + 2.5 + 5.0 + 1.0 - 2.4 + 0.5$$

$$= 7.0 - 0.1P \qquad \text{(Equation 6-8)}$$

This is presented graphically as Demand Curve A in Figure 6-2 (page 70). The horizontal trips intercept is given by the demand equation which indicates that the representative individual demands seven trips when the direct cost or price is zero. The demand equation also indicates that the quantity demanded decreases by 0.1 of a trip with each $1 increase in price. Consequently, the vertical price intercept of this ordinary demand curve can be calculated as 7 ÷ 0.1 = 70. The graphic representation of this linear demand curve is obtained by drawing a straight line between the two intercept points, i.e., seven trips and $70.

As is typical of most demand curves, a reduction in direct cost or price causes an increase in quantity demanded, and, conversely, an increase in price leads to a decrease in quantity demanded. For example, when the average price of visiting the recreation site is $20 per trip, five trips per year are demanded by the representative consumer. If the average price of visiting the site increases to $40 per trip, demand would fall to three trips per year. This would also be the effect on demand of doubling travel costs, as a result of increased energy prices. Changes such as these are defined as movements along a demand curve.

## *Nonprice Variables Shift the Demand Curve*

A change in demand—a shift from one demand curve to another—indicates a change in one or more of the other determinants of demand, the nonprice variables in the demand function. This means that at each price the number of trips demanded is either more or less than before, depending on whether the demand curve has shifted to the right or to the left. For example, consider again the effects of changes in consumer income presented in Figure 6-2 (page 70). You will recall that Demand Curve A holds income at $25,000, which is the average value estimated for users of the recreation site. Individuals with $35,000 annual income, or $10,000 more than the average user, would demand one trip more, as shown by Demand Curve C. Those with $15,000 annual income would demand one less trip per year as shown by Demand Curve B. The result of income shifts in the demand curve is that, at a direct cost or price per trip of $20, those with $10,000 less income than the average demand four trips per year compared with six trips per year for those with $10,000 more income than the average. Alternately, if individual use of the recreation area is five trips per year, those with the lower income would be willing to pay $10 per trip compared with $30 per trip by those with the higher income.

The rule to calculate the shift in the demand curve caused by a change in any of the nonprice variables included in the demand function is simply to multiply the regression coefficient for the nonprice variable by its change in value. For example, if average consumer income is assumed to change by $10,000 dollars per year and the regression coefficient for income (in thousands) is 0.1, then the income shift in demand is 10 x 0.1 = 1 trip per year. This represents the effect of a change in income on demand for trips to the recreation site, holding constant the effect of all other variables included in the demand function. These so-called partial effects of each nonprice variable on demand can be estimated by applying the same rule.

# Understanding Regression Analysis

Mansfield (1980), a noted authority on statistical applications in economics, cautions us to remember that regression analysis, like any tool, should not be applied blindly. It is important to check whether the assumptions underlying the approach are at least approximately correct, and to be aware of the problems that may arise in applications to recreation economic decisions. Although the assumptions underlying regression analysis are unlikely to be met completely, they are close enough in a sufficiently large number of cases that regression analysis is a powerful technique.

## *Potential Problems in Regression Analysis*

There are a number of potential pitfalls that should be emphasized. First, it is by no means true that a high correlation between an independent and a dependent variable means that the former "causes" the latter to vary. For example, if we regress travel cost on travel time to a recreation site, the correlation is bound to be high. But this does not mean that travel time causes travel cost to be as large or as small as it is. Two variables can be highly correlated without causation being implied. In this case, both travel cost and travel time are caused by a third variable, travel distance. Computer programs allow us to include dozens of independent variables with relative ease, which makes it extremely important that our reasons for including each of them be based on economic theory or on knowledge of the recreation economic behavior of consumers.

Second, even if an observed correlation is due to a causal relationship, the direction of causation may be the reverse of that implied by the regression. For example, suppose that we regress the profit of a recreation equipment manufacturer on its advertising expenditures, where profit is the dependent variable to be explained and advertising expenditure the independent variable. If the correlation between these two variables turns out to be high, does this imply that high advertising expenditures produce high profits? Obviously not. The line of causation could run the other way: High profits could enable management to spend more on advertising. Thus, in interpreting the results of regression studies, it is important to ask ourselves whether the line of causation assumed in the studies is correct.

Third, regressions are sometimes used to forecast values of the dependent variable lying beyond the range of sample data. For example, a scatter diagram of observations of direct cost or price and trips may show that the data for the dependent variable, trips to a recreation site, range from three to five (see Figure 6-4, page 76). But the regression is used to forecast the dependent variable, number of trips per year, from zero to seven trips, both ends of which are outside this range. This procedure, known as *extrapolation,* is dangerous because the available data provide no evidence that the true regression is linear beyond the range of the sample data. The true regression may be a curve, rather than a straight line.

Fourth, you should be careful to avoid creating a spurious correlation by dividing or multiplying both the dependent variable and an independent variable by the same quantity. For example, we might want to determine whether a distance zone's trips to a particular recreation site is related to its trips to all recreation sites. To normalize for differences in population among distance zones, it may seem sensible to use trips per capita to a recreation site as one variable and trips per capita to all recreation sites as the other. This procedure may result in these ratios being highly correlated (because the denominator of the ratio is the same for both variables), even if there is little or no relationship between the number of trips to a particular recreation site and trips to all recreation sites.

Fifth, it is important to recognize that a regression is based on past data, and may not be a good predictor of future values due to changes in the relationships between the variables. For example, past data indicates that age has a negative effect. However, with earlier retirement, better healthcare and greater physical fitness, trips may not fall as fast with age as it did in the past when the data was collected. Thus, predictions based on historic data prior to the 1970s are likely to underestimate the number of future recreation trips as the population ages.

## *Assumptions of Regression Techniques*

When we undertake a regression analysis of survey information, it is important to check whether the assumptions underlying the approach are at least approximately met. Essentially, this involves tests of misspecification of the model, heteroscedasticity, multicollinearity, and nonnormal distribution of the sample values. Regression analysis makes the following assumptions.

First, the average value of the dependent variable, number of trips, is assumed to be a linear function of the independent variables, or it can be transformed (using logarithms) to a linear function. This was discussed in the previous section.

Second, the distribution of sample observations around the predicted value of the dependent variable, number of trips, is the same for all values of an independent variable. This characteristic is called **homoscedasticity,** and its violation, **heteroscedasticity.** Correcting for this problem often involves weighting the data or observations.

Third, the values of a variable are independent of one another and independent of the values of other variables. The individual values of a variable are generally independent of one another in the case of recreation trips by hundreds of individuals. However, the values of a single variable are not always independent of the values of other variables. Violation of this assumption is called **multicollinearity,** to be discussed further.

Fourth, the values of the dependent variable, number of trips, are normally distributed (bell shaped) around their average values, although not all aspects of regression analysis require this assumption. It is worth noting that only the dependent variable, number of trips, is regarded as a random variable. The values of the independent variables are assumed to be fixed. For example if regression analysis is used to estimate the number of trips when direct cost or price is $20, the true number of trips taken at this price can be predicted subject to confidence limits, but the direct cost or price ($20) is known precisely.

One important problem that can arise in multiple regression studies is multicollinearity, which is defined as a situation in which two or more of the independent variables are very highly correlated. This violates the basic purpose of multiple regression to estimate the effect of one independent variable, holding the other independent variables constant. When multicollinearity is present, there is no way to tell how much effect each has separately when two independent variables move together in rigid, lockstep fashion. Their effects are hopelessly confounded. For example, researchers in outdoor recreation often encounter cases where the independent variables, travel cost and travel time, are so highly correlated that, although it is possible to estimate a regression coefficient for each variable, they cannot be estimated at all accurately.

To determine whether multicollinearity is high, we can have the computer print out the simple correlations among pairs of independent variables and the multiple correlation coefficients of each of the independent variables on all of the others. If some of these correlation coefficients are close to 1.0 (or –1.0), multicollinearity is likely to be a problem. As a general rule, correlation coefficients of 0.8 (or –0.8) or higher indicate the problem exists.

In cases where multicollinearity exists, it is sometimes possible to alter the independent variables in such a way as to reduce the correlation between them to an acceptable level. For example, suppose that a researcher wants to estimate a regression equation where the number of trips per capita to a recreation site is the dependent variable, with travel cost and travel time as two of the independent variables. If travel cost is measured as round-trip miles times average travel costs of $0.20 per mile, and time cost is measured as round-trip miles divided by 45 miles per hour times $3 per hour (that is, without adjustment for individual variations), there may be a high correlation between the two independent variables. The values of both variables are extensions of distance traveled. But if travel cost per mile and time cost per hour are measured for each individual consumer, this correlation may be reduced considerably. Costs per mile vary among types of vehicle: standard, compact and small cars, pickup truck, van, and motor home. Time costs vary among individuals depending on the proportion of the trip that provides sightseeing benefits and the opportunity cost of work foregone, if any. There may be good reasons to measure transportation and travel time costs for individuals rather than to estimate them for large groups in distance zones. Another solution is to combine travel cost and time cost into a single price variable, since the disutility of overcoming distance is not travel cost alone but also the disutility of travel time involved in making the trip.

If multicollinearity cannot be avoided, there may be no alternative than to use only one of the variables in the regression analysis. Researchers in outdoor recreation often find that when income and education are both included as independent socioeconomic variables in the multiple regression equation, they are highly intercorrelated. Education provides the skills that determine employment opportunities and income levels. Also, individuals born to higher income families can afford more education and often inherit wealth, which contributes to income levels.

Our purpose here is simply to expose the reader to the usefulness of multiple regression for analyzing recreation demand data. But anyone who uses regression techniques should appreciate the importance of testing the assumptions on which these techniques are based, while realizing that when these tests indicate that the assumptions are violated, a variety of methods exist that are aimed at handling the problem. Descriptions of these methods can be found in more advanced books on statistical techniques.

*Chapter 7*

# Determinants of Demand

This chapter discusses the present state of knowledge about the determinants of demand: socioeconomic characteristics of users; attractiveness of recreation sites; availability of substitutes; travel time; congestion; and preferences. It also illustrates the effect of these nonprice variables in shifting the demand curve for recreation.

Increased attention has focused in recent years on improving our understanding of the determinants of demand for recreation. This is important because a change in any of the nonprice variables that influence quantity demanded will produce a shift of the demand curve. A positive relationship indicates that consumers want to buy more at any given price than they wanted previously, causing the demand curve to shift to the right (or outward). A negative relationship indicates that consumers desire less at any given price, causing the demand curve to shift to the left (or inward). Learning how to accurately measure nonprice variables will enable you to provide useful information for recreation economic decisions.

The people involved, both recreation managers and researchers, are interested in what can be learned from recent experience to help formulate realistic measures of the determinants of demand in the future. The purpose of this chapter is to describe the nature of several innovations in the specification of variables included in statistical demand functions, and to assess their effects on empirical estimates of demand for recreation. The important nonprice determinants of demand must be correctly measured and included in demand functions if they are to explain demand and estimate benefits accurately.

Important nonprice determinants of demand include:

1. socioeconomic characteristics of the user population, notably income, education, age, gender, and ethnicity;
2. attractiveness or quality of recreation sites;

3. the availability of substitutes or alternative recreation opportunities in the market area;
4. travel time;
5. congestion or crowding at recreation sites; and
6. tastes and preferences.

We will show that notable improvements have occurred in measuring the nonprice variables included in recreation demand functions.

## Socioeconomic Variables

Individuals vary in their response to recreation opportunities. In an attempt to account for these differences, demand functions usually have included one or more socioeconomic (demographic) measures such as age, education, income, ethnicity, gender, vacation time, and size of city (to reflect differences in preferences between rural and urban residents) as independent variables. Often, several demographic variables are tested in a regression model, and only those that are found to be significantly related to demand are retained in the demand function for a specific recreation site. National household surveys of the entire population show that a number of socioeconomic variables affect participation in particular recreation activities. However, surveys of visitors at recreation sites do not always find a statistically significant relationship with trip frequency. Sometimes this is due to insufficient variation in the characteristics of small samples of on-site users already participating in a given activity.

Table 7-1 suggests that several important socioeconomic variables are related to the decision to participate in outdoor recreation. The table shows the results of a national survey of nearly 3,000 adults in the United States by the Heritage Conservation and Recreation Service (1980). Individual participation in recreation is the dependent variable in a multiple correlation analysis that included 11 socioeconomic factors as independent variables. The correlation coefficients shown indicate the strength of the relationship between participation and each of the factors when all other determinants of participation included in the equation are held at their mean values.

### Age

The most important socioeconomic variable appears to be age. Age accounts for 51% of the variation in participation by all adults (over age 18) and 43% by working adults. The sign of the coefficient is negative, indicating that the relationship is inverse—an increase in age results in a decrease in participation. Each of the other variables in Table 7-1 accounts for less than 10% of the variation in participation. The coefficients for each of the socioeconomic variables overstate somewhat the true correlation. Because they are unadjusted for degrees of freedom, their sum would exceed the coefficient of determination, $R^2$, for the

**Table 7-1. Socioeconomic Determinants of Adult Participation in Outdoor Recreation, United States**

| | Strength of the Relationship[a] | |
|---|---|---|
| Socioeconomic Variables | All Adults | Working Adults |
| Age | −0.51*** | −0.43*** |
| Education | 0.09*** | 0.09*** |
| Income | 0.08*** | 0.06* |
| Race | 0.07* | 0.10** |
| Sex | 0.08*** | 0.09*** |
| Size of City | −0.06*** | 0.07* |
| Hours Worked | 0.02 | 0.01 |
| Vacation Time | n.c. | 0.08*** |
| Have Yard | 0.07*** | 0.06** |
| Have Park Nearby | 0.09*** | 0.08*** |
| Coefficient of Determination, $R^2$ | 0.63 | 0.51 |
| Sample Size | 2,970 | 1,709 |

[a]Significance: * = 0.05; ** = 0.01; *** = 0.001.
n.c. = Value not calculated because vacation time data were not available for those not employed in a paid job.

Source: Heritage Conservation and Recreation Service, 1980.

combined socioeconomic variables included in the multiple correlation. The 11 socioeconomic variables explain 63% of the variation in participation by all adults and 51% by working adults.

Age is negatively related to participation in most recreation activities. Table 7-2 (page 90) shows that young people are more apt to participate in recreation activities than older people. In particular, more youth participate in physically strenuous activities, such as skiing, hiking, backpacking, horseback riding, sailing, water-skiing, driving off-road vehicles, playing tennis, and other outdoor games. Although these activities are clearly youth-oriented, participation in many others is only moderately related to age. Some recreation activities remain important in the lives of many people until late middle age, in particular: fishing, picnicking, sightseeing, driving for pleasure, nature walks, bird-watching, photography, visiting zoos and amusement parks, and attending outdoor sports events.

The cross-sectional data and simple correlation coefficients presented in Table 7-2 (page 90) show the relationship between participation in recreation activities and age, where no other variables are held constant. This represents the total effect of individuals in a particular age group; it includes a number of related conditions, such as education, income, patterns of preference, and position in society. Earlier (in Chapter 6) we looked at the effect of age with all other socioeconomic variables held constant. The last column in Table 7-2 shows the strength of the relationship between age and participation when all other socioeconomic determinants of participation are held at their mean values.

**Table 7-2. Effect of Age on Participation in Outdoor Recreation, United States**

| Activity | Age Group 12–17 | 18–24 | 25–34 | 35–44 | 45–54 | 55–64 | 65+ | Strength of Relationship[a] Simple Correlation | Multiple Correlation |
|---|---|---|---|---|---|---|---|---|---|
| Camping in Developed Area | 40% | 45% | 38% | 34% | 23% | 21% | 8% | –0.23 | –0.26 |
| Camping in Primitive Area | 31 | 36 | 27 | 24 | 13 | 7 | 5 | –0.23 | –0.24 |
| Canoeing, Kayaking, River Running | 29 | 27 | 19 | 14 | 14 | 3 | 2 | –0.21 | –0.20 |
| Sailing | 19 | 17 | 13 | 12 | 8 | 4 | 2 | –0.17 | –0.10 |
| Water-Skiing | 23 | 31 | 21 | 17 | 9 | 3 | 0 | –0.25 | –0.28 |
| Fishing | 72 | 60 | 57 | 56 | 52 | 46 | 30 | –0.20 | –0.20 |
| Other Boating | 48 | 39 | 41 | 37 | 31 | 19 | 17 | –0.19 | –0.16 |
| Outdoor Pool Swimming/Sunbathing | 90 | 82 | 78 | 73 | 51 | 41 | 19 | –0.48 | –0.39 |
| Other Outdoor Swimming/Sunbathing | 64 | 61 | 61 | 51 | 37 | 24 | 11 | –0.37 | –0.34 |
| Nature Walks, Bird-Watching, Photography | 54 | 47 | 60 | 62 | 48 | 43 | 33 | –0.11 | n.c. |
| Hiking or Backpacking | 41 | 40 | 38 | 32 | 19 | 14 | 7 | –0.24 | –0.25 |
| Other Walking or Jogging | 87 | 79 | 78 | 62 | 57 | 53 | 53 | –0.27 | –0.22 |
| Bicycling | 89 | 67 | 59 | 46 | 32 | 16 | 10 | –0.49 | –0.39 |
| Horseback Riding | 30 | 23 | 20 | 15 | 9 | 2 | 1 | –0.26 | –0.21 |
| Driving Off-Road Vehicles | 43 | 46 | 31 | 28 | 15 | 11 | 2 | –0.32 | –0.31 |
| Hunting | 24 | 25 | 18 | 27 | 17 | 15 | 8 | –0.11 | –0.10 |
| Picnicking | 77 | 74 | 84 | 81 | 75 | 64 | 47 | –0.21 | –0.18 |
| Golf | 21 | 18 | 17 | 15 | 14 | 19 | 8 | –0.05 | –0.02 |
| Tennis Outdoors | 65 | 53 | 43 | 34 | 18 | 7 | 2 | –0.43 | –0.36 |
| Cross-Country Skiing | 5 | 4 | 3 | 3 | 1 | 1 | 0 | –0.09 | n.c. |
| Downhill Skiing | 13 | 14 | 8 | 7 | 4 | 1 | 0 | –0.19 | –0.17 |
| Ice-Skating Outdoors | 33 | 22 | 22 | 18 | 1 | 4 | 1 | –0.25 | –0.18 |
| Sledding | 46 | 31 | 28 | 22 | 10 | 4 | 2 | –0.33 | –0.29 |
| Snowmobiling | 14 | 15 | 10 | 6 | 5 | 4 | 1 | –0.15 | –0.15 |
| Playing Other Sports or Games | 87 | 73 | 69 | 62 | 45 | 30 | 15 | –0.47 | –0.37 |
| Sightseeing | 61 | 63 | 70 | 73 | 64 | 59 | 44 | –0.10 | –0.07 |
| Driving for Pleasure | 52 | 83 | 80 | 79 | 67 | 66 | 51 | –0.13 | –0.18 |
| Visiting Zoos, Aquariums, Carnivals, etc. | 86 | 87 | 87 | 80 | 66 | 53 | 38 | –0.37 | –0.31 |
| Attending Outdoor Sports Events | 82 | 74 | 66 | 67 | 59 | 49 | 30 | –0.31 | –0.19 |
| Attending Outdoor Concerts, Plays | 57 | 62 | 45 | 36 | 31 | 21 | 18 | –0.28 | n.c. |

[a]All variables are significant at the 0.001 level; n.c. = value not calculated.

Source: Heritage Conservation and Recreation Service, 1980.

## *Education*

Education is positively related to participation in many recreation activities. Table 7-3 (page 92) shows that more educated people generally participate in physically strenuous activities such as canoeing, sailing, swimming, hiking, backpacking, jogging, skiing, and playing golf and tennis. Although physically strenuous activities are clearly favored by those with higher education, participation in less active pursuits is only moderately related to education, for example, camping in developed areas, motorboating, driving for pleasure, and visiting zoos and amusement parks. In some cases, demand falls when education rises, all other things being equal. People with higher education levels generally reduce participation in activities such as fishing, hunting, snowmobiling and sledding.

Years of experience participating in a recreation activity or at a site can be used as a proxy for knowledge and skill. In a study of whitewater boating, Munley and Smith (1976) conclude that past experience tends to increase a participant's skill, which has been called **learning by doing.** They reported a shift in the individual demand for recreation services as a result of the acquired skill.

## *Income*

Normally, the more income consumers have to spend, the more they are willing and able to buy. For most recreation activities this is true, but there appear to be exceptions. Table 7-4 (page 93) shows that the correlation between income and participation is usually positive, although not statistically significant in nearly two-thirds of the cases. The correlation is positive and statistically significant for sailing, motorboating, canoeing and whitewater boating, swimming in outdoor pools and beaches, sightseeing, playing tennis, bicycling, and attending outdoor sports events.

An **inferior good** is defined as one whose demand falls when consumer income rises, all other things remaining equal. The reason is clear enough. As people become wealthier they generally reduce their purchases of inferior goods because a more desirable alternative is available. Examples include secondhand clothing and bus tickets. For most recreation activities, if incomes rise and prices do not change, there will be an increase in participation. But for a few inferior activities there will be a decrease. For example, the correlation between income and participation is negative and statistically significant for hiking and backpacking. It is also negative, although not statistically significant, for camping in primitive areas, driving off-road vehicles, and playing outdoor sports and games.

## *Other Socioeconomic Variables*

Generally, whites are more likely to participate in outdoor recreation activities than blacks or other ethnic groups. Table 7-5 (page 94) shows that more whites participate in canoeing, whitewater boating, camping, golfing,

**Table 7-3. Effect of Education on Participation in Outdoor Recreation, United States**

| | Years of Education | | | | | | Strength of Relationship[a] | |
|---|---|---|---|---|---|---|---|---|
| Activity | 8 & below | 9–11 | 12 | 13–15 | 16 | 17 & Over | Simple Correlation | Multiple Correlation |
| Camping in Developed Area | 9% | 23% | 33% | 37% | 30% | 33% | 0.08 | 0.00 |
| Camping in Primitive Area | 5 | 14 | 22 | 27 | 22 | 25 | 0.06 | 0.02 |
| Canoeing, Kayaking, River Running | 3 | 7 | 15 | 20 | 21 | 22 | 0.08 | 0.09*** |
| Sailing | 2 | 3 | 8 | 15 | 24 | 24 | 0.13 | 0.13*** |
| Water-Skiing | 2 | 6 | 16 | 23 | 19 | 21 | 0.13 | 0.02 |
| Fishing | 47 | 49 | 53 | 58 | 47 | 43 | –0.04 | –0.09*** |
| Other Boating | 15 | 24 | 32 | 43 | 40 | 40 | 0.10 | 0.01 |
| Outdoor Pool Swimming and Sunbathing | 25 | 43 | 63 | 74 | 74 | 77 | 0.18 | 0.09*** |
| Other Outdoor Swimming and Sunbathing | 16 | 31 | 45 | 58 | 55 | 57 | 0.16 | 0.10*** |
| Nature Walks, Bird-Watching, Photography | 29 | 38 | 51 | 59 | 60 | 70 | 0.16 | n.c. |
| Hiking or Backpacking | 8 | 14 | 27 | 36 | 36 | 45 | 0.14 | 0.15*** |
| Other Walking or Jogging | 48 | 61 | 65 | 75 | 76 | 77 | 0.11 | 0.12*** |
| Bicycling | 15 | 27 | 42 | 55 | 52 | 48 | 0.06 | 0.08** |
| Horseback Riding | 4 | 8 | 14 | 18 | 15 | 19 | 0.04 | 0.03 |
| Driving Off-Road Vehicles | 9 | 24 | 27 | 28 | 20 | 17 | 0.02 | –0.06** |
| Hunting | 22 | 15 | 20 | 20 | 13 | 11 | –0.06 | 0.14*** |
| Picnicking | 52 | 69 | 74 | 78 | 77 | 82 | 0.14 | 0.08*** |
| Golf | 3 | 8 | 14 | 23 | 25 | 28 | 0.16 | 0.08*** |
| Tennis Outdoors | 6 | 16 | 28 | 40 | 45 | 48 | 0.16 | 0.15*** |
| Cross-Country Skiing | 0[b] | 2 | 2 | 3 | 3 | 8 | 0.08 | n.c. |
| Downhill Skiing | 2 | 1 | 5 | 10 | 11 | 14 | 0.09 | 0.09*** |
| Ice-Skating Outdoors | 3 | 7 | 16 | 18 | 17 | 18 | 0.03 | 0.05* |
| Sledding | 7 | 6 | 21 | 22 | 19 | 19 | –0.01 | –0.01 |
| Snowmobiling | 3 | 6 | 9 | 9 | 6 | 5 | 0.00 | –0.05 |
| Playing Other Sports or Games | 24 | 47 | 54 | 63 | 57 | 60 | 0.08 | 0.09*** |
| Sightseeing | 37 | 49 | 64 | 72 | 81 | 84 | 0.22 | 0.15*** |
| Driving for Pleasure | 46 | 69 | 76 | 77 | 75 | 76 | 0.20 | 0.04 |
| Visiting Zoos, Aquariums, Carnivals, etc. | 39 | 63 | 76 | 77 | 78 | 79 | 0.15 | 0.13 |
| Attending Outdoor Sports Events | 27 | 49 | 63 | 67 | 66 | 70 | 0.13 | 0.05** |
| Attending Outdoor Concerts, Plays | 17 | 31 | 40 | 47 | 49 | 59 | 0.15 | n.c. |

[a]Significance: * = 0.05; ** = 0.01; *** = 0.001; n.c. = value not calculated.

[b]Less than 0.5%.

Source: Heritage Conservation and Recreation Service, 1980.

**Table 7-4. Effect of Income on Participation in Outdoor Recreation, United States**

| Activity | Annual Household Income: Under $6,000 | $6,001 –$10,000 | $10,001 –$15,000 | $15,001 –$25,000 | $25,001 –$50,000 | Over $50,000 | Strength of Relationship[a]: Simple Correlation | Multiple Correlation |
|---|---|---|---|---|---|---|---|---|
| Camping in Developed Area | 17% | 30% | 36% | 36% | 32% | 31% | 0.11 | 0.02 |
| Camping in Primitive Area | 12 | 25 | 21 | 25 | 19 | 26 | 0.05 | –0.03 |
| Canoeing, River Running | 7 | 16 | 14 | 19 | 26 | 30 | 0.12 | 0.04* |
| Sailing | 4 | 8 | 8 | 15 | 26 | 27 | 0.19 | 0.10*** |
| Water-Skiing | 7 | 11 | 18 | 20 | 27 | 30 | 0.17 | 0.02 |
| Fishing | 40 | 55 | 61 | 58 | 52 | 49 | 0.07 | 0.02 |
| Other Boating | 18 | 30 | 35 | 42 | 46 | 51 | 0.18 | 0.09*** |
| Outdoor Pool Swimming | 37 | 60 | 68 | 73 | 80 | 78 | 0.29 | 0.12*** |
| Other Outdoor Swimming | 26 | 44 | 52 | 53 | 54 | 52 | 0.19 | 0.05** |
| Nature Walks, Bird-Watching, Photography | 39 | 50 | 50 | 57 | 55 | 51 | 0.11 | n.c. |
| Hiking or Backpacking | 16 | 26 | 32 | 33 | 33 | 36 | 0.12 | –0.04* |
| Walking or Jogging | 59 | 68 | 70 | 70 | 76 | 70 | 0.09 | 0.01 |
| Bicycling | 27 | 43 | 52 | 55 | 53 | 58 | 0.18 | 0.05** |
| Horseback Riding | 7 | 15 | 17 | 16 | 18 | 17 | 0.08 | 0.00 |
| Driving Off-Road Vehicles | 16 | 28 | 29 | 28 | 26 | 25 | 0.06 | –0.02 |
| Hunting | 14 | 19 | 20 | 22 | 18 | 23 | 0.04 | 0.03 |
| Picnicking | 55 | 74 | 79 | 80 | 74 | 67 | 0.14 | 0.02 |
| Golf | 6 | 11 | 13 | 22 | 34 | 26 | 0.23 | 0.18*** |
| Tennis Outdoors | 17 | 29 | 35 | 39 | 45 | 41 | 0.19 | 0.08*** |
| Cross-Country Skiing | 1 | 2 | 3 | 2 | 4 | 6 | 0.05 | 0.00 |
| Downhill Skiing | 2 | 5 | 5 | 10 | 13 | 19 | 0.13 | 0.02 |
| Ice-Skating Outdoors | 6 | 12 | 19 | 21 | 25 | 19 | 0.17 | 0.04* |
| Sledding | 9 | 16 | 25 | 26 | 29 | 20 | 0.16 | 0.04 |
| Snowmobiling | 4 | 7 | 9 | 9 | 11 | 13 | 0.08 | 0.00 |
| Other Sports or Games | 36 | 57 | 62 | 62 | 58 | 61 | 0.15 | –0.02 |
| Sightseeing | 42 | 59 | 66 | 74 | 73 | 81 | 0.21 | 0.11*** |
| Driving for Pleasure | 54 | 69 | 78 | 76 | 75 | 75 | 0.15 | 0.04 |
| Visiting Zoos, Aquariums, Carnivals, etc. | 52 | 71 | 80 | 80 | 82 | 79 | 0.21 | 0.07*** |
| Attending Outdoor Sports Events | 39 | 59 | 65 | 70 | 74 | 76 | 0.21 | 0.06** |
| Attending Outdoor Concerts, Plays | 30 | 45 | 42 | 42 | 44 | 58 | 0.08 | n.c. |

[a]Significance: * = 0.05; ** = 0.01; *** = 0.001; n.c. = value not calculated.

Source: Heritage Conservation and Recreation Service, 1980.

**Table 7-5. Participation in Outdoor Recreation According to Race, United States**

| Activity | Ethnicity (Race) | | | Strength of Relationship[a] | |
|---|---|---|---|---|---|
| | White | Black | Other | Simple Correlation | Multiple Correlation |
| Camping in Developed Area | 33% | 11% | 29% | 0.13 | 0.07* |
| Camping in Primitive Area | 23 | 8 | 20 | 0.10 | 0.10** |
| Canoeing, Kayaking, River Running | 17 | 11 | 8 | 0.06 | 0.11** |
| Sailing | 12 | 8 | 8 | 0.04 | 0.02 |
| Water-Skiing | 18 | 3 | 14 | 0.12 | 0.04 |
| Fishing | 54 | 48 | 53 | 0.04 | 0.01 |
| Other Boating | 36 | 18 | 30 | 0.11 | 0.04 |
| Outdoor Pool Swimming and Sunbathing | 48 | 27 | 48 | 0.13 | 0.05 |
| Nature Walks, Bird-Watching, Photography | 51 | 45 | 39 | 0.05 | n.c. |
| Hiking or Backpacking | 30 | 16 | 27 | 0.08 | 0.05 |
| Other Walking or Jogging | 68 | 69 | 70 | −0.02 | 0.01 |
| Bicycling | 46 | 51 | 56 | −0.06 | 0.01 |
| Horseback Riding | 15 | 13 | 19 | 0.01 | 0.04 |
| Driving Off-Road Vehicles | 26 | 25 | 27 | 0.00 | −0.03 |
| Hunting | 20 | 8 | 18 | 0.09 | 0.04 |
| Picnicking | 73 | 71 | 78 | 0.01 | −0.03 |
| Golf | 17 | 6 | 10 | −0.10 | 0.06* |
| Tennis Outdoors | 33 | 31 | 36 | 0.01 | 0.04 |
| Cross-Country Skiing | 3 | 2 | 4 | 0.01 | n.c. |
| Downhill Skiing | 8 | 1 | 6 | 0.08 | 0.04 |
| Ice-Skating Outdoors | 18 | 6 | 13 | 0.09 | 0.06* |
| Sledding | 22 | 7 | 18 | 0.11 | 0.07* |
| Snowmobiling | 9 | 3 | 3 | 0.09 | 0.05 |
| Other Sports or Games | 55 | 60 | 64 | −0.05 | −0.01 |
| Sightseeing | 55 | 43 | 62 | 0.10 | 0.00 |
| Driving for Pleasure | 70 | 64 | 66 | 0.05 | −0.01 |
| Visiting Zoos, Carnivals, etc. | 73 | 70 | 84 | −0.02 | −0.03 |
| Attending Outdoor Sports Events | 61 | 60 | 72 | −0.02 | 0.00 |
| Attending Outdoor Concerts, Plays | 40 | 49 | 55 | −0.09 | n.c. |

[a]Significance: * = 0.05; ** = 0.01; n.c. = value not calculated.

Source: Heritage Conservation and Recreation Service, 1980.

sledding, and ice-skating. It appears that more whites participate in other activities also, although the strength of the relationship is not statistically significant. More nonwhites appear to participate in picnicking; playing outdoor sports and games; visiting zoos, carnivals, and amusement parks; driving for pleasure; and driving off-road vehicles, although the relationship is also not statistically significant.

Table 7-6 shows that men are more likely than women to participate in most recreation activities. In particular, more men participate in consumptive activities—hunting and fishing—and in physically strenuous activities like hiking, backpacking, camping in primitive areas, outdoor sports and games, driving off-road vehicles, motorboating, and water-skiing.

**Table 7-6. Participation in Outdoor Recreation According to Gender, United States**

| | Gender | | Strength of Relationship[a] | |
|---|---|---|---|---|
| Activity | Male | Female | Simple Correlation | Multiple Correlation |
| Camping in Developed Area | 35% | 26% | 0.09 | 0.05* |
| Camping in Primitive Area | 29 | 18 | 0.18 | 0.11*** |
| Canoeing, Kayaking, River Running | 18 | 14 | 0.07 | 0.06** |
| Sailing | 11 | 11 | 0.00 | 0.02 |
| Water-Skiing | 20 | 12 | 0.10 | 0.08*** |
| Fishing | 65 | 43 | 0.25 | 0.18*** |
| Other Boating | 38 | 30 | 0.10 | 0.06 |
| Outdoor Pool Swimming and Sunbathing | 62 | 64 | –0.02 | 0.03 |
| Other Outdoor Swimming and Sunbathing | 48 | 44 | 0.05 | 0.00 |
| Nature Walks, Bird-Watching Photography | 47 | 53 | –0.05 | n.c. |
| Hiking or Backpacking | 34 | 23 | 0.12 | 0.07*** |
| Other Walking or Jogging | 65 | 71 | –0.06 | –0.05** |
| Bicycling | 46 | 47 | –0.01 | –0.03 |
| Horseback Riding | 16 | 14 | 0.04 | 0.02 |
| Driving Off-Road Vehicles | 31 | 21 | 0.13 | 0.06** |
| Hunting | 33 | 7 | 0.03 | 0.26*** |
| Picnicking | 71 | 74 | –0.03 | –0.06*** |
| Golf | 22 | 11 | 0.15 | 0.15*** |
| Tennis Outdoors | 33 | 32 | 0.00 | 0.06** |
| Cross-Country Skiing | 3 | 2 | 0.03 | n.c. |
| Downhill Skiing | 8 | 6 | 0.04 | 0.03 |
| Ice-Skating Outdoors | 17 | 16 | 0.03 | 0.01 |
| Sledding | 21 | 20 | 0.03 | 0.00 |
| Snowmobiling | 10 | 7 | 0.06 | 0.02 |
| Other Sports or Games | 62 | 50 | 0.13 | 0.09*** |
| Sightseeing | 63 | 62 | 0.02 | –0.03 |
| Driving for Pleasure | 69 | 70 | –0.01 | –0.05* |
| Visiting Zoos, Carnivals, etc. | 73 | 72 | 0.00 | –0.05* |
| Attending Outdoor Sports Events | 67 | 56 | 0.12 | –0.01 |
| Attending Outdoor Concerts, Plays | 42 | 40 | 0.05 | n.c. |

[a]Significance: * = 0.05; ** = 0.01; *** = 0.001; n.c. = value not calculated.

Source: Heritage Conservation and Recreation Service, 1980.

There is little or no significant difference between the sexes with respect to participation in beach swimming and sunbathing, sailing, snow sledding, attending outdoor concerts and plays, horseback riding, and bicycling. Significantly more women than men engage in the less strenuous activities of picnicking and walking.

Several other socioeconomic variables have been used in demand functions for recreation. For example, participation in 30 different recreation activities is sometimes related to number of vacation days per year, hours worked per week, occupation, region of the United States, and size of family. Annual vacation time appears to be positively related to participation in most activities except fishing, hunting, driving off-road vehicles, and sledding. Annual vacation is statistically significant for sightseeing, driving for pleasure, hiking, backpacking, camping in developed areas, motorboating, and downhill skiing. The differences in participation rates among people working less than and more than a 40-hour week are generally mixed.

Participation by people engaged in different occupations is related to available leisure time, income and age. Students (over 18 years of age) are more likely to participate in outdoor recreation activities than other adults. Retired persons are least likely to participate followed by those unemployed. Those with managerial and professional occupations are more likely to participate than farmers, except for hunting. People in all occupations participate at about the same rate in walking or jogging; picnicking; sightseeing; driving for pleasure; visiting zoos, carnivals, and amusement parks; and attending outdoor concerts and plays. Participation by people living in different regions of the United States generally reflect differences in opportunities. The relationship between population and participation in recreation tends to be one to one; that is, a 1% increase in population results in a 1% increase in participation, other things being equal. Single-person households generally are less likely to participate in recreation activities than are married couples, particularly couples with one to four children. Participation tends to decline for families with five or more children.

It should be noted however, the variables explaining whether a person is a participant in outdoor recreation may differ from those determining the level of participation, i.e., number of recreation days or trips per year. Therefore, the tables in this section should be considered suggestive of the possible socioeconomic determinants of demand for recreation to include in an empirical demand function, which would provide an acceptable test of their effects and significance.

## Travel Time

It can be reasonably argued that at least for some individuals, the value of travel time and on-site recreation time are important determinants of demand for recreation. The effects of both time variables is to shift the demand curve for a recreation site outward to the right and often to change its slope. Clawson and Knetsch (1966) observe that those who travel greater distances, and thereby incur higher direct costs or price, also have more travel time. If willingness to pay to avoid an hour of travel time is uniform per mile or increasing with miles traveled, those who travel greater distances also have proportionately higher travel time costs, and the demand curve will shift and become more negatively sloped. Figure 7-1 illustrates this effect. Note that the consumer surplus measure of benefits will change when time costs are included in the demand function. Whether consumer surplus increases will depend on the proportion of travel time devoted to sightseeing.

There is little or no reason to believe that the opportunity cost per hour of on-site recreation time of individuals will vary with distance traveled, i.e., the level of direct costs or price. However, those who incur larger direct costs or price per trip have an incentive to increase their length of stay at the recreation site to economize on the number of long distance trips to the site.

**Figure 7-1. Effect of Travel Time Costs on Demand for a Recreation Site**

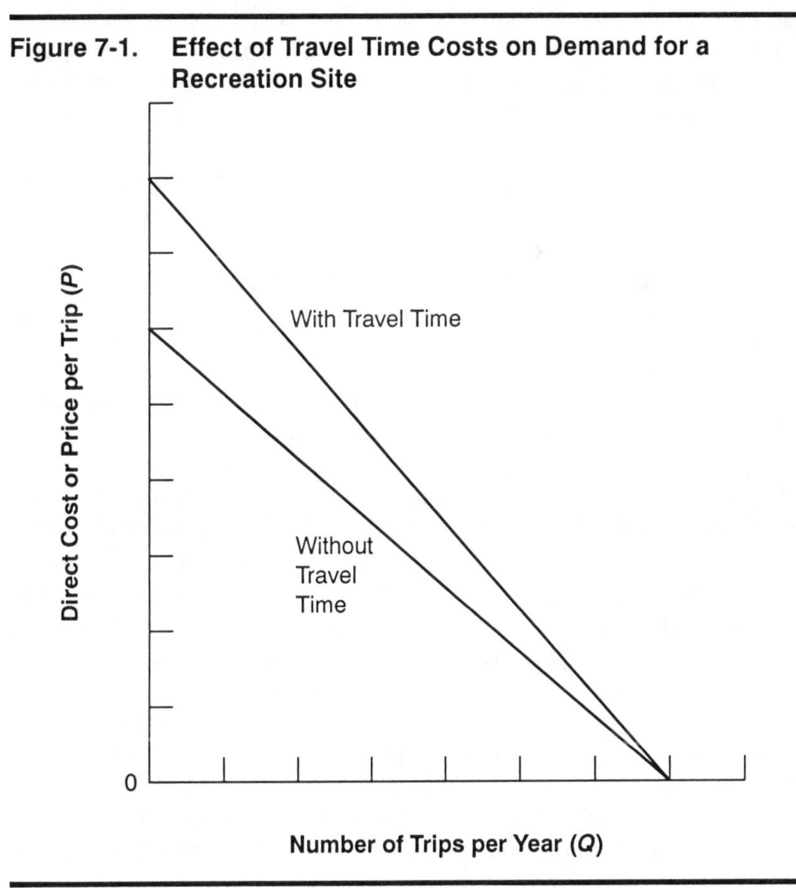

Dwyer, Kelly and Bowes (1977) observe that the travel time problem has been more easily recognized than solved. Thus far, there have been two main lines of approach. The first has been to include time as a separate independent variable in the regression equation in order to separate the effect of money and time costs on the number of trips to a recreation site. This approach has often been frustrated by high correlation between money and time costs of travel, precluding an accurate estimate of the effect of each variable. Brown and Nawas (1973) and many others since then overcame this problem by measuring travel cost and time cost for each individual consumer using survey responses rather than estimating them on the basis of distance traveled.

The second approach has been to assume a monetary value of travel time and to add this to the direct money cost of auto travel to obtain a single combined price variable. While the procedure appears to have provided acceptable results, an accurate estimate of the monetary value of travel time has yet to be established in empirical work. So far the value of travel time has been assumed to be some fraction (25%–50%) of individual wage rates, as recommended by the federal guidelines. Wilman (1980) suggests that a more accurate estimate of the value of travel time would be to ask individuals their willingness to pay to avoid it. Also she recommends that on-site recreation time be valued in terms of opportunity cost in its best alternative use. For individuals whose work time is variable, the opportunity cost of on-site recreation time could be measured as income actually foregone while on site. It seems likely that the value per hour of travel time is a function of distance and other variables, rather than a constant per mile traveled.

## Substitutes and Complements

When substitute sites are available, it is likely that they will have a significant influence on demand for a particular recreation site. If individuals have a wide choice of substitute or alternative recreation sites, then the demand curve will have a flatter negative slope, as illustrated in Figure 7-2. On the other hand, if individuals have fewer substitutes, then the demand curve has a steeper negative slope. The reason is that the observed demand curve includes the effect of the availability of substitutes as well as the price of visiting the study site. If there are reservoirs in the county where one lives, one is less likely to go fishing at a site located in the next county. When the entrance fee to that reservoir rises, demand goes up for trips to reservoirs that are substitutes. When the price of downhill skiing at popular resorts goes up, people demand less downhill skiing; instead, they go cross-country skiing closer to home.

Certain recreation goods and services make one another more desirable. For example, restaurants and lodges increase the desirability of skiing at some resorts and vice versa. The same is true of reservoirs and campgrounds. In some extreme cases, neither of the two has any use

**Figure 7-2. Effect of Substitute Sites on Demand for a Recreation Site**

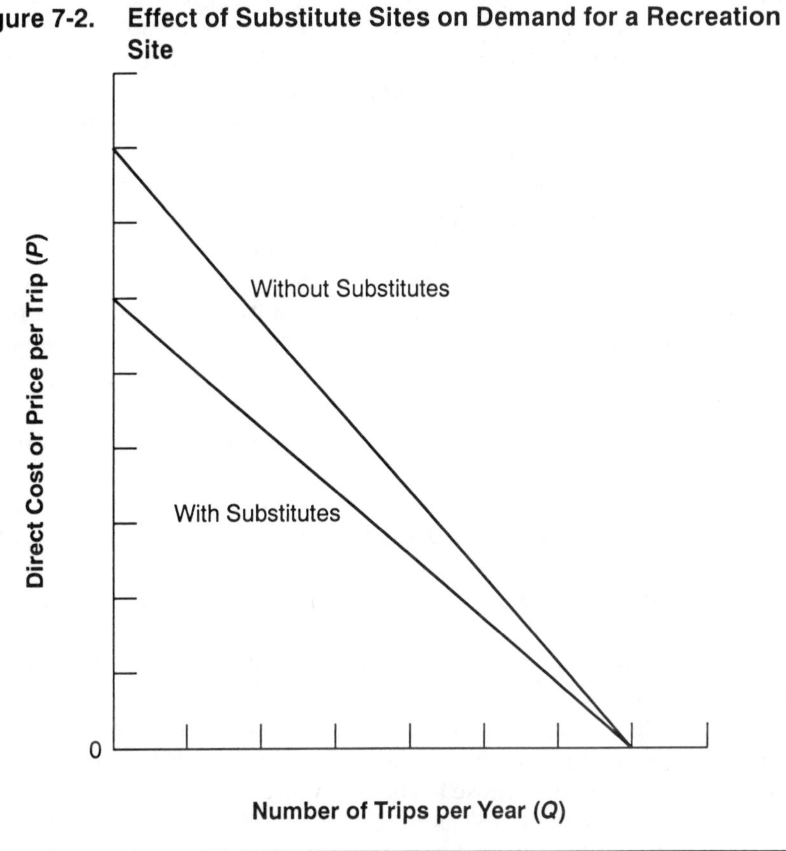


without the other—four-wheel-drive vehicles and mud tires, a pair of skis and ski boots, and so on. Such things, each of which makes the other more valuable, are called complements. The demand curves of complements are interrelated, meaning that a rise in the direct cost or price of skiing is likely to affect the quantity of restaurant meals and lodge rooms demanded. Why? When the direct cost or price of skiing at a site rises, less skiing will be demanded and therefore less overnight lodging and other services will be demanded at the ski site. A similar relationship holds for other complementary goods.

This result is really a matter of common sense. If the direct cost or price of anything goes up and there is a substitute available, some people will tend to switch to the substitute. On the other hand, if two goods or services are complements, a rise in the price of one will discourage its own use and will also discourage use of the complementary item. Two recreation sites are called substitutes if an increase in the direct cost or price of trips to one increases the number of trips demanded to the other, all other things remaining constant. Two recreation sites are called complements if an increase in the direct cost or price of trips to one reduces the number of trips demanded to both sites. Kurtz and King (1980) show that some reservoirs in Arizona are substitutes and others are complements. One plausible explanation of a complementary relationship between reservoirs is the desire of individuals with motorboats to visit a variety of recreation sites each year. Caulkins, Bishop and Bouwes (1985) suggest that the existence of two or more excellent bass fishing lakes may induce an angler to invest in more expensive equipment and fish more often, whereas the existence of only one such lake may not justify the investment.

The federal guidelines recommend that demand functions for recreation include a variable that takes into account substitutes in the form of competition from other recreational opportunities within the area influenced by a recreation site. Early efforts characterized the recreation opportunities in counties of the United States in terms of water acreage, recreation land area, and miles to the nearest large body of water. Another early attempt to incorporate the substitution variable into a recreation demand function was a study of eight reservoirs in Texas by Grubb and Goodwin (1968). The size of alternative reservoirs in surface acres of minimum pool was weighted by distance in miles to each reservoir within 100 miles of the center of counties where users live. In its simplest application, surface acres were divided by distance. To adjust for quality of substitute sites, fish catch at substitute sites has been divided by distance to the substitute sites. The substitution variable was the sum of catch per mile driven for all sites exceeding the catch per mile of the study site. These are proxy measures of the capacity of the existing stock of recreation facilities in the market area centered at the respondent's home that are similar to those at the study site. They have been characterized by McConnell (1975) as rough measures which may not capture all of the substitution effects.

The substitution price variable has been measured as the distance from the home of each respondent to the nearest existing alternative facility offering recreation opportunities similar to those at the study site. Alternately, this variable has been measured from survey questions on the willingness to drive to the next most preferred recreation facility offering similar recreation opportunities if the study site became unavailable. In regional demand functions, the direct cost of trips to other sites in the region has been used as a proxy for the price of substitutes.

There is some dispute as to whether a quantity or a price measure is more appropriate. In theory, a distance or travel cost variable is most appropriate to estimate the substitution effects in an ordinary demand curve. Unfortunately, the travel cost to the study site and the substitute site may be highly correlated, making it difficult to isolate the effect of the substitute site. In addition, the quantity of available substitutes may also influence actual user substitution. It seems likely that the supply of recreation resources and whether users consider them substitutes or complements may have an important influence on the demand for study sites. Work by social psychologists (Vaske, Donnelly and Tweed, 1983), shows that researcher-defined substitutes are not statistically related to recreation user-defined substitutes. We conclude that more emphasis needs to be placed on consumer perceptions of suitable substitute sites and activities.

## Attractiveness or Quality

The attractiveness of the site or the quality of the resource constitutes another important determinant of demand for recreation. In the past, a useful measure of attractiveness was simply size—for example, the surface area of a lake or park in acres (Grubb and Goodwin, 1968). Experience has shown size to be an effective proxy for other variables that affect site attractiveness, such as campsites, length of beach, acres of picnic area, miles of hiking trail, and boat-launching ramps. Loomis, Roach, Ward and Ready (1995) found that size is a sufficiently good measure of attractiveness for purposes of estimating demand functions for Corps of Engineers reservoirs where construction of recreation facilities tends to be related to size. However, it is too general a measure to effectively estimate the demand effects of specific site quality and design alternatives.

Recently, several measures of the quality of recreation resources have been included in demand functions in an effort to estimate their specific effects on demand and willingness to pay. Variables that have been tried include air quality and visibility (Randall, Ives and Eastman, 1974), water quality (Bouwes and Schneider, 1979), water level (Daubert and Young, 1981), forest quality (Walsh and Olienyk, 1981), game and fish harvest (Loomis and Cooper, 1990), weather conditions (McConnell, 1977), noise (McMillan, Reed and Gillen, 1980), and congestion (discussed in the following section). Wherever possible, these quality variables have been measured in physical units (e.g., cubic feet of instream flow, temperature, number of trees, number of persons, number and pounds of fish caught). In other cases, quality has been estimated by experts or visitors, using a 10-point scale. Visitors may be asked to rate the quality of the physical characteristics of facilities and resources available at the recreation site or of color photos illustrating a range of quality.

There are a large number of physical and biological characteristics of recreation sites that may influence recreation demand. Brown, Haas and Manfredo (1977) have studied consumer preferences for attributes of wilderness in the Rocky Mountains of the United States. They asked users of Wilderness Areas to rate each of the physical attributes shown in Table 7-7 (page 102) on a Likert scale of satisfaction, from most strongly adds (1) to most strongly detracts (9). Attributes of the resource were grouped into eight categories. Attributes of the meadow, forest, water, and wildlife contributed most to the satisfaction of using the recreation area. Nuisances and intrusions detracted from user satisfaction.

Interest in the study of the effects of site attractiveness has been stimulated by the development of a procedure to classify the supply of recreation land and related resources into six broad categories ranging from

**Table 7-7. Consumer Ratings of the Quality of Resource Attributes at Indian Peaks Wilderness Area, Colorado.**

| Resource Attribute | Value | Contribution to Satisfaction Mean Score[a] |
|---|---|---|
| Meadow-Forest | Strongly Adds | 1.85 |
| Water Related | Strongly Adds | 1.87 |
| Abundant Sources of Water | | 1.95 |
| Waterfalls | | 1.63 |
| Lake Views | | 1.87 |
| Large Roaring Streams | | 2.17 |
| Wildlife | Moderately/ Strongly Adds | 2.48 |
| Dense Vegetation | Moderately Adds | 2.62 |
| Rugged Topography | Moderately Adds | 2.64 |
| Rare or Unique Natural Features | Moderately Adds | 2.84 |
| Rock Towers | | 2.83 |
| Unusually Shaped Rocks | | 2.77 |
| Rare Plants | | 2.81 |
| Indian Artifacts | | 3.01 |
| Hot Springs | | 2.89 |
| Fish Related | Moderately Adds | 3.20 |
| Nuisances (e.g., insects) | Neither Adds nor Detracts | 5.37 |
| Intrusions | Slightly Detracts | 5.82 |
| Evidence of Logging Activity | | 6.81 |
| Evidence of Mining Activity | | 6.18 |
| Reservoirs in the Backcountry | | 4.46 |

[a]Nine point scale with 1 = most strongly adds, 9 = most strongly detracts.

Source: Adapted from Brown, Haas and Manfredo, 1977.

primitive to urban. The classification system, referred to as the Recreation Opportunity Spectrum (ROS), has been adopted by the U.S. Forest Service and the Bureau of Land Management. Table 7-8 illustrates the essential elements of the system including distance from a road, size in square miles, presence of buildings and other improvements, number of persons encountered, and visible management practices. These general indicators measure the naturalness of the setting in which recreation takes place. Essentially, larger and more remote sites that are less developed with lower density and less evidence of management are more likely to be classified toward the primitive end of the ROS scale. Thus, for those who desire a natural environment, hiking in a primitive roadless zone is expected to be more beneficial than hiking in a roaded or urban zone.

**Table 7-8. Characteristics of Recreation Resources in a National Forest**

| Variable | Unit | Recreation Opportunity (ROS) Zones<br>Semiprimitive,<br>Primitive | Nonmotorized | Motorized |
|---|---|---|---|---|
| Buildings and Improvements | Number | None | Rare | Frequent |
| Distance from Roads | Miles | Over 3.0 | 0.5–3.0 | Less Than 0.5 |
| Size of Sites | Acres | Over 5,000 | 2,500–5,000 | Any Size |
| Congestion on Trails | Parties Encountered /Day | Less Than 6 | 6–15 | Over 15 |
| Persons at One Time, Maximum | Persons/Acre | 0.025 | 0.083 | 0.083–7.6 |
| Management Controls | Scale | Low | Moderate | High |

Source: U.S. Forest Service, 1981.

Studies of the demand for recreation sites should include the physical characteristics that are relevant. For downhill skiing, Morey (1981) observes that the physical characteristics most useful to individual skiers depend on ability (beginner, intermediate or advanced), as they are not capable of skiing terrain that is more difficult than their ability allows. The appropriate measure of characteristics becomes the acres of terrain at the site suitable for the individual's skiing ability and the lift capacity (vertical transport feet) serving these ski runs. Other physical characteristics that affect demand for skiing include annual snowfall, snow quality, and weather conditions such as sun, temperature and wind.

In visiting a recreation site, a user acquires a bundle of physical services. Different recreation sites have different bundles of physical characteristics associated with them, and the user's demand and willingness to pay is a function of the physical services associated with the site. When there is a sufficient range of data on quality for different days at the same site or among a number of study sites, the effect of the quality variable on demand can be estimated statistically. The regression coefficient indicates the effect of one additional unit of quality on demand, all else held constant. Alternately, the value of an increment of quality can be estimated directly by asking users their willingness to pay or to participate with hypothetical changes in quality of the resource.

Leuschner and Young (1978) estimated the effect of southern pine beetle damage to ponderosa pine trees on demand for recreation use of 19 campgrounds located on the shore of two reservoirs in Texas. The demand function included pine tree density from aerial photos as one of the independent variables. The effect of the proportion of the recreation sites covered by pine crowns was isolated from other site characteristics such as the presence of hardwood trees, size of campground, facilities available, quality of access, and number of substitute sites available. They estimated the elasticity of demand (change in quantity consumed caused by change in a determinant of demand) with respect to pine trees as 0.64 to 0.68, nearly double the effect of number of pine trees at recreation sites in the northern Rocky Mountains. The variation in results may reflect differences in the value of shade from trees in the relatively cooler mountain states.

An example of the second approach is a study of forest quality at recreation sites in the Rocky Mountains. Walsh and Olienyk (1981) found that forest quality has a significant effect on demand for developed camping, semideveloped camping, backpacking, hiking, fishing, picnicking, driving off-road vehicles, and staying at resorts. Based on interviews with 435 users at six forest recreation sites, the relationship apparently is an inverted-U. Annual recreation use increases from nine days per year with no trees to nearly 19 days with 225 trees per acre. Beyond this level, participation decreases with additional trees.

## Congestion

The level of congestion or crowding at a recreation site may have a significant effect on individual demand and willingness to pay. Congestion occurs when an individual user of a recreation area encounters increasing numbers of other users. Congestion enters the individual's demand function like any other nonprice variable. When congestion adversely affects the quality of the recreation experience, a downward shift in the demand curve results. The effect of incremental congestion can be estimated directly by asking users their willingness to pay or participate with hypothetical changes in congestion as for any quality variable.

Several alternative measures of congestion at recreation sites have been included in demand functions. Measures that have been tried include:

1. actual number of users per acre per day or at one time (McConnell, 1977);
2. number of encounters per day or per hour on the trail and in backcountry campsites (Walsh and Gilliam, 1982);
3. number of minutes of lift line wait (Walsh, Miller and Gilliam, 1983); and
4. utilization of capacity, defined as a ratio of users per day to physical capacity.

Table 7-9 illustrates the rate at which individual benefits diminish as the number of people encountered increases. When visitors are few, encountering other people provides a sense of safety, does not interfere appreciably with the quality of the experience, and benefits fall off slowly.

**Table 7-9. Effect of Number of Other Parties Encountered per Activity Day on an Index of Individual Benefits From Wilderness Hiking, Camping, Fishing and Boating, United States**

| Index of Benefits per Day of Recreation Activity | Number of Other Parties Encountered per Day[a] 0 | 5 | 10 | 15 | 20 | 25 | 30 | 35 | 40 |
|---|---|---|---|---|---|---|---|---|---|
| Wilderness Areas | | | | | | | | | |
| Trails | 1.00 | 0.89 | 0.79 | 0.70 | 0.60 | 0.00 | 0.00 | 0.00 | 0.00 |
| Campsites | 1.00 | 0.81 | 0.79 | 0.53 | 0.00 | 0.00 | 0.00 | 0.00 | 0.00 |
| River Fishing | 1.00 | 0.89 | 0.79 | 0.71 | 0.55 | 0.38 | 0.33 | 0.27 | 0.12 |
| Homestake Creek | 1.00 | 0.97 | 0.95 | 0.92 | 0.88 | 0.80 | 0.70 | 0.59 | 0.32 |
| Frying Pan River | 1.00 | 0.88 | 0.78 | 0.72 | 0.60 | 0.44 | 0.38 | 0.31 | 0.12 |
| Eagle River | 1.00 | 0.83 | 0.68 | 0.55 | 0.27 | 0.00 | 0.00 | 0.00 | 0.00 |
| River Kayaking | 1.00 | 0.95 | 0.89 | 0.83 | 0.75 | 0.66 | 0.53 | 0.31 | 0.15 |
| Crystal River | 1.00 | 0.91 | 0.81 | 0.69 | 0.51 | 0.35 | 0.15 | 0.00 | 0.00 |
| Roaring Fork River | 1.00 | 0.95 | 0.88 | 0.86 | 0.84 | 0.81 | 0.77 | 0.71 | 0.64 |
| Colorado at Glenwood | 1.00 | 0.98 | 0.96 | 0.93 | 0.90 | 0.84 | 0.72 | 0.36 | 0.00 |
| River Rafting | 1.00 | 0.98 | 0.65 | 0.56 | 0.33 | 0.31 | 0.25 | 0.18 | 0.16 |
| Colorado—State Bridge | 1.00 | 0.95 | 0.89 | 0.81 | 0.69 | 0.60 | 0.29 | 0.00 | 0.00 |
| Roaring Fork River | 1.00 | 0.99 | 0.98 | 0.97 | 0.94 | 0.90 | 0.87 | 0.80 | 0.72 |
| Yampa River | 1.00 | 0.95 | 0.80 | 0.67 | 0.00 | 0.00 | 0.00 | 0.00 | 0.00 |
| Colorado at Westwater | 1.00 | 1.00 | 0.13 | 0.00 | 0.00 | 0.00 | 0.00 | 0.00 | 0.00 |
| Total, Western Rivers | 1.00 | 0.94 | 0.74 | 0.66 | 0.49 | 0.40 | 0.33 | 0.24 | 0.15 |
| Reservoir Fishing | 1.00 | 0.94 | 0.88 | 0.78 | 0.55 | 0.17 | 0.00 | 0.00 | 0.00 |
| Small, 1–50 Acres | 1.00 | 0.82 | 0.61 | 0.24 | 0.00 | 0.00 | 0.00 | 0.00 | 0.00 |
| Medium, 51–150 Acres | 1.00 | 0.93 | 0.81 | 0.65 | 0.49 | 0.22 | 0.00 | 0.00 | 0.00 |
| Large, 151–400 Acres | 1.00 | 0.97 | 0.92 | 0.85 | 0.72 | 0.51 | 0.11 | 0.00 | 0.00 |
| Reservoir Power Boating[b] | 1.00 | 0.96 | 0.92 | 0.88 | 0.83 | 0.77 | 0.72 | 0.66 | 0.59 |

[a]A party was defined as one fisherman, one power boater, one kayaker, one hiker, one camper, and one raft containing an average of five persons.

[b]Large, over 400 acres.

Source: Wilderness data are from Fisher and Krutilla, 1972; other data from studies by Walsh, Ericson, Arosteguy and Hanson, 1980; and Walsh and Gilliam, 1982.

Further increases in the number of people in a given space eventually result in crowding, a reduction in the quality of the experience, and benefits decrease more rapidly. This is true of most recreation activities for which data is available. With no encounters assigned a value of 1.0, individual benefits of wilderness camping decline by half to 0.5 when 15 other persons are encountered. Encountering the same number of persons on a trail reduces benefits by about one-third to an index of 0.7. This illustrates the fact that wilderness campers tend to be more sensitive to congestion than hikers.

Perhaps it would be useful to consider a concrete example of a congestion survey. In a study of excess demand for the Indian Peaks Wilderness Area in the Rocky Mountains, a representative sample of 126 hikers and backpackers were asked to report the maximum amount of money they would be willing to pay rather than forego the experience. From this was subtracted direct costs or price to obtain consumer surplus. The number of persons (other than members of their own party) encountered in the Wilderness Area on the day of the interview was recorded as one of four observations. Willingness to pay also was reported when the number of persons encountered was zero, for an intermediate level, and for the maximum level of crowding that individuals would tolerate before discontinuing recreation use of the site. These four observations trace out the relationship between congestion and willingness to pay.

Congestion may reduce the benefits received by individuals using the recreation area but it usually will not change the direct monetary costs or price to individual users. Each additional user considers his or her individual benefits of the experience, that is, net of the loss in benefits imposed by the presence of other users. But individuals ignore the fact that their presence increases congestion and reduces the benefits for other users, which creates a divergence between individual and social (or group) effects of congestion. As is generally true in cases of external effects, this will eventually result in overuse of the recreation site, reducing aggregate total satisfaction and benefits of the experience below efficient levels. Thus, the presence of congestion has implications for estimating the capacity of recreation areas.

As long as the gains from additional users exceed the losses due to congestion, aggregate total benefits increase. Beyond some point, the loss in benefits resulting from congestion exceed the gains experienced by additional users, and aggregate total benefits fall. Aggregate total benefits of a recreation area are maximized where the loss in benefits from incremental congestion equals the gain in benefits from incremental use. If there were no other effects of congestion, the recommended carrying capacity would be at this level. With the introduction of the costs of recreation use management and environmental degradation, the recommended carrying capacity would fall to a point where marginal benefits would equal marginal costs (see Figure 7-3, page 108).

The economic carrying capacity of recreation sites is the number of users where aggregate total benefits are maximized. There are two points that should be made about its implications for managers. Economic studies of congestion show that serving the most people would eventually push benefits to zero. Providing the highest quality experience to each individual would limit participation to fewer users than would provide the greatest benefit in total. The economic capacity of a recreation site represents a compromise solution in between these two extreme objectives.

Congestion is an important consideration not only in estimating the benefits of an existing recreation site and its carrying capacity, but also in estimating the benefits of a new or expanded site. The regression coefficients for congestion at existing sites allow us to estimate the external benefits of reducing congestion to optimal levels at these sites as part of the benefits of the substitution of a new or expanded site. Also, if congestion is taken into account when a demand function derived from an existing site is applied to a new site, it is no longer necessary to assume that congestion affects both sites in a similar manner. If the level of congestion is expected to be different at the new site, the demand curve would be shifted to reflect the change.

The influence of congestion on demand and willingness to pay depends on the perception of individual users. Thus, recreation sites may be similar in physical characteristics and still have different congestion effects. For example, McConnell (1977) found substantially different congestion effects at each of six Rhode Island beaches. On average, an extra 100 people per acre reduced the average individual's consumer surplus per day by about 25%. However, he calculated the optimal number of users per acre (at maximum total benefits) based on the congestion effects and found a wide range: from 59 people per acre for a beach near a wildlife sanctuary to a whopping 2,400 people per acre for a "singles" beach. The reason for this large divergence seems to be that the clientele of the two beaches differ greatly in their attitudes regarding the effect of crowding on their recreation benefits.

We can compare the economic capacity of several Wilderness Areas in the western United States. The number of encounters, expressed as parties per day, which would maximize aggregate total benefits varies as follows:

| | |
|---|---|
| Indian Peaks, Colorado | 12–15 |
| Other Colorado areas | 6–8 |
| Desolation, California | 7–8 |
| Spanish Peaks, Montana | 4–7 |

These estimates suggest that if preferences for congestion avoidance were the same across Wilderness Areas in the West, the economic capacity of Indian Peaks would be nearly half the level estimated. Its higher capacity is associated with scarcity of wilderness recreation opportunities near large population centers where users have learned to accept higher levels of congestion.

It is interesting to compare the effect of congestion on demand and willingness to pay for lift tickets at a small and a large ski area in the Rocky Mountains. On average, an additional one-minute wait in a lift line decreases individual skier's demand by 0.25 of a day at the small ski area compared with 0.47 of a day at the large. An additional one-minute wait in lift lines also decreases willingness to pay for lift tickets by $0.27 per day at the small ski area compared with $0.34 at the large area (Figure 7-3, page 108). Also, an extra skier per acre on the slopes decreases

**Figure 7-3. Effect of Number of Skiers per Day on Aggregate and Marginal Willingness to Pay for Lift Tickets**

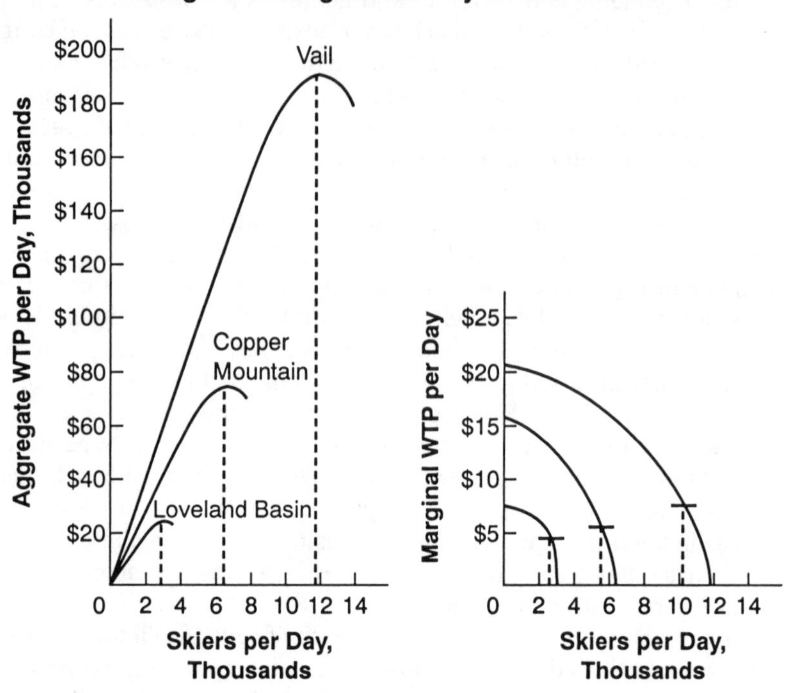


Source: Walsh, Richard G., Nicole P. Miller, and Lynde O. Gilliam. (1983, May). Congestion and Willingness to Pay for Expansion of Skiing Capacity. *Land Economics* 59:205. Reprinted by permission of the University of Wisconsin Press.

willingness to pay by $0.90 per day at the small ski area compared with $0.22 at the large. The reason for these differences seems to be that the clientele of the large ski area expect more services for the higher prices that they pay. The optimum capacity when variable management costs are introduced is illustrated in the right-hand portion of Figure 7-3. The small horizontal lines represent marginal costs. Including these reduces economic capacity.

The results of these studies should be viewed as tentative and first approximations, subject to further study. Much more research is needed before we will understand the relevant economic and noneconomic questions concerning congestion. We measured the effect of two important variables—lift line and slope congestion—on willingness to pay for lift tickets, and estimated the marginal costs of the ski areas from secondary data. As intensity of recreation resource use increases, congestion also occurs in the parking lot, lodge, restaurant, highway and airport. Congestion research in the future should encompass all possible relevant variables and postpone the decision about which ones warrant consideration in the final analysis until knowledge of their relative significance has been developed. Also, there is a need to study the marginal costs of operating recreation sites and the external costs of environmental damages. The economic capacity of recreation sites may prove much less than the available evidence suggests at the present time.

## Tastes and Preferences

Tastes and preferences of individual consumers have been considered important nonprice variables in demand functions. Unfortunately, most empirical demand studies of recreation activities in the past have not included effective taste and preference variables. The omission is due to the lack of an accurate general measure, rather than any conscious decision by economists that the variable is unimportant as a determinant of demand. In the past the federal guidelines have recommended that demand functions for recreation include the important socioeconomic characteristics of the user population as a proxy for taste and preference variables. While income and age tend to be related to variations in tastes and preferences, they are indirect measures of tastes. The task remains to integrate direct measures into demand functions for recreation.

Tastes and preferences refer to the basic characteristics of individual's personality. For example some people like active or physically strenuous activities, such as hiking in a recreation area, while others prefer more passive or comfortable activities. Should many individuals suddenly decide that they like active recreation better, the demand curve for such recreation will shift to the right. This preference variable can be categorical, meaning that one equals active and zero equals passive. A regression coefficient of 1.25 indicates that individuals who prefer active recreation demand 1.25 trips more than those who prefer passive recreation.

Alternatively, should physical activity go out of style, the demand curve for such recreation would shift to the left. Again, these are quite general phenomena. If consumer preferences shift in favor of a particular activity, that activity's demand curve will shift outward to the right, as quantity demanded rises. Conversely, if consumer preferences go against a particular activity, that activity's demand curve will shift inward to the left, as quantity demanded falls.

A number of social scientists working in recreation, particularly Driver and Brown (1975), have studied consumer preferences for recreation experiences. Driver (1977) found that patterns of individual preferences for recreation activities can be classified into the 19 categories illustrated in Figure 7-4 (page 110). They asked individuals participating in a wide variety of recreation activities to rate each of the preference variables on a Likert scale of satisfaction. The possible responses typically range from strongly adds to strongly detracts.

It is readily apparent that there are a large number of preference variables that can be significantly related to the recreation experience. Attempts have been made to combine these variables into meaningful groups

**Figure 7-4. Questions About Preference for Outdoor Recreation Experiences**

1. Developing, applying, and testing skills and abilities for a better sense of self-worth and self-development.
2. Exercising to feel good physically.
3. Resting, both physically and mentally.
4. Associating with close friends and other users to develop new friendships.
5. Obtaining privacy, solitude, and tranquillity in an outdoor setting.
6. Experiencing natural ecosystems in environments which are largely unmodified by human activity.
7. Gaining social recognition to enhance self-esteem.
8. Enhancing a feeling of family, kinship or solidarity.
9. Teaching and leading others, especially to help direct the growth, learning, and development of one's children.
10. Reflecting on personal values and growing spiritually.
11. Feeling free, independent, and more in control than is possible in more structured home and work environments.
12. Enjoyment of scenic beauty.
13. Gaining a new mental perspective in a tranquil outdoor setting.
14. Self-testing and risk taking for self-development and sense of accomplishment.
15. Applying and developing creative abilities.
16. Learning more about nature, especially natural processes, human dependence on them, and how to live in greater harmony with nature.
17. Gaining a greater appreciation of the nation's cultural heritage and resource endowment, which can contribute to development of more pride in that nation.
18. Exploring and being stimulated, to satisfy curiosity needs, and to meet the need for exploration.
19. Replenishing adaptive energies and abilities by temporarily escaping adverse social and physical conditions experienced in home, neighborhood, and work environments. These conditions include noise, too many things to do, demands of others, time pressures, crowdedness, insufficient green or open space, lack of privacy, pollution, unsafe environments, and demanding jobs.

Source: Driver, 1977.

reflecting types of individual personality groups, so-called O-types, such as passive, extractive, social, and nature (Brown, Hautaluoma and McPhail, 1977). Thus far, grouped preference scores by personality types have provided encouraging results when included in demand functions for recreation. However, the complexity of the approach and the somewhat mixed results suggest that a simplifying modification must be developed before it will receive widespread adoption. Miller, Prato and Young (1977) report that eight types of personalities explain 15% of the variation in willingness to pay for deer hunting. For example, values range from $29 per year for the group with minimum gratification to $108 for a group of gung-ho hunters who score highest on every attribute of the experience.

It may be possible to obtain direct estimates of willingness to pay for one or another of these psychological outcomes of the recreation experience. Recently, we asked a representative sample of 285 forest recreation users in the Rocky Mountains their willingness to drive additional miles to try a new recreation site. Figure 7-4 describes this motivation as "exploring and being stimulated, to satisfy curiosity needs, and to meet the need for exploration" (item 18), which is identical to Scitovsky's definition of novelty. We found that novelty shifted the demand curve outward and to the right for a substantial proportion of recreation users. Consumers reported that they were willing to drive about 30% more miles to try a new recreation site.

There may be other significant preference variables that are not included on this list and about which we know very little. For example, Leibenstein (1950) observed that a "bandwagon" effect—desire for social conformity—may make some recreation activities more desirable, and that a "snob" effect—desire for exclusivity—may favor other activities. This is an extension of the ideas of Thorstein Veblen in his earlier book, *The Theory of the Leisure Class.* Thus, if the bandwagon effect applies, the individual's demand curve will shift outward at all price levels as market demand in total increases. On the other hand, if the snob effect applies to an individual, his or her demand curve will shift back at all price levels as more and more consumers participate in the activity. As a recreation activity loses appeal with increased participation, some consumers will find the activity less desirable and take fewer trips than they would have if participation of others had been less. To estimate either the bandwagon or snob effect, a sample survey of consumers would be asked how much they would participate in a particular recreation activity when site or market demand is at various levels. Some consumers may exhibit bandwagon effects at the same time that others demonstrate snob effects.

Gibson (1980) was apparently the first economist to develop a general measure of the preference for the public good aspect of parks and recreation. She hypothesized that those who believe they do not have to use governmental services to derive benefits from them are more willing to pay taxes for the support of parks and recreational areas. She asked 182 registered voters in Santa Clara County, California, five questions including, "Some think that the only people who really benefit from state parks are people who use them. How much truth do you think there is to this way of thinking?" The possible responses were (1) very little, (2) little, (3) some, (4) pretty much, and (5) a great deal. Responses to the five questions were combined, with scores summed into a single taste variable.

Then, two demand functions were estimated. In both, the dependent variable to be explained was willingness to pay taxes to support parks and recreational areas. One equation included price and income as independent variables, and the other, these two variables plus the preference variable. The results showed that the variable explained 15% of the variation in willingness to pay, with price and income effects held constant. On average, a 1% change in the preference variable resulted in a positive 0.32% change in willingness to pay taxes to support parks and recreational areas. We can conclude that general adoption of effective taste and preference measures would substantially increase our ability to explain willingness to pay for recreation.

## *Chapter 8*

# Elasticity of Demand

This chapter shows how to calculate the three most important elasticities of demand (i.e., price, income, and cross elasticity), summarizes the results of recent studies, and illustrates how elasticities can be applied to recreation economic decisions.

The concept is simple and straightforward. Elasticity of demand is defined as the percentage change in quantity consumed that is caused by a percentage change in a determinant of demand. Price elasticity of demand, for example, is a convenient way of comparing how price changes affect the quantity consumed. It is the ratio of two percentages—the change in quantity consumed that results from a change in price. When the percentage change in price results in a larger percentage change in quantity demanded, the demand is said to be elastic. By elastic we mean that the quantity demanded is quite sensitive or very responsive to price changes. Conversely, when the percentage change in price results in a smaller percentage change in quantity demanded it is said to be inelastic, i.e., the quantity is not very sensitive to changes in the price.

Elasticity of demand has been widely used in recreation economic decisions because of its simplicity and convenience. When an elasticity is multiplied by an expected percentage change in a variable, it gives an estimate of the expected percentage change in demand. Thus, it is clear that estimates of elasticities of demand can play an important role in understanding the consequences of socioeconomic trends and management alternatives. Whether, and to what extent, entrance fees will help ease the deficits of city and state parks departments are questions that cannot be answered correctly without a knowledge of the price elasticity of demand. When managers of private or public recreation resources want to estimate demand for specific recreation activities and sites, they need to know the elasticities of demand with respect to price, income, substitution, and other variables. Many resort operators need to know the cross elasticities of demand for their resorts and those offering similar activities. Reliable measurements of demand elasticities would be valuable in a wide variety of applications involving recreation decisions.

Fortunately, a great deal of information is available on elasticities of demand from statistical studies of recreation demand. In this chapter, we will look at some of the estimates that have been made over the last couple of decades. Even where information is not already available, it is often possible to obtain it without great cost or difficulty. The appropriate methods have been carefully worked out to calculate elasticities of demand.

If you have access to the computer printout of a demand function for a recreation site, elasticities of demand can usually be calculated at the point where the quantity demanded and each independent variable are at their mean values. In this case, no additional computation is necessary when expected changes in the independent variables are small. However, you are more likely to have access to a published work showing the demand function for the study site or a similar site. In this case, you probably will need to compute elasticities from the information that is available. The first thing to do is check the functional form of the demand function, whether it is linear, quadratic, semilog, or double-log (both the dependent and independent variables are natural log transformations). When the functional form is double-log, no additional computation is necessary, because the regression coefficients are also the elasticities. The following section illustrates how to compute elasticities when the demand function is linear.

## Price Elasticity of Demand

Price elasticity of demand is a measure of the responsiveness of quantity demanded to changes in the direct cost or price of trips to a recreation site, holding constant the values of all other variables. Price elasticity of demand is defined as the percentage change in quantity demanded resulting from a 1% change in price. For example, suppose that a 1% increase in the direct cost or price of recreation trips results in a 0.4% decrease in number of trips. Then the price elasticity of demand for recreation trips is –0.4. The general formula for the price elasticity follows from its definition:

$$\text{Price elasticity} = \frac{\text{Percent change in quantity}}{\text{Percent change in price}}$$

$$= \frac{\text{Change in quantity} \div \text{Original quantity}}{\text{Change in price} \div \text{Original price}} \qquad \text{(Equation 8-1)}$$

Note that the price elasticity of demand will always be negative, since price and quantity change in opposite directions. However, you will notice that when economists discuss elasticities, they use the absolute value of the elasticity. Thus, economists say an elasticity of –1.0 is greater than an elasticity of –0.5, and an elasticity of –2.0 is greater than an elasticity of –1.0.

## *Calculating the Price Elasticity of Demand*

There are many equivalent formulas for calculating the elasticity of demand and the choice among them will depend on the information available to you. First, suppose that you have access to a linear demand function for a recreation site as presented in Table 8-1. In this case, you can algebraically rearrange Equation 8-1 to estimate the price elasticity of demand for any point on the demand curve using the following formula:

$$\text{Price elasticity} = \frac{\Delta Q}{\Delta P} \times \frac{P_0}{Q_0} \qquad \text{(Equation 8-2)}$$

The first expression in this formula, change in quantity demanded divided by change in price, is equivalent to the regression coefficient for price. Thus, the formula can be rewritten as:

$$\text{Price elasticity} = \text{Regression coefficient for price} \times \frac{P_0}{Q_0} \qquad \text{(Equation 8-3)}$$

The regression coefficient for direct cost or price per trip is shown in Table 8-1 (page 116) as –0.1 for recreation trips. The average direct cost or price is shown as $20 per trip; at this price, the representative individual user takes five trips per year. If we insert these values in the formula:

$$\text{Price elasticity} = -0.1 \times \frac{\$20}{5} = -0.4 \qquad \text{(Equation 8-4)}$$

Thus, dividing the original price ($20) by the original quantity demanded (5 trips) equals 4, and multiplying this by the regression coefficient (–0.1) equals –0.4 price elasticity of demand. This means that a 1% increase in price from the original level results in a 0.4% decrease in quantity demanded, or conversely for a price decrease. Now you are familiar with the preferred procedure when statistical demand functions are available; however, this may not always be the case.

For many recreation areas, managers do not have access to the necessary data to calculate price elasticity for a single point on the demand curve for their sites. Often only a few years worth of data points are available. Fortunately, you can estimate an "arc" or average elasticity of demand between any two of these points. Arc elasticities provide a useful approximation of the responsiveness of demand to price changes, providing all other variables that influence demand remain unchanged.

**Table 8-1. Estimating Elasticity of Demand for Trips to a Recreation Site Using Regression Coefficients from a Demand Function, $Q = 5$**

| | Units | Estimated Mean Values of the Variables (1) | Regression Coefficients for the Independent Variables (2) | Elasticities of Demand $\frac{(\text{Col. 1})}{Q} \times \text{Col. 2}$ (3) |
|---|---|---|---|---|
| Direct Cost or Price | Dollars/Trip | 20.0 | –0.100 | –0.40 |
| Consumer Income | Thousand Dollars | 25.0 | 0.100 | 0.50 |
| Travel Time | Hours Round Trip | 3.0 | –0.400 | –0.24 |
| Price of Substitute Sites | Dollars Direct Cost/Trip | 24.0 | 0.054 | 0.26 |
| Age | Years | 25.0 | –0.088 | –0.44 |
| Quality of the Site | 5-Point Scale | 4.0 | 0.625 | 0.50 |
| County Population | Thousand Persons | 200.0 | 0.025 | 1.00 |
| Taste or Preference | 1 = Active 0 = Passive | 0.8 | 1.250 | 0.20 |
| Daily Utilization/ Capacity Ratio | 1 = Optimal | 0.9 | –2.667 | –0.48 |
| Constant | | | 0.5 | |

For example, Table 8-2 shows the number of visits to a recreation site demanded at various levels of direct cost or price. Given these data, how do you go about computing the price elasticity of demand? Because the price elasticity of any site generally varies from point to point on a linear demand curve, you must first determine between what two points on the demand curve you want to measure the price elasticity of demand.

Let us assume that you want to estimate the price elasticity of demand for this site when the direct cost or price is between $20 and $30 per visit. Table 8-2 shows that the quantity demanded equals 500,000 visits when the price is $20 per visit, and that it equals 400,000 visits when the price is $30. The generally accepted procedure to calculate the elasticity is to use the average values of price and quantity as the original price and quantity in Equation 8-1. In other words, we use as an estimate of the price elasticity of demand called the **arc elasticity:**

**Table 8-2. Effect of Direct Cost or Price on the Number of Visits to a Recreation Site**

| Number of Visits per Year | Direct Cost or Price per Visit (Dollars) |
|---|---|
| 0 | $70 |
| 100,000 | 60 |
| 200,000 | 50 |
| 300,000 | 40 |
| 400,000 | 30 |
| 500,000 | 20 |
| 600,000 | 10 |
| 700,000 | 0 |

$$\text{Arc elasticity} = \frac{\Delta Q}{\sum \text{quantities} \div 2} \div \frac{\Delta P}{\sum \text{prices} \div 2}$$

(Equation 8-5)

This arc elasticity of demand uses the average of two points. In the specific case we are considering, the average arc elasticity is:

$$\text{Arc elasticity} = \frac{400 - 500}{(400 + 500) \div 2} \div \frac{30 - 20}{(30 + 20) \div 2} = -0.56$$

(Equation 8-6)

The answer to our problem is –0.56. Thus –0.56 is the average elasticity between the prices of $30 and $20. Since our elasticity is less than one, the demand curve is inelastic between $20 and $30. Thus the number of visits is not very sensitive to price in this range. As will be discussed later, this has implications for estimating the change in revenue from a change in fees.

Arc elasticity between two different points on a demand curve represents an approximation. As the two points between which arc elasticity is measured are moved closer and closer together, they merge into a single point. **Point elasticity** is simply arc elasticity when the distance between the two points approaches zero. Proper use of point elasticity is limited to cases of very small changes in price and other variables. Arc elasticity is a better approach for measuring the average elasticity over an extended range of the demand curve.

## *Elastic and Inelastic Demand*

In applying price elasticity of demand, economists use three terms—price elastic, price inelastic and unitary elasticity. The demand for a recreation site is **price elastic** if the elasticity is greater than one. The demand is

**price inelastic** if it is less than one. And the demand is of **unitary elasticity** if it equals one. Figure 8-1 illustrates these three concepts with each line passing through the same mean value of price and quantity.

Another problem in using elasticities is that they generally vary from point to point along the demand curve. Therefore, you must first determine at what point you want to measure the price elasticity of demand. For example, the price elasticity of demand for recreation trips may be higher when a trip costs $40 than when it costs $10. Note on Figure 8-2 that if a price of $50 falls to $40—a drop of 20%—quantity demanded increases from two to three trips, or 50%. That's certainly an elastic demand, 50% ÷ –20% = –2.5. But, if the price falls from $20 to $10—a drop of 50%—the quantity demanded increases only from five trips to six, or a rise of 20%. That's an inelastic demand, 20% ÷ –50% = –0.4. In other words, the relation between proportional changes in price and corresponding proportional changes in quantity varies according to where you are on the demand curve. At the top of any straight line demand curve, demand is always more elastic than at the bottom.

## *Determinants of the Price Elasticity of Demand*

Many studies have been made of the price elasticity of demand for particular recreation goods and services. Tables 8-3 and 8-4 (pages 120 and 121) present the results of some of them. Note the substantial differences

**Figure 8-1. Price Elasticities of Demand**

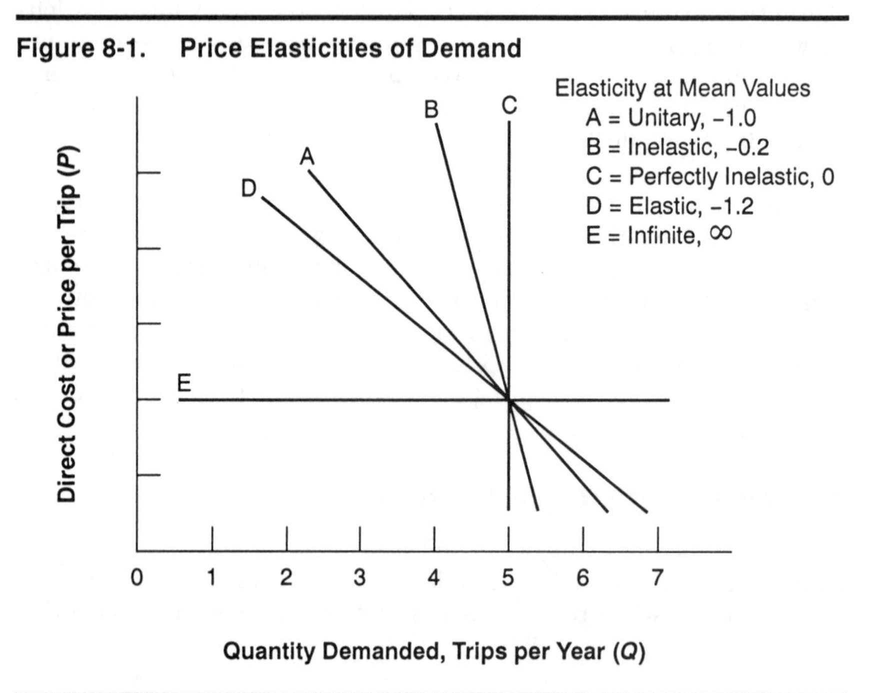

**Figure 8-2. Demand Curve for Recreation Trips by Individual Users**

among them. For example, the estimated price elasticity of demand for 23 outdoor recreation *activities* in the United States generally appears to be quite inelastic, ranging from –0.06 to –0.40. By comparison, Table 8-4 shows that the estimated price elasticity of demand for many recreation *goods and services* is elastic, for example pleasure boats, –1.3; airline travel, –2.4; radio and TV sets, –1.2; and automobiles, –1.2 to –2.1.

The purpose of this section is to explore the reasons why the price elasticity of demand is low for one product and high for another. Price elasticity of demand for recreation is generally low when it is considered a necessity, when substitutes are not available to satisfy the perceived need, when the proportion of income spent on it is low, or when it is purchased frequently. Economic studies have identified other determinants of the price elasticity of demand for particular products, including number of uses and quality of the product. The more specialized the use and the higher the quality of the experience, the lower the price elasticity of demand.

Similarly, the demand for high-priced goods and services which account for a large portion of purchasers' incomes will be relatively sensitive to price. The price elasticity of demand for boats, automobiles, and air

**Table 8-3. Estimated Price Elasticity of Demand for Selected Outdoor Recreation Activities, United States**

| Recreation Activity | Occasion | Average Number of Days per Participant | Price Elasticity of Demand |
|---|---|---|---|
| Sightseeing | Vacation | 5.42 | –0.21 |
| | Weekend Trip | 3.89 | –0.17 |
| | Day Outing | 3.51 | |
| Picnicking | Vacation | 4.67 | –0.21 |
| | Weekend Trip | 4.55 | –0.26 |
| | Day Outing | 4.05 | |
| Camping in Developed | Vacation | 7.99 | –0.16 |
| Campgrounds | Weekend Trip | 6.52 | –0.15 |
| Camping in Remote | Vacation | 5.26 | –0.14 |
| Areas, Wilderness | Weekend Trip | 7.19 | –0.18 |
| Walking for Pleasure | Vacation | 6.35 | –0.22 |
| | Weekend Trip | 4.43 | –0.19 |
| | Day Outing | 7.73 | –0.20 |
| Nature Walks | Vacation | 7.48 | –0.22 |
| | Weekend Trip | 4.73 | –0.18 |
| | Day Outing | 4.27 | –0.07 |
| Bird-Watching | Vacation | 6.55 | –0.32 |
| | Weekend Trip | 6.30 | –0.32 |
| | Day Outing | 3.52 | |
| Fishing | Vacation | 4.63 | –0.24 |
| | Weekend Trip | 5.06 | –0.27 |
| | Day Outing | 6.79 | |
| Water-Skiing | Vacation | 3.34 | –0.20 |
| | Weekend Trip | 5.02 | –0.17 |
| | Day Outing | 8.75 | –0.32 |
| Canoeing | Vacation | 5.17 | –0.29 |
| | Weekend Trip | 2.58 | –0.19 |
| | Day Outing | 2.54 | –0.16 |
| Sailing | Vacation | 4.96 | –0.25 |
| | Weekend Trip | 3.44 | –0.11 |
| | Day Outing | 10.07 | –0.40 |
| Other Boating | Vacation | 3.87 | –0.23 |
| | Weekend Trip | 5.76 | –0.18 |
| | Day Outing | 3.95 | |

| Recreation Activity | Occasion | Average Number of Days per Participant | Price Elasticity of Demand |
|---|---|---|---|
| Outdoor Pool | Vacation | 5.16 | –0.23 |
| Swimming | Weekend Trip | 5.33 | –0.23 |
| | Day Outing | 8.72 | |
| Natural Beach | Vacation | 5.87 | –0.24 |
| Swimming | Weekend Trip | 5.21 | –0.20 |
| | Day Outing | 7.52 | |
| Horseback Riding | Vacation | 4.69 | –0.20 |
| | Weekend Trip | 1.02 | |
| | Day Outing | 7.18 | |
| Bicycling | Vacation | 5.55 | –0.23 |
| | Weekend Trip | 3.22 | –0.25 |
| | Day Outing | 15.26 | |
| Riding Motorcycles | Vacation | 5.83 | –0.27 |
| Off-Road | Weekend Trip | 3.90 | –0.35 |
| | Day Outing | 7.48 | |
| Golf | Vacation | 4.72 | –0.12 |
| | Weekend Trip | | |
| | Day Outing | 9.05 | |
| Tennis | Vacation | 3.88 | –0.20 |
| | Weekend Trip | 3.35 | |
| | Day Outing | 12.08 | |
| Playing Other Outdoor | Vacation | 6.15 | –0.21 |
| Games or Sports | Weekend Trip | 4.76 | –0.22 |
| | Day Outing | 9.01 | |
| Going to Outdoor | Vacation | 1.96 | –0.17 |
| Concerts, Plays | Weekend Trip | 2.07 | |
| | Day Outing | 2.47 | |
| Going to Outdoor | Vacation | 2.37 | –0.14 |
| Sports Events | Weekend Trip | 2.99 | –0.33 |
| | Day Outing | 5.61 | –0.16 |
| Visiting Zoos, Fairs, | Vacation | 2.59 | –0.19 |
| Amusement Parks | Weekend Trip | 2.12 | –0.20 |
| | Day Outing | 2.29 | –0.06 |

Source: Adams, Lewis and Drake, 1973.

**Table 8-4. Estimated Price Elasticities of Demand for Selected Recreation Products and Services, United States**

| Product or Service | Price Elasticity |
|---|---|
| Automobiles | –1.2 to –2.1 |
| Gasoline | –0.2 to –0.6 |
| Tires | –0.6 |
| Public Transportation | –0.4 |
| Airline Travel | –2.4 |
| Electricity | –1.3 |
| Shoes | –0.4 |
| All Clothing | –0.6 |
| Pleasure Boats | –1.3 |
| Radio and TV Sets | –1.2 |
| Furniture | –1.2 |
| Newspapers | –0.1 |
| All Food | –0.4 |
| Beer | –0.9 to 1.1 |
| Cigarettes | –0.5 |
| Golfing, Club Members | –0.7 |
| Camping, Rocky Mountains | –0.4 |
| Skiing, Aspen | –0.7 |

Source: Walsh, 1986.

travel is higher than that for matches to light a campfire. The demand for less expensive products will not be so sensitive to prices. The small percentage of income spent on these goods and services means that it simply will not be worthwhile to waste time and energy worrying about their prices.

How then, can we explain the relatively low price elasticity of demand for most recreation activities? First, most are unique, having few nearby substitutes or opportunities that satisfy similar desires (e.g., bowling may be a poor substitute for tennis, since one is played indoors and the other out-of-doors in the fresh air and sunshine).

Second, the price elasticity of demand for a recreation activity is not the same as the elasticity of demand for the opportunities provided by a single recreation site. Since each recreation industry includes a large number of sites where the activity can take place, the price elasticity of demand for each site providing the opportunity will usually be less inelastic than for the activity in the national market. This is because most recreation sites have some close substitutes in the regional market. Trout fishing at Rocky Mountain sites, for example, has been estimated to have a price elasticity of –0.4. In contrast, all fishing tends to be even less price elastic, –0.2.

Price elasticity of demand is related to the quality of the resource. Price elasticities for deer hunting in Arizona are low in all regions except the rather poor hunting central region surrounding Phoenix, the population center of the state. Similarly, elasticities for cold-water fishing are lowest in the northern regions, which include the high mountain areas of the state with high catch rates.

It is often asserted that the price elasticity of demand for recreation activities also depends on the importance of the recreation expenditure in consumer budgets. Typical consumers spend a very small portion of their income for recreation activities on day outings near home, and the quantity they demand may not be influenced much by changes in price within a reasonable range. The price elasticity of demand for recreation activities is often more for weekend or vacation trips in the United States. For example, the price elasticity of demand for nature walks was estimated as -0.07 for day outings, compared with -0.18 while on weekend trips and -0.22 on vacation trips. This relationship may result in the fact that the direct cost or price of nature walks on day outings is usually lower than for nature walks on weekend or vacation trips and, thus, are less important in the consumer's budget.

## *Price Elasticity, Total Expenditures and Revenue*

Many important decisions depend on the price elasticity of demand for recreation. One reason why this is so, is that the price elasticity of demand determines whether a given change in price or entrance fees will increase or decrease the total amount of money spent on a recreation activity—often a matter of basic importance to consumers and managers of private and public recreation resources. In this section, we show how the price elasticity of demand determines the effect of a price change on total expenditures for a recreation activity.

First, consider a recreation activity where demand is price elastic. In this case, if the price is reduced, the total amount spent on the activity will increase. To see why, suppose that the price elasticity of demand for outdoor jazz concerts at a site near where you live is -2.0 and that the price of concerts is reduced by 1%. Because the price elasticity of demand is -2.0, the 1% reduction in price results in a 2% increase in attendance at jazz concerts. Because the total revenue on concerts equals the quantity demanded times the price, the 1% reduction in price will more than offset the 2% increase in quantity demanded. The result of the price cut will be an increase in the total revenue.

On the other hand, if the price of a recreation activity is increased, the total amount spent on the activity will fall. For example, if the price of outdoor jazz concerts is raised by 1%, this will reduce the quantity demanded by 2%. The 2% reduction in the quantity demanded will offset the 1% increase in price, the result being a decrease in total revenues.

Next, consider a recreation site where demand is price inelastic. In this case, if the price or entrance fee is reduced, the total revenue will decrease. To see why, suppose that the price elasticity of demand for recreation activity is –0.5 and the entrance fee is reduced by 1%. Because the price elasticity of demand is –0.5, the 1% price reduction results in only a 0.5% increase in the number of trips demanded. Since the total amount spent on trips equals the quantity demanded times the price, the 0.5% increase in the quantity demanded will not offset the 1% reduction in price. The result of the price cut will be a decrease in the total revenues.

On the other hand, if the price or entrance fee is increased, the total revenue will increase. For example, if the entrance fee or price of visiting the site is raised by 10%, this will reduce the number of trips demanded by 5%. The 10% price increase will offset the 5% reduction in quantity demanded, the result being an increase in total revenue.

Finally, consider a recreation activity where demand is of unitary elasticity. In this case, a price increase or decrease results in no difference in the total amount spent on the activity. Why? Because a price decrease (increase) of a certain percentage always results in a quantity increase (decrease) of the same percentage, so that the product of the price times quantity is the same.

## *Why Elasticities Are Useful*

It may initially appear, based on the discussion in Chapters 5 and 6, that the regression coefficients for the independent variables included in a demand function are sufficient measures of the responsiveness of the quantity demanded to changes in the determinants of demand. For example, the regression coefficient for direct cost or price of –0.1 when multiplied by a $10 increase in the price of recreation trips tells us that individual demand will decrease by one trip per year. The regression coefficient for price represents the slope of the demand curve for recreation trips (i.e., the change in quantity demanded resulting from each $1 change in price).

However, it may be difficult to compare slopes or price coefficients directly between two different demand curves. The first reason for this is the fact the two demand curves may have been estimated using different functional forms (i.e., one may be linear and the other double-log). Second, the units of the dependent variables may be different (trips in thousands versus trips per capita). Thus, elasticities provide useful measures of the responsiveness to price and nonprice variables included in a demand function for a recreation site, as well as facilitating comparisons between recreation sites and activities. This is because elasticities are in comparable units—percentage change. Thus, elasticities are standardized to represent the effect of a 1% change in that variable on the percentage change in the dependent variable. Regardless of the magnitude of the units, the variables or the functional form, once the elasticities are computed they can be directly compared.

## Income Elasticity of Demand

So far this chapter has dealt almost exclusively with the price elasticity of demand. But price is not, of course, the only variable that influences the demand for recreation. Another important variable is the level of money income among consumers in the market. The income elasticity of demand is a measure of the sensitivity of quantity demanded to the money income of consumers. Income elasticity of demand is defined as the percentage change in the quantity demanded resulting from a 1% change in consumer income, holding constant the effect of all other variables that influence demand.

The income elasticity of demand for recreation is a basic concept used by economists. Fortunately, it is calculated in the same way as price elasticity. First, suppose that you have access to a statistical demand function for a recreation site as presented in Table 8-1 (page 116). In this case, the income elasticity of demand can be estimated using the following formula:

$$\text{Income elasticity} = \begin{matrix}\text{Regression coefficient}\\ \text{for income}\end{matrix} \times \frac{\text{Original income}}{\text{Original quantity demanded}}$$

(Equation 8-7)

The regression coefficient for income (in thousands) is shown in Table 8-1 (page 116) as 0.1 for trips to a recreation site. The average household income is shown as $25 thousand and, at this income level, the representative individual user takes five trips per year. If we insert these values in the formula:

$$\text{Income elasticity} = 0.1 \times \frac{\$25}{5} = 0.5$$

(Equation 8-8)

Thus, dividing household income ($25 thousand) by the original quantity demanded (5 trips) equals five, and multiplying this by the regression coefficient for household income (0.1) equals 0.5 income elasticity of demand. This means that a 1% increase in household income from the average level results in a 0.5% increase in quantity demanded, or conversely for a decrease in income.

When information is available on the original and ending incomes and quantities ($I_O$, $I_E$, $Q_O$, and $Q_E$, respectively), the generally accepted procedure is to use the average income and quantity demanded. In other words, we use as an estimate of the income elasticity of demand:

$$\text{Income elasticity} = \frac{\Delta Q}{(Q_O + Q_E) + 2} \div \frac{\Delta I}{(I_O + I_E) + 2}$$

(Equation 8-9)

This provides a measure of the average responsiveness of demand to the change in income.

For most recreation goods and services, increases in income lead to increases in demand and income elasticity will be positive. These are called **normal goods**. Those few for which consumption decreases in response to a rise in income have negative income elasticities and are called **inferior goods**. The income elasticity of normal goods is considered low (inelastic) when it is between zero and one, or high (elastic) when it is greater than one. Elasticity is defined as unitary when a 1% increase in income leads to a 1% increase in the quantity demanded.

It should not be surprising that different recreation goods and services have different income elasticities (as shown in the studies summarized in Table 8-5). Those that consumers regard as necessities tend to have lower income elasticities than do luxuries. The reason is that as incomes rise it becomes possible for households to devote a smaller proportion of their income to meeting basic needs and a larger proportion to buying things they have always wanted but could not afford. Indeed, one way to define luxuries and necessities is to say that luxuries have high-income elasticities of demand and necessities have low-income elasticities of demand.

Examples of recreational luxuries include African safaris, yachting, foreign travel, recreational vehicle camping, owning condominiums at ski areas and ocean beaches, and possibly vacation trips to National Parks in the western states. Many other recreation activities are not very responsive to income changes, rather participation is a fairly constant proportion regardless of changes in income (e.g., jogging, picnicking). If the income elasticity of demand for a recreation site is close to zero, we would not expect recreation use to increase very much on account of increases in income.

The reaction of demand to changes in income is extremely important. In most Western economies, growth in productivity has caused the level

**Table 8-5. Estimated Income Elasticities of Demand for Selected Recreation Goods and Services, United States**

| Goods and Services | Income Elasticity | Goods and Services | Income Elasticity |
|---|---|---|---|
| Swimming Trips | 0.31 | Restaurant Meals | 1.48 |
| Boating Trips | 0.34 | Liquor | 1.00 |
| Camping Trips | 0.42 | Wine | 1.40 |
| Fishing Trips | 0.47 | Automobiles | 3.00 |
| Skiing | 0.50 | Gasoline | 1.10 |
| Recreation Expenditures | 1.40 | Housing | 0.60 |
| Theater, Live | 1.98 | Cigarettes | 0.80 |
| All Food | 0.20 | Consumer Durables | 1.80 |

Source: Walsh, 1986.

of income to double every 20 to 30 years over a sustained period of at least a century. Until recently, this rise in income is shared to some extent by most households, regardless of initial income level. As they find their incomes increasing, they demand more recreation goods and services.

As household incomes rise, causing demand for a particular recreation activity to increase rapidly, demand for the recreation equipment and services necessary to participate also increases rapidly. However, once the growth in demand for the activity levels off (matures), the demand for durable recreation equipment falls sharply, while the demand for services may level off or continue to grow at a more moderate level. Thus, the uneven impact of increased income on the demand for different recreation goods and services has important effects on different groups in the economy.

Many studies have been made of the income elasticity of demand for particular recreation activities and sites. Generally, they have found that the effect of income on demand for recreation activities is inelastic, less than one. Studies of demand for some particular recreation sites show that income elasticity is zero with no measurable effect on site demand, since income may not be a limiting factor for nearby recreation sites and inexpensive activities such as hiking.

Consider the results obtained by Kalter and Gosse (1969). Based on a U.S. census survey, the income elasticity of demand in the United States is estimated as 0.31 for swimming, 0.34 for boating, 0.42 for camping, and 0.47 for fishing trips on weekends. These estimates seem reasonable. We would expect the income elasticity of demand to be lower for swimming than for other water-based recreation activities that may require substantial investments in recreation equipment.

How can the income elasticity of expenditure for recreation be elastic, and the income elasticity of demand be inelastic for specific recreation activities? The reasons are straightforward. First, as incomes rise, households participate in additional recreation activities, while the number of days per year in any one activity remains about the same for most activities. Second, with higher income, they tend to spend more money per day on overnight recreation trips and on recreation equipment.

For most recreation activities, the income elasticity of demand is positive, indicating that as the economy expands and national income increases, demand for recreation will also increase. However, the actual size of the elasticity coefficient is also important. A recreation site might have an income elasticity of 1.5. For this destination, demand will increase 1.5 times as fast as income. We see, then, that if the income elasticity is less than 1.0 for a particular recreation resource, the operator will not share proportionately in increases in national income. On the other hand, if income elasticity is greater than 1.0, the operator will gain more than a proportionate share of increases in income.

These relationships have important policy implications for both private and public managers. Recreation resources whose demand functions have high-income elasticities will have good growth opportunities in an expanding economy. Recreation resources with low-income elasticities, on the other hand, are not so sensitive to the level of economic activity. This may be desirable in that such an economic activity is, to a large extent, recession proof.

## Cross Elasticity of Demand

Besides the direct cost or price of recreation and the level of consumer income—the factors discussed in previous sections of this chapter—the demand for recreation also depends on the price of other related goods and services. Suppose the direct cost or price of camping is held constant. The amount of camping demanded will be influenced by the price of commercial accommodations, such as motels and lodges in the region of the campground. For some people a drastic reduction in the price of resort accommodations might induce them or allow them to switch from camping to staying at resorts for their vacations. Cross elasticity of demand is used to measure the sensitivity of the former's demand to changes in the latter's price. Cross elasticity is defined as the percent change in the quantity demanded of one good or service resulting from a 1% change in the price of another good or service.

The distinguishing characteristic of cross elasticity is that the direct cost or price of trips to the second site is substituted for price of trips to the study site.

First, suppose that you have access to a statistical demand function for a recreation site as presented in Table 8-1 (page 116). In this case, the cross elasticity of demand for recreation can be estimated using the following formula:

$$\text{Cross elasticity} = \begin{matrix}\text{Regression coefficient} \\ \text{for substitutes}\end{matrix} \times \frac{\text{Original price of substitutes}}{\text{Original quantity demanded at this site}} \quad \text{(Equation 8-10)}$$

The regression coefficient for cross elasticity is shown in Table 8-1 (page 116) as 0.054 for trips to a recreation site. The average direct cost or price of substitute sites is shown as $24 per trip and, at this price, the representative individual user takes 5 trips per year to this site. If we insert these values in the formula:

$$\text{Cross elasticity} = 0.054 \times \frac{\$24}{5} = 0.26 \quad \text{(Equation 8-11)}$$

Thus, dividing the original price of substitute sites ($24) by the original quantity demanded for this site (5 trips) equals 4.8, and multiplying this by the regression coefficient for substitution (0.054) equals 0.26 cross elasticity of demand. This means that a 1% increase in the price of substitutes from the original level results in a 0.26% increase in quantity demanded at the site, or conversely for a price decrease.

When information is available on the original and ending prices of trips to the second site and the number of trips to the study site, the generally accepted procedure is to use the average price of substitutes and quantity demanded. In other words, we use as an estimate of the cross elasticity of demand:

$$\text{Cross elasticity} = \frac{\Delta Q}{(Q_O + Q_E) \div 2} \div \frac{\Delta P}{(P_O + P_E) \div 2} \qquad \text{(Equation 8-12)}$$

This provides a measure of the average responsiveness of demand at the study site to the change in price of substitutes.

Pairs of goods and services are classified as substitutes or complements, depending on whether the cross elasticity of demand is positive or negative. If the cross elasticity of demand is positive, two goods or services are substitutes because a decrease in the price of motels, for example, will result in a decrease in the demand for camping—many campers may really prefer the more comfortable motel accommodations.

On the other hand, if the cross elasticity of demand is negative, two goods or services are complements. For example, camping and fishing may be complements since an increase in the price of fishing licenses will decrease the demand for camping because people often camp near their favorite fishing areas.

When cross elasticity of demand is zero, or nearly zero, we can conclude that the goods or services are unrelated and in separate and distinct markets. We would know this because variations in the price of one good or service would have no effect on demand for the second.

Many studies have been made of the cross elasticity of demand for various pairs of goods or services. According to a study by Kurtz and King (1980) of motorboating on large reservoirs in Arizona, the cross elasticity of demand between pairs of reservoirs is sometimes positive and sometimes negative, depending on the characteristics of the reservoirs and the preferences of recreation users.

Table 8-6 illustrates the relationships that may occur. The negative elasticity of demand for the relationship between Bartlett and Canyon reservoirs indicates that a 1% increase in the price of trips to one of these reservoirs reduces the number of trips demanded for recreation use of the other reservoir by –2.98% to –4.40%. This complementary relationship indicates that users desire a variety of motorboating opportunities at both reservoirs.

On the other hand, the positive elasticity of demand suggests that a substitute relationship exists between Apache and Canyon reservoirs. A

**Table 8-6. Estimated Cross Elasticity of Demand for Motorboating on Selected Reservoirs in Arizona**

| Pairs of Reservoirs | Cross Elasticity of Demand[a] | Relationship |
|---|---|---|
| Canyon to Bartlett | –4.40 | Complement |
| Bartlett to Canyon | –2.98 | Complement |
| Canyon to Apache | 1.87 | Substitute |
| Apache to Canyon | 2.60 | Substitute |
| Saguaro to Carl Pleasant | 3.44 | Substitute |
| Carl Pleasant to Saguaro | –1.54 | Complement |

[a]Cross elasticity of demand is defined as the percentage change in the number of trips demanded to the first reservoir listed, resulting from a 1% change in the direct cost or price of trips to the second reservoir listed.

Source: Adapted from Kurtz and King, 1980

1% increase in the price of trips to one of these reservoirs increases the number of trips demanded for recreation use of the other reservoir by 1.87% to 2.6%. For substitutes, recreation opportunities provided by the respective reservoirs are perceived by consumers to be reasonably comparable (the same), so that they will tend to use the least-cost resource.

## Long-Run Elasticity of Demand

Time may have an important effect on elasticity of demand for recreation. One of the general characteristics of consumer demand is the lack of an instantaneous response. Individuals often react slowly to changes in price and other conditions. To illustrate this delayed (or lagged) effect, consider the demand for recreation travel. Suppose the direct cost or price of a trip increased by 10% relative to the price of other goods and services, primarily owing to the increased price of gasoline. What effect will this have on demand for recreation travel? In the very short run, the effect will be slight. Tourists may be more careful to avoid unneeded side trips, but total demand for recreation travel, which is highly dependent on the established patterns of recreation behavior and recreation equipment owned, will probably not be greatly affected. Prices will go up and demand will not fall very much. In other words, the short-run demand for recreation travel is relatively inelastic.

Over the long run, however, the increase in direct costs of travel has more substantial effects. Consumers will reduce their purchases of travel trailers and other recreation equipment, and those products that are purchased will be more energy efficient. When their present auto is replaced, it may well be by a more economical model. Similarly, the travel industry itself will tend to switch to other energy sources, will employ less energy-intensive methods, or will relocate in areas where energy requirements are less.

Consumer adjustments to changes in the price and nonprice determinants of demand for recreation often takes time to accomplish. We have seen instances in which individuals seem to respond to price increases by apparently not reducing consumption very much, if at all. Obviously, tastes and preferences differ substantially among consumers, causing the initial response of some people to be a very slight adjustment in number of trips demanded. Another reason for this slow response is a phenomenon called "habit formation," whereby it takes individuals several periods to change past habits even in response to changes in real or relative prices or income.

Every empirical demand curve in recreation pertains to a certain time interval such as the summer season or, at most, a calendar year. In general, demand is likely to be more sensitive to price over a long period of time than a short one. Thus, the ultimate effect of a price increase on quantity demanded may be substantial, but it will take a number of years before the full impact is felt. For example, an increase in one site's entrance fee may result in the user learning more about other sites and visiting them to determine their suitability. Once he or she finds a comparable substitute, use at the original site will drop even more. Another example might be significant increases in lift ticket prices. This will cause an initial reduction in number of ski trips, but in the long run, the person may not replace his or her worn-out skis when the time comes to replace them. Thus, in the long run the person will completely stop skiing at the higher lift ticket prices. The phenomenon of long-run elasticity exceeding short-run elasticity is typical for most determinants of demand.

When time-series data are used in demand analysis, the year can be entered as a separate independent variable to account for long-term trends in demand, such as might result from changing consumer preferences or technological change of equipment. The effect of time can also be estimated for specific conditions by the use of lagged variables such as the previous year's direct costs to explain this year's demand.

Cross-sectional data from a sample of individual consumers in a single year are usually used in recreation demand analysis, and it is even more difficult to include an effective measure of time. Respondents sometimes have difficulty recalling the direct costs of recreation trips during the past 12 months and would be unable to accurately report direct costs for the past five to 10 years. There are two approaches to overcome this problem. The most frequently used is to pool data from different cross sections of visitors obtained over several years. For example, Peterson, Stynes and Arnold (1985) pooled annually collected permit data at the Boundary Water Canoe Area in Minnesota to investigate the stability of recreation demand over a five-year period. A more powerful, but more data demanding, technique is to develop a panel of respondents who would report their direct costs and trips each month for five to 10 years, similar to the pioneering study by LaPage and Ragain (1974) of demand for camping in the northeastern region of the United States. Their work suggests that long-run demand is more sensitive to changes in direct costs than data on the trends in aggregate demand for camping would suggest.

## Price Elasticity for Derived Demand Products

The demand functions for some goods and services are derived from the demand for a final product, so we use the term **derived demand.** The demand for air transportation is an example. The quantity of air transportation to major resort areas is not a direct demand but rather is derived from the demand for recreation. The consumer demand for recreation equipment such as skis, boots, and poles is derived from the final demand for skiing. The final demand for recreation determines, in large part, the demand for the goods and services used as inputs in the production process. None of these goods and services is demanded because of its direct value to consumers but rather because of the role it plays in the production of recreation activity.

The price elasticity of demand for skiing may appear to be misleadingly low if measured simply in terms of ski-lift ticket prices, since skiers could be more sensitive to changes in total direct costs. A skier pays for a ski-lift ticket but also has to pay for travel, added food, overnight accommodations, equipment rental, and the like. Since the price of the ski-lift ticket is often only a relatively small part of the total direct cost of skiing, the skier may not be particularly sensitive to the cost of the ticket.

This relationship can be illustrated by looking at the demand for lift tickets used in the production of downhill skiing in the United States. Assume the total direct cost to consumers of vacation ski trips to major winter resorts is $160 per day, and $20 of this is the cost of lift tickets. Assume the price of lift tickets is doubled (a 100% increase) so that it now requires $40 of this input for each recreation day of skiing produced. In this situation, the total direct cost of the final product—and presumably its price—will increase by only 12.5% (= $20 ÷ $160). If the price elasticity of demand for an additional day of downhill skiing is –0.7 (as reported by Walsh and Davitt, 1983), this 12.5% increase in price would result in an 8.75% reduction in final demand. Assuming that the 100% increase in the price of lift tickets would result in only an 8.75% reduction in its demand, the price elasticity is little more than –0.08% (= –8.75 ÷ 100). In other words, a 1% increase in the price of lift tickets would cause vacation skier's demand for them to decline by only eight-hundredths of 1%. The vacation skier's demand for lift tickets is extremely price inelastic even though the demand for the final product is much less so.

Contrast this with the price elasticity of derived demand for lift tickets by day users who live in the region of the ski resort. In this case, assume the total direct cost to consumers of one-day ski trips to winter resorts is $40 per day, and $20 of this is the cost of lift tickets. If the price of lift tickets is doubled (a 100% increase), it now requires $40 of this input plus $20 direct cost of travel for each recreation day of skiing produced. This means that the total direct cost of the final product will increase by 50% (= $20 ÷ $40). If the price elasticity of demand for one-day ski trips is also –0.7, this 50% increase in price would result in a 35% reduction in final demand. Assuming that the purchase of a daily lift ticket is necessary to ski, the 100% increase in the price of lift tickets would result in a 35% reduction in its demand. That implies a price elasticity of –0.35% (= –35 ÷ 100). In other words, a 1% increase in the price of lift tickets would cause day user demand for them to decline by thirty-five hundredths of 1%. The day user demand for lift tickets is not as price inelastic as that for vacation skiers. This is because its cost represents a major part of the total direct cost of the final product—one day of skiing. The total direct cost of the final product, skiing, is one-fourth as much for day users as for vacation skiers; thus the price of a lift ticket accounts for four times more of the total direct cost or price of the final product, and the derived price elasticity of demand for lift tickets is four times greater.

## Other Elasticities of Demand

The concept of elasticity is a useful way to measure the effect of a change in any of the independent variables on the dependent variable in a demand function. The dependent variable in an ordinary demand function is the quantity demanded or number of trips, so it is possible to calculate the demand elasticity of any variable in the function.

We have emphasized the three most common demand elasticities—price, income, and cross elasticity—but other demand elasticities are also important to recreation economic decisions. For example, Table 8-1 (page 116) illustrates the elasticities of demand for the age of participants, quality of the site, population, taste and preference, and congestion or crowding. The elasticity for any determinant of demand is defined as the percentage change in quantity demanded resulting from a 1% change in the variable, holding constant the effect of all other variables that influence demand. These elasticities are calculated in the same manner as price and income. The same formulas can be used by replacing the price regression coefficient and original-ending price variable with the regression coefficient and original-ending variable of interest (e.g., age, education).

Many studies have been made of other elasticities of demand for recreation. Table 8-7 summarizes the results of a U.S. census survey of several thousand participants in hiking, camping, boating, fishing and swimming. Note the substantial differences among elasticities of demand with respect to age, education and gender. For example, age elasticity of demand is inelastic and positive for hiking, camping and swimming. However, it is negative for fishing and boating. Education is inelastic and positive for all of these recreation activities, especially fishing and boating. Elasticity of demand with respect to gender (male) is inelastic and positive for camping, fishing and boating, while it is negative for swimming and hiking.

**Table 8-7. Other Elasticities of Demand for Outdoor Recreation**

| Independent Variable | Activity | Elasticity of Demand |
|---|---|---|
| Population | Outdoor Recreation | 1.00 |
| Age | Hiking, Vacation | 0.98 |
| | Camping, Trip | 0.37 |
| | Boating, Trip | –0.37 |
| | Fishing, Overall | –0.41 |
| | Swimming, Trip | 0.89 |
| Education | Hiking, Overall | 0.33 |
| | Camping, Vacation | 0.39 |
| | Boating, Overall | 0.51 |
| | Fishing, Vacation | 0.58 |
| | Swimming, Overall | 0.44 |
| Gender, Male | Hiking, Vacation | –0.14 |
| | Camping, Trip | 0.19 |
| | Boating, Trip | 0.32 |
| | Fishing, Overall | 0.10 |
| | Swimming, Overall | –0.07 |

Source: Adapted from Kalter and Gosse, 1969.

A number of studies have been made of the elasticity of demand with respect to quality of recreation resources. For example, consider three studies that estimated the effect of forest quality on demand for recreation in the United States. The first study is by Michaelson (1975) who applied the travel cost approach in a study of the demand effect of mountain pine beetle damage to ponderosa pine at campgrounds in Idaho forests. The average elasticity of demand with respect to trees on forest campgrounds was estimated as 0.27, which is comparable to the effect of number of trees at recreation sites in Colorado. The elasticity of demand with respect to trees also varies among recreation activities and over the range of the functions.

A second study, by Leuschner and Young, applied a travel cost demand estimating method to calculate the elasticity of demand with respect to pine tree cover as 0.64 to 0.68 at campgrounds located at reservoirs in Texas, nearly double the elasticity in Colorado. The variation in results may reflect differences in the value of shade from trees in the relatively hot southern state compared to the cooler mountain region. Walsh and Olienyk (1981) interviewed a sample of 500 households at forest recreation sites on the Front Range of the Rocky Mountains. The study estimated the demand effect of the number of live ponderosa pine trees six-inches dbh (diameter breast high) or more per acre surviving mountain pine beetle infestation. Results of the analysis show the elasticity of demand with respect to trees was estimated at between 0.28 and 0.34 depending on the demand estimating technique employed.

Bouwes and Schneider (1979) used the travel cost approach to estimate the shift in demand for water-based recreation with pollution from a storm sewer at Pike Lake in southeastern Wisconsin. It is one of many small lakes in the state less than one square mile in size that are suitable for day use, with boat-launching facilities and swimming beaches with lifeguards. The elasticity of demand with respect to water quality was estimated as 0.31 which means that a 1% change in lake water quality results in a 0.31% change in the number of trips demanded to Pike Lake.

Information on elasticities of demand can help a ski resort make effective operating and planning decisions. What the ski resort needs to know is: How sensitive is demand to changes in the independent variables in the demand function? A sample of 837 skiers were interviewed in Aspen, Colorado, on vacation trips averaging eight days with expenditures of $96 per day (Walsh and Davitt, 1983). Elasticities of demand for an additional day of skiing are estimated as: -0.73 with respect to price, 0.53 income, 0.37 skiing ability, 1.50 distance traveled, 0.11 state population, 0.18 preference for Aspen relative to substitute ski areas, -0.11 party size, and -0.34 package plan.

Some of these variables can be controlled by the ski resort—the range in prices and quality of services offered, for example—and it is important to know the effects of altering them if effective price and service decisions are to be made. Although other variables are outside the control of the ski resort, they can be influenced by effective promotional programs. For example, advertising can be directed to particular groups of skiers: smaller parties, advanced skiing ability, higher income, living in more populous states, located farther from Aspen. In addition, estimates of the sensitivity of demand to long-run trends in population, family size, and income can enhance a ski resort's ability to predict future growth potential and to establish effective long-run programs.

## *Chapter 9*

# Travel Cost Method

This chapter describes how to estimate the demand curve for recreation based on actual travel behavior and how to calculate the economic benefits of recreation activities and resources from the demand curve. Also discussed are implications of valuing changes in resource quality for recreation economic decisions.

The travel cost method (TCM) has been preferred by most economists, as it is based on observed market behavior of a cross section of users in response to direct out-of-pocket and time cost of travel. The basic premise of the approach is that the number of trips to a recreation site will decrease with increases in distance traveled, other things remaining equal. By calculating (i.e., integrating) the area under the demand curve for the site or resource, the travel cost approach provides an indirect measure of consumer surplus benefits. The travel cost method represents an empirical application of the household production approach to consumer economic decisions. The household production approach was pioneered by Becker (1965) and further developed by Bockstael and McConnell (1981) in the case of outdoor recreation.

While we will refer to the travel cost method, this term also refers to several closely related methods that have at their core, use of travel cost (i.e., transportation cost and travel time) as a measure of price. The dependent variable (i.e., what the analyst is trying to predict and explain using travel cost) is some form of quantity of recreation. Typically this will be trips taken by each person over a year or season, or trips per capita from a county to a recreation site. These models may be estimated for a single site, or to better allow for incorporation of how visitation changes with changes in recreation quality, estimated for multiple recreation sites in one regression equation. The single site TCM models are the most straightforward models and the one we will start with.

However, we will also note more recently developed statistical models that are in the spirit of TCM. These models predict and explain how people decide which particular site to visit out of the many available substitute sites and how the quality of that site influences which site to visit. We will briefly discuss these at the end of the chapter.

## Individual Observation Versus Zonal Methods

Two types of travel cost methods can be distinguished by how we define the dependent variable, quantity of trips. In the individual observation approach, the dependent variable in the demand function is the number of trips per year by individual users of a recreation site. This is an acceptable approach whenever most individuals take more than one trip per year and the objective is to estimate demand by the current population of participants. Individuals typically take several trips to recreation sites located within 100–150 miles from where they live. With this method, each data point or observation is a different individual. This means that the independent variables are the individual's measure of income, education, skill, equipment ownership, and so forth. When this level of detail is available from survey data, the individual observation model provides greater precision in estimation of the coefficients. As we will see below, this method also better allows for incorporation of travel time as a separate variable in the demand equation. This avoids a degree of subjectivity when incorporating travel time in the zonal TCM.

However, the individual observation model requires two conditions to be applicable. First, most visitors to the site under study must make more than one trip per year. If nearly all individuals take only a single trip per year, then the observations of the dependent variable are ones, and a demand curve cannot be estimated. Examples where each visitor only makes one trip per year includes distant National Parks, rafting trips such as through the Grand Canyon or on the Middle Fork of the Salmon River, and Wilderness Areas remote from population centers. In these cases, the dependent variable does not exhibit sufficient variation to estimate a statistical demand function based on individual observations. When individuals take, at most, one trip per year, the dependent variable must be either the probability of participation or rate of participation per capita of some residential area such as a county. The second requirement is that survey data be available that records the number of visits a person takes to the site each year. Thus, the individual observation model only can be implemented with visitor survey data.

Often recreation economists must estimate demand curves using existing (i.e., secondary) data from sources such as trail registers, campground or wilderness or hunting permits, creel census, and the like. These data sources usually only record whether a person from a particular zip code or county has visited the site, not how many times they have visited each year. If four visits from a certain zip code are observed, the analyst has no idea if this is four different people each taking one trip, or two people taking two trips. Thus, the zonal or aggregate TCM is of broader applicability. Hellerstein (1995) has shown the zonal travel cost method is more robust, that is, less susceptible to errors from using the wrong functional form or distributional assumptions than is the individual observation approach.

Thus, the zonal approach is more versatile than the individual observation approach. It can accommodate situations where participants take either one or several trips per year. In addition, the zonal approach introduces the effects of population, which is an important determinant of demand for recreation activities and resources. If some nonusers would become participants when prices fall or the quality of the resource improves, then the use of data on current visitors to estimate demand provides only part of the necessary information (Ribaudo and Epp, 1984). Essentially we need the product of two types of demand: (1) the number of trips per participant and (2) the proportion of the population participating, or:

$$\text{Quantity demanded} = \frac{\text{Trips}}{\text{Participants}} \times \frac{\text{Participants}}{\text{Population}} \qquad \text{(Equation 9-1)}$$

This states that demand for a site is a product of the number of trips per individual participant times the number of participants in the population. The zonal travel cost approach combines these two types of demand into a single variable. Note that the number of participants appears in both terms, and thus cancels out. The dependent variable in the zonal travel cost method becomes trips per capita:

$$\text{Quantity demanded} = \frac{\text{Trips}}{\text{Population}} \qquad \text{(Equation 9-2)}$$

This is certainly a useful feature of the zonal travel cost model when the analyst only has existing permit data. If household survey data that includes nonparticipants is available, it is possible to augment the individual observation travel cost demand equation to account for the participation effect. The statistical technique involves use of a two-equation sample selection model (often referred to as a Heckman model, after its originator). The first equation is a binary regression model (called a probit) that calculates the probability that a person will participate. A variable from this probit model is then included in the individual observation demand curve model to account for this probability. Generally speaking, only advanced statistical packages contain routines for such sample selection models. Thus, the zonal model provides a simple means to account for the net effect of both the probability of participation and the frequency of trips per participant. However, the individual observation travel cost method has advantages over the zonal in certain situations. These will be pointed out later in this chapter.

### *An Overview of the First Stage and Second Stage TCM Demand Curves*

To estimate the first stage of the travel cost method, a regression equation is run with annual trips (per individual or per county of visitor origin) as a function of the distance or monetary plus time cost of travel (which is the proxy for the independent variable, price). Other independent variables that should be included in the multiple regression are socioeconomic characteristics of the individual or county of origin if individual data are not available, and travel cost to substitute recreation opportunities. These variables are the minimum necessary to estimate a correct individual or per capita demand curve. In the second stage of the travel cost method, the statistical coefficients from the first stage are used to calculate each individual's or zonal population's demand for trips to the study site with increments in prices starting from the current price of each individual or zone and continuing until the estimated number of trips falls to zero. The observed number of trips by all individuals or from all distance zones represents the quantity demanded at current travel costs. Summed, this becomes one point on the total demand curve for the site or resource (i.e., the number of trips with no price increase). The remainder of the demand curve for the site is estimated by calculating the number of trips by all individuals or zonal populations at each of several incremental prices. The area under the site demand curve plus any entrance fee measures the visitors' net willingness to pay or consumer surplus attributed to the site or resource.

## Illustration of the Zonal Method

The essentials of the zonal travel cost approach can be illustrated by using a simple hypothetical example involving recreation trips to a site from each of three zones of varying populations and distances from the site entrance.

Frequently the only information available is that provided by campground fee receipts or visitor permits which indicate the zip code or county where the visitor lives. From the U.S. census, one can identify the current population of each of these zip codes or counties. Combining these two pieces of information provides our quantity variable (i.e., the number of visits or trips per capita or per 1,000 persons living in the counties of origin). The reason the number of visits is divided from each zone by population is to obtain a visit rate that puts the number of visits from each zone on a comparable basis.

The federal guidelines recommend distance traveled as an acceptable proxy for the independent variable, direct cost or price per trip to the recreation site. This is particularly important because the number of miles from the population center of each county to the recreation site can be estimated from road maps which are readily available. Later, one-way distance traveled can be converted to round-trip miles then multiplied by travel and time cost per mile. For now, it is convenient to use one-way distance traveled.

Suppose that the number of trips per year taken by visitors to a recreation site from counties in three zones of origin with population centers located 50, 100, and 150 miles from the site entrance is known. Dividing the number of trips in each zone by its population determines the visit rate (i.e., the number of trips per capita shown in Table 9-1). These visit rates for each zone are related to distance in Figure 9-1 (page 140), that shows a demand curve for trips per capita to the recreation site.

The next step is to calculate total use for increments in distance as illustrated in Table 9-2 (page 141). The estimate of 35,000 trips from Table 9-1 represents the initial point of the demand curve for the recreation site or resource with zero increase in distance. To find sufficient points to determine the entire demand curve, it is necessary to make several increases in distance and measure the number of trips that would be demanded, given these changes. This is equivalent to asking how many of the users would pay more than their current travel costs so as to be able to continue to visit the site. We have used increments of 50, 100, and 150 miles in Table 9-2 to keep the illustration simple.

First, an added distance of 50 miles is assumed for each trip to the site from each zone of origin. The travel distance from the closest zone, County A, was originally 50 miles, and an added 50 miles would make a total of 100 miles. The question is, how many trips would visitors living in County A make if they had to travel 100 miles? There are several ways to answer this question and they all yield the same answer. First is to recognize that we have data from County B which is *actually* located 100 miles from this site. How many trips per capita did people in County B take? The answer from Table 9-1 is 0.2 visits per capita. If everything else is

**Table 9-1. Per Capita Demand for Visits to a Single Recreation Site**

| Origin Zone | Population | Trips per Year | Trips per Capita | One-Way Distance (Miles) |
|---|---|---|---|---|
| County A | 100,000 | 30,000 | 0.3 | 50 |
| County B | 10,000 | 2,000 | 0.2 | 100 |
| County C | 30,000 | 3,000 | 0.1 | 150 |
| Total | | 35,000 | | |

**Figure 9-1. Trips per Capita From Distance Zones to a Recreation Site**

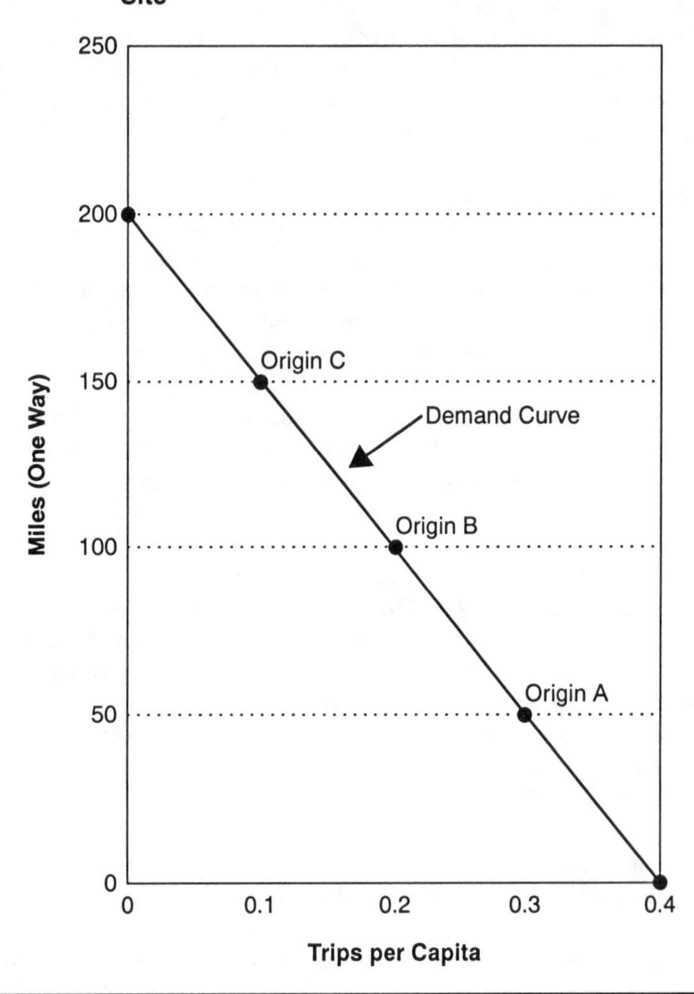


similar between people in County A and County B (or has been adjusted for by including other independent variables as demand shifters), then we can be fairly certain that the visitation rate of people living in County A, if they had to incur the dollar equivalent of driving 100 miles, would be the same as County B, that is 0.2 visits per capita. The other way to answer this question is to refer to Figure 9-1. If we read over from 100 miles on the vertical axis to the per capita demand curve, we see at 100 miles that 0.2 trips per capita are predicted (which is the amount for County B).

Using either approach, the trips per capita are predicted to be 0.2. To calculate total trips from County A at 100 miles, we must multiply their trips *per capita* by their county (zone) population. Thus, 0.2 trips per capita times the 100,000 population of County A equals 20,000 trips per year.

**Table 9-2. Calculating the Site Demand Curve Using Estimated Total Trips at Increased Distances.**

| Added Distance | County A | County B | County C | Total |
|---|---|---|---|---|
| 0 Miles | 30,000 | 2,000 | 3,000 | 35,000 |
| 50 Miles | 20,000 | 1,000 | 0 | 21,000 |
| 100 Miles | 10,000 | 0 | 0 | 10,000 |
| 150 Miles | 0 | 0 | 0 | 0 |

Now we repeat this logic and approach to estimate the trips per capita from the next distance zone, County B. Adding 50 miles to their current 100 mile distance would put them at a distance of 150 miles. How many trips per capita would we predict people in County B to take? Using the logic above, we would look at the trips per capita for County C, which actually faced a 150 mile distance. We see 0.1 trips per capita from both Table 9-1 (page 139) and Figure 9-1. Multiplying 0.1 trips per capita by the 10,000 population of County B equals 1,000 trips per year at the 50 mile increment. The trips per capita from the last distance zone, County C, would fall from 0.1 of a trip per capita to zero as a result of the added 50 miles, since we do not observe anyone willing to travel 200 miles to this site. This is consistent with the vertical intercept of Figure 9-1 indicating zero trips per capita. The total number of trips that would be expected with an added distance of 50 miles would be 21,000, including 20,000 trips from County A, 1,000 trips from County B, and none from County C. This represents a second point on the demand curve for the recreation site or resources at an added distance of 50 miles.

To obtain the next point on the second stage demand curve, a distance of 100 miles is added for each trip to the site from each zone of origin. The travel distance from the closest zone, County A, was originally 50 miles, and an added 100 miles would make a total of 150 miles. The visit rate from County A, given this added 100 miles, can be read from Figure 9-1, in this case 0.1 of a trip per capita, down from the original 0.3 of a trip per capita. Thus, 0.1 of a trip per capita times the 100,000 population of County A equals 10,000 trips per year. Similarly, the visit rates from Counties B and C would fall to zero with an added distance of 100 miles because Table 9-1 (page 139) and Figure 9-1 show that no trips are made by persons living 200 and 250 miles from the recreation site. Thus, the total number of trips that would be expected with an added distance of 100 miles would be 10,000, all from County A. This represents a third point on the demand curve for the recreation site.

Last, an added distance of 150 miles is assumed for each trip to the site from each zone of origin. The travel distance from the closest zone, County A, was originally 50 miles, and an added 150 miles would make a total of 200 miles. The travel distance from Counties B and C would become 250 and 300 miles, respectively. As a result, the visit rate from all zones would fall to zero, because Table 9-1 (page 139) implies that no trips are made by persons living 200 to 300 miles from the recreation site. This represents a fourth point on the demand curve for the recreation site, the added distance that results in a visit rate of zero from all origin zones.

## *Using the TCM Regression Equation*

Now we want to relate the discussion of regression in the previous chapters to the travel cost method. The data in Table 9-1 (page 139) can be input into a spreadsheet or statistics package to estimate the regression equation equivalent to the demand curve in Figure 9-1 (page 140). This regression equation is:

$$\text{Trips/Population} = 0.4 + (-0.002 \times \text{Distance}) \qquad \text{(Equation 9-3)}$$

The amount 0.4 is the constant and is graphically represented as the horizontal intercept in Figure 9-1. The slope coefficient tells us that each additional mile causes trips per capita to go down by 0.002 (this seems like a small number because the dependent variable is trips per person and not everyone in these counties visits the site).

When recreation economists actually compute the second stage or site demand curve, they typically use the regression equation to predict visits at each distance increment. This has several advantages over the graphical or tabular approach when there are numerous counties or the best fitting demand function is nonlinear. (If you know calculus, you can integrate the demand equation directly to calculate consumer surplus for each county and then add them up. However, with nonlinear demand equations, the calculus can become complicated. In addition, calculation of the resource demand equation provides an opportunity to check the prediction of the regression equation against actual visitation as well as providing the data necessary to make a graph of the resource demand curve. This graph is quite useful in communicating your results to managers.)

We will illustrate use of the regression equation for predicting trips per capita for County A. We need to know how many trips per capita the residents of County A would take if they had to pay the equivalent of 100 miles *more* to visit the site. As before, we add this 100 mile increment to their current 50 mile distance, equaling 150 miles. How many trips per capita would people in County A take at 150 miles? We can use the regression equation to answer this. If we multiply 150 miles by the slope coefficient that tells us how much their trips per capita fall with increasing distance, we get $-0.3$ ($= -0.002 \times 150$ miles). This $-0.3$ is then added to the constant term (0.4) to calculate the 0.1 trips per capita. This is the same result as with the graph, but it is much quicker to perform in a spreadsheet with hundreds of counties that are typical of most zonal TCM applications.

## *Construction of the Second Stage or Resource Demand Curve*

Horizontally summing trips from the three counties (i.e., that is adding up visits from the three counties *at a given distance*) yields the total in Table 9-2 (page 141). Figure 9-2 graphically illustrates this second stage or site demand curve. Note that at the current distance (zero added distance), predicted trips in Table 9-2 (35,000) equals the observed total number of trips that we started with in Table 9-1 (page 139). This is what we would expect, since the total in Table 9-2 is nothing more than a statistical estimate using the data we started with in Table 9-1.

**Figure 9-2. Aggregate Demand Curve for Recreation Resource or Site**

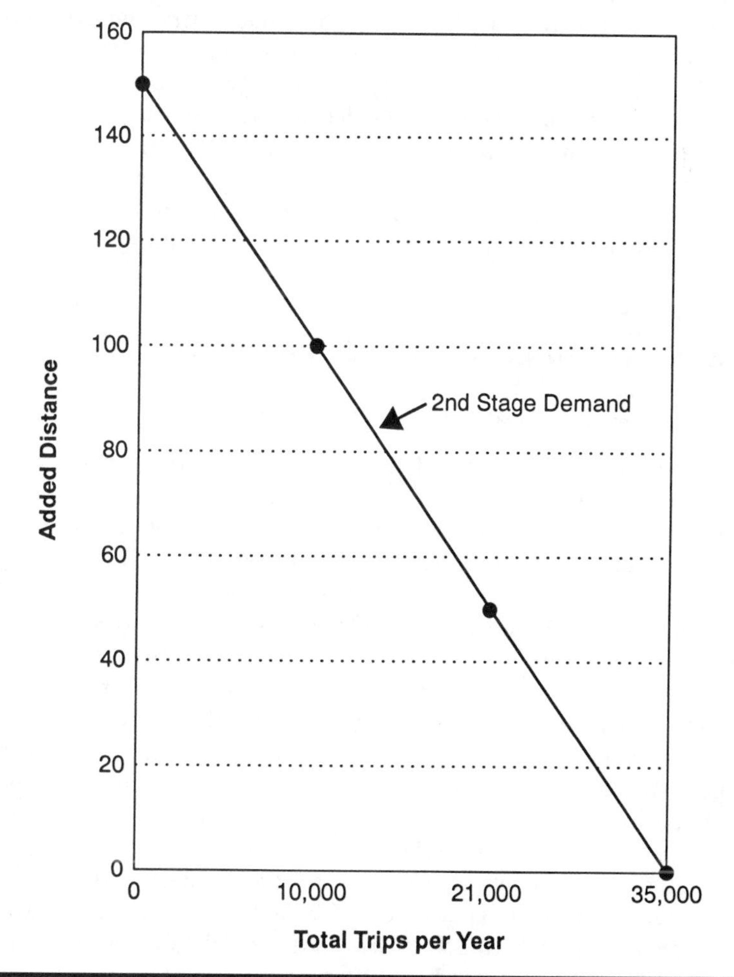

In practice, the equality of the predicted visits with the actual visits is rare for two reasons. First, unlike the demand curve in Figure 9-1 (page 140) where all of the data points lie along the line (implying an $R^2$ equal to one), data points in real studies lie above and below the regression line, as shown in Figure 6-4 (page 76) (implying more realistic $R^2$ of 0.3 to 0.7). With a linear regression and equal populations in each county the over-estimates and underestimates would cancel out. But in practice, county populations are usually not equal in most zonal TCMs. Second, we often use nonlinear functional forms, where the error of the natural logarithm of trips per capita or trips per person (in the individual observation model) does balance out, but the errors surrounding the retransformed trips do not (see Stynes, Peterson and Rosenthal, 1986). As a rule of thumb, if the total of predicted visits (across all zones or individuals) is within 20% or so of the actual total visits, this may be adequate for most purposes.

If the prediction is off by more than 20%, several options are available. The most obvious is to check for data coding, data entry and calculation errors. These often arise in the long chain of events from raw data to final results. The second is to include additional independent variables to improve the correspondence between the data and the regression. The third is to try alternative functional forms such as double-log or semilog. Systematic over- and underprediction may be due to a poor match between the visitor behavior represented by the data and the *implied* behavior represented by the functional form of the demand equation.

## *Converting Travel Distances to Dollars in the Zonal TCM*

### Transportation Costs

The next step is to estimate the dollar price at which the various quantities of use are demanded. The increases in distance are simply converted to the dollars recreation users would pay if they were required to travel the additional distance. This allows us to calculate the willingness to pay over and above current costs (remember, what is plotted in Table 9-2 [page 141] and shown in Figure 9-2 [page 143] are the amounts over and above their current distance). The variable, or out-of-pocket travel costs, are used as the proxy for money price since these are the dollars that users would have to pay to visit the site at greater travel distances. The preferred way to convert miles to dollars is to use data on the cost per mile from the visitor survey. However, when using secondary data on visitation (e.g., permits), sample specific information on travel cost is often not available. In this case, the federal guidelines recommend that the conversion of distance to money price should use the most current published results of studies conducted periodically by the U.S. Department of Transportation or American Automobile Association on the average cost of operating standard, compact, and subcompact automobiles. For example, we will use a cost per mile of $0.12.

Two adjustments must be made, however, before travel cost can be used as the proxy for money price. The first adjustment is to account for round-trip miles. The distance measure used in Table 9-2 (page 141) on per capita use was one-way miles, while recreation users must travel to and from the recreation site. So either the number of one-way miles must be doubled or the cost per mile doubled. A second adjustment is made to distribute the travel costs of a trip between the number of users traveling in each vehicle. This is usually done by taking the average number of recreation users per vehicle from entrance station reports or from a sample survey. Thus, the estimated money price for a simulated increase in distance of 50 miles in the previous example would be equal to $4. This is derived as follows: 50 miles times two for round trip miles, times $0.12 per mile divided by three persons (average number of users per vehicle).

## Travel Time

The final adjustment in travel cost recommended by the federal guidelines is to account for travel time. When we observed the trips per capita from County C were 150 miles, it was much lower than that of the nearby County A. Besides the deterrent effect of higher transportation costs, residents of County C also had to withstand longer travel times. Thus, not all of the decrease in trips per capita is simply due to transportation cost, some is due to the disutility of riding in the car for long distances. Ideally, the way to account for this, is to include travel time (in hours or hours times the wage rate) as a separate variable in the demand equation or regression. If this is done, then we know the regression coefficient on transportation cost is likely to provide an unbiased estimate of the price slope of the regression equation.

However, there is a statistical problem that arises in trying to include travel time as a separate variable in a zonal TCM. Generally speaking, people who live in distant counties have simultaneously higher transportation costs and travel times, conversely, for residents in nearby counties. Essentially the data have pairs of high cost–high travel times and low cost–low travel times, but no observations of high cost–low travel times and low cost–high travel times. We cannot ask a regression to estimate the separate effect of transportation cost and travel time when we provide only data pairing high cost–high travel times and low cost–low travel times. The regression simply cannot disentangle the separate effect of transportation cost and travel time from each other. This is a result of the naturally high correlation between transportation cost and travel times as distance increases. The resulting statistical problem is called *multicollinearity.* This problem is particularly troublesome in zonal TCMs because we are using the zone's average distance or transportation costs paired with the zone's average travel time. There is often a nearly one to one relationship between the averages, because all of the individual variability in transportation costs and travel time has been averaged out.

At this point we have two choices. If most visitors take more than one trip and visitor survey data is available, an individual observation model may be a better choice. When estimating an individual observation TCM it is often possible to estimate separate variables for transportation cost and travel time. This is because there is often a fair amount of individual variability between transportation costs and travel times that breaks down the high correlation observed in zonal TCMs. For example, people who like to speed up to the mountains, will have higher transportation costs due to rapidly increased gasoline consumption from "flooring it" up the mountains, but significantly shorter travel times. Cautious drivers will have lower travel costs but much longer travel times. This is just the type of data needed to estimate the separate effect of increased travel time in reducing the number of trips taken.

In fact, an individual observation TCM can allow us to infer the implicit value or deterrent effect of travel time on trips. For this example we will use the following individual observation TCM demand equation:

$$\text{Trips} = 20 + (-0.1 \times \text{Travel cost}) + (-1 \times \text{Hours travel time}) \quad \text{(Equation 9-4)}$$

Interpretation of the travel cost coefficient suggests that a $10 increase in travel cost reduces trips by one (= $10 x –0.1). Similarly, a one hour increase in travel time will reduce trips by one (= 1 hour x –1). What is the dollar equivalent of an additional hour of travel time? It is $10 an hour. The reason is that $10 of added travel cost and 1 hour of added travel time both result in exactly the same reduction in trips.

Unfortunately, the zonal model is usually estimated because the recreation economist does not have visitor survey data, but rather just permit or register data. In these circumstances, the U.S. Water Resources Council (1983) provides a conventional approach to include the effect of travel time in a zonal TCM: Calculate the dollar equivalent of the travel time and add it to the travel cost. As discussed in Chapter 4 on costs and price, the transportation planning literature suggests that drivers appear to value their travel time at one-quarter to one-half the wage rate. Given that this was the data available to the U.S. Water Resources Council, they suggest using one-third the wage rate to convert travel time to dollars. More recent work by Smith, Desvouges and McGivney (1983) suggests the full wage rate may be a better indicator, while McConnell and Strand (1981) use an individual observation TCM similar to Equation 9-4 to determine that Rhode Island anglers value their travel time at approximately 60% of the wage rate.

Following the U.S. Water Resources Council (1983) approach, distances should be converted to dollar values, including both out-of-pocket and time costs per mile. For purposes of this illustration, we use a third of an assumed wage rate of $4.50 per hour (approximate minimum wage), yielding a cost of travel time of $1.50 an hour. Thus, the individual time cost for a simulated increase in distance of 50 miles in the above example would equal $3. This is derived as follows: 50 miles times two for round trip miles, divided by 50 miles per hour, times $1.50 per hour.

## Final Benefit Calculations

Distances are converted to dollar values by summing out-of-pocket costs of $4 and time costs of $3 for 50-mile increments, equal to $7, illustrated in Figure 9-3. This allows us to make the final computation in the travel cost approach, which is to measure the area under the demand curve in Figure 9-3. Integration of the area can be approximated by breaking it up into a complete series of triangles and rectangles. Once this is done, basic

**Figure 9-3. Aggregate Monetary Demand Curve for Resource or Site**

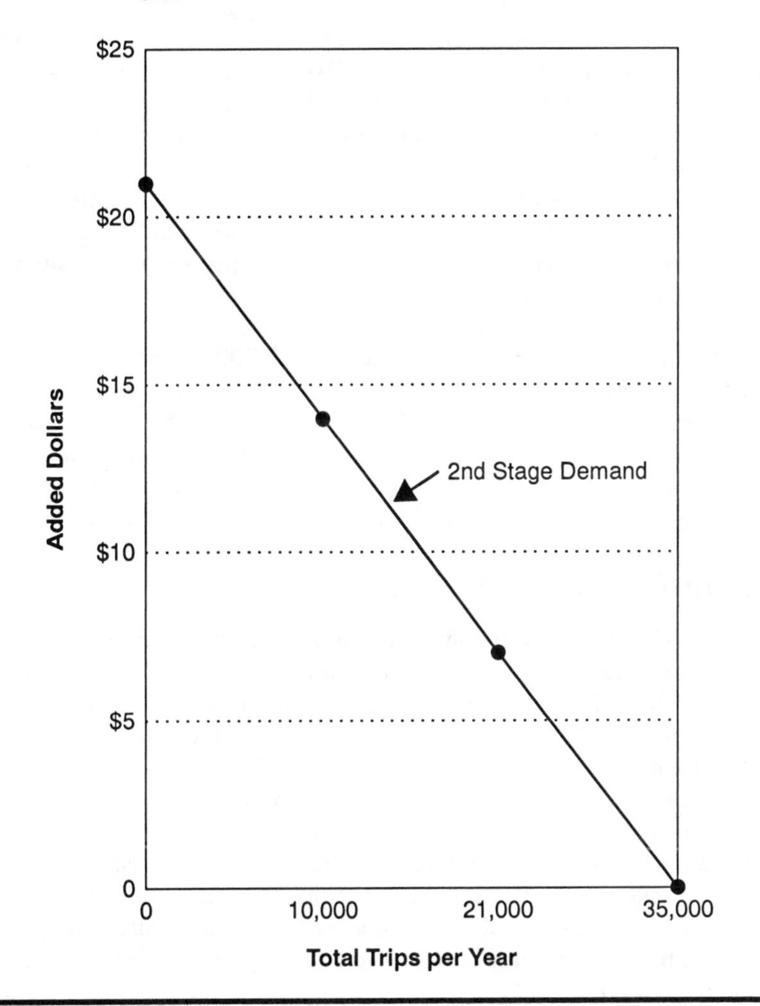

geometry will allow you to calculate the areas. Adding the dollar amount of these areas together yields total net willingness to pay (WTP) of the sample of visitors to the recreation site. (If the data used to estimate the TCM demand curves had not already been expanded from the sample of visitors to the total population of visitors, then the sample total net WTP must be expanded to the total population of visitors at this point.) The area under the second stage TCM demand curve is equal to the amount users would be willing to pay, but do not have to pay, for the opportunity to participate in recreation at the study site.

The estimated benefits of the recreation site, represented by the area under this demand curve, are $367,500 per year, equal to $10.50 per individual recreation trip. This means that the average visitor would pay $10.50 more than his or her current costs to be able to visit this site and participate in his or her particular recreation activity. Note, that this does *not* mean the agency could charge each visitor $10.50 more. Since the $10.50 is an average net WTP, half the visitors would pay more than $10.50, but half would pay less. The half that would pay less than $10.50 would no longer visit if a uniform entrance fee of $10.50 were imposed on all visitors. This annual benefit can be used to evaluate the economic efficiency of keeping the site open. For example, if the cost of managing the site ($80,000) plus the annualized opportunity cost ($60,000) is $140,000 each year, there is a net gain to society of $227,500 from keeping this recreation site open and retaining it in public ownership. Another use of the annual benefit figure is to compare the benefits of preserving the site versus allowing a proposed development at the site. For example, if a company wishes to mine at the site, its annual *net benefits* (i.e., total revenues *minus* mining costs) must be greater than $227,500 a year.

In this simple TCM demand curve example, the visit rate from distance zones was considered to be a function of the distance-related travel costs and time. Actually, other variables would also influence trips per capita and would need to be considered in applications of the method. These include the determinants of demand discussed in Chapter 7.

## Assumptions of the Simple TCM

Like any model, the TCM involves several simplifying assumptions so as to make data collection less burdensome and keep the statistical analysis tractable. Since all models are necessarily simplifications of reality, the use of assumptions is a necessary feature of any conceptual or statistical model. The assumptions of the simple TCM follow. More sophisticated statistical analysis and very thorough visitor surveys can reduce reliance on some, but not all of the assumptions. The proper use of assumptions is to tell the analyst when the model is applicable. In some cases one can check for or test for violations of the assumptions. When the assumptions of the TCM are met, it should provide a reasonably accurate estimate of the use and benefits of outdoor recreation at the particular site where the data were collected.

There are three categories: (1) assumptions necessary to interpret travel cost as the price paid to visit the site; (2) assumptions associated with simplifications that can be relaxed with better data; and (3) assumptions necessary to estimate the statistical regression.

## Assumptions Needed to Interpret Travel Cost as Price

### *Single Destination Trips*

If the individual leaves home and drives directly to the recreation site and then returns directly home, we can be pretty certain the transportation and travel time were incurred exclusively to gain access to the site. In contrast, if he or she left home and visited an aunt who lives very near the recreation site, we do not know how much of the transportation cost and travel time is related to visiting the recreation site and how much is related to visiting the aunt. The same is true if the individual visits several National Parks on a single trip from home. For example, people often visit both the Grand Teton and Yellowstone National Parks on the same trip. How much of the travel cost from home is for each park? To the extent the data fails to account for multidestination trips such as these (i.e., recording the full, round-trip cost from the visitor's home to *each* of the National Parks, that is, double counting the travel costs), TCM will overstate the benefits attributable to the recreation area.

Unfortunately there is not a theoretically correct answer to the allocation of joint trip costs among multiple destinations. The analyst is left with two choices. The first is to drop these observations and estimate the demand curve with just the single destination users and then apply the average consumer surplus per trip to these multidestination users. The second is to ask the visitors what proportion of trip cost is attributable to visiting each destination. A variant of this is to use the proportion of visitor's on-site time to apportion total trip costs to each site. These approaches are intuitively appealing and will work mechanically with the individual observation TCM, but do not work well with the zonal TCM (essentially these adjustments add noise to the measurement of the price variable when only a portion of the travel cost to the site is included for some visitors from that zone).

Luckily, for the vast majority of recreation users visiting the majority of recreation sites, single destination trips are the rule rather than the exception. For most day and weekend hiking, skiing, fishing, hunting and rafting trips, the recreation site is the sole or primary purpose of the trip so little data is lost.

Often a key to meeting the assumption of single destination trips is in choosing the geographic boundary of the relevant market area for the recreation site. Frequently, many of the people that are multidestination users are visitors who have come great distances from home and are on vacation trips rather than typical weekend trips. A market area that includes these distant users may throw off the vertical intercept or choke price of the demand curve, defined as the point where the demand curve cuts the price axis. It represents the maximum direct cost or price anyone will pay for use of the recreation site and is based on the maximum distance people are willing to travel for single destination trips. The problem occurs when a few recreation users come a great distance and when nonlinear demand curves do not cut the vertical axis. Otherwise acceptable functional forms for the demand curve may imply unrealistic travel behavior and lead to gross overestimation of consumer surplus.

However, reasonable assumptions can be incorporated into the calculation of consumer surplus. For example, the Corps of Engineers uses distance zones that include approximately 95% of all visitors to the study site as the cutoff for single destination users. Thus, roughly 5% live beyond the most distant zone, which represents the price intercept of the demand curve. These users are excluded from the analysis, and their benefits are assumed equal to the average consumer surplus of those included. This is an acceptable procedure according to the federal guidelines. Other studies have limited the boundary of the relevant market so as to exclude out-of-state users who generally will have traveled farther than in-state users. This practice has often underestimated benefits of big-game hunting, waterfowl hunting, cold-water fishing, and boating. Further research on this problem may provide a more acceptable solution in the future.

### *No Benefits From Travel*

An assumption related to single destination trips is that the costs of travel and the travel time are incurred to gain access to the recreation site and that no benefits are received from the travel itself. If the individual obtained substantial benefits from sightseeing while driving to the site, then the travel cost and travel time produced a joint benefit: access to the recreation site and sightseeing. Once again we do not know how much of the benefit is related to sightseeing on the drive versus visiting the site itself. Wilman (1980) has proposed a series of questions that can be asked of the visitor to help sort this out. For example, one can simply ask visitors if sightseeing was the main purpose of their trip. Alternatively, if the visitor spent three hours driving to the site, but only one hour at the site, most likely it was a sightseeing trip. Once again, we could exclude this observation from the data but account for the individual's benefit by applying the sample average consumer surplus estimated from individuals whose trip was for the primary purpose of visiting the site.

For many frequently visited recreation sites the assumption of no benefits of travel is often met. An individual that makes multiple trips per year to the same site, or to sites that require driving the same road, the benefits of the travel are probably quite minimal. The visitor sees the route several times per year and weekend traffic to major recreation sites often mimics urban rush-hour traffic. Nonetheless, to the extent the assumption is violated, TCM will overstate the benefits of recreation at a particular site.

## Assumptions Which Can Be Relaxed

In our simple example of the zonal TCM we assumed (1) the characteristics of the population are the same from one distance zone to another; (2) trips are of uniform duration and for the single purpose of visiting the recreation site; and (3) individuals travel the same speed regardless of road conditions, pay the same direct costs to operate private autos, and experience uniform opportunity costs of time.

Where direct survey data are available or can be collected on individual visitors, any one or all of the assumptions may be avoided. Even if survey data are not available, secondary data such as demographics from the U.S. census allow us to account for differences among population zones. For example, income, wage rates, education, and percent urban are available from census data and can be used as independent variables to control for differences between zones of origin or counties. Permit data frequently contains information on length of stay, so this too can be entered as a separate variable in the regression, rather than assuming it is the same for all users. Standard statistical procedures are used to hold these other variables constant in the demand function, and show the single effect of travel cost or price on quantity demanded. This means that the slope and location of the demand curve can be automatically corrected for variations in the characteristics of the population from one distance zone to another.

However, even when direct survey data are available, the zonal per capita approach aggregates individual consumers by residence into origin zones. This means that each zone is associated with a single average travel cost or price, opportunity cost of time, income per household, age, and the like. Individual variations are averaged out. The resulting zonal values for travel cost and time cost are more highly correlated with quantity demanded than are these values for individuals within zones. Thus, the zonal approach may appear to "explain" more of the variation in quantity demanded than the individual approach. This occurs because there is less variation to explain rather than because the approach is in any way superior in this respect.

When individual consumers are aggregated by residence location into origin zones, the socioeconomic variables usually have shown little or no significant relationship to quantity demanded. This results, in part, from the fact that averaging data by counties or zip codes tends to eliminate variability in the data, making it less likely that the variables will have a statistically significant influence on demand. In general, tests of the influence of the socioeconomic characteristics of individual users, such as tastes and preferences, income, and age will be more precise and significant in studies using individual observations rather than zonal averages. For example, Martin, Gum and Smith (1974) used the individual travel cost approach to test the effect of 20 independent variables on demand for fishing, hunting, and other outdoor recreation in Arizona.

The travel cost approach is designed to estimate demand for the recreation activities at a specific site. For a resource that provides a single recreation activity—for example, a campground—site demand is equivalent to demand for the recreation activity. However, most sites provide opportunities for more than a single recreation activity—a reservoir may provide fishing, motorboating, water-skiing, sailing, swimming, camping, picnicking, and sightseeing. When information is desired on the demand for a specific recreation activity at a multipurpose site, studies have been limited to users who are primarily engaged in the activity of interest to the study (i.e., more than 50% of on-site time). This approach may not be sufficiently precise when information is desired on demand by all users who engage in a single activity at the study site. The problem can be resolved by asking a sample of users to allocate total on-site time and travel cost among their various recreation activities at the study site. With this information, separate travel cost demand curves can be estimated for each recreation activity and summed to obtain demand for the site.

## Assumptions Necessary to Estimate Demand Function

### *Sufficient Variation in Travel Costs to Trace out a Demand Curve*

The key requirement is there must be variation in travel costs in order to estimate the demand curve. If all visitors come from the same city, then only one price data point is likely to be observed. As one can visualize, it is possible to fit any number of curves through one price point. Any demand curve needs at least two distinct prices. Thus, at least two distinctively different travel costs are needed to trace out a demand curve.

The implication of this assumption is that TCM will not work well for most urban recreation sites, since travel costs will often be the same for all users and travel costs are often close to zero. In this situation, a TCM demand curve for the park cannot be estimated, and the contingent valuation method must be employed.

### *All Relevant Variables Affecting Trip Making Behavior Are Included*

This is a common assumption in regression analysis to avoid omitted variable bias. We need to include in the demand equation all of the determinants discussed in Chapter 7, particularly those that might be correlated with our price variable, travel cost. Omission of variables not correlated with the price variable is not as crucial since their effect will often be reflected in the constant term. However, omission of any variable, such as the price of substitutes, that is correlated with travel cost to the study site will bias the size of the coefficient on travel cost. Since it is this coefficient that determines the benefits per day, bias here may cause serious error in our estimate of recreation benefits. Thus, it is important to include as many determinants of demand as is feasible (given budget and study time constraints), particularly variables such as price of substitutes. Travel time should be included as a separate variable or converted to dollars and added to the transportation cost variable.

Costs, in addition to automobile costs of the trip, should be included when they vary either among origin zones in relation to distance traveled or among individuals. Such costs will change the slope and the area under the demand curve above price. This may occur when some more distant or less frequent individual users are on overnight weekend trips, where payments for camping or resort lodging represent a substantial part of the necessary costs of the trip. In this case, lodging and related costs, such as air fare or rental cars, should be added to the direct cost of auto operations. An alternative procedure recommended by federal guidelines is to separate the sample into day users and overnight users, and to estimate separate demand functions for each group.

It is not necessary to include an item of cost that does not vary either among origin zones in relation to distance traveled or among individuals in relation to number of trips; it will not change either the slope or the area under the demand curve. For example, if all users of a campground pay a daily fee of $10 for a campsite, the estimate of consumer surplus will not be affected, because both price and the demand curve shift upward by the same amount. Thus, the slope and the area under the demand curve above price remains the same. Where these costs are not known, reasonably accurate results often can be obtained by omitting them.

## Reliability of the Approach

When assumptions of the travel cost method have been reasonably well met, the model's predictions of trips and recreation benefits should be reasonably accurate. The travel cost method has been thoroughly investigated and improved upon over more than 35 years and refinement continues today. Much of this discussion has taken place in the scientific or peer reviewed economic journals. Readers interested in the latest advances can consult with recent issues of journals such as *Land Economics, American Journal of Agricultural Economics, Journal of Environmental Economics and Management,* and *Journal of Leisure Research,* to name just a few.

# Regional Multisite Models to Incorporate Site Quality

So far we have focused on estimating the demand to a single site from data for that one site. To estimate the value of recreation with current quality levels, this is sufficient. But often the policy question is, what happens to recreation benefits if quality is improved with better management or degraded by incompatible resource uses, such as water pollution by mining or other developments? How trips and benefits change cannot be answered using a demand curve estimated for a single site. The reason is that we observe the current demand curve just for the current conditions at the site. We have no information on how trips change with improved water quality or more boat ramps. Every person visiting the site, no matter from what county or distance zone, receives the same water quality or has the same number of boat ramps available to him or her. Thus, if we tried to include a variable for boat ramps, the quantity of this variable would be the same for all observations. Therefore, it logically (and statistically) cannot tell us anything about how visitation *varies* when we add another boat ramp.

To observe how visits change when another boat ramp is added or the reservoir is kept full (as compared to drawdowns during irrigation releases), we must look at visitation levels at sites that have more and less boat ramps or larger surface area of lake. If larger lakes are more attractive to visitors because they allow users freedom to spread out, then this effect should be reflected in more visits per capita (for the same distance traveled) at larger lakes. Conversely, smaller lakes, with all else being equal, should have fewer visitors per capita or visits per year from a given individual.

The modeling strategy is to pool or combine visitation data from multiple sites that have different levels of the site quality variable of interest. Thus, we might pool data from three lakes, one smaller than our study lake and one with larger surface area. Table 9-3 illustrates this pooling.

We can now estimate a regression across the combined data set. Doing so results in the following regression:

$$\text{Trips/Population} = 0.196 + (-0.00089 \times \text{Distance}) + (0.000098 \times \text{Surface acres}) \quad \text{(Equation 9-5)}$$

This equation shows that for every additional 1,000 surface acres of reservoir, trips per capita increase by 0.098. For a county with 10,000 people, that translates into 980 more visits. If we were evaluating a proposal to maintain Site 1 at its full reservoir storage capacity of 2,000 surface acres instead of the current drawdown reservoir of 1,000 surface acres, we could use this regression equation to predict the increase in visitation. Since an additional 1,000 surface acres results in 0.098 more trips per capita, this

**Table 9-3. Per Capita Demand for Visits to Three Recreation Sites**

| Site | Origin Zone | Population | Trips per Year | Trips per Capita | One-Way Distance (Miles) | Lake Surface Acres |
|---|---|---|---|---|---|---|
| 1 | A | 100,000 | 30,000 | 0.30 | 50 | 1,000 |
| 1 | B | 10,000 | 2,000 | 0.20 | 100 | 1,000 |
| 1 | C | 30,000 | 3,000 | 0.10 | 150 | 1,000 |
| 2 | B | 10,000 | 4,000 | 0.40 | 60 | 1,500 |
| 2 | D | 20,000 | 5,000 | 0.25 | 120 | 1,500 |
| 2 | E | 10,000 | 1,000 | 0.10 | 200 | 1,500 |
| 2 | F | 40,000 | 2,000 | 0.05 | 300 | 1,500 |
| 3 | E | 10,000 | 2,000 | 0.20 | 175 | 2,000 |
| 3 | F | 40,000 | 4,000 | 0.10 | 250 | 2,000 |
| 3 | G | 50,000 | 1,000 | 0.02 | 500 | 2,000 |
| 3 | H | 70,000 | 3,500 | 0.05 | 400 | 2,000 |

will translate into 9,800 more visits from Zone A, 980 from Zone B, and 2,940 from Zone C. The total increase in recreation use would be 13,720 visits. For purposes of illustration, we will use the original benefits per trip of $10 that we calculated for Site 1 using the second stage demand curve in Figure 9-2 (page 143). The annual benefits of keeping the reservoir full to provide 2,000 surface acres instead of the existing 1,000 surface acres is worth $137,200 (= 13,720 added visits x the $10 consumer surplus per visit). In Figure 9-4 (page 156) the $137,200 is equal to the shaded area between the current site demand curve and the site demand curve with increased surface acres. The difference is the gain in net WTP since the vertical axis is added dollars. This is illustrated in Figure 9-4.

This annual benefit can be compared to the costs of retaining water in the reservoir during the recreation season. The opportunity cost might be reduced irrigated agricultural output. As long as the reduced net benefits in agriculture (i.e., crop revenues minus farming costs) are less than the gain in recreation, retaining water to keep the reservoir full during the recreation season would increase the overall benefits to society.

It is worth noting that the prediction of increased visitation will also be of great use for estimating the local tourism benefits based on the input-output modeling approach described in Chapter 14.

The multiple-site method is preferred in the federal guidelines because it economizes on costs required for site-specific studies. The multiple-site methods are also more effective in measuring the effects of variation in resource quality and opportunities to substitute alternative sites (Sutherland, 1982).

**Figure 9-4. Shift in Demand Curve with Improvement in Quality**

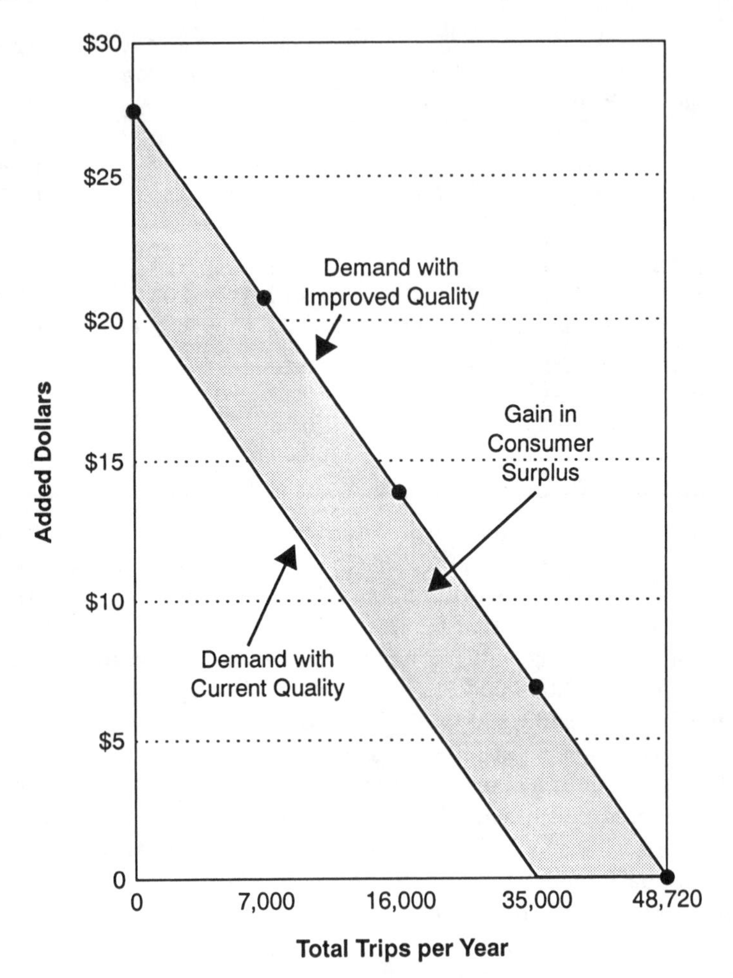


# Hedonic TCM

The federal guidelines do not preclude the use of new techniques as, for example, the hedonic method (Brookshire, Thayer, Schulze and d'Arge, 1982) or a combination of the hedonic and travel cost methods. Another multisite TCM model is a hybrid hedonic travel cost method developed by Brown and Mendelsohn (1984). This method combines the hedonic procedures from the household production approach with the traditional travel cost method. The distinguishing characteristic of the approach is that travel cost is the dependent variable in the first step of a two-step process. The first step is to estimate the price individuals from each origin zone must pay to obtain each characteristic of the experience or recreation activity. A separate regression is run for each of 10 or more origin zones in which the quantity of characteristics and recreation activities are independent variables. The resulting regression coefficients for marginal prices of the characteristics and recreation activities, along with the mean quantities, are assigned to all individuals from each zone. When there is sufficient range in the prices and quantities of characteristics and activities between zones, it is possible in the second step to estimate a demand curve for each characteristic and activity for all individuals from the 10 or more zones. The hedonic travel cost approach has been used to estimate the effects of fish catch, congestion, scenic quality, and for the characteristics of hiking trails in Olympic National Park in Washington state. Although the hedonic approach has provided some useful results with respect to the quality of recreation sites, its application has been limited to situations where the most distant sites are also the highest quality with respect to the important characteristics. Otherwise, studies find a puzzling large number of the regression coefficients for the marginal prices of characteristics have the wrong sign.

## *Multisite Selection Models*

Models that predict which site individuals will go to on any particular recreation trip are often called **site selection models.** These models still use travel cost as a price variable, but the dependent variable is now a qualitative variable, equaling one if a particular site is visited and zero if not. Similar to regional models, the site selection models pool data across multiple sites. As with regional models, this allows the analyst to quantify how the probability of visiting a particular site changes with the quality of the site.

Site selection models are estimated with a technique known as **multinomial logit regression.** While this is a rather complicated statistical technique, the intuition behind it is straightforward. An individual is assumed to compare the net benefits (e.g., utility of visiting a site minus the travel cost) of visiting each possible site and to select the one to visit which gives the highest net benefits. The quality of the site (e.g., the quality of facilities, fishing, forests) increases the benefits. The distance the individual lives from the site increases the cost. Individuals balance these two opposing forces in choosing which site is best for them. Of course, an analyst could not possibly include all of the variables in the regression model for all of the factors that individuals balance when they assess benefits of visiting a site (e.g., number of insect bites on their last visit). Thus, some individuals might be observed choosing a site that is further away that does not, using the limited number of variables in the analyst's model, indicate higher quality. But the site surely does have higher quality to the recreationist. Viewed from the analyst's point of view, there appears to be a random element in some visitors' choices. As such, we often see multinomial logit models of site selection called Random Utility Models (RUMs). While the name is not completely accurate, it is simply a type of travel cost model.

Because travel cost is a price variable in the multinomial logit model, formulas exist to calculate the net WTP for maintaining the existing site and improving its quality. There are numerous applications of the technique, the most common include freshwater recreational fishing (Parsons and Kealy, 1992) and saltwater recreational fishing (Kling and Thomson, 1996). The technique is useful to evaluate quality improvements at recreation sites in which most people make at most one visit a year or none at all. Examples include remote recreation areas such as the Grand Canyon and Yellowstone National Parks, and rafting the Middle Fork of the Salmon River in Idaho.

# *Chapter 10*

# Contingent Valuation Method

This chapter reviews a survey-based approach that directly elicits an individual's willingness to pay for recreation and environmental quality. The strengths and weaknesses of the method are discussed.

The Contingent Valuation Method (CVM) is a direct interview (survey) approach that can be used to provide acceptable measures of the economic value of recreation opportunities as well as preservation of natural resources. This latter use is unique to contingent valuation. In particular, contingent valuation can value the benefits to nonvisiting households from simply knowing that a natural environment exists as habitat for fish and wildlife or as a geological and ecological resource. Some households may be motivated by this **existence value** to pay for protection of a resource they do not plan to use, but derive satisfaction from knowing that it exists (Krutilla, 1967). Other households that have no intention of visiting may also be willing to pay to protect a resource for future generations. This **bequest value** toward ones own children, grandchildren or future generations is a frequent motivation expressed in many contingent valuation surveys. Together, these existence and bequest values are sometimes referred to as preservation values, passive use values, or nonuse values.

The U.S. Water Resources guidelines authorized use of the contingent valuation method in 1979 and established procedures for its application to recreation problems. In this approach, a sample of the affected population is asked to report its maximum willingness to pay, contingent on hypothetical changes in recreation opportunities or resources. This is the basis for the term contingent valuation. In 1986 the U.S. Department of the Interior began recommending contingent valuation for measuring existence and bequest values.

# Characteristics of the Approach

Contingent valuation methods use simulated (hypothetical) markets to identify values similar to actual markets, if they existed. The reliability of the estimates depends, in part, on the care with which the interviewer describes the nature of the hypothetical market; the change in the recreation activities or resources to be valued; the time period for which the valuation applies; the method of hypothetical payment; and the type of value question asked. The basics of each of these issues is discussed here. Details can be found in Mitchell and Carson (1989).

## *Hypothetical Market Rules*

The institutional rules pertaining to the hypothetical market should be described in sufficient detail so that the respondent knows his or her rights and the rights of all others in the market. These rules should be realistic and credible; they should encourage market behavior with which consumers are familiar; and they should be viewed as just, fair, and ethically sound. Situations that threaten the respondents with losing what they already have, may be viewed as unfair and should be avoided unless this is actually the policy under evaluation. The rule that relates responses in the survey to provision of the recreational resource should be spelled out. For example, stating "If willingness to pay [WTP] of users for the addition of a boat ramp exceeds the cost, it will be provided." The question asked should be of a type that suggests the pragmatic "take it or leave it" atmosphere of the marketplace. The wording, "Would you be willing to pay . . . ?" should be avoided because some respondents may interpret it as an appeal for voluntary contributions, and the reported value would understate total willingness to pay. Respondents should be asked, "Would you pay a maximum of . . . ?" with the clear understanding that, "if not, you would go without" the recreation activity or resource.

## *Description of the Resource to Be Valued*

The recreation activities or resources to be evaluated should be carefully described as to quantity, quality, time and location. The description should be realistic and precise enough to give the respondent adequate information on which to base a valuation. To estimate the effect of possible changes in the availability of recreation opportunities and resources, the descriptions may be hypothetical in the sense that they may not precisely describe features of actual activities or resources. Still, they should be plausible, that is, within the realm of possibility. Also, the alternatives should be displayed in color photos, drawings, or maps. These should be selected with care to assure that the relevant attributes of the recreation activities or resources are clearly distinguishable while other possible variations (such as clouds) are held to a minimum.

For example, Walsh, Loomis and Gillman's (1984) study of the value of wilderness in the Rocky Mountains provided respondents with maps depicting four levels of wilderness designation. These included the 1.2 million acres of wilderness at the time of the study; the 2.6 million acres proposed (and subsequently designated); double this amount or 5.0 million acres; and the 10.0 million acres of potential wilderness. These amounts were described as equivalent to about 2%, 4%, 8%, and 15% of the surface land area of the state. Their general location and quality was familiar to most residents. Respondents were asked to assume that potential Wilderness Areas would be similar in quality to existing wilderness and would be designated for protection at the time of payment. Recently, photo simulations have been used in CVM surveys to depict the changes in lake water levels, forest density or crowding levels.

## *Valuation Measure*

Ideally, respondents would be asked their WTP for an increase (or increment) in a recreation opportunity or resource. It is an appropriate measure for enhancement in the recreation resource such as providing new access, facilities, or improving quality of the site. Asking WTP for alternative levels of improvement is the preferred approach for determining economic benefits, as compared to asking respondents their WTP to avoid a threatened decrease in a recreation opportunity or resource. Valuing improvements offers respondents the chance to value something they desire, and thus it is unlikely to provoke an offended reaction. On the other hand, asking respondents how much they would pay to avoid a change they do not want, may seem unfair or morally offensive to some, and thus, may result in unreliable values.

All existing federal guidelines recommend asking the maximum willingness to pay measure of value over the alternative, minimum willingness to sell or to accept compensation (WTA) for reduced recreation opportunities and resources. The appropriate question depends on property rights and the resource decision to be made. If the public holds the property right as it does for fish and wildlife, then the question of the minimum level of compensation would normally be the appropriate valuation measure required. Legislation such as the Endangered Species Act, Clean Water Act, Clean Air Act, Superfund Act for clean up of hazardous waste sites, and the Oil Pollution Act all assign property rights to the public. Since minimum WTA is not directly constrained by income, it would be expected to be greater than WTP, which is constrained by income. However, the difference between WTP and WTA for most recreational resources should be small because households spend a small percentage of their income to visit, and there may often be good substitutes for the recreational resource under study.

Unfortunately a number of studies, including Bishop and Heberlein (1979), have found that willingness to sell values including actual cash sales are far higher than willingness to pay, whether the latter is measured by the contingent valuation or the travel cost approach. This has cast doubt on the ability of CVM to accurately measure WTA as compared to WTP. A great deal of research is underway to understand if the high WTA values reflect some form of loss aversion, not accounted for in standard economic theory, artifacts of the experiments which have been conducted to date or the fact that WTA questions are frequently unfamiliar and unrealistic to most visitors. That is, most consumers and visitors are used to paying, not being compensated. We act as consumers daily, frequently determining whether we will pay a given price or not. It is far more rare that we act as sellers, determining the minimum we will accept. Further compounding the problem is the fact that government frequently asks on referenda and in polls whether we would pay more in taxes for a given program, but rarely asks what we would accept as compensation for eliminating an existing program. Thus, asking WTP is believed to be a more valid measure of benefits. However, it is very important to recognize and communicate to decision makers that WTP is a *conservative* measure of losses to individuals for reduction in the quality or quantity of recreation.

## *Time Frame of Valuation Responses*

Contingent valuation studies can obtain measures of individual or household willingness to pay for almost any time period. Frequently the time period is the amount he or she would pay annually. Thus, respondents usually should be informed that what is being valued is the right to have or to use the recreation resource for one year. In some cases, however, it may be more realistic for respondents to value changes in the availability of recreation opportunities per day or per trip (when of uniform duration), given the continued availability of existing sites. Where willingness to pay per day or per trip is more appropriate, it can be used so long as information is available on the total number of recreation days or trips to permit the calculation of annual values. Also, estimates of recreation use may be collected as part of a contingent valuation survey. To do so, the question should include how many trips were taken in the past 12 months; how many days were spent per trip to existing recreation sites similar to the proposed site; and how many household members participated in each trip. These questions should be followed with one asking for the same use information if the proposed increment in recreation opportunity or resource were made available. The difference between number of trips with and without the proposed additional recreation opportunity or resource is the use attributed to it.

## *Method of Payment*

The method of payment (called payment vehicle) which should be selected is one that is most likely to lead to honest evaluation by respondents. A number of alternative methods have been used in past studies.

For valuing a recreation trip, the most familiar and direct payment vehicle is to ask how much of an increased trip cost visitors would pay so as to be able to have made this trip to this site. Other payment vehicles for recreation include higher entrance fees or fishing and hunting license fees. The drawback to fees as a payment vehicle is that visitors may use their answer to signal their dissatisfaction with the agency, rather than provide an indication of the benefits they receive from recreation at the site.

For valuing preservation of natural resources that have little use value (a strong suit of the CVM as we will see), useful payment vehicles include payments into special trust funds, taxes (e.g., sales, property or income), utility bills (e.g., water, sewer or electricity), as well as general prices of goods and services purchased. The federal guidelines suggest that several methods of payment should be tried in the survey pretest, including a neutral method, e.g., "The money collected will be placed in a trust fund and devoted entirely to providing the recreation opportunity or resource." This last statement is important to assure users that money paid will be used to provide the good described in the survey, rather than have the money going into the general treasury (which they rightly believe reduces the likelihood of the resource being supplied or protected).

For recreation, the U.S. Water Resources Council guidelines (1983) suggest that methods of payment such as taxes, utility bills, and hunting or fishing license fees usually should be avoided because they may result in a symbolic reaction against the agency or utility company. More recently, a "blue ribbon" panel suggested that for preservation studies such as overall wilderness or open space protection, it may be appropriate to cast the CVM question as a voter referendum. In this case, they further recommended that taxes would be the appropriate payment vehicle. Thus, each method of payment may be used when it is the most realistic and promotes honest evaluations by respondents in particular situations.

Davis (1963), who originated the contingent valuation approach (then called "bidding game") more than three decades ago, initially used an entrance fee but abandoned it after a pretest showed that willingness to pay direct trip expenses proved more realistic and acceptable to households engaged in fishing, hunting, and camping in the Maine woods. Concepts of "reasonable" and "proper" which may apply to entrance permits, taxes, and utility bills are diffused when applied to transportation, lodging, added food, and miscellaneous trip expenses. Direct trip costs also have been used successfully in studies of hiking, backpacking and other recreation activities. Figure 10-1 (page 164) presents sample questions from a study of the benefits of wilderness recreation, using direct trip costs as the method of payment.

Entrance permits have been used with apparent success to estimate changes in willingness to pay, even though they appear to be deficient in estimating total willingness to pay for the recreation experience. Examples include studies of the effect of instream flow of water (Daubert and Young, 1981), natural forest scenery (Thayer, 1981), congestion in

**Figure 10-1. Contingent Valuation Questions About Recreational Use of Wilderness**

1. Please estimate what your last trip to Wilderness Area X cost in total including transportation, food, accommodations and miscellaneous expenses. $______.
2. How many people in your party shared this cost? ________# persons.
3. How much did you value this trip? Was it worth more than you actually spent? YES NO
4. Assume that your trip became more expensive due perhaps to increased travel costs. What is the maximum you would have paid for this trip rather than not visit this site? $______.

downhill skiing (Walsh, Miller and Gilliam, 1983), and propagation of such endangered wildlife species as grizzly bear and mountain sheep (Brookshire, Eubanks and Randall, 1983).

The first study of the contingent value of environmental quality (Randall, Ives and Eastman, 1974) found that households in New Mexico were willing to pay only about one-fourth as much for air quality (visibility) when the method of payment used was electric utility bills as compared to sales tax ($23 versus $85 per year). A similar study also reported that households in Colorado (Greenley, Walsh and Young, 1982) were willing to pay only about one-fourth as much for water quality when the method of payment used was a water bill compared to a sales tax ($26 versus $91 per year). Thus, the payment vehicle must be pretested for acceptability. If no single payment vehicle is widely accepted by respondents, multiple payment vehicles can be used in split samples and the results compared.

## *Question Format*

There are several ways in which to ask the WTP question. The most obvious might be as shown in Figure 10-1, where the visitor is asked to write down the highest dollar amount he or she would pay rather than stop visiting this site for a given period of time (e.g., one trip). This is called the **open-ended** question format. It is the simplest to ask in a mail survey, where interaction with the respondent is not possible. This question format also provides the easiest data to analyze, since the exact dollar amount of WTP is provided by the respondent.

Unfortunately, while it is an easy question to ask, it is one of the more difficult for the visitor to answer. If the respondents infrequently participate in this activity or rarely visit this site, it may be hard for them to determine a specific dollar amount that is their maximum WTP. As a result, these infrequent visitors or users may leave the question blank. Alternatively, they may write down a dollar amount they are quite certain they would pay, but it may not truly represent the maximum they would pay (Hoehn and Randall, 1987). Nonetheless, the open-ended question format is still sometimes used today in mail questionnaires when the typical user is quite familiar with the site and activity.

A **payment card** has been developed to overcome the concerns about open-ended questions, yet allow for their use in mail questionnaires. An unanchored payment card approach asks respondents to select their maximum willingness to pay from a list of alternative values shown or to write down their own maximum amount. An anchored payment card provides an indication of what the respondent's household is likely already spending on other public programs, so as to provide some context to the program being asked in the survey. Figure 10-2 illustrates an anchored payment card.

While there have been concerns raised that the range and midpoint of the dollar amounts shown on the card might influence a respondent's WTP, recent research by Rowe, Schulze and Breffle (1996) suggests that respondents reported WTP is not significantly related to the range or midpoint of the payment card, within reasonable ranges. The range can be set from open-ended WTP responses obtained in pretest surveys.

An **iterative bidding** technique was recommended by federal guidelines in 1983 to encourage respondents to report maximum values, representing the point of indifference between having the amount of money (income) stated versus the recreation opportunity. Following a description of the market and the recreation opportunity or resource to be valued, the respondent is asked to react to a series of dollar values posed by the interviewer. Respondents answer yes or no to whether they are willing to pay the stated amount of money to obtain the increment in recreation opportunity or resource. The interviewer increases or decreases the dollar value until the highest amount the respondent is willing to pay is identified.

The starting price (called *starting point*) of the iterative process should be varied from one respondent to another on a random basis, to reduce the possibility that this initial bid may influence individual values. Early increases (or decreases) in the dollar value may be large (e.g., double the initial starting price) until the interviewer senses that the value is approaching the respondent's point of indifference; final changes in price

**Figure 10-2. Example Anchored Payment Card for Annual WTP**

Please circle your maximum willingness to pay

| | | | |
|---|---|---|---|
| $0 | $50 | $250 | $700 |
| $2 | Police and Fire | $300 | $800 |
| $5 | $70 | $350 | Defense Program |
| $10 | $90 | Public Education | $900 |
| Space Program | $120 | $400 | $1,000 |
| $15 | $150 | $500 | $1,500 |
| $25 | $200 | $600 | $2,000 |

Source: Adapted from Mitchell and Carson, 1989.

should become smaller (e.g., $1 increments). This will avoid the possibility that respondents will get tired of answering yes or no to an excessive number of small price changes and end the process before their total willingness to pay is reached. Iterative bidding questions are most effective in personal or telephone interviews. Due to concern over the influence of starting point on final WTP responses, iterative bidding is not frequently used today.

**Dichotomous choice and referenda** question formats became quite popular in the 1990s. With this question format, respondents answer yes or no to whether they would pay a single incremental price that is varied across respondents. While close-ended questions do not provide a direct estimate of maximum willingness to pay, data on the proportion of the sample answering yes or no to each of a range of dollar values can be used to estimate a value function or demand function from which net benefits can be derived (Bishop and Heberlein, 1979).

The dichotomous choice question format has a number of advantages. First, it mimics price taking behavior consumers are familiar with in a market. Here the choice is simply "buy it or not at the price marked on the item." Thus, a dichotomous choice CVM question is a format familiar to consumers. The dichotomous choice question can also be framed as a yes or no vote on a referenda to provide the recreational resource. Again, this is familiar to most people as we often vote, at least every two years, on school bond and other public project issues. Hoehn and Randall (1987) suggest that dichotomous choice questions provide incentives compatible with truth telling. That is, if you value provision of the resource less than the amount you are asked to pay, you have no incentive to misstate your preferences and say yes. If the CVM market is framed in such a way as to suggest that the survey responses will influence delivery and financing of the good, the respondents will reduce their potential benefits by not telling the truth. The dichotomous choice format also minimizes the respondents' opportunity to overstate their valuation, hoping to encourage provision since they can only respond yes or no to the stated price. Dichotomous choice questions can be used in mail surveys as well. The dichotomous choice format has been recommended by the blue ribbon panel on CVM as the preferred question format (Arrow, Solow, Portney, Leamer, Radner and Schuman, 1993).

The primary drawbacks to dichotomous choice CVM lie in the design of the range of bid amounts and the greater difficulty in estimating WTP. Designing the bid amounts requires determining the range and increment of specific dollar amounts to ask and how many respondents get which dollar amounts. In essence, the range of dollar amounts to be picked must allow the analyst to trace out a probability of paying curve for the recreational resource. Therefore, at least one price low enough that most people would say yes is needed, to identify the horizontal intercept. Conversely, at least one dollar amount high enough that no one would be expected to pay that amount is needed, to identify the vertical intercept. Since regression-like techniques called logit and probit are used to estimate the valuation equation, there should be multiple observations spaced throughout the rest of the probability curve. Figure 10-3 illustrates a typical relationship between bid amount respondents were asked to pay and the percent who answered yes for elk hunting in Montana, with current conditions and a doubling of the chance of harvesting a trophy elk.

The other difficulty is that a regression analysis is needed to infer WTP. While this is no different than the travel cost method, many of the issues of functional form and variable specification may become more important with dichotomous choice CVM than with open-ended questions. Thus, dichotomous choice CVM gives up a few of the advantages of being a direct approach to elicit WTP for its ease on the respondent.

More recently, studies have compared various WTP question formats. The values obtained have been analyzed to determine if the different approaches significantly influence the results. Several studies have shown

**Figure 10-3. Elk Hunting Logit Curve and Willingness to Pay**

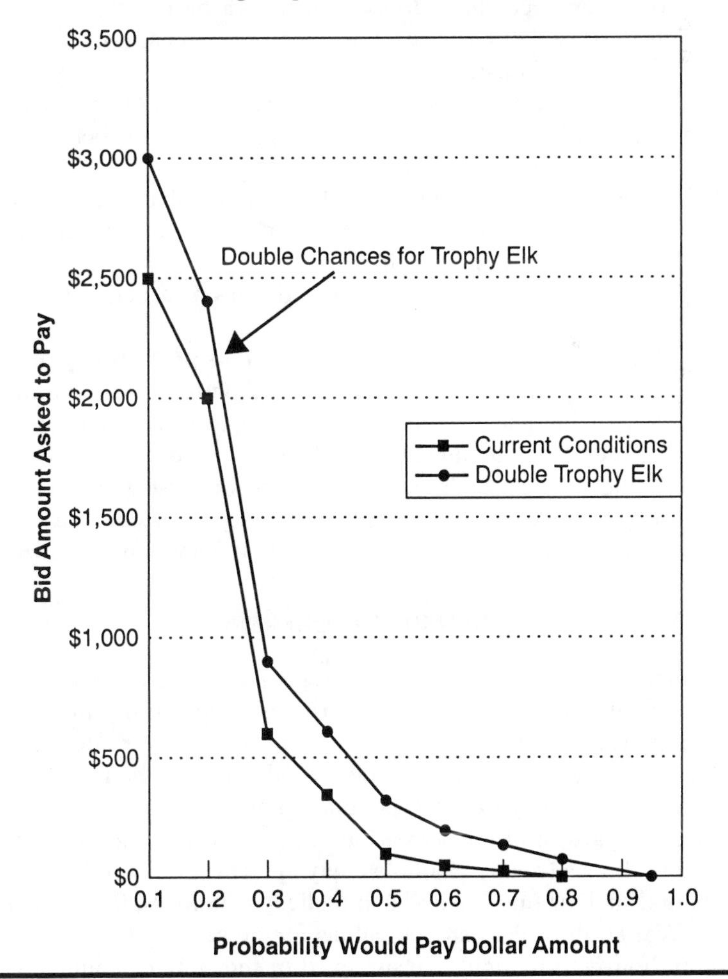

that open-ended direct (noniterative) questions yield noticeably lower values. While these tests are not conclusive, it appears that future studies using noniterative questions may provide somewhat lower, more conservative estimates than the dichotomous choice or iterative approach.

### *Identifying Protest Responses*

Some respondents are likely to report that they are not willing to pay for a proposed change in recreation opportunity or resource. Thus, it is important to identify which of these represent true zero valuations and which, if any, represent a protest against the hypothetical market or method of payment. Questions should always be included in contingent valuation studies that ask:

Did you answer zero because (check one):

a. You do not receive any benefits from the recreation opportunity or resource and therefore see no reason to pay?
b. Your cost of living is already too high or you cannot afford it (i.e., income constraint)?
c. You believe the method of payment (e.g., sales tax, property tax, utility bill) is not fair or equitable (in that some beneficiaries do not pay)?
d. You have a right to the recreation opportunity or resource, and it is unfair to expect you (as a utility customer, a fishing license holder) to pay for it.
e. You do not think the program would work as described.

Answers to *c*, *d* and *e* above should be recorded as protesting against the method of payment or hypothetical market and omitted from the calculation of average willingness to pay for the sample of respondents. The federal guidelines recommend that surveys with more than a 15% protest response should not be used in decision making because a high incidence of protest may indicate that other values are also distorted. Most contingent valuation studies have recorded protests that fall within this 15% limit.

## Survey Design

The population to be sampled should be people in the market area who would be affected by the change in recreation opportunity or resource. For recreation studies, the basic sampling unit is the visitor, such as campers, hikers, hunters and anglers. Samples of individuals or household groups may be drawn randomly from the population of on-site users (i.e., as they depart from a park or other recreation area) to avoid length of stay bias discussed by Lucas (1963). Samples may be drawn from reliable lists of participants, such as hunting and fishing license holders, if available.

For CVM studies of existence values for preserving a resource, at a minimum, households should be surveyed in the state or country where the resource is located. Recent studies have shown nationwide concern for preservation of even local natural resources such as old growth forests in Oregon that are habitat for the northern spotted owl.

Samples such as households may be randomly or systematically drawn from the regional population of households, as listed in phone directories, if the issue involves improvements in site quality that might induce participation or passive use values. Randomized cluster sampling is permissible to save travel time between interviews, provided that no cluster is larger than one-thirtieth of the sample size. Sample size should be no less than 200 households or individuals and upwards of 1,000 may be desirable to provide sufficient precision in WTP estimates for constructing meaningful confidence intervals. The respondent selected to answer on behalf of the household should, preferably be, the head of the household or spouse of the head. Another adult member of the household may be interviewed, provided he or she is sufficiently informed about household values.

## *Structure of Interview or Questionnaire*

Contingent valuation questionnaires should usually contain at least three sections, one to measure a respondents preferences in a nonmonetary way, one for obtaining use and valuation of the recreation opportunity or resource, and one for collecting appropriate demographic data on income, age, and the like. The complete interview usually should not require more than 30 minutes in order to minimize inconvenience and fatigue of the respondent. If the CVM is being performed via personal or telephone interview, each interviewer should be given the complete script to assure consistency in application.

## *Importance of Pretesting*

Small discussion groups (called focus groups) can help in determining the method of payment and appropriate visual aids. The entire questionnaire or script should be pretested, using a sample of at least 30 respondents to uncover misinterpretation of the questions, ambiguity in response categories and clarity of any visual aids, such as graphs and photos. Ideally, the sample selected for pretest would be drawn from the same population as the subsequent study, although budget limitations sometimes make this difficult. Sampling procedures for the pretest are not especially crucial, but an attempt should be made to obtain a cross section of users, with respect to demographic characteristics. The key purpose of the pretest is to check whether the questions are worded correctly (i.e., does the visitor interpret the question as intended by the analyst). Misinterpretation can sometimes be identified by debriefing the respondent after each major section of the questionnaire. The number of nonresponses and protest zero responses should be tabulated; if they are equal to more than 15% of the sample, the questions should be redesigned and retested.

## *Factors Potentially Influencing CVM Responses*

Statistical tests should be made for possible problems that may arise from the hypothetical information provided, the method of payment used, the starting points for the iterative process, and over- or underreporting of true values (called *strategic behavior*). When tests indicate the presence of any of these problems, the pretest questions should be redesigned and retested. Also, the final results of the sample survey should be tested later for the same types of problems, and any that remain should be reported along with the findings of the study. Users of contingent valuation techniques should appreciate the importance of testing for possible problems. The particular statistical tests are straightforward, and if the problem is detected, there are methods for coping with the problem. Descriptions of some methods of identifying problems can be found in Schulze, d'Arge and Brookshire (1981) and Thayer (1981). These articles review six contingent value studies and conclude that problems such as bias is not likely to be a major problem in carefully designed studies.

The particular tests for these possible problems include the following:

1. **Hypothetical.** To test whether individuals respond as they would to an actual market situation; compare the results to other methods based on actual behavior, such as the travel cost or hedonic methods; and to assess convergent validity. Unfortunately, this test is limited to the use value of recreation activities and environmental resources. There are currently no behavior-based methods of estimating existence, or bequest values. In these applications, hypothetical bias is reduced if the contingent situation is realistic. To test for the theoretical validity of the results, a regression of WTP on preference, attitude and demographic variables can be performed to determine if WTP varies in a manner consistent with economic theory (e.g., does WTP go up with the strength of preference for the site or activity). Finally, the reliability of WTP results can be assessed by retesting the same population at a later date, using the same questions, as long as there has been no radical changes in circumstances surrounding site use (e.g., a severe drought, oil spill).
2. **Payment method.** To determine the effects of the payment vehicle, one can ask about WTP using two or three of the most likely payment vehicles with three pretest subsamples and then test for statistical difference in mean values. It is also important to ask pretest respondents about the acceptability of each type of payment. The influence of the payment vehicle is reduced if it seems appropriate to respondents.

3. **Bid design or starting points.** The range of dichotomous choice bid amounts or the iterative bidding starting points need to be determined in the pretest. If iterative bidding is used, the starting point should be included as an independent variable in the statistical WTP function. If the starting point is significant, its effect may be corrected for by setting the starting point equal to zero when calculating WTP from the estimated WTP function.
4. **Protest bidding.** The federal guidelines suggest that we include a question asking respondents their reasons for answering zero to the value questions. Then, we should remove those respondents who object to the hypothetical market or payment vehicle, not to exceed 15% of the sample.
5. **Strategic behavior.** To obtain an indication of whether some respondents try to influence the outcome of the study, prepare a frequency distribution of dollar values to test for the possibility of bimodal clustering of very high or very low values. Also, Randall (1987) suggests that we remove any very high outlying bids to obtain a solid core of estimates. Outlying bids may include WTP in excess of 5%–10% of income for a particular activity or site.
6. **Order effects.** To test for the effect of the order in which several value questions are asked, start with the most important attributes of environmental resources or recreation activities for half of the sample and reverse the order for the other half. Then, test for statistical differences in mean values. This test is appropriate if the programs being valued are truly independent of one another and the respondent is told to treat them as independent. If the programs are related or the second WTP amount is in addition to the first, then economic theory would suggest an ordering effect is appropriate and this is not a sign of poor design. Therefore it is sometimes suggested that we provide respondents the opportunity to go back and correct any prior values on telephone or in person surveys to reduce order efforts. Of course, when the order in which environmental improvement programs will be implemented is known, then that would determine the proper order of the value questions and no adjustment is needed.
7. **Scope effects or absence of embedding.** Economic theory suggests that visitors should be willing to pay greater amounts for larger quantities of recreation resources or greater improvements in quality. There are two ways to test this. The preferred way is to ask separate samples of visitors their WTP for meaningfully different increases in quantity or quality of recreation resources. It is important to provide the overall context in which the improvement takes place or provide a

supplementary, relative measure of the improvement as well. Maps of the region or graphs illustrating the improvement relative to the current situation are often quite helpful. If this approach is used, it is critical that there be random assignment of quality and quantity levels to respondents and that demographic variables be collected to allow comparison across samples. A less powerful approach for testing for scope is to ask the same individual to value multiple levels of quantity or quality improvements. This change in quality is then entered into the WTP function. If the variable is statistically significant it indicates that visitors have differentiated their answers between the different scenarios or levels of resource quality.

8. **Interviewer.** If in-person interviews are used and there are multiple interviewers, it is desirable to test for possible influence of the interviewer on the values reported. Statistical tests of equality of interviewer elicited WTP values are possible. If one interviewer is found to result in higher WTP values, it may be possible in a regression to control for this by including a shifter variable equal to one for his or her observations. Then to calculate WTP, the shifter variable can be set to zero. Alternatively, the regression coefficient for each interviewer indicates the amount of adjustment in the values. Interviewer bias can be reduced by careful training and supervision or by using professional interviewers.
9. **Survey response rates and nonresponse bias.** Several tests are recommended to determine the possible influence of the sampling procedure and the nonresponse of some individuals. Ideally, response rates of 70% are desired to provide a sample that represents the population of interest. Obtaining such high response rates involves several strategies, although given the length and complexity of most CVM surveys, responses rates of 40%–60% are more common (which is equivalent to voter turnout in real elections). Tests include comparing the sample characteristics to known characteristics of the population obtained from U.S. census reports or high response rate surveys of visitors, such as the U.S. Fish and Wildlife Service National Survey (1988, 1993) of fishing, hunting and wildlife associated recreation. If differences are found, the sample WTP values can be reweighed using population proportions as weights.
10. **Effects of survey mode.** When a mail survey is used for a contingent valuation study, the guidelines developed by Dillman (1978) should be followed insofar as possible. Random sampling methods should be used and at least one follow-up mailing is necessary to reduce nonresponse. In addition, the federal guidelines recommend that after the follow-up mailing, a random sample of 10% of the nonrespondents be

contacted by phone. Responses to the telephone survey should be analyzed separately in order to test whether they are significantly different from the responses to the mail survey. There is some concern that mail and telephone surveys overrepresent more interested or avid users or households with more time to complete surveys (e.g., retired persons). Surveys also tend to be filled out more frequently by people with higher education levels than the rest of the U.S. population. Therefore, it is often useful in the case of state and national household surveys to compare sample demographics against the population demographics. Socioeconomic (demographic) information on the general population is available from the U.S. census and can be compared to the socioeconomic characteristics of responses to the mail survey. The regression coefficients for socioeconomic variables included in the value function can be used to adjust sample values to represent the intended population.

Dillman (1978) recommends three mailings, including a third certified mailing, rather than the two recommended by the federal guidelines. He has obtained response rates of 70%–75% in statewide surveys by following the original mailing with a postcard reminder, a second letter and replacement questionnaire, and a final certified letter with replacement questionnaire. Many surveys omit the final certified mailing recommended by Dillman because of time and budget constraints. Moreover, a certified mailing may irritate persons who prefer not to participate and consider repeated requests an intrusion on their privacy.

The authors have found that including a $1 bill attached to the cover letter of the first mailing increases the response rate by 10%–15%. Using the $1 bill and two survey mailings resulted in response rates between 50% and 65% in several CVM surveys.

Dillman (1978) recommends that mail questionnaires be designed and pretested for clarity and ease of answering. They should be printed on good quality paper, photo-reproduced, visually uncluttered, and bound in booklet form. Letters should be typed individually and addressed to the individual by name. They should be individually signed by the project leader. In addition, the cover letter should be designed to motivate respondents by explaining the usefulness of the research and the importance of participation in the study. Interest may be stimulated by newspaper articles about the nature of the study. The reader is referred to the guidebook by Dillman for other helpful suggestions in designing mail surveys.

Telephone interviewing procedures also are described in the guidebook by Dillman (1978). With improved telephone and computer equipment, the method is becoming more widely used for contingent valuation studies. Computer-aided telephone interviewing (CATI) allows for random digit dialing of respondents insuring a more representative sample frame as well as allowing for complex questionship patterns and branching. Several studies have successfully combined a mail booklet with telephone interviews. A description of the legitimate scientific purpose of the study and the questions and visual aids are mailed to a random sample. Respondents are asked to read and think about the material in the booklet and answer as many questions as possible. They are then called at an agreed upon time and the interview is conducted over the phone. The advantage of combining the two methods is that maps and other information can be supplied by mail. Then, any problems can be clarified by telephone interviews. Answers can be typed directly into a computer during the telephone interview. Also, the urgency of a phone call encourages more people to participate in the survey. However, the increased use of phones for telemarketing has reduced phone survey response rates. In addition the increased reliance on answering machines to screen phone calls requires that the first few seconds of the call clearly identify the legitimate nature of the interview.

Both Mitchell and Carson's comprehensive book on CVM (1989) and the blue ribbon panel on CVM recommend personal interviews as the most accurate way to conduct a CVM survey. The presence of the interviewer provides motivation to the respondent to pay attention to details and more elaborate visual aids can be used. Reliance on the reading comprehension of respondents is also reduced with an in-person interviewer. The drawback to the use of in-person interviews is largely the much higher cost, relative to telephone (about one-half to one-tenth the cost of in person) and mail (about one-tenth to one-twentieth the cost of in person). Another concern with in-person interviews is that the presence of the interviewer may elicit more socially desirable responses, rather than honest answers. Detailed discussion can be found in Mitchell and Carson (1989).

## Accuracy of CVM

Economists who are trained to rely on actual behavior to make inferences about values are often hesitant to accept what people say they would pay. The heart of this issue is the validity (sometimes mistakenly referred to as reliability) of CVM responses. The key issue is whether visitors would pay the amounts they state in answers to questionnaires. There are two aspects of this. First is whether people have a realistic sense of how much more they would actually pay if they were forced to. The second is whether they have the incentive to honestly report this amount. If individuals believe that their answers might affect provision of additional recreation facilities and that these facilities will be paid for from general taxes, they may respond in ways to maximize the likelihood of a preferred policy. Individuals may overstate true willingness to pay in order to gain a desired change or they may understate values in order to prevent a change they oppose. In addition, Samuelson (1954) has warned that ". . . it is in the selfish interest of each person to give false signals, to pretend to have less interest . . ." when he or she suspects that he or she may actually have to pay the amount revealed as his or her willingness to pay. However, respondents usually are asked to reveal their willingness to pay in what is clearly a hypothetical situation. While this hypothetical nature of the survey reduces incentives to purposefully misstate their WTP, it may increase the possibility that the individuals do not put sufficient thought into their answers so as to report their true WTP. That is, if I do not have to live with (via higher taxes or entrance fees) my response, I also may not be as careful in reporting my WTP as I would be if I had to pay it. Balancing these two opposing influences on respondents is a delicate art.

To reduce the tendency of people to "free ride" on the payment of others, willingness to pay questions can specify that all households using a resource will pay. While there has been much debate about strategic behavior, Schulze, d'Arge and Brookshire (1981) reviewed six contingent valuation studies and tentatively concluded that "strategic bias in revealing consumer preferences is not likely to be a major problem."

It is notable that objections to the contingent valuation approach have been primarily theoretical, as empirical evidence of systematic bias is at best inconclusive. There have been multiple testing strategies. One is to compare CVM-derived values to those based on actual behavior such as the travel cost method. A summary of all of the actual behavior-CVM comparisons across nearly 80 studies that provided over 500 comparisons, found that average CVM-WTP estimates were slightly *lower* than actual behavior estimates. Specifically, CVM estimates were about 90% that of actual behavior methods such as TCM. As further evidence of the convergent validity of CVM, the actual behavior and CVM values had a correlation of 0.40 which is significant at the 0.01 level (see Carson, Flores, Martin and Wright, 1996, for more details).

There also have been a series of laboratory and field experiments comparing actual cash payments and stated WTP in CVM surveys. Bohm (1972) conducted a controlled experiment comparing five alternative measures of willingness to pay for a closed circuit public TV program, including actual payment in cash of the stated willingness to pay. He found no significant difference in values reported by five of the six groups, each presented with an alternative willingness to pay question. Bohm concluded that the theoretical objections to the contingent valuation approach could be resolved by application of an interval method. Two questions would be asked with incentives to under- and overstate willingness to pay. The midpoint of the interval would represent the most acceptable value. More recent experiments have found that CVM may overstate WTP by a factor of at least two and as much as 5–10 times, depending on whether subjects in the experiments were students and the nature of the good (Loomis, Brown, Lucero and Peterson, 1996).

A very thorough field experiment with deer hunters was performed by Bishop, Heberlein and Welsh at the University of Wisconsin (reported in Mitchell and Carson, 1989, p. 201). They compared hypothetical and actual cash WTP using open-ended, iterative bidding and the dichotomous choice question formats. The iterative bidding approach to valuation of a one-day deer permit produced a hypothetical WTP of $43, while the cash value was about $22. The dichotomous choice question format produced greater correspondence, with the cash value equal to $31, while hypothetical WTP was $25. The open-ended WTP question produced a cash WTP of $24 while the open-ended hypothetical WTP was $32. Given this limited information, dichotomous choice CVM appears to have greater criterion validity than open-ended and iterative bidding question formats. More recent experiments however, have shown similar correspondence of dichotomous choice and open-ended response formats in comparing hypothetical and actual WTP. Many more replications are necessary before this can be taken as a firm conclusion.

Given the difficulty in conducting actual cash experiments, several researchers have evaluated the test-retest reliability of CVM answers. Retesting the same subjects two weeks to eight months later has uniformly shown that CVM responses are reliable indicators of WTP (Reiling, Boyle, Phillips and Anderson, 1990; Loomis, 1989, 1990).

While it is easy to create CVM surveys that yield bizarre results (and many critics of CVM have done just that), carefully designed and pretested CVM surveys appear capable of providing a reasonably accurate measure of the economic value of recreation and protecting natural environments. While the estimates from CVM may not be perfect, neither are estimates from any other economic or physical science models. Recreation management and resource policy decisions are often made with less than perfect data about many factors and economic values is no exception. Nonetheless, CVM has been upheld by the U.S. District Court of Appeals and endorsed by the blue ribbon panel on CVM that was co-chaired by two Nobel laureates in economics (Arrow et al., 1993). As the panel concluded, CVM provides value estimates that are comparable to what courts rely upon as starting points in judicial and administrative determinations. At present, CVM provides one of the best methods to value natural resource quality before degradation occurs. To wait until after unique environmental resources are destroyed to measure the actual change in recreation behavior of users would be an unnecessarily costly form of social experimentation and often useless for making policy decisions.

Next we compare the relative merits of TCM and CVM to the unit day value and benefit-transfer approaches introduced in the next chapter.

*Chapter 11*

# Other Valuation Methods

This chapter presents alternative approaches to valuing outdoor recreation that rely upon existing studies or published values. These shortcut methods may be useful to provide rough estimates of recreation values when there is insufficient time or budget to perform an original travel cost method or contingent valuation method study.

There are several shortcut valuation methods used by federal agencies. They rely on expert judgment to develop an approximation of the average net willingness to pay (WTP) for recreation activities. These methods do not require site-specific data collection and statistical analysis, other than knowing visitor use levels. The unit day value (UDV) approach involves selecting an estimate from a table or range of values approved by the federal agencies. More recently, the practice of transferring benefit estimates from existing sites to other sites without values has become a subfield called **benefit transfer.** Benefit transfer can incorporate UDV approaches as well as transfer the entire demand function from a travel cost method (TCM) study or a willingness to pay function from a contingent valuation method (CVM) study. We will describe all of these approaches in this chapter. Also, we will discuss the new hybrid approach of combining actual visitation data with intended visitation data to better estimate the value of outdoor recreation.

## U.S. Water Resources Council Unit Day Values

The U.S. Water Resources Council's UDVs are probably the most well-known. Initially based on a survey of entrance fees at private recreation areas in 1962, the UDVs recommended by the guidelines have been adjusted for changes in the consumer price index since then. Subsequently, the Council revised the UDVs in 1973 and again in 1979. The bipartisan political support for the guidelines in the past indicates their broad acceptability within and outside of government.

The UDV approach may be used if application of the travel cost or contingent valuation methods would exceed study budget constraints and if the recreation site studied is relatively small, with fewer than 750,000 recreation days per year. The method relies on expert judgment to develop an approximation of the average net willingness to pay for recreation use. The values selected are considered to be equivalent to consumer surplus (i.e., net of travel cost or price).

The U.S. Water Resources Council (1983) guidelines classify recreation into two categories: general and specialized. **General recreation** includes the majority of activities requiring the development and maintenance of convenient access and developed facilities. Included are most picnicking, tent and trailer camping, flat-water boating, warm-water fishing, swimming, and small-game hunting. **Specialized recreation** opportunities are more limited; intensity of use is low; and more skill, knowledge, and appreciation are required. Recreation use of Wilderness Areas is considered specialized, as are trout fishing, big-game hunting, upland bird and waterfowl hunting, pack trips, whitewater boating, canoeing, and specialized nature photography.

The guidelines recommended a range in value of $9 to $27 per day of specialized recreation, including wilderness use, in fiscal year 1997. General recreation values are much lower, $2 to $7 per day. Unit day values have been adjusted for changes in the consumer price index to the present. For example, the recommended range of specialized recreation values was $2 to $6 in 1962, $3 to $9 in 1973, $6 to $18 in 1982, and increased to $9 to $27 in 1996. You can update these values to the present by adjusting for changes in the consumer price index.

Unit day values are adjusted to reflect quality considerations that prevail in various regions based on a point score. For example, a reservoir that carries a heavy load of suspended silt or is used beyond capacity would be less desirable, and therefore, of lower point score and hence would be at the lower end of the range of generalized recreation values than one with clear water and fewer users. The availability of substitute opportunities is also considered in assigning values. Higher values are assigned if the population served does not have similar recreation opportunities. On the other hand, if similar recreation opportunities are relatively abundant, lower unit values are assigned, even if a large number of people are expected to use a proposed site.

However, there are problems with these guidelines for rating the quality of the recreation experience. The scale for availability of substitutes assumes that alternative sites cannot be complements, however, they actually often are complements, particularly in resort areas such as in Florida, Colorado and Hawaii. The biggest problem is the subjectivity in rating the site. First, a recreation planner rather than the visitor typically does the rating. Depending on how well the preferences or knowledge of the recreation planner matches that of the majority of the visitors, there can be some differences as to the quality rating. Second, the repeatability or reliability of the rating is a problem across sites if different people are performing the rating. Also, it may be quite easy to manipulate the rating to value the recreation activity promoted by the agency higher than other types of recreation. In essence the rating is like the recreation planner trying to guess at the coefficients on quality in a regression equation.

The guidelines recommend five criteria to rate at particular sites:

1. quality of the recreation experience, as affected by congestion;
2. availability of substitute areas (in hours of travel);
3. carrying capacity, as determined by level of facility development;
4. accessibility, as affected by road and parking conditions; and
5. environmental quality, including forests, air, water, pests, climate, adjacent areas, and aesthetics of the scenery.

Individual sites are rated on a 100-point scale, in which recreation experience is assigned a weight of 30 points, availability of substitutes 18, carrying capacity 14, accessibility 18, and environmental quality 20 points. Table 11-1 (page 180) provides the rating scale and Table 11-2 (page 181) provides the federal guidelines for converting the scaled values into unit day dollars representing estimated consumer surplus. For example, a specialized recreation activity such as rafting, with a quality rating of 80 points out of a possible 100 would be assigned a value of $21 per user day, and one with a quality rating of 90 would have a value of $24 per user day.

The $24 per day value can be thought of as an approximation of the average consumer surplus per day. It is assumed to be the total area under the second stage TCM demand curve divided by total days. Alternatively, the UDV is equivalent to the net WTP per day calculated from CVM. To arrive at the total benefit estimate for a recreation site, we simply multiply the selected UDV by the total number of recreation days per year at the study site. Thus, UDVs work well when we know the total visitation at the site but not the value per day. UDV is of little use when we do not know total visitation. For if an estimate of total visitation must be developed, it is likely that the survey could provide data sufficient to conduct a TCM analysis of use and benefits with little added cost or effort.

The U.S. Water Resources Council UDVs are still used by field offices of the Corps of Engineers, Bureau of Reclamation and Natural Resources Conservation Service for small projects. However, as the expertise of economists in these agencies improves, they rely less and less on this approach.

## USDA Forest Service RPA Values

The USDA Forest Service developed its own unit day values for recreation as part of its implementation of the Resources Planning Act of 1974 (RPA).

**Table 11-1. Guidelines for Rating Quality of the Recreation Experience on a 100-Point Scale**

| Criteria | Quality of the Experience, 100-Point Scale | | | | |
|---|---|---|---|---|---|
| Recreation Experience | Heavy use or frequent crowding or other interference with use | Moderate use; other users evident and likely to interfere with use | Moderate use; some evidence of other users and occasional interference | Usually little evidence of other users; rarely, if ever crowded | Very low evidence of other users; never crowded |
| Total Points: 30 | | | | | |
| Point Value: | 0–4 | 5–10 | 11–16 | 17–23 | 24–30 |
| Availability of Substitutes | Several within 1 hour of travel time; a few within 30 minutes of travel time | Several within 1 hour of travel time; none within 30 minutes of travel time | One or two within 1 hour of travel time; none within 45 minutes of travel time | None within 1 hour of travel time | None within 2 hours of travel time |
| Total Points: 18 | | | | | |
| Point Value: | 0–3 | 4–6 | 7–10 | 11–14 | 15–18 |
| Carrying Capacity | Minimum facility development for public health and safety | Basic facilities to conduct activity(ies) | Adequate facilities to conduct activities without deterioration of the resource or activity | Optimum facilities to conduct activity at site | Ultimate facilities to achieve intent of selected alternative activity |
| Total Points: 14 | | | | | |
| Point Value: | 0–2 | 3–5 | 6–8 | 9–11 | 12–14 |
| Accessibility | Limited access by any means to site or within site | Fair access, poor quality roads to site; limited access within site | Fair access, fair road to site; fair access, good roads within site | Good access, good roads to site; fair access, good roads within site | Good access, high standard road to site; good access within site |
| Total Points: 18 | | | | | |
| Point Value: | 0–3 | 4–6 | 7–10 | 11–14 | 15–18 |
| Environmental | Low aesthetic factors[a] exist that significantly lower quality[b] | Average aesthetic quality; factors exist that lower quality to minor degree | Above average aesthetic quality; any limiting factors can be reasonably rectified | High aesthetic quality; no factors exist that lower quality | Outstanding aesthetic quality; no factors exist that lower quality |
| Total Points: 20 | | | | | |
| Point Value: | 0–2 | 3–6 | 7–10 | 11–15 | 16–20 |

[a]Major aesthetic qualities to be considered include geology and topography, water, and vegetation.
[b]Factors to be considered in lowering quality include air and water pollution, pests, poor climate, and unsightly adjacent areas.

Source: U.S. Water Resources Council, 1983.

**Table 11-2. Relation Between Quality of the Experience and Unit Day Values**

| | Quality of the Experience, 100-Point Scale | | | | | | | | | | |
|---|---|---|---|---|---|---|---|---|---|---|---|
| Recreation Activity | 0 | 10 | 20 | 30 | 40 | 50 | 60 | 70 | 80 | 90 | 100 |
| General Recreation | $2 | $3 | $3 | $4 | $4 | $5 | $5 | $6 | $6 | $7 | $7 |
| General Fishing and Hunting | $3 | $4 | $4 | $4 | $5 | $5 | $6 | $6 | $7 | $7 | $7 |
| Specialized Recreation | $9 | $10 | $11 | $11 | $12 | $14 | $15 | $18 | $21 | $24 | $27 |
| Specialized Fishing and Hunting | $16 | $16 | $17 | $17 | $18 | $19 | $21 | $22 | $24 | $26 | $27 |

Source: U.S. Water Resources Council (1983) adjusted to 1996 by consumer price index.

The values are updated every five years. The first systematic effort was in 1980 when values for forest-based recreation and fish and wildlife were established based on existing literature. This was followed by the 1985 values that were based on a comprehensive survey of the existing TCM and CVM values in the literature (Sorg and Loomis, 1984). The 1990 RPA values were further refined by including the values from numerous TCM and CVM studies conducted between 1985 and 1990. Walsh, Johnson and McKean's (1992) effort in this area established a solid empirical foundation for the 1990 RPA values. With minor refinements, the 1990 values were used by the U.S. Forest Service for the 1995 RPA Program Environmental Impact Statement. Consult the U.S. Forest Service's latest RPA Program Environmental Impact Statement for updates to these values every five years.

Table 11-3 (page 182) presents a simple national average of the RPA values for recreation in the eight regions of the U.S. Forest Service. Note these numbers represent what the U.S. Forest Service calls market clearing price plus consumer surplus (MCP+CS). However, the terminology is confusing since there is no market clearing price for recreation in the estimates for two reasons. First, there really is no such thing as a market clearing price for recreation at most Forest Service sites since the agency has not historically charged anything for entry to the National Forest to hike, backpack, picnic or fish. Second, no single market clearing price exists, since each visitor pays a different price depending on how far he or she travels. Finally, the values in the MCP+CS were derived by Walsh, Johnson and McKean (1992) from estimates of consumer surplus from

**Table 11-3. Net Willingness to Pay for Forest-Based Recreation, 1990 U.S. Forest Service Resource Planning Act Values**

| Activity | Activity Day | 12-Hour RVD |
|---|---|---|
| Camping | $13.33 | $14.56 |
| Picnicking | $2.89 | $12.78 |
| Swimming | $3.33 | $16.00 |
| Hiking/Horseback Riding | $6.56 | $21.67 |
| Nonmotorized Boating | $5.56 | $20.11 |
| Mechanized Land Travel | $3.11 | $14.89 |
| Motorized Boating | $4.11 | $14.78 |
| Big-Game Hunting | $44.33 | $77.00 |
| Small-Game Hunting | $19.44 | $57.33 |
| Upland-Game Hunting | $27.67 | $78.56 |
| Waterfowl Hunting | $33.22 | $98.89 |
| Cold-Water Fishing | $39.78 | $110.78 |
| Warm-Water Fishing | $33.44 | $92.78 |
| Winter Sports | $33.69 | $77.50 |
| Resorts | $21.25 | $23.38 |
| Wilderness | $28.99 | $32.75 |

Source: Averages calculated from U.S. Forest Service, 1990.

120 updated TCM and CVM studies. Thus, for economic valuation purposes, MCP+CS really represents just the conceptually correct benefits—consumer surplus. Also note that activity day values are equivalent to visitor days in UDVs, while recreation visitor days (RVDs) represent 12-hour visitor days which usually reflects two to four activity days depending on the length of a typical visit for each activity (see Chapter 3 for more details on converting from visitor days to recreation visitor days).

Reliance on unit day values can be expected to decrease as federal agencies gradually adopt such alternative methods as the travel cost and contingent valuation approaches. Both the U.S. Forest Service and Environmental Protection Agency have built databases of existing studies that allow for formal benefit-transfer procedures. In recent years, greater reliance on travel cost and contingent valuation methods has been encouraged through agency review procedures, demonstration projects, and educational workshops.

## Benefit Transfer

For a number of years, economists performing small scale benefit-cost analyses often were forced by time and budget limitations to adopt values already reported in the existing literature rather than perform their own studies. They used simple adjustments to the values in the literature to account for differences in location and recreation quality levels. Two significant advances have markedly improved the practice of transferring values from the existing literature to sites where management or policy decisions must be made, but for which no values, nor time to perform a study is available. The first advancement was the application of meta-analysis to estimate a regression equation, relating average consumer surplus per day from past studies to a host of explanatory variables. These include (a) the type of recreation activity, (b) location of the recreation area, and (c) details of the valuation method employed (e.g., TCM, CVM). Pioneered by Walsh, Johnson and McKean (1992) and Smith and Karou (1990), these regression equations make possible a more systematic approach to estimating the value per day of a given outdoor recreation activity without performing a site-specific study. The analyst simply needs to insert the values of the explanatory variables for the site of interest into the meta-analysis regression and perform the multiplications to arrive at an estimate of the value per day. To date, there has been little published use of this new approach, nor has there been any formal evaluation of its accuracy relative to site-specific studies. Our opinion (reinforced by the following two studies) is that while it is more accurate than just picking values from the literature, it is likely to provide only a rough approximation of the value per day than a site-specific study would. However, for some management decisions or policy issues, the approximate nature of the value estimated from a meta-analysis may be sufficient.

The second major advance in the area of benefit transfer has been the application of benefit-function transfer. Using this technique, the demand function from an existing TCM study or a WTP function from an existing CVM study, performed for a similar activity but in a different location, is applied to the recreation area under study. Like meta-analysis, this approach requires that estimates of the independent variables are obtain from sources such as the U.S. census and distance is calculated from maps. These are inserted into the demand or WTP function to estimate value per day. Since the demand or WTP functions are specific to a particular activity or type of recreation resource (e.g., a Wilderness Area or a reservoir), the approach is likely to be more accurate than meta-analysis. However, formal comparison of the benefit-function transfer to an original, site-specific study illustrates some degree of error for this improved approach. For transferring TCM demand functions that include site characteristics for a general recreation resource, like reservoir recreation (e.g., boating, fishing, swimming) between two similar geographic regions (e.g., within the Midwest), the errors in the consumer surplus per trip average 5%–10% which is an acceptable range. However, transferring TCM demand functions across the country (e.g., from the Midwest to the West coast) the errors were an unacceptable 250% (see Loomis, Roach, Ward and Ready, 1995, for more details). Statistically significant different estimates of WTP between the original site and the transfer site were shown for a dichotomous choice CVM-WTP function from a logit model of saltwater fishing without site characteristics among different bays in Texas (Downing and Ozuna, 1996).

At present, benefit transfer is an active area of research. This should be accelerated by the recent assembly of large databases of existing studies. Both Environment Canada (the Canadian equivalent of the U.S. Environmental Protection Agency) and several U.S. federal agencies as well as consulting firms have assembled estimates of the value of recreation and the associated demand and WTP functions from hundreds of studies. Combining the growth in number of original studies with the database and benefit-transfer protocols may make it easier to estimate recreation benefits when time and budgets do not permit a site-specific study and accuracy is not critical.

## New Techniques to Combine TCM and CVM Data

The view of the first thirty years of recreation economics was that TCM and CVM were two alternative approaches to estimating the value of outdoor recreation. However, recently several economists have developed hybrid models that combine TCM and CVM data together. There are basically two approaches. The first is sometimes called the trip response model, since it supplements the observed number of trips associated with current quality and price with survey responses regarding "intended" number of trips if quality or price (e.g., travel costs) were changed. These models combine the strengths of both the TCM and CVM. For example, the trip response model is well-suited to analyzing the demand for and benefits of management changes that have not occurred at a site. TCM would not work, since the management action has not taken place, so there is no way to observe the change in actual trips with the management action. While CVM-WTP could be estimated, some economists believe visitors have an easier time stating how they will change their trip-making behavior, rather than their value per trip. Studies have shown that responses to intended behavior questions are both reliable and valid (Loomis, 1993).

The second hybrid approach is to combine responses to CVM-WTP questions with both actual trip behavior and intended trip behavior. In essence the individual is asked a minimum of three questions:

a. Do you currently visit the site? (those currently visiting the site are then asked),
b. If the cost of visiting the site were $\$y$ higher, would you still visit? (and finally),
c. Would you visit the site if quality were improved by $x$? (costs can be left at the current level or raised).

Answers to this series of questions can be analyzed using a variety of panel data estimators available in advanced statistics packages.

By pooling actual and intended behavior, the economist now has the ability to more fully trace out how the demand curve shifts with alternative quality changes (e.g., intended visitation), as well as how the vertical intercept of the demand curve changes (e.g., WTP) with the same improvements in quality.

# Comparing the Results From the Different Methods

## *Travel Cost Method*

The objective of each of the four approaches is to estimate net willingness to pay for recreation activities at a specific site. We have defined net WTP or consumer surplus as the area below a demand curve above price, or the willingness to pay above actual payment. Thus, it is useful to estimate empirical demand curves for recreation sites. Statistical demand curves can be estimated using both the travel cost and the contingent valuation methods. Application of either method can yield an identical demand curve. However, it is important to remember that the dependent variables, and therefore the intercepts, are reversed for the two approaches.

The individual travel cost method results in an ordinary demand curve in which the number of trips demanded ($Q$) is dependent upon price ($P$). Assume the equation for an ordinary demand curve is:

$$Q = 7 - 0.1P \quad \text{(Equation 11-1)}$$

The equation indicates that if $P = \$60$, individuals are willing to pay this amount for a single trip per year. By inserting other values for P, we can trace out the demand curve. It shows that the average individual will take five trips per year at a price of $20 per trip. Total consumer surplus of each individual is the sum of consumer surplus for all trips per year that would be taken at a given price. This can also be found by integrating (calculating) the area of the right triangle under the demand curve and above the average direct cost or price.

## *Contingent Valuation Method*

The contingent valuation approach can provide an inverse demand curve, either directly or indirectly, depending on how the valuation questions are worded. The federal guidelines recommend that questions be worded to obtain the added WTP or marginal values per trip. Usually we ask individuals to report their added willingness to pay for the current trip or all trips to a specific recreation site that year. It is possible to ask a question sequence about WTP for each trip so as to provide a direct estimate of an inverse demand curve in which change in WTP is dependent on the change in number of trips ($Q$). The inverse demand equation for our representative individual's trips is:

$$\text{WTP} = 70 - 10Q \qquad \text{(Equation 11-2)}$$

The equation indicates that if $Q = 1$, individuals are willing to pay $60 for a single trip per year, just as with TCM. By inserting other values for $Q$, we can trace out the demand curve. Such a demand curve would show that the average individual is willing to pay $20 for the fifth trip per year. Just as with TCM, total consumer surplus of each individual is the sum of consumer surplus for all trips per year.

The contingent valuation approach also can provide a direct measure of total consumer surplus—one that can be calculate by hand. Suppose the question asked is, "What is the largest sum of money you would be willing to pay each year, rather than give up visiting this site?" You can sum the answers to this question from a random sample of recreation users at a site. You find the average individual is willing to pay a maximum of $200 for five trips per year, and that at this level of use, total direct costs are $50 annually. The consumer surplus of the average individual user of the site is simply the difference between total willingness to pay and total direct cost. Consumer surplus, as you can see, is $200 willingness to pay minus $50 direct cost which equals $150. Total consumer surplus from recreation use of the site is obtained by multiplying total consumer surplus of the average individual in your sample by the total number of users of the site.

## Empirical Estimates of Benefits

The purpose of this section is to present the results of recent benefit studies and their implications for recreation economic decisions. Case studies of the net WTP of recreation activities at particular recreation sites are too numerous to review here. In the interest of brevity, Table 11-4 summarizes the results of 120 studies with 287 studies for various recreation activities.

Across the 287 estimates there is a wide range of values, largely explained by type of recreation activity. Saltwater fishing, anadromous fishing (e.g., salmon), and rafting major rivers have the highest values. These are followed by big-game hunting and waterfowl hunting. At the low end is picnicking, sightseeing, driving off-road vehicles and warm-water fishing (which is typically done at reservoirs). This table is useful for two major types of recreation economic decisions. First, if conflicts among recreation activities take place, this table may give some indication of the relative values of one activity versus the other. Multiplying use levels by their respective economic values per day would give an indication, from the economic efficiency view, as to which activity should be restricted. Second, the values give an indication of the relative values for estimating recreation benefits versus incompatible development such as mining.

In addition to the benefits of actual recreation use reported here, the general public may be willing to pay for the preservation of recreation

**Table 11-4. Net Economic Values per Recreation Day Reported by TCM and CVM Demand Studies From 1968 to 1988, United States (1987 Dollars)**

| Activity | Number of Estimates | Mean | Median | Standard Error of the Mean | 95% Confidence Interval |
|---|---|---|---|---|---|
| Total | 287 | $33.95 | $27.02 | 1.67 | 30.68 – 37.22 |
| Camping | 18 | 19.50 | 18.92 | 2.03 | 15.52 – 23.48 |
| Picnicking | 7 | 17.33 | 12.82 | 5.08 | 7.37 – 27.29 |
| Swimming | 11 | 22.97 | 18.60 | 3.79 | 15.54 – 30.40 |
| Sightseeing and Off-Road Driving | 6 | 20.29 | 19.72 | 3.73 | 12.98 – 27.60 |
| Boating, | | | | | |
| Motorized | 5 | 31.56 | 25.67 | 10.36 | 11.25 – 51.87 |
| Nonmotorized | 11 | 48.68 | 25.36 | 15.85 | 17.61 – 79.75 |
| Hiking | 6 | 29.08 | 23.62 | 5.82 | 17.67 – 40.49 |
| Winter Sports | 12 | 28.50 | 24.39 | 4.48 | 19.72 – 37.28 |
| Hunting, | | | | | |
| Big-Game | 56 | 45.47 | 37.87 | 3.47 | 38.67 – 52.27 |
| Small-Game | 10 | 30.82 | 27.48 | 3.51 | 23.94 – 37.70 |
| Migratory Waterfowl | 17 | 35.64 | 25.27 | 5.87 | 24.13 – 47.15 |
| Fishing, | | | | | |
| Cold-Water | 39 | 30.62 | 28.49 | 3.24 | 24.27 – 36.97 |
| Anadromous[a] | 9 | 54.01 | 46.24 | 11.01 | 32.43 – 75.59 |
| Warm-Water | 23 | 23.55 | 22.50 | 2.46 | 18.73 – 23.87 |
| Saltwater | 17 | 72.49 | 53.35 | 14.05 | 44.95 –100.03 |
| Nonconsumptive Fish and Wildlife | 14 | 22.20 | 20.49 | 2.30 | 17.69 – 26.71 |
| Wilderness | 15 | 24.58 | 19.26 | 6.10 | 12.62 – 36.54 |
| Other Recreation Activities | 9 | 18.82 | 16.06 | 3.65 | 11.67 – 25.97 |

[a]Anadromous fishing estimates included in cold-water fishing; estimated as roughly 5%.

Source: Adapted from Walsh, Johnson and McKean, 1992.

resources. The environmental economics literature identifies several possibilities of willingness to pay for the preservation of natural resources, in addition to consumer surplus from recreation use. Preservation values include option, existence, and bequest demands of the general public. Option value is defined as the willingness to pay to guarantee the opportunity for future access to resources of a given quality for recreation use. Existence value is the willingness to pay for the knowledge that a natural environment is protected for itself even though no recreation use is contemplated. Bequest value is defined as the satisfaction derived from endowing future generations with a natural environment. These preservation values are nonmarket and public goods, which means their consumption is both nonrival and nonexcludable. Additional beneficiaries can be added without diminishing the benefits of recreation users.

Table 11-5 summarizes estimates of the preservation or passive use values and recreation use values for several recreational resources. Note that while the annual recreation value per visiting household is often larger than the preservation value of a nonvisiting household, in the aggregate for the nation as a whole, total preservation values often are at least as large and often two to 10 times larger than recreation use values. This may not be surprising since all members of the general public, whether they visit the site or not, may receive existence and bequest values. Since there are often a thousand times more nonvisiting households that care about the continued protection of the natural environment than there are visitors to the site, even small preservation values per household add up to large aggregate values.

During the 1970s the benefit estimating procedures of the U.S. Water Resources Council and U.S. Forest Service did not include preservation values. The agency guidelines should be enlarged to include them since both the U.S. Department of the Interior (1994) and U.S. National Oceanic and Atmospheric Administration (1996) have included such values in their assessment of natural resource damages. In the absence of information on preservation values to all of the people, insufficient public land will be protected in a pristine state. The problem is especially acute in states where future development of subdivisions, roads, timber, minerals, energy, and water may irreversibly degrade environmental quality. Governments throughout the world face a similar problem of how much natural environment they can afford to protect as wildlife sanctuaries, National Parks, and Wilderness Areas. Recently, more federal agencies are including empirical estimates from their own original studies. One recent example includes the U.S. Fish and Wildlife Service (1994)

**Table 11-5. Annual per Household Preservation and Use Values for Recreational Resources**

| Resource | Preservation Value | Use Value |
|---|---|---|
| Bald Eagles | $28 | $47 |
| Forest Protection | 51 | 8 |
| Salmon/Steelhead | 26 | 48 |
| Water Quality | | |
| (Colorado) | 67 | 79 |
| (Entire U.S.) | 111 | 126 |
| Wilderness | | |
| (Colorado) | 22 | 23 |
| (Eastern United States) | 6 | 8 |
| Whooping Cranes | 1 | 10 |

Source: Adapted from Brown, 1993.

inclusion of existence values to United States households for reintroducing wolves into Yellowstone National Park. Another recent study performed for the U.S. Bureau of Reclamation estimated the value that U.S. nonvisiting households place on maintaining more natural river flow patterns in the Colorado River through Grand Canyon National Park to improve the quality of rafting experienced by others, as well as habitat for endangered (and nongame) fish (Welsh, Bishop, Phillips and Baumgartner, 1995). We hope this is a trend that continues.

There are two additional points that should be made about the limitations of the economic measures of the benefits of recreation activities and resources presented in this chapter. First, there may be psychological values associated with the preservation of recreation resources that exceed the economic measure of values reported here. The demand for recreation use of resources, and therefore our benefit estimates, is constrained by limited consumer income, availability of leisure time, and other variables. However, psychological values may not be constrained (i.e., demands for recreation use and preservation may be worth more than people are able to pay). This suggests that alternative measures, such as willingness to accept, may be more appropriate when managers are evaluating reductions in recreation programs, facilities or areas currently accessible to the public.

Second, there may be long-run ecological values of preserving natural resources that are not included here. It is difficult for biologists to predict what these might be, let alone for economists to translate them into an economic value. For this reason, it seems that the benefits of recreation opportunities represent a conservative estimate of the total benefits to society from protecting recreation resources. The inability of economics to estimate a dollar value for many ecological values should be recognized in making decisions about recreation resource programs.

## Suggestions for Determining Which Valuation Technique to Apply

The first step in deciding which techniques are appropriate to any given study is to determine the management or policy question to be answered by the study. There are three basic evaluation problems in recreation to estimate: (1) the benefits of recreation activities at existing sites of given quality; (2) the benefits of recreation activities with changes in the quantity and quality of the resource; and (3) the public benefits from preservation of resource quality.

The travel cost method is the preferred approach for estimating the benefits from recreation activities at existing sites. Also, it is often an acceptable approach for estimating the recreation benefits from changes in the quality of resources at recreation sites as long as the change in quality is within the range observed in the data. If changes in quality are so large as to be well outside the range of the existing quality, then either the trip response approach or CVM would likely be more appropriate. CVM is also more useful for estimating the value of reducing congestion. TCM has difficulty in empirically measuring the benefits of reduced congestion, since the number of trips taken is at once the dependent variable in TCM and an indicator of congestion.

In addition, TCM is not capable of estimating the benefits to nonusers, from the preservation of the quality of the resource. At present, only the CVM is capable of measuring the existence and bequest values to the general population.

The travel cost method has been successfully applied to intermediate recreation areas located within 150 miles from the homes of most users (e.g., state parks and reservoirs). TCM is unlikely to be useful for estimating the value of urban recreation sites, since travel cost is often unimportant and there is little or no variation in travel costs across most visitors. Thus, there usually is insufficient variation in travel distances to urban sites to allow statistical estimation of the relationship between distance (or price) and number of trips. Therefore, CVM may be most appropriate in this situation.

For sites such as National Parks where several parks are usually visited on a single vacation trip, the distance-traveled proxy for price cannot be assigned to a single destination. Thus, for such areas as remote National Parks, TCM may not be appropriate and CVM may be more useful for valuing recreation there.

As can be seen the limited applicability of the travel cost approach is a continuing problem in recreation economics. However, when there are existing visitor permit data or data indicating visitor residence locations (e.g., zip code or county), a simple zonal TCM can be applied without having to perform a time-consuming and costly CVM survey. In addition, the strength of TCM is its reliance on actual behavior for estimating visitor use levels with changes in recreation site characteristics as well as recreation benefits. The actual behavior base gives TCM wide acceptability among managers and many economists.

While CVM is able to value a much wider range of recreation experiences (e.g., multidestination, urban, reduced congestion), the method requires development and implementation of a survey instrument. It is generally recognized that the method requires careful wording of questions and well-defined hypothetical market situations with which respondents are familiar. It often takes several months to develop, pretest and administer a CVM survey. As noted in the previous chapter, while CVM responses may be hypothetical, there is strong evidence that the estimated recreation values are valid and reliable. Carson, Flores, Martin and Wright (1996) found that, if anything, TCM tends to give slightly *higher* values than CVM. In general, values from the behavior-based TCM tend to be quite similar to CVM. Nonetheless, many managers and economists unfamiliar with CVM sometimes discount the value estimates because of the hypothetical nature of the answers.

The UDV method is considered an acceptable approach for estimating the benefits from recreation activities at small sites. The guidelines recommend that its use be limited to general recreation activities at sites with fewer than 750,000 annual visits, where recreation specific costs do not exceed 25% of the expected total costs of multiple-purpose projects, and where annual costs to the agency for recreation management are less than $1 million. The U.S. Forest Service (1990) has prepared unit day values for regions of the United States and does not restrict their use to small projects. One limitation is that expert evaluations of changes in resource quality are not testable by accepted statistical methods, as are quality effects developed by the TCM and CVM. Also, UDVs do not presently exist for estimating the public benefits from preservation of resource quality. However, as a number of contingent valuation studies are completed on the public benefits of various types of resource quality, benefit-transfer methods may soon be developed to measure existence value to the general population, including users and nonusers, for protecting natural environments used in recreation. Similar meta-analysis has been successful in valuing endangered species and ground water.

At present, available meta-analyses for recreation are available in publications of Walsh, Johnson and McKean (1992) and Smith and Karou (1990). These may provide rough estimates of value when neither UDVs or RPA values seem appropriate.

In the end, the choice of technique to value recreation involves balancing of practical issues regarding available budget and time to perform the study with the desire to be as accurate as possible. Most recreation economists (including both authors) have used all of the techniques for one type of study or another. Each technique is a potential tool. The hallmark of a skilled professional is knowing when to use the right tool.

*Chapter 12*

# Risk, Uncertainty and Information

This chapter reviews existing knowledge about the extent of risk and uncertainty in recreation and shows how to apply it to decision making by consumers and managers.

In previous chapters it was implicitly assumed that individuals make recreation economic decisions in an environment characterized as risk free. That is, when individuals decide to take a recreation trip they know what they are getting, what it will cost, and how much benefit it will yield. Substantial insight into decision making was gained by treating the problem as though individuals and managers had reasonably complete information concerning the outcomes of possible alternative decisions. Recreation economic decisions are somewhat more complex under conditions of risk and uncertainty.

In this chapter we will see how recreation economic decisions are based on the "expected value" of alternatives. Expected value depends on the uncertainty of trip conditions and is adjusted for the decision maker's attitude toward risk. The riskiness of a decision depends, in part, on the information available to the decision maker. We consider the manager's problem of how much information service to provide at a recreation site.

## Perceptions of Risk

Existing knowledge about the extent of risk and uncertainty in recreation suggests that it is pervasive. Vacation travel, for example, is riskier than the purchase of many other goods and services. It takes considerable discretionary dollars and time. The recreation experience cannot be examined before purchase as would be true for most other goods and services. Travelers tend to visit new destinations and try new things in the search for variety in recreation. This increases the uncertainty regarding the outcome and the risk of being disappointed. Yet, there is also the possibility that the new experience will exceed expectations. This illustrates two important features about risk. First, for some people this uncertainty is what they seek in traveling to new and exotic locations. These people are risk seeking or risk lovers, at least within reasonable bounds of risk. People who like rock climbing are another example of risk seekers. Second, the same objective measure of risk will be perceived differently by some people as compared to others. Some people are natural worriers and pessimists who will perceive much larger risk from the same activity (e.g., travel on an airplane) than others. However, often it is the perceived risk that motivates visitors' behavior, not some actuarially correct objective measure of risk.

Making recreation economic decisions under conditions of risk and uncertainty is difficult. Uncertainty regarding the weather is a common example. If individuals do not know if it will snow or not, they are likely to make a bad decision and this often results in reduced benefits. For example, they may decide to go skiing and it snows. In which case, they are stuck in traffic and they cannot see well when skiing, resulting in negative net benefits being realized (total cost exceeds the benefits). Alternatively, they may decide not to go and the weather could turn out just fine. In this case, they have foregone the positive net benefits they would have realized had they known the weather was going to be nice.

Another common risk in recreation is physical. We know more about the physical risks of recreation than other types. A national survey of 750 participants in selected recreation activities found that 80% suffered frequent physical accidents and illnesses during recreation trips. The sample was limited to individuals who participated in at least two of the following recreation activities for three weeks or more per year: hunting, hiking, angling, backpacking, canoeing, mountain climbing, biking, and skiing.

However, economics is primarily concerned with the risk and uncertainty of future benefits and costs. We have seen that benefits represent the willingness to pay for the satisfaction of the recreation experience. The economic meaning of the term "satisfaction" includes all of the physical, psychological, social, leisure, and technological aspects of recreation. Consider a study that related individual perceptions of economic or financial risk to the other measures. Cheron and Ritchie (1982) studied seven types of risk perceived by participants in 20 recreation activities in Alberta, Canada. Because the authors interviewed a nonrandom sample of 68 college graduates, the findings of the study cannot be generalized to a broader population. Nonetheless, they are indicative of the types of perceived risks associated with different recreation activities. Individual risk was measured on a nine-point scale with one equaling the lowest and nine equaling the highest. The seven types of risk considered were:

1. **financial,** the possibility that the activity will not provide value for the money spent;
2. **time,** the possibility that the activity will take too much time or will waste time;
3. **satisfaction,** the possibility that the activity will not provide personal satisfaction or self-actualization;
4. **functional,** the possibility of problems with mechanical equipment or the organization while performing the activity;
5. **physical,** the possibility of physical danger or injury (i.e., detrimental to health);
6. **psychological,** the possibility that the activity will not be consistent with the individual's self-image, lifestyle, or personality; and
7. **social,** the possibility that participation will adversely affect others' opinions of the individual.

An overall risk, the possibility that when all types of risk are considered, participation will result in disappointment, was also considered.

Snowmobiling was viewed as the recreation activity having the highest overall risk (6.1) and cross-country skiing was viewed as the lowest (2.4). There were a number of variations for specific activities. For example, downhill or alpine skiing was considered the second most risky activity with respect to the possibility of physical injury, yet it was rated medium to low for other types of risk.

Results of this study suggest that an economic measure of risk can provide an effective proxy for the psychological and social perceptions of risk by individuals participating in recreation activities. Cheron and Ritchie (1982) tested the correlation between overall risk and each of the seven types perceived by participants in the 20 recreation activities. They found that financial risk—the possibility that the activity would not provide value for the money spent—was highly correlated (0.94) with overall risk, as were personal satisfaction (0.94), psychological self-image (0.96), social opinion (0.95), and use of time (0.85). Such high correlation between two or more variables suggests that they are measuring the same thing, and it is acceptable practice to adopt a single proxy, such as the expected economic value measure introduced in this chapter.

## Understanding Risk in Decisions

All recreation economic decisions are made in the present based on expectations about the future. The actual experience will seldom turn out exactly as expected when a decision is made. Since no one knows for certain what the future holds, we are all forced to guess what the most likely outcome of any of our decisions will be. Though we may not explicitly think of a decision in these terms, what we often do when we guess is to assign a statistical probability to the likelihood that future events will occur, based on our knowledge and experience of the situation. You may prefer to talk about "the odds" or "chances" or "degrees of belief" instead of probabilities. For this chapter we will use these terms as working synonyms. To say that you believe an event has a high or low probability is simply to make a statement that forecasts the future. Probability may range between zero and one. Zero means you estimate that there is no chance of the event happening, and one means you are sure it will happen.

Probability is defined as the chances, odds, or frequency that an event will occur. For example, an individual consumer may read the weather forecast in a local paper and conclude that the odds are three in 10 it will rain during a softball game and seven in 10 it will not. If all possible relevant outcomes are considered, and if the probability is assigned to each possible outcome, then this is defined as a probability distribution. For our softball example, we could set up the following probability distribution:

| Outcome | Probability of Occurrence |
|---|---|
| Rain | 3 in 10 = 0.3 = 30% |
| No rain | 7 in 10 = 0.7 = 70% |
| Total | 10 in 10 = 1.0 = 100% |

The possible outcomes are listed in the first column, and the probability of each, expressed as chances, decimals, and percentages are given in the second column. Notice that the probabilities sum to one, or 100% as they must if the probability distribution is complete. A probability estimate of 0.30 means that you think the chances are three in 10 that the event will happen. A probability estimate of 0.30 indicates that you think there is twice as great a chance of the event happening than if you had estimated a probability of 0.15.

**Certainty** is defined as knowing the outcome of a decision in advance. For many simple recreation economic decisions, the outcomes are known with certainty. In these cases, the expected value is equal to the actual consumer surplus realized when the event occurs. For example, you may observe as you walk out the door with a picnic lunch under your arm that there is not a cloud in the sky. You may conclude that there is virtually a 100% chance that sunny skies will prevail while you are picnicking at a city park during the next two hours. The probability of a single "state of nature" is equal to one. Thus, the expected value of picnicking is equal to the full value of the experience under sunny skies. If the consumer surplus of picnicking at the city park is $15 with sunny skies, then its expected value is $15 x 1 = $15. In some cases, such as this, the amount of risk is so small that it can be ignored. You are sure that the event will happen as expected. However, in reality the vast majority of consumer and managerial decisions are made under conditions of risk or uncertainty where benefits and costs cannot be predicted exactly. Consumers and managers must select a course of action from the alternatives available, with less than full knowledge about the events affecting the outcome.

**Uncertainty** is defined as a situation in which two or more possible outcomes may result from a decision, but the precise nature of these outcomes is not known, or the probability of each occurring cannot be assigned objectively. That is, not all of the possible outcomes can be accurately foreseen; and their probabilities cannot be based on previous empirical data. Instead, the decision maker must use intuition, judgment, experience, and whatever other information is available to assign probabilities to the outcomes considered possible in such a situation.

Most individual consumers and managers of private and public recreation resources operate in a continuing state of uncertainty. With uncertainty, consumers and managers have no information concerning the probabilities of possible outcomes of alternative decisions. The expected value of a recreation activity with a number of uncertain outcomes is simply the consumer surplus that the individual will realize, on average, if the decision is repeated many times. Suppose, for example, that we have no information at all about the probability that it will rain or not during a softball game. In this case, we must proceed on a subjective basis, and the most simple method of assigning probabilities when there is no information is to assume "equi-probability of the unknown." That is, since we are uncertain about the relative likelihood that it will rain or not, we assign equal probabilities of each occurring. We assume that there is a 50% chance that it will rain and a 50% chance that it will not. If there are two or more possible outcomes ($n$), the probability of each outcome under the equi-probability method is $1 \div n$. Thus, with two possible outcomes, the probability of each outcome is $1 \div 2 = 0.5$; with three possible outcomes, the probability of each is $1 \div 3 = 0.33$; with four possible outcomes, the probability of each is $1 \div 4 = 0.25$.

**Risk** is defined as a situation in which two or more possible outcomes may result from a decision and the probability of each occurring is known to the decision maker. The actual outcome of a particular decision is not known in advance, of course. But given a sufficiently large number of decisions, the proportion of each possible outcome is known. This objective knowledge is based either on mathematical and physical principles or on past experience under similar circumstances. Thus, the major distinction between risk and uncertainty is that probability has an objective basis in the case of risk, rather than a subjective basis in the case of uncertainty.

For example, the National Weather Service keeps extensive data on previous wind patterns, temperatures, cloud formations and rainfall. Meteorological data show the relative incidence of various outcomes in past situations. On finding that a particular weather pattern is similar in all major respects to those of the database, the service is able to assign a probability to the chances of a particular event (state of nature) occurring in the near future. On this basis, the probability of snow, rain, wind, and flood is forecast daily by the service. Similarly, the probabilities of personal injury and death are prepared by insurance companies as actuarial tables. Risk of personal injury to downhill skiers has been calculated for ski areas by the U.S. Forest Service. State wildlife management agencies have developed a historic database on hunting and fishing success in each region of their states. If hunting and fishing conditions are similar to those of the database, recreation decision makers can assign a probability to the chance of a successful hunt in a particular hunting zone during the next season.

Any decision is only as good as the information on which it is based, in particular, the accuracy of the probability of the event occurring. There is no logical difference between the probabilities that an insurance company estimates on the basis of the frequency of past death rates or weather service estimates on the basis of past weather patterns, and the individual angler's seat-of-the-pants estimate of whether the fish will be biting. No frequency data can speak for itself in a perfectly objective manner. Many judgments go into compiling every frequency series, in deciding which series to use for an estimate, and in choosing which part of the data to use. For example, should anglers use only their recorded catch from last year, which will be too few observations to give as much data as they would like, or should they also use catch records from years further back, when conditions were different? They can ask friends and acquaintances and rely on the judgment of the most experienced among them. But in the end, their own subjective estimate of the likely variability in the expected outcome of the decision is all that they have upon which to base a recreation economic decision. Tourists may purchase a five-day fishing license only to find that the fish are not biting during August when they are on vacation at a resort area. Similarly, the weather forecast may be for scattered showers, but the microclimate where they choose to fish may have heavy rain all afternoon. Tens of thousands of deer and elk hunters have an unsuccessful hunt each year because of unforeseen circumstances.

## Decision-Making Process

We can now outline the major steps involved in decision making under conditions of risk and uncertainty. The decision maker should develop an understanding of the (1) alternatives, (2) outcomes, (3) economic benefits, (4) probabilities, (5) expected values, and (6) adjustments for the decision maker's attitude toward risk. First, because all decisions involve a choice among alternatives, we must have at least two possible alternatives or projects between which to choose. If there is only one possible course of action available, then obviously no decision is necessary. Second, for each alternative recreation activity or program, we have a number of possible outcomes that may occur depending on the "state of nature," or other conditions encountered. Only one of these outcomes will occur, although we do not know which one. Third, we have estimates of the economic benefits associated with each possible outcome for each alternative recreation activity or program. Fourth, we have estimates of the likelihood or probability of each particular outcome occurring. Fifth, we calculate the expected value of consumer surplus at the time the decision is made, which equals the weighted average value of possible outcomes for each alternative considered. Finally, we adjust the expected value for the decision maker's attitude toward risk, whether he or she tends to be neutral, cautious or a gambler.

We can illustrate the approach by applying it to a simple recreation economic problem in which a consumer must decide whether to take a trip or to devote the equivalent leisure time to some other unspecified alternative activity. The treatment of two or more alternative activities will be considered in subsequent cases in this chapter. This initial problem is purposely limited in order to emphasize the other important steps in decision making under conditions of risk and uncertainty.

Brookshire and Crocker (1981) present an example of the effects of visibility (as measured by the distance that users can see in and around a National Park) on demand for recreation use. A coal-fired power plant nearby either operates effective air quality control devices or shuts them down for maintenance periodically during the recreation season of park use. As a result, visibility in and around the park will be clear (c) or murky (m) during an individual recreation trip. The direct costs of trips to the park are not affected by the availability of atmospheric visibility in the park. However, how dramatic the vista, how photogenic, and the ability to observe distant snowcapped mountains from the site enhances individual satisfaction and benefits from recreation use. Economists depict such effects as shifts in the demand curve for trips to the park. If the relationship between a nonprice variable, such as visibility, and demand is not familiar to you, review the first section of Chapter 6 on shifts in the demand curve.

Figure 12-1 (page 200) reproduces our representative individual's demand curve (D) for trips to a recreation site from Chapters 5 and 6. With seasonal average conditions as to visibility, users would demand five trips per year at a price of $20 per trip. Net benefits to consumers would equal the area below the demand curve above price. The total consumer surplus for five trips would be $100 which, divided by five trips, yields average consumer surplus of $20 per trip with average visibility. With clear visibility, consumers would be willing to take more trips for the same travel costs or price. That is, magnificent vistas normally shift the demand curve outward to the right, as depicted by demand curve $D_c$ with clear skies. Demand would increase from five to seven trips per year and total consumer surplus for seven trips per year becomes $210 which, divided by seven trips, yields an average consumer surplus of $30 per trip with clear skies. However, when skies are murky with low visibility, the demand curve ($D_m$) for trips shifts inward to the left. At the same direct costs or price of trips, demand would decrease from five to three trips per year. Total consumer surplus for three trips becomes $30 which, divided by three trips, yields an average consumer surplus of $10 per trip with a murky sky.

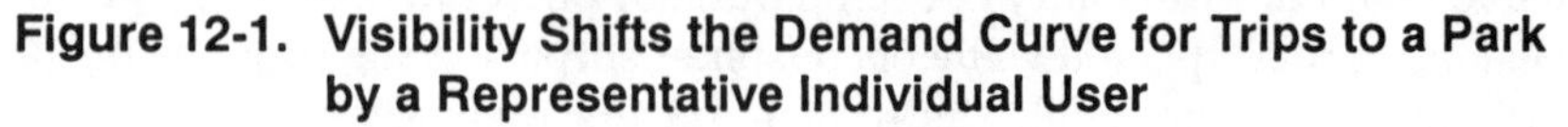

**Figure 12-1. Visibility Shifts the Demand Curve for Trips to a Park by a Representative Individual User**

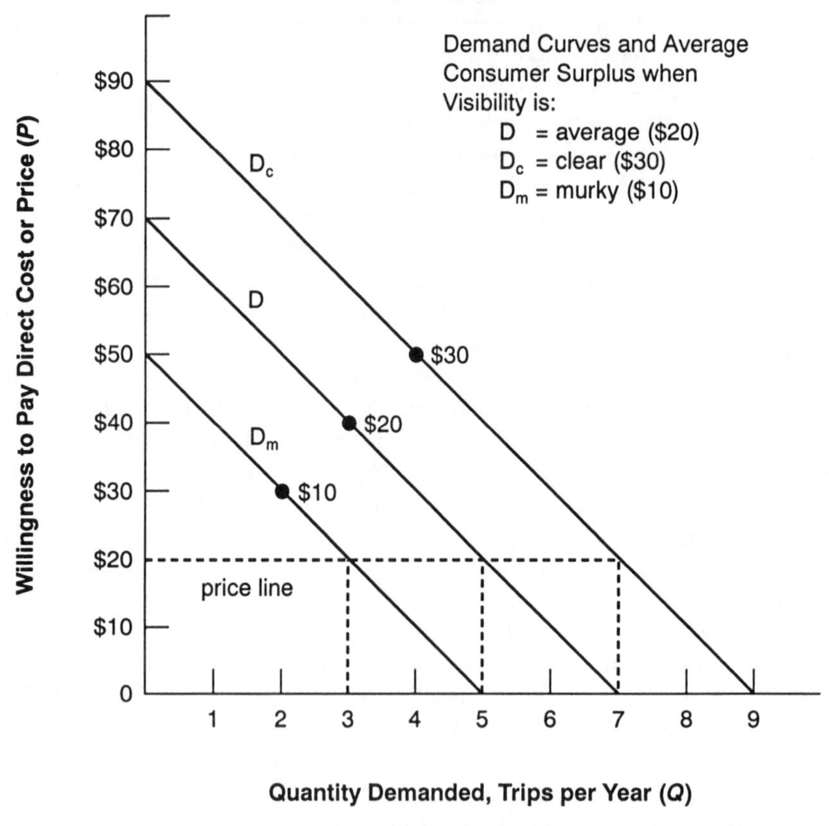


Recreation economic decisions under conditions of risk and uncertainty are based on the **expected value of consumer surplus** ($E_{CS}$) which is defined as the average benefits that individuals will end up with when they take repeated trips to a recreation site. To estimate this weighted average expected value, economists multiply the consumer surplus for each possible outcome by its probability of occurrence and then add these products. For example, if individuals contemplating trips do not have access to information about visibility at the park, they may be assumed to have a fair chance with a 50-50 probability of obtaining clear vistas valued at \$30 or murky visibility valued at \$10. The calculation of expected value becomes:

$\$30 \times 0.5 = \$15$ (Equation 12-1)
$\$10 \times 0.5 = \$5$ (Equation 12-2)
$E_{CS} = \$20$ (Equation 12-3)

For uncertain park users, the recreation economic decision would be to take five trips per year with an expected value of $20 per trip. As shown in Figure 12-1 this is the average consumer surplus of individual users who take repeated recreation trips if half are clear and half are murky.

Now assume that park managers initiate a program to supply prospective park users with visibility forecasts. Individuals considering trips are provided with the information that there is a 75% chance of clear visibility and a 25% chance of murky skies. The calculation of expected value becomes:

$$\$30 \times 0.75 = \$22.50 \quad \text{(Equation 12-4)}$$
$$\$10 \times 0.25 = \$2.50 \quad \text{(Equation 12-5)}$$
$$E_{CS} = \$25.00 \quad \text{(Equation 12-6)}$$

The improvement in knowledge converted the decision from one of uncertainty to one of risk. Now the recreation economic decision by informed park users would be to take six trips per year with an expected value of $25 per trip. This is the average consumer surplus of individual users who take repeated trips if 75% of the trips are under clear skies and 25% murky. Six trips is the optimum number of trips to take at a cost of $20 a trip when there is a 75% chance of clear weather and a 25% chance of murky weather. The optimum number of trips is calculated as:

$$7 \text{ Trips} \times 0.75 = 5.25 \text{ Trips} \quad \text{(Equation 12-7)}$$
$$3 \text{ Trips} \times 0.25 = 0.75 \text{ Trips} \quad \text{(Equation 12-8)}$$
$$E_{Trips} = 6.0 \text{ Trips} \quad \text{(Equation 12-9)}$$

The recreation benefits of the park are increased as a result of the improved information. Now individuals choose to visit on days when the probability of clear vistas is high. In fact, users may be willing to pay considerably more for the opportunities to realize improved visibility. The benefits of the visibility forecasting program are equal to the increase in the expected value of recreation use, $5 (= $25 – $20) per trip, and the increase in individual demand for use of the park, from five to six trips per year, or by 20%. Users might even be willing to pay as much as $50 per year for the site improvement (= $25 for the one additional trip + [$5 gain on previous trips x 5 trips]). This $50 is a measure of the improvement in the welfare of recreation users by the introduction of the improved resource management program, assuming they have a neutral attitude toward risk.

The final step involved in decision making under conditions of risk and uncertainty is to adjust the expected value to users for their attitude toward risk—whether risk neutral, risk averse, or risk seeking. This is based on Bernoulli's insight that individuals are usually risk averse (1954); thus, high-risk recreation activities and programs have an expected value that is less for individuals who have an averse attitude toward risk. Individuals who are neutral toward risk, value a dollar gained equal to a dollar lost (as assumed in the visibility example above) and thus expected value calculations are appropriate for them. Individuals who tend to be risk averse, value a dollar gained less than a dollar lost, and those who are risk seeking, value a dollar gained more than a dollar lost. For these individuals we must adjust the expected value calculation for this differential weighting of gains and losses.

Figure 12-2 illustrates the three possible attitudes toward risk. The expected value of each outcome is shown on the horizontal axis and the "adjusted" expected value of each outcome (for individual attitudes toward risk), on the vertical axis. Note that the relationship is linear for risk-neutral individuals, as represented by a straight line drawn at a 45° angle from the origin at zero. The relationship is nonlinear for risk-averse and risk-seeking individuals, represented by a curve drawn convex from the origin for risk aversion and by a curve drawn concave from the origin for risk seeking. The illustration assumes equal probabilities (i.e., a 50-50 chance) for each of the two possible outcomes (states of nature) for trips to a park, continuing the previous example.

Suppose that we ask recreation users how much they would be prepared to pay to take recreation trips offering a 50-50 chance of realizing outcomes with benefits of either $10 or $30 per day. If they are "neutral" in their attitudes toward risk, they might reply that they would be prepared to pay $20 per day, because the $20 is a "bird in the hand," which they are prepared to give up in the hope of gaining the "two in the bush" on average. Then we can say that they regard $20 as being equivalent to a 50-50 chance of realizing outputs with benefits of either $30 or $10. It is possible to offer individuals a number of 50-50 chances, such as the previous one, in order to construct the functions shown in Figure 12-2. The neutral attitude toward risk is depicted in Panel 1.

If recreation users are risk seekers, who in fact gain a positive consumer surplus from taking a chance on visibility, then they might regard a 50-50 chance of gaining outcomes with benefits of $30 or $10 as being the equivalent to, say, $24 with certainty. The $4 difference between the $20 expected value of risk-neutral individuals and the $24 willingness to pay of risk-seeking individuals represents a risk premium that gamblers would be willing to pay for the thrill of the gamble or uncertainty of the outcome. This is shown in Panel 3 of Figure 12-2. Similarly, risk-seeking anglers on trips to high mountain rivers and lakes in the park may value a dollar of consumer surplus gained from catching one large fish more highly than a dollar of consumer surplus lost by not catching a fish of any size. This attitude toward risk was clearly the central plot in Hemingway's last novel, *The Old Man and the Sea,* in which the many dreary days the old man and the boy fished without success were more than offset by the satisfaction of a final solitary catch of a very large fish.

Conversely, if individuals are to some extent averse to risk, then they might be prepared to pay only $16 to take recreation trips offering a 50-50 chance of outcomes with benefits of either $30 or $10. This is shown as

**Figure 12-2. Adjusting the Expected Value of Consumer Surplus for Individual Attitudes Toward Risk**

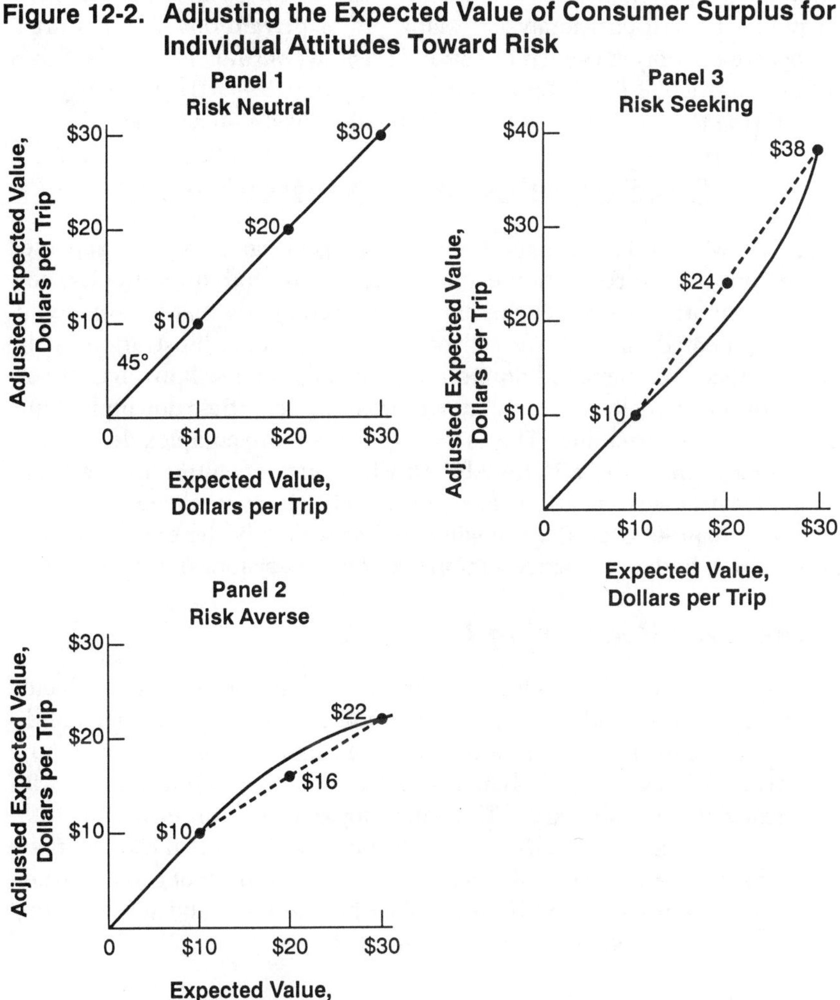


Panel 2 of Figure 12-2. The $4 difference between the $20 expected value of risk-neutral individuals and the $16 willingness to pay by risk-averse individuals represents a premium which cautious individuals would be willing to pay to avoid the risk, that is, the 50-50 chance of realizing clear or murky skies on trips to the park. Economists refer to this $4 risk premium as the **option value** of air quality to risk-averse users of the park. Option value is defined as a kind of insurance premium that is in addition to the $16 expected value of recreation use of the park. The purchase of options is a common practice in real estate and securities markets. The same kind of individual motivations exist for environmental and recreational resources, even though markets are absent. Randall (1987)

concludes that it makes sense to quantify these values and to include them in public benefit-cost analysis. Managers of private downhill ski areas recognize the option value motivation of risk-averse individuals when they lower the price of lift tickets to encourage skiers to participate early and late during the ski season when snow conditions are most risky.

## Case Studies of Risky Decisions

Next, we will see how consumers and managers can apply the expected value approach to recreation economic decisions and, in particular, how risk-averse attitudes affect the choice of alternatives that maximize adjusted expected values. We will begin with a simple illustration of the effect of risky weather conditions on consumer decisions. It involves choosing between two alternative winter recreation activities, downhill skiing and cross-country skiing. This is followed by a more complex decision by the superintendent of a National Park who considers alternative ways to expand visitor services in the face of variability in general economic conditions (business cycles). You will see that we apply the expected value approach to both of these recreation economic decisions in the same way.

### *Consumer Recreation Decision*

A skier is making plans for a weekend trip. The problem is to decide between downhill and cross-country skiing under risky weather conditions. Recreation benefits of downhill skiing are $60 with sun and a negative $30 in a blizzard. Benefits of cross-country skiing are $40 with sun and $30 in a blizzard. The morning weather forecast is an 80% chance of sun and a 20% chance of a blizzard. The problem is to estimate the expected value of each alternative with (1) certainty of good weather, (2) risk as defined by the National Weather Service, and (3) adjusting expected value for an averse attitude toward risk:

1. Certainty of good weather:
   Choose the highest net benefits of $60 for downhill skiing.

2. Risk with a 0.8 probability of good weather and a 0.2 probability of a blizzard:
   Downhill skiing: ($60 x 0.8) + (–$30 x 0.2) = $48 – $6 = $42 (Equation 12-10)
   Cross-country skiing: ($40 x 0.8) + ($30 x 0.2) = $32 + $6 = $38 (Equation 12-11)

   Downhill skiing has the higher expected value.

3. Adjusting expected value for an averse attitude toward risk:
   For example, $60 of expected value contributes only $45 of benefits for a 25% risk aversion reduction. Roughly $48 of

gain becomes $36. For the risk averse, the pleasure of gain contributes less benefits than the pain of loss. Therefore the $6 loss would be valued more than $6, say as a $9 loss.

Downhill skiing: if +$48 = +$36 and –$6 = –$9
then $36 – $9 = $27
Cross-country skiing: if $32 = $24 and $6 = $4.50
then $24 + $4.50 = $28.50

Cross-country skiing has the highest expected value, adjusted for risk aversion of this particular person. Since different risk averse people will place different weights on gains and losses than others, what is important is the process, not the specific values of this example.

## *Public Recreation Agency Decision*

Suppose that the superintendent of Yosemite National Park in California is considering alternative programs to increase public recreation use and benefits. The agency has limited resources and is preparing a risk analysis of its management plan. Suppose park managers are considering three alternative programs which would result in more recreation opportunities: (1) expand the size of the park by the acquisition of land; (2) rehabilitate facilities to provide more intensive park use for existing recreation activities; or (3) construct new facilities to provide a greater variety of recreation activities.

The park managers would like to know what the public use and benefits will be from each alternative. How will these effects change with variability in economic conditions of normal economy, boom economy, or recession? What is the probability that each of these conditions will occur in the future 10 years? With this information, they could adjust the expected recreation benefits from each management program for risk. Knowing something about the economic health of the U.S. economy may lead to different recreation economic decisions by the agency.

Begin the analysis by assuming the park staff used the travel cost method to estimate the public use and benefits of each alternative program under different economic conditions, as shown in Table 12-1 (page 206). Set up the problem with the alternatives you want to consider displayed on the left margin, and the possible economic conditions horizontally along the top. The recommended structure of the decision is shown in Table 12-1.

Suppose that a recent empirical study of the demand for recreation use of the park provides forecasts of net benefits (total benefits minus total costs) in millions of dollars. The park will receive more use and public benefits will be higher when the national economy is booming, and less when the national economy is in a recession. If future prosperity of the economy is a certainty, the alternative that would maximize benefits of $200 million is to rehabilitate existing facilities. Rehabilitation and

**Table 12-1. Estimated Public Use and Benefits of Alternative Programs**

| Alternative Management Programs | Normal | Boom | Recession |
|---|---|---|---|
| | Conditions in U.S. Economy: (Public Benefits in Million Dollars) | | |
| Land Acquisition, Park Expansion | $60 | $125 | –$10 |
| Rehabilitation of Existing Facilities | $10 | $200 | –$5 |
| Construction of New Facilities | $50 | $140 | $10 |

expansion of facilities for existing uses, such as sightseeing by car or bus, staying at a resort lodge, pool swimming, and playing golf, would meet the needs for developed recreation by a growing population in the California market area served. The recreation economic decision is to rehabilitate existing facilities under risk-free conditions of prosperity in the economy. Public benefits exceed that of either alternative. Of course, the risk-free decision would change if it were certain the economy would be either normal or in a recession.

Suppose an economic forecast by the U.S. Department of Commerce shows that, given current trends in economic indicators, the odds are only one in 10 that a recession will occur, six in 10 that the economy will be normal, and three in 10 that there will be a boom. Redefining these odds as probabilities, we estimate that the probability of a recession is 0.1 or 10%. The probability of normal times is 0.6 or 60%, and the probability of a boom is 0.3 or 30%. Note that the probabilities add up to 1.0 or 100%.

Next, calculate the expected value of benefits from each alternative by multiplying each benefit by its probability of occurrence. When the values for each alternative are summed, the result represents a weighted average of the outcomes under variable conditions in the U.S. economy. This weighted average is defined as the expected value of benefits from each alternative park program adjusted for risk:

Land acquisition, park expansion:

$$\$60(0.6) + \$125(0.3) - \$10(0.1) = \$36.00 + \$37.50 - \$1.00 = \$72.50 \quad \text{(Equation 12-12)}$$

Rehabilitation of existing facilities:

$$\$10(0.6) + \$200(0.3) - \$5(0.1) = \$6.00 + \$60.00 - \$0.50 = \$65.50 \quad \text{(Equation 12-13)}$$

Construction of new facilities:

$$\$50(0.6) + \$140(0.3) + \$10(0.1) = \$30.00 + \$42.00 + \$1.00 = \$73.00 \quad \text{(Equation 12-14)}$$

When adjusted for risk, the construction of new facilities has the highest expected value of $73 million compared with $72.5 million for land acquisition and $65.5 million for rehabilitation of existing facilities. The recreation economic decision, adjusted for the risk of variability in the economy, would be to construct new facilities.

## Other Approaches to the Problem

So far, we have illustrated the basic principles of decision making with risk and how to apply them without presenting the details of all possible approaches to the problem. The reader is referred to any managerial economics book for a discussion of the several approaches that have been used to estimate the effect of risk and uncertainty on decision making by consumers and managers. Among these are degree of risk, decision tree, maximin and minimax strategies, risk premium, and simulation.

The degree of risk is indicated by the spread or variation in the probability distribution of the possible outcomes for each alternative. A useful statistical measure of the degree of risk for each alternative activity or project is to calculate the coefficient of variation, which is the ratio of the standard deviation to the mean, expressed as a percentage. Activities that have a wide spread or variation in distribution of possible outcomes may be rejected in favor of those with a narrower range.

When a sequence or series of decisions is to be made, a decision tree enables the decision maker to visualize the ultimate outcome of all possible alternative activities or projects. It shows the sequence over time of the possible choices open to consumers or managers of private and public recreation resources.

The maximin strategy is to choose the activity or project that yields the best of the worst possible outcomes. It is designed to avoid a possible catastrophic outcome that might endanger the survival of the individual, corporation, or government agency. The minimax regret strategy is to choose that activity or project whose expected value is least different from the highest possible benefit. It is designed to minimize the regret or opportunity cost of incorrect decisions. Managers of private recreation resources will make risky decisions only if there is a commensurate risk premium. Investors adjust interest rates to reflect perceived risk. A risk premium is the difference between the expected profit on a risky activity or project and profit on one that is risk free.

Finally, another approach is simulation, in which a computer is used to generate random distributions of costs and benefits for each alternative activity or project and to estimate the probability distribution of possible outcomes. Computer programs such as @Risk have been developed to allow analysts to visualize the distribution of risk with different alternatives.

It is rarely possible to avoid risk and uncertainty in recreation. Weather conditions and the biological nature of the production process cannot be controlled, particularly in the case of fishing and hunting. There are, however, a number of approaches that consumers and managers commonly use to reduce risk and uncertainty. Among these are acquiring additional information, attempting to control the environment, modifying goals, introducing flexibility into plans, diversifying interests, and purchasing trip insurance.

Gathering information on the consequences of each alternative outcome will often reduce uncertainty about outcomes into a situation where the consumer or manager at least knows the probabilities. Thus, the more information gathered about the future, the less uncertain it will be. However, this is only true up to a point, after which the law of diminishing returns takes over. The collection of information is costly, and the benefits to be derived from additional information must be weighed against the additional cost of obtaining it. Hasty decisions made before sufficient information is gathered can be very costly. On the other hand, a recreation economic decision delayed too long in the pursuit of information may put the consumer or manager in the position of "too little, too late."

## Waiting Time or Queuing

Many problems of consumers and recreation resource managers involve waiting time or queuing. The two terms may be used interchangeably. Europeans prefer the word *queuing,* while in the United States, we use the phrase *waiting time.* It is defined as time, beginning when you enter a waiting line and ending when services begin. Waiting-time or queuing problems occur whenever there is (1) variation in the number of people arriving for service; (2) variation in the time required to provide the service; or (3) an arrival rate that exceeds the capacity of the resource, so that a bottleneck is created. These conditions are characteristic of many recreation activities. People often wait for service at a park entrance, visitor center, restaurant, grocery store, hotel, airline, gas station, repair shop, stop sign, train station, bus depot, golf course, tennis court, boat ramp, and ski lift. For example, people wait in line at restaurants during meal time on peak demand days, and they experience delays in receiving their food order from the kitchen. Similarly, people wait to tee off at a golf course and wait for the foursome ahead to clear the green before continuing play.

Becker (1976) has suggested that a reservation or appointment system is a type of queue, in which the waiting is done at home rather than in line. Examples include making advance reservations at campgrounds, theaters, and airlines. People reserve tennis courts to minimize the time waiting their turn to play. Limits on playing time are often set to allow more people to use the facilities and to minimize the wait. Advance purchase of hunting licenses is a form of reservation, and limitations on the number of licenses sold are designed to provide sustained yield management of the herd. The state of California and several other states use a campsite reservation system. The National Park Service experimented with a national reservation system for campsites, as has the U.S. Forest Service. Hotels, motels, and lodges routinely accept advance reservations.

Airlines encourage advance reservations, but 30-minute check-in lines are still common during the peak holiday season. Planes themselves often wait in a holding pattern for their turn to land at large airports.

How many rangers should be employed by managers to obtain the best economic balance between the cost of idle employee and/or facility time, and delay in serving visitors who line up and wait for service? How long should consumers wait in line for a recreation service? The answer depends on the balance between the costs of waiting time and the benefits of the recreation service. An entrance station to a park can become a bottleneck, even though sufficient capacity for additional visitors is available inside the park. In this case, additional booths and standby employees may be provided to handle peak demand at additional cost to the park but with considerable benefit to park visitors. Time costs are especially burdensome to society because they are a *deadweight* loss. Time is a cost to people who wait in line, but it is not a revenue to the suppliers of the service. Charging a higher price and providing the associated higher level of service often reduces this deadweight loss.

There are several alternative solutions to queuing problems, including changes in the:

1. number of service employees;
2. number of service stations or counters;
3. queue discipline, such as first-class and second-class airline ticket counters; and
4. self-service, to reduce employee time per customer.

## *Waiting Time at a Park Information Center*

Consider individuals on recreation trips to Yellowstone National Park. Suppose as they approach the entrance, they consider the possibility of stopping at the headquarters building where there is an information booth that provides, free of charge, a brochure containing a map of the park and advice about where to go and what to see. Increased knowledge of geysers, flora, fauna, trails, and other features of the park would enhance their enjoyment. However, road traffic has been relatively heavy, and it is expected that there will be many other visitors present. The problem is to decide whether or not to visit the information center. They would like to know what the chances are that they will have to wait in line; how many people will be in line and what the average waiting time is. With this information, they could estimate their own waiting-time cost and compare that to their expected benefits from the added information about the park.

Begin the analysis by estimating the number of visitors to the information booth and its capacity per day. Any convenient unit of time could be used, but park visitor centers are known to be staffed from 8 A.M. to 5 P.M. for a nine-hour day. A recent study of the operation of the information booth shows that visitors arrive at an average rate of 60 visitors per day and that service time per visitor averages 5.4 minutes. To calculate capacity of the information booth, divide total time available in a day by the service time per visitor. Multiplying nine hours by 60 minutes per hour equals 540 minutes of total operating time per day. Dividing the 540 minutes of total time available by 5.4 minutes per visitor served equals 100 possible visitor contacts. Thus, capacity of the information booth is 100 visitors per day.

What are the chances that visitors have to wait in line? Obviously, they will have to wait if they arrive when the information center is occupied, serving other visitors. To calculate the proportion of time the information booth is occupied, simply divide the number of visitors in a day by capacity. Dividing 60 visitors by the capacity of 100 equals 0.6. Thus, the information booth will be occupied serving visitors 60% of the time. The chance they will have to wait in line is 60 out of 100.

How long will visitors have to wait in line? To calculate the average waiting time, first divide the number of visits per day by the result of daily capacity times idle capacity:

$$\frac{60}{100(100 - 60)} = 0.015 \text{ Day} \qquad \text{(Equation 12-15)}$$

Then, convert the 0.015 proportion of a day to minutes of waiting time. Multiplying the 540 minutes in a nine-hour day by 0.015 of a day equals 8.1 minutes. Visitors can expect to wait an average of 8.1 minutes to be served by the information center.

How many people will be waiting in line? To calculate the average number of persons waiting in line, multiply the visitor arrival rate by the average waiting time per visitor. Multiplying the arrival rate of 60 persons per day by the average waiting time of 0.015 day equals 0.9 persons. Thus, the average number of people waiting in line is slightly less than one.

What are visitors' waiting-time costs? A useful approximation is their opportunity costs. This means their waiting-time costs are equal to the loss in benefits from recreation opportunities given up to wait in line. Assume they are typical users with three persons per household and individual benefits equal to approximately $20 per five-hour day spent in the park. Dividing $60 by 300 minutes in a five-hour day equals benefits valued at $0.20 per minute. Thus, their opportunity costs of waiting time equals $1.62 (= 8.1 minutes x $0.20). Their opportunity costs of 13.5 minutes at the visitor center (including waiting time of 8.1 minutes and service time of 5.4 minutes) are found by multiplying 13.5 minutes by $0.20 per minute, which equals $2.70.

What are the visitors' expected benefits from the added information? With such a small proportion of their available recreation time at stake (13.5 minutes out of 300 minutes, or 4.5%), it may be sufficient to ask whether benefits are expected to exceed waiting and service time costs of

$2.70. A missed turn on a trail or road could easily waste 10 to 15 minutes of time, and a good map and information about road and trail conditions could prevent this. Some consumers would estimate the expected dollar value of the benefits from the additional information. They may estimate that with the additional information, the total benefits of a party of three persons visiting the park would amount to $66 per day compared with $60 without the added information. Thus, benefits increase by $6 per day with additional information from the visitor center.

What is the recreation economic decision? Should visitors decide to wait at the information booth? To make a decision, review the findings of the previous analysis. Although the chances are 6 out of 10 that visitors will have to wait in line, the average length of the waiting time is approximately one person. They can expect to wait an average of 8.1 minutes, which is probably within their range of tolerance, even when we add 5.4 minutes for receiving the information, for a total time at the visitor center of 13.5 minutes. This is a small proportion (4.5%) of their total available time in the park. Benefits were estimated at $6, compared with the opportunity cost (or disbenefits) of $2.70. Dividing benefits by costs ($6 ÷ $2.70) results in a benefit-cost (B:C) ratio of 2.2. Chances are that this B:C ratio for stopping at the visitor center would exceed the B:C ratio of using the 13.5 minutes in any practical alternative recreation activity in the park. Their recreation economic decision would be to stop at the visitor center for additional information.

How sensitive are the results to changes in the variables? For example, what if visitors underestimated the number of other people who want to visit the information center? What if the number of people arriving at the information center increases from 60 to 80 to 90 or even 95 on a holiday weekend with peak demand? If capacity of the information center remains unchanged at 100 visitors per day, utilization of capacity would increase from 60% to 80%, 90%, and 95%. It is a simple task to calculate the effect of these changes in this key variable on the chances that visitors have to wait in line, number of people in line, and waiting time. Table 12-2 was prepared using these procedures.

**Table 12-2. Effects of Capacity Utilization on Average Waiting-Time Cost to Visitors at an Information Center, Yellowstone National Park**

| Rate of Capacity Utilization | Probability Visitors Will Have to Wait in Line | Average Number of Visitors Waiting in Line | Average Waiting per Visitor (Minutes) | Waiting-Time Plus Service-Time Cost |
|---|---|---|---|---|
| 60% | 0.60 | 1 | 8.1 | $2.70 |
| 80% | 0.80 | 3 | 21.6 | $5.40 |
| 90% | 0.90 | 8 | 48.6 | $10.80 |
| 95% | 0.95 | 18 | 102.6 | $21.60 |

Note that the probability that visitors will have to wait in line increases from 60 in 100 to 80 in 100, and so on and is identical to the rate of capacity utilization of the information center. At 90% utilization, the average number of people in line is eight and the average waiting time becomes 48.6 minutes (Table 12-2, page 211). It seems that most people would not wait when waiting time ranges from 20 to 50 minutes, or between 80% and 90% utilization of capacity. Multiplying average waiting time plus service time of 5.4 minutes by time costs of $0.20 per minute equals $5.40 at 80% utilization, and rises to $10.80 at 90% utilization. The point at which benefits of $6 equals costs (or disbenefits) of $6 occurs at around 80% utilization, where the average wait equals 21.6 minutes plus service time of 5.4 minutes. However, many people would leave the line before this point is reached, simply because their B:C ratio from using the time in any practical alternative recreation activity in the park would exceed unity or 1.1 (= $6 ÷ $5.40). It seems unreasonable to expect that 95% utilization of capacity could occur, because it would result in an average of 18 visitors waiting in line at an information center for 1 hour and 42 minutes plus a service time of 5.4 minutes. Waiting-time costs of $21.60 result in an unacceptable B:C ratio of only 0.3 (= $6 ÷ $21.60).

Changes in other variables may alter the results of the analysis. If this is the visitors' first trip to the park, the information provided may be more critical to their beneficial use of its facilities, than if they have accumulated some knowledge from previous visits. Thus, their benefit from waiting in line may exceed $6 on their first visit. Moreover, they may realize that knowledge gained now has a holdover effect and will contribute to benefits from future park visits. But knowledge gained does not last forever; thus, benefits to future visits will decay more or less rapidly as they lose maps, conditions change, and they forget what they once could easily recall. Perhaps their benefits from information now would be $8 on this visit, totaling $16 for five visits over the following year. In this case, their recreation economic decision would be to wait in line longer than the average visitor, who has been to the park many times before.

What if some visitors are unlucky and invariably arrive when the service counter is occupied and a waiting line exists? In the initial problem, they had lots of company, as 60% of the users arrived when the visitor center was occupied serving other visitors. It is important to note here that the average waiting time of 8.1 minutes included the zero waiting time of the lucky ones (the 40% of the visitors who did not wait at all). What you have intuitively sensed is confirmed. The waiting time when the visitor center is serving others will be substantially longer than the average. This can be shown by dividing the average waiting time of all visitors by the proportion of visitors who have to wait. This shows that their average wait increases from the user average of 8.1 minutes to 13.5 minutes (= 8.1 ÷ 0.60), or two-thirds, because they arrive when the service counter is serving other visitors. Their waiting-time costs increase from $1.62 to $2.70 or by $1.08.

## *Waiting-Time Costs and Alternative Levels of Park Information Service*

Assume that the superintendent of Yellowstone National Park is concerned about waiting time at the visitor information center in the park headquarters building. Park managers wish to investigate the severity of the problem and to consider alternative levels of information service to provide an efficient level of public recreation use and benefit. The agency is considering three alternative staffing levels to increase the output of information services: (1) continue the current program with increased utilization of idle time of the single employee assigned to the information desk from 8 A.M. to 5 P.M. daily; (2) double the capacity by increasing the number of employees assigned to the information desk from one to two; and (3) triple the capacity by increasing the number of employees assigned to the information desk from one to three. Under all three alternatives, the information center would continue to have one line for all customers, perhaps marked out with metal posts on stands and nylon rope. Visitors would be serviced by the first available employee in the order of first-come first-served.

The problem, in brief, is to decide how to expand visitor information services to provide an efficient level of public use and benefits. When the waiting is done by the agency's employees, the cost is more easily calculated than when the waiting is done by visitors. In the latter case, the cost of waiting time and of the visitor information and visitor goodwill of those who refuse to wait is harder to estimate. We need to know the effects of the number of visitors and the number of service employees on the waiting-time costs of visitors. A useful approach is to hold one of these variables constant and to calculate the effect of changes in the other on waiting-time costs. Holding number of visitors constant, what is the effect of changes in the number of service employees? With this information we could estimate the total or social cost of waiting time and compare that to the benefits from the information provided by the park program. Waiting in line does not usually change the direct cost or price of a recreation activity, but it has the same effect on the number of visitors, because it increases the indirect time costs until demand for the resource or program is curtailed to the limited supply.

## *Changes in Size of Staff*

Begin the analysis by adopting a simplifying assumption that the visitor center staffing does not have an effect on overall park visitation or visitors coming to the information center. This will show the effects of the second and third alternatives—changing service capacity by increasing the number of employees assigned to the information desk from one to two or three persons, holding the number of visitors constant.

What is the effect of the number of service employees at the information center on the proportion of visitors who will have to wait in line? When visitors arrive, they will receive immediate service if one of the employees present is not occupied serving other visitors. Visitors will have to wait if all employees present are occupied serving other visitors. Table 12-3 shows that the probability that visitors will have to wait in line is 0.6 when a single service employee is at the information center. Assume that with two service employees, the probability of waiting falls to 0.3, and with three employees, to 0.2. Thus, the chances of a waiting line forming at the information center are nearly one-half as great with two employees as with a single employee.

What is the effect of number of service employees at the information center on visitor waiting time? Table 12-3 shows that the average waiting time per visitor is 8.1 minutes when a single service employee is at the information center. With two employees, average waiting time is cut in half to 4 minutes, and with three employees to 2.6 minutes. A procedure for calculating the effects of number of employees on waiting time is illustrated in Barish (1962).

Multiplying average waiting time of all visitors (this is an average across all visitors including the 40% that have no wait) by number of visitors equals total waiting time. With a single service employee, the total waiting time of 60 visitors is 486 minutes per day. When the number of service employees is increased to two, the total waiting time of 60 visitors is 240 minutes per day. Increasing the number of service employees to three reduces the total waiting time of 60 visitors to 156 minutes per day.

**Table 12-3. Effect of Increases in the Size of Staff on Waiting-Time Costs of Visitors to an Information Center, Yellowstone National Park**

| | Number of Employees Present at One Time | | |
|---|---|---|---|
| Variables | One | Two | Three |
| Average Number of Visitors per Day | 60.00 | 60.00 | 60.00 |
| Proportion of Visitors That Wait | 0.60 | 0.30 | 0.20 |
| Average Waiting Time of all Visitors (Minutes) | 8.10 | 4.00 | 2.60 |
| Total Visitor Time | 486.00 | 240.00 | 156.00 |
| Total Visitor Waiting Time Costs (@$12/Hour) | $97.20 | $48.00 | $31.20 |
| Visitor Time Cost Saving With Additional Employees | | $49.20 | $16.80 |

What is the effect of the number of service employees at the information center on waiting-time costs? Table 12-3 shows that the average waiting-time cost per visitor declines at the same rate as waiting time. When waiting-time costs are valued at a typical wage rate of $12.00 an hour or $0.20 a minute, the total waiting costs are $97.20 per day (= 486 minutes x $0.20 per minute). This falls to $48.00 per day with two service employees and to $31.20 per day with three service employees.

What are the expected benefits from increasing the number of service employees at the information center? Table 12-3 shows benefits to visitors as the difference in waiting time with and without the added service employees. Subtracting $48.00 from $97.20, yields a benefit per day (cost saving to visitors) of $49.20 per day for the second employee. If a summer temporary employee can be hired for less than $49.20 a day, total social benefits will be improved. Thus if a person is hired at $5.50 an hour for eight hours per day this costs $44.00, while he or she would produce a time saving of $49.20 to visitors. The gain of $5.00 a day over a 120-day summer season is $6,000.

The benefits from adding a third service employee to the visitor information center are similarly calculated. The time cost savings from adding the third employee is just $16.80 (= $48 – $31.20). Unless the third employee is a volunteer, it is very likely that the costs to society from hiring the third person is greater than the incremental waiting-time cost savings to visitors.

*Chapter 13*

# Forecasting Future Consumption

This chapter introduces several important methods of forecasting future levels of recreation use, including extrapolation or trend projection, and forecasting demand from multiple regression coefficients and elasticities of demand. It summarizes recent trends and forecasts of the future consumption of recreation, and discusses implications for improving the application of forecasting techniques to recreation economic decisions.

Up to now we have assumed that the consequences of most recreation economic decisions occur in the short run rather than long run, a simplification that was useful for purposes of understanding decisions with immediate effects. At this point we modify this assumption in order to consider important long-run recreation economic problems. Decisions made now by managers of private and public recreation resources will have consequences next year and in the decades that follow. Most facilities such as campgrounds have a 10- to 20-year lifetime. Whether building a new campground is justified depends as much on what we think future use will be as current use. More important, how large to make the campground depends on our estimate of future use. The very type of facilities to provide depends on the relative growth of different recreation activities over time. For example, should more land and other resources be devoted to cross-country or downhill skiing? It is useful to consider the problem of forecasting the future effects of current recreation economic decisions.

In this chapter, we will describe alternative approaches to forecasting future recreation use. No single approach to forecasting future participation has been developed that is suitable for all purposes. Thus, we will examine a variety of methods that are used, including time-series, simple regression, multiple regression, resource capacity, expert judgment, and market survey. Although each of these approaches has provided satisfactory estimates of the amount of recreation that will be consumed in future years under particular conditions, each also has its drawbacks. We will discuss the problems of each approach and demonstrate under what conditions it should be used. Accuracy of the alternative forecasting methods is a continuing problem, although considerable progress has been made in recent years.

The purpose of forecasting is to estimate what future benefits and costs would be with a proposed project compared to what they would be without it. The difference is the increment in net benefits of the proposal. Thus, we forecast consumption both with and without a project. Such estimates are useful to anyone planning future development of recreation resources. The availability of private financing depends on reliable forecasts of future revenues and costs of proposed projects in order to determine if they will be financially feasible. The availability of public financing also depends on reliable forecasts of future benefits and costs of proposed public projects in order to determine if they will be socially beneficial. With the renewed emphasis on accountability in government, there is a special concern about the expected benefits of expenditures on recreation programs.

## Historic Trends

Total recreation use is five to 10 times greater than it was in 1950. Increases in recreation use have been substantially faster than the population growth during that time. Table 13-1 illustrates the high absolute level and change over the last four decades.

This table illustrates the growth in recreational demand for lands and activities provided by the National Park Service, U.S. Forest Service and U.S. Fish and Wildlife Service. Their recreation settings are primarily natural rather than facility oriented, and the activities are largely nonconsumptive, such as hiking and wildlife viewing. Reservoir recreation use has fluctuated at both the Bureau of Reclamation and Corps of Engineers sites. There has been a 19% overall gain at the Corps of Engineers reservoirs but no significant change in the pattern of use at Bureau of Reclamation reservoirs.

While the absolute level of use generally has been increasing, the rate of growth in many recreation activities has been slowing. Annual growth rates exceeding 10% per year were typical of the period from 1950 to 1960. Rapid growth was due to increases in leisure time, income and greater automobile ownership. It also resulted from expanded opportunities provided by government recreation development and subsidization of recreation via free access. Development of new technology and commercial production was also important, particularly for skiing, snowmobiling, whitewater boating, camping and backpacking.

Annual growth rates declined from more than 10% during the early postwar period to about 5% in the 1970s, then to approximately 2% in the 1980s and 1990s. There are many reasons for the slowdown in the rate of growth. One is the rapid rise in gasoline prices during the late 1970s and early 1980s arising from two oil embargoes. Second is that visitor use had

**Table 13-1. Trend in Recreation Visitation on Federal Lands**

| Agency | 1950[a] | 1960[a] | 1980 | 1984 | 1987 | 1993 |
|---|---|---|---|---|---|---|
| | | | Millions of Visitor Days | | | |
| Forest Service | 16.4 | 55.5 | 234.9 | 227.5 | 238.4 | 287.7 |
| Corps of Engineers | 9.6 | 63.6 | 160.5 | 137.7 | 148.6 | 192.2 |
| National Park Service | 19.6 | 43.7 | 86.8 | 103.3 | 114.7 | 115.8 |
| Bureau of Land Management | n.d. | n.d. | 5.7 | 17.4 | 43.1 | 46.9 |
| Tennessee Valley Authority | 9.9 | 25.4 | 7.2 | 6.6 | 6.5 | 11.4 |
| Bureau of Reclamation | 3.9 | 14.5 | 33.9 | 23.5 | 31.7 | 22.4 |
| Fish and Wildlife Service | 3.2 | 6.4 | 1.4 | 4.7 | 5.9 | 17.7[a] |

[a]Estimated from recreation visits; n.d. = no data.

Source: Years 1950–1984: Walsh, 1986; years 1987–1993: U.S. Department of the Interior, 1993, p. 22.

reached the capacity of most National Parks, Wilderness Areas, and other recreation facilities. With a slowdown in expansion of National Parks in the lower 48 states and failure to construct new recreation facilities to meet the increase in demand, there was simply no capacity to absorb even a 2% growth rate, let alone historic growth rates of 5% or 10%. Underlying demographic conditions have also changed. For example, the rate of population growth declined by nearly half, from 1.8% per year in the early postwar baby boom years to a rate of less than 1.0% The rate of increase in real household income (adjusted to remove inflation) fell from an average increase of about 3% per year in the early postwar years to near zero. The average number of hours in the workweek tended to stabilize at about 40 hours. However, the rise of two-income households with long commutes tended to reduce discretionary time.

## Future Prospects

Table 13-2 (page 220) illustrates the results of a forecast by Cordell, Bergstrom, Hartmann and English (1990) for use in long-run planning by the U.S. Forest Service. The authors used multiple regression to forecast the number of participants in 32 outdoor recreation activities for 10-year intervals to the year 2040. Their data involved more than 30,000 interviews with visitors to state and federal recreation areas nationwide as part of the Public Area Recreation Visitor Study (PARVS). The results are presented as an index (or percent), with 1987 equal to 100. For example, an index of 161 for day hiking in the year 2010 means that participation in the activity is forecast to increase to 61% over its level in 1987.

It is clear from the results presented in Table 13-2 (page 220) that substantial increases in participation are expected in all of the recreation activities studied. There are noticeable differences in the size of projected increases for land-based, water-based, and snow- and ice-based activities. Downhill skiing, day hiking, visiting prehistoric sites and pool swimming

**Table 13-2. Maximum Preferred Demand for Recreational Trips Away From Home and Indices of Future Demand Growth to 2040**

| Resource Category and Activity | Trips in 1987 (Millions) | Future Number of Trips as Percentage of 1987 Demand | | | |
|---|---|---|---|---|---|
| | | 2010 | 2020 | 2030 | 2040 |
| **Land** | | | | | |
| Wildlife Observation and Photography | 69.5 | 131 | 146 | 162 | 174 |
| Camping in Primitive Campgrounds | 38.1 | 127 | 140 | 154 | 164 |
| Backpacking | 26.0 | 164 | 196 | 230 | 255 |
| Nature Study | 70.8 | 113 | 120 | 131 | 138 |
| Horseback Riding | 63.2 | 141 | 160 | 177 | 190 |
| Day Hiking | 91.2 | 161 | 198 | 244 | 293 |
| Photography | 42.0 | 143 | 165 | 188 | 205 |
| Visiting Prehistoric Sites | 16.7 | 160 | 192 | 233 | 278 |
| Collecting Berries | 19.0 | 126 | 143 | 166 | 192 |
| Collecting Firewood | 30.3 | 124 | 138 | 157 | 178 |
| Walking for Pleasure | 266.5 | 131 | 146 | 164 | 177 |
| Running/Jogging | 83.7 | 163 | 197 | 234 | 262 |
| Bicycle Riding | 114.6 | 148 | 173 | 202 | 222 |
| Driving Vehicles or Motorcycles Off-Road | 80.2 | 111 | 118 | 125 | 130 |
| Visiting Museums or Information Centers | 9.7 | 136 | 153 | 174 | 188 |
| Attending Special Events | 73.7 | 127 | 141 | 157 | 168 |
| Visiting Historic Sites | 73.1 | 143 | 169 | 203 | 241 |
| Driving for Pleasure | 421.6 | 128 | 142 | 157 | 167 |
| Family Gatherings | 74.4 | 135 | 152 | 170 | 182 |
| Sightseeing | 292.7 | 136 | 156 | 183 | 212 |
| Picnicking | 262.0 | 117 | 126 | 136 | 144 |
| Camping in Developed Campgrounds | 60.6 | 137 | 155 | 173 | 186 |
| **Water** | | | | | |
| Canoeing/Kayaking | 39.8 | 126 | 140 | 157 | 169 |
| Stream, Lake, or Ocean Swimming | 238.8 | 110 | 117 | 124 | 129 |
| Rafting/Tubing | 8.9 | 136 | 164 | 215 | 255 |
| Rowing, Paddling, or Other Boating | 61.8 | 124 | 136 | 150 | 159 |
| Motorboating | 219.5 | 111 | 117 | 123 | 127 |
| Water-Skiing | 107.5 | 121 | 131 | 141 | 148 |
| Pool Swimming | 221.0 | 169 | 205 | 242 | 269 |
| **Snow and Ice** | | | | | |
| Cross-Country Skiing | 9.7 | 177 | 199 | 212 | 195 |
| Downhill Skiing | 64.3 | 197 | 247 | 298 | 333 |

Source: Cordell, Bergstrom, Hartmann, and English, 1990.

are forecast to have the largest increase in demand by the year 2040. Participation in motorboating is expected to increase at a somewhat lower rate than for most other watersports, however, large increases are forecast for participation in whitewater rafting. Participation in land-based activities is expected to increase at a rate of 1.0% per year, a somewhat slower rate than the other activities. Those with the smallest increase in participation are driving off-road vehicles and nature study. Note that considering only percentage increases can be somewhat misleading. Land-based activities include larger numbers of participants. Thus, the smaller percentage growth will still mean much larger absolute growth in numbers of participants in land-based activities than for either winter sports or water-based activities.

# Explanatory Variables for Estimating Future Use

Nearly all of the methods used to forecast future recreation use are based, either explicitly or implicitly, on expected future changes in key demand shifters. Thus, it is important to investigate these in some detail.

## *Population*

One of the major determinants of future recreation is the overall level of population. Since market or site demand curves are the summation of individual demand curves, the more individuals there are, other things remaining equal, the larger the market or site demand. Future population is predictable for many recreation activities. New boaters and skiers in the next decade have already been born. People have both predictably long life spans as well as reasonably predictable recreation patterns with age.

The relevant population to use for forecasts depends on the nature of the recreation site. For a city park, clearly future population in the town and county is most relevant. For a nationally recognized recreation area such as a Yellowstone National Park, the growth pattern for the entire U.S. population is relevant. Looking at the geographic distribution of current visitors can help to identify from which counties and states to collect future population data.

Population projections based on three different population series—high, medium and low—from the U.S. census are commonly used to make forecasts by recreation planners. States often perform their own population forecasts providing estimates by county. City planning offices usually have population forecasts useful for local park planning.

## *Geographic Distribution of Population*

The longtime trend is population shifts to the West and South, closer to more public recreation land than when individuals were residents of the East or Midwest. This tends to lower average travel cost, making recreation trips more frequent. Thus, when forecasting future use, it is important to account for shifts in population toward or away from the recreation area of interest.

## Age Distribution of Population

In addition to total population, another predictable influence on recreation demand is the age structure of the population. The U.S. population is forecast to have an aging population for the next two decades based on aging of the large segment of the population called baby boomers. While it is hazardous to use recreation participation and activity patterns of previous 60- to 70-year-old persons to infer what those who will be 60 to 70 in the future will demand, there are some underlying trends. A very young population of many new families with young children will likely demand more city parks with playground equipment than downhill ski areas. Alternatively, an aging population will likely demand fewer areas for rock climbing and more areas for day hikes, golf and resorts.

Average age in the medium census projection is expected to increase from 38.5 years in the base year (1977) to 45.8 years in 2000, and to 48.9 years in 2030. In the short run, the distribution of population among age categories may be more important than the average age. The aging American population may actually stimulate some areas of recreation participation as a result of better healthcare, concern for fitness, and greater lifelong commitments to recreation activity.

## Income

The level and distribution of income also has a significant influence on certain types of recreation activities. As discussed in Chapter 8, the income elasticity of demand measures how sensitive participation and trip frequency is to income. Perhaps the best measure of income available for recreation is disposable per capita income. Disposable means income after taxes and per capita is per person. Thus, a large family will have lower per capita income and is likely to not be able to afford downhill skiing where a lift ticket must be purchased for each person versus affording camping, where the site fee is fixed regardless of the number in the family. Income influences participation far more strongly than trip frequency. Studies show that income influences decisions as to whether to participate in downhill skiing, motorized boating, snowmobiling, horseback riding, and other high-cost activities.

In addition to the average level of income in the population, income distribution may be quite important. During the 1980s and 1990s, more and more income became concentrated in the upper income groups while the lowest income group saw its real income fall. This growing disparity has two implications: Expensive recreation activities preferred by high-income households would tend to grow, while low-income households would increase participation in inexpensive recreation such as visiting city parks, reservoir fishing, and camping.

## *Availability of Time*

A key determinant of the type of recreation activities that will be demanded in the future is the amount and type of time available for recreation. As discussed in Chapter 2, total leisure time as measured by paid vacation and number of paid holidays may be an important predictor of visits to resource-based sites such as distant National Parks and Wilderness Areas. Visits to city and state parks may be driven by number of hours in the workweek. Studies of time budgets are frequently made by both private firms and government agencies. It is useful to consult these latest studies when developing forecasts of different types of recreation activities.

## *Ethnicity*

The United States is rapidly becoming a more pluralistic society. Many states such as California will soon have multiple racial groups (e.g., white, Hispanic, Black, Asian) none of which are in the majority. Population growth rates are higher for Hispanics than whites, which will lead to a larger relative proportion of the population in the future being Hispanic. Several studies have indicated that preferences for recreation are quite different among ethnic groups. Studies from southern California suggest Hispanics tend to participate in activities related to picnicking and do so in large groups or extended families. This suggests the demand for group picnic sites would likely increase in areas with large Hispanic populations. When forecasting recreation use, including variables for percent of the population that is nonwhite or of particular ethnic background may improve the accuracy of forecasts of future use.

## *Rural Versus Urban*

Differences exist in recreation preferences between those living in an urban or suburban environment and those living in rural, farm and ranch areas. Consumptive recreation activities such as hunting and fishing are frequently traditional in rural areas, while nonconsumptive activities such as observing wildlife, tend to be favored by urban residents. When forecasting future use, it is important to include a variable for degree of urbanization (e.g., percent of relevant population living in urban and suburban areas).

## *Incorporating Future Values of Explanatory Variables Into Forecasts*

Multiple regression forecasting depends on the accuracy of future projections of the explanatory variables. Projections of per capita income are often based on gross domestic product forecasts by the Bureau of Economic Analysis of the U.S. Department of Commerce. The U.S. Census

Bureau's projections of population, age distribution, and ethnicity are usually reasonably good. Long-term (e.g., more than 10 years into the future) projections of other explanatory variables such as availability of time or geographic distribution of the population are more prone to error as demographic or technological changes are difficult to foresee (e.g., rise of single parent families, telecommuting, availability of microwave ovens). Forecasting the future prices of gasoline is also quite uncertain. Nonetheless, it is important to include these variables in forecasts. The sensitivity of future use estimates can be evaluated by performing the forecast using alternative assumptions about variables such as the future price of gasoline to see if project feasibility is altered.

### *Accounting for Supply Availability When Forecasting Use*

Most of the factors discussed previously are known to influence the demand for outdoor recreation. However, for that demand to be realized as actual visitation, there must be an adequate supply of facilities to accommodate that demand. Often this is not the case. Reservations for campgrounds and whitewater boating permits are often hard to obtain. The result is unmet demand that does not show up in any commonly kept use statistics (which is a major limitation of current visitor use statistics when it comes to facility planning). Thus, the availability of recreation facilities is an important determinant of actual participation in general; it is especially important to those activities that require specialized facilities. As noted in the section that follows on recreation capacity, forecasted recreation demand may need to be capped at the use limit of the site or area.

As illustrated in Table 13-3, future supply is not expected to be adequate to accommodate the expected increase in demand for several recreation activities. While raising fees can ration the quantity demanded down to the available supply, the foregone benefits of the displaced use often exceed the costs of augmenting the available supply of recreation facilities. As shown in Table 13-3, the largest shortfalls are in areas for wildlife observation, backpacking, horseback riding, day hiking and cross-country skiing. Thus for these activities, it is important to compare demand forecasts with the current or expected future supply of opportunities to participate.

## With-and-Without Comparison

The basic purpose of forecasting is to identify what the future benefits and costs would be with a proposed project compared to what they would be without it. The difference is the increment in net benefits of the proposed project. For example, if we forecast consumption both with and without a project, the difference represents the effects of the proposal. Note that these with-and-without comparisons are not the same as comparing the

**Table 13-3. Projected Excess Demand Relative to Expected Supply**

| Recreation Activity | Percent Excess Demand Year: 2020 | 2040 |
|---|---|---|
| Wildlife Viewing | 26% | 44% |
| Backpacking | 31 | 57 |
| Horseback Riding | 25 | 41 |
| Day Hiking | 30 | 64 |
| Picnicking | 0 | 0 |
| Driving Off-Road | 6 | 9 |
| Canoeing/Kayaking | 2 | 6 |
| Stream/Lake/Ocean Swimming | 0 | 0 |
| Motorboating/Water-Skiing | 0 | 0 |
| Cross-Country Skiing | 57 | 69 |
| Downhill Skiing | 0 | 0 |

Source: Cordell, Bergstrom, Hartmann and English, 1990.

situation before and after the project. The before-and-after comparison does not account for changes in future recreation demand that would occur without the project and thus, may lead to an over- or understatement of the benefits attributable to it. This point has been developed by the federal guidelines (U.S. Water Resources Council, 1983).

Figure 13-1 (page 226) illustrates the five situations likely to be encountered in forecasting the consequences of alternative recreation programs:

1. consumption is growing without the project, which will provide additional growth;
2. consumption is declining without the project, which will restore consumption to its former level;
3. consumption is declining without the project, which will avoid the loss and increase recreation use;
4. consumption is stable without the project, which will increase recreation use; and
5. there is little or no consumption without the project, which will initiate growing recreation use.

The most common (see Panel 1 of Figure 13-1, page 226) is when recreation demand in the area is already growing, if only slowly, and would probably continue to grow during the life of the proposed project. The objective is to increase benefits by providing additional opportunities to participate in recreation activities. For example, in a mountain region, participation in recreation in primitive roadless areas was forecast to grow at about 2% a year without designation of the areas as wilderness. It was proposed to designate and manage these areas as wilderness to protect the natural environment and to increase recreation benefits. If, with

**Figure 13-1. Variations in Net Benefits With and Without Proposed Projects**

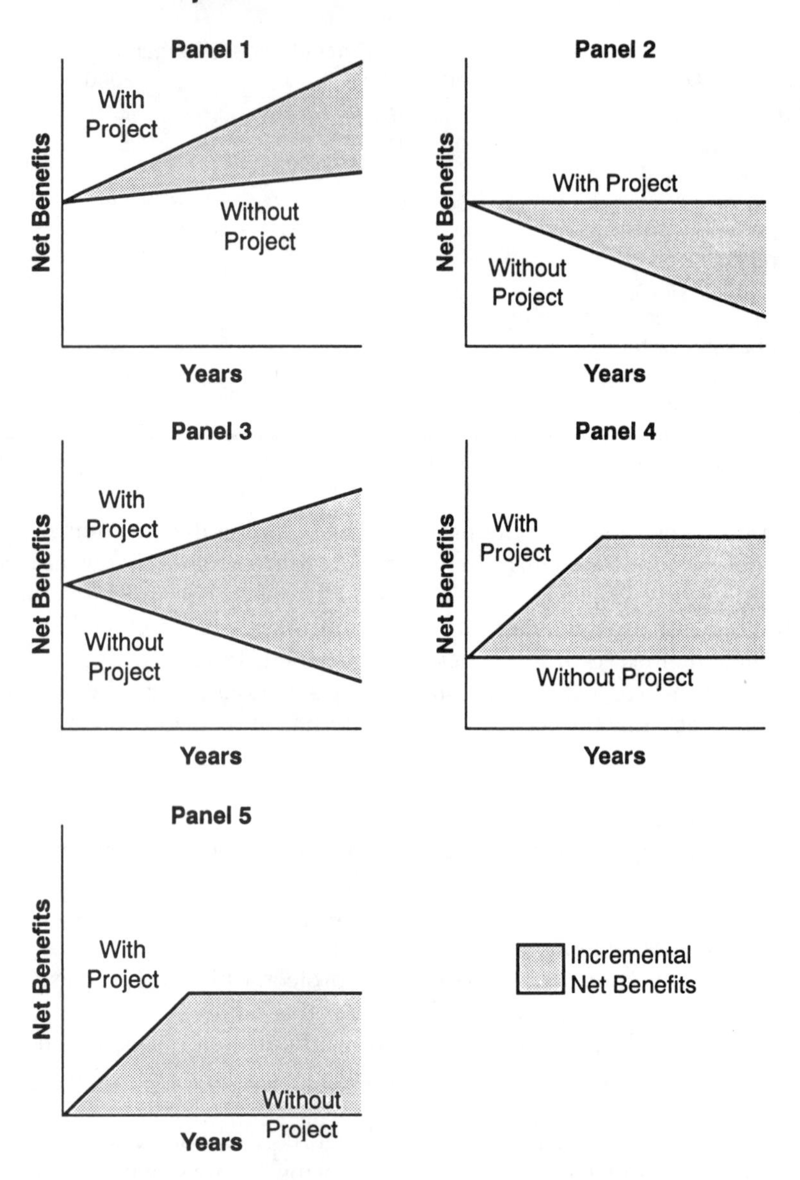


Source: Adapted from Gittinger, 1982.

designation, recreation use is forecast to grow at a rate of 5% a year and the project analysts simply compare the recreation use before and after the project, they would erroneously attribute the total increase to wilderness designation. Actually, what can be attributed to the proposal is only the 3% increase in recreation use in excess of the 2% that would have occurred anyway. Net recreation benefits equal with-project use levels minus the without-project use levels.

The federal guidelines caution that many proposed projects involve both recreation gains and recreation losses. Consider the following examples of existing site use displaced or destroyed by new project facilities. River use, such as for hiking, fly-fishing and whitewater boating, may be lost because of a proposed reservoir that would flood many miles of river. Or the development of a large ski resort may result in the loss of the habitat of an elk herd with the subsequent loss of elk hunting opportunities over the life of the ski area. In the case of wilderness expansion, the prohibition of motorized use would result in the loss of opportunity for off-road vehicle use in the designated area.

A second situation (see Panel 2 of Figure 13-1) occurs when recreation use would actually fall in the absence of the proposed project. Near Chicago, on the south shore of Lake Michigan, the Indiana Dunes National Lakeshore is located on a 20-mile strip of sand edging the lake. The shoreline has been subject to erosion from wave action. Under a federal project, the government has built sea walls to prevent the erosion. The benefits from this project, then, are not from increased recreation use but from avoiding the loss in recreation opportunity resulting from erosion of the swimming beach and scenic highway. A similar situation may characterize state wildlife management programs, where recreation opportunities would actually fall without the regulation of annual harvest and other management programs. A simple before-and-after comparison would fail to identify these benefits.

A third situation (see Panel 3 of Figure 13-1) occurs when a proposal to increase recreation use also avoids a loss. In this case, benefits would include both the increased use and the loss avoided. In many areas, river fishing and boating opportunities are diminished during the late summer months. This is in part attributable to the natural reduction in flow such as what occurs with the end of the snowmelt and runoff but is exacerbated by water diverted from rivers for irrigation. If nothing is done, recreation use will decline. Consider a proposal to purchase irrigation water rights to maintain instream flow. This would provide sufficient instream flow for fishing and boating in the river to extend through the late summer months of peak tourist demand. The proposal would not only increase recreation opportunity but also avoid a loss. A simple before-and-after comparison would fail to identify the benefits realized by avoiding the loss from reduced instream flow.

There is a more general situation in which projects that increase recreation use may also avoid a loss. Demand often exceeds supply of existing sites in regions where new or expanded capacity is proposed. Availability of the new or expanded recreation site would encourage some participants to substitute the new site for the old. This would reduce congestion at existing sites with excess demand at those sites. Reduced congestion would increase willingness to pay by those who continue to use the existing sites. Since reducing the use of existing sites toward benefit-maximizing levels would be a consequence of the new or expanded site, the increased willingness to pay would be counted as an external benefit and added to the benefits from recreation use of the proposed project.

Panels 4 and 5 of Figure 13-1 (page 226) illustrate a situation where existing use is either minimal (Panel 4) or essentially zero (Panel 5) in absence of the recreation project. These cases might be illustrated by the purchase of private land for public recreation. A private ranch that is presently fenced and heavily grazed provides little or no direct recreational use except to the owners. Purchasing this land to prevent development and provide public access and trails for hiking, horseback riding and mountain biking would result in net benefits as illustrated in either Panel 4 or 5.

In the Alaska Lands Bill, National Parks were established in many areas where there had been virtually no prior development for recreational use. Nor was there likely to be significant recreation use, at least for many years, in the absence of the National Parks. With the National Park designation, the government will develop access and visitor facilities to provide opportunities for sightseeing, fishing, hiking, camping, and related uses. In this case, recreation use without the project would be virtually the same as the output before the project.

## Simple Methods of Forecasting

Several simplistic methods have been used to forecast future consumption of recreation. These include (1) time series or extension of past trends in use; (2) resource capacity which provides an upper limit on recreation consumption; (3) informed judgment of those directly involved in management; and (4) market surveys of user intentions and preferences. Although each of these approaches has provided satisfactory estimates of the amount of recreation which may be consumed in future years under particular circumstances, each also has its drawbacks. In this section, we will discuss these problems and demonstrate under what conditions each approach can be used. We look at the principal methods of forecasting and show how to apply them without presenting the details of all possible approaches to the problem. Any marketing research book will provide a discussion of the several approaches that have been used to estimate future consumption of goods and services.

### *Resource Capacity Approach*

The use of this approach is authorized by the federal guidelines when it can be demonstrated that sufficient excess demand exists in the market area of a recreation site to fully utilize the additional capacity supplied by a proposed project. This means that the forecast of future consumption is assumed to be equal to the maximum practical capacity of recreation sites. As unique recreation resources become increasingly scarce, the resource capacity approach will become more and more applicable. There are many National Parks in which recreation use exceeds carrying capacity (for example, Yosemite), and it is well-known to decision makers that expanding supply would increase use up to the new capacity.

Application of the resource capacity approach usually begins with the preparation of an inventory of the resource to determine its physical development potential. This establishes an upper limit on the amount of recreation use that a site can sustain based on the amount of physical resource that can be developed for recreational purposes. Once the carrying capacity is established and resources are developed to that level, recreation use is kept within resource capability limits. This means that user controls are initiated to maintain the quality of the resource. Thus, in this approach, forecasts of recreation consumption in the usual sense are simply not needed.

Problems arise when the resource capacity approach is applied to situations where it is inappropriate. It is important to remember that the approach applies only when known excess demand is greater than the capacity of proposed projects. However, if new sites are poorly located and equipped they may receive very low levels of use, even when there is excess demand for conveniently located or high amenity sites. In addition, the method is potentially subject to abuse whereby the agency simply *assumes* there will be excess demand in the future to justify building the site now.

## *Informed Judgment Approach*

The informed judgment approach to forecasting utilizes all of the data and analysis available, but the final estimates also are based on subjective appraisal of variables that are not measured. The resulting forecasts depend on the personality and experience of the individuals involved. At its best, the approach brings to bear the accumulated knowledge of managers and administrators. The approach was developed because quantitative methods often cannot directly incorporate the special insights and the informed judgments of those involved with management of recreation sites. No statistical method can forecast the influence of variables explicitly excluded from the analysis. Managers can contribute a great deal to forecasting the use of a recreation site or planning unit. They often know the history of the particular recreation site and region, observe changing recreation use patterns, understand resource capabilities, and can subjectively evaluate regional political and economic conditions that are likely to prevail at some future time.

The essential advantage of the approach is that forecasts of recreation use derived from quantitative methods can be tempered by informed judgments and special individual insights. For example, informed judgment can be used to incorporate into national forecasts those regional changes that are likely to occur and to identify realistic limits such as the practical carrying capacity of resources. Moeller and Echelberger (1974) reviewed past applications of forecasting methods and concluded that the quantitative methods should take advantage of informed judgment whenever possible. For example, Hof and Kaiser (1983) relied on informed judgment in estimating some of the high, medium, and low projections of explanatory variables. All empirical approaches require informed judgment at numerous points—which data to use, what model is appropriate, how to interpret statistical results, and the like.

The Delphi method is one form of the judgment approach. It consists of a systematic survey of a group of experts asked about the determinants of future demand. The results of the first round are reported to each member of the group, and values are reestimated in subsequent rounds. A final consensus is reached, based on the most persuasive reasoning within the group. Unpredictable variables, such as the fuel situation, changes in preferences, amounts of leisure, and the effectiveness of promotion programs, obviously have an impact on future demand.

Informed judgment, by itself, is not a reliable approach to forecasting recreation consumption, and it can create special problems if relied upon too much. Individual biases can easily enter into the process, and past short-term use trends can be misinterpreted as long-run trends. Evidence also suggests that resource managers are not always able to accurately perceive consumer preferences and behavior. Moreover, rapid turnover in management personnel means that reliable, informed judgment is not always available.

## Market Survey Approach

One of the obvious methods of short-run forecasting is to ask people what they are going to do. For example, commercial market survey organizations ask households what trips they intend to take and recreation equipment they intend to purchase over the next six months or one year. These surveys can often provide a reasonable indicator of future use, but they are not as precise as quantitative forecasts. The intentions of recreation consumers seldom require much advance planning, and proposed trips are easily postponed. Nonetheless, market surveys are often useful for monitoring trends, as long as this bias is constant across survey periods.

Test marketing is another way to forecast the demand for recreation. In this approach, new recreation facilities and opportunities are introduced at a typical site, and the results analyzed to see if they are likely to be acceptable nationally. Similarly, one could test the reaction of consumers to changes in entrance fees, and thus obtain direct estimates of the price elasticity of demand. The problem is that most users of a recreation site will have chosen it without prior knowledge of the change in facilities, services, or entrance fees. Rather than change destinations, they will tend to accept the experimental conditions in the short run. One cannot be sure that the long run will show the same pattern as the two- or three-month experiments. Test marketing experiments in recreation often must be continued over two or three years to allow sufficient time for consumers to change their decisions about subsequent trips to the site with experimental conditions.

## *Extension of Past Trends*

Extension of past recreation use trends has been widely adopted as a method of forecasting future use of local, regional, and national recreation resources. The method assumes that whatever has caused recreation consumption in the past will continue to operate in the same way in the future. A time series is a set of observations of a variable, such as the number of recreation visitor days at a campground over time (number of years or months). If a time series shows regularity, we may expect that it would continue in the same manner next year and the years that follow. Using the trend in past visitor rates, we can extrapolate the series into the future. Computer programs are available that fit a curve to time-series data fed into the computer, and then produce extrapolations for future years.

A **linear trend line** means that the variable increases by a constant amount each year. For example, assume that visits to a city's parks 20 years ago were 500,000 and have increased to 1,000,000 today. Growth in number of visits from 20 years ago to the present would be 25,000 per year (= 500,000 total additional visits ÷ 20 years). With growth calculated as an annual increase by a constant absolute amount of 25,000, projected growth 10 years in the future would be a straight line drawn from 1,000,000 in the present to 1,250,000 (= [25,000 additional visits per year x 10 years] + 1,000,000 visits in the current year).

Successful forecasting requires that there be enough information within the time series to explain its behavior. Many methods of time-series analysis are extremely sophisticated, but they only use information within the series itself. Looking for regular patterns in recreation behavior is, of course, quite sensible. The method assumes that past growth trends will continue without change in the future. Clawson and Knetsch (1966) conclude that where past growth has been relatively stable, the method has often been both useful and reliable. Whatever variables are operating to produce a regular trend, the assumption is that they will continue to be effective in the future. However, the method should not be relied upon for long-run projections. Estimates based on a constant growth rate tend to become unrealistic in the long run, due to changes in the determinants of demand. However, for short-run forecasts, up to perhaps five years, linear trend analysis may yield more accurate estimates than other methods, and its simplicity has much to commend it.

# Advanced Statistical and Demand-Based Forecasting Methods

There are several techniques which make more systematic use of a wider range of variables including single variable and multiple variable regression. A particularly powerful multiple regression approach is to estimate a TCM demand curve and use that to forecast future visitation as well as benefits.

## *Single Variable Regression Method*

A parsimonious statistical approach to forecasting is to look for a variable that acts as a good barometer for all of the determinants of demand that influences future consumption of recreation. A barometer measures the changes in atmospheric pressure which takes place *before* the weather changes. Similarly, some economic variables are considered **leading indicators** which change direction before consumption of recreation. For example, changes in population, income, leisure time, and travel have been used to forecast upswings or downswings in recreation demand. To apply this method, information on the level of consumption for a series of past years is plotted against one important determinant of demand, such as income. Then, through the application of a statistical technique known as least squares regression, we obtain a line that "best fits" the relationship between consumption and income.

A number of past studies have used this approach, as it does have a distinct advantage over simple trend analysis. For example, one might estimate that use has been increasing at 10% a year in the past. With trend analysis, one would simply use this as the estimate for future use. However, if use was rising at 10% a year due to rapid in-migration of population, and that migration was expected to slow down, this trend forecast would be in error. The simple regression approach would estimate an explicit relationship between population growth rate and past visitation. Once this regression is estimated, then separately obtained estimates of future population growth would be input into the regression equation. From this, a forecast of future use that explicitly accounts for a slowing in population growth would be calculated. The major drawback of simple regression is that only one explanatory variable can be considered at a time. Often, more than just one variable is changing in ways that could either reinforce the other variable or partially offset it. For example, while population growth rate may be slowing, income might be increasing. Thus, the forecasting model needs to expand to incorporate this complexity.

## *Multiple Regression Method of Forecasting*

The federal guidelines recommend that forecasts of future recreation use be based on multiple regressions, which provide coefficients indicating how much each of the explanatory variables causes demand to vary. Chapter 6 provided a detailed discussion of multiple regression and the approach was used in Chapter 9 in the TCM. Multiplying the projected values of the explanatory variables by their regression coefficients and summing the results often provides the best available forecasts of future demand. The approach provides decision makers with reasonably accurate predictions of the amount and type of recreation use that an area is likely to receive at a particular level of facility development and price. Changes in several socioeconomic characteristics of the population, user preferences, facilities, management policy, recreation supply, price, and other variables can be incorporated into the model to determine their potential effects on consumption. In short, the approach shows the reasons why future demand will change. This means that if one or more of the determinants of demand is expected to change in future years, its effect on consumption can be easily estimated.

The technique relies upon projections of the determinants of demand, such as population, income, age, price of substitutes, tastes and preferences, and other traditional demand shifters. The Bureau of the Census, U.S. Department of Commerce, routinely prepares long-run forecasts for some of these values. An advantage of the uniform application of recognized and acceptable sources is that any two studies can be compared. However, other values are less readily available and must be estimated by the individuals conducting the studies. Faulty projections of explanatory variables may introduce some error in the forecasts of recreation consumption. The following provides an example of forecasting future visitation using a demand equation.

The approach basically assumes that the relationship between demand and its determinants, as shown by their regression coefficients, will remain sufficiently stable so that inserted changes in their values will accurately predict the future. These models implicitly assume that the variables determining recreation behavior in the future will be the same as those at the time of the study. Most models also implicitly assume a constant relationship between demand and recreation facility supply over time. Thus, the method cannot foresee the effect of large changes in preferences and technology. Technological advance will continue to influence recreation consumption. Major breakthroughs are possible in clothing and equipment. Entire new sports will develop. This was evident with the emergence of windsurfing in the 1980s and mountain biking in the 1990s. While it is important to make careful forecasts to guide recreation economic decisions, forecasts of visitor use more than 20 years out into the future provide, at best, order of magnitude estimates of likely use levels.

Also, it is important to remember that forecasts based on national participation in recreation activities cannot be used to estimate the recreation use of particular recreation sites. It would not be correct to assume that all recreation areas providing facilities for a particular activity will receive an identical proportion of use. There are several reasons why facilities do not receive similar use intensity. The amount of recreation consumed differs between areas depending on characteristics of the population served, climatic variation, and transportation available. Different recreation areas vary in quality which affects their attractiveness. Finally, the supply of substitute recreation facilities within a particular region will influence the use of a particular recreation site.

## Single Equation Multiple Regression Approaches

There are basically two steps in this approach. In the first step, a time-series regression is estimated where visitation to an existing site over time is used as the dependent variable in the multiple regression. Explanatory variables should include all of the determinants of demand described previously. The regression can be estimated with a linear or log form of the independent variables. Variables consistently insignificant may be dropped to simplify the second step. In this second step, future values of the independent variables are multiplied by the coefficients to arrive at a future use estimate:

Step 1 (regression estimate):

$$\text{Annual trips} = 10{,}000 + 1.5(\text{County population}) + 0.001(\text{Per capita income}) - 5(\text{Average age})$$

(Equation 13-1)

Step 2 (insert future values and calculate use):

$$\text{Year 2020} = 10{,}000 + 1.5(100{,}000) + 0.001(15{,}000) - 5(30) = 159{,}865$$
$$\text{Year 2040} = 10{,}000 + 1.5(130{,}000) + 0.001(17{,}000) - 5(35) = 204{,}842$$

(Equation 13-2)

### *Forecasting From an Individual Observation Travel Cost Method Demand Function*

In multiple regression forecasting, one simply predicts shifts in the demand curve for a recreation site or activity. If incomes increase, for example, consumers may decide that they can afford to engage in more recreation and thus, increase the number of recreation trips, even if travel cost and other determinants of demand remain the same. Increases in income normally shift demand curves outward to the right. Figure 13-2 shows two demand curves for the recreation use of a recreation area: (1) demand in the current year (from Chapter 6), and (2) demand forecast 25 years in the future. A shift from one demand curve to another indicates a change in one or more of the nonprice variables in the demand function. The forecasted shift in the demand curve would be caused by the expected changes in all of the independent variables.

You will recall from the discussion in Chapter 6 that demand functions for recreation sites are estimated using standard statistical procedures for multiple regression. This approach is used because it fits an equation to a set of observed data providing statistical estimates of the effect of each variable, holding other variables in the demand function constant. The most valuable information provided by statistical demand functions is the regression coefficient for each of the determinants of demand. The regression coefficients provide an estimate of the change

**Figure 13-2. Forecasting Shifts in the Demand for Trips to a Recreation Area by a Representative Individual User**

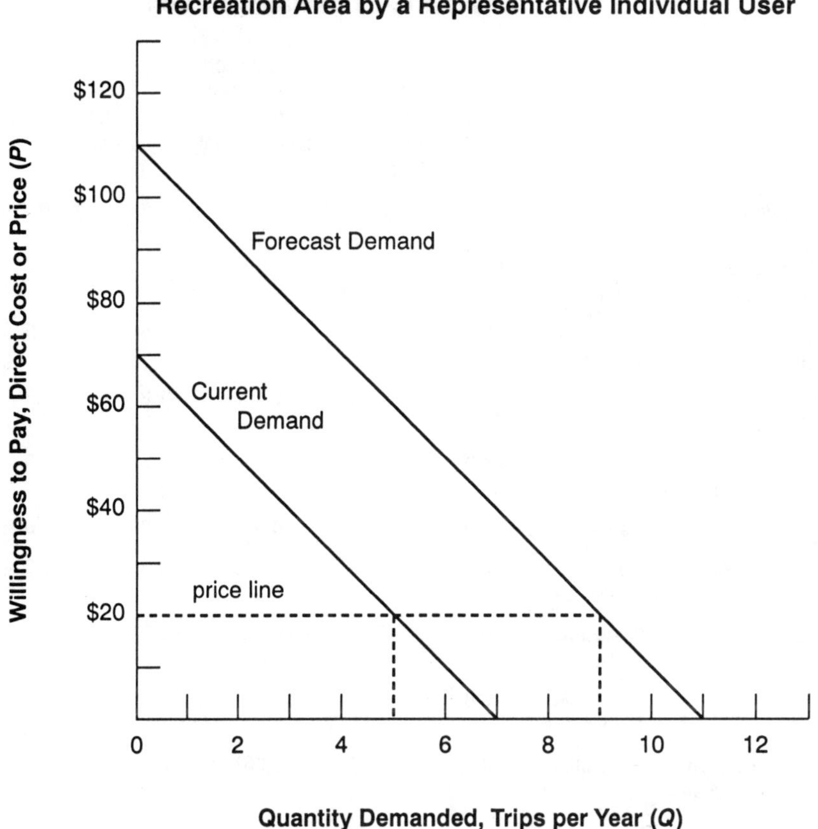


in number of trips to the recreation site associated with a one-unit change in each of these independent variables. For example, Column 3 of Table 13-4 (page 236) indicates that individual demand for trips to a recreation site falls by 0.1 with each $1 increase in average direct cost or price. The coefficient for income indicates that when all other variables are constant, a $1,000 increase in income will cause the quantity demanded to increase by 0.1 per year.

The first step in forecasting future consumption from a demand function is to estimate the expected changes in the average values of each of the determinants of demand. Assume that careful long-run forecasts of these values are available from the Bureau of Census and other agencies. On this basis, the direct cost or price is expected to increase from $20 to $24 per trip in constant dollars. Consumer income is expected to increase from $25,000 to $30,000 in constant dollars. Travel time is expected to fall from three to two hours with improved roads, autos, and increased speed limits. The price of substitutes is expected to increase

**Table 13-4. Forecasting Individual Demand for Trips to a Recreation Area Using a Demand Function**

| Independent Variables | Units | Estimated Mean Values of the Independent Variables: Current (1) | Forecast (2) | Regression Coefficients for the Independent Variables (3) | Estimated Total Demand, Trips per Year: Current (4) | Forecast (5) |
|---|---|---|---|---|---|---|
| Direct Cost or Price | Dollars per Trip | 20.0 | 24.0 | –0.100 | –2.0 | –2.4 |
| Consumer Income | Thousand Dollars | 25.0 | 30.0 | 0.100 | 2.5 | 3.0 |
| Travel Time Round Trip | Hours | 3.0 | 2.0 | –0.400 | –1.2 | –0.8 |
| Price of Substitute Sites | Dollars per Trip | 24.0 | 30.0 | 0.054 | 1.3 | 1.6 |
| Age | Years | 25.0 | 30.0 | –0.088 | –2.2 | –2.6 |
| Quality of Site | 5-Point Scale | 4.0 | 3.0 | 0.625 | 2.5 | 1.8 |
| County Population | Thousand Persons | 200.0 | 400.0 | 0.025 | 5.0 | 10.0 |
| Taste or Preference | 1 = Active 0 = Passive | 0.8 | 0.9 | 1.250 | 1.0 | 1.1 |
| Daily Utilization Capacity Ratio | 1 = Optimal | 0.9 | 1.2 | –2.667 | –2.4 | –3.2 |
| Constant | | | | | 0.5 | 0.5 |
| Total Demand | | | | | 5.0 | 9.1 |

from $24 to $30 per trip in constant dollars. The average age of users is expected to increase from 25 to 30 years, with the gradual aging of the population. Quality of the site is expected to deteriorate somewhat with the number of users exceeding the biological carrying capacity of the natural environment. Daily utilization of capacity is expected to exceed the economic optimum by 20%. The population of counties where users reside is expected to double in the next 25 years. Individual preferences for active recreation are expected to increase with the rising concern for physical fitness and personal health. These forecasted values are shown in Column 2 of Table 13-4.

The second step in forecasting future consumption from a demand function is to multiply the average values for each of the determinants of demand by their regression coefficients and sum them all (including the value of the constant term in the demand function, which does not change). The result of this procedure is shown as Column 5 in Table 13-4. The bottom line (sum) shows that demand for trips to the site is forecast to increase from five trips per year per visitor currently to nine trips per year per visitor 25 years in the future.

The final step in forecasting future consumption from a demand function is to convert this estimate for the representative individual user to total annual use by multiplying it by the total number of users. For example, if it is known that 100,000 individuals currently use the site, total demand is estimated as 500,000 recreation days per year. Assume that a separate study has estimated that 100,000 individuals will use the site in 25 years; then the combined demand forecast is 910,000 recreation days (= 9.1 x 100,000).

## *Forecasting From Elasticities*

Table 13-5 (page 238) illustrates an alternative procedure to the one just described. Identical results can be obtained by forecasting individual demand for trips to a recreation area using elasticities of demand. Instead of using the average values and regression coefficients, the average values are converted to percentage changes and the regression coefficients are converted to elasticities. You will recall from the discussion in Chapter 8 that elasticity of demand is defined as the percentage change in quantity consumed (number of trips) that is caused by a percentage change in each of the determinants of demand. It is a ratio of two percentages—the change in demand that results from a change in an independent variable.

Elasticities for each of the variables in the demand function for trips to an area are shown in Column 2 of Table 13-5 (page 238). The percentage change in the average value of each of the variables in the next 25 years is shown in Column 1 of the table. The procedure is to add one to the forecasted percentage and multiply this sum by the elasticity to obtain the percentage change in demand caused by each variable. (One is added so that the resulting product yields the new total, not just the change from the previous total.) This is shown in Column 3. The next step is to multiply the percentage change in demand attributed to each variable by the current five trips per year and sum them all, as shown in Column 4. The bottom line of this column is nine trips per year for the representative individual. This result is identical to the previous procedure presented in Table 13-4.

Much information is available on elasticities of demand. Many of the major statistical problems associated with the measurement of demand for recreation were solved early in the 1960s. Since that time, large quantities of data on demand elasticities have been accumulated. Even where information is not already available, it is often possible to obtain it without great cost or difficulty. The appropriate methods for calculating elasticities of demand were presented in Chapter 8. If you have access to the computer printout of a demand function for a recreation site, elasticities of demand are usually shown for each independent variable, at the point

**Table 13-5. Forecasting Individual Demand for Trips to a Recreation Area Using Elasticities of Demand**

| Independent Variables | Units | Forecast Percent Change in Mean Values of the Variables (1) | Elasticities of Demand (2) | Estimated Percent Change in Total Demand, Trips Per Year (3) | Estimated Total Demand, Trips Per Year (4) |
|---|---|---|---|---|---|
| Direct Cost or Price | Dollars per Trip | 0.200 | –0.40 | –0.480 | –2.4 |
| Consumer Income | Thousand Dollars | 0.200 | 0.50 | 0.600 | 3.0 |
| Travel Time Round Trip | Hours | –0.330 | –0.24 | –0.160 | –0.8 |
| Price of Substitute Sites | Dollars per Trip | 0.250 | 0.26 | 0.325 | 1.6 |
| Age | Years | 0.200 | –0.44 | –0.528 | –2.6 |
| Quality of Site | 5-Point Scale | –0.250 | 0.50 | 0.375 | 1.8 |
| County Population | Thousand Persons | 1.000 | 1.00 | 2.000 | 10.0 |
| Taste or Preference | 1 = Active 0 = Passive | 0.125 | 0.20 | 0.225 | 1.1 |
| Daily Utilization Capacity Ratio | 1 = Optimal | 0.330 | –0.48 | –0.638 | –3.2 |
| Constant | | | | | 0.5 |
| Total Demand | | | | | 9.1 |

where the quantity demanded and each independent variable are at their mean values. No additional computation is necessary when expected changes in the independent variables are small. However, you are more likely to have access to a published work showing the demand function for the study site or a similar site. In this case, you probably will need to compute elasticities from the information that is available.

## *Forecasting From a Zonal Travel Cost Demand Function*

The best way to forecast the future recreation use of a *new* park or existing recreation site is a zonal travel cost demand function for the region or for a similar site. This is known in the profession as forecasting from an econometric model, participation function, or use-estimating model. Potential use of a new site is the expected quantity demanded at given travel costs to the new site and the characteristics (including capacity) of the new site. Forecasts of the total recreation use should be made for each activity currently provided at other sites in the region that will be provided at the new site. The recreation use of the proposed site will depend not only on the quality of its resources and its proximity to population centers, but also on its location in relation to other sites providing similar types of recreation within the region.

Such an estimate is best made using a regional multisite travel cost method (TCM) demand equation described in Chapter 9. It can also be made by transferring a demand curve (like Equation 13-3) from an existing recreation site that is similar to the site under study (see Chapter 11 for a discussion of such benefit transfer approaches). Essentially, the coefficients from the existing site are used with the values of the independent variables for the new proposed site. The calculation is identical to the approach to calculate initial and future use.

In the zonal model, the dependent variable is trips from origin $i$ divided by the population of origin $i$ (i.e., trips per capita). In Chapter 9 we demonstrated how to use this model to estimate current recreation use and economic benefits. The model can also be used to forecast future visitation and future benefits at an existing, new or proposed site. To illustrate, consider the following equation which is a zonal travel cost model with income as a demographic variable:

$$\text{Trips}_i/\text{Pop}_i = 1 - 0.075(\text{Dist}_i) + 0.001Y \qquad \text{(Equation 13-3)}$$

where $\text{Trips}_i$ is trips from county $i$, $\text{Pop}_i$ is population of county $i$, $\text{Dist}_i$ is round trip distance from county $i$ to the recreation site, and $Y$ is county per capita income.

To apply this equation to forecast future use to the year 2030, the analyst would insert an estimate of each county's income in the year 2030 (which might be obtained from the state demographer's office). For each county, future income would be multiplied by the coefficient for income (0.001), added to the product of their distance to the site times the distance coefficient and then added to the constant term. For example, if per capita income in County A is expected to be $19,000 in 2030 and this county is 100 miles from the site we would calculate:

$$\text{Trips}_i/\text{Pop}_i = 1 - [0.075(100 \times 2)] + 0.001(19{,}000) = 1 - 15 + 19 = 5 \qquad \text{(Equation 13-4)}$$

Therefore, we would predict trips per capita from County A of five in the year 2030. To convert trips per capita into trips from County A, we must multiply by the population of County A. Since we desire an estimate of trips in the year 2030 we would multiply by the estimated county population in 2030.

Thus, if the county population is expected to be 10,000 in the year 2030 our estimate of trips from this county would be 50,000. This process would be repeated for each county in the market area and the result summed to arrive at an estimate of total site use in the year 2030. Benefits in the year 2030 can be calculated using the second stage demand curve approach discussed in Chapter 9.

Reasonably accurate forecasts of future consumption can probably be obtained from a zonal travel cost demand function. Cicchetti (1973) correctly observes that the decision-making process of consumers involves two steps: (1) whether to participate in a particular recreation activity, and (2) how much to participate per year. He suggests that we adopt a two-step approach to forecasting recreation consumption. The first equation would predict the probability of an individual's choosing to participate in a particular recreation activity. The second would predict the number of trips per year by the average individual participant. This two-step approach may improve future applications of the multiple regression approach to forecasting consumption of recreation. The reason is that different variables are likely to influence one decision more than the other. For example, age and income influence the decision whether to participate at all. But price, leisure time, and the availability of substitutes may be more important in determining the number of trips to a recreation site. In the application of this approach, the forecast would represent the sum of the two multiple regressions.

## *Chapter 14*

# Regional Economic Impact

This chapter introduces the concept of regional economic impact of recreation management and allocation decisions on business sales, jobs, net income and tax revenues; summarizes the results of empirical studies of the regional economic impact of recreation; and discusses policy implications for recreation economic decisions.

Economists distinguish between the primary benefits and secondary impacts of recreation economic decisions. In previous chapters, we considered the primary benefits to individual users of recreation programs. Substantial insight into decision making was gained by treating the problem as though there were no other effects. Understanding recreation economic decisions of individual consumers provides the foundation for comparing benefits and costs. The net benefits of individual consumers represents the social benefits of public recreation programs. The consumer surplus of individual users may not be spent in the region of the recreation site, as it is real income retained by the recreationists. Consumer surplus is a measure of the economic value that people receive from recreation activities and resources.

In this chapter, we introduce another related concept—regional economic impact. It is defined as the economic activity generated by the recreational use of resources. It is a measure of the secondary effects of the actual expenditures by individual consumers and managers of private and public recreation resources. These are the regional economic impacts on sales revenue, jobs, net income and tax revenues. The essential idea is that the primary costs to individual consumers and managers become secondary gains, in part, to the regional economy supplying recreation goods and services. Studies of regional economic impact do not measure the value to the primary users of a recreation site, but rather the gains to those who are involved in supplying the primary users with goods and services.

Every local community is concerned about regional economic development to create job opportunities, raise incomes, and contribute to the community's social viability and general economic prosperity. The hundreds of local economic development organizations in each state are testimony to the importance local business owners place on regional economic impacts. These organizations cooperate with the state and federal government in programs aimed at attracting new employers and retaining current ones. Examples of economic development activities in resort areas include acquiring parks, open space, upgrading sewer and water systems, roads, labor training, small business assistance, theme zoning, and storefront renovation. The goal of these efforts is to promote business growth. This traditional, or what Power (1996) calls the "rearview mirror" approach, is summarized in Figure 14-1.

In this chapter, we will examine the traditional methods used in conducting empirical studies of the regional economic impact of outdoor recreation. We also will present the results of these studies, and in particular, the policy implications for recreation economic decisions. We will close with a more recent view of what determines local economic activity.

## Impacts Versus Benefits

Economic theory and federal guidelines proscribe that regional economic impacts should be treated as income transfers in a separate account, to distinguish them from benefits that contribute to gains in economic efficiency of resource use or national economic development. Conceptually, gains of employment in one county, must be offset by reductions of employment elsewhere in the country, if there is full employment (e.g., full employment involves an unemployment rate around 3%–5%, most of this unemployment is frictional; i.e., people temporarily unemployed while they look for better jobs or move to a new job).

To see how the transfer of income and employment works, consider the decision of whether an agency should approve a proposed ski area. The developer will always tout the direct jobs the ski area "creates." The ski area will have to hire people as lift operators, ski instructors, parking lot attendants, food service personnel, and the like. But are these really new jobs to the country's economy? There are several reasons the answer to this question is no. First, where will the workers come from to work at this ski area? If there is full employment, the ski area workers will probably come from other existing (but perhaps less interesting) jobs elsewhere. Now, think about what happens if the ski area is not approved. Does it mean that all of the people who would have been employed at the ski area will not have jobs for the proposed 50-year life of the ski area? Probably not. Most of people have some kind of job to feed themselves and pay their rent.

**Figure 14-1. Traditional View of the Flow of Regional Economic Activity**

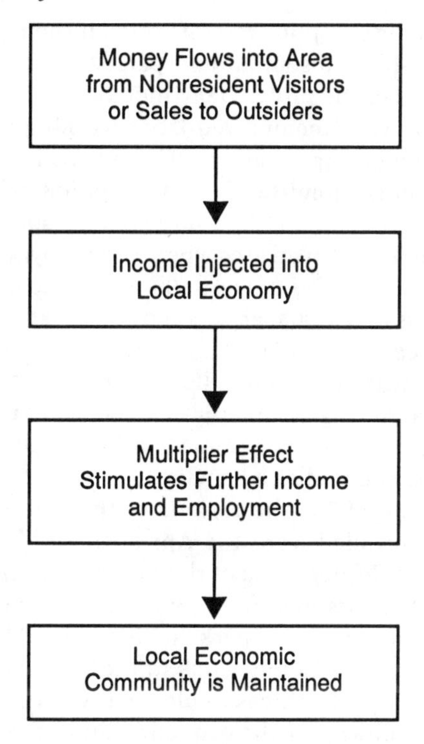


Source: Adapted from Power, 1996.

To make the transfer even more obvious, think about what happens if the new ski area is approved. Skiers will come to this new area and spend money for the services of workers employed there. But, where did the skiers' money come from? It came from reduced spending at some other ski area or in some other activity. Regions where the expenditures are withdrawn from will now need fewer workers than before the new ski area opened. The opening of a new ski area (or shopping center) simply rearranges existing spending, there is really no net gain in spending or employment in the country's economy. There may be a net gain in the community that has the new ski area, but it is an incomplete analysis to focus on that gain without recognizing there is a perfectly offsetting loss dispersed throughout the rest of the economy. Unless there is an explicit political judgment that the gain of one job in a particular county is worth more than a job lost in another county, generally employment gains "net out" in benefit-cost analysis.

## *When Impacts May Also Be Economic Benefits*

There are a few major exceptions to this rule. If the regional economy of a proposed project has substantial and persistent unemployment, then the primary benefits of the project may include the income (i.e., salaries and wages) of otherwise unemployed labor working on site in the construction of a project or improvement. These benefits will be determined at the time a project is submitted for authorization and appropriation of funds to begin construction. In the United States, substantial and persistent unemployment exists in an area when unemployment in the previous year was 6% or more; and was at least 50% above the national average for three of the previous four years, or 75% above the national average for two of the previous three years, or 100% above the national average for one of the previous two years (U.S. Water Resources Council, 1983). Even in regions qualifying as having substantial and persistent unemployment, not more than half of the labor is assumed to be supplied by unemployed workers and can be counted as a benefit.

In the 1960s and 1970s the regions of the United States in which these conditions prevailed were the Appalachian Mountains and rural portions of the Four Corners area of the Southwest. In these cases, secondary economic benefits measured by direct and indirect gains in net income from the construction of park facilities would be counted as benefits, representing real economic gains to the national economy. Aside from these regions, few other areas would qualify in most developed countries. This is not to downplay the economic importance of regional economic impacts to the economic and political considerations in the region of a park or other recreation area. Much of the political motivation for the development of public and private recreation resources represents an attempt to capture regional gains, which in many cases are reflected in large increases in property values for commercial landowners. From the viewpoint of the region in which a proposed recreation project will be located, the residents affected are concerned about the gains and losses to themselves, not to other regions or the nation as a whole. But, when federal taxpayer financing or federal lands are involved, the analysis must take a national viewpoint.

Another important exception to the rule of excluding job gains is the role of tourism in developing countries throughout the world. Eco-tourism, in particular, holds the hope of providing higher incomes to people living in poverty in Third World countries. But, for this promise to be realized, the tourist industry must make use of local labor and materials. Building a few large resort hotels with United States–based construction crews and imported materials will contribute little to the local economy. Operating large resort hotels that import all their food and supplies from the United States will do little to stimulate local economies in undeveloped countries. Dispersed eco-tourism that utilizes local foods, labor and materials will have a higher local value added. This will make a sizeable difference in the local income generated and in the spin-off effects (called multiplier effects) on the rest of the local economy.

However, on a global scale most secondary gains to a particular region or country will be offset by actual or potential losses elsewhere, because these projects do not affect the total amount of consumer spending. This means that recreation programs redistribute income from other regions, consumption sectors, and the nation, to the regional economy with the parks and other recreation sites. Whether such redistribution is desirable is a political decision beyond the scope of economics. The essential point is that these changes in the distribution of income represent transfers of income and not social benefits. What is a gain to the local region may be a loss to another region, and the national economic well-being may not change. Economists refer to such transfers of income as pecuniary impacts. This transfer also illustrates the zero-sum nature of chamber of commerce–like promotions in one town versus another: One's gain is often the other's loss.

## Usefulness of Regional Economic Impact Studies

Nonetheless, regional economic impact studies provide the states with useful information about the social and economic effects of proposed new projects and programs. Beginning in the 1970s, many such regional economic studies were undertaken as part of Environmental Impact Statements to comply with the National Environmental Protection Act (NEPA). The law requires that all major projects, defined as those having a significant effect on environmental quality, include information on social and economic effects. As a result, environmental impact studies have included a study of the regional economic impact in the immediate vicinity of the project or park. These studies show the effect of the construction and operation of the proposed project and of the change in tourist consumption. Included are the estimated changes in direct and indirect output or sales of each industry and trade in the region. Income and employment effects are either estimated directly or as a proportion of the added output or sales. Population effects are estimated on the basis of the number of new jobs created. The effects on tax revenues and expenditures for social services are estimated from changes in population or in output. Effects on environmental quality, such as air and water pollution, can be estimated from technical studies of the effect of changes in population and output on aspects of environmental quality.

The distinguishing characteristic of a regional economic impact study is that it is one approach to answer questions about the distribution of economic gains and losses. How much does an industry gain or lose? How is the change in income to various economic groups affected by alternative park development proposals? Thus, a regional economic impact study answers a different question than does a benefit-cost study. Managers and officials often confuse the two types of studies because both report results in dollars. But it is important to remember the dollars from a regional impact study are a measure of effects on local businesses, whereas dollars from a benefit-cost analysis measures the effect on the visitors.

Regional economic studies are also needed to counter similar studies by those wishing to develop natural resources in a way that would preclude recreation. It is common for logging, mining or real estate companies to use models described in this chapter to claim their activity creates or supports $x$ number of jobs. As discussed previously, this is quite misleading. Unfortunately, the myth of *job creation* is often influential with local county commissioners who either do not recognize it is just a transfer or do not care if their county happens to be on the gaining end of the transfer. In these situations, it is important for recreation managers to be able to provide comparable estimates of jobs supported by the recreational use of natural resources, such as standing forests or instream flow. To this end, the National Park Service has developed a Money Generation Model that will be reviewed later in this chapter.

Studies of regional economic impacts have often emphasized the secondary gains and failed to count the secondary losses or costs. We should remember that local economic impacts involve not only pluses (gains) but also minuses (losses), which should be subtracted from the gains to find the net regional impact. Millard and Fischer (1979) reviewed several categories of local secondary costs. First, development of a recreation site usually means that the natural resources cannot be used for other purposes, such as agriculture and forestry. These lost opportunities lead to foregone local income and employment in those industries. Second, increases in local tax rates may be necessary to provide medical, fire protection, and police services to the additional tourists entering the area. The seasonal nature of tourist demand for these public services may lead to underutilization by regional residents during the balance of the year. Third, the markets for private recreation land, housing, repair and maintenance, food, clothing, and general merchandise may be bid up by tourists who are willing to pay higher prices than local residents can afford to pay. Fourth, increased congestion on the roads and in local businesses may result in inconvenience and frustration to local residents and adversely alter local lifestyles. Finally, many individuals affected by higher rents, congestion, and poorer public services may not gain from the additional employment opportunities, increased business sales, larger profits, and rising property values. In fact, growth may destroy the very qualities that attracted current residents to the area in the first place. Thus, regional economic studies should provide a balanced accounting of positive and negative effects of tourism.

## Size of the Impact Region

Obviously the relevant region of economic impact extends beyond the boundary of the park or recreation site. The geographic area depends on the type of park decision, its magnitude, and the size of the relevant regional economy associated with a particular site. The geographic extent of the appropriate region depends on the policy question and from where a bulk of the tourist support services are coming. In most cases the minimum size area is the county or group of counties surrounding the site that contain the major cities providing lodging, food services, equipment rental and transportation (e.g., airport, rental cars). In the case of a state park, the state legislature or governor's office may primarily be interested in impacts to the entire state economy as a whole, even though a majority of the impacts occur in the counties surrounding the site. As shown in the following impact models developed, the larger the impact area, the larger will be the multiplier effects, as a greater proportion of the transactions occur within a larger impact region.

In practical applications, it has been shown that little is lost by defining functional economic areas to include combinations of two to six entire counties, thus making standard census data sources useful to the analysis. The functional economic area for Yosemite National Park, for example, includes the five counties immediately adjacent to and surrounding its perimeter.

## Traditional Regional Economic Analysis and Multipliers

The most important concept, with respect to regional economic impact, and the most elusive, is the multiplier. It is defined simply as the total effects (direct plus indirect) divided by the direct effects:

$$\text{Multiplier} = \frac{\text{Direct + Indirect effects}}{\text{Direct effects}} \qquad \text{(Equation 14-1)}$$

It is not difficult to comprehend the direct effect on the sales of businesses from which park visitors and the park agency purchase goods and services. However, the concept of indirect effects may be more elusive. It is simply the effect on the sales of these and other businesses in the region, as a portion of the recreation dollars are spent and respent, leading to a multiple increase in the sales of all businesses in the region. For example, as a rafting business expands to meet increased tourist demand (the direct effect), it must purchase more sandwiches from local supermarkets (indirect effect). This causes local supermarkets to purchase more bread from bakeries and bakeries to purchase more flour from grain mills, which are further indirect effects.

Each industry or sector of the economy has its own output multiplier effect. The size of that multiplier will depend on how much of its inputs it purchases locally from other businesses. The Type I industry multiplier is defined as:

$$\text{Type I industry multiplier} = \frac{1}{1 - (\text{Fraction of industry } i\text{'s inputs from all other industries in the area})} \quad \text{(Equation 14-2)}$$

The Type II industry multiplier adds in the effect of purchases from local households in the form of labor (e.g., wages):

$$\text{Type II industry multiplier} = \frac{1}{1 - (\text{Fraction of industry } i\text{'s inputs from all other industries + Households in the area})} \quad \text{(Equation 14-3)}$$

One can also develop an approximate general income multiplier for a local economy. As a general rule (Coppedge, 1977), the income multiplier is determined by three factors:

a. percentage of new income a consumer will spend rather than save;
b. percentage of consumer expenditures made in the local area; and
c. percentage of business expenditures made in the local area.

Thus, the formula for this general income multiplier is:

$$\text{General income multiplier} = \frac{1}{1 - abc} \quad \text{(Equation 14-4)}$$

If $a$ equals 90%, as is typically the case, and $b$ equals 70% and c equals 40% then the general income multiplier is:

$$\text{General income multiplier} = \frac{1}{1 - (0.90 \times 0.70 \times 0.40)} = 1.34 \quad \text{(Equation 14-5)}$$

This means that each $1 of new income injected into this local economy from outside the area will generate a total of $1.34 of income once it is spent and respent.

The difference between total sales and local value added is defined as **leakage,** which is the payment for wholesale and retail products and services brought in from outside the region, plus the interest, profits, rents, and taxes paid outside the region. Of course, only part of the income earned by residents of the region is respent locally. Some is saved, taxed away, or spent outside the region. Thus, we could also say that the multiplier is equal to one divided by the percent of regional sales that are leaked outside the region (i.e., lost to businesses in the region).

If firms buy more of their inputs locally, the multiplier will increase. For example, if local businesses made 60% of their purchases locally, then the multiplier would increase to 1.60. From these examples, you can see that you should be quite suspicious of anyone suggesting multiplier effects larger than two in rural counties (Coppedge, 1977). Multipliers as large as two or three are possible at the state level, since a majority of businesses and households spend nearly all of their discretionary incomes within their own state (especially in the West, where states are quite large).

Figure 14-2 (page 250) illustrates the multiplier process. It shows the direct and indirect impact on regional output of an increase of $100 in direct demand for recreation goods and services when 40% of the output is produced from inputs purchased locally. The important thing to note is that the portion of recreation dollars that becomes local income is spent and respent through six rounds, at which time their effect approaches zero. Most of the indirect effect of tourist spending occurs during the first calendar year in about five to six rounds. The first-round direct impact on the regional economy is an increase of $100 in demand for recreation goods and services.

Note that the income multiplier in this example is 1.66, which is equal to what would have been calculated had we taken $1 \div (1 - 0.4)$. Actual studies of the regional economic impact of recreation development rely on input-output analysis to obtain a more precise estimate of the multiplier effect. Input-output procedures will be illustrated in a later section of this chapter. It is sufficient here to understand the concept and how it operates.

## *A Multitude of Multipliers*

There are several different types of multipliers. Three general categories are (a) output multipliers, (b) income multipliers, and (c) employment multipliers. While all three of these are the ratio of total effects to direct effects, the numerical values pertain to their respective concepts of output, income and employment respectively. Thus, an employment multiplier would be applied if the analyst wished to know the total number of jobs generated from a park hiring a given number of additional year-round employees. Bergstrom, Cordell, Watson and Ashely (1990) in their study of state parks found employment multipliers (ranging from 1.37 to 1.81) were considerably less than income multipliers (ranging from 2.01 to 2.83).

**Figure 14-2. Direct and Indirect Impact on Regional Economy From Increase in $100 in Demand for Recreation Goods and Services**

| Round | Expenditure (1) | Paid to Nonlocal Suppliers (2 = 60% x Col. 1) | Local Production (Income) (3 = 40% x Col. 1) |
|---|---|---|---|
| 1st | $100.00 | $60.00 | $40.00 |
| 2nd | $40.00 | $24.00 | $16.00 |
| 3rd | $16.00 | $9.60 | $6.40 |
| 4th | $6.40 | $3.84 | $2.56 |
| 5th | $2.56 | $1.53 | $1.02 |
| 6th | $1.02 | $0.61 | $0.41 |
| | Total Income | | $66.39 |
| | Income Multiplier | | $66.39 ÷ $40 = 1.66 |

In addition, some employment multipliers are actually coefficients that show the total effect (direct and indirect) from an additional $1 million in sales. These are typical of the U.S. Department of Commerce's Bureau of Economic Analysis Regional Multipliers. Thus, if the analyst estimated that a new park would generate $10 million in sales, then the employment coefficient would be multiplied by $10 million.

Output multipliers are primarily useful for estimating changes in sales tax revenue. Otherwise, knowing how total sales volume in a county changes with a proposal is not very informative, since it tells us little about how much of that sales volume is actually retained as income in the local community.

## *Estimates of Recreation Multipliers*

State level output or sales multipliers for expenditures on recreation goods and services average about 2.0 and range from 1.5 to 2.6 in the United States. Table 14-1 shows the results of several regional economic impact studies conducted during the last three decades.

**Table 14-1. Regional Output or Sales Multipliers for Expenditures on Recreation Goods and Services, United States**

| Regions | Sources | Types of Recreation Development | Output or Sales Multipliers |
|---|---|---|---|
| Teton County, Wyoming | Rajender, Harston and Blood (1967) | Tourism | 1.46 |
| Southwest Counties, Wyoming | Kite and Schulze (1967) | Fishing at Flaming Gorge Reservoir | 2.07 |
| Sullivan County, Pennsylvania | Gamble (1965) | Summer Homes | 1.60 |
| Itasca County, Minnesota | Hughes (1970) | Summer Resorts | 2.23 |
| Ely County, Minnesota | Lichty and Steinnes (1982) | Boundary Waters Canoe Area, Tourism | 2.23 |
| Wadsworth County, Wisconsin | Kalter and Lord (1968) | Tourism | 1.87 |
| Baldwin County, Alabama | Main (1971) | Tourism | 2.58 |
| Montana | Haroldson (1975) | Winter Resorts | 2.40 |
| Grand County, Colorado | Rhody and Lovegrove (1970) | Hunting and Fishing | 2.00 |
| Colorado Counties | McKean and Nobe (1984) | Nonresident and Resident Hunting and Fishing | 1.75<br>2.60 |
| Yaquina Bay, Oregon | Stoevener, Retting, and Reiling (1974) | Fishing | 2.06 |
| Texas | Goldbloom (1988) | State Parks | 2.70 |
| North Carolina | Bergstrom, Cordell, Watson and Ashley (1990) | Hanging Rock Park | 1.92 |
| Georgia | Bergstrom, Cordell, Watson and Ashley (1990) | Unicoi Park | 1.85 |
| South Carolina | Bergstrom, Cordell, Watson and Ashley (1990) | Myrtle Beach | 1.80 |
| Tennessee | Bergstrom, Cordell, Watson and Ashley (1990) | 3 State Parks | 2.37 |

Since regional multipliers are expressed as a ratio, changes in the general price level do not appreciably affect their application to current regional economic development problems. Thus, we would not expect a regional output multiplier from an input-output study in 1970 to be significantly different from a study in 1980 or 1990 for the same recreation activity and region. However, some resort areas have experienced substantial growth, causing the relationships between industries and multipliers to change. In areas where recreation visitation is growing, local value added will increase, as it will become profitable to meet this growing demand locally. Thus, the tourist multipliers will also rise over time. This is probably best illustrated in the case of Moab, Utah. When the area's primary attractions were the National Parks and rafting, a great deal of food and beverage was imported. As mountain biking gained popularity, resulting in several hundred thousand more visitors each year, two microbreweries opened in Moab. The reverse would be expected for declining areas.

The empirical results of past studies provide several clues to the reasons multipliers vary in amount. Size of the region has an important effect; for example, a typical county may have a recreation multiplier of 1.6 compared to a five-county region with 1.9; the entire state, 2.7; and the United States, 3.0. This reflects the fact that the value added within a region rises as its geographic area is increased and a smaller proportion of the expenditures on recreation goods and services are purchased outside of the region. Wholesalers are more likely to be located within a region as its size increases. The manufacture and processing of recreation goods and services also are more likely to be included in the region, as are the individual owners of business outlets, and corporate headquarters.

Table 14-2 illustrates another important reason why regional multipliers vary. They represent a weighted average of the multipliers for each type of business from which tourists purchase goods and services. Over half of the direct spending by recreation visitors is typically for retail (food in stores, miscellaneous supplies such as film or sunscreen) and automotive products (gasoline). Businesses selling these products to recreation visitors purchase more of their inputs outside of the county than do some other businesses (e.g., very few recreation areas have oil refineries producing gasoline). Consequently, their business output or sales multipliers (1.80 and 1.76) are low. If a large proportion of expenditures by recreation visitors is for services, such as lodging, restaurant-prepared food and beverages, which have higher output or sales multipliers (2.41, 2.19 and 2.18 respectively), then the regional multiplier will be higher because it represents a weighted average for all recreation expenditures.

Thus, regional multipliers vary among types of recreation activities. Day users of a park who bring a picnic lunch from home have very low impact on regional output or sales multipliers. Recreation visitors who stay overnight in campgrounds typically spend little or no money for services, lodging, or restaurant meals, and as a result, have low regional

**Table 14-2. Distribution of Direct Expenditures for Hunting and Fishing Among Industries With Multipliers for Output and Employment**

| Industries | Percent of Direct Expenditures | Output or Sales Multiplier | Employment Multiplier (Jobs per $1 Million) |
|---|---|---|---|
| Retail & Wholesale Trade | 27.8 | 1.80 | 59 |
| Services | 15.1 | 2.41 | 44 |
| Lodging | 8.5 | 2.19 | 97 |
| Eating & Drinking | 20.3 | 2.18 | 97 |
| Automotive | 27.8 | 1.76 | 63 |
| Communication & Transportation | 0.5 | 2.05 | 31 |
| Total | 100.0 | 2.00 | 69 |

Source: Rhody and Lovegrove, 1970.

multipliers. Tourists who stay overnight in resort lodges, eat in restaurants, and purchase local services have much higher regional multiplier effects. Owners of seasonal homes have higher multipliers because they purchase repairs from the local construction industry and they pay local property taxes. Downhill ski resorts have higher regional multipliers than Wilderness Areas. This difference illustrates the distinction between benefits to the user versus economic activity in the economy. Cross-country skiers in Wilderness Areas spend very little money, and hence retain most of the benefit of cross-country skiing as consumer surplus (i.e., as real income). Downhill skiers pay for everything from parking, lift tickets, lunches, lessons, and equipment rental. They generate a great deal of economic activity, but often have very little consumer surplus left over. That is, downhill skiers' net willingness to pay may in fact be much smaller (e.g., $150 – $140 = $10) than cross-country skiers' (e.g., $60 – $10 = $50). Economic benefits to the participants may be higher for cross-country skiing than for downhill skiing, even though more economic activity is stimulated at the downhill ski area.

The recreation industry tends to have somewhat lower income multipliers than agriculture, forestry, or light manufacturing industry. For example, logging multipliers range from 2.2 to 3.0 and average about 2.5, while sawmill multipliers range from 2.5 to 3.1. However, in many rural counties with substantial recreation industries, the somewhat lower regional multiplier effect of tourist spending is more than offset by the large absolute level of tourist expenditures. For example, in Teton County, Wyoming, tourist spending to visit Jackson Hole Ski Area and Teton National Park accounts for nearly two-thirds of the regional economy. Ranching and forestry are relatively minor, despite their more favorable regional multipliers. In addition, employment multipliers are often much higher for recreation, since it requires more labor per dollar of expenditures than does mining, which is quite capital intensive (Douglas and Harpman, 1995).

To obtain an accurate estimate of the total effect, the multiplier must be applied to the appropriate sales or spending figure. Johnson and Moore (1993), as well as the National Park Service, point out that only expenditures of nonlocal visitors should be counted. It is the nonlocal visitors who bring new money into the impact region. When local residents visit the park, often they have simply reallocated spending from one location or industry in the impact region to visiting the park. Thus, their spending does not represent a new final demand in the regional economy. It is also important to apply the multiplier only to visitor expenditures that occur in the impact region. Thus, expenditures by nonlocal visitors for gasoline, food and supplies purchased at or near home, would have no effect on the impact region. Therefore, visitor expenditure surveys must delineate expenditures made at home from expenditures made en route versus those made within the impact region.

## Input-Output Method

The purpose of this section is to describe briefly the input-output method of estimating the multiplier. The distinguishing characteristic of the method is that it provides information on the direct and indirect impact of tourist spending on the output or sales of each industry in the local economy. This provides a more precise calculation of the regional tourist multiplier, as a weighted average of the multipliers for each local industry where tourists purchase goods and services. A regional economy consists of a number of businesses, which are classified into industries according to type of output or sales. These industries buy from and sell to each other and to industries in other regions. They also sell goods and services for household consumption. Input-output analysis involves the development of an interindustry table, showing the distribution of all purchases and sales. An input-output table is a set of double-entry accounts for the regional economy. It maps the interconnections among various lines of businesses. The essential idea is that part of the output of one business becomes input to another.

The input-output method has a long history. In 1758, French economist Francois Quesnay developed a table to trace the flow of money and goods in a nation. The first empirical input-output study in the United States was published by Wassily Leontief in 1936. A Harvard economist, Leontief won the Nobel Prize in economics for his pioneering effort, which described the structure of the U.S. economy for 1919. It has been followed by other studies for the years 1947, 1958, 1968, 1972, and subsequent years. Since then, the method has been used to describe the economies of most nations and of smaller regional economies within their borders. The method has become an important tool for studying such economic problems as energy development, water use, and recreation demand in the United States, Europe, and other countries.

Table 14-3 illustrates the first step in applying the input-output method, to assemble the basic transactions table used in the analysis. This includes the transactions identified as (1) intermediate sales between industries A, B and C in the region; (2) payments for capital, labor, and other inputs; and (3) sales to final buyers, such as resident consumers, and tourists. The table identifies each industry's annual dollar value of sales to other industries, and each industry's purchases of inputs from the other industries. Thus, the table represents a system of double-entry accounts, in which every sale constitutes a purchase, and the total output or sales of each industry equals the total inputs purchased. In many cases, states will have already developed such an interindustry table in their state input-output model or it can be constructed for a given impact region, using the IMPLAN input-output model described later in this chapter.

Reading across a row in Table 14-3 shows the total dollar value of output or sales by each industry, including the intermediate sales to other industries and to final buyers. For example, if Industry B represents the food and lodging industry, the table shows total annual sales of $25 million, including sales to Industry A, $2 million; Industry B, $6 million; Industry C, $1 million; and to consumers, $16 million. Reading down the column shows the total dollar value of inputs each industry buys from other industries and payments for capital, labor, and other inputs. Thus, if Industry B is producing $25 million, the column of this table shows that Industry B must purchase inputs equaling $25 million as well. This includes purchases from Industry A, $2.25 million; purchases from other firms in Industry B, $6 million; Industry C, $3 million; and payments for capital, labor, and other inputs, $13.75 million.

Table 14-4 (page 256) illustrates the second and simplest step in input-output analysis. This is to estimate the direct inputs required per dollar of output or sales by each industry. These coefficients are calculated from the information contained in Table 14-3. The procedure is straightforward in that each entry in a column for a single industry is divided by its column total. The resulting coefficients show the direct purchases necessary from each supplier (at the left of the table) in order for the industry (at the head of the column) to produce one dollar's worth of output or sales. For example, if Industry B represents the food and

**Table 14-3. Interindustry Transactions in a Regional Economy**

| Output or Sales by Industry | Purchases by Industry (Million Dollars) A | B | C | Final Demand | Total Output or Sales |
|---|---|---|---|---|---|
| A | $1.00 | $2.25 | $0.20 | $1.55 | $5.00 |
| B | 2.00 | 6.00 | 1.00 | 16.00 | 25.00 |
| C | 0.20 | 3.00 | 1.80 | 15.00 | 20.00 |
| Payments | 1.80 | 13.75 | 17.00 | 3.00 | 35.55 |
| Total Input | 5.00 | 25.00 | 20.00 | 35.55 | 85.55 |

**Table 14-4. Coefficients of Direct Inputs Required per Dollar of Output or Sales in a Regional Economy**

| | Direct Purchases by Industry (Cents per Dollar Sales) | | |
|---|---|---|---|
| Output or Sales by Industry | A | B | C |
| A | $0.20 | $0.09 | $0.01 |
| B | 0.40 | 0.24 | 0.05 |
| C | 0.04 | 0.12 | 0.09 |
| Payments | 0.36 | 0.55 | 0.85 |
| Total Input | 1.00 | 1.00 | 1.00 |

lodging industry, the table shows for each dollar of output or sales, the industry must buy inputs from Industry A valued at $0.09; Industry B, $0.24; Industry C, $0.12; plus capital, labor, and other inputs, $0.55. Thus, Table 14-4 converts the dollar information in Table 14-3 (page 255) to the equivalent percentages.

Table 14-5 illustrates the third step in applying the input-output method. This is to calculate the multipliers for each industry in the region. The sum of each column shows the direct plus indirect impacts of $1 of output or sales by each industry. Multipliers can be calculated by taking the inverse of the direct coefficients matrix or computed based on computer iterations of successive rounds of transactions in the region. For example, from Table 14-4, we see that if Industry B increases output by $1, it must buy $0.09 of input from Industry A. In turn, Industry A must buy inputs from other industries such as C, as well as labor. As a result, Industry A eventually will supply $0.16 of direct and indirect inputs. This figure is noticeably larger than the $0.09 of direct inputs, because industries depend on each other. Table 14-5 shows that the total business or sales multiplier for Industry B is 1.76, which indicates that, as tourist spending for food and lodging increases by $1, total sales of $1.76 are generated in the regional economy. The recreation multiplier would be the weighted average of multipliers for each industry from which tourists purchase goods and services.

In this example, we see a highly aggregated version of a transaction table for a regional economy. Headings for three industries, plus aggregate payments and aggregate final demand, are sufficient to illustrate the input-output method. In empirical studies of regional economies, the extent of disaggregation will depend on the purpose of the study, the availability of data, and the time and resources budgeted for the study. It is common practice to have 20 or more industries and five to 10 payment and final demand categories.

The payments row in Table 14-3 (page 255) represents the value added by the regional economy. These are the payments to the factors of production that contribute to the output of goods and services. Labor is paid wages and salaries; capital is depreciated and receives interest; land is

**Table 14-5. Output or Sales Multipliers, Total Direct and Indirect Impact per Dollar of Final Demand in a Regional Economy**

| | Direct and Indirect Purchases (Cents per Dollar Final Demand) | | |
|---|---|---|---|
| Output or Sales by Industry | A | B | C |
| A | $1.33 | $0.16 | $0.02 |
| B | 0.71 | 1.41 | 0.09 |
| C | 0.15 | 0.19 | 1.11 |
| Output or Sales Multipliers | 2.19 | 1.76 | 1.22 |

Source: Adapted from McKean, 1981.

paid rent; and entrepreneurs (or owners) are paid profits or dividends based on profitability. Also included are payments of taxes to governments in and outside the region and payments for goods and services imported from outside the region. The latter represents leakage from the regional economy.

Regional economic development is based on changes in final demand, such as tourist spending. An increase in final demand stimulates the economy and leads to increased output or sales, income and employment. Final demand includes sales for end use. Included in end use sales are tourist spending in the region, nonlocal government expenditures for construction and operation of parks in the region; new private investments, and other sales of products and services outside the region. Final demand also consists of sales to regional households for consumption, sales to regional governments, sales of goods and services outside the region (exports), inventory changes, and investments.

Other effects can be estimated from the interindustry transactions table (Table 14-3, page 255). For example, there are three types of income multipliers. Type I is the ratio of the direct plus indirect income to the direct income paid to households in the region, primarily in the form of wages and salaries. Type II or III multipliers show not only the direct plus indirect changes in income but also the induced increases in income generated by additional consumer spending. These multipliers capture the chain reaction, beginning with increased demands, increased output, increased income, increased household purchases induced by increased household income, increased output, and so on. The Type II or III multiplier is obtained by including households as an "industry" in the input-output table. Note that the income multipliers are sometimes reported as a per dollar change in direct income paid to households, and sometimes as a per dollar change in direct business output or sales.

Employment multipliers are closely related to business output or sales multipliers. If the direct labor inputs required per dollar of sales are measured for each industry, it is simply a matter of multiplication to find the direct employment effects of a change in output or sales for each industry. Suppose that the direct labor inputs per $1,000 of sales for Industry A are 0.06 of a work year, compared with 0.02 for Industry B and 0.01 for Industry C. For example, assume a $100,000 increase in sales to tourists (final demand) by Industry B, food and lodging. Table 14-5 (page 257) shows that output or sales by Industry A will rise by $16,000 (= $100,000 x 0.16), output or sales by Industry B will rise by $141,000 (= $100,000 x 1.41), and Industry C sells an added $19,000 (= $100,000 x 0.19). In this case, where sales to tourists increase by $100,000 per year, employment will rise by four workers [= (0.06 x $16) + (0.02 x $141) + (0.01 x $19)].

# Obtaining Input-Output Models and Multipliers

## *Survey-Based State Models*

Until recently, the input-output method was often an expensive and time-consuming process. States that developed their own input-output models had to develop their own transactions table, showing the sales and purchases of each local industry. This involved collecting data from businesses, governments, and consumers using interviews and surveys. Once the data is collected, it must be cross-checked and verified to assure reliable results. For example, one test of consistency is the requirement that industry sales equal purchases. This is still the most accurate way of developing an input-output model. However, if the state for which a person is working has already developed such an input-output model for the state, it makes sense to use it unless the impact region affected by the recreation site is quite small, relative to the state. Thus using the Texas input-output model for evaluating a small park in rural Texas may well overstate the effect of the park on the local rural economy, since most of the income and employment effects reflected in the multiplier occur in the regional supply centers, such as Dallas–Fort Worth or Houston, not surrounding the park. This is especially true when visitors are from the larger cities and they purchase most of their supplies at home. If the survey does not account for the fact that most of the purchases do not take place at the site (since often there are few stores there), the income and employment effects of the park on the local rural economy will be erroneously overstated.

## *U.S. Department of Commerce's Bureau of Economic Analysis RIMS Multipliers*

The U.S. Department of Commerce's Bureau of Economic Analysis produces a set of output multipliers and income-employment coefficients at a state level for every state in the United States. The multipliers are derived from the agency's Regional Input-Output Modeling System or RIMS. These multipliers are useful if the analyst knows the change in final demand from recreation by sector and wants an estimate of the effect on the state economy. These multipliers will overstate the effect on any county or group of rural counties in the state from a recreation site since their multipliers are much smaller than the state-level multipliers (due to greater leakages at the county level). The agency also produces an employment coefficient, defined as jobs per million dollars of output for each major sector in each state economy. This coefficient contains both the direct and indirect effect of an initial change in expenditures.

## National Park Service Money Generation Model

A simple paper-and-pencil work sheet approach to apply the RIMS multipliers and estimate effects of National Parks on state economies can be performed using the Money Generation Model (National Park Service, 1995). This short report provides average expenditures per day and the RIMS multipliers and employment coefficients for each state. The park analyst simply multiplies by the number of visitor days of nonlocal visitors. Nonlocal visitors are used, since their spending represents new money injected into the area, as compared to spending by residents. The work sheet also allows calculation of total sales, added sales tax revenue and jobs supported.

## IMPLAN Input-Output Model

An attractive alternative to either collecting detailed regional data to build an input-output (I-O) model or using simple state averages is to use national data and develop a region-specific multiplier using a computer software model called IMPLAN. While this model assumes that the average relationships between industries will be approximately the same in each county or regional economy, it allows for county or multicounty region-specific leakages and therefore is more accurate than using state level multipliers, if the analyst desires the effect on the local economy rather than the state as a whole. The IMPLAN input-output model was originally developed by the U.S. Forest Service and is available through the Minnesota IMPLAN Group[1]. National data provides the basis for IMPLAN, a 466 industry input-output model. It is used to produce detailed estimates of the direct, indirect, and induced economic impacts on regional economies that result from alternative resource management plans for any county or group of counties in the United States. The model can be run on a desktop computer and has been used in hundreds of applications. IMPLAN appears to slightly overstate the multiplier effects that would occur in rural economies (Radtke, Detering and Brokken, 1985; Johnson, Obermiller

[1]IMPLAN data and computer software are available from Minnesota IMPLAN Group, Inc., 1940 S. Greeley Ave., Suite 101, Stillwater, MN 55082-6059; 612-439-4421.

and Radtke, 1988), but is far more accurate than using Department of Commerce RIMS multipliers, since RIMS multipliers are published at the state level (or using the National Park Service Money Generation Model which depends on RIMS multipliers).

# Regional Economic Impact Analysis Examples

## *Economic Impact of Mountain Biking at Slickrock in Moab, Utah*

To illustrate the steps for applying the IMPLAN input-output model in a real case study, data on expenditures was collected for mountain biking at the Slickrock bike trail in Moab, Utah. To answer the policy question of what effect does providing a designated area for mountain biking have on the economy of Moab, Fix (1996) chose the county level (Grand County) to be the impact area. A sample of people returning from mountain biking at the site were met at the parking lot and asked to fill out a survey. Relevant expenditures to assess the impact on the Moab area were expenditures in Moab, not their entire trip expenditures. Thus, any gasoline or food purchased at home, typically Salt Lake City or Denver, has no impact on the Moab area.

To facilitate recall, categories of typical visitor expenditures were listed. The average trip expenditures per person (group expenditures divided by average party size) were divided by length of stay in the Moab area to arrive at expenditures per day. The conversion to per day is needed, since the visitor statistics for the Slickrock bike trail are on a per day basis. Total expenditures are daily per person expenditures in each category times 158,681 total visitor days. To estimate total annual spending by visitor day requires an average expenditure across all visitors, not just the people who purchased that service. This explains why the average cost for lodging is $1.71 per person in Table 14-6. Even with four people to a room, this amount is insufficient. But only 89 people out of more than 300 had any lodging expenses. The average across people with lodging expenses is $76. But it would be wrong to multiply the $76 by the 158,861 visitor days since the vast majority did not incur lodging expenses. The same explanation applies to bike rental (which very few people reported).

The next step is to create a linkage between the categories of visitor spending and the industrial and service sectors tabulated by the U.S. Department of Commerce that are used in the IMPLAN model. As shown in Table 14-7, for sectors such as lodging the match is obvious. For others, assumptions must be made regarding a typical bill of sale from the miscellaneous category. That is, what proportion of miscellaneous spending is on souvenir T-shirts versus replacement bike parts? Nonetheless, the entire $1,366,244 of visitor expenditure is allocated to one of the IMPLAN industries or **personal consumption expenditure categories.**

**Table 14-6. Mountain Biking Trip Expenditures in Moab, Utah**

| Expenditure Profile | Trip Expenses per Person | Trip Expenses per Visitor Day per Person | Total Annual Spending |
|---|---|---|---|
| Lodging | $6.09 | $1.71 | $271,345 |
| Camp Fees | $0.96 | $0.27 | $42,844 |
| Bike Rental | $0.96 | $0.27 | $42,844 |
| Entrance Fees | $0.82 | $0.23 | $36,497 |
| Misc. Expenditures | $4.24 | $1.19 | $188,830 |
| Gasoline | $2.60 | $0.73 | $115,837 |
| Food—Grocery | $4.98 | $1.40 | $222,153 |
| Food—Restaurant | $10.00 | $2.81 | $445,894 |
| Total | $30.65 | $8.61 | $1,366,244 |

Once these are input into IMPLAN, the model performs several calculations. First, it looks to see if the final demand can be met by the local economy of Grand County. Some leakages occur there. Second, it disaggregates grocery store purchases into a typical grocery basket of meat, dairy, vegetables and fruits. We have grouped those together in Table 14-8 (page 262) as agriculture. But at this stage when the model is attempting to have industries produce these goods, leakages can also occur if, for example, there are no dairies in Grand County. Thus, milk must be imported. The bottom of Table 14-8 shows the leakages are $191,543. This amount is not included in the Grand County multipliers, as it is spent outside the impact area.

Next, the model computes the indirect or interindustry purchases from all of the sectors to meet final demand. This series of iterations accounts

**Table 14-7. Allocation of Expenditures to IMPLAN Sectors**

| Survey Category | IMPLAN Personal Consumption & Industry Sector | |
|---|---|---|
| Lodging | Hotels & Lodging | $271,345 |
| Camp Fees | Recreation Services | $42,844 |
| Bike Rental | Recreation Services | $42,844 |
| Entrance Fees | State & Local Government | $36,497 |
| Misc. Expenditures | Film & Developing | $18,883 |
| | Clothing (T-shirts) | $75,532 |
| | Beverages | $56,649 |
| | Wheeled Goods (Bike Parts) | $37,766 |
| Gasoline | Fuel | $115,837 |
| Food—Grocery | Food in Off-Premise Consumption | $222,153 |
| Food—Restaurant | Eating and Drinking | $445,894 |
| | Direct Effects | $1,366,244 |

**Table 14-8. Input-Output Model Results of Interindustry Effects**

| Major Sectors | Direct Effect | Total Output Effect | Jobs Coefficient | Direct Jobs/ $1000s | Jobs Multiplier | Total Jobs |
|---|---|---|---|---|---|---|
| Agriculture | $31,900 | $49,400 | 0.02024 | 0.645 | 1.5486 | 1.00 |
| Oil & Gas | $82,400 | $91,700 | 0.00174 | 0.143 | 1.1129 | 0.16 |
| Beverages | $23,600 | $23,900 | 0.02218 | 0.523 | 1.0127 | 0.53 |
| Wholesale Trade | $49,400 | $73,800 | 0.02453 | 1.211 | 1.4939 | 1.81 |
| General Retail Store | $11,800 | $14,500 | 0.05655 | 0.667 | 1.2288 | 0.82 |
| Food Stores | $47,000 | $77,200 | 0.03472 | 1.631 | 1.6426 | 2.68 |
| Auto Services | $25,500 | $54,500 | 0.03651 | 0.931 | 2.1373 | 1.99 |
| Apparel | $7,700 | $14,100 | 0.06596 | 0.508 | 1.8312 | 0.93 |
| Eating & Drinking | $393,500 | $441,200 | 0.04259 | 16.758 | 1.1212 | 18.79 |
| Hotels & Lodging | $245,400 | $259,200 | 0.04842 | 11.880 | 1.0562 | 12.55 |
| Film, Photo | $42,300 | $47,100 | 0.02357 | 0.997 | 1.1135 | 1.11 |
| Recreation Services | $84,300 | $89,000 | 0.01326 | 1.117 | 1.0558 | 1.18 |
| Other Misc. | $129,900 | $402,000 | 0.03779 | 4.908 | 3.0947 | 15.19 |
| Subtotal in Region | $1,174,700 | $1,637,600 | 0.03587 | 42.136 | 1.3941 | 58.74 |
| Leakages out of Region | $191,543 | | | | | |
| Total | $1,366,243 | | | | | |

for the interindustry linkages, as each sector attempts to produce the increase in final demand for its output brought about by mountain bikers visiting the Slickrock area in Moab. In addition, the induced effect of increased number of workers and increased incomes to workers is reflected as further stimulating spending. Thus, the other miscellaneous category reflects stimulation of such sectors as additional medical and dental services now demanded by new workers and their families. In addition, other sectors such as apparel get further stimulated since the new workers and their families buy more clothes.

Thus, the difference in Table 14-8 in going from direct effects to total effects is that total effects incorporates the direct, indirect and induced effects. Applying the labor requirements coefficients for each sector (jobs per thousand dollars of output) times the direct effect, we can calculate the direct jobs brought about by the initial spending by 158,681 visitor days of mountain biking at the Slickrock area. Applying the jobs multiplier captures the indirect and induced effects of this spending on the rest of the economy. Thus, 42.1 jobs are directly supported by mountain biker expenditures on food, gasoline and retail goods. However, for the industries to produce these goods and to support the added workers, another 16.6 jobs are generated in other industries. Thus, a total 58.7 jobs are supported by mountain biking at the Slickrock bike trail in Moab.

The gain in employment is also reflected in increased wage income. But this is just part of the income gain, as there is also an increase in profits and rents to businesses located in Moab. Using the more detailed tables produced by IMPLAN (not shown), direct income to workers is $388,000 which, with the overall average income multiplier (1.45), results in $562,300 in total income to workers. There is also $211,300 of direct income by self-employed proprietors, business owners and landowners that increases to $384,400 with the multiplier effect (an overall average of 1.82). Thus, total personal income in Grand County is estimated to have increased by $946,700 as a result of the presence of the designated mountain biking trails and facilities at the Slickrock bike trail in Moab. The model estimates that this increase in income will result in about 100 more people moving into the Grand County area. In contrast to the nearly $1 million in local income is the nearly $9 million in visitor benefits from mountain biking at Slickrock.

## *Impacts Versus Efficiency in Wilderness Designation*

The relationship between economic benefits and economic impacts can be highlighted by a realistic example. Following the analysis of Stewart, Browder and Covault (1992), we compare the net economic benefits and economic impacts (local income and jobs) from timber production versus wilderness designation on the Lolo National Forest in Montana.

The three roadless areas considered for Wilderness Area designation have about half their lands suitable for timber production. However, since they are roadless, roads would have to be built into these areas to harvest the timber. Given the steep terrain and miles of road involved, it would cost $6.5 million dollars more to harvest the trees than the trees are worth (Stewart, Browder and Covault, 1992, p. 160). Companies would only find it profitable to build the roads and harvest the trees if the U.S. Forest Service (i.e., the taxpayers who pay funds into the U.S. Treasury) provides a purchaser road credit that reimburses the company for building the roads, by deducting the road building costs from the timber sale payments the company would make to the U.S. Forest Service (i.e., the U.S. Treasury). The bottom line is that it is very costly to society to build the road and harvest the trees. Even without considering the foregone wilderness recreation and preservation benefits, it is economically wasteful to allocate these public lands to timber production since the costs outweigh the timber benefits (this is why these are called below-cost timber sales).

But, the fact that it is very costly to build the roads and harvest the timber results in the need to hire many workers each year. In particular, the direct and indirect labor required per million board feet is 13.2. Given that 10.3 million board feet could be harvested annually from the roadless areas, this translates into total employment of 136 workers per year. Using IMPLAN, the U.S. Forest Service estimates that direct plus indirect income in this region of Montana would be $3 million (Stewart, Browder and Covault, 1992, p. 160). Designation of the three roadless areas totaling 206,000 acres as Wilderness would likely provide only a small fraction of the jobs that timber harvesting would provide.

In this case the economic impact analysis paints quite a different picture than the benefit-cost analysis. Can we resolve this conflict? Of course we can. Remember, the 136 jobs gained in this region of Montana from harvesting timber in these roadless areas is just a transfer of jobs from somewhere else. If the Wilderness Area is designated, the 10.3 million board feet of timber will be produced somewhere else. Wherever it is produced, loggers will be needed there. So there really is no net benefit to the U.S. economy from the timber jobs since they are really not lost in the first place.

The loss of $6.5 million from incurring road building and timber harvesting expenses in excess of the value of the trees is a net loss to the U.S. economy that is not offset anywhere else. It is a real opportunity cost. Society gave up more valuable uses for the road construction crews, diesel fuel and trucks than it received in timber output. Power (1996) points out that the intact standing forest may be a more powerful long-run attraction to cause business owners, skilled workers and retirees to relocate to the area, bringing in more long-term jobs than timber harvesting would.

This example also illustrates a very important point about regional economic impact studies: The more wasteful the project the more likely it is to generate large local employment effects. Having workers build hiking trails with small garden shovels would increase employment, but is a wasteful use of labor. Regional economic analysis is a potentially powerful and influential tool in recreation economic decisions. However, it should be used as a supplement to benefit-cost analysis, not a substitute for it.

## Progressive View of Regional Economic Analysis

The misplaced emphasis on timber harvesting to generate jobs, even when it is uneconomic has been questioned by two economists. First, Burton and Berck (1996) show that the level of National Forest timber sales has no persistent effect on the long-term level of employment in the timber industry in Oregon. Second, Power's research (1996) has noted that the traditional view of regional economic analysis, as depicted in Figure 14-1 (page 243), is somewhat anachronistic and inconsistent with the facts in the western United States. Most western states have seen a drop in employment in industries such as mining, timber harvesting and agriculture. According to the traditional view, the regional economy of these areas should be in decline. However, the opposite is true. Employment, income

**Figure 14-3. Progressive View of the Flow of Regional Economic Activity**

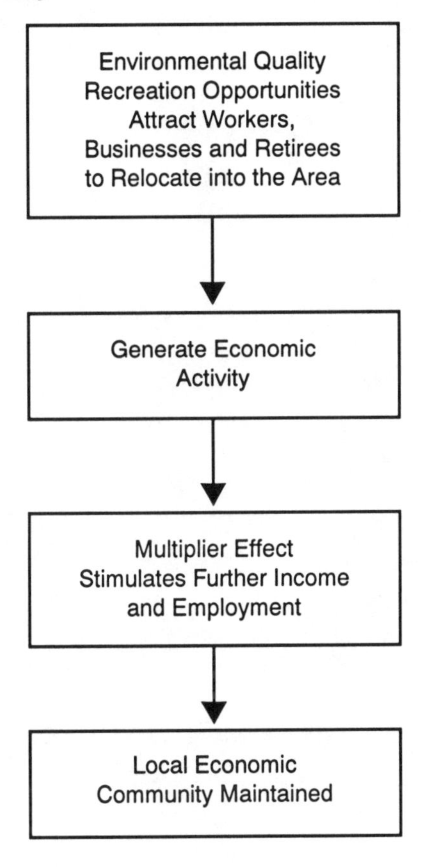


Source: Adapted from Power, 1996.

and population are flourishing. The reason is the quality of natural resources, such as forests, are drawing entrepreneurs, business owners, skilled workers and retirees to the area. His progressive model of regional economics is illustrated in Figure 14-3.

It is the new businesses, skilled workers and retirees, attracted by the quality of the natural environment and outdoor recreation opportunities, who bring their incomes into these economies that further stimulate existing businesses via the multiplier effects. Income flows in and is retained because the area is an attractive place to live. This view can explain why states like Montana have seen significant growth in personal income and employment while traditional extractive industries have declined. We hope this alternative view will provide some balance to the traditional view that only through resource extraction can a community's economic base be maintained.

# *Chapter 15*

# Resource Supply and Costs

This chapter introduces the theory of recreation resource supply, and the various types of fixed and variable costs including capital construction, land, operation, maintenance, external costs, and associated costs; and describes the three sources of cost information: engineering-economic, cross-sectional, and time-series methods.

Resource supply and costs are important in recreation economics, because decisions by private and public managers require a comparison between the costs of alternative courses of action and their benefits. For example, the expected benefits of a program to upgrade services provided at a campground are compared with the costs of the program. Likewise, a decision to expand a boat marina or campground involves a comparison of the benefits expected from the capital improvement with its costs. Even a decision about whether to improve park employees' living quarters requires a comparison between the cost of the project and the subjectively estimated benefits expected to result from improved employee morale. In each case, the benefits resulting from the decision are compared with its costs.

In this chapter, we introduce the concept of economic costs. We show that the distinction between financial costs and economic or social costs is based on the idea of opportunity costs. You will see what economists mean by short-run, long-run, fixed, variable, and marginal costs. The latter is the supply curve for outdoor recreation.

## Short-Run and Long-Run Costs

The supply of parks and other recreation resources is primarily determined by the cost of production. Supply is also affected by other variables, of course, such as availability of public funds, quality of potential sites, the price of inputs such as labor, energy, and other factors of production. But for now, we will consider cost and quantity supplied. The purpose of this section is to introduce the concepts of short-run and long-run production costs. In the short run, costs of production vary with changes in the rate of utilization of capacity of facilities, such as the proportion of existing campsites occupied. In the long run, costs of production vary with changes in the size of facilities, such as the number of campsites in a campground, which defines maximum capacity. In addition, long-run costs of production vary with changes in the level of technology or development. For example, there are three basic levels of technology in campgrounds: fully developed with utility hookups, primitive with pit toilets, and undeveloped backcountry sites where everything is carried in and out by the user. If the relationship of short-run to long-run costs is not familiar to you, review the microeconomic theory section of any economic textbook.

**Total cost** (TC) means the total cost of producing any given level of output. Total cost is divided into two parts, **total fixed costs** (TFC) and **total variable costs** (TVC). **Fixed costs** are those that do not vary with changes in the recreation use of a site in the short run. They will be the same if output is 100 visits or 10,000. Managers often refer to fixed costs as overhead costs or unavoidable costs. Fixed costs include capital investment, general administration, and external costs. **Variable costs** are those that vary directly with changes in the recreation use of a site, rising with more visits and falling with less. Managers often refer to variable costs as direct costs or avoidable costs. Variable costs cover operation and maintenance (O&M) including direct labor, expendable supplies, and utilities. Panel 1 of Figure 15-1 illustrates these concepts. Note that total fixed cost does not vary with output, while total variable cost and total costs (TC = TFC + TVC) rise with more visits, first at a decreasing rate, and then at an increasing rate.

**Average total cost** (ATC), also called average cost (AC), is the cost per visit. Average total cost may be separated into **average fixed costs** (AFC) and **average variable costs** (AVC) in the same way that total costs were divided. Thus, the total cost curves in Panel 1 of Figure 15-1 provide the basis for the average cost curves shown in Panel 2. AFC declines continuously as output increases. A doubling of output always leads to a halving of fixed costs per unit of output. This is the process popularly known as spreading the overhead. ATC curves are usually U-shaped; they fall and then rise as output increases. This reflects the fact that productivity is increasing when output is low, but at some level of output, productivity begins to fall enough to cause AVC to increase faster than AFC falls. When this happens, ATC increases.

**Marginal cost** (MC), sometimes called incremental cost, is the increase in total cost resulting from increasing production by one visit. Marginal costs are necessarily variable costs, and changes in fixed costs will not affect marginal costs. For example, the marginal cost of producing a few more skier days by utilizing a given ski site more intensively is

**Figure 15-1. Total, Average and Marginal Cost Curves for Park and Recreation Programs in the Short Run**

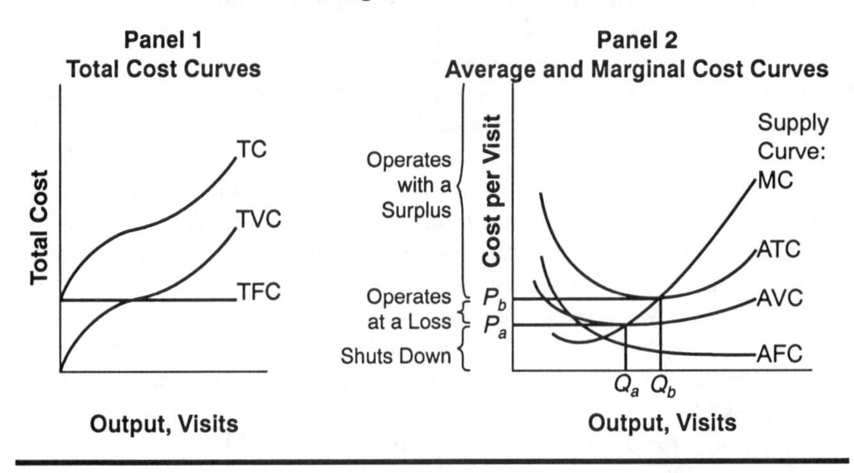


the same, whatever the rent paid for the fixed amount of land in the ski slope. Panel 2 of Figure 15-1 shows that MC falls and then rises as output increases and intersects the ATC and AVC at their minimum points. The intersection of the MC and AVC curves defines the shutdown point ($Q_a$ visits), below which there is no incentive to continue operation of the site. Note that above this point, the MC curve represents the supply curve for the site.

Economic capacity of a park or other outdoor recreation site is defined as the level of output at the minimum ATC. This is not an upper limit on what can be produced. Instead, it is the largest output that can be produced without encountering rising average total costs per visit. In Figure 15-1, economic capacity output is $Q_b$ visits, but output could be higher, provided the manager is willing to accept the higher costs per visit that accompany output above economic capacity. For outputs less than the point of minimum average total cost, the site is said to have extra or excess capacity. This definition of capacity may differ from that in everyday speech, but it is widely used in economic and financial discussions.

**Short-run cost curves** show how costs vary with the number of visits to a park or other recreation site of a given size. There is always some limiting factor of production that is fixed, such as acres of land or size of facilities. In any regional market for outdoor recreation, there is a different short-run average cost curve for each park or other recreation site of a given size. A small city park will have its own short-run cost curve. A medium-sized state park and a very large National Park will each have its own short-run cost curve. If a park or recreation program expands and replaces a small site with a medium-sized one, it will move from one short-run cost curve to another. The change from one size to another is a long-run change. How short-run average cost (SRAC) curves for sites of different sizes are related to each other is shown in Figure 15-2. Economists define the **long-run cost curve** as a situation in which all factors of production can be varied, i.e., all costs become variable costs.

The long-run planning decisions are important because once a new recreation site is acquired and new facilities constructed, it becomes fixed for a long time. The decisions are also difficult because managers must estimate how many visitors will use the facilities. The long-run average cost (LRAC) curve shown in Figure 15-2 falls at first and then rises. This curve is often described as saucer shaped. Over the range of output from zero to *Q*, the industry has falling long-run average costs. An expansion in size of facilities results in a reduction of costs per visit. Over the range of size greater than *Q*, the industry encounters rising costs. An expansion in size of facilities will be accompanied by a rise in average cost per visit. Such an industry is said to suffer long-run increasing costs or diseconomy of scale (or size). At output *Q* in Figure 15-2, the industry has reached its lowest possible long-run costs per visit. In a competitive industry, each supplier would produce at the minimum point on its LRAC curve.

## *Changes in the Determinants of Supply*

The discussion so far, shows how cost varies with changes in output and size, assuming constant prices of the factors of production and fixed technology. Changes in either technological knowledge or factor prices will cause the short-run and long-run cost curves to shift. Technological change normally works in only one direction, to shift cost curves downward. Improved ways of providing existing recreation opportunities will mean that lower cost methods of production become available. Changes in the price of the factors of production can exert an influence in either direction. If an agency has to pay more for any input, the cost of producing each level of output will rise; if the agency has to pay less, costs will fall.

**Figure 15-2. Relationship Between the Long-Run Average Cost Curve and Short-Run Average Cost Curves for Park and Recreation Programs**

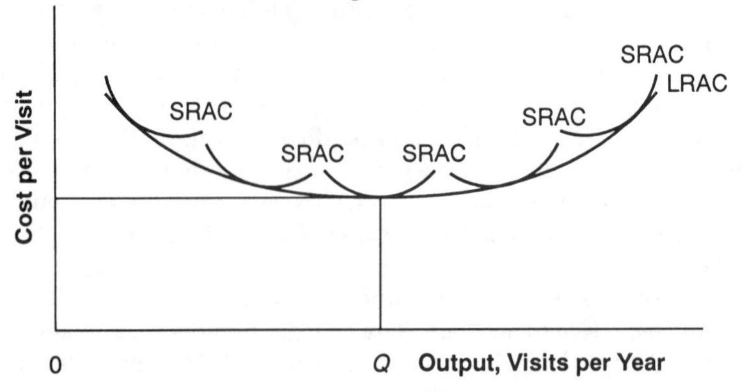

Lipsey and Steiner (1981) reviewed major changes that have affected production costs in the long run. All are related to technology, broadly defined. The first is the change in the techniques available for producing existing recreation opportunities, products, and services. Over an average person's lifetime, these changes often can be dramatic. Seventy years ago, recreation roads were built by crews of workers using buckets, spades, and draft horses; today bulldozers, front-end loaders, and other specialized equipment build miles of roads quite efficiently. Second is the change in new products and services that become available. Portable computers allow parks to have computerized reservation and check-in systems. Photovoltaic panels allow lights in areas where no electrical lines exist. Cellular phones allow rangers to be in contact with the office while on patrol. Many of these inventions allow a given amount of labor (e.g., rangers) to produce more output.

# Types of Fixed and Variable Costs

To economists, the total cost of a park or recreation program includes the cost of program planning or design; the cost of land and related natural resources; the cost of capital construction or installation; operation and maintenance costs; external costs to other agencies and individuals; and the associated cost to users. The purpose of this section is to review these types of fixed and variable cost and to distinguish social costs from the financial costs of private and public agencies.

The economic evaluation of public recreation projects differs from financial analysis in that social costs rather than accounting costs are used. The social cost of producing recreation is what must be given up by society as a whole to make that production possible. To economists, the concept of social cost always means opportunity cost. The **opportunity cost** of using a resource is the value of the resource in its next best alternative use. When measuring the opportunity cost of recreation, all consequences of its production must be identified and incorporated into the measurement. Economists estimate the opportunity costs for all inputs, whether they are correctly or incorrectly priced by markets or not priced at all.

There are a number of reasons why financial cost differs from economic cost. The standard accounting practice in both private and public agencies is to record only the costs of those inputs purchased from others. This can lead to a substantial divergence between accounting measures of financial cost and social cost. For example, accountants often fail to measure the implicit costs of factors of production owned by the firm or public. Certain planning and overhead costs may be paid by other agencies that do not require reimbursement by the agency operating the park or recreation program. Alternatively, financial cost incurred by the park may benefit others, for example, when a low-quality road to the site is replaced with a high-quality access road that reduces dust and speeds access to unrelated destinations along the road.

Although economists and accountants define costs differently, both definitions are correct since they are used for different purposes. To determine the financial feasibility of the project (e.g., whether entrance fee revenues will cover the agency's direct costs) accounting procedures are often most appropriate. However, in helping public managers make the best decisions they can using public tax money and using scarce public lands and natural resources, economists should substitute social cost rather than financial or accounting costs. There is of course some overlap as well. In smoothly functioning markets, wage rates and the prices of material and equipment are a close approximation of the opportunity cost of resources. Some possible exceptions are noted here.

## *Capital Construction Costs*

Parks and other recreation programs usually require the construction of facilities such as buildings, roads, campgrounds and trails. Preconstruction costs include design, contract preparation, environmental assessment, site survey and feasibility analysis. Construction costs include clearing and grading, roads, spurs and barriers; water development and distribution; wastewater disposal, signs and bulletin boards; visitor information facilities, electrical connections, fee collection facilities, campsite facilities, trails, contract administration and inspection; and other construction costs.

Estimating the social costs of capital construction is relatively straightforward. Well-established markets usually exist for construction material, equipment and services. Thus, information on market prices is generally available or can be obtained through estimating procedures based on past construction costs in the region of the site. The National Park Service publishes *Construction Cost* guidelines for long-run planning.

Administration costs associated with construction include review of the engineering plans and inspection during construction, to ensure that facilities are installed in accordance with the plans and specifications. Also included are the administrative services to secure the necessary permits for construction and costs of public meetings to solicit input.

The costs of construction are usually based on current contract bids in the region of the proposed project or on the current market value of purchased materials and services to install the facilities. Contingency costs are normally added, to allow for unforeseen construction problems. These funds are set aside to allow for the uncertainty of project cost estimates. They help insure that funds will be adequate to complete the project. They are not an allowance for inflation or for the omission of the costs of facilities that are known to be required.

Economists distinguish between explicit and implicit costs. Explicit costs are the costs of inputs purchased from others such as direct labor, expendable supplies, rent and general administration. Implicit costs are capital or labor services purchased during an earlier accounting period. Capital investment forgoes interest and loses value, i.e., depreciates. This distinction has important implications because public agencies own land, buildings, and equipment that they use in production of recreation opportunities. The conventional practice is that if they were purchased in the past, there is no payment during this year to show up on the accounting records. This means that there is no explicit cost associated with the use of existing land and capital improvements by public agencies. Also, if some of these assets are purchased during the current accounting period (one year), the expenditure to acquire them is not a valid explicit cost of this period's production of recreation opportunities, because the assets will still be able to contribute to the production of recreation opportunities in future periods. Thus, government accounting procedures that emphasize actual cash expenditures may provide a distorted view of the true social cost of producing recreation, since some historic costs are ignored.

Problems may arise when converting the initial capital investment costs to annual fixed costs over the life of the facility. Depreciation and interest on capital investment are generally overlooked by public agencies. Managers of private recreation sites realize that depreciation, which means setting aside enough money to replace facilities when they wear out, is a cost which must be recovered if they are to continue to operate. Depreciation includes both the loss in value due to physical wear and that due to obsolescence. Accountants use several conventional methods of depreciation based on the price originally paid for the asset. One of the most common is straight-line depreciation, in which the same amount of historical cost is deducted in every year of useful life of the asset. While historical costs are often useful approximations, they may differ from depreciation required by the opportunity cost principle. The economic cost of using an asset for a year, is the loss in value of the asset during the year or its replacement cost. Economists consider interest on the value of assets as the opportunity cost of capital necessary to keep the assets employed.

There are several additional points that should be made with respect to depreciation and interest on capital investment. They should be counted as an economic cost when (1) they are part of a proposed new facility and have not yet been expended; and (2) when their value is reduced by continuing to use them. On the other hand, depreciation and interest on capital investment should not be counted as an economic cost when facilities have already been installed and they will have the same value, whether or not they continue to be used.

Managers should not overlook the fact that when parks and other recreation facilities are established on what was formerly private land, there is a loss of property tax base to the community. For example, a city operating its own golf course forgoes the tax revenue it could have earned if the golf course were supplied by private operators who pay property taxes. Since a public recreation facility consumes municipal services in much the same way as a private one, the costs of services provided results in a higher tax load on the rest of the community. Economists consider the foregone tax as an economic cost of the capital investment by the public recreation agency. As a result, a number of states and federal agencies make annual payment to local units of government in lieu of taxes.

Another challenge to managers is to phase investment in capital improvements consistent with growth. For example, construction of campgrounds could be phased with the first loop built in year one, the second loop in year five, the third and final loop in year 10. Managers could install the first loop of a second campground in year 15, and continuing so long as demand is growing.

## *Opportunity Cost of Land*

Parks and other recreation programs usually require a substantial amount of land and related natural resources such as forests, rivers and lakes. Estimating the social costs of these natural resources is one of the most difficult problems in recreation economics. Land set aside for public recreation use has an opportunity cost. Often it could be devoted to other productive uses if it were not set aside. The value of the land in the best alternative use represents the economic cost of land for recreation use.

Land used for publicly provided recreation may have been acquired in several ways. It may be land that has been in state or federal ownership for decades. It may be purchased from private landowners at market prices or what similar parcels have sold for in the area. Some land used for recreation sites may have been donated to government for the expressed purpose of recreation. Reiling and Anderson (1983) suggest that in the case of donation, its opportunity cost is not clear. In principle, it has an opportunity cost; however, the donor has sacrificed the potential return from alternative use in exchange for the satisfaction of knowing the land will be preserved for the recreation enjoyment of future generations. They argue that alternative uses of the land have been rejected by the donor, and the agency cannot consider alternative uses under terms of the bequest. So its opportunity cost may be zero. Land may or may not have an opportunity cost, depending on whether it would have been used for other productive uses or would have been an unemployed resource if the agency had not accepted the gift.

If, as is usually the case, the recreation site is already publicly owned, no capital outlay is required, but valuable alternative uses may be foregone. If alternative uses of the land are sacrificed for recreation uses, estimates of the value of the land in previously allowable uses should approximate its opportunity cost. For example, the opportunity cost of land set aside as part of the National Wilderness Preservation System should be based on the alternative uses that were previously allowed under the multiple-use concept of management, but are disallowed with wilderness designation. The social opportunity cost of land removed from timber harvesting for wilderness use may range from zero for lands that are at the margin for timber harvesting (e.g., below-cost timber sales), to an upper limit represented by the annualized stumpage value of timber net of access road construction costs. Reiling and Anderson (1983) suggest that the correct measure of the social opportunity cost of wilderness is equal to this economic rent or net benefit associated with the removal of land from timber harvesting plus the loss of consumer surplus from motorized recreation which is no longer allowed.

Land that is already part of the public domain may have very little opportunity cost when used for recreation purposes other than wilderness. On land managed for multiple use, dispersed recreation such as mountain biking or driving off-road vehicles may impose almost no opportunity cost on other uses such as mining, grazing, water developments or timber harvesting. Roads established for timber management may be used by off-road vehicles and mountain bikes as well as snowmobiles.

Previous studies have estimated the opportunity cost of land in a number of ways. One study used total acquisition costs, including purchase price and closing costs, to estimate the opportunity cost of private land purchased in Eastern states for inclusion in the Wilderness system (Guldin, 1980). For existing public lands that were designated as Wilderness, he based the land value on current stumpage value of timber production and net of road construction costs. Others have also used timber production on U.S. Forest Service land as a basis for estimating the opportunity cost of recreation use (Gibbs and Reed, 1983; Gibbs and van Hees, 1981; and Tyre, 1975). However, using the proposition that most recreation activities generally do not exclude other uses under the multiple-use concept of National Forest management, the opportunity cost of land was not included in a few studies of recreation use of U.S. Forest Service land (Reiling and Anderson, 1983; Downing, 1979; and Manthy and Tucker, 1972). In these cases, the opportunity cost of the land may be very low. Also, many of these studies were designed, for the most part, to measure the financial costs of the agency rather than social costs.

## Operation and Maintenance Costs

Parks and other recreation programs usually require expenditures for the operation and maintenance of facilities. They include both variable and fixed costs. Variable costs are for cleaning, contacts with visitors, collection of fees, law enforcement, repairing vandalism, utilities, and maintenance that depends on the amount of use of the facilities. Fixed costs are for annual opening and closing of facilities, scheduled maintenance not dependent on the amount of use, and administration. These costs include the current value of materials and services needed to operate the facility and to make repairs necessary to maintain it in good condition during its useful life. Included are the salaries and fringe benefits of operating personnel, custodial services, repairs, replacements, inspection, supervision, and administrative overhead. Also included are the costs of vehicles, travel time, training, vacation, housing, and other incidental costs. If road maintenance or fire patrols in the vicinity of the site will be increased because of visitor use, then these increased costs should be included in the costs of operation and maintenance. When any of these tasks are contracted outside of the agency, the costs should include an allowance for contingencies.

In most cases, accurate estimates of operation and maintenance costs for a recreation site can be obtained from historical records and the knowledge of agency employees. Labor costs may be obtained for a facility from employee logs of their time, and the actual use of supplies, materials, and equipment. However, these costs are often difficult to estimate for a specific facility such as a campground or trail located in a larger management unit, such as a ranger district in a National Forest. Costs to be included are those that are incurred only if the park or other recreation site is opened for visitor use. Costs that would be incurred whether or not the site is open should not be included. If costs of general administration would be increased by opening the site to visitors, then these added costs should be included.

Generally, administrative overhead costs do not vary with the level of output and are considered fixed costs. Administrative overhead includes an allocated portion of the agency supervisory services, personnel services, legal services, computer services, accounting and budget services, purchasing division, motor pool, and other general expenses. Problems may arise in estimating the costs of administrative overhead for a recreation site. How far up the administrative structure of the agency should we go? For example, should a fraction of the cost associated with recreation planning by the National Park Service staff in Washington, D.C., be allocated to a specific camping facility in a National Park? Reiling and Anderson (1983) suggest that managers are in the best position to resolve this problem. Some administrative services are always shared with other recreation sites. They have the same directors, auditors, training programs, computer services, and the like.

Some of these common or joint costs could be allocated on the basis of time studies, in which employees would keep an hourly time diary during several typical weeks of the year. Other common costs could be allocated on the basis of the agency budget for direct operation and maintenance costs. If the O&M costs of a recreation site accounted for 10% of total O&M costs of the agency, 10% of the administrative overhead costs would be allocated to the site. Shabman and Kalter (1969) applied this procedure to allocate the general administrative costs of recreation programs in New York state. The federal guidelines recommend the separable costs remaining benefits method (U.S. Water Resources Council, 1983). In this case, the direct O&M costs of each recreation site would be subtracted from the benefits of each site. Then the administrative overhead of the agency would be allocated to each site on the basis of its remaining benefits as a proportion of the total remaining benefits of all sites operated by the agency. Allocating costs on this basis appeals to many because of the inherent fairness of each site's users paying in proportion to benefits.

The contribution of different types of fixed and variable costs to total cost varies for specific park and recreation programs, but labor cost comprises the largest share. Labor cost typically accounts for over 80% of O&M cost, and over 50% of total cost. Market wage rates generally provide an acceptable measure of the opportunity cost of labor. The reason is that in competitive markets, workers tend to be paid the value they produce (the marginal revenue product). Both public and private employers have to pay the going market wage rates to hire workers. Of course, minimum wage laws, union bargaining, or exploitation by employers may cause the earnings of some workers to differ from their true social contribution. Moreover, unpaid family workers and volunteers may have a social opportunity cost if they forego other jobs or devote less time to other enterprises. Nonetheless, the operational rule is: In the absence of clear-cut market imperfections, actual wage rates may be assumed to be the true social costs of labor. As discussed in Chapter 14, the opportunity cost of unemployed labor would be less than the market wage rate since little or no production would be foregone if they were employed in the recreation project. However, for most recreation projects, it is unlikely that unemployed labor will be available on a continuing basis over the life of the project, thus labor should be costed at its prevailing wage rate.

Not all variable costs are directly proportional to changes in the number of visits. As buildings and equipment age, maintenance and repair costs rise. This is particularly important in the case of recreation facilities where the preservation of historic buildings can override efficiency goals. Historic buildings may be maintained well beyond a point in time when it would be more economical to replace them. It is not unusual to have higher O&M costs for equipment and buildings as they get older. Taking a simple arithmetic average of these costs may sometimes overstate the value. This is especially true when there is a sharply increasing pattern in later years. For example, assume that the anticipated maintenance costs of a proposed visitor center are as follows:

| Year | Anticipated Maintenance |
|---|---|
| 1 | $0 |
| 2 | 0 |
| 3 | 0 |
| 4 | 0 |
| 5 | 1,000 |
| 6 | 1,000 |
| 7 | 2,000 |
| 8 | 2,000 |
| 9 | 3,000 |
| 10 | 3,000 |
| Total | $12,000 |

Total anticipated maintenance over the 10-year period is $12,000, or an arithmetic average of $1,200 per year. The equivalent annual cost, taking time into account, would be considerably less than the simple arithmetic average because it discounts future payments, giving them less value than the current one. In this case, the present value of the total maintenance cost over the 10-year period would be only $5,574 with a 10% discount rate, and the equivalent annual cost becomes $907 per year. Discounting and present value concepts are discussed in Chapter 19.

O&M costs cannot be classified as permanently fixed or variable. Any cost can be altered by a decisive manager, or become fixed as the result of failure to act. For example, the park supervisory work force is usually not reduced or increased with fluctuations in the number of visits. However, given a large enough or long enough decrease in number of visits, the supervisory work force may be intentionally reduced. Similarly, the costs of heat and light can be reduced by closing sections of park facilities, such as some toilets or part of the visitor center building. Direct labor is considered a variable cost, however, it becomes temporarily fixed in a situation where a cutback in number of visits owing to adverse weather conditions, cannot be accompanied by a reduction in the direct labor force. When sunny weather returns, a full complement of direct labor will be needed. Also, some costs are partly fixed and partly variable. For example, part of the maintenance costs of a trail may be proportional to its use, whereas certain routine inspection and maintenance costs may continue so long as it is open regardless of the level of use.

The definition of fixed and variable cost depends entirely on the planning horizon, i.e., the time period over which managers make decisions. In the short run, during a skiing season for example, some costs are usually fixed while others are variable. In the long run, all costs are variable since individuals could simply liquidate the resources they use for the recreation enterprise and invest them in some entirely different enterprise. Whether an item of cost is fixed or variable is all a matter of time. If ski resorts have already prepared for opening day by cleaning and repairing equipment and other facilities, the costs of performing those tasks are no longer relevant to any decisions during the operating season. For the rest of the year, the costs of initial cleaning and repairing equipment must be considered fixed. As the season progresses, managers will make many more decisions, one by one. They will decide how much to spend on artificial snowmaking, at what time and manner to groom the slopes, and how much to invest in marketing strategies that may increase the total revenue they receive. After each of these various tasks is completed, the expenditures for them must be considered fixed for that operating season. Decisions of managers will be based only on the costs that face them in the future, that is, those costs that are still variable in that operating season.

If they encounter adverse climatic conditions or a sharp fall in the demand for their services, it may become apparent to them that the total revenue they can expect during the entire season will be less than the total costs, fixed plus variable, of operations. However, they will continue to operate as long as the total revenue from current operations seems likely to exceed the current direct costs. At any point in the ski season, they will base operating decisions on incremental total revenue and variable costs. Only if their expected total revenue over the remainder of the season is so low that they cannot recover daily direct costs will they simply close for the season to minimize their losses.

But what about next year's ski season? Before they begin to prepare the ski facility for opening day, they will make their best estimate of the total revenue from the season. They will perform the first task of the new ski season if, and only if, the expected total revenue exceeds its total direct costs. At the very start of the skiing season, all the direct costs of the season are variable. However, they still have some fixed costs; for example, the costs of owning the land, facilities, and equipment. Those costs are fixed, until such time as they seriously consider whether to sell out. If they take a very long view of their decision problem, even the costs of owning the land, facilities, and equipment are variable.

## *External Costs and Benefits*

The social costs of recreation programs often include external costs, defined as those costs of production that fall on others and for which the agency bears no responsibility. These are the uncompensated adverse effects. A recreation area may result in a decrease in the output or additional costs to continue production of livestock grazing or timber production on nearby public lands. Also included are increases in the cost of local governmental services directly resulting from the recreation program, and adverse effects on the local economy such as increased transportation costs resulting from road congestion. The recreational agency is not legally required to reimburse those individuals and agencies that bear these external costs. Alternatively, the presence of a preserved recreation area or National Park tends to drive up land values surrounding the area bestowing a windfall gain. Many homeowners like to live adjacent to such areas since they know they will stay relatively natural and not be developed into subdivisions or shopping centers.

External costs and benefits are outside of the financial accounting and decision-making framework of the agency whose actions cause them. As a result, the recorded accounting costs of recreation agencies may not fully reflect the true social costs and benefits. The social cost of producing recreation should include all of the consequences of its production. Thus, all external costs should be identified and incorporated into the measurement of total social costs.

Fishing and hunting opportunities are produced by internal costs of the wildlife agency in each of the states and external costs to individual landowners and other government agencies. The supply cost of big-game hunting in a western state, for example, was estimated to include the following internal and external costs per hunter day:

| | |
|---|---|
| Internal cost, state wildlife agency | $13 |
| External cost, federal feed and habitat | 9 |
| External cost, private feed and habitat | 9 |
| Total internal and external costs | $31 |

Although the responsibility for wildlife management lies with the state, few of the costs of land, food, and habitat are paid by the state. The majority of habitat both in terms of acreage and animal unit months of food consumed is provided by private and federal land. Of the total land in the state of Colorado, 95% is used by wildlife for feed and habitat. About 60% is privately owned compared to about 4% owned by the state. Some 36% is in federal ownership, nearly all of which is used by big game. More than 80% of the food supply for deer and elk is provided by federal land, compared to about 20% for waterfowl and upland game birds.

In some cases, the development of park and other recreation sites may damage fish and wildlife habitat. For example, a ski resort or reservoir may result in the permanent loss of wildlife habitat and wildlife. Also, during construction of facilities, water pollution may damage the fishery. If the developer of the recreation site is a federal agency, mitigation measures must be included in project plans. The Fish and Wildlife Coordination Act (PL 85-625) requires the recreation agency to coordinate with the federal and state fish and wildlife agencies in either redesigning the project or developing mitigation programs to reduce external costs. For example, a ski resort or reservoir development might include the cost of purchasing a nearby ranch with sufficient habitat to support wildlife populations equal to the expected loss. Providing public access for hunting and fishing could fully compensate for the loss resulting from the ski resort or reservoir development.

Another important external cost is congestion. It occurs when individual users of a recreation site encounter increasing numbers of other users on site or create traffic congestion in the vicinity. Sometimes local residents oppose establishment of a new recreation facility unless the transportation infrastructure (e.g., roads, buses, parking) is expanded to handle the additional use. If the agency pays to expand the infrastructure, this partially converts what was an external cost of the project (e.g., crowding) into an internal cost of the project (e.g., cost of building additional parking facilities).

## Associated Visitor Costs

The social cost of parks and other recreation programs also includes the associated cost of users. Associated costs are defined as the costs of goods and services that must be incurred by the visitor to use the facilities provided by the agency. These are the costs which must be incurred before consumer benefits can be realized from the project. The associated costs of using recreation sites include transportation to the site, and lodging at or near the recreation site that would not otherwise have been incurred.

In addition, uses of recreation sites may incur time costs of traveling to and from the sites and while engaged in on-site recreation activities. Also, to become recreation participants, consumers must obtain the minimum amount of equipment necessary, either through rental or purchase. When the agency or a concessionaire supplies recreation equipment, the consumer has the option of rental which would be an associated cost.

There are two approaches to the treatment of associated costs. Some observers have noted that the associated cost of recreation users has already been subtracted from total benefit to obtain an estimate of *net* benefit for purposes of benefit-cost studies of the recreation programs of public agencies. Thus, they argue that associated costs have been accounted for in the benefit estimate and need not be reintroduced in the estimation of cost. This would be an acceptable procedure when savings in associated user costs of visiting a new recreation site are considered benefits of the project. For example, if one proposed site is located nearer its user clientele than an alternative site, decreased travel costs will accrue as benefits of the nearer site. When users save travel time, the value of time saved is another measure of benefits. If travel time of a successful fishing trip formerly taking 12 hours can be compressed into 10 hours without loss of fishing success, then savings in income foregone are additional benefits. As a result, the net benefits of recreation sites located closer to where users live should have higher net benefits, all else equal, than sites located more distant.

Others have noted that the associated costs of recreation users are often ignored in benefit estimation. This would occur whenever estimates of net benefits per recreation visitor day do not take into account effects of the location of recreation sites. In this event, it would be appropriate to estimate the associated cost of users and include it in total social costs of sites. This would be especially important when decisions are being made about the location of sites. The reason is that the minimum cost facility based solely on agency costs will not be the same location and size as the minimum cost facility based on total social cost, including the travel cost of users.

There are two examples where failure to minimize the sum of visitor and agency costs will lead to inefficient resource allocation decisions. In the first case, economies of scale in production of recreation sites often make it appear efficient to have a few large recreation sites. But with few sites, many people will be located quite a distance from these few recreation areas. The transportation economic literature has shown that the minimum cost location and size of recreation sites is really a function of optimizing the sum of agency costs and associated user travel costs. As a result, it is often more efficient for recreation sites to be small and, for any given density of population, located closer to where users live.

The second case involves trading off agency land cost versus visitors' transportation costs. Often the direct purchase price of land or its opportunity cost might be lower for parcels of land in remote areas. Agencies seemed to be easily deceived into thinking it is cheaper to buy land in these remote areas than pay more for land closer to where the visitors live. But when it is recognized that the savings to the agency may be offset by much larger travel costs of the visitors, the true social cost of remote recreation areas may be higher than nearby areas. Hof and Loomis (1983) provide an approach that combines a linear programming optimization model with a travel cost demand equation of wilderness visitation to maximize the net benefits of designating Wilderness Areas located at different distances from urban areas.

# Sources of Cost Information

Several methods have been used to measure the costs of developing and operating parks and other recreation sites. These include the following: (1) engineering-economic estimates of the optimum combination of inputs to produce a range of output levels; (2) cross-sectional comparison of the costs of several existing facilities with varying output levels at one point in time; and (3) time-series observations of costs for varying output levels of a single recreation site over a period of time. While each of these methods has provided satisfactory estimates of costs under particular circumstances, each also has its drawbacks. In this section, we will discuss the problems of each approach and demonstrate under what conditions they can be used successfully. In the next chapter, we will illustrate the principle methods of cost analysis and show how to apply them to recreation economic decisions. Accuracy of the alternative methods is a continuing problem, although considerable progress is evident in recent years.

## *Engineering-Economic Method*

The engineering-economic approach probably comes closest to the least-cost combination of inputs expressed in economic cost functions. Conditions that affect costs, such as the quality of management and age of facilities, can be held constant to show the separable effects of size or capacity, rate of capacity utilization, changes in technology, and the quality of services provided. The engineering-economic approach avoids the potential drawbacks of inconsistent cost accounting data over time (e.g., time series) or across recreation sites with different cost accounting definitions.

The engineering-economic method is based on the physical relationships expressed in the production function. Costs represent engineering estimates of the optimum combination of inputs to produce a range of output levels, with each quantity of input multiplied by its cost or price per unit and the results summed for each output level. The technique is discussed in federal guidelines (U.S. Water Resources Council) as cost estimating from engineering-economic, synthetic, or budgeted data. The method is particularly useful for estimating costs for new parks or recreation facilities where the historical data necessary for statistical cost analysis are unavailable. The technique, in all of its forms, assumes that the relationship between the inputs and outputs will remain sufficiently stable, so that inserting expected changes in their values into the cost function will accurately predict future costs.

Anyone can apply the engineering-economic method with little or no training in economics and statistics. The first step is to determine the physical dimensions of the project. That is, how many acres are involved, miles of roads to be built, (as well as the type of road—asphalt, gravel or dirt), number of picnic units, whether there will be a water system, and so on. Engineering estimates of the per unit (e.g., per picnic table, per mile of road) facility construction costs may be available to recreation managers from recent contract construction bids or from the record of construction costs for similar facilities, or even construction material price lists. These can be supplemented by interviewing a sample of engineers with construction companies and equipment suppliers who have been involved in planning recreation facilities near the study area. The interviews can verify whether past contract costs still reflect current costs and to cover items that may be unique to the site under study. Physical conditions, such as location, elevation, topography, and soil type, should be specified when performing the interviews.

The engineering-economic approach comes the closest of any of the estimation procedures to reflecting the theoretical cost function. It abstracts from all of the complications of existing operations in favor of engineering estimates of the required quantities of various inputs and current price quotations from suppliers. This, however, may result in underestimates of the cost because it reflects an ideal operation rather than the actual level of performance that has been realized at existing sites. Thus the engineering-economic method can provide a useful alternative to statistical cost estimation (which is discussed next) but its limitations must be kept in mind.

## *Cross-Sectional Method*

The cross-sectional approach is used by public agencies to compare the operating costs of existing parks and other recreation areas. It is also used by trade associations of private recreation companies. For example, the National Ski Area Operators Association compares the average costs of small, medium, and large ski sites each year. With available computer software, it is possible to estimate statistical functions showing the relationship between costs and a set of independent variables determining costs. A multiple regression can show the effect of recreation output, input prices, facility capacity, level of service, quality of natural resources, weather conditions, and the like. Multiple regression can account for the effect on costs of factors other than level of output.

The cross-sectional method is based on the accounting records of public agencies and private companies. Thus it relies on costs that have actually occurred in the past. Usually a sample of 30 or more similar recreation sites are selected to represent small, medium, and large operations. Cost-accounting data is classified into categories of fixed, variable, and semivariable costs. From this basic data, statistical cost functions are estimated using variation in the price of inputs and other conditions that may affect costs. Because the empirical cost curve is an average of past relationships, it is not an exact replica of the theoretical cost curves discussed in economics.

Problems may arise when input prices vary in different recreation areas and regions of the nation. Labor and fuel costs, for example, should be adjusted using the U.S. Department of Commerce index of input prices and wage rates in the various states. A second problem can be traced to variations in accounting procedures. This is less likely to be a problem in comparing sites managed by a single recreation agency, such as the U.S. Forest Service, with uniform accounting practices. However, differing depreciation schedules among private ski site operators and varying techniques for amortizing major expenses, such as development costs, can substantially distort the true cost-output relationship. A similar distortion can arise if the recreation sites that are compared use different means of paying for land, labor or capital.

Finally, a basic assumption of the cross-sectional method is that all recreation sites are operating at points along the long-run cost curve at which costs are minimized. That is, the cross-sectional technique assumes that all recreation areas are operating in an efficient manner and are using the latest technology available, whatever their output. If this assumption is violated, the regression line will lie above the true long-run average cost curve, and recreation costs will be overstated. Moreover, it is possible that the true curvature in the long-run cost curve may be accentuated and thereby overstate any economies or diseconomies of scale available to recreation areas. For example, if more of the smaller recreation areas are operating well below their optimum output, the estimated long-run average cost curve will have a downward slope much steeper than the true long-run average cost curve, and this will lead to an overestimation of economies of scale in recreation facilities and parks. It is possible to overcome this problem by including both capacity and output as independent variables in the cost function. Then, the long-run average cost curve can be estimated for the optimum output of each site.

## Time-Series Method

The time-series method is based on observations of the costs of a single park or other recreation site over a given period of time. Thus, monthly costs over a period of five years would provide 60 observations of costs if the park operates year-round. Although the best length of time will vary from situation to situation, monthly data is the time period most frequently used. In other words, the various costs incurred during each month are collected and related to the number of visits during the month. A total period of perhaps 30 months can provide enough observations for statistical analysis, yet still be short enough that the recreation activities provided have remained relatively unchanged.

This approach is the most popular method used to estimate the short-run cost functions for private recreation companies. Variable costs are regressed on output, in a cost function that typically includes a number of other variables affecting cost, such as wage rates, material prices, weather, fuel costs, input quality, and so on. Including these variables in the model allows us to isolate their effects and obtain a better estimate of the relationship between variable costs and output. The time-series method uses recorded historical data, and during most of the period for which data are available, the costs of labor, raw materials, and other items may have been rising. To remove this bias, historic data are deflated for price level changes. The time-series method is usually applied to variable costs rather than fixed costs. This has the advantage of avoiding the difficult problem of allocating fixed costs to a particular recreation activity. Moreover, it is a relatively simple matter to add alternative estimates of fixed costs to the basic variable cost function.

Problems may arise when an increase in the number of visits during one time period causes additional maintenance expenses not in that period but, rather, in subsequent periods. During a period of high production, actual maintenance expenditures will be unusually low because the recreation facilities are being used at full capacity, so that maintenance must be postponed when possible. Repairs that are made will usually be temporary in nature, aimed at getting the facilities back into operation rapidly, until a period when some slack exists in the number of visits. Without careful adjustment, this problem can cause errors in statistically estimated cost functions from time-series data.

Another problem is that accounting data usually fail to record opportunity costs, which may be the largest and the most important costs for future decisions. Because managerial decisions pertain to future operations, the relevant costs are future costs, as opposed to current or historical costs found in accounting records. Accounting costs usually should be modified to reflect likely changes before they are used for making important decisions about future operations.

The three approaches discussed in this section should not be regarded as mutually exclusive or even competitive in all cases, but rather as generally complementary to one another. For example, in some cases time-series and cross-section data can be combined to obtain a more robust estimate of the cost function. As always, the emphasis placed on any one method depends on the purpose of the study, that is, determining what management really needs and wants, as well as the time and expense involved, considering the availability of data.

*Chapter 16*

# Empirical Cost Studies

This chapter summarizes the results of several cost studies; illustrates the principles of empirical cost analysis for boat marinas and campgrounds; shows how managers simplify cost studies with break-even charts; illustrates how to apply cost-effectiveness to recreation economic decisions when costs can be measured but benefits are in physical units or effectiveness scores; shows how to adjust inflating costs over the life of a project to constant dollars.

The widespread availability of computer software enables us to show how the costs change with improvement in design, size, utilization of capacity, and level of service provided. Such studies are particularly useful in recreation economic decisions because they show how future costs are expected to change with alternative policies.

## Some Cost Studies

In the past, most cost studies by state and federal agencies were cross-sectional. Their objective was to provide summaries of the average costs of recreation programs of an agency for one point in time. Considerable progress has been made in improving the traditional public cost-accounting procedures so that they show the operating costs associated with each major type of recreation activity. Historical line-item accounting practices show types of expenses, such as total agency or park labor, materials, maintenance and repair, and contract services. Functional accounting practices are an improvement over line-item accounting, in that they show expenses by type of program. Typically, these include total agency or park fire control, safety, conservation, visitor interpretation, recreation services, and the like. However, neither line-item nor functional accounting reveals the costs allocated to each recreation activity, nor how costs vary with changes in design, size, utilization of capacity, or level of services provided. Now, some cost studies have begun to remedy these deficiencies in the available cost information.

Here we present examples of the many average cost studies by state and federal agencies. Also, we will examine the few studies that have developed cost functions or supply curves. These studies are particularly useful in recreation economic decision making, for they show how future costs are expected to change with alternative levels of the program or budget.

## *Average Costs per User Day*

An interesting example of the cross-sectional method is a study of the average costs of recreation activities at state parks in Pennsylvania by Strauss (1975). Table 16-1 shows the average costs statewide for 17 recreation activities. Included are the costs in 110 parks for direct and indirect labor allocated on a time basis and contract services for operation, maintenance, and minor development. These costs represent the essential variable costs of park operations. Strauss purposely omitted fixed costs, in the belief that they might be used as a convenient catchall for many park expenditures, resulting in an inaccurate allocation of total costs. Note that output is measured in activity days of service, which represent use by one person for any portion of a given day.

The results of the study show that average variable costs range from $0.07 per activity day of pleasure driving to $2.77 for lodging in primitive cabins. Picnicking was the most popular activity in the state parks with

**Table 16-1. Average Annual Operating and Maintenance Costs per Recreation Activity Day, Pennsylvania State Parks**

| Recreation Activity | Percent of Annual Operation & Maintenance Costs | Percent of Annual Activity | Costs per Day (1974 Dollars) |
|---|---|---|---|
| Tent and Trailer Camping | 21.8 | 6.7 | $1.30 |
| Group Tent Camping | 2.4 | 0.3 | 2.71 |
| Group Camping | 2.4 | 0.5 | 1.87 |
| Primitive Cabin | 3.6 | 0.5 | 2.77 |
| Swimming, Beach | 13.2 | 16.7 | 0.32 |
| Swimming, Pool | 4.7 | 3.4 | 0.56 |
| Picnicking | 22.2 | 38.3 | 0.23 |
| Boating | 7.8 | 6.7 | 0.47 |
| Fishing | 7.4 | 11.8 | 0.25 |
| Environmental Education | 4.6 | 4.9 | 0.38 |
| Hiking | 3.6 | 8.6 | 0.17 |
| Hunting | 1.7 | 1.0 | 0.66 |
| Pleasure Driving | | | 0.07 |
| Ice Sports | 0.9 | 0.2 | |
| Snowmobiling | 0.7 | 0.1 | 2.16 |
| Sledding | 0.2 | 1.1 | |
| Skiing | 2.7 | 1.1 | |

Source: Adapted from Strauss, 1975

average costs of $0.23 per day, followed by beach swimming, $0.32; fishing, $0.25; hiking, $0.17; tent and trailer camping, $1.30; and boating, $0.47. The average costs for all recreation uses of the state parks were not reported, but appear to have been less than $0.50 per day at the time of the study. These costs have increased substantially to the present time; however, the relationships would probably remain much the same. You can estimate how much these costs have increased by referring to a later section of this chapter, for changes in the general price level.

A number of studies have attempted to calculate the average fixed costs as well as the variable costs of recreation activities. Table 16-2 shows average fixed and variable costs for several recreation activities in two regions of the U.S. Forest Service. Variable costs include operation and maintenance, similar to the Pennsylvania state parks study. Because output is measured in 12-hour recreation visitor days (RVDs), the variable cost results are not directly comparable to the state data. For example, it would take nearly two RVDs to equal one activity day of camping. This means that the variable costs of camping in the northern Rocky Mountains reported as $0.66 per RVD should be doubled to $1.32 per activity day. This compares favorably with the state data for camping of $1.30 per activity day. In the case of picnicking, nearly four activity days are required to equal one 12-hour RVD. This means that variable costs of picnicking in the northern Rocky Mountains reported as $1.11 per RVD should

**Table 16-2. Average Annual Fixed and Variable Costs of Recreation Activities in the National Forests**

| | Costs per Recreation Visitor Day | | |
|---|---|---|---|
| Region and Activity | Variable Costs | Fixed Costs | Total Costs |
| **Northern Rocky Mountain Region** | | | |
| Camping, Total | $0.66 | $1.08 | $1.74 |
| Wilderness | 0.14 | 0.14 | 0.28 |
| Semiprimitive Motorized | 0.79 | 0.86 | 1.65 |
| Roaded Natural | 0.68 | 1.05 | 1.73 |
| Semiurban | 0.59 | 1.27 | 1.86 |
| Picnicking | 1.11 | 1.80 | 2.91 |
| Boating | 0.76 | 2.29 | 3.05 |
| Swimming | 0.73 | 1.57 | 2.30 |
| Interpretation Minor | 0.15 | 1.31 | 1.46 |
| Observation | 0.48 | 0.82 | 1.30 |
| **Southern Region** | | | |
| Camping | 0.74 | 0.54 | 1.28 |
| Picnicking | 1.31 | 0.83 | 2.14 |
| Boating | 2.11 | 1.26 | 3.37 |
| Swimming | 2.50 | 1.76 | 4.26 |
| Observation | 1.04 | 0.58 | 1.62 |

Source: Tyre, 1975; Gibbs and Reed, 1983; Gibbs and van Hees, 1981.

be divided by four to equal about $0.28 per activity day. This compares favorably with the state data for picnicking of $0.23 per activity day.

Fixed costs include the opportunity cost of foregone timber harvests, overhead, and the amortized construction costs of facilities at replacement cost. As you can see by reading down the fixed cost column of Table 16-2 (page 289), if we have to replace all of our capital investment in outdoor recreation facilities on federal land, costs would increase by a substantial amount. For example, in the case of camping in the northern Rocky Mountains, fixed costs would be $1.08 per RVD and would account for nearly two-thirds of total camping costs of $1.74 per RVD with all new facilities. Including fixed costs does illustrate the magnitude of the long-run costs when new facilities are added as demand increases in future years.

## Incremental Cost Functions

The best example of an application of the engineering-economic method is a study of pleasure boat marinas on the Chesapeake Bay, Maryland, by Lyon, Tuthill and Matthews (1969). It shows costs for marinas with capacities of 50, 100, 150, 200, and 300 boats, and costs for rates of utilization from 50% to 100% of capacity (see Table 16-3). The marinas are standardized in all respects except size. Each provides the same services—dock rental, fuel, showers, rest rooms, and hookups for electricity and drinking water. The study excludes the maintenance and repair of boats, dry storage, hauling and launching services, restaurant operations, and boat sales.

Information on necessary investment costs was obtained from marina engineering and construction firms based on uniform specifications of materials used in the construction of piers, docks, electrical systems, water systems, and buildings for the office, equipment, showers, and rest rooms. Commercial companies serving marinas provided information on the prices of necessary marina equipment, materials, and insurance. Public utilities in the area provided information on electricity, natural gas, water, and sewage rate schedules and use by marinas. A survey of the operating costs of 17 marinas provided information on average wages and miscellaneous expenses (see the footnotes to Table 16-3 for additional information).

Most of the 308 marinas in Maryland at the time of the study were small, with an average capacity of 64 boats. Pleasure boating on the Chesapeake Bay occurred during a six-month period between May and November. Most boats were stored at marinas during winter months, so marina utilization was year-round. Annual marina charges averaged $167 per boat. Marinas were operating at nearly 90% of capacity and, with rapid increases in the demand for marina services, operators reported they would need 30% more capacity in the next five years. Thus, the problem was to estimate the effect on costs of changes in the utilization and size of marinas.

Table 16-3 shows the effect of size on average annual fixed and variable costs per boat. Note that the data are for 100% capacity operation.

**Table 16-3. Effect of Size on Average Annual Fixed and Variable Costs per Boat for Recreation Marinas, Chesapeake Bay, Maryland**

| Costs per Boat | Marina Size, Number of Boats at Capacity 50 | 100 | 150 | 200 |
|---|---|---|---|---|
| **Fixed Costs** | | | | |
| Buildings[a] | $5.37 | $3.07 | $2.34 | $1.98 |
| Piers[a] | 26.22 | 19.85 | 19.78 | 19.75 |
| Bulkheading[a] | 12.31 | 7.47 | 6.29 | 5.11 |
| Equipmenta | 12.17 | 6.26 | 4.67 | 4.97 |
| Water System[a] | 1.46 | 1.36 | 1.35 | 1.32 |
| Electrical System[a] | 3.15 | 2.87 | 2.90 | 2.75 |
| Taxes[b] | 9.58 | 8.09 | 7.91 | 7.85 |
| Insurance | 8.31 | 5.99 | 5.52 | 5.13 |
| Maintenance[c] | 2.91 | 2.16 | 2.04 | 2.03 |
| Interest[d] | 43.97 | 36.38 | 35.20 | 34.40 |
| Subtotal | 125.45 | 93.50 | 88.00 | 85.29 |
| **Variable Costs** | | | | |
| Labor[e] | 61.75 | 42.30 | 31.84 | 41.37 |
| Electricity[f] | 14.40 | 12.64 | 11.54 | 10.75 |
| Water-Sewer[f] | 1.04 | 0.59 | 0.58 | 0.53 |
| Telephone[g] | 4.50 | 4.50 | 4.50 | 4.50 |
| Fuel for Heat[h] | 2.43 | 1.33 | 0.98 | 0.80 |
| Miscellaneous[i] | 3.03 | 3.27 | 4.22 | 3.83 |
| Subtotal | 87.15 | 64.63 | 53.66 | 61.78 |
| **Average Total Costs[k]** | **$213.00** | **$158.00** | **$142.00** | **$147.00** |

[a]Depreciation was calculated by the straight line method, assuming a 20-year life for buildings, piers, and bulkhead; 10 years for the water and electrical systems; and 5 years for equipment.
[b]Average tax of $9.58 per $10,000 of investment for the 50-slip marina, declining $0.0073 per slip for the larger size marinas.
[c]Maintenance at 5% of investment.
[d]Interest at 5% of one-half of facilities investment and all of land investment.
[e]Labor based on survey of 17 marinas. Manager salary was omitted as a cost because managers are assumed to receive a share of profits.
[f]Public utility services for electricity, fresh water, and sewage were available to marinas.
[g]Based on average telephone costs of 17 marinas adjusted for marina size.
[h]Based on average heat costs of 17 marinas adjusted for building volume.
[i]Includes office supplies, toilet supplies, laundry, rags, legal fees, and other minor supplies.
[k]Average total costs are rounded to nearest dollar.

Source: Lyon, Tuthill and Matthews, 1969.

Fixed costs fall continuously from $125.45 for marinas with 50-boat capacity to $85.29 for 200 boats. Variable costs fall from $87.15 for marinas with 50-boat capacity to $53.66 for 150 boats and then rise to $61.78 for 200 boats. Total costs, which are the sum of fixed and variable costs, fall from $212.60 for marinas with 50-boat capacity to $141.66 for 150 boats and then rise to $147.07 for 200 boats. The authors also included costs for a 300-boat marina, which are omitted here to simplify the example without changing the results.

Table 16-4 shows the effect on costs of rate of capacity utilization. Average total costs increase sharply as utilization of capacity falls from 100% to 50%. For example, costs of the 150-boat marina rise from $142 at 100% capacity utilization to $230 at 50%, or by 62%. You can verify this result by multiplying average fixed costs of $88 by 150 boats ($13,200; Table 16-3, page 291), dividing by 75 boats ($176), and adding variable costs of $53, which vary directly with output and do not change ($230, rounded). Similar procedures were used to estimate the effect on costs of rate of capacity utilization for each marina.

Figure 16-1 illustrates the relationship between marina size and rate of capacity utilization. The short-run average cost curves are formed by varying the utilization of marinas from 50% to 100% of capacity. Costs decline sharply over this range. The long-run average cost function represents the effect of varying the size of marinas from 50 to 200 boats. Drawing a line through the minimum cost points of the short-run average cost curves for each marina provides a close approximation of the long-run average cost curve for the marina industry.

The long-run average cost curve is characterized by three distinct phases—decreasing, constant, and increasing costs. The initial phase of the curve shows decreasing costs resulting from more efficient use of capital equipment as size of the enterprise increases. Also, expansion allows more labor specialization, which increases labor efficiency and reduces average costs. Constant costs along the horizontal segment of the curve indicate that costs cannot be decreased through improved management

**Table 16-4. Effect of the Rate of Capacity Utilization on Average Total Costs for Recreation Boating Marinas, Chesapeake Bay, Maryland**

| Marina Size | Percent of Capacity Utilization 50 | 60 | 70 | 80 | 90 | 100 |
|---|---|---|---|---|---|---|
| **50 Boats** | | | | | | |
| Number of Slips Rented | 25 | 30 | 35 | 40 | 45 | 50 |
| Average Cost | $338 | $296 | $266 | $244 | $227 | $212 |
| **100 Boats** | | | | | | |
| Number of Slips Rented | 50 | 60 | 70 | 80 | 90 | 100 |
| Average Cost | $252 | $220 | $198 | $182 | $169 | $158 |
| **150 Boats** | | | | | | |
| Number of Slips Rented | 75 | 90 | 105 | 120 | 135 | 150 |
| Average Cost | $230 | $200 | $179 | $164 | $151 | $142 |
| **200 Boats** | | | | | | |
| Number of Slips Rented | 100 | 120 | 140 | 160 | 180 | 200 |
| Average Cost | $232 | $204 | $184 | $168 | $157 | $147 |

Source: Lyon, Tuthill and Matthews, 1969.

**Figure 16-1. Short-Run and Long-Run Average Cost Curves for Recreation Boat Marinas, Chesapeake Bay, Maryland**

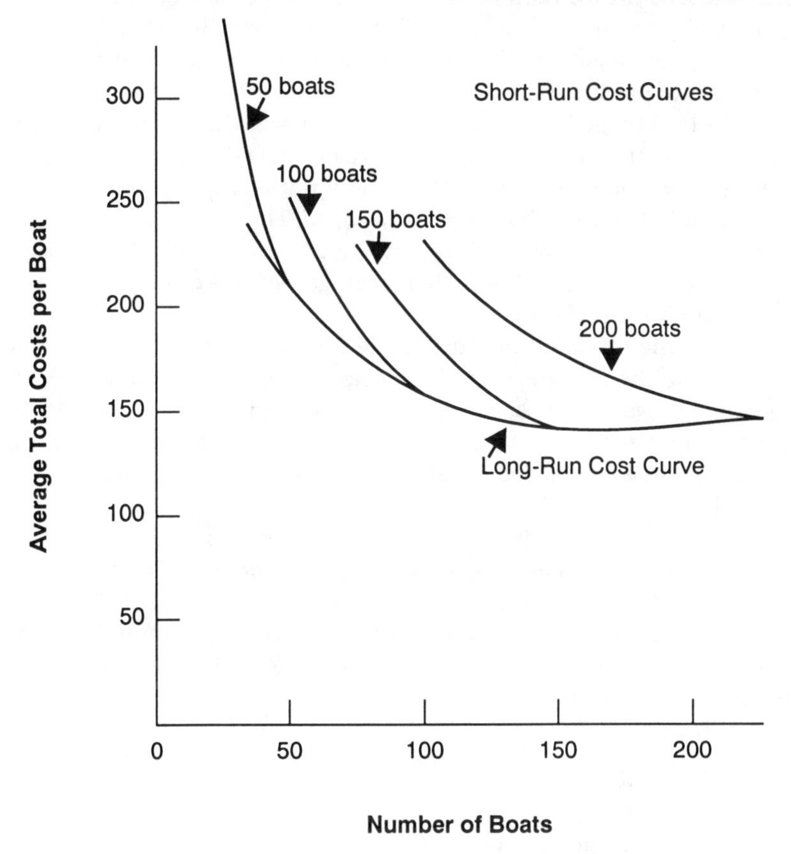


organization or techniques of operation to reduce material inputs. The final phase of the curve shows increasing costs, which result from decreases in labor efficiency as employees are required to walk greater distances to perform their work in larger marinas. Marinas extend their operations either along the waterfront or perpendicular to the waterfront. In either case, expansion adds to the distance that personnel cover when going back and forth between their central station and the boat docks, resulting in additional labor costs per boat.

Engineering-economic cost information can help managers make several important recreation economic decisions. For example, what dock rental fee would be required to cover the total costs of a small 50-boat marina? This depends on the capacity utilization. Unfortunately, capacity utilization depends, in part, on the fee to be charged. Thus, Table 16-4 shows that a fee of $244 per boat would cover total costs with 80% utilization, which is considerably more than the average fee of $167 at the time of the study. If utilization of capacity of the large 200-boat slip capacity marina fell to 50%, a fee of $232 would be required to cover total costs, which exceeds the fee required to cover the total costs of the smaller 100-boat capacity marina operating at 100% of capacity. Similar comparisons suggest that a smaller marina operated at higher capacity typically has lower costs of production.

Table 16-3 (page 291) also allows us to answer the management question of at what price would small and large marinas shut down? The smallest marinas would shut down if they could not charge a price of $87 per boat and fill all of their boat docks or slips. The largest marinas would shut down at a price of $62 if they could not fill all of their slips. Continuing to operate when price is less than average variable costs, increases the losses over shutting down.

What is the optimum or most efficient number of boat docks or slips per marina in the long run? Optimum size occurs at the minimum of the long-run average total cost curve. A 150-boat marina has average total costs of $142, the lowest of the four marinas shown. However, Figure 16-1 (page 293) suggests that the lowest cost marina may be somewhat larger, as the following discussion demonstrates.

Many managers of private and public recreation resources are developing computerized management information systems. To illustrate the possible use of engineering-economic data in statistical cost analysis, four points were estimated on the long-run average cost function shown in Table 16-3 (page 291) and Figure 16-1 (page 293). Ordinary least-squares regression procedures were used to estimate the following quadratic cost curve:

$$AC = a - bQ + cQ^2 \qquad \text{(Equation 16-1)}$$

$$AC = 291.25 - 1.897Q + 0.0059Q^2$$
$$\text{(t-value)} \quad (-9.82) \quad (7.76) \quad R^2 = 0.99 \quad \text{Cases} = 4 \qquad \text{(Equation 16-2)}$$

where AC refers to average costs per boat; $Q$ is the size of marinas or the quantity of boats at capacity; and $a$, $b$, and $c$ are the regression coefficients determined by the statistical analysis. T-values are shown in parenthesis and indicate that all coefficients are highly significant. A comparison of the actual and statistical (in parentheses) estimates of average costs for 50 boats were $213 ($211); for 100 boats, $158 ($161); for 150 boats, $142 ($139); and 200 boats, $147 ($148). This represents a close relationship which is not surprising since the data points were all generated from the same deterministic engineering model, and do not contain the variation that would be observed if data were collected from different marinas or the same marina over time.

The quadratic form is widely used in empirical cost studies, because it is a relatively simple matter to derive the cubic total cost function once a quadratic average cost function is known by multiplying the AC function by $Q$. The cubic total cost (TC) function becomes:

$$TC = aQ - bQ^2 + cQ^3 \qquad \text{(Equation 16-3)}$$
$$TC = 291.25Q - 1.897Q^2 + 0.0059Q^3 \qquad \text{(Equation 16-4)}$$

Note that the quadratic form includes both a linear and a squared term for the size of marina. Figure 16-2 depicts the average, total, and marginal costs per boat for recreation marinas in the long run. The curves were all derived from the regression results for total costs.

**Figure 16-2. Total, Average and Marginal Costs per Boat at Recreation Marinas, Chesapeake Bay, Maryland**

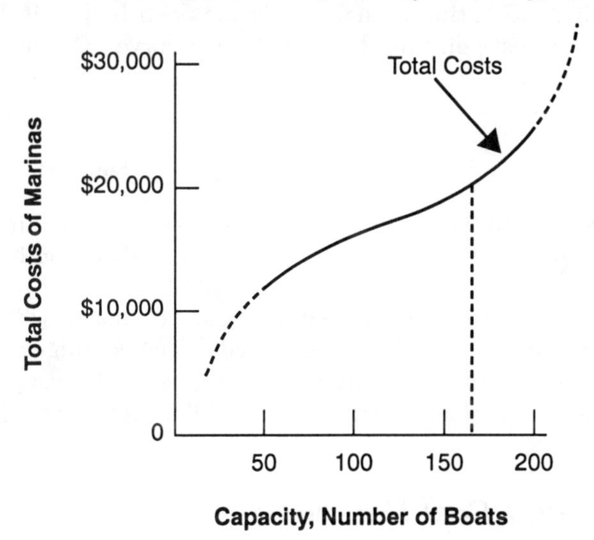


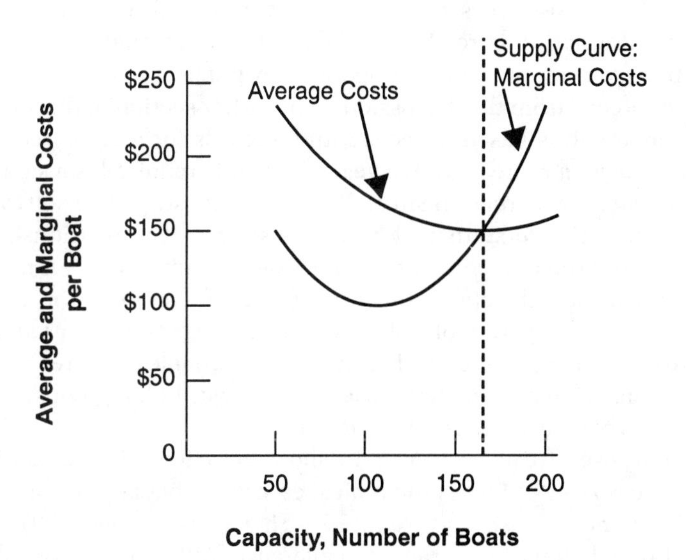

The total cost curve shows that the first dollars spent on providing boat marina services produce a large output of boating opportunities. However, as more and more dollars are spent, less additional output is produced by each additional dollar, i.e., increasing marginal costs. The marginal cost function can be derived from a total cost function by taking the first derivative. The marginal cost (MC) function becomes:

$$\text{MC} = a - 2bQ + 3cQ^2 \qquad \text{(Equation 16-5)}$$
$$\text{MC} = 291.25 - 3.8Q + 0.0177Q^2 \qquad \text{(Equation 16-6)}$$

The marginal cost curve represents the long-run supply curve for boat marinas. Finally, the optimum size of marinas can be precisely estimated as the least-cost point on the average cost curve. Optimum size ($S_{\text{Optimum}}$) becomes:

$$S_{\text{Optimum}} = \frac{b}{2c} \qquad \text{(Equation 16-7)}$$

$$S_{\text{Optimum}} = 1.897 \div 0.0118 \qquad \text{(Equation 16-8)}$$
$$S_{\text{Optimum}} = 160.76 \qquad \text{(Equation 16-9)}$$

The optimum size marina is estimated at about 161 boats, which is a more precise estimate than the 150 boats, based on engineering-economic budgets for the four marinas. Optimum size occurs at the lowest point on the long-run average total cost curve where marginal cost is equal to average cost.

## *Cross-Sectional Cost Functions*

Managers also can use cross-sectional data in statistical cost analysis. The necessary information is readily available. Often, all that is required is information from a sample of sites operated by public agencies in the state of interest. Recall from the discussion in an earlier section of this chapter, that the approach is based on accounting records for a cross section of sites operating in a representative year. All that is required is a sample of 30 or more similar recreation sites. With available statistical software, it is possible to estimate statistical functions showing the relationship between costs and the independent variables determining costs. A multiple regression can show the effects on costs of level of technology or development, size or capacity, rate of utilization of capacity, and other variables. The regression coefficient for each independent variable indicates the marginal relationship between that variable and cost, holding constant the effect of all other variables in the function.

The purpose of this section is to show the effect of a reduction in campground services. This is the typical case when budgets for operation and maintenance are sharply reduced. Figure 16-3 (page 300) shows empirical-based shifts in average variable cost (AVC) and marginal cost

(MC) curves for campgrounds with changes in the level of management service (note the MC curve is darker above AVC since this is the range where MC is the supply curve—above the shutdown point). This illustrates a possible application of the computerized information system of the U.S. Forest Service. The cross-sectional data are from the Recreation Information Management (RIM) system for campgrounds in the Arapaho and Roosevelt National Forests in the Rocky Mountains of the United States. By using data for one region from a single agency, it is possible to avoid several potential problems of cross-sectional analysis.

First, the variable costs reported in RIM appear to be reasonably complete. In this study, AVC includes unadjusted RIM data for operation, maintenance, roads, trails, and administration of the campgrounds. The agency's accounts include the cost of cleaning, contact with visitors, collection of fees, law enforcement, vandalism, utilities, and materials to operate the campgrounds and to make repairs necessary to maintain standard service. Not included in the agency's accounts are the external costs of unpaid labor such as volunteers, fire control, and other off-site costs. Omitting them here does not preclude meaningful analysis.

Second, the prices of inputs such as labor, fuel, and repairs are generally the same across the sample of campgrounds. Third, several important problems of cross-sectional analysis can be avoided in selecting the sample. The possible effect of environmental quality, in particular the location of campgrounds along the shore of a river or lake, is controlled by excluding the few sites otherwise located. Also, the sample is limited to the agency's Roaded Natural (Class 3) campgrounds. This means that capital improvements at all of the sites are rustic, being constructed of native materials. Visitor information services are informal. Access is by gravel or hard surface roads. As a result of these two adjustments, the sample is limited to 47 of the 58 campgrounds located in the two National Forests.

Fourth, there is sufficient variation in output (recreation visitor days or RVDs) that the effects of capacity and its utilization can be estimated by including them as independent variables in the cost function. Output of individual campgrounds varies from a low of five RVDs to nearly 900 RVDs per day. The size distribution is:

| Number of campsites | Number of campgrounds |
|---|---|
| Less than 10 | 15 |
| 10–19 | 17 |
| 20–29 | 5 |
| 30–39 | 4 |
| 40 and Over | 6 |

The average campground is small with 22.8 campsites and capacity of 228 RVDs at one time (i.e., 10 RVDs per campsite). Overall, 14.4 campsites are occupied per day which represents 63.2% utilization of capacity during the 142-day summer season. This is reasonably efficient, given the peak use on weekends, holidays, and during the months of July and August.

Fifth, there is sufficient variation in the quality of service, so that its effects can be estimated by including it as an independent variable in the cost function. The sample includes 21 campgrounds with standard service and 26 without. The categorical variable is set equal to one if standard services are provided, and equal to zero if less than standard services are provided. The campground service variable is specified as the attractiveness of a recreation site in terms of management service level including capital improvements. Standard service is defined to include the availability of drinking water, toilets, tables, fireplaces, trash removal, tent pads, parking spaces, and access roads to developed campgrounds where fees are charged. Less than standard service omits drinking water, with other services at minimal levels. No camping fees are charged at less than standard service campgrounds.

Last, one problem that could not be avoided is the possibility that some or all of the sites are not operating efficiently. For example, they may not be using the optimum combination of resources. If this is the case, the regression line for existing campgrounds will lie above the potential efficient cost curve and recreation costs will be overstated. This is an inherent limitation of the cross-sectional approach. However, violation of the assumption of optimum combination of resources does not preclude meaningful analysis. When the purpose of the study is to describe or predict the actual behavior of managers, we should use the accounting information that managers actually use.

Once the information is prepared and put into the computer, statistical packages are available to quickly perform the analysis. Following the usual procedure in recreation cost analysis, we use the multiple regression statistical method to estimate the relationship of costs to output and other important variables including size and services provided. The general form of the average cost function to be estimated with the data is:

$$\text{AVC} = a - bQ + cQ^2 + dS - eS^2 + fM \qquad \text{(Equation 16-10)}$$

where AVC refers to average variable costs per RVD; $Q$ is utilization of capacity in RVDs per day; $S$ is size or capacity in RVDs per day; $M$ is a categorical variable for standard service of management; and $a$, $b$, $c$, $d$, $e$, and $f$ are the regression coefficients determined by the statistical analysis.

The statistical regression is:

$$\text{AVC} = 0.6666 - 0.0843Q + 0.00013Q^2 + 0.0322S - 0.000015S^2 + 0.3471M$$

(t-values) (4.7) (3.7) (6.5) (2.5) (2.1) (1.65)

Sample Size ($N$)=47 $R^2 = 0.60$ $F = 14.98$ (Equation 16-11)

Note that the quadratic form of the equation includes both a linear and a squared term for the rate of utilization and capacity of the campgrounds. It provided the best fit of the actual data points.

The coefficient of determination, $R^2$, adjusted for degrees of freedom, indicates that 60% of the total variation in average variable costs is explained by the variables included in the function, which is considered a satisfactory level of explanation for cross-sectional data from operating sites. The overall equation is significant at the 0.01 level, as indicated by an $F$ value of 14.98.

Furthermore, the regression coefficients for each independent variable are highly significant. The numbers in parentheses below each regression coefficient represent the t-statistics on the coefficients. The regression coefficients included in the equation are significantly different from zero at the 0.01 level except for capacity squared at the 0.06 level and standard service at the 0.11 level. That is, we can reject the hypothesis that the independent variables are unrelated to cost at the 99% significance level, except capacity squared at the 94% confidence level and standard service at the 88% confidence level. This is an acceptable level of significance.

The cost curves shown in Figure 16-3 (page 300) can be easily derived from the statistical cost function. The short-run AVC curve is that part of the AVC function that expresses the relation between cost and rate of utilization of capacity, holding constant the effects of all other independent variables. For example, if we hold constant size or capacity ($S$ = 32.3 campsites) and level of service ($M$ = 1 for standard, 0 for less than standard), we can reduce the multivariate statistical cost function into a two dimensional AVC curve. This procedure results in the following condensed equations:

With standard service:

$$\text{AVC} = 1.89 - 0.0843Q + 0.00013Q^2 \quad \text{(Equation 16-12)}$$

With less than standard service:

$$\text{AVC} = 1.54 - 0.0843Q + 0.00013Q^2 \quad \text{(Equation 16-13)}$$

Figure 16-3 (page 300) depicts how short-run AVC varies with the number of visits to a campground of a given size. Note that the curves are U-shaped; they fall at first and then rise as output increases.

The marginal cost equation can be easily derived from the quadratic AVC equations by first multiplying it by $Q$ to make it a total variable cost function and then taking the first derivative. The marginal cost (MC) equations become:

$$\text{MC} = a - 2bQ + 3cQ^2 \quad \text{(Equation 16-14)}$$

With standard service:

$$\text{MC} = 1.89 - 0.1686Q + 0.00039Q^2 \quad \text{(Equation 16-15)}$$

With less than standard service:

$$\text{MC} = 1.54 - 0.1686Q + 0.00039Q^2 \quad \text{(Equation 16-16)}$$

**Figure 16-3. Shifts in the Short-Run Costs of Campgrounds in the Arapaho and Roosevelt National Forests, Colorado**

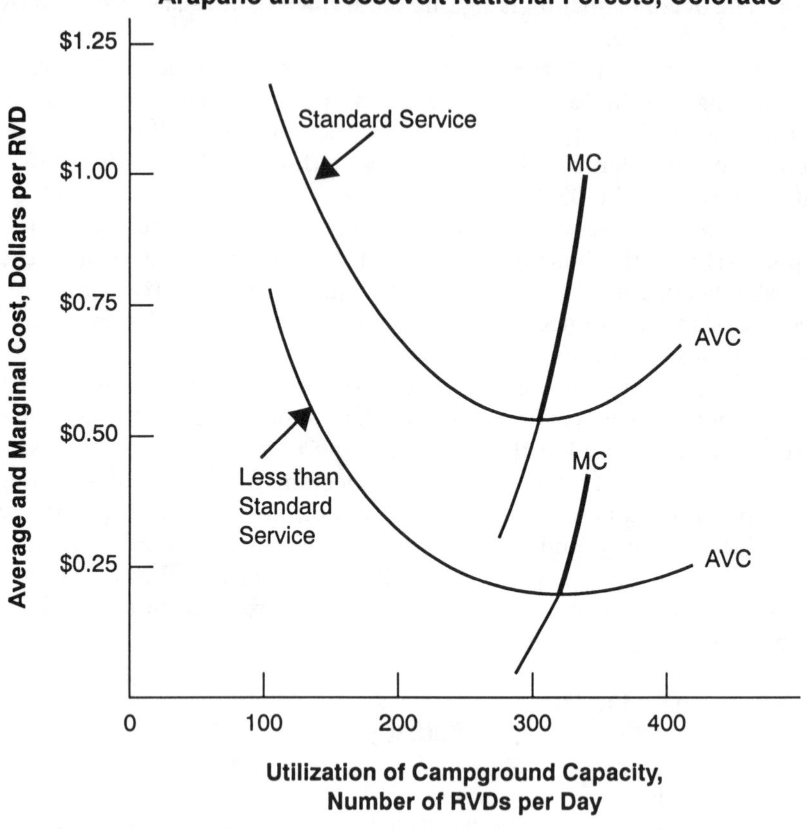


The marginal cost curves represent the short-run supply curves, indicated by the heavy portion of the curves above the point of intersection with the average variable cost curves. As is typical for the supply curve for most goods and services, we see that an increase in supply is associated with an increase in marginal cost. Changes such as this represent movements along the supply curves.

Figure 16-3 also shows the shift from one supply curve to another for campgrounds with and without standard service. The regression coefficient indicates that AVC and MC increase by $0.3471 per RVD with standard service. Thus, the constant or *a* terms in the condensed AVC and MC equations are increased by $0.35 from 1.54 to 1.89 as shown here. This means that the level of service results in parallel shifts in the AVC and MC curves. We can test for the possibility that the effect of service may vary with level of output by including interactive variables in the cost function. In this case, the interactive variables are not statistically significant and therefore are omitted from the final function. We conclude that the shift is parallel in the vicinity of mean values, which is the important area of decision making.

Figure 16-3 shows that at its lowest point the AVC of standard service campgrounds is $0.54 per RVD, compared with $0.19 per RVD for campgrounds with less than standard service, or $0.35 per RVD lower. This provides managers with a more accurate estimate of the cost of standard service than could be obtained by alternative procedures. For example, taking the difference between the simple average costs of campgrounds grouped by level of service, we would have concluded that standard service costs about $0.43 rather than $0.35 per RVD. This would overstate the cost of providing standard service by about 23% because the difference in AVC also is caused by differences in size or capacity and utilization of campground capacity. The average campground with standard service contains 36 campsites compared with only 12 campsites in campgrounds with less than standard service. Standard service campgrounds utilize 70% of capacity, compared with 45% for campgrounds with less than standard service. The chief advantage of using a statistical cost function is that it can show the cost of standard service with these other determinants of costs held constant.

For other applications of cross-sectional data to statistical cost analysis, see the pioneering study by Gibbs and van Hees of 47 campgrounds in roaded natural forests of Oregon and Washington (1981) and the study by Gibbs and Reed of 94 roaded natural campgrounds in northern Idaho, Montana, and North and South Dakota (1983). The authors adjusted labor costs to account for the contribution of trainees, volunteers, and shared workers. In their northern Rocky Mountain study (Gibbs and Reed, 1983) the opportunity costs of this unbudgeted labor was estimated as $0.11 compared to budgeted labor costs of $0.30 per RVD. Total variable costs were $0.68, including contract services, $0.11; vehicles, $0.09; and materials, $0.05 per RVD.

## Break-Even Charts

Empirical cost functions are used in a variety of ways in making recreation economic decisions. One important practical application by managers of private companies and government agencies is to prepare linear break-even charts. They are a simplification of the nonlinear total cost and total revenue functions shown previously. The charts are used to estimate the number of customers necessary to break even. They simply show that if recreation sites are going to break even or make a profit, total revenue must rise fast enough to get above total cost, before running out of customers. This is an important consideration for recreation sites. By the time most sites are set up to open for visitors, they have already incurred substantial fixed cost. So the sites must serve a lot of customers to break even. But beyond the break-even point, additional customers add to profits. There is nothing new or novel about this basic idea; the first such chart was developed in the early 1900s at Columbia University in New York City.

A break-even chart is a graphic representation of the relationship between total cost and total revenue for all levels of output or sales. As shown in Figure 16-4, output is measured on the horizontal axis, with total revenue and total cost shown on the vertical axis. Since fixed costs are constant regardless of output, they are indicated by a horizontal line. Variable costs at each level of output are measured by the distance between the total cost and the constant fixed costs.

The total cost function is simply a straight line drawn from fixed cost at zero output through total cost at current output. Since total revenue is proportional to output, it is usually shown as a 45° straight line from zero to current output. The break-even point is depicted as the level of output and sales where total revenue equals total cost.

Linear analysis is appropriate for many uses. To assume a linear total revenue function means that all units of output can be sold at the same price. A constant price per unit of output would be true of companies in a competitive industry, and for many other companies in situations where the product can be sold without a break in price over a wide range of output. To assume a linear total cost function means that additional units of each input can be purchased at the same price and the production function also is linear. These assumptions may be reasonable for a wide range of output for most recreation goods and services, as shown by a number of empirical studies of costs. Finally, it should be noted that even though the charts are drawn from zero output to current output, managers who use them would not ordinarily consider the high and the low extremes. Linear functions are probably reasonably accurate within the relevant range near current output.

## *A Break-Even Chart for Skiing*

The ski industry provides a good example of the effective use of break-even analysis. Figure 16-4 shows a typical linear break-even chart for large ski areas in North America, based on the data contained in Table 16-5 (page 306). Fixed costs of $3.4 million are represented by a horizontal line. Variable costs are estimated to be $5.50 per skier day, so total costs rise by $5.50 for each additional skier day of output. At the time of the study, average revenue was reported to be $16.50 per skier day, so total revenue is a 45° straight line through the origin. The slope of the total revenue line is steeper than of the total cost line. This follows from the fact that large ski areas receive $16.50 in revenue for every $5.50 spent on labor, materials, and other variable costs.

The break-even point is found at the intersection of the total revenue line and the total cost line. Figure 16-4 indicates a break-even point at a sales and cost level of slightly over $5.0 million which occurs at an output level of roughly 300,000 skiers per year. Up to this point, the ski area suffers losses. Beyond this point, it begins to make a profit or cash flow. Both gains and losses are shown as the shaded areas in Figure 16-4. For example, if large ski areas had only 200,000 skier days of output in a year

**Figure 16-4. Break-Even Chart for Large Ski Areas in North America**

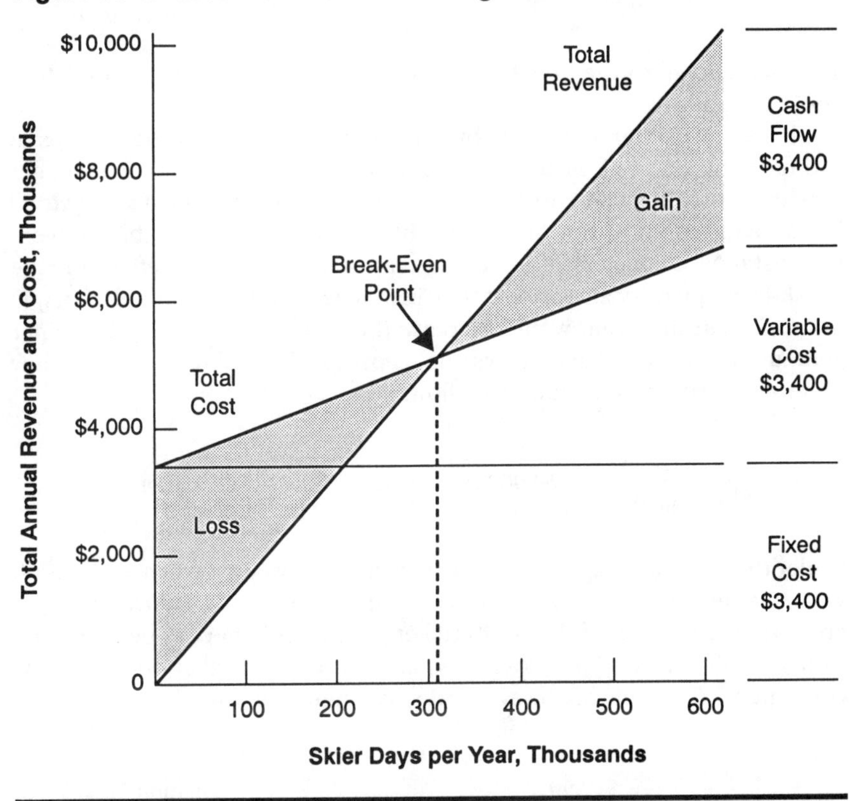


of very poor snow, they would have lost an average of \$0.5 million. On the other hand, if fair snow conditions increased demand to 400,000 skier days, they would have made a profit of \$0.5 million. With fair to good snow conditions, demand increased to more than 600,000 skier days, and large ski areas made a profit (or cash flow) of \$3.4 million. In this way, the break-even chart shows approximately how much profit or loss will result from each output level.

An algebraic technique for solving break-even problems can be illustrated using the cost and revenue shown in Figure 16-4. The break-even output, defined as that quantity at which total revenue is exactly equal to total cost, is found as follows:

$$Q = \frac{\text{TFC}}{P - \text{AVC}} \qquad \text{(Equation 16-17)}$$

where $P$ is price per unit of output; $Q$ is quantity of output; TFC is total fixed cost; and AVC is average variable cost per unit of output. In the example illustrated in Figure 16-4, $P$ = \$16.50, AVC = \$5.50, and TFC = \$3.4 million. So the break-even quantity is found as follows:

$$Q = \frac{\$3,400,000}{\$16.50 - \$5.50} = 310,000 \text{ Skier days (rounded to nearest 10,000)} \quad \text{(Equation 16-18)}$$

This is identical to the break-even output shown geometrically in Figure 16-4 (page 303).

Break-even charts are used by private companies and other groups to estimate the effect of output on revenues, costs, and profits. A manager may use a break-even chart to estimate the effect on profits of a projected increase in output or how much output must be produced to break even. For instance, managers of ski areas may want to find the effect on the break-even quantity and price if they install new equipment (such as triple or quad chair lifts) that would increase their fixed costs to $4 million per year and reduce their average variable cost to $5 per skier day. The new break-even quantity is found as follows:

$$Q = \frac{\$4,000,000}{\$16.50 - \$5.00} = 350,000 \text{ (rounded)} \quad \text{(Equation 16-19)}$$

Under these circumstances, the break-even point would be nearly 350,000 skiers rather than 310,000, a growth of more than 10%. Without an increase in the number of skiers, lift ticket prices would have to be increased from $16.50 to $17.90 per skier to equal costs after installation of the new equipment. The new break-even price is found as follows:

$$P = \frac{\$4,000,000}{310,000} = \$12.90 \quad \text{(Equation 16-20)}$$

$$P = \$12.90 + \$5.00 = \$17.90 \quad \text{(Equation 16-21)}$$

This information is of considerable value to managers of ski companies. It means that, if they install the new equipment, they must sell at least 40,000 more ski tickets or increase the price of each ticket by $1.40 to stay in the black.

Operating leverage is a useful concept which refers to the profit contribution of increased output and sales. The degree of operating leverage is defined as the percentage change in profit resulting from a percentage change in number of skiers. Algebraically, this may be expressed as:

$$\text{Operating leverage} = \frac{\text{Percentage change in profit}}{\text{Percentage change in output}} \quad \text{(Equation 16-22)}$$

For large ski areas in Figure 16-4 (page 303), the degree of operating leverage at 620,000 skiers is calculated as follows: To calculate percentage change in profit, the profit contribution of an additional 6,200 skiers is divided by cash flow with 620,000 skiers; profit contribution is defined as the difference between total revenue and variable cost; it is therefore equal to the price of a lift ticket minus average variable cost per skier [($16.50 – 5.50) x 6,200 skiers].

$$\text{Operating leverage} = \frac{\$68,200 + \$3,400,000}{6,200 + 620,000} = \frac{0.2}{0.1} = 2.0 \text{ (Equation 16-23)}$$

This means that a 1% increase in output would result in a 2% increase in cash flow. This elasticity represents a substantial incentive for growth.

One of the challenges in developing an accurate break-even chart is estimating which costs are fixed and which are variable with changes in output. Fixed cost will not be affected by short-run changes in the number of skiers within the relevant range of operation. Table 16-5 (page 306) shows that fixed cost in the ski industry includes the usual elements—general administrative, marketing, rent and property taxes. Variable cost includes ski lift direct expenses such as wages, payroll taxes and property operation (e.g., materials, electricity, fuel).

The accuracy of the allocation of costs into fixed and variable categories varies from industry to industry. In the ski industry, some types of costs are neither fully fixed nor fully variable. Take, for example, insurance costs. Normal accounting practice would probably lump property and liability insurance together as a fixed expense. Actually, however, property insurance is a fixed cost and liability insurance tends to be a variable cost since rates vary with the level of liability which is a function of output, i.e., number of skiers. Constructing an accurate break-even chart then is largely dependent upon proper cost allocation. As a first approximation, we estimate that semivariable cost includes insurance, land use fees, snowmaking, snow removal, and miscellaneous expenses. We assume for illustrative purposes that semivariable costs are allocated one-half to fixed costs and one-half to variable costs. This means that fixed cost includes one-half of semivariable costs or $450,000. Variable cost includes one-half of semivariable cost or $0.72 per skier day (= $450,000 ÷ 623,000).

Managers usually think of profit as cash flow rather than as simply total revenues minus total costs. For short-run decisions where a portion of the company's capital is already an allocated investment and hence immobile, the appropriate profit concept is known as contribution margin or cash flow. This is defined in various ways for different purposes. One useful approach is to define cash flow as equal to total revenue minus total cash outlay for fixed, semivariable and variable costs. In other words, cash flow is the cash available to owners as profit on their investment, depreciation on fixed assets, and interest to debt holders. Thus, unprofitable ski areas in Table 16-5 (page 306) may continue to operate because their cash flow equals 15% to 20% of total revenue. This contribution to the cost of capital may be considered superior to shutting down which would provide no contribution.

**Table 16-5. Total Revenue and Cost of North American Ski Areas, 1983**

| Revenue and Cost, Thousand Dollars | Size, Vertical Transport Feet (1,000 VTF/Hour) Under 2,500 | 2,500 –3,999 | 4,000 –5,499 | 5,500 –9,999 | Over 10,000 |
|---|---|---|---|---|---|
| Sample Size | 31 | 25 | 19 | 22 | 21 |
| **Revenue** | | | | | |
| Ski Lift Gross—Winter | $376 | $910 | $1,296 | $3,047 | $8,057 |
| Ski Lift Gross—Summer | 1 | 4 | 45 | 20 | 58 |
| Supporting Margin—Winter | 179 | 245 | 368 | 471 | 1,172 |
| Supporting Margin—Summer | 61 | 40 | 50 | 21 | 30 |
| Year-Round Margin | 18 | 22 | 29 | 282 | 949 |
| Total Revenue | $635 | $1,221 | $1,788 | $3,841 | $10,266 |
| **Variable Cost** | | | | | |
| Ski Lift Direct Expense | $101 | $289 | $387 | $887 | $2,206 |
| Payroll Taxes | 35 | 63 | 77 | 178 | 242 |
| Property Operation | 84 | 123 | 196 | 228 | 542 |
| Total Variable Cost | $220 | $475 | $660 | $1,293 | $2,990 |
| **Semivariable Cost** | | | | | |
| Insurance (Property, Liability) | $36 | $64 | $80 | $127 | $301 |
| Land Use Fees (Public) | 12 | 21 | 26 | 67 | 220 |
| Snowmaking | 58 | 88 | 103 | 101 | 252 |
| Snow Removal | 4 | 3 | 5 | 21 | 34 |
| Miscellaneous | 2 | 16 | 15 | 18 | 100 |
| Total Semivariable Cost | $112 | $192 | $229 | $334 | $907 |
| **Fixed Cost** | | | | | |
| General & Administrative | $120 | $205 | $335 | $712 | $1,870 |
| Marketing (Advertising, Public Relations, Promotion, etc.) | 47 | 71 | 121 | 261 | 601 |
| Land Rent (Private) | 15 | 4 | 23 | 14 | 49 |
| Property Taxes | 15 | 15 | 28 | 68 | 214 |
| Other Taxes (Except Income) | 7 | 19 | 12 | 36 | 233 |
| Total Fixed Cost | $204 | $314 | $519 | $1,091 | $2,967 |
| **Cash Flow** | | | | | |
| Interest | $102 | $93 | $198 | $297 | $931 |
| Depreciation & Amortization | 104 | 171 | 258 | 613 | 1,638 |
| Profit (Loss) Before Taxes | (107) | (24) | (76) | 213 | 833 |
| Total Cash Flow | $99 | $240 | $380 | $1,123 | $3,402 |
| **Profitability** | | | | | |
| Cash Flow on Sales | 15.59% | 19.66% | 21.25% | 29.24% | 33.14% |
| Profit (Before Taxes) on Equity | Loss | Loss | Loss | 3.74% | 8.33% |

Source: Adapted from Goeldner, Buchaman and Duea, 1984.

Profitability of all ski areas is an increasing function of size. The larger the ski area, the larger the profit and cash flow. This conclusion is based on financial data presented in Table 16-5 for a sample of 118 North American ski areas grouped into five size classes ranging from about 1,500 to 10,000 skiers on peak days of operation. An interesting exercise would be to draw new break-even charts for small and medium-sized ski areas.

The charts would show that the increase in cash flow with size is related to price and revenue rather than cost or efficiency. Apparently, large ski areas have been able to command a premium price by differentiating their product.

The effect of size is also shown in Table 16-6 (pages 308–309) where the total revenue and cost information from Table 16-5 is converted to the equivalent average values per skier. On this basis, the cash flow of large ski areas averaged about $5.50, considerably more than small ski areas. The profit of large ski areas averaged $1.33 while small ski areas experienced a loss.

Prices of lift tickets were an increasing function of size—the larger the ski area, the higher the price. Lift ticket prices of large ski areas averaged nearly $20 in 1983, which was one-third more than small areas. After discounts, average lift ticket revenue for all ski areas was about $5 per skier less than list price. But, ski areas received an additional margin of $2 to $3 per skier for other services such as food and beverage, ski school, ski rental, and ski shop.

## Cost-Effectiveness

Cost-effectiveness is a way to make recreation economic decisions when costs can be measured but benefits cannot be measured in dollar values. It is usually presented as a ratio in which the nonmonetary measure of effectiveness is divided by the costs. Measures of cost are the same as for benefit-cost studies, although measures of benefits may be in physical units or effectiveness scores. In the past, benefit-cost studies defined some benefits from nonmarket output, such as historic and environmental preservation, as intangible and not quantifiable in dollar terms; and thus, they were omitted from the benefit-cost ratio. Cost-effectiveness is a way to study the most efficient way to achieve such objectives.

The National Park Service authorized use of the cost-effectiveness method in 1976. Since then, it has been applied to the evaluation of alternative park management plans. Its ready acceptance by park managers should not be surprising. Our ability to measure the benefit of recreation programs varies and is possible to different degrees for different programs. There are three types of programs or services. The output of Type I programs has a market value, or if nonmarket, dollar values can be calculated. Either the service is sold, as overnight camping in the parks, or the service increases the value of other outputs, as a visitor interpretation program or backcountry camper registration, which increases the willingness to pay of park users. Or the service may reduce the costs associated with other activities, as development of parks programs near population centers saves visitors' travel time and costs. The output of Type II programs can be measured in physical terms but no market or nonmarket valuation procedure has been developed. Examples include site beautification through revegetation, road maintenance, law enforcement, and so

**Table 16-6. Economic Characteristics of North America Ski Areas, 1983**

| Revenue and Cost/Skier | Size, Vertical Transport Feet (1,000 VTF/Hour) Under 2,500 | 2,500 –3,999 | 4,000 –5,499 | 5,500 –9,999 | Over 10,000 |
|---|---|---|---|---|---|
| Sample Size | 31 | 25 | 19 | 22 | 21 |
| **Size** | | | | | |
| VTF/Hour, Thousands | 1,579 | 3,282 | 4,534 | 7,400 | 16,785 |
| Skiable Acres | 67 | 295 | 514 | 930 | 1,239 |
| Gross Fixed Assets (1000s) | $1,878 | $3,591 | $3,786 | $9,532 | $22,840 |
| Net Worth (1000s) | $132 | $899 | $1,203 | $5,691 | $9,999 |
| **Business Characteristics** | | | | | |
| Operating With USFS Permit | 19% | 44% | 74% | 68% | 68% |
| Engaged in Land Development | 20% | 16% | 39% | 46% | 52% |
| **Operational Characteristics** | | | | | |
| Average Days of Operation/ Year | 83 | 110 | 128 | 141 | 138 |
| Average Peak Day Use/Day | 1,446 | 2,870 | 3,314 | 4,893 | 9,701 |
| Average Skier Visits/Year[a] | 52,000 | 99,000 | 141,000 | 262,000 | 623,000 |
| **Economic Characteristics** | | | | | |
| Average Revenue/Skier Visit | $12.32 | $12.38 | $12.69 | $14.68 | $16.49 |
| Average Lift Ticket Revenue/ Skier Visit | $8.83 | $9.76 | $10.13 | $12.83 | $14.56 |
| **Average Adult Lift Ticket Price** | | | | | |
| Weekend | $14.36 | $14.87 | $16.63 | $17.73 | $19.77 |
| Weekday | $12.02 | $12.86 | $14.50 | $17.14 | $19.12 |
| Average Adult Season | $217.00 | $264.00 | $335.00 | $381.00 | $499.00 |
| **Revenue/Skier** | | | | | |
| Ski Lift Gross | $8.83 | $9.76 | $10.13 | $12.83 | $14.56 |
| Ski School Margin | 0.43 | 0.44 | 0.53 | 0.36 | 0.51 |
| Food Service Margin | 0.66 | 0.53 | 0.61 | 0.52 | 0.61 |
| Bar Margin | 0.31 | 0.29 | 0.34 | 0.21 | 0.20 |
| Ski Shop Margin | 0.35 | 0.22 | 0.22 | 0.26 | 0.28 |
| Ski Rental Margin | 1.44 | 0.81 | 0.60 | 0.51 | 0.25 |
| Other Margin | 0.30 | 0.33 | 0.26 | (0.01) | 0.08 |
| Total Revenue/Skier | $12.32 | $12.38 | $12.69 | $14.68 | $16.49 |
| **Ski Lift Department Direct Labor/Skier** | | | | | |
| Ski Lift | $0.59 | $0.85 | $0.75 | $0.85 | $0.88 |
| Ski Patrol | 0.12 | 0.40 | 0.23 | 0.50 | 0.46 |
| Slope Maintenance | 0.13 | 0.29 | 0.30 | 0.40 | 0.32 |
| Maintenance and Repair | 0.38 | 0.56 | 0.49 | 0.51 | 0.54 |
| Ticket Sales | 0.14 | 0.19 | 0.16 | 0.21 | 0.20 |
| Other Payroll | 0.13 | 0.13 | 0.12 | 0.05 | 0.22 |
| Total Direct Cost/Skier | $1.48 | $2.42 | $2.04 | $2.52 | $2.62 |
| Other Direct Cost/Skier | 0.96 | 0.76 | 0.88 | 1.26 | 1.19 |
| [a]Total Direct Cost/Skier | 2.44 | 3.18 | 2.92 | 3.78 | 3.81 |
| Gross Margin/Skier | 6.39 | 6.58 | 7.20 | 9.05 | 10.75 |
| **Variable Cost/Skier** | | | | | |
| Ski Lift Direct Expense | $1.96 | $2.93 | $1.60 | $3.39 | $3.54 |
| Payroll Taxes | 0.68 | 0.64 | 0.55 | 0.68 | 0.39 |
| Property Operation | 1.63 | 1.25 | 1.39 | 0.87 | 0.87 |

**Table 16-6. Continued**

| Revenue and Cost/Skier | Size, Vertical Transport Feet (1,000 VTF/Hour) Under 2,500 | 2,500 –3,999 | 4,000 –5,499 | 5,500 –9,999 | Over 10,000 |
|---|---|---|---|---|---|
| Sample Size | 31 | 25 | 19 | 22 | 21 |
| **Variable Cost/Skier (Cont.)** | | | | | |
| Total Variable Cost | $4.27 | $4.82 | $3.54 | $4.94 | $4.80 |
| Gross Margin/Skier | $8.05 | $7.56 | $8.01 | $9.74 | $11.69 |
| **Semivariable Cost/Skier** | | | | | |
| Insurance (Liability) | $0.70 | $0.65 | $0.57 | $0.49 | $0.48 |
| Land Use Fees (Public) | 0.23 | 0.21 | 0.18 | 0.26 | 0.35 |
| Snowmaking | 1.13 | 0.89 | 0.73 | 0.39 | 0.40 |
| Snow Removal | 0.08 | 0.03 | 0.04 | 0.08 | 0.05 |
| Miscellaneous | 0.04 | 0.16 | 0.11 | 0.07 | 0.16 |
| Total Semivariable Cost | $2.18 | $1.94 | $1.63 | $1.29 | $1.44 |
| **Fixed Cost/Skier** | | | | | |
| General & Administrative | $2.33 | $2.08 | $2.38 | $2.72 | $3.01 |
| Marketing (Advertising, Public Relations, Promotion) | 0.91 | 0.72 | 0.86 | 1.00 | 0.97 |
| Land Rent (Private) | 0.29 | 0.04 | 0.16 | 0.05 | 0.08 |
| Property Taxes | 0.29 | 0.15 | 0.20 | 0.26 | 0.34 |
| Other Taxes (Except Income) | 0.14 | 0.19 | 0.08 | 0.14 | 0.37 |
| Total Fixed Cost | $3.96 | $3.18 | $3.68 | $4.17 | $4.76 |
| **Cash Flow/Skier** | | | | | |
| Interest | $1.98 | $0.94 | $1.40 | $1.13 | $1.49 |
| Depreciation & Amortization | 2.02 | 1.73 | 1.83 | 2.34 | 2.63 |
| Profit (Loss) Before Taxes | (2.08) | (0.24) | (0.54) | 0.81 | 1.33 |
| Total Cash Flow | $1.92 | $2.43 | $2.69 | $4.28 | $5.45 |

[a]Adjusted.

Source: Adapted from Goeldner, Buchanan and Duea, 1984.

forth. Type III programs are those for which no useful estimate can be made of either the level of output or its value. Program objectives can be defined and the level of activity of such programs can be measured only in terms of costs or work-hours. Examples include some of the programs undertaken to protect a natural environment or historic site. The general public benefits from Type III programs, although there is no market in which demands of the general public can be expressed.

The distinguishing characteristic of the cost-effectiveness approach to decision making is that measures of benefits may be in units other than dollar values, such as physical units of output or a scale of effectiveness prepared by informed managers. For example, different freshwater wetland restoration alternatives might be compared on the basis of acres of wetlands restored per dollar of costs. The only physical measure of the output of historic site preservation devised so far is the square footage of buildings preserved and the number of acres of battleground protected. These measures do not differentiate between the value of preserving relatively minor sites compared to those of national historic significance, such as Plymouth Rock or the Gettysburg battleground. To account for this, areas of different significance might be assigned weights, based on how old they are or their uniqueness.

## *Least-Cost and Constant-Cost Methods*

Cost-effectiveness is a way to compare alternative recreation projects and programs by (1) minimizing dollar cost subject to some required output level that is not measurable in dollar terms, or (2) maximizing some output level of a recreation program subject to a fixed budget constraint, such as appropriation levels. These are the least-cost and constant-cost methods of cost-effectiveness analysis.

A typical least-cost-effectiveness study begins with a statement of an objective, such as the protection of a viable herd of bighorn sheep, then estimates the costs of achieving this objective under different management systems. Some of the alternatives that might be examined in this case would include zoning of habitat area to prevent the intrusion of people, hunting restrictions and disease control. The problem is to determine the effectiveness of each alternative and then to calculate the cost of the program needed to reach the objective.

For example, let's simplify the problem of preserving bighorn sheep. Assume there are two alternative projects with the following costs and effectiveness scores:

| | Effectiveness, number of sheep protected | Costs, thousand dollars | Cost-effectiveness (sheep/cost) |
|---|---|---|---|
| Project A | 100 | $100 | 1.0 |
| Project B | 100 | 50 | 2.0 |

We see that Project B has a cost-effectiveness ratio of 2.0 compared with 1.0 for Project A. Project B is the preferred alternative with the highest cost-effectiveness score. In essence, we get the same number of sheep for half the cost with Project B.

A constant cost-effectiveness study tells a decision maker what he or she can buy for the same amount of money. The objective is to determine the maximum level of output that can be produced with different systems, all of which require the same commitment of resources. This shows the consequences of alternative policies with fixed budget appropriations. For example, continuing the example of the problem of preserving a herd of bighorn sheep, the cost-effectiveness scores are the same, but compare costs and output levels:

| | Effectiveness, number of sheep protected | Costs, thousand dollars | Cost-effectiveness (sheep/cost) |
|---|---|---|---|
| Project A | 100 | $100 | 1.0 |
| Project B | 200 | 100 | 2.0 |

We see that Project B again has the highest cost-effectiveness score—2.0 compared with 1.0 for Project A. We get twice as many sheep for the same cost with Project B.

Many government agencies find themselves asked to provide more recreation services without proportionate increases in budget and under conditions of inflating costs. Thus, they have no alternative but to seek ways to improve efficiency, that is, to reduce the costs of providing existing services as well as new ones. Cost-effectiveness is a technique to evaluate alternative systems or to determine whether a new design can provide the same benefits as other alternatives and at reduced costs.

A third type of cost-effectiveness analysis is to estimate the costs of achieving several alternative levels of effectiveness for a single objective. This again may be illustrated with the case of preserving a herd of bighorn sheep. Assume that the budget for Project A, disease control, can be varied as:

| Effectiveness, number of sheep protected | Costs, thousand dollars | Cost-effectiveness (sheep/cost) |
|---|---|---|
| 50 | $75 | 0.67 |
| 100 | 100 | 1.00 |
| 150 | 200 | 0.75 |
| 200 | 400 | 0.50 |

Protecting a herd of 100 sheep is the most cost-effective level of operation for the disease control program. As the size of the herd is increased above 100 sheep, the costs of disease control increase at a much more rapid rate than does the level of effectiveness.

This illustrates an important economic fact of life for many programs. The added costs of increasing the sheep population from 100 to 150 is as great as the cost of protecting the first 100. This may give the decision maker the information needed to make expenditure decisions. For example, it may be clear that the $100,000 expenditure needed to protect the first 100 sheep is reasonable. It may be far less clear that protecting an additional 100 sheep is worth the required incremental expenditure of $300,000. Thus, we can see that cost-effectiveness studies provide decision makers with studies of program costs in relation to measurable but unvalued estimates of program outputs. This modest accomplishment may be of substantial aid in the decision-making process.

## *A Case Study of Cost-Effectiveness*

Let's consider a case study drawn from the real world in which cost-effectiveness played a decisive role in the final outcome of an important decision about the use of natural resources. The problem is whether to route a section of the Interstate Highway System through an environmentally sensitive area. Figure 16-5 shows two alternative routes for Interstate 70 just west of the Continental Divide in the Rocky Mountains about 75 miles west of Denver. The Vail Pass route would, for the most part, follow the existing U.S. Highway 6 right of way. The Red Buffalo route, farther north, would cut through what is now the Eagles Nest Wilderness Area. It would take about 7,000 acres for actual construction, and it would destroy the wilderness quality of nearly 25,000 acres.

Table 16-7 summarizes the design characteristics and costs of the two alternatives presented by Neuzil (1968). The Red Buffalo route is nearly 11 miles shorter than the Vail Pass route but has steeper grades. Both routes were designed for speeds of 50–60 miles per hour. The net effect is that auto driving costs would be about $1.14 per trip less for the Red Buffalo route. The Red Buffalo route would cost $40 million more, nearly three times as costly to construct as the Vail Pass route. The difference is attributed to the need to construct a twin-bore tunnel. Construction costs were converted to annual equivalent costs using a discount rate of 3.5% and useful lives of 20 years for the pavement, 40 years for the roadway, and 60 years for the tunnel and right of way. Road user costs were based on 20-year projections of 10.8 to 12.4 thousand vehicles per day and standard auto costs per mile.

Note that a unique contribution of this cost study is that the state highway department included external costs as well as costs internal to the agency, that is, road user costs as well as agency costs of construction and maintenance. Recreation agencies, such as the National Park Service and U.S. Forest Service, could learn an important lesson from these highway engineers. The travel costs of recreation users should be included as an external cost in planning the location of parks and other recreation sites.

Normally, the route with the lowest highway cost is assumed to be the most economically desirable unless it can be shown that a more expensive alternative would produce offsetting savings in the form of lower user costs. Using the information in the lower half of Table 16-7 the state highway department prepared a benefit-cost ratio for the Red Buffalo route in which social benefits were the lower annual road user costs ($11.8 versus $8.5), and social costs were the higher annualized costs of construction and maintenance, as compared to the Vail Pass route ($1.2 versus $2.9). The benefit-cost (B:C) ratio of the Red Buffalo alternative was calculated to be:

$$\text{B:C ratio} = \frac{\$3.3 \text{ million}}{\$1.7 \text{ million}} = 1.94 \qquad \text{(Equation 16-24)}$$

**Figure 16-5. Map of Alternative Routes for Interstate Highway 70**

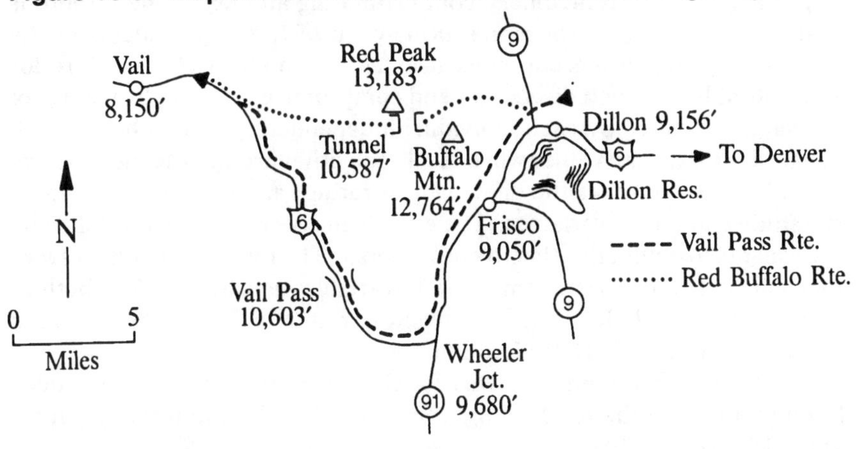


This means that for each additional dollar of annual highway costs, over and above the annual highway costs of the Vail Pass alternative, the Red Buffalo route is expected to save motorists $1.94 in user costs. On this basis, the state highway department recommended construction of the Red Buffalo route.

The Red Buffalo route was opposed by many citizens of the state. As a result, the U.S. Forest Service decided to study the cost-effectiveness of the two routes. Each was evaluated by a study team on the basis of environmental impacts, recreation, regional economic impact, and highway efficiency. The interdisciplinary study team included experts in engineering, economics, fish and wildlife biology, recreation resource management, and community impacts. They prepared a report which rated the effect of

**Table 16-7. Design Characteristics and Costs of Alternative Routes for Interstate 70 via Vail Pass or Red Buffalo Gap**

| Variable | Vail Pass | Red Buffalo |
|---|---|---|
| Length, Miles | 27.30 | 16.50 |
| Average Grade, Percent | 3.10 | 5.10 |
| Average Daily Traffic, Thousand Vehicles | 12.40 | 10.80 |
| Auto Driving Costs, Dollars per Trip | 2.90 | 1.76 |
| Construction Costs, Millions of Dollars | 22.80 | 63.10 |
| **Annual Costs, Millions of Dollars:** | | |
| Construction Costs | 1.10 | 2.70 |
| Maintenance Costs | 0.10 | 0.20 |
| Total | 1.20 | 2.90 |
| Road Users Costs | 11.80 | 8.50 |
| Total, Highway Department and User | 13.00 | 11.40 |

Source: Adapted from Neuzil, 1968.

alternative routes on a scale from plus-seven to minus-seven. The most important point to remember about estimating an effectiveness score is that the panel of experts representing each of the major effects of the project must reach a group consensus as to the effectiveness score for each variable (through discussion and compromise). A simple average of the values assigned by each individual independently should be avoided, because the extreme values will cancel each other around the mean score. Table 16-8 summarizes the effectiveness ratings and weights assigned by the study team to 11 variables. The effectiveness ratings are multiplied by the weights to obtain the effectiveness scores. The total effectiveness score for each alternative is the sum of the 11 variables considered. The bottom line in Table 16-8 shows an effectiveness rating of 53 for the Vail Pass route compared with 15 for Red Buffalo.

The cost-effectiveness ratios for the alternative routes are calculated by dividing the total rating from Table 16-8 by the total cost from Table 16-7 (page 313):

$$\text{Vail Pass} = \frac{53 \text{ points}}{\$13.0} = 4.1$$

$$\text{Red Buffalo} = \frac{15 \text{ points}}{\$11.4} = 1.3$$

**Table 16-8. Effectiveness Ratings for Alternative Routes of Interstate 70 via Vail Pass or Red Buffalo Gap**

| | Rating of Alternatives | | | Weighted Effectiveness Rating | |
|---|---|---|---|---|---|
| Variable | Vail Pass | Red Buffalo | Weight Factor | Vail Pass | Red Buffalo |
| **Environmental and Recreational** | | | | | |
| Wilderness Loss | −1 | −3 | 5 | −5 | −15 |
| Driving for Pleasure | +7 | +6 | 1 | +7 | +6 |
| Physical Environment Damage | −1 | −3 | 5 | −5 | −15 |
| Fish and Wildlife Damage | −1 | −4 | 2 | −2 | −8 |
| Other Recreational Effects | +2 | +1 | 2 | +4 | +2 |
| **Impacts on Economy** | | | | | |
| Local | +3 | +2 | 3 | +9 | +6 |
| State | +3 | +3 | 4 | +12 | +12 |
| National | +2 | +1 | 5 | +10 | +5 |
| **Roadway Efficiency** | | | | | |
| Annual Direct Cost | +1 | +1 | 5 | +5 | +5 |
| Traffic-Carrying Ability | +2 | +1 | 1 | +2 | +1 |
| Safety | +4 | +4 | 4 | +16 | +16 |
| **Total, Effectiveness Rating** | | | | **+53** | **+15** |

Source: Libeau, 1969.

This means that for each $1 million of annual cost for highway construction, maintenance, and road user costs, Vail Pass has an effectiveness score of 4.1 compared with 1.3 for Red Buffalo. The cost-effectiveness of Vail Pass in terms of attributes per dollar is higher than that of Red Buffalo.

As a result of this cost-effectiveness study and other evidence prepared by citizens opposed to the Red Buffalo route, the Vail Pass route was chosen by the governor of the state. The Red Buffalo route is now part of the Eagles Nest Wilderness Area. This result should not be surprising. The Vail Pass route results in a small loss of natural resources compared to Red Buffalo and this was weighted quite heavily. This example illustrates the importance of the relative weights in trading off between different qualitative factors.

## Treatment of Inflation

In the 1970s and early 1980s inflation became a fact of life in most nations. Very likely, inflationary pressures will return, and we should learn how to measure its effects. Table 16-9 shows two measures of the annual rate of inflation in the general price level in the United States. The consumer price index increased at a compound annual rate of 4% per year between 1983 and 1990. Since many recreation benefits and costs are outputs of government agencies, the U.S. Forest Service considers the gross

**Table 16-9. Annual Rate of Inflation in the General Price Level, United States, 1980–1995**

| Year | Gross Domestic Product Price Index (1992 = 100) | Inflation Rate Index (1982–84 = 100) | Consumer Price (1982–84 = 100) | Inflation Rate | Consumer Price Index Energy |
|---|---|---|---|---|---|
| 1980 | 60.4 | | 82.4 | | 86.1 |
| 1981 | 66.1 | 9.4% | 90.9 | 10.4% | 97.7 |
| 1982 | 70.2 | 6.2% | 96.5 | 6.2% | 99.2 |
| 1983 | 73.2 | 4.3% | 99.6 | 3.2% | 99.9 |
| 1984 | 75.9 | 3.7% | 103.9 | 4.4% | 100.9 |
| 1985 | 78.6 | 3.6% | 107.6 | 3.5% | 101.6 |
| 1986 | 80.6 | 2.5% | 109.7 | 1.9% | 88.2 |
| 1987 | 83.1 | 3.1% | 113.7 | 3.7% | 88.3 |
| 1988 | 86.1 | 3.6% | 118.4 | 4.1% | 88.9 |
| 1989 | 89.7 | 4.2% | 124.0 | 4.8% | 94.0 |
| 1990 | 93.6 | 4.3% | 130.8 | 5.4% | 101.7 |
| 1991 | 97.3 | 4.0% | 136.3 | 4.2% | 102.1 |
| 1992 | 100.0 | 2.8% | 140.4 | 3.0% | 102.6 |
| 1993 | 102.6 | 2.6% | 144.6 | 3.0% | 103.8 |
| 1994 | 105.0 | 2.3% | 148.3 | 2.6% | 104.3 |
| 1995 | 107.6 | 2.5% | 152.5 | 2.8% | 104.9 |

Source: Federal Reserve Bank of St. Louis, 1995.

domestic product price index more appropriate than the consumer price index for converting recreation values to constant dollars.

In forecasting future costs or adjusting costs to a common price index, sometimes it is more useful to apply an industry or product specific price index. For example, the U.S. Department of Commerce publishes price indices for construction costs. There are also indices for energy prices, road construction and for labor costs. These specific indices are often more appropriate when costs in these industries are changing at a different rate than the overall inflation rate. Table 16-9 (page 315) provides examples of indices for inflation and for energy prices, which are often important since recreation requires travel. As you can see, real energy prices, such as gasoline, have changed at quite a different rate than overall inflation.

Inflation may create an illusion of high interest rates. For example, from 1960 to 1980, market interest rates on private recreation investments doubled, increasing from less than 8% to 15% and more. Yet in real terms, the 1980 interest rate of 15% was much lower than the 1960 interest rate of 8%. The reason is that in 1960, there was virtually no inflation, with prices typically rising at less than 2% a year; however, in 1980 inflation was rampant, with consumer prices rising over 13% in a single year. The real interest rate is simply the market rate of interest divided by the rate of inflation (adding one to each variable). For example, the precise calculation of the real interest rates for 1960 would be:

$$1.0588 = \frac{1.08}{1.02} \qquad \text{(Equation 16-25)}$$

or 5.88%, rather than 8% nominal rate. In 1980, it would be:

$$1.0177 = \frac{1.15}{1.13} \qquad \text{(Equation 16-26)}$$

or 1.77%, rather than the 15% nominal rate.

Economists distinguish between nominal or market dollar values and real or constant values. In benefit-cost studies, we assume a stable price level for the life of the project. Usually all estimates of the costs and benefits for each year of the planning period of a proposed project are in constant (current or present) dollars, i.e., the purchasing power of the dollar at the time of the decision. So long as future benefits and costs of public projects are valued at constant prices, the social discount rate should be the real rate of interest, before inflation, not the monetary (nominal or market) rate. The President's Office of Management and Budget has established this policy for treatment of inflation in benefit-cost studies.

Use of constant or current dollars in benefit-cost studies provides satisfactory results when the value of benefits and costs changes at approximately the same rate over the life of the project. The relative values of inputs and outputs do not change with a uniform rise in the price level. Using current prices is equivalent to deflating all prices to the present. Howe (1971) demonstrated that in the case of general inflation, it makes no difference whether we use (1) benefits and costs in constant (current) dollars and a discount without inflation, or (2) benefits and costs in inflating dollars of the year in which they are incurred and a discount rate that fully compensates for the expected rate of inflation. Assuming a rate of general inflation of 5%, then the value of benefits and costs each year of the expected life of the project would be multiplied by the sum of 1 + 0.05. Also, the discount rate will be multiplied by the sum of 1 + 0.05 to incorporate an inflationary premium because interest rates will increase to protect lenders from a loss of purchasing power on the funds they lend. Because the inflationary adjustment is introduced into both the numerator and denominator, they cancel out, and leaving the same present value calculation as without inflation.

On the other hand, if the relative prices of some inputs or outputs are expected to change, with some prices expected to rise more than others, their prices may be increased over the life of the project. This practice is authorized by the Office of Management and Budget when there is a reasonable basis for estimating such changes. For example, early in the 1980s camping fees increased more than the general price level. From 1979 to 1982, the average fee at over 7,500 private campgrounds in the United States increased from $5.39 to $7.28 per campsite, or 35%. During the same period of time, the gross national product price deflator increased 26.8%. Thus, the real rate of increase in fees for camping averaged nearly 2.7% per year. If this relative price increase continues for a 5- to 10-year period and is expected to continue during the 20-year life of a proposed campground project, it could be included in the calculation of benefits. However, it is unlikely that this is a long-run trend, rather it probably represents a lagged adjustment to the business cycle. Over time, campground fees will likely rise and fall relative to the general price level. Given the difficulty in forecasting future prices of specific items such as energy or road costs, use of their current costs is likely to be the most defensible approach.

## *Chapter 17*

# Price Practices of Public Agencies

This chapter introduces the problem of charging users for the cost of park and recreation programs; evaluates pricing patterns in terms of agency policy, costs, benefits, comparable prices, feasibility of collection, and public health and safety; summarizes the results of recent studies of user fee policies in public agencies; and makes recommendations for improving future fee practices.

This chapter describes recent studies of cost recovery by user charges for local, state, and federal government park and recreation programs. Local government provides most of the public supply of outdoor recreation opportunities in the United States. State government has been the lead organization in the national effort to supply recreation resources since passage of the Land and Water Conservation Fund Act. User charges recover over one-third of state park costs. State hunting and fishing license fees recover more than half of the costs of state wildlife management programs with federal grants being the next largest source at 25%.

Historically, federal expenditures on park and recreation programs have ranked third behind the cities and states. The Forest Service recovers about 15% of the cost of providing recreation programs from visitors to the National Forests. However, in the National Park Service, user charges recover less than 5% of the operating costs. Overall, the federal government recovers less than 10% of costs from users of recreation facilities. This situation prompted President Ronald Reagan's Task Force on User Charges (the Grace committee) to recommend substantial increases in user fees to recover a greater percentage of the cost. While their ideal solution would be to achieve complete cost recovery through a user fee system, they conclude that public policy would be served by some general funding of programs that protect the "public good" benefits that many park and recreation resources provide present and future members of society.

# Multipurpose User Fees

Economists generally recommend that user fees be set where the added costs of producing recreation opportunities equal the added benefits. This means that prices equal the point of intersection of the demand and supply curve. In other words, the efficient pricing solution for a government agency would be to attempt to provide the competitive industry result. In this way, public recreation opportunities would be supplied at efficient minimum-cost levels, that is, at the lowest point on the average total cost curve. Resources would be efficiently used, as subsidies would be kept to a minimum and excess demand would be reduced.

In a broad social context, there are other goals that we expect to be served by pricing policy. While most people think fee decisions are driven by revenue goals of the agency, this is only half true. Pricing is a very powerful management tool to influence the overall level of recreation use and the timing of that use. As will be shown, a coordinated set of differential fees for different days of the week and different sites can spread out visitor use more evenly and reduce congestion. In addition to these economic efficiency concerns, pricing policies can be designed to contribute to equity in recreation opportunity; fairness in apportioning joint fixed costs among users; community stability through promoting the tourist industry; conservation of natural resources; protection of environmental quality; and other external effects. A number of studies, notably the work of Clawson and Knetsch (1966), reviewed these and related arguments that have been put forward with respect to pricing policy.

First, charging a user fee contributes to economic efficiency because it insures that only those who value participation at least as high as the fee, use the limited facilities. Economic efficiency can be reduced by fee collection in some cases if the cost of collecting user fees is more than the value of the fees collected.

Second, user fees contribute to a **benefits received concept** of equity because those who participate pay and nonusers avoid payment. However, if user fees are set at high levels, they may exclude some people with low income, reducing an **ability to pay concept** of equity.

Third, user fees contribute to fairness because fees are charged for other resource uses such as livestock grazing, timber harvesting, and mining. However, these other resource users often do not pay the market clearing price and are subsidized by the general treasury. Under these conditions, charging full market price recreation fees would discriminate against recreation users.

Fourth, user fees contribute to regional economic development because they encourage private companies to compete with government in providing facilities such as campgrounds when government prices are not artificially low. However, if user fees are increased when the local tourist industry provides ancillary services such as lodging and food to users of public recreation sites, consumers would have less left over to purchase the goods and services provided by private companies or may visit the area less.

Finally, when the external benefits to nonusers of publicly provided recreation resources are low, costs should be recovered by user fees rather than by taxing the general public. However, user fees should be low when external benefits to the public are high. External benefits of park and recreation programs include environmental protection, reduced crime, and increased work productivity. If recreation is a merit good, then children, the aged, the disabled, and the poor should pay reduced fees. However, the defenders of pricing argue that these groups can be helped without lowering user charges for everyone else.

The pricing decision of most park and recreation agencies is no longer, "Should we charge a fee?" Rather it is, "How much should we charge?" Managers are required to justify their pricing decisions by demonstrating that they are neither arbitrary nor inequitable. For example, the Land and Water Conservation Fund Act authorized user fees at federal recreation sites provided that they are consistent with:

1. the public policy or interest served by the agency;
2. the direct and indirect costs to the government and the general public;
3. the benefits to users and the general public;
4. comparable prices charged by private, other federal, and nonfederal public agencies;
5. the economic and administrative feasibility of fee collection; and
6. other pertinent matters such as effects on public health and safety.

Properly interpreted, this enabling legislation provides the necessary criteria to evaluate the pricing practices of recreation and park agencies at the state and local levels of government, as well as federal agencies. The purpose of this chapter and Chapter 18 is to illustrate how to apply these pricing criteria. We will draw on several studies of user fee policies in public agencies and discuss implications for improving fee practices in the future.

We will adopt the term **user fee** to refer to all types of charges paid by users of parks and other recreation sites. These include direct user charges such as entrance fees, admission fees, rental fees, licenses and permits, and payment for special services. Also included are the revenues from the sale of retail products, although this is not strictly a user fee, and indirect user charges such as rental income from concessionaires sales to visitors.

The National Recreation and Parks Association has adopted the following classification of charges:

1. entrance fees to enter a park, botanical, or zoological garden, historical area or other developed recreation area;
2. admission fees to enter a building or structure offering an exhibit, show, or demonstration including grandstand, museum, zoo, monument, and historic building;
3. rental fees for use of equipment such as boats, golf clubs, lawn chairs and meeting rooms; user fees for use of a facility such as golf course, campsite, swimming pool, boat-launching ramp, and trapshooting range;
4. sales revenues from the operation of retail stores and rental income from concessionaires selling food, beverage, souvenirs, fireplace wood, educational materials, sports equipment, and photo supplies;
5. licenses and permits for fishing, hunting, cutting firewood, exhibiting, hang gliding and rafting; and
6. special service fees for instruction and materials, making reservations, equipment storage, night lighting, and pay telephone booths.

As you can see, our concept of user fees is a broad one. We intend it to include all of the types of fees collected by park and recreation agencies.

## Price Practices and Costs

The pricing guidelines recommend that recreation agencies compare user charges to direct and indirect costs. While cost recovery from recreation user fees is not the only basis for pricing decisions by public agencies, it is obviously the most important. Managers of city, county, and state park and recreation programs rank costs of operation and maintenance as the most important consideration in making decisions about user charges. Capital investment costs rank fifth behind costs of operation, user benefits, comparable public fees, and collection costs. The five most important variables for city and county managers are the following:

| | City | County | State |
|---|---|---|---|
| Costs of operation | 1 | 1 | 1 |
| User benefits | 2 | 2 | 5 |
| Comparable public charges | 4 | 3 | 2 |
| Fee collection costs | 3 | 4 | 6 |
| Capital investment costs | 5 | 5 | 7 |

This is based on a survey of 36 California recreation agencies by Economic Research Associates (1975).

The purpose of this section is to discuss the results of several studies of user charges and costs of government provided recreation programs. According to the U.S. census, total government expenditures on park and recreation programs amounted to $17.7 billion in 1992. This was equal to about 0.71% of the total spending by all levels of government in the United States in 1992. Recreation spending was $8.2 billion or 3.75% of all spending by cities; state governments spent $3 billion which represents just 0.4% of total state expenditures; and the federal government spent $2 billion on recreation programs, representing just 0.1% of all federal expenditures. Total government spending on park and recreation programs was equivalent to a cost per capita of $70. Data on the trend in per capita expenditures indicate that government recreation programs grew rapidly during the 1960s. Growth slowed in the 1970s, followed by no growth since the early 1980s. The slow down was of major concern to recreation consumers and managers. In a period of inflating costs and growing scarcity of tax revenues to support park and recreation programs, there was increased interest in user charges.

In the past, most observers of public pricing practices in the United States and elsewhere throughout the world concluded that user charges were "excessively low or zero" (Vickerman, 1975), with virtually all of the costs of public recreation programs paid by general tax revenues rather than user fees. There were many cases where this was true in the past and continues to the present time. However, since their beginning, park and recreation programs have paid a part of their costs from entrance fees, licenses, permits, and other kinds of charges, particularly for special services such as camping. In the 1970s and 1980s, public agencies began to rely on recreation use fees to cover a larger proportion of their costs.

States recover more of the costs of park and recreation programs from users than did either local or federal government. User charges pay 34% of state operating costs; compared with local government, 18%; U.S. Forest Service, 15%; Corps of Engineers, 10%; and National Park Service, less than 5%. This may be related to the suitability of user fee collection at well-defined and regulated state recreation facilities, as compared to relatively open access parks of local government, and with remote and dispersed resource-based facilities of the federal government.

## *Local Government Park and Recreation Programs*

The modern parks movement began with the industrial revolution in the growing urban centers of Europe during the late eighteenth and early nineteenth centuries. The word *parc* originally meant enclosure of animals for hunting by the nobility, but most of them were later converted to parks for the people. Investigations by the British Parliament emphasized the benefits of parks to industrial workers. In North America, public squares were set aside in the earliest settlements. The Boston Commons, established in 1634, is one of the oldest parks in the United States. Central Park was established in New York City in 1858. Local parks were developed in most cities during the latter half of the nineteenth century.

Many public works programs benefited city parks during the economic depression of the 1930s. After World War II, the sustained period of economic prosperity led to renewed interest in the balanced growth of urban and suburban parks. With the migration of many middle-income and upper-income people to the suburbs, more recreation programs in the large cities served low-income people who could least afford to pay user fees.

Local government park and recreation sites vary in size, design, facilities, and programs. They are planned to meet the needs of the people of a neighborhood or section of town rather than the state or nation. They include vest-pocket parks on 30-foot lots between two large buildings with playground equipment, concrete surfaces, and a minimum of landscaping. They also include large parks (3,000 to 14,000 acres) with a natural environment except for access roads, trails, and picnic sites. Despite the unique nature of each park, some recreation facilities are common to most park systems. Verhoven and Lancaster (1976) surveyed 1,123 cities with a majority of parks having tennis courts, baseball and softball diamonds, basketball courts, recreation centers, athletic fields and outdoor swimming pools. About one-quarter of parks had outdoor ice-skating rinks, boat-launching facilities, day camps, bathing beaches, golf courses and outdoor theaters.

The park and recreation programs of local government represent the most important public supply of recreation opportunities in the United States. Total expenditures of local government was $13 billion in 1992. Cities are the most important, accounting for about 62% of this amount; compared with counties, 20%; special recreation districts, 10%; and townships, 5%. This was equivalent to a per capita cost of $51 for all park and recreation programs of local government including cities. This compares to a per capita cost of nearly $12 for state programs and $8 for federal programs. Local government spending is higher because three-fourths of all participation in recreation occurs close to where people live.

There has been a general upward trend in user charges for the park and recreation programs of city governments from the 1960s to the 1990s. User fees averaged 15% of total cost from 1967 to 1972. After 1972 fees began a rising trend over the next 20 years. User fees increased to 18% in 1982 and to 22% in 1992. The trend is for the user fees of city parks to increase in more and more states. From 1972 to 1977 user fees rose in 19 of the 50 states, while from 1977 to 1982 they increased in 35 states.

There is considerable variation among the states in revenue earned from user fees as a proportion of expenditures for city park and recreation programs. The states where user fees of city programs are the highest included North Dakota, 43.0%; and West Virginia, 42.2%. The states where user fees of city programs were the lowest included Alaska, 2.9%; and Delaware, 3.7%. It was reported that the park and recreation department of the industrial city of Wheeling, West Virginia, is 98% self-sufficient.

Within large metropolitan areas, smaller suburban cities and counties recover more of costs from user fees than does the large central city, according to a national urban recreation study. The city of Denver, for example, recovers only about 4% of the cost of city park and recreation programs, compared with an average of 40% in smaller cities within the metropolitan area and 100% in a suburban recreation district.

In the past, the primary reason that user fees did not equal the cost of local government programs was that most managers believed they should not do so. This was the finding of an Economic Research Associates survey of a sample of managers about agency user fee policies and practices (1975). They reported that the pricing structure preferred by a majority of local government agencies was to offer resource-based activities free and to charge user fees for selected recreation activities requiring developed facilities. Fifty-five percent of the managers believed that users should pay only for special facilities such as golf courses, campgrounds, and boat-launching ramps. About 20% reported users should not pay any of the costs. As a result, entrance fees were charged at only 16% of the large multiple-use parks operated by cities and 14% of the counties. In 36% of the cities and 53% of the counties, user fees were charged for some recreation activities at developed sites.

For example, in Oakland, California, Odell (1972) reported that historically, the city subsidized children's recreation activities from general tax revenues on the principle that recreation activities are wholesome and build character. Also, several of the programs for senior citizens were fully supported through general tax revenues. Overall, the recreation and parks department recovered one-third of total expenditures. The balance was subsidized from general tax revenue and grants from federal and state government. There was considerable variation among recreation activities in the proportion of costs recovered by user fees. Golf courses were operated on a self-supporting basis, which means that golfers of working age subsidized persons under 18 and over 65, who paid reduced green fees.

For neighborhood parks, which are used mostly by local residents, general tax revenue from local sources may be viewed as an indirect form of user fee because participation in the service hinges on local residence for the most part. A substantial portion of the costs of park operation and maintenance are paid from the general funds of local government, which are financed by property and sales taxes paid by local residents. Often, the capital costs of new neighborhood parks can be paid by the developer of new residential units based on the value of each residence. But many cities also provide park and recreation services to persons who reside and pay taxes in the suburbs. User fees can recoup some of the costs of serving suburban users and tourists by charging higher rates for nonresidents and during the peak tourist season. Thus, some observers believe that from a practical viewpoint, most of the costs of local park and recreation facilities can be recovered by a combination of local tax assessments and user fees. Unlike most state and federal recreation programs, local park and recreation programs can be financed largely by either direct or indirect user charges.

Intergovernmental transfers or grants from state and federal government also help local government finance park and recreation programs. Their purpose has been to cover the capital costs of construction and rehabilitation of neighborhood park and recreation facilities, and to pay some of the costs of serving nonresidential users and tourists. The trend in total intergovernmental transfers suggests that federal and state grants to local government continue to be a substantial source of revenue for park and recreation programs.

## State Park and Recreation Programs

The first state recreation areas were set aside by the Massachusetts Bay Colony in 1641. Public rights were established for access to 2,000 lakes with 90,000 surface acres for recreation use by the people. The California state parks system may be the earliest in the nation. Yosemite was granted to the state in 1864 for preservation and public recreation use. In 1905, the state returned Yosemite Valley and Mariposa Grove to the federal government as part of Yosemite National Park.

Until the 1930s state park and recreation programs were relatively minor. Some recreation sites were located on land originally held by the colonies and not turned over to the federal government, federal school land turned over to the states, tax-delinquent private land, and land received as gifts. For example, Pennsylvania obtained nearly 3 million acres of tax-delinquent forest and wildlife lands.

After World War II state park and recreation programs expanded rapidly. During the 40 years from 1950 to 1990, state recreation land nearly tripled from about 4 million acres to over 11 million acres. States acquired the additional recreation land primarily with special bond issues and special taxes which provided matching funds for federal grants. During the same time period, recreation use increased from 114 million to 725 million visits. We can gain some perspective as to the important role of states by comparing them to National Park and forest recreation programs, as follows:

| | Surface acres, million | Recreation visitor days, million | Recreation visitor days per acre |
|---|---|---|---|
| State park and recreation areas | 11 | 302 | 27.5 |
| National Park Service | 57 | 106 | 1.9 |
| U.S. Forest Service | 185 | 230 | 1.2 |

This shows that with considerably less land area, the states provide more recreation use than either of the federal agencies. Apparently, the state acreage is much more intensely used, with 27.5 recreation visitor days per acre compared to only 1.9 for the National Park Service and 1.2 for the

U.S. Forest Service. But contrary to popular belief, state lands do not provide more total recreation than the federal lands.

As is true for all functions of state government, the management of park and recreation programs differs among the states. Most state parks are managed solely for the dual purpose of recreation use and preservation of the resource, similar to the National Parks. Others are managed for multiple use including recreation, timber, range, and wildlife, similar to the National Forests. Others are highly developed resort communities with lodges, golf courses, and marinas, such as in Kentucky.

All 50 states have some state parks. They range from small highway rest stops of a few acres to huge natural areas, such as in Alaska. State parks are especially important in the eastern part of the United States where there is very little federal park and recreation land. In the state of New York, for example, Adirondack State Park was established in 1892 and includes 3.4 million acres of state, local government, and private land. As such, it is several times larger than any of the National Parks. It includes the 2.0-million acre, state-owned Adirondack Forest Preserve. In addition, there are 3.7 million acres of private land over which the state maintains land use controls to keep the park attractive while allowing logging, mining, and continued operation of resorts such as Lake Placid. Even in the western United States, where federal parks and forests offer extensive opportunities for recreation, state parks are important. They often are located on the plains or in the foothills around small reservoirs or lakes. State parks provide warm-water fishing, camping, picnicking, and other recreation activities within one- or two-hours drive from the larger cities in the region.

Historically, expenditures on state park and recreation programs have been second only to city government, according to the census. Table 17-1 (page 328) shows that total park and recreation spending by the states was $1.48 billion in 1993. Data indicate that state recreation expenditures grew moderately during the 1960s. Growth slowed in the 1970s, but was at the same rate as total government expenditures for park and recreation programs. State spending fell sharply in the early 1980s, but increased slowly in the 1990s. After removing the effects of inflation, the annual change in spending per capita was 4.5% from 1967 to 1972, 3.5% from 1972 to 1977, –3.6% from 1977 to 1982, and 0.7% from 1983 to 1993. Note that per capita spending for state park and recreation programs decreased by an average of 3.6 per year from 1977 to 1982 and increased by only an average of 0.7% each year from 1982 to 1993.

Table 17-1 (page 328) summarizes information on the number of visits, costs, and user charges for state parks in each of the 50 states in 1993. The data are not directly comparable to census data on state park and recreation programs. In some states, the data were only for state parks. Some states omitted expenditures for fixed capital investments. In other states, the agency included forestry, fish and wildlife, and other functions. Total expenditures on state park and recreation programs were reported

**Table 17-1. State Park Acres, Visitation, and User Fee Revenues, 1993**

| | | | Expenditures | | | | User Fees | | |
|---|---|---|---|---|---|---|---|---|---|
| | Total | Total | Budget | | | Expenditures | | User Fee as Percent of | |
| | Acres | Visitors | Operating | Capital | Total | Per | Revenues | Operating | Total |
| State | (1,000s) | (1,000s) | ($1,000s) | ($1,000s) | ($1,000s) | Visitor | ($1,000s) | Costs | Costs |
| Alabama | 50 | 6,198 | 28,547 | 84 | 28,631 | $4.62 | 23,912 | 83.8% | 83.5% |
| Alaska | 3,240 | 6,590 | 4,968 | 2,431 | 7,399 | $1.12 | 1,156 | 23.3% | 15.6% |
| Arizona | 45 | 1,858 | 9,702 | 5,085 | 14,787 | $7.96 | 2,912 | 30.0% | 19.7% |
| Arkansas | 48 | 7,257 | 21,012 | 2,323 | 23,335 | $3.22 | 12,661 | 60.3% | 54.3% |
| California | 1,330 | 66,674 | 152,137 | 47,892 | 200,029 | $3.00 | 79,065 | 52.0% | 39.5% |
| Colorado | 342 | 10,137 | 12,732 | 5,002 | 17,734 | $1.75 | 7,258 | 57.0% | 40.9% |
| Connecticut | 174 | 7,314 | 9,735 | 11,809 | 21,544 | $2.95 | 3,536 | 36.3% | 16.4% |
| Delaware | 14 | 3,151 | 9,480 | 6,313 | 15,793 | $5.01 | 4,029 | 42.5% | 25.5% |
| Florida | 428 | 11,416 | 43,858 | 14,100 | 57,958 | $5.08 | 19,196 | 43.8% | 33.1% |
| Georgia | 57 | 15,637 | 37,832 | 4,525 | 42,357 | $2.71 | 18,475 | 48.8% | 43.6% |
| Hawaii | 25 | 15,178 | 7,808 | 5,977 | 13,785 | $0.91 | 1,100 | 14.1% | 8.0% |
| Idaho | 42 | 2,701 | 5,390 | 1,195 | 6,585 | $2.44 | 2,271 | 42.1% | 34.5% |
| Illinois | 391 | 35,851 | 31,182 | 33,715 | 64,897 | $1.81 | 3,978 | 12.8% | 6.1% |
| Indiana | 54 | 10,381 | 12,653 | 186 | 12,839 | $1.24 | 9,323 | 73.7% | 72.6% |
| Iowa | 54 | 9,794 | 8,000 | 2,000 | 10,000 | $1.02 | 2,500 | 31.3% | 25.0% |
| Kansas | 324 | 3,930 | 7,458 | 3,723 | 11,181 | $2.85 | 2,367 | 31.7% | 21.2% |
| Kentucky | 43 | 28,396 | 57,672 | 10,906 | 68,578 | $2.42 | 40,800 | 70.7% | 59.5% |
| Louisiana | 39 | 1,221 | 6,511 | 2,675 | 9,186 | $7.52 | 2,141 | 32.9% | 23.3% |
| Maine | 75 | 1,942 | 4,412 | 1,240 | 5,652 | $2.91 | 1,621 | 36.7% | 28.7% |
| Maryland | 242 | 9,666 | 23,142 | 7,160 | 30,302 | $3.13 | 8,266 | 35.7% | 27.3% |
| Massachusetts | 292 | 15,139 | 23,900 | 4,800 | 28,700 | $1.90 | 7,686 | 32.2% | 26.8% |
| Michigan | 288 | 21,228 | 27,806 | 15,000 | 42,806 | $2.02 | 22,862 | 82.2% | 53.4% |
| Minnesota | 234 | 7,492 | 19,300 | 2,100 | 21,400 | $2.86 | 7,600 | 39.4% | 35.5% |
| Mississippi | 22 | 3,913 | 11,909 | 1,562 | 13,471 | $3.44 | 5,196 | 43.6% | 38.6% |
| Missouri | 126 | 16,216 | 18,777 | 4,816 | 23,593 | $1.45 | 4,636 | 24.7% | 19.6% |
| Montana | 44 | 4,153 | 2,141 | 423 | 2,564 | $0.62 | 1,501 | 70.1% | 58.5% |
| Nebraska | 142 | 8,858 | 14,200 | 860 | 15,060 | $1.70 | 8,729 | 61.5% | 58.0% |
| Nevada | 146 | 2,600 | 4,472 | 3,912 | 8,384 | $3.22 | 700 | 15.7% | 8.3% |
| New Hampshire | 75 | 1,158 | 4,738 | 1,500 | 6,238 | $5.39 | 4,225 | 89.2% | 67.7% |
| New Jersey | 305 | 11,643 | 26,373 | 5,000 | 31,373 | $2.69 | 6,573 | 24.9% | 21.0% |
| New Mexico | 121 | 4,174 | 11,078 | 1,314 | 12,392 | $2.97 | 3,026 | 27.3% | 24.4% |
| New York | 260 | 62,376 | 111,380 | 32,300 | 143,680 | $2.30 | 18,052 | 16.2% | 12.5% |
| North Carolina | 35 | 11,830 | 11,956 | 2,839 | 14,795 | $1.25 | 2,238 | 18.7% | 15.1% |
| North Dakota | 19 | 1,043 | 1,897 | 532 | 2,429 | $2.33 | 799 | 42.1% | 32.9% |
| Ohio | 209 | 56,908 | 45,314 | 470 | 45,784 | $0.80 | 6,707 | 36.9% | 36.5% |
| Oklahoma | 72 | 16,049 | 27,664 | 1,349 | 29,013 | $1.81 | 17,240 | 62.3% | 59.4% |
| Oregon | 91 | 40,236 | 27,080 | 590 | 27,670 | $0.69 | 9,437 | 34.8% | 34.1% |
| Pennsylvania | 276 | 35,641 | 54,344 | 0 | 54,344 | $1.52 | 8,975 | 16.5% | 16.5% |
| Rhode Island | 9 | 3,515 | 6,395 | 0 | 6,395 | $1.82 | 2,789 | 43.6% | 43.6% |
| South Carolina | 80 | 8,189 | 19,919 | 3,871 | 23,790 | $2.91 | 12,034 | 60.4% | 50.6% |
| South Dakota | 93 | 6,200 | 6,460 | 2,882 | 9,342 | $1.51 | 4,201 | 65.0% | 45.0% |
| Tennessee | 133 | 28,701 | 36,216 | 0 | 36,216 | $1.20 | 21,033 | 58.1% | 58.1% |
| Texas | 499 | 25,368 | 36,093 | 10,289 | 46,382 | $1.83 | 15,178 | 42.1% | 32.7% |
| Utah | 97 | 6,607 | 14,058 | 3,704 | 17,762 | $2.69 | 3,724 | 26.5% | 21.0% |
| Vermont | 64 | 765 | 4,920 | 584 | 5,504 | $7.19 | 4,246 | 86.3% | 77.1% |
| Virginia | 67 | 3,779 | 11,122 | 5,767 | 16,889 | $4.47 | 2,350 | 21.1% | 13.9% |
| Washington | 247 | 45,114 | 30,000 | 47,455 | 77,455 | $1.72 | 7,577 | 25.3% | 9.8% |
| West Virginia | 199 | 7,822 | 23,304 | 2,748 | 26,052 | $3.33 | 14,937 | 64.1% | 57.3% |
| Wisconsin | 127 | 11,481 | 13,354 | 6,217 | 19,571 | $1.70 | 8,184 | 61.3% | 41.8% |
| Wyoming | 120 | 2,010 | 3,192 | 1,014 | 4,206 | $2.09 | 378 | 11.8% | 9.0% |
| Total | 11,509 | 725,500 | 1,143,593 | 332,239 | 1,475,832 | | 479,380 | | |
| Average | 230 | 14,510 | 22,872 | 6,645 | 29,517 | $2.03 | 9,590 | 40.5% | 33.6% |

Source: Adapted from O'Toole, 1995.

as nearly $1.48 billion. Of this amount, direct operating costs were 77%, and capital investments, 23%. With 725.5 million visits, operating costs averaged nearly $1.58 per visit and total expenditures, including capital investment averaged $2.03 per visit. There was a large difference among the states in average total expenditures per visit. For example, Louisiana reported expenditures of $7.52 per visit and Iowa about $1 per visit.

There is evidence to suggest that the proportion of costs recovered by the states from user charges has increased over the last 40 years. Table 17-1 shows that user charges were 34% of total expenditures in 1993. This is a significant increase from the 23% cost recovery in the 1950s.

Many of the state park and recreation agencies have made considerable progress toward the objective of users paying for the costs, although Table 17-1 shows that considerable variation remains. User charges are the highest percentage of total costs in Alabama, Vermont and Indiana. User charges are the lowest in Illinois at 6.1% and under 10.0% in Hawaii, Nevada, Washington and Wyoming. The 12 western states averaged 24% recovery of total costs from user charges as compared to the United States average of 34%.

Nearly all states report one or more types of user charge. These included entrance fee, 37 states; camping fee, 46; camping reservation fee, 26; cabin and lodge room rental, 36; concessionaires, 50; beach and pool, 18; golf courses, 17; and revenue from other operations, 43 states.

There are a number of important points that should be made about the role of states in recreation. The first is that state government has been the lead organization in the national effort to supply recreation resources since passage of the Land and Water Conservation Fund Act of 1965. In most states, a division of planning for recreation has prepared State Comprehensive Outdoor Recreation Plans (SCORP) and coordinates the distribution of grants to agencies of the state and local government. The Land and Water Conservation Act provided each of the states with matching funds. The states have allocated these financial resources to acquire land, develop facilities and improve programs. The states have provided technical assistance to local government agencies preparing proposed projects to receive grant money. Eligibility of the proposed projects has been evaluated in terms of their contribution to state comprehensive recreation plans. In addition, the states have received historic preservation funds. State agencies have reviewed federal environmental impact statements, and their comments have affected federal natural resource and recreation programs within the states.

Second, most states have had tourist promotion divisions to advertise recreation opportunities, both public and private. Budgets for tourism promotion increased dramatically as many states have turned to tourism to spur rural development. The state agencies coordinate their television and print ads with chambers of commerce and private companies in tourist areas. But problems of coordination between agencies may develop. One agency promoted additional recreation use of state parks, for example, while managers of the parks lacked sufficient revenue to cope with the effects of the resulting overuse.

Third, the states have land that is used for recreation, although it was acquired for other purposes. In addition to the 11 million acres of state park and recreation areas, the states have more than 9 million acres of fish and wildlife areas and over 10 million acres of forests. In the past, the recreation use of state forests was often considered secondary to timber production. Access was usually by unimproved fire lanes and logging roads. Campgrounds were primitive with few developed sites. More recently, state forest managers have begun to consider the aesthetic and recreation effects of timber production, especially in the Northeast and Midwest where public recreation lands are particularly scarce. Some observers have suggested that recreation user fees should be charged at state forests to compensate for the reduced revenue from timber sales. Although acquisition and maintenance of fish and wildlife areas are paid mainly by hunters and anglers, the areas are sometimes used less for hunting and fishing than for other recreation activities, such as wildlife observation, photography, hiking, picnicking, and camping. Although many of the individuals who engage in these activities are also hunters and anglers, some observers have suggested that user fees should be charged in the interest of fairness. They believe that all recreation users should share in the costs of fish and wildlife areas.

## State Fish and Wildlife Programs

According to common law, fish and wildlife are property of the states until they are captured, and become the private property of individual anglers and hunters. For this reason, economists refer to wildlife as a fugitive resource. Although some migratory birds and endangered species are controlled by federal law and by international treaty, the states have the principal responsibility for controlling wildlife, hunting, and fishing, whether it be on private, state or federal land. As a result, each state has a wildlife agency responsible for the management of fish and game. The agencies regulate fishing and hunting, conduct research and stocking programs, and manage fish and wildlife populations on public lands. In addition, wildlife agencies assist landowners in the management of habitat and wildlife populations on private land.

The states began issuing licenses and imposing seasons to protect game animals from indiscriminate killing in the middle of the nineteenth century. Today, a fishing license permits the holder to engage in fishing in the particular state for one year. A license usually must be purchased in the state where an individual fishes. A hunting license may be for an entire year, but is usually restricted to a shorter period of time, such as a two-week period of authorized deer hunting, or a three-month period of pheasant hunting. Usually, a separate license is required for big-game hunting (i.e., deer, elk and bear) and for small-game hunting (i.e., upland birds, waterfowl, rabbits and squirrels). The purchase of a federal duck stamp is required for hunting certain migratory waterfowl.

Total revenue from the sale of fishing and hunting licenses was $904 million in 1993. The average price of a license to fish was $11, while to hunt was $16. There are considerable differences among states in the level of license fees. Fishing licenses ranged from $7 in five states to $20 in Maine. Hunting licenses ranged from $7 in Massachusetts to $73 in Colorado. Differences in license fees reflect differences in the costs of fish and wildlife management programs. For example, big game are usually more costly to manage than small game and cold-water fishing programs are more costly than warm-water fishing programs. Also, average license fees in some states are affected by the proportion of resident and nonresident licenses, since the latter are typically higher priced. About one-third of Colorado hunters are nonresidents.

It is important to note that not all individuals who participate in fishing and hunting purchase licenses. Exempt were children under 16 years of age, those over 65, and disabled persons. Marine fishing was exempt, except for some states on the East Coast. In addition, there is always some illegal fishing and hunting.

License fees and other user charges provide more than half and often 90% or more of most fish and game agencies' budgets. For example, license fees plus other user fees accounted for 76% of the California wildlife budget in 1993, with nearly all of the rest from federal Dingell-Johnson and Pittman-Robertson excise tax revenues on fishing and hunting equipment and other taxes. In Canada license fees and other user charges in the 1960s were equal to expenditures on wildlife programs in the province of Alberta, according to Neave and Goulden (1983). By 1982, the proportion of license fees to the total costs of the Alberta wildlife program had declined to 33%. This was not unique to Alberta; license fees accounted for about 40% of the Manitoba wildlife budget in the same year.

Some state wildlife agencies have been more successful than others in obtaining state tax revenues to pay the costs of free fishing and hunting by children, retired, and disabled persons, nongame wildlife programs, and environmental protection programs. Unlike other state agencies, the wildlife programs of many states have not received revenues from their general tax fund. For example, license fees accounted for 58% of the Washington state wildlife budget in 1982, while 38% came from federal funds and 4% from such miscellaneous sources as mitigation damages and private donations. As a result, the state of Washington could support only one wildlife enforcement agent per 230,000 days of fishing and hunting in the state, compared with an average of one agent per 75,000 days in eight other western states. Contrast this experience with the state of Missouri, where license fees accounted for 23% of the wildlife budget in 1982, while over half came from a 0.125% sales tax, with the balance from federal excise tax revenues and miscellaneous sources. The broader funding base provided by the special sales tax was passed by vote of the people in 1976.

Other state fish and wildlife agencies have been successful in obtaining a broader funding base in numerous ways. The most popular is the nongame checkoff program. This program allows state residents to donate a portion of their state tax refund to a fund targeted at enhancing nongame wildlife populations in the state. Over thirty states have this program. Still, in many states when license fee revenues went up, the wildlife agencies were required to reduce reliance on tax funds.

The traditional federal sources of funds for state fish and wildlife management provided 24% of the total revenues in 1993. The majority of this money came from Pittman-Robertson funds for wildlife management and Dingell-Johnson funds for fish management. These funds represent a user fee in the form of excise taxes on sporting arms, ammunition and fishing tackle. The wildlife program is financed by excise taxes of 11% on sporting arms, ammunition, and certain archery equipment, and 10% on pistols and revolvers. The industries whose products are taxed and the hunters who ultimately pay the taxes, have consistently supported this program. A similar act was passed for sport fisheries. The Dingell-Johnson Act derived all its funding from a manufacturer and importer excise tax of 10% on fishing rods, reels, creels, and lures until 1984, when an amendment extended the tax to additional items of sport fishing tackle, yachts and other pleasure craft, and part of the motorboat fuel tax. The programs provide assistance for managing fish and wildlife species, hunters and anglers.

However, species that can be harvested through hunting and fishing constitute no more than 10% of America's vertebrate fauna. The remaining 90% are nongame species and receive only peripheral management even though they are of value to an even larger number of Americans. The Fish and Wildlife Conservation Act of 1980, although not fully funded, provided about $4.5 million in grants to the states for the management of nongame species. Funding of nongame wildlife programs is expected to increase as a majority of states have adopted a nongame checkoff program. Federal and state agencies continue to struggle with ways to raise money for funding nongame wildlife.

Several points should be made about the sale of licenses to fish and hunt. First, the most important recreation economic decision of wildlife managers is how to allocate the limited supply of fish and game when there is excess demand for fishing and hunting. The number of licenses available is determined by estimating sustainable harvests and relating that to the number of hunters that can be accommodated. Excess demand refers to a situation where there are more applications for a license to fish and hunt than can be issued because of the limited supply of fish and game. For example, Sandry, Buccola and Brown (1983) reported that the excess demand for cow and calf elk licenses was more than double the 15,600 licenses available in Oregon. In Montana, nearly 36,000 applications were received for 7,360 elk hunting permits, and in the state of Washington, there were about 24,000 applications for the 3,300 elk hunting licenses available. Excess demand is expected to increase in the future.

Increasingly, state wildlife agencies have used a combination of fees, drawings, and waiting lines to allocate big-game hunting permits. The price of nonresident licenses usually has been set closer to market clearing levels than for residents. For example, nonresident licenses to hunt elk in Colorado were $210 compared with $25 for residents. Typically, if applications exceed the number of licenses available in a region, a random drawing is conducted to determine which individuals will be allowed to hunt. Often the winners are required to surrender the right to apply for licenses to hunt the species for a number of years. Unfortunately, when permits are allocated by a drawing rather than by market clearing prices of the licenses, the benefits from big-game hunting are reduced by about 40%. Loomis (1982) has shown that the primary losers from higher license prices would be hunters with relatively low willingness to pay who were winners in the drawing, but who would not pay higher license prices. Those who would benefit from higher license prices would be those with greater demand who were losers in the drawing and denied access to hunt at prices they were more than willing to pay (Sandry, Buccola and Brown, 1983).

Second, it is important to distinguish between licenses which are usually issued by public agencies, and access permits to public or private property which are usually obtained from landowners. State licenses ordinarily authorize the holders to perform the act of fishing or hunting during a specified period of time, but seldom authorize them to do so at a specific site. More and more states have required individuals to obtain written permission from landowners to fish and hunt on private property. Access fees of $25 or more have been paid to private landowners. However, entrance fees seldom have been charged for fishing and hunting on public land. Congress has been reluctant to authorize federal agencies to charge for fishing and hunting. Representatives of the states believed that federal entrance fees for fishing and hunting would adversely affect state license sales.

The third and final point is that the experience of wildlife agencies with fee collection has important implications for other recreation programs. The states appear to have developed one of the most efficient user fee collection systems in the United States. Licenses to fish and hunt are sold by sporting goods stores for a small commission, usually 5% of the purchase price. For example, retailers receive $0.50 for selling a license costing resident anglers $10. For nonresident deer hunting licenses costing $100, the retailer receives $5. The retail stores purchase bonds to protect the wildlife agency against loss, if for some reason a store fails to turn in the money from license sales. In a typical year the state of Colorado had to recover less than 1% of license sales from the bonding company. With more than 1,000 license agents in the state, the system is convenient for anglers and hunters. Wildlife enforcement agents verify the purchase of licenses by making spot checks of anglers and operating highway check stations for big game such as deer and elk.

## *Federal Park and Recreation Programs*

Historically, federal expenditures on park and recreation programs have ranked third behind the cities and states. Park and recreation spending by the federal government was about $2 billion in 1992, according to the census. This was equivalent to a cost per capita of nearly $8. Park and recreation programs accounted for only about 0.10% of total spending by the federal government. The trend in per capita expenditures indicate that federal recreation expenditures grew moderately during the 1960s, and then declined with the advent of the energy crisis during the 1970s. Growth accelerated with the start of a park rehabilitation program. After removing the effects of inflation, *annual* growth in spending per capita was estimated as 2.60% from 1967 to 1972, –2.20% from 1972 to 1977, averaged 3.50% from 1977 to 1982, but slowed to 0.35% from 1982 to 1992.

The federal government administers one-third of the land area of the United States and another 2% is held in trust for Native Americans. This compares with about 5% managed by the states and about 1% by local government. Although the supply of recreation opportunities on federal land is influenced by more than 100 agencies, seven have been designated the principal land management agencies offering recreation opportunities. The National Park Service and the Fish and Wildlife Service administer lands reserved for these purposes. The Forest Service and Bureau of Land Management have the largest area of multiple-use lands. The Corps of Engineers, Bureau of Reclamation, and Tennessee Valley Authority manage reservoirs and other water projects.

Federal collection of user fees began at Mount Rainier National Park, Washington, in 1908. In 1916 entrance fees were also collected at Yosemite and Yellowstone National Parks. From this early beginning until the present time, a part of costs has been paid from entrance fees, licenses, permits, and other kinds of user charges.

The recent history of user charges began with passage of the Land and Water Conservation Fund Act (LWCFA) in 1965. The act authorized the Interior Department to manage a coordinated federal recreation fee program. The LWCFA authorized the seven agencies to charge fees at sites where specialized outdoor recreation facilities, equipment, or services were provided at federal expense. The agencies were authorized to collect three types of recreation revenue: entrance fees, user fees and special permits.

User charges have been a constant subject of controversy since passage of the LWCFA legislation. Six of the seven federal recreation agencies limited their user fee program almost entirely to campgrounds that require personal supervision by agency employees and maintenance expenses for developed facilities. Campgrounds that lacked essential services, in particular drinking water, were exempt from the collection of user fees.

Beginning in the early 1980s, a concerted effort was made to increase the proportion of costs recovered from recreation users. President Reagan's Task Force on User Charges recommended substantial increases in user fees to recover a greater percentage of the cost of operating the facilities. Although the task force's ideal solution was to achieve complete cost recovery through a user fee system, it concluded that public policy is served by some tax-subsidized programs that protect natural areas for the benefit of present and future society. It seemed reasonable that user fees should reflect the direct costs of the services provided by the public agencies.

Table 17-2 provides data on user fee revenues at federal park and recreation sites. This is based on data from Federal Recreation Fee Reports prepared by the U.S. Department of the Interior (1992). User fees increased from $32.2 million in 1981 to $104.5 million in 1992. This was equal to an average of $0.60 per recreation visitor day at fee sites. However, user fees were charged at only about one-quarter of the federal sites.

The increase in user charges during the 1980s was a marked change from the fee policies during the previous decade. The seven federal agencies reported that recreation user fee revenues increased from $20.6 million in 1975 to $104.4 million in 1992. Average user fees at the sites of the three most important federal recreation agencies were:

| | 1975 | 1979 | 1984 | 1992 |
|---|---|---|---|---|
| National Park Service | $0.11 | $0.20 | $0.24 | $0.67 |
| Forest Service | 0.18 | 0.30 | 0.47 | 0.48 |
| Corps of Engineers | 0.08 | 0.42 | 0.93 | 0.43 |
| Total Federal | 0.11 | 0.23 | 0.36 | 0.60 |

Total fee revenues increased less than average fees because users were charged at fewer and fewer sites. For example, the Corps of Engineers reported that visitors subject to payment of user fees decreased by nearly two-thirds from 1975 to 1979. This trend was reversed during the 1980s

**Table 17-2. User Fee Revenues at Federal Recreation Sites**

| Federal Agency | Percent Fee Sites | Total Receipts (Millions) | Receipts Per Visitor Day at Fee Site |
|---|---|---|---|
| National Park Service | 51% | $64.40 | $0.67 |
| Forest Service | 21% | $14.90 | $0.48 |
| Corps of Engineers | 36% | $19.50 | $0.43 |
| Bureau of Land Management | 17% | $1.95 | $1.52 |
| Fish and Wildlife Service | 16% | $1.85 | n.a. |
| Bureau of Reclamation | 2% | $0.70 | $0.91 |
| Tennessee Valley Authority | 25% | $1.10 | $0.97 |
| Total Federal | 27% | $104.40 | $0.60 |

n.a. = Not applicable.

Source: U.S. Department of the Interior, National Park Service, 1992.

and 1990s, when the Corps of Engineers increased the number of visitors subject to the payment of user fees from 5% in 1981 to 23% in 1992.

## Forest Service

Of the federal agencies, the Forest Service made the most progress in shifting the cost of financing recreation programs from the general tax base to recreation user fees and permits during the early 1980s. The trend in receipts from recreation user fees and special use permits of the Forest Service from these two sources increased from $16.9 million in 1980 to $49.3 million in 1993. However, these recreation user fee and permit revenues have consistently accounted for about 15% of the agency's expenditures on the recreation program over this time period (U.S. Forest Service, 1995, p. E-2). Camping fees accounted for much of the rise in user charges. Fees increased at 1,900 campgrounds from an average of about $2.80 per campsite in 1980 to $5.50 in 1985. The number of fee campsites increased slightly during the same time period. Fees were related to the quality of service provided. Few campgrounds were highly developed with flush toilets and utility hookups. Generally, camping fees ranged from $3 to $10 per night. In addition revenues from special use permits for ski areas and summer homes doubled from 1980 to 1985. Permit revenues from outfitters and guides increased from $0.5 million to $4.6 million.

The Forest Service estimated that user fee revenues could have been increased with added authority from Congress to charge user fees at developed recreation sites without standard facilities or drinking water. In 1996 the U.S. Forest Service received authority to begin charging recreation fees at selected recreation areas throughout the United States as part of the demonstration project to test the effectiveness and acceptability of fee collection to visitors. The innovative feature of this program is that 80% of the new fees collected will go into the recreation maintenance budget of the National Forest where the money is collected (U.S. Forest Service, 1996b). This greatly improves the user-pay linkage which should increase acceptability to the visitor as well as reduce the backlog of deferred maintenance at many of the agency's recreation facilities. The other 20% of the revenue will go to maintenance of recreation areas where fee collection would not be feasible.

## National Park Service

The National Park Service collected more than one-half of the total user fees of federal agencies. The agency reported entrance fees of $51 million at 184 parks and recreation areas in 1995. Entrance fees of $4–$5 per vehicle were charged at 133 National Parks, monuments, recreation areas, seashores, historic sites, and memorial parks. Grand Teton, Yellowstone and Grand Canyon National Parks had entrance fees of $10 in 1995, which were increased to $20 in 1997 as part of the fee demonstration program. In 1995 the National Park Service also collected $29 million in recreation user fees, primarily for camping. Examples of other user fees include boat launching and parking. Special permit fees were generally considered a type of user fee. Examples include renting a picnic shelter for a group activity, or a site for a special recreation event such as an off-road vehicle race. Special permit fees were charged to outfitters and guides of horseback excursions and river rafting. Omitted from the Federal Recreation Fee Report was $5 million of other indirect fees for recreation use, such as lease revenues from concession operations at ski sites, resorts, campgrounds, and boat marinas. Also omitted were special use permits, such as for summer home sites.

A federal task force concluded that user fees should not be expected to recover the total cost of operating the National Park Service. More than any other federal agency, the National Park Service is charged with protecting natural, cultural, and historic resources as well as providing opportunities for recreation use. The task force recommended that National Park Service recreation receipts be increased by $30 million in the first year and slightly higher thereafter. They reported that the increase in receipts would enable the agency to recover 27% of the cost of operating and maintaining the fee sites, significantly more than the current 10% recovery. Subsequently, the Secretary of Interior requested that Congress authorize increasing user fees from 7% to 25% of the costs of maintaining and operating National Parks, national monuments, wildlife refuges, and other recreation areas under the department's jurisdiction.

One reason that the task force's recommended increase was not higher is the little known fact that the National Park Service operates large recreation areas in and near the central cities. It manages the oldest urban park system in the United States, the National Capital Parks in Washington, D.C., which, as a courtesy to visitors, does not charge user fees. In 1984 the National Parks, monuments, historic sites, and recreation areas in the large cities accounted for 37% of total visits to the agency's facilities. These urban sites provided recreation opportunities at significantly lower costs per visitor than did large parks in the rural areas of the western states. For example, in 1977 costs per visit at Gateway in New York City were $0.75; Golden Gate in San Francisco, $0.57; and Jefferson National Expansion Memorial in Saint Louis, $0.52. This compares with costs per visit at Yellowstone in Wyoming of $3.03; Yosemite in rural California, $2.14; and Grand Canyon in Northern Arizona, $1.92.

## *Recommendations for Increasing Federal Fees*

Large increases in federal recreation fee revenues were recommended by the President's Task Force on User Charges. The task force recommended that user charges of $31.2 million in 1982 be increased to $157 million in the first year, $176.3 million in the second year, and to $193.8 million in the third year. More than two-thirds of the increase in user charges would be collected by the Forest Service, nearly 20% by the National Park Service, and about 10% would come from the initiation of entrance fees at Corps of Engineers reservoirs.

How would the additional revenue be obtained? The task force recommended increasing the price of the annual Golden Eagle pass from $10 to $25 to raise an additional $2 million. Increasing entrance fees at 25 sites from an average of $2 ($1–$3 range) in 1980 to $5 ($2–$7 range) per vehicle would increase revenues by about $11 million. Initiating entrance fees at 23 sites where entry was free (thereby charging fees at all 48 National Parks) would increase revenues by $7 million. Extending the hours during the day when fees are collected would increase revenues by approximately $5 million. Finally, the task force recommended increasing revenues by $5 million through increased fees for such services as camping and boat launching and indirect recreation fees paid by concessionaires from visitor expenditures for food, lodging, swimming, and equipment rentals.

About 530 concessionaires operating in 333 National Park areas reported total sales of $266 million in 1981, with profits of $24 million or 9% of sales. The government received franchise fees of $5.2 million or 2% of sales. Concessionaire fees were based on a weighted average percentage of sales depending on the category of goods. The task force recommended that concessionaire fees be increased from 2% to 4% of sales. This would be closer to private franchise fees outside of the parks.

The task force concluded that U.S. Forest Service recreation user charges should be increased to recover much more than the 18% of total expenditures to operate and maintain recreation sites. They recommended that recreation use receipts be increased by $112 million in the first year and slightly more after that. They apparently considered it appropriate for recreation use revenues to cover virtually all of the costs of recreation management. The Forest Service expenditures for recreation management were approximately $119 million at the time. The task force anticipated that the agency's recreation budget, which had been declining in real dollars during the previous years (MacCleery, 1981), would be increased, consistent with increases in recreation user revenues.

The task force recommended that Congress amend the 1965 Land and Water Conservation Fund Act to enable the Forest Service to charge entrance fees for access to all recreation land and water administered by the agency. They estimated that entrance fees of the Forest Service would produce net revenues of $100 million per year based on an annual entrance fee equivalent to $0.50 per 12-hour recreation visitor day. The task force concluded that gross entrance fee receipts would be at least $125 million per year, less $25 million collection costs. They noted that collection costs of 20% represent the historic level for the Forest Service and should not be considered the most acceptable target level (see the section on collection costs in Chapter 18).

The federal recreation agencies would institute comparable cost-accounting procedures and other management information systems and they would account for all costs attributed to provision of recreation facilities. These costs would include operation and maintenance; capital costs of equipment, buildings, and land acquisition; and personnel costs including payroll overhead, training, and retirement benefits. To this list should be added the opportunity costs of foregone development, external costs such as may be shifted to private firms or other governmental agencies, and costs of environmental protection. A shortcoming of the task force report is its nearly complete orientation toward internal cost accounting to the exclusion of important external costs and benefits.

The task force also recommended that more precise fee-collection cost data be developed. They recommended that all federal recreation user fees be earmarked for payment of the recreation management costs of the collecting agency. A marketing program should inform the consuming public that the fee revenues would be used to pay the costs of the recreation services received.

The mistaken belief that highly developed camping was virtually the only service provided by six of the seven federal recreation agencies has had several unfortunate consequences. For example, because developed recreation facilities are excluded by law from designated Wilderness Areas, entrance fees are not charged at Wilderness Areas. In addition, activities such as backpacking and camping in undeveloped sites in the backcountry are exempt because it is erroneously believed that no services are provided. However, during the early 1980s, a few Wilderness Areas experimented with backpacking permits for which $3 per party was charged to cover the costs of administering the permit program, including private sales of the permits at convenient locations in the region. This program demonstrated the feasibility of charging user fees for camping in Wilderness Areas.

The costs of providing opportunities for wilderness recreation have included significant levels of direct personal services for safety patrol, trash removal, and maintenance of trails and signs within the sites. Wilderness Areas also require substantial investments in access roads, parking lots, and toilets at trailheads in the National Forests on the border of Wilderness Areas. Wilderness resource protection programs should not be paid for solely from user fees. One acceptable basis for allocating the costs of recreation use and resource protection programs would be based on the proportion of benefits received by users compared to the general public. This will be illustrated in Chapter 19.

Estimating the revenue to be obtained from a given fee increase can be difficult for several reasons. Often some users, such as senior citizens or tour groups, pay a fee lower than the standard fee. If the fee is set on a per vehicle basis, it must be prorated to the number of people per vehicle. Thus, one usually cannot take total visitation times the entrance fee. Second, problems may arise when entrance fees are set on a per unit basis, such as per vehicle or per person entering the park. Most National Parks charge for an entry which is good for seven days. However, daily fees make more sense from a marginal cost standpoint. In addition, fees are often the same during peak holiday periods when there is excess demand as they are in the middle of April when there is no excess demand. It is at times of peak demand when prices should be the highest to ration use. This is a point we will return to in Chapter 18.

Current government cost accounting practices often make it hard to determine exactly what the operating and capital costs of recreation are. For example, many of the park's costs are capital investments that provide outputs for 20 years or more. Capital costs, most observers would agree, should properly be amortized over time. Government accounting procedures typically have not adequately addressed this issue. The full costs of facility construction are often charged against recreation user fees during the year of construction. For example, annual Forest Service budgets include the total expenditures for recreation use management, site operation, maintenance, rehabilitation, and construction of capital facilities.

Finally, there are problems in setting fees for recreation use when, unlike most goods and services, there is no standard unit of measurement. Reiling and Anderson (1983) point out that user fees are usually assessed per car, per party, and per person entering a park or other recreation site. However, the most widely used measure of recreation use is the recreation visitor day (RVD) which is one person for 12 hours, 12 persons for one hour each, or any combination totaling 12 hours. A family of four persons using a campsite for 24 hours accounts for eight RVDs but the user fee is for one occupied site for one night. In contrast, 96 persons (equaling eight RVDs) who arrive at a picnic site at the same time and use it for an hour may have a very different effect on costs than the family of four persons for one overnight stay. Thus, the RVD measure of use may not accurately relate to costs. Reiling and Anderson recommend that user fees be based on a measure of use that accurately reflects costs of service. In spite of these difficulties Congress passed a Recreation Fee Demonstration Program in 1996. Eighty percent of additional revenue will be used for maintenance, repair and improvements at the federal recreation area (e.g., National Park unit, Forest, or Refuge) where it was collected, with the other 20% being distributed to other federal recreation areas. The National Park Service has raised fees by $5–$10 at its most popular parks and anticipates raising $40 million per year in additional revenue.

*Chapter 18*

# Market Structure and Price Behavior

This chapter illustrates the effect of alternative levels of demand on the three basic pricing problems, namely, when marginal costs are less than, equal to, or exceed average costs; distinguishes between several types of differential pricing and related practices such as peak load pricing; evaluates pricing patterns in terms of agency policy, costs, benefits, comparable prices and feasibility of collection; introduces the problem of charging users and nonusers for the cost of park and recreation programs, and a portion of the cost of protecting natural, historic and cultural resources.

If the issues of scarcity and choice are the basic problems of economics, demand and supply functions are the basic empirical tools. In this chapter demand curves will be used not for valuation, but to estimate the relationship between the entry prices to a recreation site and the quantity that consumers demand. Supply curves will be used to provide information on agency costs of providing alternative quantities of recreation resources and facilities.

## Marginal Cost Pricing

Economists generally recommend that user fees be set where the added costs of producing recreation opportunities (i.e., the marginal cost of another visit) equal the added benefits. This means that price would be set were marginal cost equals (i.e., intersects) the demand (or marginal benefit) curve. However, such a price may not cover average total costs or may exceed it. To understand the relationship between the principle of marginal cost pricing and the accountant's tendency toward average cost pricing, it is helpful to review the effect of alternative levels of demand on marginal and average total costs of production. Look at the panels in Figure 18-1 (page 343). Note that there are only three possible situations. Park and recreation agencies exhibit either:

1. **Minimum cost production:** with demand equal to supply, marginal cost prices equal average total costs including investment costs, resulting in pay-as-you-go operations (Panel 1).
2. **Decreasing cost of production:** with economies of scale in supplying recreation, the marginal cost prices are less than average total costs. Therefore marginal cost pricing will result in a need for subsidies to cover losses (Panel 2).
3. **Increasing cost of production:** with excess demand relative to supply or rapidly rising costs of meeting increased visitor use, marginal cost prices are greater than average total costs, resulting in surplus revenues to expand operations (Panel 3).

Each of these situations will be explained here, but first, it is important to understand the dynamic relationship between marginal cost prices and demand. Krutilla (1967) has observed that initially when park and other recreation sites are developed, there is excess capacity of facilities, justifying a low marginal cost pricing policy in the short run, which does not recover average total costs including investment costs (Panel 2). However, as use of capacity increases in a growing economy, marginal cost prices would rise until a point is reached where the revenue from user fees covers average total costs including investment costs. User fees would be equivalent to the competitive equilibrium price in the long run (Panel 1). Where excess demand for use of capacity develops, marginal cost prices would rise still further, demonstrating sufficient willingness to pay to justify an expansion of facilities (Panel 3). This illustrates the fact that the problem of efficient pricing is twofold: in the short run to encourage the best use of existing facilities, and in the long run to find the optimum level of investment in capacity.

## *Minimum Cost Production*

The efficient pricing solution for a government agency is to attempt to provide the competitive industry result. Effective price competition among private suppliers would drive user fees to minimum cost levels. However, without the discipline of competitive markets, it may be difficult for managers of government agencies to find the competitive solution. As a result, the efficient operation of recreation programs by public agencies is likely to depend on the ability of managers to adopt the correct least-cost price policy.

The recreation economic decision would be to set user fees at the intersection of the demand curve ($D_b$) with the marginal cost (MC) and average cost (AC) curves. This is shown in Panel 1 of Figure 18-1. Public recreation opportunities would be supplied at minimum cost, i.e., at the lowest point on the average total cost curve. User fees would equal marginal cost as well as average total cost, resources would be efficiently used, and no operating deficits or surpluses would occur. If demand at this

**Figure 18-1. Effect of Demand on Marginal Cost Pricing**

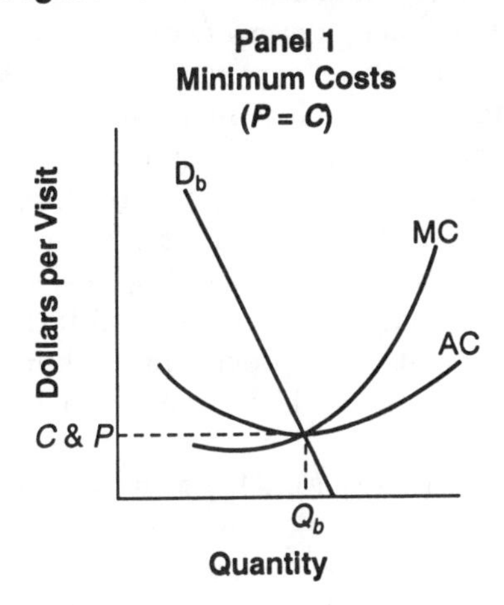


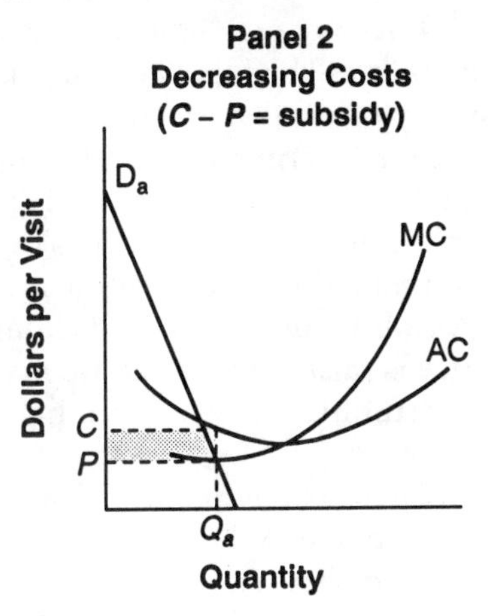


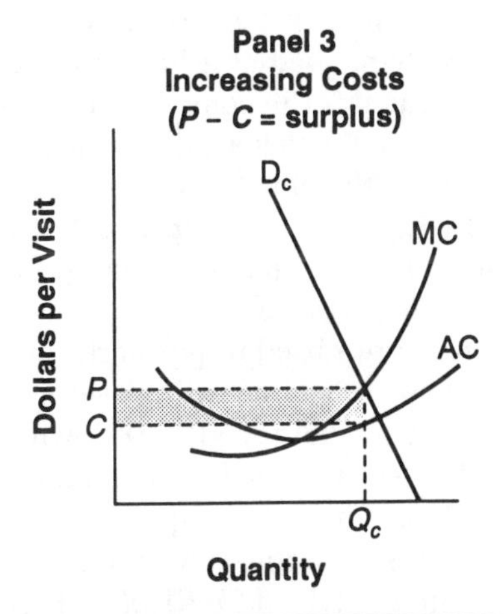


price turns out to be less than the quantity which would yield minimum average total cost, the losses would be avoided by reducing the capacity of park and recreation programs. Some recreation sites or facilities would be closed. On the other hand, when demand at this price turns out to be in excess of supply, an expansion of capacity would be recommended.

To see that this would be equivalent to the competitive industry result, consider the market for ski-lift tickets. The first panel in Figure 18-1 illustrates a typical demand curve for ski-lift tickets ($D_b$) with a series of alternative quantities demanded at different prices moving along the demand curve. If lift tickets are offered at an exorbitant price, the market potential of downhill skiing may decline sharply because skiers are apt to find it cheaper to go cross-country skiing instead. If the price is lowered to more reasonable levels, downhill skiing will attract many skiers who find it much more exciting than cross-country skiing.

Price not only influences quantity demanded, it also affects the quantity that will be supplied. This has always been true for private companies supplying outdoor recreation goods and services. It is increasingly the case for government agencies supplying outdoor recreation opportunities. The first panel in Figure 18-1 (page 343) displays the supply curve (MC) for our illustrative downhill skiing market. If the price of lift tickets is so low that it does not cover the average total cost (AC) of operating most ski areas, little or no downhill skiing will be provided in the long run. If the price is raised somewhat, we may expect suppliers to provide more skiing opportunities. And at even higher prices, they may be willing to provide still more.

There is one point in Panel 1 (Figure 18-1, page 343) at which the supply curve (MC), average total cost curve (AC), and the demand curve ($D_b$) intersect. At the price corresponding to that point, the quantity supplied is equal to the quantity demanded. Prices should be set at this point if recreation resources are to be managed efficiently in the long run. The quantity demanded will exceed the quantity supplied at a lower price and the quantity supplied will exceed quantity demanded at a higher price. The price at which supply and demand are equal is the competitive long-run equilibrium price. In this market, it is the lift ticket price at which willing sellers exchange skiing opportunities with willing buyers. This is not the whole story, of course, because the demand and supply of downhill skiing are affected by other things, for example, changes in travel costs and other variables that were discussed in Chapters 7 and 13.

Problems may occur when low user fees are raised to put parks and other recreation programs on a pay-as-you-go basis. Increasing user fees can be a costly source of revenue, according to Vickrey (1972). Swimming pools are a case in point. Suppose that a city-owned pool increases the adult daily user fee from $1.50 to $2.00 per person to equal average total costs under least-cost operation. As a result of this 33% increase in user fees, assume that the number of swimmers falls off by 10%. Then, for every 100 swimmers per day who previously paid $1.50, yielding $150.00 of total revenue, there will be 90 swimmers per day paying $2.00 and yielding $180.00, a net increase of $30.00. The increase in user fees paid by the 90 persons who continue to swim will be $0.50 each, or a total of $45.00. The loss in benefits to 10 former swimmers, who chose an alternative form of recreation they considered inferior to the $1.50 swim but preferable to the $2.00 swim, would range from zero to $0.50, or an average of $0.25. This totals $2.50 per day for all 10 persons excluded from the pool by the price increase. Thus, the burden on recreation users, both continuing and former swimmers combined, totals $47.50 per day (= $45.00 + $2.50) compared to increased revenue of $30.00. This is equivalent to a user cost of $1.58 for each $1.00 of new revenue for pool operations. If costs are not appreciably changed by a 10% lower use of pool capacity, as seems likely, then this $1.58 is a reasonable approximation of the marginal cost of the added revenue.

Another objection to pricing recreation appropriately is that higher user fees would hurt the poor. This is especially pertinent to city park and recreation programs, such as swimming pools, because an increase in user fees is regressive, imposing approximately the same dollar burden on adults drawn from a wide range of income levels. The poor, along with everyone else, would pay more if user fees were raised. The challenge is to devise special user fee schedules for those who cannot pay. A study by Economic Research Associates (1975) found that nearly 25% of a sample of city park and recreation departments reported charging low-income and welfare families reduced or no user fees. Other groups that were charged reduced or no fees included more than 55% of the children and students, over 50% of the elderly, and 14% of young adults. As a result of these and related programs, only 8% of the managers of city park and recreation departments reported that fewer lower income families would participate in outdoor recreation with increased user fees. In addition, there may be more direct and efficient ways of helping the poor than to underprice outdoor recreation for all users. Perhaps an income supplement or subsidized housing, better education, job opportunities, special counseling, and similar programs would serve the targeted groups more effectively without inducing wasteful recreation resource use practices in all of the population.

## Decreasing Costs of Production

In the past, studies of most park and recreation programs concluded that average total costs were decreasing. Panel 2 in Figure 18-1 (page 343) illustrates this case of decreasing costs. The important difference from the competitive solution illustrated in the first panel is that with the efficient quantity (price equals marginal cost), marginal costs are less than average total costs. Marginal costs are always below average total costs when average costs are declining. Thus, there is a trade-off between economic efficiency and revenue self-sufficiency.

Since the principle of marginal cost pricing was first developed, its advocates generally have held that it is the proper solution to the problem of achieving economic efficiency under conditions of decreasing costs, such as occur in public recreation. They would set user fees at marginal cost. Because the intersection of the demand curve and the marginal cost curve would occur at a price ($P$) where marginal cost is below the average cost of production ($C$), the result would be a net loss from operating recreation programs ($C - P$) shown as the shaded rectangle in Panel 2 of Figure 18-1 (page 343). The deficit would be subsidized from taxes or other sources that are not related to participation rates, in order to avoid interfering with efficient pricing.

Under conditions of decreasing costs of production, the most important advantage of marginal cost pricing is that it would result in larger output and lower average total cost per visit than would average cost pricing, which recovers all operating and capital costs. You can verify that this is the case by drawing a line in Panel 2 of Figure 18-1 (page 343) from the intersection of the demand curve ($D_a$) and the average cost curve (AC) down to the horizontal axis, and compare that output level to the marginal cost price solution shown in the panel. The inefficiencies resulting from average cost pricing under conditions of decreasing costs of production are readily apparent. The output would be overpriced, underproduced and underconsumed.

It is often argued that when a recreation site has excess capacity, managers should price services at the marginal cost of serving additional users, which may be very low. Restricting use by charging visitors the average total costs, including cost of the allocated investment, would lead to a misallocation of resources. This marginal cost pricing suggestion has a few drawbacks, however.

One possible problem is that recreation users may regard the low price early in the history of recreation sites as the long-term price and make recreation plans accordingly. If price is kept low during a period of excess capacity, users are likely to make long-lived decisions such as purchase of equipment based on the low entrance fee. Once a low price is established, groups who benefit will often be able to bring political pressure to bear on public agencies to maintain the low price for the services of existing facilities and to extend the same low pricing practice to new facilities.

With decreasing costs, pricing at marginal costs results in an operating loss to the agency. This loss must be subsidized from the general taxpayer. Thus a decision to engage in marginal cost pricing in the face of decreasing costs should be made on the basis of weighing the previously mentioned considerations against the loss of economic efficiency from average cost pricing. In spite of these limitations, the economic efficiency gains with marginal cost pricing may outweigh these concerns.

## Increasing Costs of Production

Since the 1980s the logic of decreasing costs of production seemed less compelling. Several developments in the preceding decade contributed to the realization that more and more public recreation sites experienced increasing costs, especially on weekends and holidays. Suitable sites for many kinds of recreation were increasingly scarce and land costs were rising rapidly. The costs of new facility construction rose significantly to meet new legal requirements that all facilities be fully accessible to all persons regardless of disability. Demand continued to increase at a rate in excess of population growth, and shortages of facilities resulted in rising congestion on peak days of use. Managers became more aware of the environmental damages of excess demand for some types of recreation. As a result, emphasis shifted toward the case of increasing costs.

Panel 3 of Figure 18-1 (page 343) illustrates the effect of these increasing costs on marginal cost prices. The important thing to note when resources are very scarce relative to demand is that marginal costs are above average total costs. Thus, the recreation economic decision to set user fees (*P*) at the intersection of the demand curve ($D_c$) and the marginal cost curve (MC) has two effects. First, it yields the surplus revenue (*P* – *C*) needed to expand recreation programs. When users demonstrate they are willing to pay more for recreation opportunities than the average total cost of existing programs, this would be clear evidence of the need for expansion, and the surplus revenue available would enable this expansion to occur without government subsidies. Second, it restricts output to the point where marginal costs intersect the demand curve even though average total costs could be recovered at a lower price and larger output. Thus, it correctly rations the use of existing capacity to the users who value the experience more highly than the added costs of providing the recreation opportunity. A lower price equal to average total cost would violate this principle.

In other words, marginal cost pricing in the face of rising costs solves both problems of efficient pricing faced by public agencies producing recreation opportunities: in the short run to encourage the best use of existing facilities, and in the long run to find the optimum level of investment in capacity. Under conditions of increasing costs, the chief advantage of marginal cost pricing is that it serves these two basic purposes: first, to discourage excess demand (i.e., more recreation use than the optimum carrying capacity of existing facilities in the short run), and second, to generate surplus revenue for capital investment to expand recreation programs in the long run.

In a competitive industry, increasing cost of production would not be a stable situation. In the long run, new investment would expand capacity which shifts the cost functions for recreation to the right. The objective of managers of public agencies should be to expand recreation opportunities until the demand curve (D) equals the new marginal cost curve where it intersects the new average total cost curve. You will recall that in the long run, the recreation economic decision would be to set user fees at this level. Public recreation opportunities would be supplied at least cost, i.e., at the lowest point on the new average total cost curve.

Unfortunately, prices that correctly ration the use of capacity and deal with congestion may or may not provide sufficient revenues for expansion. Expansion decisions should be based on whether the revenues are sufficient to cover the costs of expansion at the time in the future when they are contemplated. In an inflationary era, future replacement or expansion costs may bear little relation to investment costs at an earlier period. Thus, deciding whether the revenues generated by user fees justify an expansion of facilities cannot be determined by covering the historical capital costs, although that may be required for legal purposes. Applying the opportunity cost principle to long-run investment decisions in an inflationary era would shift the long-run marginal cost curve to a higher level than for the cost reimbursement problem of current recreation programs (Reiling, Anderson and Gibbs, 1983). Long-run marginal cost is set at replacement cost not historic costs.

Problems may arise in the definition of increasing marginal cost. If marginal cost pricing is to be effectively applied by government agencies under conditions of increasing costs, more recreation economic research is needed to define and measure marginal cost itself. In the past, much of the discussion of marginal cost pricing under conditions of decreasing internal costs of recreation agencies missed the essential point. That is, the relevant costs should include more than the internal operation and maintenance costs of the public agencies administering recreation programs. For many recreation facilities one of the greatest influences on long-run marginal cost, properly conceived, are often two external effects: congestion and opportunity costs. Congestion results when too many users impose external costs on each other. Opportunity costs may result from using natural resources for recreation at the expense of another purpose. An example would be the opportunity cost of foregoing the diversion of water from a reservoir during the recreation season to generate hydroelectric power, which would adversely affect boating and fishing on the reservoir and downstream.

In order to make appropriate recreation economic decisions with respect to prices, they should be related to appropriate measures of cost. In the usual recreation supply situation, there are:

1. capital costs to acquire land and to develop access roads and facilities;
2. environmental resource protection costs;
3. agency operation, maintenance, and replacement costs;
4. administrative overhead costs;
5. congestion costs of users;
6. other associated costs; and
7. opportunity costs of foregone resource development.

The shape of the marginal cost curve depends on the number of these inputs, which vary as the level of output is increased. As discussed in Chapter 15, this depends in part on the length of the planning period to which the marginal cost refers. While it is apparent that in the very short run, some internal costs of the agency may decline with increased use of a site owing to the fixed nature of their recreation inputs, costs external to the agency often increase in the long run.

## Peak Load Pricing

The application of marginal cost pricing by managers of parks and other recreation sites often results in variable user fees at different times of the day, week, or season of the year. Economists use the term *peak load pricing* when they refer to the practice of charging different prices for the same services demanded at different points in time. It makes sense to charge higher prices during peak periods of demand and lower prices during off-peak periods. Since the demand for most recreation opportunities is higher at some times than others, capacity has to be large enough to accommodate demand during the peak periods. This results in substantial excess capacity during off-peak periods. The costs of this capacity can be covered by adoption of a marginal cost pricing policy that charges peak users more than off-peak users. In addition, higher prices are needed during peak periods to ration what would be excess demand to the available supply. Downhill ski areas, airlines, hotels and movie theaters are examples of situations where higher prices for peak holiday periods is quite common to ration use to available capacity.

Peak load pricing can be illustrated by referring to Figure 18-2. Assume that the demand curve $D_{peak}$ represents the weighted average demand curve for all peak days and $D_{off\text{-}peak}$ all off-peak days. During the off-peak period, low user fees are set at $P_o$ where supply is equal to the marginal benefit of off-peak users. During the peak period, high user fees are set where marginal cost is equal to the marginal benefit of peak users. As a result, off-peak users pay only the lower operating costs to provide the recreation opportunities they consume. However, peak users pay both

**Figure 18-2. Peak Load Pricing**

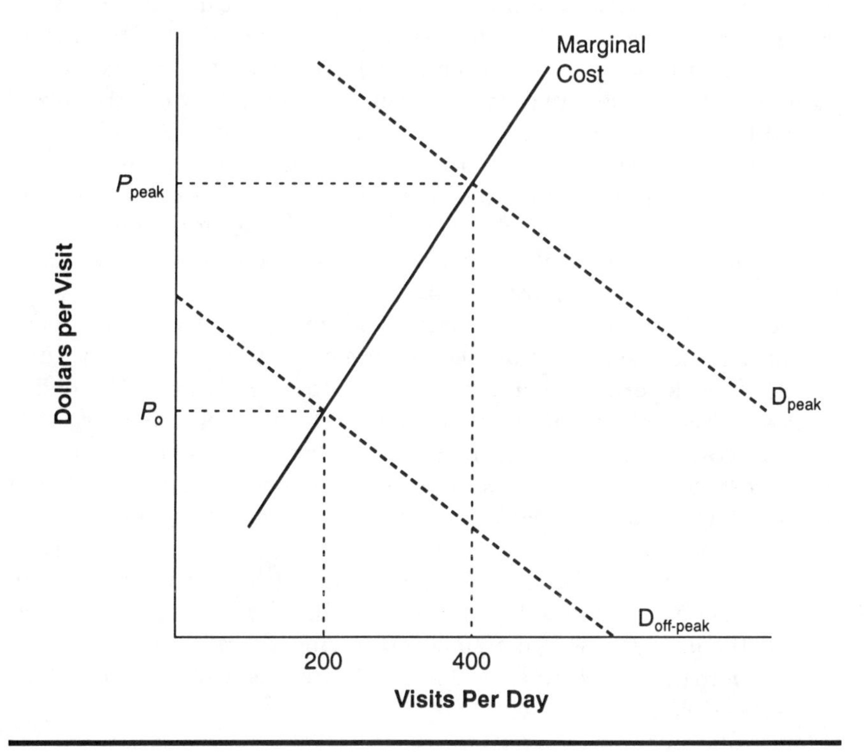

the operating costs and the costs of increased capacity to provide the additional recreation opportunities.

For example, a peak price of $6 and an off-peak price of $2 would cover average total costs of $4 when one-half of the annual use of a site occurs on peak days and one-half on off-peak days. Figure 18-2 (page 349) illustrates the situation where the quantity demanded on peak days is double that on off-peak days. But there are roughly twice as many off-peak days in the midweek as peak days on weekends and holidays, so that approximately one-half of the annual recreation use occurs on peak days and one-half on off-peak days. Of course, if annual peak and off-peak use differs, then they must be weighted accordingly.

The difference between the $6 peak and $2 off-peak period prices represents two types of costs: (1) increased operating costs incurred to provide services to large numbers of visitors when operating at high levels of output; and (2) a capacity charge, representing the annualized value of capital expansion at the site to accommodate peak periods, divided by the number of users in the peak period. This means that a capacity charge is added to the operating cost in the peak period so that demand and supply will be in equilibrium.

In the long run the value of the capacity charge takes on added significance. As the demand for recreation use increases over time, the capacity charge also increases to maintain the equilibrium between quantity demanded and capacity of the park. If the number of visitors in the peak period is known, then multiplying peak usage by the capacity charge per user represents the total revenue remaining after payment of the cost of operation. If this remaining revenue is greater than the annual capital costs of new construction, then expansion of park capacity is justified and should be done. This means that additions to capacity should be made until the daily capacity charge, multiplied by the number of users in the peak period, equals the annual capital costs associated with expansion. Hence, the value of the capacity charge required to clear the market during the peak period indicates whether expansion of park facilities is justified from an economic viewpoint.

Peak load pricing has two additional advantages. First, the approach provides casual users with an economic incentive to visit the facilities during off-peak periods when entrance fees are lower. This would tend to reduce the seasonal variation in the number of daily users and to partially equalize costs over time. Second, when peak period users pay an additional cost to reflect the scarcity of recreation opportunities during peak periods, this guarantees that those users who place the highest value on recreation use of the site at that time are the ones that actually are admitted. This is important because as a result, only those persons whose benefits equal or exceed the added costs of providing the recreation resources will use them. In this way, marginal cost pricing will result in the production of recreation opportunities that maximize total user benefits at the lowest possible cost.

Peak load pricing may reduce equity problems associated with pricing since low-income users (e.g., college students, retired persons) can go during off-peak periods when charges are less. Thus, the imposition of peak load pricing may lead to desirable distribution results. However, if low-income workers can only visit on peak weekends and holidays due to fixed work schedules, then peak load pricing could worsen equity. Thus equity may require a dual system whereby half the sites are allocated using peak load pricing and the other half at low fees using a lottery.

Implementation of peak period pricing would require information that should not be difficult to obtain. First, the number of users during peak and off-peak days should be readily available from fee receipts. More difficult to obtain is information regarding the number of potential users turned away from the site on peak days. This would be needed to accurately estimate the quantity of use demanded at the given user fees. Peak load pricing would be contrary to many existing pricing practices where unrestricted annual passes result in decreasing prices with increased use, even on peak days. Examples include the Golden Eagle pass at federal recreation areas, and annual passes at state parks and municipal facilities, such as swimming pools and golf courses. Daily user fees should be charged, in addition, to reflect marginal costs. Alternatively, passes would not be honored at peak periods.

## Comparable Pricing and Market Structure

The pricing guidelines of the federal government recommend that recreation agencies compare their own user fees to charges by other federal agencies, nonfederal public agencies, and private enterprises which provide similar facilities and services in the region. Differences not explained by the level of development and amount of service should be noted and user fees adjusted accordingly. In practice, comparable pricing represents charging the average of user fees charged by other organizations for equivalent services. Managers of public campgrounds periodically take surveys of public and private camping fees in the region, and attempt to charge the average user fee. For example, the U.S. Forest Service compares the average camping fees at private campgrounds to fees at its own campgrounds and adjusts its camping fees in subsequent fiscal years.

Pricing public recreation opportunities at the going market rate has several advantages. Perhaps the most important observation is that the market establishes the range of prices that are acceptable to users. Thus, it would tend to avoid controversy because the agency's prices would be consistent with those charged by other suppliers. Moreover, the market price represents the collective wisdom of suppliers in the region concerning what is fair and efficient. Thus, the practice would ensure that the public operation of recreation sites such as campgrounds would not impede the success of private campgrounds and reduce the range of camping opportunities available. If public campgrounds charged lower prices, it could be detrimental to commercial campgrounds and result in congestion and turn aways at the public campground.

Problems may arise in applying the comparable pricing standard. First, where public facilities are new or unique, there may be no similar sites in the region from which to draw market prices for comparison. For example, the so-called "crown jewels" of our National Park system, such as Grand Canyon, Yellowstone, and Yosemite, are unique and no similar recreation sites exist. However, the user fees at these parks can be compared to those at other unique recreation sites with a large amount of use such as Disneyland and Marineworld.

Where public facilities are not new or unique, comparable prices in the region may still not accurately reflect social values. It is a common situation for comparable market prices to underestimate or overestimate social values. Either the user fees charged by other public agencies do not cover the social cost of all inputs used in the production process, or excess user fees are charged by private producers who have a substantial degree of market power.

Managers should consider the direction and likely magnitude of the divergence from social values in estimating the upper and lower bounds of the comparative price estimate. Comparable prices charged by private suppliers may need to be adjusted when competitive market forces are weak, to ensure effective competition, or to establish minimum standards of performance. The purpose of this section is to discuss some important effects of market structure and behavior on the practice of comparable pricing by government agencies.

## *Monopoly and Competition*

You will remember that the efficient pricing solution for a government agency is to attempt to provide the competitive industry result. The recreation economic decision of a public agency would be to set user fees at the intersection of the demand curve with the marginal cost and average cost curves. Under competitive conditions, markets have so many sellers that no single one's supply decision has any appreciable effect on the price of their output. All sellers are price takers, not price makers. The price is determined in a competitive market through the impersonal forces of supply and demand. Individual operators would take price as given, confident that with a very small share of the market, they would be able to sell whatever services they can supply at that price. In competitive markets, private suppliers of recreation opportunities would charge comparable prices.

Where one or a few suppliers have control over the available supply of recreation opportunities or sites, the market structure is said to be monopolistic. Suppliers have the ability to raise price, lower recreation use to an inefficiently low level and earn profits in excess of the opportunity cost of capital employed. Thus, the market price may not be a satisfactory indicator of an efficient price (price equals marginal cost) when recreation facilities are provided by one or a few producers, i.e., when monopoly or oligopoly is present.

Economists define the term *oligopoly* as markets with a few dominant sellers in which mutual interdependence is recognized. A competitive fringe of small sellers follows the price leadership of the dominant firms. There are high barriers to the entry of new firms, and products or services are usually highly differentiated. As a result, average revenue is consistently above average cost in the long run. These conditions are present in some regional markets for skiing. Under these and related market structures, private market prices would not provide a suitable standard for comparable pricing by public agencies.

Market power may develop for several reasons. Most producers have locational advantages; a single site or perhaps a few sites provide the only opportunity for a particular recreation activity in a local or regional market. Others operate sites that provide a truly different recreation experience; some have been endowed with unique natural, historical, and cultural resources; others have simulated these site characteristics by artistic design and capital improvements, as for example, theme parks. The government awards concessionaires an exclusive right to operate recreation businesses in a particular park or recreation site. These concessionaires may gain substantial control over lodging, food service, equipment rental, and related services at the site. In other cases, decreasing costs of producing recreation services may allow a single company or perhaps a few companies, to have lower costs than potential producers who might contemplate entering. Callahan and Knudson (1966) studied the structure of the private recreation market in southern Indiana. They found considerable seller concentration and product differentiation resulting from location, quality of service, and advertising.

When entry is discouraged, for whatever reasons, then one or a few existing producers may be free to set the prices of recreation opportunities at profit maximizing levels that restrict use to an inefficiently low level. The producers are constrained only by the demand for the recreation opportunity at the price they set and not by any threat that competitors will undercut their prices and lure their customers away.

A comparison of Panels 1 and 2 of Figure 18-3 (page 354) illustrates the effect of market structure on the prices of private recreation suppliers. Panel 1 represents the case of a monopoly. Shown are the usual average total cost (AC) curve, marginal cost (MC) curve, demand (D) curve or average revenue curve, and the marginal revenue (MR) curve for a typical monopoly. Notice that the marginal revenue curve is below the demand curve. When monopolies lower their price to increase sales, then the additional revenue that they take in is the price they collect from their new customers minus the revenue they lose by cutting the price paid by all of their old customers.

**Figure 18-3. Effects of Market Structure and Costs on User Fees of Private Suppliers of Recreation Services**

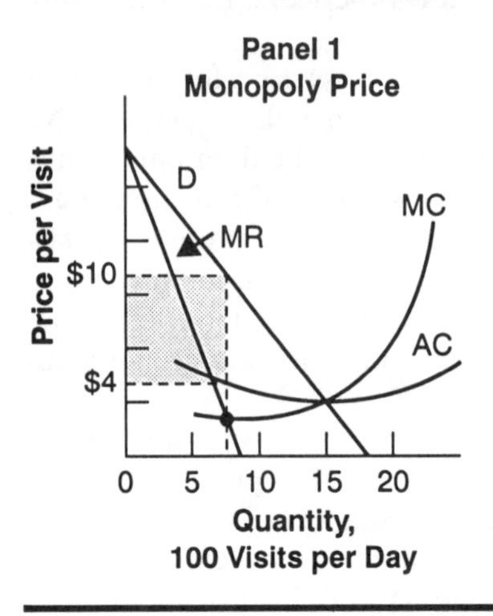


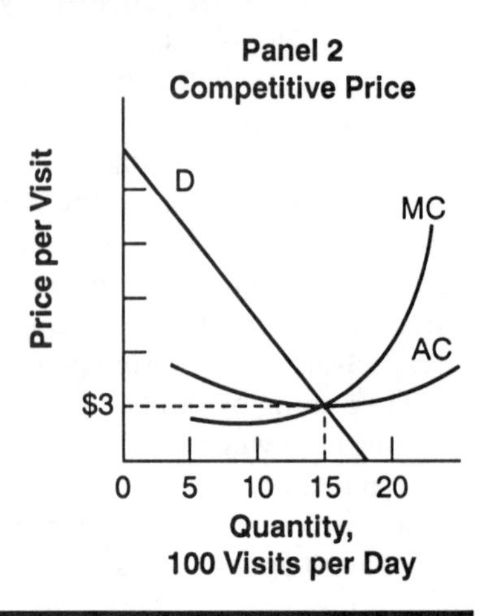


Like other private companies, monopolies maximize their profits by setting marginal revenue (MR) equal to marginal cost (MC). They would select the point in the diagram where output is 750 visits. But that point does not indicate the monopoly price because price exceeds MR for a monopolist. To learn what price the monopolist charges, we must use the demand curve to find the price at which consumers are willing to make 750 visits. The answer, we see, is that the monopoly price is $10 per visit, which exceeds both MR and AC (which is equal to $4). The monopoly depicted in Panel 1 is earning an economic profit (i.e., profit in excess of the normal rate of return on capital and management). This profit is shown as the shaded rectangle whose height is the difference between price and average cost, and whose width is the quantity produced (750 visits). In this example, profits are $6 per visit times 750 visits, or $4,500 per day.

Panel 2 represents the case of a competitive market which, you will remember, provides a suitable standard for comparable pricing by public agencies. The average total cost (AC) curve, marginal cost (MC) curve, and demand (D) curve are identical to those shown in Panel 1 for monopolies. The competitive equilibrium would occur where price equals $3 per visit and quantity equals 1,500 visits per day. This is the point where the quantity demanded (which we read from the demand curve) and quantity supplied (which we read from the MC or supply curve) are equal. By comparing this competitive result with Panel 1, we can see that monopolies would produce fewer recreation opportunities than would a competitive industry with the same demand and cost conditions. The monopoly output at which MC equals MR falls from 1,500 to 750 visits per day. Note that the monopoly price of $10 per visit exceeds the $3 price that would result from competition by $7 per visit.

The monopoly price is inefficiently high because consumers who would pay an amount for an additional visit that exceeds what it costs to produce that visit (its MC) are turned away since they will not pay the monopolist price. The monopolist refuses to lower prices to marginal cost and increase production, for if it raises output by one unit, the revenue it will collect (MR) will be less than the price that consumers will pay for the additional visit. So monopolies do not increase their production and resources are not allocated efficiently.

The comparison between monopoly and competition in the real world is not quite as simple as in our example. In practice, price is usually set at a level somewhere between monopoly and competition. With more market power, the price will be closer to the monopoly level. With less market power, price will approach the competitive level. In addition, we have assumed that the cost curves are the same whether the industry is competitive or a monopoly. This may not always be the case as a monopolist may be able to utilize economies of scale, which lower costs below that of a smaller competitive firm.

## *Price Discrimination*

Generally, economists assume that sellers of comparable services in the region of a park or other public recreation facility can charge only a single price to all buyers. However, price differences can be found almost everywhere in the recreation industry. Sellers vary prices according to the buyer's age, location, income, time of use, and other reasons. The young pay less than adults to enter zoos and parks, attend outdoor theater and concerts, and buy licenses to fish and hunt. Retired persons either pay lower fees or are exempt from the payment of fees.

State wildlife agencies charge nonresident anglers and hunters higher license fees than residents, who often pay state taxes in support of wildlife programs. Some campgrounds charge more for campsites located on the edge of a lake or stream than for interior sites. Recreation condominiums located on the side of a building with the most favorable view are higher priced. Airlines have first-class fares for higher income travelers. Quantity discounts are often available for groups of 10 or more persons. Peak load pricing is a type of price discrimination. For example, municipal golf courses charge higher green fees per round of golf after 4 P.M. on weekdays and on weekends and holidays. Resort hotels and restaurants charge more during the peak season than the off-peak season.

Price discrimination is defined as charging different prices for the same goods and services where the price differences are not proportional to differences in costs. Either different buyers are charged different prices or each buyer is charged different prices for succeeding units purchased. Not all price differences represent price discrimination. When price differences are proportional to cost differences, they represent the competitive market result. Common usage of the term price discrimination by economists has no odious connotation, although the antitrust laws make certain kinds of price discrimination illegal.

The purpose of price discrimination is to capture as much of the buyer's consumer surplus as possible as revenue. If some buyers would pay more than the market price rather than go without, most sellers wouldn't mind trying to exploit this. Few sellers are likely to succeed in getting all of the consumer's surplus. But some probably get quite a lot of it. Price discrimination of one kind or another can be found almost everywhere because it increases profit.

Economists refer to three degrees of price discrimination. First degree or "perfect" price discrimination occurs when a seller extracts all of the potential consumer surplus by charging buyers a price equal to their maximum willingness to pay for each unit purchased. Second degree or "imperfect" price discrimination occurs when a seller extracts some but not all of the potential consumer surplus with discounts for blocks of units rather than individual units. Third degree price discrimination involves separating buyers into groups with different elasticities of demand and setting prices so that marginal revenue equals marginal cost in each.

Panel 1 of Figure 18-4, allows us to compare uniform pricing to perfect price discrimination. With uniform pricing, 10 units would be sold at a price of $20 each. Total revenue would be $200 (= 10 x $20) as represented by the rectangle determined by these values. With perfect price discrimination, sellers turn the entire area under the demand curve into total revenue. The perfectly discriminating monopolists establish prices so as to extract from each consumer the full value of his or her consumer surplus. If a ski area, for example, could sell some lift tickets for $40, while also selling others for $38, $36, $34, and $32, the total revenue the seller could collect would be much larger. Total revenue for the 10 units becomes the sum of all the revenue received for all of the prices shown on the vertical axis: $40 + $38 + $36 + . . . + $24 + $22 = $310. This is $110 or 55% more than the $200 the seller can get without price discrimination. In practice, perfect price discrimination is rare because it is difficult to segment the market and to know the preference structure of potential buyers. It is most likely to occur in markets with a small number of buyers of a specialized product.

Second degree price discrimination involves sellers taking part, but not all, of consumer surplus. With imperfect price discrimination, sellers turn some of the area under the demand curve into total revenue. Different prices are established for two or more blocks of units rather than for each individual unit. The result is a stairstep pricing effect illustrated in Panel 2 of Figure 18-4.

For example, a ski area could offer the first five days of skiing for sale to each individual at a price of $30 per day. If skiers wish to purchase more than five days of skiing, the additional days can be purchased at a lower price, say $20. The total revenue the seller collects from 10 days of individual skiing per year becomes $250 [= (5 x $30) + (5 x $20)]. This is $50 or 25% more than the $200 the seller can get without this type of price

**Figure 18-4. Perfect and Imperfect Price Discrimination**

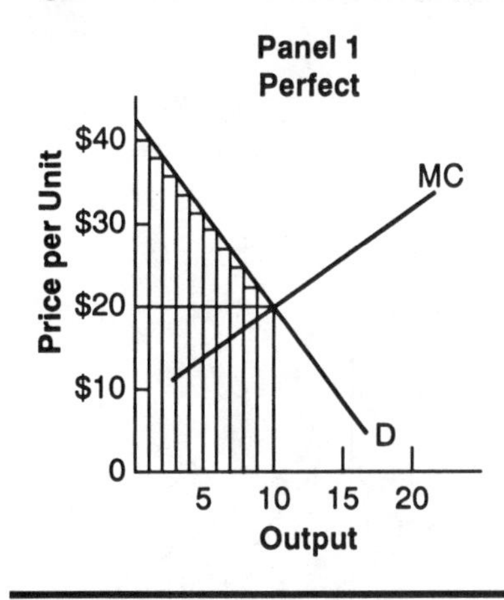


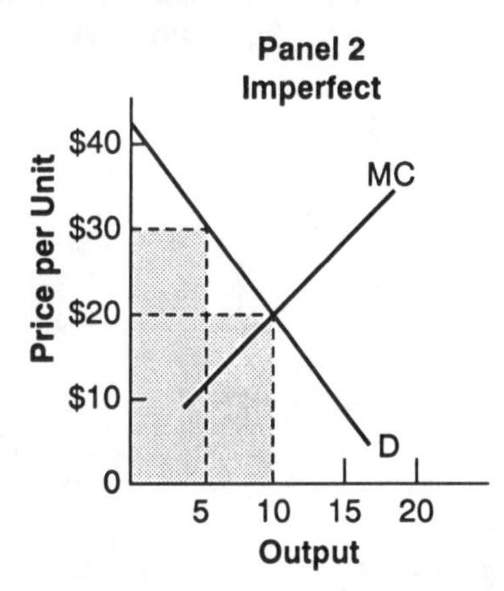


discrimination. However, some of the consumer surplus ($60) remains, as indicated by the unshaded triangles above the two price lines.

In this example of less than perfect price discrimination, only two price lines (known as block rates) are set to illustrate the method. In practice, the number of price lines could be increased to approach the results of perfect price discrimination. As the number of price lines is increased, more and more of the consumer surplus would be captured by the seller as additional revenue.

Third degree price discrimination is the maximization of total profits by setting prices of a product or service in two or more different submarkets so that marginal revenue equals marginal cost in each. To practice third degree price discrimination, sellers must have sufficient market power to set their own prices, serve two or more submarkets with different elasticities of demand, and be able to prevent transfers among customers in different submarkets. This can be demonstrated by an example.

Suppose a ski area is selling the same service—downhill skiing—to two separate submarkets of skiers—youth and adult. These two groups can be easily identified and segregated at moderate cost. Buyers are unable to transfer lift tickets easily from youth to adults, as the tickets are two distinct colors and age is a readily observable characteristic. Otherwise it would be possible for skiers to make money by buying the lower price youth lift tickets and selling them at a higher price to adults, thus making it difficult to maintain the price differentials between the two groups of customers.

Figure 18-5 (page 358) illustrates the separate submarkets for skiing. The elastic demand curve for youths is shown in Panel 1, and the inelastic demand curve for adults in Panel 2. The aggregate demand curve for the ski site is shown in Panel 3. It represents the horizontal sum of the number of skier days demanded at each price in the two submarkets. The marginal cost curve shown in Panel 3 is applicable to both submarkets.

**Figure 18-5. Price Discrimination for an Identical Product Sold in Two Submarkets**

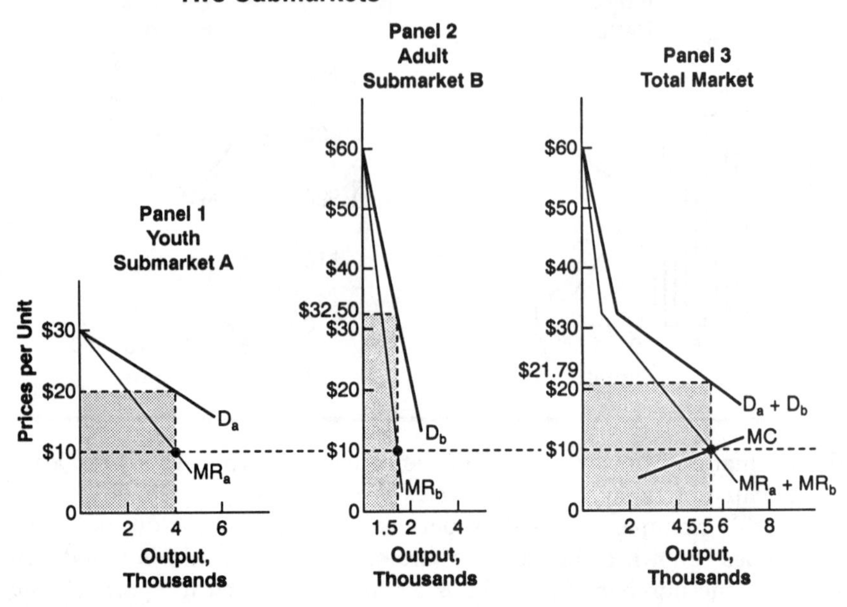


Costs of serving youth and adult skiers are virtually identical. Thus, from a production standpoint, it does not matter which submarket purchases a lift ticket. Of course, if production costs differ between the two submarkets, this fact would have to be taken into account.

The solution to this pricing problem is a two-part process. First, the ski site must determine the optimum total output level. Profit maximization occurs at that aggregate output where marginal cost and marginal revenue are equal. As shown in Panel 3 of Figure 18-5, the optimum output is 5,500 skiers per day where marginal cost and marginal revenue are both equal to $10 per skier. Second, the managers of the ski site must allocate this output between the two submarkets. Proper allocation of the total output between the two submarkets can be illustrated graphically by drawing a horizontal line through Panels 1 and 2 at $10 to indicate that this is the marginal cost in each market at the indicated aggregate output. The intersection of this horizontal line with the marginal revenue curve in each submarket indicates the optimum distribution of sales of lift tickets to youth and adults and the appropriate discriminating price levels.

According to Figure 18-5, the ski site maximizes total revenue by selling a total of 5,500 ski-lift tickets per day, including 4,000 tickets to youths at a price of $20 and 1,500 tickets to adults at a price of $32.50. The profit-maximizing price of lift tickets in the inelastic adult skier submarket is over 50% higher than the price charged in the youth submarket where demand is relatively elastic. The effects on total revenue of the ski corporation are summarized as follows:

1. With Price Discrimination:

| | | |
|---|---|---|
| Youth, Market A: | $80,000 | (= 4,000 skiers x $20) |
| Adult, Market B: | 48,750 | (= 1,500 skiers x $32.50) |
| Total Market | $128,750 | |

2. Without Price Discrimination:

| | | |
|---|---|---|
| Total Market: | $119,845 | (= 5,500 skiers x $21.79) |

Thus, price discrimination increases total revenue by $8,905 per day or 7%. This could be the difference between making a profit or loss.

One important reason for having public recreation facilities is to protect the consumer from the more damaging effects of price discrimination. For example, when one group of consumers consistently pays higher prices than do other groups, the result can be a redistribution of recreation opportunities from those who would receive more benefits to those with less. The total welfare of society may be reduced accordingly. For this and other reasons, comparable prices charged by private suppliers may need to be adjusted to bring about more effective competition and performance.

## An Example of Using Differential Pricing for Management and Revenue

As is evident, pricing can be used as a management tool as well as to raise revenue. An example of this is the field experiment conducted by Bamford, Manning, Forcier and Koenemann (1988) at 14 Vermont state parks. The parks' current pricing system charged the same fee for high amenity campsites such as those adjacent to lakes and streams, and less desirable sites located elsewhere in the campground (e.g., by the main road). The natural result is competition and overuse of the desirable sites and underutilization of the other sites.

To evaluate the effect of a fee differential to spread use more evenly among sites, a price differential ranging from $1 to $5 was instituted at selected Vermont state park campgrounds. The prices for the different types of campsites was displayed at the entrance station map so that campers knew the prices for various locations of sites when they were making their campsite selection. Visitor use before and after the fee was monitored, and a sample of campers was sent a survey to record their socioeconomic characteristics.

Regression and correlation analysis showed that the fee differential resulted in a strong and statistically significant shift in visitor use away from prime campsites as the fee differential increased between prime and nonprime campsites. Over half the variation in the demand for prime campsites can be explained solely by the fee differential.

Since the demand for prime sites was found to be slightly price inelastic, increases in fees resulted in small (5%–20%) increases in fee revenue. Bamford, Manning, Forcier and Koenemann (1988) also noted a small, but consistent effect of visitor income on campsite choice with the fee differential. However, while the *presence* of a differential caused fewer low-income households to choose prime sites, the *amount* of the differential did not further reduce the percentage of low-income households choosing prime sites. Nonetheless, it appears that fee differentials could be used as a potent alternative to simply closing prime sites to rest them from overuse.

## Feasibility of Fee Collection

In the past, most observers considered the economic and administrative feasibility of fee collection to be the most important pricing problem of public agencies supplying recreation opportunities. Economists refer to any cost associated with the sale of permits to users and their purchase by users as **transaction costs.** Studies of transaction costs traditionally focused on the investment in collection booths, in building a fence around the site, and the salaries of ticket takers and guards. As a result, it should not be surprising that many managers have concluded they would not be able to collect sufficient revenue to offset collection costs at sites with low annual use and/or a large number of entrances.

Consider the findings of a report to Congress by the U.S. General Accounting Office in 1982. The study was based on a 20% sample of the 330 recreation areas administered by the National Park Service, 26 sites with entrance fees and 45 without. The authors found that revenues from entrance fees exceeded collection costs at all existing fee sites. The report recommended that Congress authorize the National Park Service to increase entrance fees and collection hours at existing fee sites, representing about 20% of all sites; begin charging entrance fees at 40% of the sites; and maintain 40% of the sites as nonfee sites. The economic and administrative reasons for recommending against entrance fees is especially relevant to this discussion. The report concluded that collecting entrance fees would not be economical at 30% of the sites and not administratively feasible at nearly 10%.

The most important reason why collection costs would exceed fee revenue was the presence of too many access points to control entry. For example, the report recommended against charging entrance fees of more than two million visitors per year to Olympic National Park, located 60 miles northwest of Seattle, Washington. The park has 14 entrances rather than the usual one or two entrances at most recreation sites with a single access road. The report concluded that the cost of constructing and operating 14 entrance fee collection stations would exceed the revenue obtained.

The second reason collection costs would exceed fee revenue was low annual recreation use. Nine percent of the recreation sites did not have a sufficient number of visitors to allow the revenues from user fees to equal or exceed the cost of constructing and operating entrance fee collection stations. The third reason why collection costs would exceed fee revenue was the high cost of capital investment in collection facilities. Five percent of the recreation sites did not have existing entrance stations where park employees provided information to visitors. The costs of road widening and construction of a booth (or kiosk) would exceed the revenue collected as user fees.

Finally, the report concluded that collecting entrance fees would not be administratively feasible at nearly 10% of the sites. In some cases (6%), the initial legislation authorizing the recreation site or the covenants of property deeded to the agency required free access. For example, Congress prohibited charging entrance fees at Alaska units of the National Park system. Similar restrictions were made in the case of Acadia, Mount Rushmore, Gateway, Golden Gate and Lincoln Home. At Great Smoky Mountain, the state of North Carolina deeded land to the federal government with the provision of free access by its citizens. At other sites (4%) visitors were already charged user fees for special transportation or a tour to see the main attraction at the site and it was not considered feasible to add an entrance fee. For example, Mammoth Cave charged $3 per person for a guided tour.

## Trend in Collection Costs

The trend in collection costs as a proportion of total revenues from recreation user fees has been sharply down with few exceptions. Data available from the *Federal Recreation Fee Report to Congress* prepared by the U.S. Department of the Interior (1993) indicated that in 1976 an average of 43% of total fee revenue was spent collecting the fees. By 1984 this had fallen to 26% with the Corps of Engineers having the lowest collection costs, accounting for 21% of user fee revenues. The Forest Service and the National Park Service had the highest collection costs, nearly 30% of user fee revenues. One reason for the drop in costs was the increase in the level of entrance and camping fees. Increasing the amount of the fee adds to revenue without resulting in any additional collection costs. While campground fee increases were substantial, visitation fell only slightly. This indicates that in the current range of fees, the demand curve for developed camping is price inelastic. Thus, it is not surprising that increased user fees resulted in a substantial growth in total revenue from user charges.

Park managers estimate that initiating user fees at nonfee sites would decrease the number of visits for about two years. Once visitors become accustomed to paying a reasonable entrance fee, recreation use is expected to increase above preentrance fee levels.

## Costs of Alternative Methods of Collection

Managers of some recreation sites have little or no experience in charging user fees. The problem is to decide whether or not it is efficient to initiate user fees, and if so, what method of collection would be the most cost effective. One improvement which shows promise to dramatically reduce collection costs is the self-service system. Indications are that the costs of collecting campground fees can be reduced to less than one-half the cost of entrance booths manned during daylight hours. Thus, the choice is between two alternatives: (1) a self-service collection system at each relevant recreation entrance or (2) a manned collection booth.

In the past, most parks and other recreation sites that charged entrance fees had entrance booths occupied by employees during daylight hours located at each of the primary entrances to the parks. This fee collection system was favored by managers because it allowed employees to provide maps and other information, to observe individuals as they enter the park, and to remind them of park rules concerning alcohol consumption, the leashing of dogs, and the like. More recently, some observers have begun to question whether staffed entrance stations are always a cost-effective use of employee time. Self-service fee collection at the entrance to some state parks and federal campgrounds have advantages beyond just reduced collection costs. Self-service fee stations free employees to patrol several recreation sites, and to provide both random checks of fee compliance and information on the spot of the recreation activity where it would be most useful to visitors.

Experience with both fee collection systems indicates compliance may be greater with self-service than entrance booths. The term compliance refers to the proportion of the total number of recreation users entering a site who are eligible to pay user fees and actually do pay. It is usually expressed as a percentage of total recreation use. For example, voluntary payment of self-service fees has been approximately 70% for vehicles entering Forest Service campgrounds in the Rocky Mountains without a resident employee or volunteer. For campgrounds with a voluntary host living on the site, compliance has approached 92%. Self-service fee collection has the advantage that it is operative 24 hours every day of the year, whereas entrance booths only collect revenue when employees are on duty. It would seem a relatively minor inconvenience to require all vehicles at a recreation site to display a receipt for payment and/or individuals to have a receipt in possession while engaging in recreation activities.

Most recreation sites are small with too little recreation use to enable managers to efficiently operate collection booths. This depends on the level of user charge, of course, and whether a given level of use is evenly spread out over the year or concentrated into just one season. When the use of a recreation site is concentrated into one or two seasons of the year, the total use necessary to efficiently operate fee collection booths is less than when use is spread over the entire year. However, even when the use of a recreation site is concentrated into a single summer or winter season, the number of users required to efficiently operate fee collection booths exceeds the use of many recreation sites.

Generally, self-service fee collection would be more efficient than collection booths. For example, with 100 vehicles per day, self-service fee collections have costs one-fifth that of collection booths. Most of the advantage of self-service results from savings in facility construction and labor costs. For example, the self-service envelope depository costs about $1,000 and the instruction signs an additional $1,000. Compare this to the collection booth (or kiosk) which often costs $25,000 including utilities and equipment. Self-service entrance fee collection costs also are expected to be somewhat lower for road widening, highway signs, and site vegetation or landscaping.

It is with respect to labor costs that self-service would be most efficient. Self-service fee collection appears to represent potential labor savings of about 90%. A single fee collection officer can service 10 fee collection stations at least every other workday traveling a round trip of approximately 100 miles.

Self-service fee collection stations may be cost effective at numerous sites where recreation use is very low. These would include remote access roads and trailheads, very small campgrounds, and where it is efficient to staff an entrance booth only during daylight hours. At such sites, the capital investment required to begin self-service fee collection would not exceed $2,000 for the signs and depository. There would be little or no added costs for road construction to allow temporary parking at the site. Also, operator salary and transportation costs could be reduced by half through the pick up of revenues from the depository every four days rather than two. This suggests that self-service fee collection can be cost effective for sites where recreation use is very low.

## Payment for Recreation Use and Environmental Protection Programs

The problem of pricing is complicated by the fact that outdoor recreation agencies produce both on-site and off-site benefits. There are benefits that accrue to individuals in addition to the values they receive from visiting a site or to individuals who may never visit the site at all. These off-site (i.e., public or external) benefits have been described as the willingness to pay for (1) the option of possibly visiting a site in the future; (2) the value from simply knowing the natural area exists and is protected for its own sake; and (3) the satisfaction from knowing the area will be available to future generations. Our purpose here is to illustrate the proportion of total recreation resource benefits that are attributable separately to recreation use and to protecting the quality of the natural resource. The pricing guidelines of the federal government recommend that recreation agencies establish user fees consistent with the benefits to users and the general public. The pricing guidelines contain the related point that recreation agencies must consider the public policy or purpose of the agency as spelled out in its enabling legislation.

## *History of the Concept*

Most parks and other recreation sites were established for two reasons: first, to preserve their unique historic, scenic, natural, and wildlife resources, and second, to make them available for the enjoyment of people. Historically, the federal government became involved with providing opportunities for recreation use as a result of policies designed to achieve other objectives, notably the protection of unique environmental resources. For example, Congress created Yellowstone National Park in 1872:

> . . . to conserve the scenery and the natural and historic objects and the wildlife, and to provide for the enjoyment of the same by such means as will leave them unimpaired for the enjoyment of future generations.

Similar language appears in legislation to establish other National Parks, separating the recreation use management contribution from natural resource protection. National Forests were established in 1891 as federal forest reserves to preserve valuable forest lands and watersheds. Recreation use programs were introduced in 1960 under the multiple-use concept. Also, the Corps of Engineers and Bureau of Reclamation undertook water resource development projects to supply electricity, flood control, navigation, and irrigation water. Prior to 1965 the recreational potential of their reservoirs was not recognized in project planning or evaluation. The multiple-use resource management objectives of these agencies require careful judgments in allocating costs to specific recreation user groups and the public at large.

Based on this experience, John Ise (1961) concludes in a critical history of *Our National Park Policy* that visitors to the parks should not pay the entire cost of their operation. Some of the agency's output benefits the general public, and not just visitors to the parks alone. Clawson and Knetsch (1966) note that if there are broad social benefits to the general population from recreation programs or park protection, then it is appropriate that much of the costs be met by taxes imposed upon all of the citizens. On the other hand, if most of the benefits of recreation resource management are received directly by users engaged in recreation activities at the site, it is appropriate that more of the costs be paid directly by user fees. Clawson and Knetsch suggest that research is needed to provide a basis for allocating the costs of recreation resource management between recreation and other outputs.

Table 18-1 shows the distinction that economists make between the outputs of recreation use and environmental programs. Economists consider the output of recreation resource management as a private good or service that has some public good characteristics. This means that part of the benefits are private, in that they are received by individual users, and part by the general public. The most important characteristic of recreation use, whether privately or publicly supplied, is that it can be divided

**Table 18-1. Payment for Recreation Use and Environmental Protection Programs**

| | Output of Recreation and Environmental Programs | | | |
|---|---|---|---|---|
| Variable | Privately Supplied Recreation Use | Publicly Supplied Recreation Use | Partial Public Goods, with External Effects | Public Goods with Jointness in Supply |
| Distinguishing Characteristic | Exclusive and divisible output | Predominantly exclusive and divisible output | Not exclusive, external costs and benefits to others are present | Not divisible, equally available to all persons, collective goods, merit goods |
| Production Process | Usually services are intangible nonstorable, with simultaneous production and consumption | Same as privately supplied recreation use | Spillovers, site congestion, associated costs | Often non-reproducible, gifts of nature, available at zero marginal cost |
| Role of Government | Protect private property rights, administer private concessionaire contracts on public land | Multiple-use management (e.g., recreation wildlife, water) | Requires government intervention | Must be provided by government agencies |
| Examples | Resort lodges, campgrounds, amusement parks, swimming pools and beaches, private hunting reserves, charter boat fishing, ski areas | Parks, trails, playgrounds, campgrounds, fishing, hunting, swimming pools, beaches | Environmental damages, wildlife on private land, site carrying capacity, location advantages | Protection of the quality of air, water, natural scenery, wilderness areas, wild and scenic endangered species of wildlife |
| Payment Policy | User fees | User fees, taxes | User fees, taxes, subsidies | General tax revenues |

Source: Adapted from Randall, 1987.

among individuals who purchase the amount desired for their individual exclusive use. The distinguishing characteristic of public benefits is that generally they are not divisible or exclusive. This means that once they are supplied, they are equally available to all individuals. Such public benefits usually are provided by government from general tax revenues, since there is no way that user fees can be charged for output that cannot be divided among individuals.

The "benefits received" principle of taxation states that the payment by individuals for government services should correspond to the benefits that individuals receive. Consider first, those who participate in recreation activities and benefit directly from improvements in recreation facilities and environmental quality at recreation sites. According to this principle, the proportion of total costs recovered as user fees would equal the proportion of total benefits received by individuals who participate in recreation activities. Second, consider the population as a whole which benefits indirectly from resource protection programs. A number of studies have shown that most people have option, existence, or bequest motives for protecting natural resources and environmental quality. But in this case, it is not feasible to charge the individual citizens who benefit from government expenditures. Thus, the portion of total cost related to resource preservation as distinct from recreation management should be paid from general taxes. This means that the proportion of total costs covered by general tax revenues would equal the proportion of total benefits received by the general public.

## *Empirical Estimate of Public Benefit*

Recreation economics has traditionally focused on the benefits of recreation use. To estimate the proportion of total resource management costs that are appropriately paid from general taxes as compared to user fees, we need to measure the preservation benefits to the general public from resource protection. Data were obtained from a household survey designed to represent the population of the state of Colorado (Aiken, 1985). Personal interviews were conducted in the homes of a subsample of 198 households. The results illustrate a practical way to measure the benefits of recreation and resource protection programs to users and to the general public. The survey design was based on the federal guidelines discussed in Chapter 10. The interagency committee recommended use of the contingent valuation method in recreation and environmental benefit studies. Thus, the research method should be acceptable and the results of this pilot study useful in future research designed to assist actual policymaking by public decision makers.

Figure 18-6 provides some tentative evidence as to the allocation of total benefits between recreation use and resource protection. For example, the pilot study suggests that recreation use benefits account for only about one-third of the total benefits from the construction and maintenance of recreation facilities (see Column G in Figure 18-6). This suggests that user fees should recover only about one-third of the costs of their construction and maintenance. The general public, including both users and nonusers, would pay about two-thirds of the costs of recreation facilities from general taxes. Most people receive satisfaction from knowing that public recreation facilities are available and in good condition. Their motivations for payment include the option of possibly using the facilities in the future, the knowledge that they exist, and the knowledge that they will be available to future generations.

The essential point is that presence of preservation benefits could justify user prices at less than the long-run marginal costs of the resource management program. This would not necessarily mean that recreation resources would be supplied free of charge to individual consumers. It is both possible and desirable to levy user charges. A proper user charge would equate marginal user benefits to marginal user cost. For example, one possibility would be to charge individual users all of the variable costs for which they are directly responsible. The proportion of the capital investment costs that should be paid by the general public depends on the extent to which the nonusing public benefits from resource protection.

Clearly, the quality of environmental resources contributes to the benefits of recreation. Figure 18-6 shows for one state, the recreation use portion of the total benefits of resource protection programs. Direct

**Figure 18-6. Average Annual Willingness to Pay per Household for Recreation Use and Environmental Protection Programs in the State of Colorado**

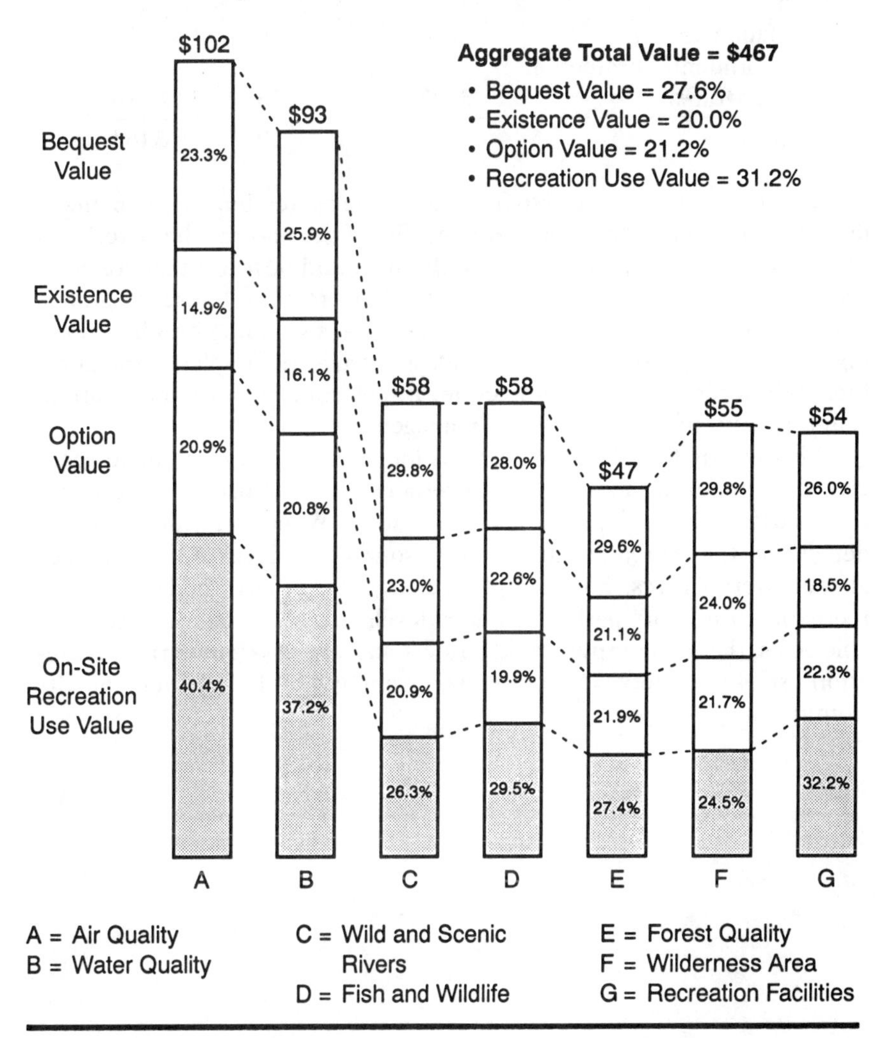

recreation benefits accounted for slightly more than 30% of total willingness to pay for six important environmental resource programs. The pilot study suggests that households were willing to pay, on average, a total of $145 per year for the recreation use value of the seven resources. This includes $18 per year to construct and maintain facilities in parks and other recreation sites located in the states where they live. However, the largest proportion of total recreation use benefit was attributed to programs that protect the quality of environmental resources such as the air, water, forest, fish, and wildlife. These annual household values are summarized here:

| | Recreation use value | Public preservation value | Total |
|---|---|---|---|
| Park and recreation facilities | $18 | $36 | $54 |
| Environmental protection programs | $127 | $283 | $410 |
| Total | $145 | $319 | $464 |

This illustrates the need to distinguish the recreation user benefits of facility management from the user benefits of the natural characteristics of recreation sites and other areas in the surrounding forest that are managed under other environmental protection or multiple-use programs. Examples of the former include campgrounds, swimming beaches, boating sites, and a portion of access roads and trails. Examples of the latter include reforestation, fire protection, insect control, soil conservation, water quality, and wildlife habitat management.

This information has implications for pricing policy by public agencies. It is important to determine whether recreation use of the resource causes external benefits to the general public. Whenever public benefits depend on the recreation use of the resource, the level of user charges affects external gains. For example, if charges for a merit good such as the recreation use of city parks were set at levels to cover total fixed and variable costs, the total output would be substantially less than current recreation use, and society would lose the advantages of the external benefits from the larger output.

*Chapter 19*

# Comparing Benefits and Costs

This chapter shows how comparing benefits and costs can help public decision makers choose among alternative recreation projects which vary in size, design, and purpose; introduces the concept of discounting and net present value in benefit-cost studies; and shows how to apply the approach to recreation economic decisions

The purpose of benefit-cost studies is to assist decision makers in improving their operations with respect to: (1) optimum size of the program; (2) design of the recreation program mix for maximum efficiency; and (3) choosing from the available alternatives those that are most productive. To achieve efficiency in government, spending on recreation programs should be increased in each area and in total until the marginal social benefits of the last recreation visitor days equal their marginal social costs. This would help managers produce the most benefits of public recreation programs for society.

In principle, the benefit-cost approach to evaluation of recreation and park programs is the same as when individual consumers compare the benefits and costs of alternative recreation activities described in Chapter 5. It differs from the individual approach to decision making in an important way. The values that count are not those of the individual manager or planner, but rather the values held by the visitors and other citizens of the nation. Two managers with different personal values should generate very similar estimates of the social benefits of a recreation project serving the same purpose.

## Public Versus Private Decisions

Benefit-cost studies of public proposals ask the question, "Do the net benefits to all the people exceed the costs required of them?" If the answer is yes, the proposal is an efficient one. If it is no, the proposal would waste resources and would not be in the public interest. Benefit-cost studies are concerned with social gains and losses, not just revenues and out-of-pocket costs.

For the evaluation of public recreation programs, the denominator in the benefit-cost ratio (B:C) is the direct agency operational costs and opportunity costs to the rest of society over the life of the project. The numerator is the net benefits (consumer surplus) to the visitors and citizens, summed over the life of the project.

Benefit-cost studies of publicly funded recreation programs consider a broader range of benefits and costs than do managers and accountants in private business. Although economic analysis asks the same question as financial analysis (Is it worth it?), the question is asked about the effects to a wider group of people (those who comprise society). Instead of asking whether the private business revenues will exceed private costs, benefit-cost studies ask whether society as a whole will be better off.

Financial analysis would only consider benefits defined as total revenue or sales divided by the direct monetary costs incurred by the company. When dealing with many nonmarketed uses of natural resources such as recreation on publicly owned lands, this definition is deficient in two ways. First, benefits to visitors and other citizens from maintaining a natural area for recreation almost always exceeds the entrance fee revenue collected. In part this is due to fees being set below market clearing prices. It also is due to the fact that visitors enjoy a consumer surplus (i.e., a value over and above what they pay, since the entry fee equals the value of just the last trip, not the first few trips). Further, many individuals receive benefits from simply knowing the natural area is preserved for their own future recreation use and for future generations. Since they currently do not visit the site, no revenue is collected from them. Thus, actual recreation area receipts miss a substantial portion of the benefits. In the case of Wilderness Areas, Congress has precluded the agency from charging any entrance fee, so revenue is essentially zero. Clearly, recreation use benefits and preservation benefits are not zero.

Second, reserving an area for recreation imposes real costs on society that may not be fully reflected in financial costs. Building a downhill ski area reduces wildlife habitat and often results in significant increase in soil erosion that can adversely affect water quality and fish habitat. Yet, there is no market charge for these negative effects. However, these are real opportunity costs to society in that they impose losses in well-being to hunters and anglers. In addition, when the land is publicly owned, there may be no financial costs of reserving the land as park, but there may be an opportunity cost of foregone timber harvesting or mining.

Thus, benefit-cost studies broaden the concept of benefits to society from the concept of total revenue or sales of the private business. For the total operating costs of the private business, benefit-cost studies broaden the concept to include opportunity cost—the social value foregone when resources are moved from alternative economic activities into the proposed project. For the profits of the firm, benefit-cost studies substitute the concept of net benefits to society (benefits minus costs).

Schultze (1977), a former chief economic advisor to the President of the United States, sees the need to compare benefits and cost as resulting from the scarcity of public resources and the nonmarket context of public decisions. The resources of the government are always less than needed to accomplish all of the useful things that we would like government to do for us. Therefore, from among the competing claims on resources, decision makers must choose those that contribute most to our national objectives, and choose efficiently in order to free scarce resources for other useful programs. Second, government programs rarely have an automatic regulator that indicates when a program has ceased to be productive, could be made more efficient, or should be replaced by another program. In private business, society relies upon profits and competition to furnish the necessary incentives and discipline and to provide a feedback on the quality of decisions. While this self-regulatory mechanism is basically sound in the private sector (if no pollution is generated by the firm), it is virtually nonexistent in the public sector. In government, we must find another tool for making choices which resource scarcity forces upon us.

In the United States, the benefit-cost approach (synonymous with cost-benefit analysis in Europe) was first authorized by the Rivers and Harbors Act of 1902 and the Flood Control Act of 1936 which provided for the comparison of benefits "to whomsoever they may accrue" (i.e., regardless of whether they live in the state where the project is located or not) with costs. Until 1965 the method was limited primarily to the Corps of Engineers and Bureau of Reclamation study of water resource development projects. Since then, with a new emphasis on accountability in government, benefit-cost studies of all social programs has flourished. Now the approach is routinely applied in such program areas as parks and recreation, environmental regulation, education, criminal justice, transportation, urban renewal and healthcare programs.

Much has been written about benefit-cost studies, both pro and con. Some have attacked them, either as an attempt to quantify what cannot be measured, or as an effort on the part of economists to usurp the decision-making function of managers and political leaders. Most observers, however, have recognized benefit-cost studies for what they are, a means of helping responsible public officials make better decisions, ones not so driven by local political constituencies (so called *pork barrel* politics, which in the recreation field have been named *park barrel* politics). Benefit-cost studies are a means to improve the decision-making process in order to assist the final judgment, not to supplant it.

While benefit-cost analysis is being used by some agencies more than others, its full potential has not been realized in natural resource and recreation agencies. In part this stems from many managers' misunderstanding of benefit-cost analysis, and performing such an analysis is sometimes seen as a costly effort to justify what the managers want to do anyway.

However, the continuing efforts to estimate the benefits and costs of recreation programs would need to result in only a small increase in the effectiveness of recreation program expenditures to justify the studies cost.

## Optimum Social Benefits and Costs as Inputs Into Three Decisions

Benefit-cost studies ask whether society is better off because of expenditures or government programs. Are the social gains greater than the social losses or less? A public recreation program can increase the well-being of society if the resources given up are used to produce greater benefits than they would produce in the absence of the government programs. Benefit-cost studies help public decision makers choose among alternative recreation programs and projects which vary in size, design and purpose. They assist decision makers in (1) developing the optimum size program or project; (2) designing the recreation program features to be of maximum benefit to the different types of visitors; and (3) choosing from the available alternative projects those that produce the most benefits over and above their costs. We will discuss each of these functions.

### *Optimum Program and Project Size*

Consider first, a fundamental recreation economic problem of governments throughout the world: How large should the program be? How much should the government tax and spend for recreation? The question of the size of the public program is a problem of resource allocation. How many of society's resources should be allocated to the production of recreation opportunities versus competing government priorities? Benefit-cost studies can assist decision makers in thinking meaningfully about this question. To achieve efficiency in government, spending on recreation programs should be increased in each area and in total until the marginal social benefits of the last recreation visitor days equal their marginal social costs. This will ensure that the net benefits of recreation programs to society are as large as possible and do not needlessly reduce benefits that other government programs, such as education and mass transit, might provide. An important related question that agency managers must frequently answer, is just how large to make a particular campground (e.g., how many individual campsites to provide), how many miles of trails to build or how many acres of wilderness to recommend to Congress.

In Figure 19-1 for example, Panel 1a shows the total social benefits of public recreation in the United States compared to the total social costs of producing these recreation opportunities. Panel 1b shows the marginal social benefits and costs derived from the totals. The marginal curves are simply the changes in value of the total curves resulting from changes in the amount of recreation opportunities provided. They may be more

**Figure 19-1. Optimum Size of Public Recreation Programs**

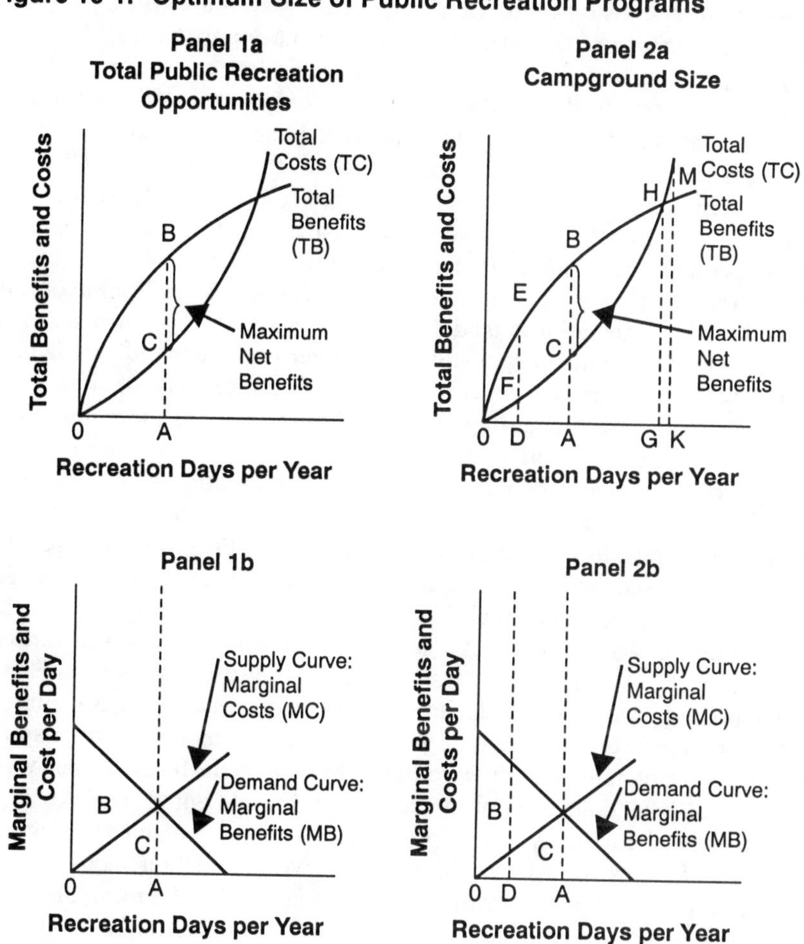


familiar to you as demand and supply curves, with optimum output occurring where the two intersect, i.e., where supply equals demand.

Assume that the government has detailed information on citizens' willingness to pay for additional recreation programs represented by recreation days on the horizontal axis. The result is the total social benefits curve (TB) shown in Panel 1a of Figure 19-1. The total social cost curve (TC) is also drawn. Land must be acquired or set aside for recreation sites and personnel must be hired for planning, supervision, and operation. In addition, some recreation programs have social opportunity costs, such as foregone production of timber, minerals, energy, and the like. All of the social costs of providing recreation opportunities are summed in the total social cost (TC) curve in Panel 1a.

The total social benefits (TB) curve shows that for the first dollars the government spends on recreation programs, citizens are willing to pay a great deal because of the scarcity of recreation opportunities; there are very large social benefits. However, as more dollars are spent and additional visitor days produced, the value generated by each additional dollar becomes smaller, i.e., diminishing marginal benefits. As individual demand for recreation activities is fully satisfied, the shape of the TB curve becomes flatter as more and more dollars are spent on public recreation. The total social costs (TC) curve shows that the first dollars the government spends on recreation programs produce a large output of recreation opportunities. However, as more dollars are spent, less additional output is produced by each additional dollar, i.e., increasing marginal costs. The reason is that the efficiency of additional government expenditure falls as less suitable sites are developed and the opportunity costs of alternative uses rise. As a result, the shape of the TC curve rises as more and more dollars are spent on public recreation.

As you will recall, economics suggest that recreation economic decision makers continue increasing the size of the program until the excess of its benefits over its costs is as large as possible. In Panel 1a of Figure 19-1 (page 373), we see that from an economic viewpoint, the government budget for recreation programs should be at output A. At an output of A, the government budget would be AC and total benefits, AB. The B:C ratio is AB divided by AC and the excess of benefits over costs (net benefits), which is the greatest vertical distance that exists between these two curves. If government recreation output were less than A, there would be some potential net benefits which were not being realized. If the output were larger than A, all dollars spent in excess of AC would entail social costs in excess of the benefits that they produced. The same result is shown in Panel 1b of Figure 19-1 for the marginal curves—marginal social benefit (MB) and marginal social cost (MC)—associated with the total curves of the upper panel. There, the familiar economic proposition is applied to the public sector; net benefits (area B) are maximized where marginal social benefits (MB) equal marginal social costs (MC).

Debate over public recreation budgets may be characterized as addressing the question of whether the agencies involved produce outputs that are less than optimum or greater than optimum. Managers of public recreation programs, in effect, argue that existing budgets are insufficient and should be increased to point A, but opponents argue that the proposed budgets are excessive and should be decreased to point A. No one knows for sure which view is correct. However, the issue could be better resolved with more accurate benefit-cost studies of the question.

For example, the 1980s government output was estimated at three billion recreation visitor days at a cost of $8 billion. On this basis, government expenditures were equal to about $2.50 per recreation visitor day. Given the mean recreation benefit per day figures presented in Table 11-4 (page 187) (the average value was $34 per day) benefits substantially exceed government costs. That is, if marginal benefits exceed costs by $31.50, it must be that we are to the left of point A in Figure 19-1, Panel 1b (page 373). If benefits per day equaled cost per day, society would be at point A in Panel 1b. Panel 1b of Figure 19-1 indicates that when benefits exceed costs by these amounts, output is less than optimum.

Panel 2a of Figure 19-1 (page 373) applies this same logic to evaluating the optimum size of a proposed campground. Assume that outputs A, D, G and K represent the only possible sizes. From the diagram, we can clearly see that size K can be ruled out because its costs exceed benefits. Similarly, size G can be excluded because benefits just equal costs; the program would have no net gain and society would be just as well-off without the program as with it.

To obtain maximum social benefits, the public decision maker should make a reasonably complete search of alternative ways to accomplish the objective, then choose the one that maximizes the excess of social benefits over social costs (net benefits). Thus, if decision makers face two alternatives, A and D, with benefits and costs as shown in Panel 2a of Figure 19-1 (page 373), they should choose alternative A, which yields the greater excess of benefits over costs. Note that both sizes A and D are worthwhile because benefits exceed costs in each case. But Panel 2b resolves the choice. At output D, the last dollar of cost generates more than a dollar of benefits, indicating that campground size should be increased until the marginal benefits equal marginal costs at size A. As you can see on Panel 2a, this is the optimum project size where net benefits (total benefits minus total costs) are the greatest.

Finally, it is important to note that although project A is the optimum size campground, project D has a greater B:C ratio (= DE ÷ DF) as shown in Panel 2a of Figure 19-1 (page 373). As you can clearly see, this exceeds project A's ratio (= AB ÷ AC). In fact, all campgrounds to the left of A would have a more favorable B:C ratio than project A because their costs are so small relative to benefits. However, the lesson, then, is that choosing the project size with the highest B:C ratio may lead to the wrong choice. For finding the optimum project size, the appropriate rule is to maximize net benefits (= TB – TC) where marginal benefits equal marginal costs (MB = MC) and not to maximize the B:C ratio. Well-being is improved from maximizing the *amount* of net benefits which can be consumed, not the rate of benefits. In a later section of this chapter, we will see that once the optimum size project has been determined for each alternative purpose or site, then B:C ratios may sometimes be useful in choosing among projects (all of which are of optimum size).

## *Efficient Project Design*

The problem of developing a particular project involves questions of design as well as size. In economics, **design** of a project means combining the available inputs of land, labor, and capital in the most efficient way, so that they yield a mix of recreation site characteristics that provide the most benefits for the costs. The question that comparisons of benefits and costs can assist in answering is: Which of the possible designs for any given project size is the optimum (i.e., yields the greatest net benefits)?

For example, if 1,000 acres are available for a park, how much of this area should be devoted to picnic sites, campsites, parking, and hiking trails? Alternatively, if 100 miles of trails can be constructed, what mix of hiking, horseback riding, mountain biking and nature trails should be provided to maximize net benefits? The different types of trails have different construction costs, just as the different activities have different benefits per day.

Consider another example of the proper design of forest campgrounds that involves the management of environmental resources, such as forests, water, fish and wildlife, and scenery. Recent studies suggest that environmental quality may contribute more to the total benefits of camping than do access roads and provision of facilities, such as tables, drinking water, toilets, and trash barrels. For example, users of developed campgrounds in the Rocky Mountains were willing to pay $5 per recreation visitor day for standard campground services compared with $6 per day for an optimum number of trees, which provide shade, seclusion, and scenic quality of the site. Project design involves using all of the available resources to the best advantage.

This leads to a time-honored rule in benefit-cost analysis: Evaluate separable project features separately to insure each passes the benefit-cost test. For example, a high standard campground with flush toilets, hot water, showers, paved parking and a nature trail may have costs in excess of benefits. This provides a feedback mechanism to the designer to scrutinize each feature. What is the added cost of the showers, relative to the increase in camper benefits from the showers? Techniques such as contingent valuation (Chapter 10) have been applied by the U.S. Army Corps of Engineers to answer facility design questions such as this. By applying benefit-cost analysis to each component, the designer can identify which components are pulling down the B:C ratio and possibly design a feasible project.

From this discussion, it should be clear that benefit-cost studies are important in both the design of projects and the choice of project size. In fact, the two decisions are interdependent. The most efficient design for each project size has to be determined before either the total benefit or the total cost curve can be estimated. The optimum size and design combination can be determined only after rather comprehensive benefit-cost calculations. Thus, there are often a series or family of total benefit and total cost curves, one for each design or service level. Choosing among them is the next topic of discussion.

## *Choosing Among Alternative Projects*

The final point is that benefit-cost analysis can help decision makers choose among worthwhile competing or mutually exclusive alternative projects with different purposes or at different sites, when all of them cannot be undertaken at once. For example, assume that a Regional Director of the National Park Service has $1 million to allocate to campground improvement projects in California this year, and is presented with the 16 alternatives shown in Table 19-1. All of these projects are of optimum size and, it will be noted, have B:C ratios greater than 1.0. The costs of the projects vary from $250,000 to $1 million. Which of the 16 projects should be undertaken this year? The decision rule is to choose the combination of projects that provides the most net benefits (total benefits minus total costs). As will be shown, this cannot be achieved by simply ranking all projects by either their net present values (net benefits) or their B:C ratios.

The decision maker should carefully search through the list of alternatives to select the few that together maximize net benefits of the $1 million budget. This is obviously superior to applying the rule of first-proposed, first-built and choosing the first four proposed projects, A, B, C and D, exhausting the budget to obtain $1.05 million net benefits. Or, the decision maker could do even better by ranking the projects according to the amount of net present value (net benefits), where project P is the highest. With costs of $1 million, project P exhausts the total budget, and provides net benefits of $1.3 million. Could the decision maker do even better? Or is $1.3 million the maximum net benefits that can be achieved? Sassone and Schaffer (1978) recommend that to maximize the total (or sum of) net benefits over several independent projects subject to a capital

**Table 19-1. Benefits and Costs of Alternative Campground Improvement Projects, National Park Service, California**

| Project | Present Value of Benefits ($1,000) | Present Value of Costs ($1,000) | Net Present Value of Net Benefits ($1,000) | Benefit-Cost Ratio |
|---|---|---|---|---|
| A | $400 | $250 | $150 | 1.60 |
| B | 800 | 250 | 550 | 3.20 |
| C | 500 | 250 | 250 | 2.00 |
| D | 350 | 250 | 100 | 1.40 |
| E | 360 | 250 | 110 | 1.44 |
| F | 1,100 | 500 | 600 | 2.20 |
| G | 800 | 500 | 300 | 1.60 |
| H | 600 | 500 | 100 | 1.20 |
| I | 1,000 | 500 | 500 | 2.00 |
| J | 1,250 | 500 | 750 | 2.50 |
| K | 800 | 750 | 50 | 1.07 |
| L | 1,000 | 750 | 250 | 1.33 |
| M | 1,500 | 750 | 750 | 2.00 |
| N | 900 | 750 | 150 | 1.20 |
| O | 1,100 | 750 | 350 | 1.47 |
| P | 2,300 | 1,000 | 1,300 | 2.30 |

budget constraint, the rule is to adopt projects based on their B:C ratios, implementing successively lower projects until the capital budget is exhausted or until the B:C ratio reaches unity. In this case, ranking by B:C ratios is equivalent to maximizing the sum of net benefits over all feasible sets of projects.

By a search and elimination process using B:C ratios as a guide, a few projects with more than $1.3 million net benefits can be found. This yields a combination of projects B, J, and C, which, taken together, exhaust the budget and provide net benefits of $1.55 million. Projects B and J are selected because they have the highest and second highest B:C ratios of 3.20 and 2.50, respectively. Note that their costs are $500,000 and $250,000, respectively, totaling $750,000. Project C is also selected because it has the highest B:C ratio (2.00) of the few projects that could be built with the remaining budget of $250,000. By choosing these three projects, net benefits are maximized. Spending $1 million generates $1.55 million of total net benefits rather than just $1.05 or $1.30 million. This is illustrated here:

| | Choices | Net benefits |
|---|---|---|
| First-proposed, first-built | A, B, C, D | $1.05 million |
| Net present value (net benefits) | P | $1.30 million |
| B:C ratios to maximize net benefits | B, J, C | $1.55 million |

It should be noted that there is some controversy among economists concerning the proper procedure to use in recommending alternative projects for funding. If you are interested in exploring the issue, consult a more detailed treatment of the subject such as contained in Sassone and Schaffer (1978).

In this illustration, we assumed that the 16 proposed projects were independent of one another. A project is independent of other projects when net benefits and costs would not change if any of the other projects were implemented. In comparing campground improvements in a single state such as California, possible interdependence may exist between project benefits. In this event, the net benefits of several projects located in the same market may not equal the sum of net benefits for the individual projects. When projects are interdependent, the proper way to proceed is to assume that all possible combinations of projects are built, then to evaluate the net benefits of each such combination. For example, Sassone and Schaffer (1978) demonstrated the interdependence of three public beaches proposed to be located within 40 miles of each other. Site A would have net benefits of $120 million when considered alone. But its net benefits would fall to $40 million if sites A and B were constructed, and to $75 million if site C were built in combination with site A.

# Discounting and Net Present Value

Discounting is essential to the comparison of benefits received and costs paid in different time periods. Its function is to convert future benefits and costs of a project into present value (today's dollars) at the time of decision. Quite simply, it telescopes to the present all the benefits and costs during the life of the project.

It makes sense to measure future benefits and costs in terms of today's dollar values, because decision makers choose between short-run recreation projects which have no future benefits and costs, and long-run projects which do. To compare the various streams of benefits and costs over time, the usual procedure is to weight the benefits received and costs incurred in the present more highly than benefits received and costs incurred in the distant future. This differential weighing of future and current benefits and costs converts them into equivalent dollars called *present values.* The sum of the discounted benefits less the sum of the discounted costs over the life of the project measures the economic value of recreation investments.

Public recreation investments produce benefits and costs for various numbers of years into the future. Figure 19-2 illustrates the typical recreation project that involves a large initial capital investment (for purchase of land or construction), low annual costs of operation and maintenance, and annual benefits that increase over the life of the project. A good example is a major downhill ski area where an expansion in facilities was planned (initial capital investment costs were incurred) in 1996, but the first skiing on the new slopes would not occur until 1999. In an example such as this, the time profile of costs in Figure 19-2 shows very high costs in the construction stages (years one, two and three) but quite modest

**Figure 19-2. Time Paths of Benefits and Costs**

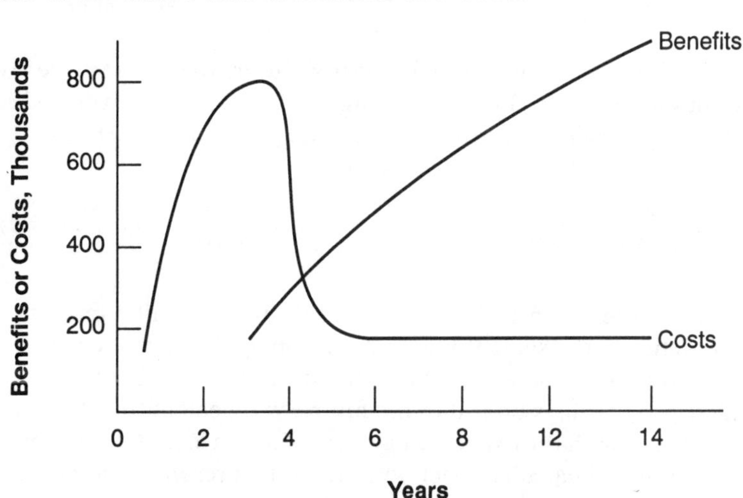

annual costs of operation, maintenance, and repair once the facility is developed. In this case, the benefits may not start until year three, but then they grow significantly until the investment matures in about 15 years.

Most of the total costs of a project occur early in the planning period and most of the total benefits in later years. As a result, the rate at which we weight or discount future benefits and costs relative to the present is critical in determining whether the future benefits offset the large up-front costs. The discount rate is like an interest rate. The higher the interest or discount rate, the less weight one places on future benefits and costs relative to the present.

Most people find compound interest and future value easier to understand than discounting and present value. Compound interest is a familiar concept. For example, if you invest money in a bank or savings institution, you can either take the interest earned on the investment each year or leave it in the account to earn more interest. If you leave the interest in the account to be added to the principal, you can calculate what the investment will be worth each year by using a compound interest formula.

In some sense, the interest rate makes current and future dollar values equivalent. For example, if the interest or discount rate is 7.125%, then $1 received 10 years from now is perceived as "worth" just $0.50 today. While this may seem arbitrary and by some as way too low (but by others as way too high), the explanation is simple. At an interest rate of 7.125%, $0.50 invested in the bank today will yield $1 ten years from now. Thus, the interest or discount rate literally makes future and present values equivalent.

When compounding, to find the future value (FV) in some future year ($t$) of a present sum (PV), multiply the present sum by one plus the interest rate ($r$):

$$FV_t = PV(1 + r)^t \qquad \text{(Equation 19-1)}$$

The formula can be easily revised to go from future to present value. When discounting, to obtain the present value of some amount expected in future year ($t$), divide the future value by one plus the interest rate:

$$PV = \frac{FV_t}{(1 + r)^t} \qquad \text{(Equation 19-2)}$$

Thus, the interest rate and the discount rate are different names for what is arithmetically the same thing. It is customary, however, to use the two terms in different contexts. When we start with a sum of money and calculate the earnings on it into the future, we speak of the interest rate. When we start with the expected payment of a sum of money at some time in the future and calculate back in time to the present to determine the present value, we speak of the discount rate.

Remember that compound interest is the amount paid on the principal and the interest earned in previous time periods. This means that $100 invested now will accumulate, at 10% interest, to $110 in a year:

$$\$110 = \$100 \times (1 + 0.10) \qquad \text{(Equation 19-3)}$$

After another year of compounding at 10% interest, the investment will become $121, and so on:

$$\$121 = \$100 \times (1 + 0.10)(1 + 0.10) \qquad \text{(Equation 19-4)}$$

Note that if we keep the $100 invested at 10% interest for two years, it is turned into $121 by going through the same calculation two times. We could conclude that individuals who invest at 10% interest consider having $100 now, $110 in one year, or $121 in two years as equivalent amounts. Because discounting corresponds to compounding, we can say that $110 in one year or $121 in two years has a present value of $100 at a discount rate of 10%. The $110 received in one year divided by 1.10 has a present value of $100:

$$\$100 = \frac{\$110}{(1 + 0.10)} \qquad \text{(Equation 19-5)}$$

Similarly, $121 two years from now divided by 1.21 has a present value of $100:

$$\$100 = \frac{\$121}{(1 + 0.10)\,(1 + 0.10)} \qquad \text{(Equation 19-6)}$$

You can check the complete correspondence of compounding and discounting by comparing Tables 19-2 and 19-3 (pages 382 and 383). Table 19-2 shows the compound factor for $1 invested for two years is 1.21, at a 10% interest rate. Table 19-3 shows that at a discount rate of 10%, the present value of $1 received two years from now is 0.826:

$$0.826 = \frac{1}{1.21} \qquad \text{(Equation 19-7)}$$

The factor for present value (0.826) is equal to one divided by the factor for compound value (1.21). Based on this mathematical rule, discount factor tables have been worked out for various discount rates and number of years, as shown in Table 19-3 (page 383). For the case considered here, look down the years column to the row for year two, discounting at 10%. The figure shown there (0.826) is the discount factor which,

**Table 19-2. Future Value of $1 With Compound Interest**

| Year | Future Value of $1 With Compound Interest of: 4% | 7% | 10% |
|---|---|---|---|
| 1 | 1.040 | 1.070 | 1.100 |
| 2 | 1.082 | 1.145 | 1.210 |
| 3 | 1.125 | 1.225 | 1.331 |
| 4 | 1.170 | 1.311 | 1.464 |
| 5 | 1.217 | 1.403 | 1.611 |
| 6 | 1.265 | 1.501 | 1.772 |
| 7 | 1.316 | 1.606 | 1.949 |
| 8 | 1.369 | 1.718 | 2.144 |
| 9 | 1.423 | 1.838 | 2.358 |
| 10 | 1.480 | 1.967 | 2.594 |
| 11 | 1.539 | 2.105 | 2.853 |
| 12 | 1.601 | 2.252 | 3.138 |
| 13 | 1.665 | 2.410 | 3.452 |
| 14 | 1.732 | 2.579 | 3.797 |
| 15 | 1.801 | 2.759 | 4.177 |
| 16 | 1.873 | 2.952 | 4.595 |
| 17 | 1.948 | 3.159 | 5.054 |
| 18 | 2.026 | 3.380 | 5.560 |
| 19 | 2.107 | 3.617 | 6.116 |
| 20 | 2.191 | 3.870 | 6.727 |
| 21 | 2.279 | 4.141 | 7.400 |
| 22 | 2.370 | 4.430 | 8.140 |
| 23 | 2.465 | 4.741 | 8.954 |
| 24 | 2.563 | 5.072 | 9.850 |
| 25 | 2.666 | 5.427 | 10.835 |
| 26 | 2.772 | 5.807 | 11.918 |
| 27 | 2.883 | 6.214 | 13.110 |
| 28 | 2.999 | 6.649 | 14.421 |
| 29 | 3.119 | 7.114 | 15.863 |
| 30 | 3.243 | 7.612 | 17.449 |
| 31 | 3.373 | 8.145 | 19.194 |
| 32 | 3.508 | 8.715 | 21.114 |
| 33 | 3.648 | 9.325 | 23.225 |
| 34 | 3.794 | 9.978 | 25.548 |
| 35 | 3.946 | 10.677 | 28.102 |
| 36 | 4.104 | 11.424 | 30.913 |
| 37 | 4.268 | 12.224 | 34.004 |
| 38 | 4.439 | 13.079 | 37.404 |
| 39 | 4.616 | 13.995 | 41.145 |
| 40 | 4.801 | 14.974 | 45.259 |
| 41 | 4.993 | 16.023 | 49.785 |
| 42 | 5.193 | 17.144 | 54.764 |
| 43 | 5.400 | 18.344 | 60.240 |
| 44 | 5.617 | 19.628 | 66.264 |
| 45 | 5.841 | 21.002 | 72.890 |
| 46 | 6.075 | 22.473 | 80.180 |
| 47 | 6.318 | 24.046 | 88.197 |
| 48 | 6.571 | 25.729 | 97.017 |
| 49 | 6.833 | 27.530 | 106.719 |
| 50 | 7.107 | 29.457 | 117.391 |

**Table 19-3. Present Value of $1 Received or Paid in Future Years**

| Year | Present Value of $1 With Discount Rate 4% | 7% | 10% |
|---|---|---|---|
| 1 | 0.962 | 0.935 | 0.909 |
| 2 | 0.925 | 0.873 | 0.826 |
| 3 | 0.889 | 0.816 | 0.751 |
| 4 | 0.855 | 0.763 | 0.683 |
| 5 | 0.822 | 0.713 | 0.621 |
| 6 | 0.790 | 0.666 | 0.564 |
| 7 | 0.760 | 0.623 | 0.513 |
| 8 | 0.731 | 0.582 | 0.467 |
| 9 | 0.703 | 0.544 | 0.424 |
| 10 | 0.676 | 0.508 | 0.386 |
| 11 | 0.650 | 0.475 | 0.350 |
| 12 | 0.625 | 0.444 | 0.319 |
| 13 | 0.601 | 0.415 | 0.290 |
| 14 | 0.577 | 0.388 | 0.263 |
| 15 | 0.555 | 0.362 | 0.239 |
| 16 | 0.534 | 0.339 | 0.218 |
| 17 | 0.513 | 0.317 | 0.198 |
| 18 | 0.494 | 0.296 | 0.180 |
| 19 | 0.475 | 0.277 | 0.164 |
| 20 | 0.456 | 0.258 | 0.149 |
| 21 | 0.439 | 0.242 | 0.135 |
| 22 | 0.422 | 0.226 | 0.123 |
| 23 | 0.406 | 0.211 | 0.112 |
| 24 | 0.390 | 0.197 | 0.102 |
| 25 | 0.375 | 0.184 | 0.092 |
| 26 | 0.361 | 0.172 | 0.084 |
| 27 | 0.347 | 0.161 | 0.076 |
| 28 | 0.333 | 0.150 | 0.069 |
| 29 | 0.321 | 0.141 | 0.063 |
| 30 | 0.308 | 0.131 | 0.057 |
| 31 | 0.296 | 0.123 | 0.052 |
| 32 | 0.285 | 0.115 | 0.047 |
| 33 | 0.274 | 0.107 | 0.043 |
| 34 | 0.264 | 0.100 | 0.039 |
| 35 | 0.253 | 0.094 | 0.036 |
| 36 | 0.244 | 0.088 | 0.032 |
| 37 | 0.234 | 0.082 | 0.029 |
| 38 | 0.225 | 0.076 | 0.027 |
| 39 | 0.217 | 0.071 | 0.024 |
| 40 | 0.208 | 0.067 | 0.022 |
| 41 | 0.200 | 0.062 | 0.020 |
| 42 | 0.193 | 0.058 | 0.018 |
| 43 | 0.185 | 0.055 | 0.017 |
| 44 | 0.178 | 0.051 | 0.015 |
| 45 | 0.171 | 0.048 | 0.014 |
| 46 | 0.165 | 0.044 | 0.012 |
| 47 | 0.158 | 0.042 | 0.011 |
| 48 | 0.152 | 0.039 | 0.010 |
| 49 | 0.146 | 0.036 | 0.009 |
| 50 | 0.141 | 0.034 | 0.009 |

when multiplied by the expected $100 benefit in two years, yields its present value (rounded to the nearest dollar):

$$\$83 = \$100 \times 0.826 \quad \text{(Equation 19-8)}$$

Note that while these discount factors are shown for three different rates, nearly all microcomputer spreadsheet programs (e.g., Lotus 1•2•3, Excel) have discounting routines built into them that will expedite computation of the present value of any stream of benefits and costs over time. It is a handy feature of spreadsheets to learn for performing benefit-cost analysis.

The essential idea is that waiting involves an opportunity cost. Nearly everyone, under almost any circumstance, would prefer $100 now to $100 a year from now. A sum of money in hand is worth more than a promise of the same sum at a specified time in the future, because the money may be invested and produce earnings in the intervening time. This is true whether the money is to be invested by an individual, business, or government which must raise the necessary funds through taxation or borrowing. Take the case of an individual who is to be paid a sum of money a year from now. There is a lesser sum that he or she can invest today, for instance by depositing it in a savings bank, that will accumulate to that amount by the time the year has passed. This lesser sum is the present value of receiving the payment one year hence.

Notice that we have not said anything about risk. We assume no risk is involved here and that the individual $100 of benefits is as certain as anything can be. Rather, we are saying that having to wait for payment means foregoing the income that could be earned on the money in the meantime. In other words, waiting carries a cost in the form of a lost opportunity. This is not to suggest that risk should be ignored in studying a project, but merely when evaluating government projects that this is not how it should be incorporated into the analysis. In the real world, uncertainty and waiting are often entangled; it is important that we understand they are separate phenomena. The effects of risk and uncertainty were considered in Chapter 12.

Figure 19-3 shows the effect of different discount rates on calculation of present values. For example, the present value of $100 in benefits expected 25 years in the future is about $38 discounted at 4%, $23 discounted at 6%, but only about $9 discounted at 10%. Thus, present values of benefits 25 years in the future can be changed by more than a factor of four, depending on the discount rate. The discount rates used in the evaluation of recreation projects will be discussed in Chapter 20.

## Benefit-Cost Ratio

Benefit-cost studies usually result in the calculation of a B:C ratio, in which the benefits of a project are divided by its costs:

**Figure 19-3. Present Value of $1 Received or Paid in Future Years Discounted at 4%, 6%, 8% and 10%**

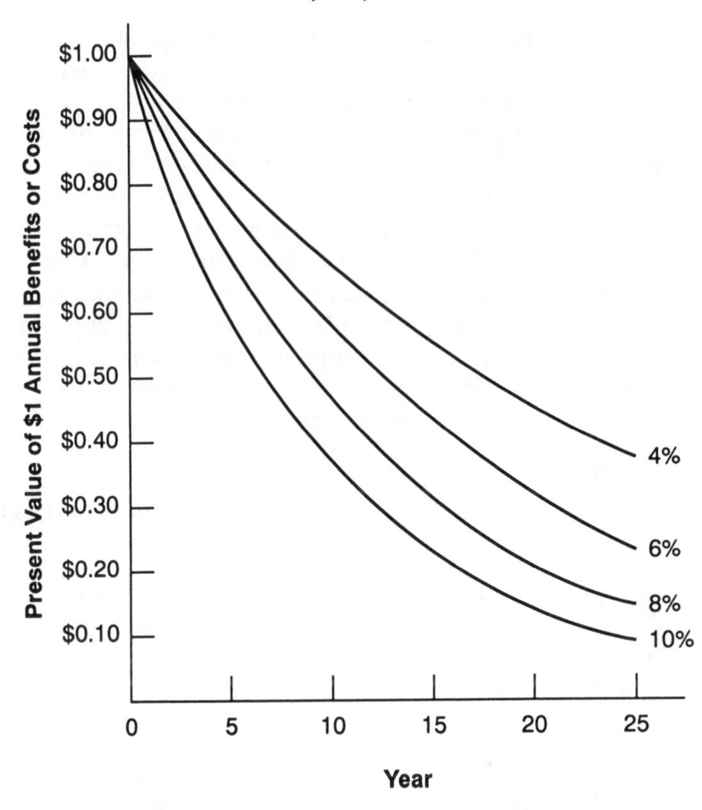


$$\text{B:C ratio} = \frac{\text{Present value of total benefits}}{\text{Present value of total costs}} \qquad \text{(Equation 19-9)}$$

If the ratio is greater than 1.0, public expenditures for the project are judged to be economically worthwhile. If it is equal to 1.0, the public expenditure adds nothing, on balance, to the nation's economic well-being. If it is below 1.0, it detracts from the economic well-being of the nation. The reason is that the ratio measures the comparative benefits of alternative projects using the same resources. If the ratio for a particular project is more than 1.0, it adds more benefits than society gives up when it pays the costs.

The numerator of this ratio is defined as the present value, expressed in dollars, of all of the expected economic benefits of the proposed project. The monetary values that are attached to these benefits are those which society has placed on them, as observed in market prices or inferred from willingness to pay studies. In symbolic terms, the numerator of the B:C ratio, the present value of total benefits, is:

$$\text{Total benefits} = \sum \frac{B_t}{(1+r)^t} \qquad \text{(Equation 19-10)}$$

in which $\sum$ means "summation over all the years," $B_t$ stands for the benefits expected in year $t$, and $1 + r$ is the discounting factor by which values expected in the future are turned into today's values.

The denominator of the B:C ratio is defined as the present value of all of the expected economic costs of undertaking and operating the project. If the project involves capital investment (a new park, campground, access highway, or a trail, for example), costs are of two types: (1) initial construction costs, and (2) operation, maintenance and repair costs. Capital construction costs usually occur before the project begins producing output of recreation opportunity. The remaining costs—operating, maintenance, and repair—are future ongoing expenses, which occur after the project is operating. In symbolic terms, the denominator of the B:C ratio, the present value of total capital and future operation costs, is:

$$\text{Total costs} = K + \sum \frac{C_t}{(1+r)^t} \qquad \text{(Equation 19-11)}$$

in which $K$ is the capital or construction costs (assumed to occur in the current year) and $C_t$ is the operation, maintenance, and repair costs expected in the year $t$.

The full B:C ratio, expressed in symbolic terms, is:

$$\text{B:C ratio} = \frac{\sum \frac{B_t}{(1+r)^t}}{K + \sum \frac{C_t}{(1+r)^t}} \qquad \text{(Equation 19-12)}$$

or, the ratio of the present value of the benefits over the present value of capital investment and future operation costs. It should be noted that these present value formulas are very close to the ones in the previous section on discounting. The main difference is that the formulas for the B:C ratio have a summation sign ($\sum$) in them. This must be included because the formula in the previous section gives the present value (PV) for some benefit or cost expected in future year $t$ ($FV_t$). Most government recreation projects have benefits that occur in each of a number of future years. The formula for the B:C ratio states that the present value of these future benefits must be added together to get the total present value of the entire stream of benefits during the expected life of the project.

Assume, for example, that a park superintendent has asked you to evaluate the benefits and costs of a proposed investment in automatic entrance fee equipment to improve the productivity of labor in park operations. The initial capital investment would be $20,000. The acquisition would commit the government to annual operation, maintenance, and repair costs of $1,000 per year during the expected life of the equipment. The project would result in annual benefits of $10,000, representing the labor savings at entrance stations to the park. Assume that the equipment has a useful life of three years and no salvage value. The discount rate is 10%.

Calculate the present value of total benefits, as illustrated in the previous section:

$$\text{Total benefits} = \frac{10{,}000}{1 + 0.10} + \frac{10{,}000}{(1 + 0.10)^2} + \frac{10{,}000}{(1 + 0.10)^3} \quad \text{(Equation 19-13)}$$

$$= 9{,}091 + 8{,}264 + 7{,}513 = 24{,}868 \quad \text{(Equation 19-14)}$$

The annual benefits of $10,000 in labor savings at entrance stations to the parks have a present value of $24,868 (rounded to the nearest dollar).

Next, calculate the present value of total costs of the project:

$$\text{Total} = 20{,}000 + \frac{1{,}000}{1 + 0.10} + \frac{1{,}000}{(1 + 0.10)^2} + \frac{1{,}000}{(1 + 0.10)^3} \quad \text{(Equation 19-15)}$$

$$= 20{,}000 + 909 + 826 + 751 = 22{,}486 \quad \text{(Equation 19-16)}$$

The $20,000 capital investment costs of the automatic equipment occurs before the project begins producing output and are not discounted. The remaining costs of $1,000 per year (for operating, maintenance, and repair) are discounted in the same way as annual benefits. The total costs of capital investment and future operation have a present value of $22,486.

The ratio of the present value of total benefits over the present value of total costs of the capital investment and future operation is:

$$\text{B:C ratio} = \frac{\$24{,}868}{\$20{,}000 + \$2{,}486} = 1.1 \quad \text{(Equation 19-17)}$$

The B:C ratio of 1.1 indicates that the public expenditures for the parks project are judged to be economically worthwhile. Each $1 of social costs generates $1.10 of social benefits, or $0.10 more. The public recreation expenditure contributes 10% more to the nation's economic well-being than the resources given up.

Most recreation projects and programs have long-run consequences with annual benefits and costs extending for 10 to 50 years (or more) into the future. Calculating the present value of long-run benefits and costs by hand, as in the previous example, would be cumbersome. Two shortcuts have been developed. Discount factor tables have been worked out for various discount rates and numbers of years, as for example, in

Table 19-3 (page 383). For the case considered here, look down the years column to the row for year three, discounting at 10%. The figure shown there, 0.751, is the discount factor which, when multiplied by the expected benefits and costs in three years, yields their present value. This is the same result we obtained in working out the present value by hand. For a large number of years it is easier to use a microcomputer spreadsheet program to perform the discounting routines.

In recent years, recreation planners and managers have compared benefits and costs of both construction and nonconstruction programs. For example, consider a proposed 10-year program to provide park visitors with interpretive services. Although the information program has no initial capital investment, it will commit the government to annual expenditures for personnel training, supervision, and operation of the program (Column 2 of Table 19-4). Costs rise during the first few years as effective procedures are being learned, then decline as the program becomes a routine part of park operations. Annual benefits of the interpretive program to park visitors are shown in Column 3 of Table 19-4. Benefits are low during the first few years of most new programs, then rise as they become a popular activity of visitors to the park. The discount factor for 10% from Table 19-3 (page 383) is reproduced as Column 4. Note that the present value of costs (Column 5) for each of the 10 years is calculated by multiplying expected annual costs (Column 2) by the discount factor (Column 4). In the same way, the present value of benefits (Column 6) for each of the 10 years is calculated by multiplying expected annual benefits (Column 3) by the discount factor (Column 4). All benefits and costs are in thousands of dollars.

The present value of total benefits ($117,600) and the present value of total costs ($95,500) are obtained by summing the present value of

**Table 19-4. Present Value of Long-Run Benefits and Costs for a Recreation Program With No Capital Investment**

| (1) Year Since Initiation | (2) Expected Annual Costs* | (3) Expected Annual Benefits* | (4) Discount Factor for 10% | (5) Present Value of Costs* (Col. 2 x Col. 4) | (6) Present Value of Benefits* (Col. 3 x Col. 4) | (7) Net Present Value (Col. 6 – Col. 5) |
|---|---|---|---|---|---|---|
| 1 | $10 | $ 0 | 0.909 | $9.1 | $ 0.0 | –$9.1 |
| 2 | 20 | 0 | 0.826 | 16.5 | 0.0 | –16.5 |
| 3 | 30 | 5 | 0.751 | 22.5 | 3.8 | –18.7 |
| 4 | 30 | 10 | 0.683 | 20.5 | 6.8 | –13.7 |
| 5 | 20 | 30 | 0.621 | 12.4 | 18.6 | 6.2 |
| 6 | 10 | 40 | 0.564 | 5.6 | 22.6 | 17.0 |
| 7 | 5 | 40 | 0.513 | 2.6 | 20.5 | 17.9 |
| 8 | 5 | 40 | 0.467 | 2.3 | 18.7 | 16.4 |
| 9 | 5 | 40 | 0.424 | 2.1 | 16.9 | 14.8 |
| 10 | 5 | 25 | 0.386 | 1.9 | 9.7 | 7.8 |
| Total | 140 | 230 | | 95.5 | 117.6 | 22.1 |

*All benefits and costs in thousand dollars.

benefits and costs for each of the 10 years (Columns 5 and 6). The ratio of the total benefits over total costs is:

$$\text{B:C ratio} = \frac{\$117{,}600}{\$95{,}500} = 1.23 \qquad \text{(Equation 19-18)}$$

The B:C ratio of 1.23 shows that the public expenditures for the interpretation program are judged to be economically worthwhile. Each $1.00 of social costs generates $1.23 of social benefits, or $0.23 more. The public recreation expenditure contributes 23% more to the nation's economic well-being than the resources withdrawn from the economy.

# *Chapter 20*

# Issues in Benefit-Cost Analysis

This chapter illustrates one of the most important issues of benefit-cost analysis, namely what discount rate to use in estimating present value of future benefits and costs; describes the alternative bases for deciding the appropriate discount rate; discusses other issues including multiple objectives in natural resource planning, choice of alternatives, determining the length of the planning period, time phasing of investments, income distribution effects, nonmonetary effects, and sensitivity of the results to possible changes in key variables.

Economists distinguish increases in real values of recreation from decreasing discounted values. This is important because it often strikes recreation managers as strange that future values of recreation are discounted to the point where they are worth less than current values. Isn't recreation becoming scarcer and more valuable over time? It may very well be that increasing demand for recreation, driven by population increases when combined with shrinking natural areas for recreation, will increase the real or relative value of recreation in the future. For example, a current day of wilderness hiking may be worth $25. Increases in demand and reductions in supply will likely increase this value over the next two decades to something much higher, say $35, adjusted for inflation. Thus, the value of wilderness recreation in the numerator of the benefit-cost (B:C) ratio should be increased to this higher, real or relative value. However, the higher value is not realized until the future, so it still must be discounted. If the real value of recreation is rising faster than the discount rate (e.g., recreation value increasing at 5% per year and the discount rate is 4%), then the real discounted value of recreation still could be increasing in the future. Agencies such as the U.S. Forest Service provide forecasts of future real increases in the value of recreation to account for this affect in their benefit-cost analysis.

## Importance of the Discount Rate

Selecting the rate of discount to use in valuation of the future consequences of projects is one of the most important issues in comparing benefits and costs. Several points should be made about its effects. First, the higher the discount rate, the lower the present value of benefits. This is illustrated in Figure 20-1 for the effect of changes in the discount rate on the present value of $1 worth of benefits received each year for 25 years. If benefits were not discounted to account for the passage of time, total benefits in the numerator of the B:C ratio would be $25 (= 25 years x $1). Using discount rates of 4% to 10%, the present value of $1 annual benefits for 25 years would range from $9.08 to $15.62.

The second point is that annual benefits received late in the planning period have very little present value. Figure 20-2 illustrates the effect of increasing the length of the planning period from 25 to 50 years on the present value of the benefits. Recall that without discounting, total benefits would be $25 for the first 25 years and an additional $25 for the second 25 years, or $50 over the total of 50 years. However, with discounting, benefits accruing only 25 to 50 years hence are reduced substantially. For example, using a discount rate of 6%, the present value of $1 of annual benefits each year for the second 25 years is only $2.98 in present value terms today. Note that the present value of benefits for the second 25 years averages about one-fourth as much as the first 25 years.

The third point is that when projects have consequences extending beyond 50 years, the discounted benefits of future generations are reduced to trivial amounts. For example, using a discount rate of 6%, the present value of $1 annual benefits for the second 50 years is about $0.86. Note that the present value of benefits for the second 50 years averages about one-twentieth as much as for the first 50 years:

| Discount rate | 4% | 6% | 8% | 10% |
|---|---|---|---|---|
| First generation, 1–50 years | $21.48 | $15.76 | $12.23 | $9.91 |
| Second generation, 51–100 years | $3.02 | $0.86 | $0.26 | $0.08 |
| Total, 100 years | $24.50 | $16.62 | $12.49 | $9.99 |

Thus far, no completely satisfactory remedy has been found for the intergenerational problem associated with very long-run projects and programs. A tentative solution has been suggested by Mishan (1976), a British economist who has written several books on comparing benefits and costs. He assumed generations of successive 50-year life spans (e.g., 1–50 and 51–100). In the real world, generations obviously overlap in time; to assume that generations are completely separate simplifies the arithmetic without changing the nature of the problem. In practice, the assumption would mean that the useful life of very long-run projects would be divided

**Figure 20-1. Effect of the Discount Rate on the Present Value of $1 Annual Benefits for 25 Years**

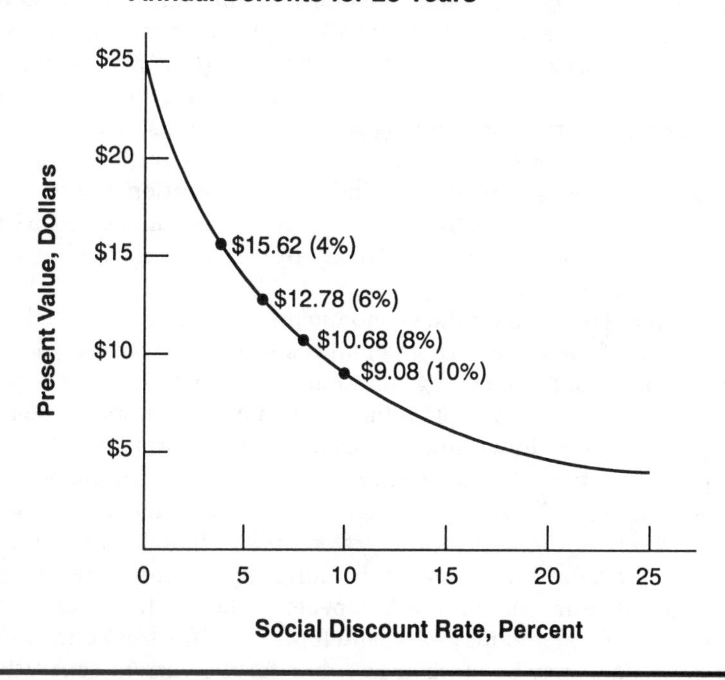


**Figure 20-2. Effect of Length of the Planning Period on the Present Value of $1 Annual Benefits**

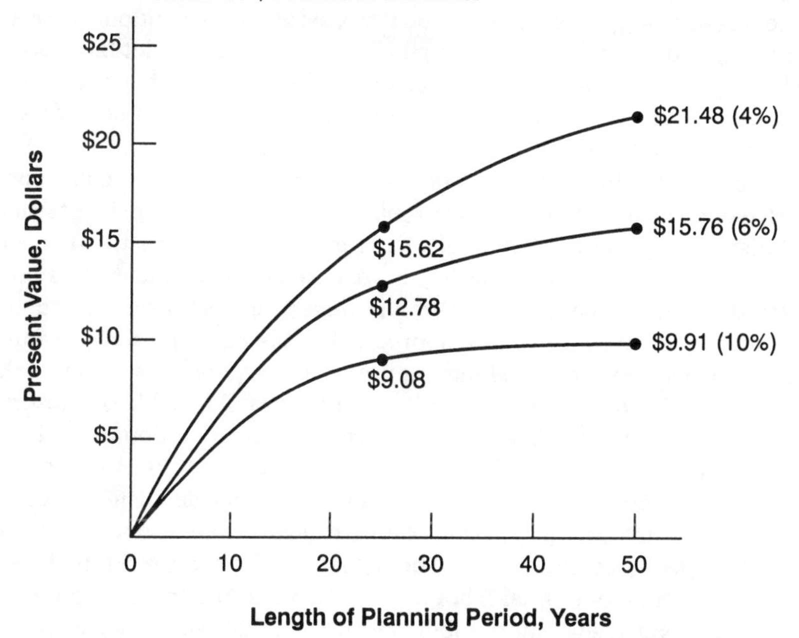

into 50-year segments, one for each generation affected. The annual benefits for years 1–50 would be discounted in the conventional way.

For example, using a discount rate of 6%, the present value of $1 annual benefits for 50 years would be $15.76. The Mishan proposal is to simply restart the discounting process at the 51st, 101st, 151st years, and so on throughout the useful life of the project. For each generation adopting a 6% discount rate and receiving $1 annual benefits, present value would be $15.76, rather than $0.86 for the second generation, and even less for each succeeding generation, under the conventional procedure. The present value of benefits for a 100-year project would be $31.52 for two generations, nearly double the $16.62 present value of benefits without the proposed procedure.

This proposal is based on the economic principle that individuals are the best judges of their own benefits and costs at a given time. Clearly, individuals born into the second generation will discount benefits to year one of the second generation's planning period, not to year one of the first generation. The procedure also is consistent with the principle of equality between generations. It seems reasonable to assume that the benefits of a recreation area will be just as valuable to the second generation of users as to the first. Of course, the preferences of individuals in future generations may differ from those of the current generation, and the per capita income of future generations is expected to be much greater. Thus, future patterns of demand may vary, and future benefits from current investment decisions may be more or less than for the current generation. Despite these limitations, the procedure would avoid the problem in which projects having large benefits to later generations and small cost to the present generation may be rejected on the basis of the conventional present value approach. Or even more tragically, projects that inflict large costs on later generations may be accepted on the basis of small benefits to the present generation. There are many choices today that can be reversed only at extremely high cost to future generations, or not at all.

The fourth point is that it would not be correct to use a zero discount rate to solve the intergenerational problem. The concepts of present value and discounting are fundamental to the evaluation of investment decisions. Because conservation decisions are basically investment decisions, it would not be correct to use a zero discount rate to achieve the protection of unique environmental resources. For the same reason, it would not be correct for water development projects in arid regions of the world to use a zero discount rate to provide water that would enable the deserts to produce essential foods and fiber, as well as recreation opportunities.

The fifth point is that the level of the interest rate used in project evaluation affects the choice of methods of production. High interest rates restrain investment by making long-run government projects more difficult to justify economically. The higher the discount rate, the lower the present value of annual labor costs relative to the initial capital investment. As a result, more labor and less capital will be used in the production of recreation opportunities. Higher discount rates, for example, favor hiring interpretive specialists rather than constructing elaborate visitor centers and acquiring mechanical displays (with the same amount spent on interpretive services). Higher discount rates favor less durable government investments and related expenditures. They also favor natural river preservation over reservoir construction, hunting and other backcountry recreation over downhill ski resorts, beach swimming over pool swimming, and scenic easements over public land acquisition.

## Which Discount Rate to Use

Economists have not been successful thus far in discovering the "correct" rate of discount. There continue to be disagreements for legitimate reasons. Because there is no consensus on the discount rate problem, benefit-cost studies should display the effects of several relevant discount rates. Typically, three discount rates should be used—high, medium and low. It is not difficult to calculate present value at various rates of discount once the benefits and costs have been forecast for each year in the planning period. In many instances, one of these discount rates will be the official or prescribed discount rate to use based on agency policy. The use of alternative discount rates helps the analyst and decision maker to see how robust the resulting benefit-cost ratio and project desirability is at different discount rates. Projects which are attractive at a wide range of discount rates would merit stronger recommendations for their funding relative to projects whose feasibility may be quite sensitive to the discount rate chosen.

The federal government uses different discount rates in benefit-cost studies of government programs including recreation. We will discuss the inefficiency of such an approach. For now, we note that the U.S. Forest Service is authorized to use a real (net of inflation) discount rate of 4% for all its programs including recreation (U.S. Forest Service, 1995, p. IV-5). Water resource agencies such as the Bureau of Reclamation, U.S. Army Corps of Engineers and USDA Natural Resource Conservation Service use a nominal (including inflation) discount rate of approximately 7.5% set by the U.S. Water Resources Council, based on the average cost of federal borrowing. All other Federal agencies are required to use one of two different rates set by the Office of Management and Budget. For the vast majority of government investment decisions for programs that provide outputs to the public a 7% real (net of inflation) discount rate is required (U.S. Office of Management and Budget, 1992). This rate is based on the view that public investments will displace both private investment and consumption (U.S. Office of Management and Budget, 1992). Public investment projects must acquire resources via increased taxes, which reduce consumption or via increased borrowing, which reduces investment or consumption. In a world with international capital flows between countries, some economists have questioned this one-for-one displacement view.

In particular, Lind (1990) recommends that the appropriate discount rate for all government programs should be the government nominal borrowing rate, which in 1996 was 5.5%. Netting out inflation converts this to a real discount rate of 2.8%, which is very low by most standards.

## Social Time Preference

The lower discount rate suggested by Lind (1990) is also consistent with the view that discounting should not be solely determined by market rates of interest but reflect a social time preference. The idea of a social rate of discount is based on the distinction between the private time preference of individuals acting on their own, and the social time preference of individuals acting collectively. When we say that individuals acting on their own have a high time preference, we mean that they want to consume now rather than defer consumption in order to provide resources for future generations. Also, future generations are unrepresented now so their interests are not adequately considered. Because government is supposed to be a representative of current and future generations we should use a low social discount rate because a lower rate gives greater weight to the future than does a higher rate. This is based on the belief that society, in its role as trustee for the future, has a longer time horizon than do individuals; therefore society's discount rate should be lower.

There is convincing evidence that individuals have more concern for the future than their savings and investment behavior as individuals indicates. Their individual behavior suggests they would choose to invest less for the future as each person's individual saving would provide little for the future. However, when we all agree to save for future generations, then we know the collective savings will be substantial.

Unfortunately, this means that the social discount rate cannot be derived from data on market interest rates, because the social discount rate is based on the social time preference of individuals acting collectively. Time preference for individuals acting on their own is most clearly seen when they have a choice between income now and income some time in the future. If we have information about past consumer investment decisions which the individuals consider satisfactory, we can calculate a time preference rate of discount. If individuals were satisfied with an additional investment of $100 at 12% interest, they apparently valued income in the future by the difference between $100 and $112, which includes the $12 interest received one year hence. Individuals estimate their real personal discount rate after inflation and personal taxes. Thus, if the inflation rate was 4% and the personal tax rate 25%, the real personal discount rate was:

$$\text{Discount rate} = 12\% - (12\% \times 0.25) - 4\% = 12\% - 3\% - 4\% = 5\% \quad \text{(Equation 20-1)}$$

This indicates that these individuals acting on their own discounted future earnings at a rate no higher than 5%. Unfortunately it is difficult to know what adjustment is necessary moving from the individual to collective action. One way to infer a social discount rate is to analyze a collective choice whereby people were asked to vote on a project that has $x$ costs now and provides well-defined benefits over the future period. If such a referendum were to pass, one could calculate an implicit social discount rate.

Another interesting approach to inferring a social discount rate is to simply ask households how they would make such trade-offs. An example of this is the work of Cropper and Portney (1992) where they ask individuals their trade-off between saving people's lives now versus in the future. When faced with the trade-off, respondents to the telephone survey made choices implying a 4% discount rate for a 100-year horizon.

## *Market Interest Rate*

In theory, capital markets determine the interest rate where the supply of loanable funds and demand for funds intersect. This means that increases in the interest rate encourage individuals to forego larger amounts of present consumption in favor of increased savings, which increases the supply of loanable funds. The lower the interest rate that firms have to pay to borrow for investment, the greater the number of investments they will make. Funds may be borrowed for private business investment, housing, car loans or general consumer loans. However, the distinction between private and social time preference represents a shift to the right in the supply of funds curve. In other words, individuals may be willing to accept a lower interest rate to forego consumption in favor of saving for long-run investments that may benefit future generations.

## *Opportunity Cost of Capital*

The rationale underlying Office of Management and Budget's (OMB) recommendation of a real rate of 7% is that it represents the foregone return that would have been earned by firms had they invested the money rather than the government. One might arrive at the opportunity cost of capital or the rate of return foregone by starting with the prime interest rate. The prime rate of interest on loans by large banks to large corporations is taken as the best available proxy for the marginal efficiency of investment, when adjusted for the rate of inflation and the corporate income tax. The prime rate of interest includes a premium for anticipated inflation during the period of the loan, removal of which is consistent with the practice of valuing future benefits and costs in constant (or current) dollars at the time of decision. When corporate income taxes approach 50%, a private corporation undertaking an investment would need to earn approximately twice the prime interest rate. Studies have shown that with the inflation rate removed, the prime lending rate has been about 2.5% to 3.0% in the long run, i.e., a period of time sufficiently long that short-run business cycles do not appreciably influence the results. This suggests that the marginal productivity of investment has been about 6% in real terms (constant dollars), not too different than the OMB recommendation of 7%.

## *Cost of Government Borrowing*

Water-based recreation projects were evaluated using a social discount rate of approximately 7.5% in 1996. The federal guidelines provide that the rate be recalculated each year based on the average yield of U.S. government securities with 15 years or more remaining to maturity. The rate has been referred to as the "risk free" social discount rate because it was based on the yield of securities that are nearly without risk to the investor. In order to dampen short-run changes in the discount rate, it could not be raised or lowered by more than 0.25% in any single year. When the average yield in the preceding year exceeded the established discount rate by more than 0.25%, the rate was raised. Whenever the average yield became less than the established discount rate by more than 0.25%, the rate was lowered.

In the past, the federal water resource agencies used rates of discount that most economists regarded as low. During the 1950s and into the 1960s, the discount rate was only 2% to 3% for the multipurpose water projects of the Corps of Engineers, Bureau of Reclamation, and Soil Conservation Service. The reason was that, in the early postwar years, Federal Reserve policy allowed the U.S. Treasury to borrow at artificially low rates of interest, by purchasing government bonds that could not be sold to private investors at the low level. As a result, the cost of government borrowing for long-term government securities was only 2.5% during the 1950s, rising gradually to 3% in 1968.

For many years, federal agencies and their clientele groups resisted increases in the discount rate because of its effect on the present value of benefits of water resource projects. For example, Fox and Herfindahl (1964) evaluated federal water projects authorized by Congress in 1962, which generally used a discount rate of 2.625%. At higher discount rates, fewer projects had benefits in excess of costs. This is illustrated here:

| Discount rate | 2.625% | 4.000% | 6.000% | 8.000% |
|---|---|---|---|---|
| Proportion of projects with benefits in excess of costs | 100% | 92% | 36% | 20% |

The effect of the low discount rate was to favor water-based recreation projects over other public and private investments using a higher discount rate. Thus, the supply of resources providing opportunities for reservoir recreation increased dramatically during the 1950s and 1960s (but at the expense of river recreation).

Since then, many states used a social discount rate of 4% to 6%, which substantially increased the present value of benefits for state water resource projects compared with the federal rate of 7% to 8%. As a result, states and municipalities provided increased opportunities for water-based recreation activities during the latter half of the 1970s and the 1980s.

In principle this cost of borrowing approach is a conceptually sound basis for calculating a discount rate in a world economy with international capital flows (Lind, 1990). However, implementation in the United States has compromised this concept. The most important problem is that the U.S. Water Resources Council requires agencies to evaluate benefits and costs in real terms (net of inflation) but then requires them to use the nominal (including inflation) discount rate. This inconsistency results in the nominal rate being treated like a real rate, far in excess of the true government cost of borrowing money.

## Steps in Benefit-Cost Analysis

There are five major steps in performing a complete benefit-cost analysis:

*Step One: Define the problem to be solved and the parameters of the analysis:*

a. Develop the range and composition of alternative solutions to the problem (i.e., what management practices and inputs will be used).
b. Determine the likely future without the project or the consequences of the no-action alternative in terms of key variables (i.e., future use levels if no action is taken).
c. Select which accounting stance will be used to measure benefits (e.g., local, state or federal).
d. Determine the overall study constraints in terms of time, personnel and budget available.
e. Choose the discount rate or range of discount rates to be used.

*Step Two: Design the analysis:*

a. Describe the problem structure. Are alternatives mutually exclusive? Is there an overall project investment budget constraint?
b. Select the benefit-cost analysis decision criterion. Is the net present value or B:C ratio to be used as the summary criterion to select the preferred alternative?
c. Identify and list all primary benefits and costs that must be included in the analysis.
d. Choose the key variables for sensitivity analysis. That is determine which variables are both fairly uncertain and likely to have a significant impact on the economic feasibility of the project (i.e., on the size of net present value or B:C ratio).
e. Develop a data collection plan.

*Step Three: Collect the data.*

*Step Four: Perform the benefit-cost analysis outlined in step two:*
a. Quantify benefits and costs.
b. Express as many benefits and costs in dollar terms as is consistent with the chosen accounting stance.
c. Compute the benefit-cost analysis decision criterion (i.e., net present value or B:C ratio) chosen in step two.
d. Perform the sensitivity analysis.

*Step Five: Present results.*

Clearly, performing a comprehensive benefit-cost analysis is a great deal of work. However, this framework can be tailored to the magnitude of the recreation resource issue to be analyzed. A simple benefit-cost analysis can be performed in a matter of weeks if the agency maintains good visitation records. Alternatively, if a visitor survey is involved, the benefit-cost analysis may take several months. Such a time consuming analysis would be worthwhile if the project costs several hundred thousand dollars or would irreversibly change a natural environment (e.g., whether to build a ski area or hydropower dam).

# Difficulties in Application

The purpose of this section is to discuss difficulties in the comparison of benefits and costs, to summarize the results of recent benefit-cost studies, and to suggest ways of improving future applications of the approach to recreation economic decisions. Challenges in conducting benefit-cost studies, include dealing with the multiobjectives in natural resource planning, choice of alternatives, determining the length of planning period, time phasing of investments, risk and uncertainty, income distribution, nonmonetary effects, and sensitivity of the results to changes in the variables.

## *Search for Alternatives*

The first and perhaps most important task in applying the benefit-cost approach is to choose relevant alternatives to be evaluated. Recreation economic decisions nearly always involve the comparison of two or more distinct possibilities. Whenever an individual consumer, private company, or government agency contemplates doing something, the alternatives of doing nothing and doing something else should be considered. The selection of alternative plans should be approached in a systematic manner to insure that all reasonable alternatives are evaluated. In practice, a number of alternative plans will usually be identified early in the planning process. Then, they will be refined as more information is developed during the study. Additional alternatives can be introduced at any time.

The federal guidelines define an alternative plan as a combination of structural and/or nonstructural measures to solve a problem or take advantage of an opportunity. Structural aspects include the capital investment costs of land, roads, facilities and equipment to maintain or increase the flow of output in the future. Nonstructural aspects include the costs of changes in existing management practices, policies, laws and regulations. When institutional barriers would prevent the initiation of an economically attractive alternative, possible changes in existing policies and regulations should be identified. Alternatives are not limited to those that the planning agency could implement directly under current authority. Alternative plans could be implemented by other public agencies of federal, state, and local governments, or by private companies and nonprofit organizations.

A reasonable number of alternatives should be evaluated. A *no-action* alternative is included to show the benefits and costs of continuing the current program without change and as a baseline by which to judge the improvement provided by the other alternatives. An alternative should be formulated which reasonably maximizes the contribution to net economic benefits, defined as the net present value of benefits to society. Subsequent alternatives may reduce net economic benefits in order to achieve other objectives. The purpose of the other alternatives is to provide decision makers the opportunity to judge whether these less tangible beneficial effects outweigh the loss in net economic benefits. For example, another alternative should be formulated to maximize the protection of environmental quality. Finally, there should be one or more significantly different alternatives in between the economic and environmental alternatives that are designed to enhance the best features of both.

There are a number of criteria that have been used to generate possible alternatives. The alternatives should represent complete plans that cover all of the necessary investments and operating programs. This includes appropriate mitigation of adverse environmental effects, as required by law. They should be effective plans, which means they can be expected to achieve their objectives. This includes considering the realistic capability of cooperating agencies and businesses to finance their proportionate share of the programs. They should be efficient plans, representing the most cost-effective (lowest cost) combination of resources to meet the objectives. They should encompass a broad range of output and expenditure levels. They should be acceptable plans, which represent politically viable, workable programs compatible with existing laws, regulations, and public policies as well as having realistic budgets for implementation.

Alternatives in a benefit-cost analysis also have been based on the objectives of the agency. Specific objectives are usually described in terms of the desired output of goods and services expected to alleviate a problem or realize an opportunity to increase the well-being of society.

Failure to include a broad enough range of alternatives limits the usefulness of the benefit-cost analysis and may create the impression that the agency had a predetermined outcome in mind prior to undertaking the analysis. In several cases, federal courts have found federal agencies' analyses incomplete and required them to redo their analysis when insufficient alternatives have been considered.

## *Choosing When to Start and End the Planning Period*

Two other important problems are when to begin and how long to continue recreation programs. When to start up is important because it defines the "present" for calculation of the present value of net benefits. Economists recommend that recreation programs should begin in the year that maximizes the present value of net benefits. Before then, postponing programs would increase their value to society. Postponing beyond that time would reduce their net benefits. For example, when a new campground is planned in anticipation of expanding demand for camping in future years, capacity of the facility will exceed demand during the early years after construction and become fully utilized during years 10 to 20, late in the life of the facility. In this case, delaying construction of the entire campground could increase net benefits. An alternative would consider phased construction with the first loop built in year one, the second loop in year five, and the third loop in year 10 consistent with the expanding demand. Thus, varying the project initiation date may be an important element of the overall project design.

How long to continue a project also is important because it defines the relevant planning period. A reasonable time horizon from beginning to end of expenditures on programs is the useful life of the most durable assets. The federal guidelines recommend that alternatives should have uniform planning periods, meaning that they begin and end in the same years. Otherwise, the alternatives would not receive a fair comparison. Most government agencies specify the length of the planning period. Recreation facilities located at reservoirs of the Corps of Engineers and Bureau of Reclamation are assumed to have a life of 50 years. However, most components of campgrounds such as roads, water systems, and picnic tables, have useful lifetimes of 10–20 years. Therefore, if one plans to provide a campground for 50 years, replacement of some facilities needs to be periodically included in the cost figures.

In contrast, a designated Wilderness Area may be assumed to have a perpetual life, in which case, the relevant planning period may be a continuous series of 50-year plans. The U.S. Forest Service prepares 50-year plans under authorization of the Forest and Rangeland Renewable Resources Planning Act (RPA) of 1974 and the National Forest Management Act of 1976.

Another problem in an era of increasing concern about efficiency in government results from the fact that more and more parks and other recreation sites are being treated as separate units for accounting purposes, and operated on a pay-as-you-go basis. This means that capital investment is converted to annual cost by amortization or some other basis of capital recovery. In this case, length of the planning period has a significant effect. Fixed assets of equal value but different useful lives will have significantly different annual costs. For example, employee vehicles are durable assets that routinely have been amortized on an annual basis. Table 20-1 (page 404) shows that the annual cost of a capital investment of $10,000 at 10% interest varies with useful life:

| | |
|---|---|
| Three years | $4,020 |
| Five years | $2,640 |

The appropriate method of converting capital investment to annual cost depends on whether investments are financed by taxes, the sale of revenue bonds, or by user fees. Amortization is recommended to estimate the full social cost of investments from tax revenues. Amortization also is an appropriate measure of the annual obligation to repay the principle plus interest on revenue bonds. However, a sinking fund would be appropriate when users are charged fees sufficient to replace recreation facilities as they wear out. These two methods are illustrated in Tables 20-1 and 20-2 (pages 404 and 405, respectively).

Amortization is defined as the annual payment to pay back an investment plus the payment of compound interest on the unpaid balance at the end of each year. The sinking fund method is defined as the annual payment that must be set aside each year to be invested at compound interest, in order to recover the original investment at the end of its useful life. The key difference is in the treatment of interest. Amortizing involves the payment of compound interest, and a sinking fund receives compound interest. For example, the annual payment into the fund could be invested in government bonds paying 10% interest. The importance of this distinction is the difference in the annual cost of investment under the two methods which increases for higher interest rates and longer planning periods.

The social cost of investment could be much lower with annual payments deposited in a sinking fund and invested in interest-bearing bonds. For example, consider a capital investment of $10,000 with a useful life of 20 years and an interest rate of 10%. The annual cost of the investment would be:

| | |
|---|---|
| Amortization | $1,175 |
| Sinking Fund | $175 |
| Saving | $1,000 |

**Table 20-1. Amortizing a $1 Investment in 1–50 Years With Payment of Compound Interest of 4%, 6%, 8% and 10%**

| Year | Annual Payment to Recover $1 With Compound Interest of[a] 4% | 6% | 8% | 10% |
|---|---|---|---|---|
| 1 | 1.040 | 1.060 | 1.080 | 1.100 |
| 2 | 0.530 | 0.545 | 0.561 | 0.576 |
| 3 | 0.360 | 0.374 | 0.388 | 0.402 |
| 4 | 0.275 | 0.289 | 0.302 | 0.315 |
| 5 | 0.226 | 0.237 | 0.250 | 0.264 |
| 6 | 0.191 | 0.203 | 0.216 | 0.230 |
| 7 | 0.166 | 0.179 | 0.192 | 0.205 |
| 8 | 0.149 | 0.161 | 0.174 | 0.187 |
| 9 | 0.134 | 0.147 | 0.160 | 0.174 |
| 10 | 0.123 | 0.136 | 0.149 | 0.163 |
| 11 | 0.114 | 0.127 | 0.140 | 0.154 |
| 12 | 0.107 | 0.119 | 0.133 | 0.147 |
| 13 | 0.100 | 0.113 | 0.127 | 0.141 |
| 14 | 0.095 | 0.106 | 0.121 | 0.136 |
| 15 | 0.090 | 0.103 | 0.117 | 0.131 |
| 16 | 0.086 | 0.099 | 0.113 | 0.128 |
| 17 | 0.082 | 0.095 | 0.110 | 0.125 |
| 18 | 0.079 | 0.092 | 0.107 | 0.122 |
| 19 | 0.076 | 0.090 | 0.104 | 0.120 |
| 20 | 0.074 | 0.087 | 0.102 | 0.118 |
| 21 | 0.071 | 0.085 | 0.100 | 0.116 |
| 22 | 0.069 | 0.083 | 0.098 | 0.115 |
| 23 | 0.067 | 0.081 | 0.096 | 0.113 |
| 24 | 0.066 | 0.080 | 0.095 | 0.111 |
| 25 | 0.640 | 0.078 | 0.094 | 0.110 |
| 26 | 0.630 | 0.077 | 0.093 | 0.109 |
| 27 | 0.061 | 0.076 | 0.091 | 0.108 |
| 28 | 0.060 | 0.075 | 0.090 | 0.107 |
| 29 | 0.059 | 0.074 | 0.090 | 0.107 |
| 30 | 0.058 | 0.073 | 0.089 | 0.106 |
| 31 | 0.057 | 0.072 | 0.088 | 0.105 |
| 32 | 0.060 | 0.071 | 0.087 | 0.105 |
| 33 | 0.055 | 0.070 | 0.087 | 0.104 |
| 34 | 0.054 | 0.070 | 0.086 | 0.104 |
| 35 | 0.054 | 0.069 | 0.086 | 0.104 |
| 36 | 0.053 | 0.068 | 0.085 | 0.103 |
| 37 | 0.052 | 0.068 | 0.085 | 0.103 |
| 38 | 0.052 | 0.067 | 0.085 | 0.103 |
| 39 | 0.051 | 0.067 | 0.084 | 0.102 |
| 40 | 0.050 | 0.066 | 0.084 | 0.102 |
| 41 | 0.050 | 0.066 | 0.084 | 0.102 |
| 42 | 0.050 | 0.066 | 0.083 | 0.102 |
| 43 | 0.049 | 0.065 | 0.083 | 0.101 |
| 44 | 0.049 | 0.065 | 0.083 | 0.101 |
| 45 | 0.048 | 0.065 | 0.083 | 0.101 |
| 46 | 0.048 | 0.064 | 0.082 | 0.101 |
| 47 | 0.048 | 0.064 | 0.082 | 0.101 |
| 48 | 0.047 | 0.064 | 0.082 | 0.101 |
| 49 | 0.047 | 0.064 | 0.082 | 0.101 |
| 50 | 0.046 | 0.063 | 0.082 | 0.101 |

[a]The capital recovery factor shows the annual payment that will repay a $1 loan in *x* years with payment of compound interest on the unpaid balance.

**Table 20-2. Sinking Fund Method of Recovering a $1 Investment in 1–50 Years With Compound Interest of 4%, 6%, 8% and 10%**

| | Annual Payment to Recover $1 With Compound Interest of[a] | | | |
|---|---|---|---|---|
| Year | 4% | 6% | 8% | 10% |
| 1 | 1.0000 | 1.0000 | 1.0000 | 1.0000 |
| 2 | 0.4902 | 0.4854 | 0.4808 | 0.4762 |
| 3 | 0.3203 | 0.3141 | 0.3080 | 0.3021 |
| 4 | 0.2355 | 0.2286 | 0.2219 | 0.2155 |
| 5 | 0.1846 | 0.1774 | 0.1705 | 0.1638 |
| 6 | 0.1508 | 0.1434 | 0.1363 | 0.1296 |
| 7 | 0.1266 | 0.1191 | 0.1121 | 0.1054 |
| 8 | 0.1085 | 0.1010 | 0.0940 | 0.0874 |
| 9 | 0.0945 | 0.0870 | 0.0801 | 0.0736 |
| 10 | 0.0833 | 0.0759 | 0.0690 | 0.0627 |
| 11 | 0.0741 | 0.0668 | 0.0600 | 0.0540 |
| 12 | 0.0666 | 0.0593 | 0.0527 | 0.0468 |
| 13 | 0.0601 | 0.0530 | 0.0465 | 0.0408 |
| 14 | 0.0547 | 0.0476 | 0.0413 | 0.0357 |
| 15 | 0.0499 | 0.0430 | 0.0368 | 0.0315 |
| 16 | 0.0458 | 0.0390 | 0.0330 | 0.0278 |
| 17 | 0.0422 | 0.0354 | 0.0296 | 0.0247 |
| 18 | 0.0390 | 0.0324 | 0.0267 | 0.0219 |
| 19 | 0.0361 | 0.0296 | 0.0241 | 0.0195 |
| 20 | 0.0336 | 0.0272 | 0.0219 | 0.0175 |
| 21 | 0.0313 | 0.0250 | 0.0198 | 0.0156 |
| 22 | 0.0292 | 0.0230 | 0.0180 | 0.0140 |
| 23 | 0.0273 | 0.0213 | 0.0164 | 0.0126 |
| 24 | 0.0256 | 0.0197 | 0.0150 | 0.0113 |
| 25 | 0.0240 | 0.0182 | 0.0137 | 0.0102 |
| 26 | 0.0226 | 0.0169 | 0.0125 | 0.0092 |
| 27 | 0.0212 | 0.0157 | 0.0114 | 0.0083 |
| 28 | 0.0200 | 0.0146 | 0.0105 | 0.0075 |
| 29 | 0.0189 | 0.0136 | 0.0096 | 0.0067 |
| 30 | 0.0178 | 0.0126 | 0.0088 | 0.0061 |
| 31 | 0.0169 | 0.0118 | 0.0081 | 0.0055 |
| 32 | 0.0159 | 0.0110 | 0.0075 | 0.0050 |
| 33 | 0.0151 | 0.0103 | 0.0069 | 0.0045 |
| 34 | 0.0143 | 0.0096 | 0.0063 | 0.0040 |
| 35 | 0.0136 | 0.0090 | 0.0058 | 0.0037 |
| 36 | 0.0129 | 0.0084 | 0.0053 | 0.0033 |
| 37 | 0.0122 | 0.0079 | 0.0049 | 0.0030 |
| 38 | 0.0116 | 0.0074 | 0.0045 | 0.0027 |
| 39 | 0.0111 | 0.0069 | 0.0042 | 0.0025 |
| 40 | 0.0105 | 0.0065 | 0.0039 | 0.0023 |
| 41 | 0.0100 | 0.0061 | 0.0036 | 0.0020 |
| 42 | 0.0095 | 0.0057 | 0.0033 | 0.0019 |
| 43 | 0.0091 | 0.0053 | 0.0030 | 0.0017 |
| 44 | 0.0087 | 0.0050 | 0.0028 | 0.0015 |
| 45 | 0.0083 | 0.0047 | 0.0026 | 0.0014 |
| 46 | 0.0079 | 0.0044 | 0.0024 | 0.0013 |
| 47 | 0.0075 | 0.0041 | 0.0022 | 0.0011 |
| 48 | 0.0072 | 0.0039 | 0.0020 | 0.0010 |
| 49 | 0.0069 | 0.0037 | 0.0019 | 0.0009 |
| 50 | 0.0060 | 0.0034 | 0.0017 | 0.0009 |

[a]The sinking fund factor shows the annual payment that will repay a $1 loan in *x* years with receipt of compound interest on investment of the accumulating fund.

This means that annual payment of $175 per year and the interest that accumulates on the payments over the 20 years will result in a balance of $10,000. With 1,000 RVDs per year, amortized investment cost would equal about $1.18 per RVD compared with only about $0.18 per RVD payment into a sinking fund. The payment of only $0.18 per RVD would be sufficient to replace existing facilities with revenues generated from user fees. As a result, the agency would be self-supporting in the provision of the existing capacity of facilities which otherwise would require a tax subsidy of $1.18 per RVD, or $1.00 per RVD more. This potential saving represents a strong case for sinking fund financing of recreation investments out of user fees.

## Other Problems in Application

Several additional points should be made about the comparison of benefits and costs. Here we will discuss four, having to do with uncertainty, sensitivity analysis, income distribution, and noneconomic effects.

After a study presents the best estimates of benefits and costs, it is important to include information on the effects of uncertainty. This refers to the absence of accurate information, or to that which is unknown. Uncertainty is an important problem when comparing benefits and costs because there is always some degree of error in the measurements. The federal guidelines recommend that studies include comparisons of the sensitivity of the results to uncertainty in the data and assumptions of future conditions. The objective is to help decision makers understand the effects of possible variation in conditions.

Sensitivity analysis should (1) vary the assumptions regarding uncertain economic, demographic, environmental, and other important conditions; and (2) report the effects on benefits and costs. Typically, benefits and costs are calculated for high, low, and medium levels of each important variable. This is an attempt to account for the variance (or degree of error) in the estimates of benefits and costs.

Also, studies should show the effects on distribution and equity. In the basic comparison of benefits and costs, it does not matter who benefits and who pays the costs. Benefit-cost studies are primarily concerned with the objective of economic efficiency, and less with other possible objectives such as income distribution. This means that we measure the net benefits to all of the people rather than to special interest groups. But after the basic comparison, studies should show decision makers how costs and benefits are distributed to different populations. With this information, they can decide whether, on equity grounds, the cost to one population is worth the benefits to another population.

Whenever government investment and operating costs are not fully reimbursed by users, they result in an income distribution effect. Many of the services of park and recreation programs are not regarded as suitable for sale on a pay-as-you-go basis. For example, it has been public policy that the youth and the aged should be entitled to the services of most park and recreation programs whether they can pay or not. Society desires that all persons have the opportunity to receive the services as a matter of principle because of distributional considerations. This results in a transfer of income in kind to those who do not pay from those who do.

When society attaches a different value to a dollar of cost or benefit for different groups of users, our unadjusted measures would need to be changed. For example, when benefits are adjusted on the basis of federal income tax weighting, those attributed to low-income users of recreation sites in Massachusetts increase by 10%–15%, according to studies in the northeastern United States. The effect of adjusting the value of benefits and costs for different income groups should be shown after the basic comparison without the adjustment.

It is important that all of the potentially significant costs and benefits be measured or at least discussed. Studies should describe any beneficial or adverse effects that cannot be quantified in monetary terms. There are two important reasons: (1) the description provides decision makers the opportunity to make their own estimates of the possible effects of the missing data on net benefits of the alternatives; and (2) it identifies the areas where additional data collection (or possibly research) is most needed for future decision making. Gaps in scientific data prevent our measuring some costs and benefits. This is a limiting factor in the case of physical and biological conditions that affect the quality of recreation experiences. For example, the relation between fish stocking programs and fishing success is not fully known. Because of limited knowledge, the term benefit-cost analysis may suggest a degree of precision that is seldom attainable.

Still, methods are available to achieve levels of accuracy in measuring benefits and costs that are reasonable and consistent with levels obtained in other areas of economics and in other disciplines. Nonetheless, it is important to check whether the assumptions underlying the approach are at least approximately correct, and to be aware of the problems that may arise in applications to recreation economic decisions. Although the assumptions underlying the comparison of benefits and costs are unlikely to be met completely, they are close enough in a sufficiently large number of cases that it is a powerful approach.

## Multiple Objective Natural Resource Planning

Benefit-cost studies are primarily designed to provide direct information on one objective: maximizing net economic benefits, i.e., to increase the economic efficiency by allocating resources among competing uses. Most public agencies must also address other objectives. Environmental impact statements consider the effect of implementing different alternatives on environmental quality (e.g., air, water, nongame wildlife).

Environmental impact statements also consider the distribution of project benefits and costs among different income classes and ethnic groups. In addition, they discuss intangible concerns such as health and safety.

This means that recreation allocation and management decisions involve more than one objective. The multiple objectives should be made explicit in the planning process and to the public. The U.S. Water Resources Council Principle and Standards established two co-equal objectives in evaluating the effects of alternative plans. They are national economic development and environmental quality. The effects on regional economic development, and other social effects must also be presented. These four are intended to include all of the significant effects of a recreation program on the human environment as required by the National Environmental Policy Act of 1969. Throughout this book we have focused on the national economic development objective, as it is synonymous with economic efficiency analysis. Chapter 14 dealt with regional economic development through discussion of input-output models and multipliers. The environmental quality objective introduces the study of biology, geology, natural history, archeology, and related subjects. The study of other social effects brings in sociology, psychology and philosophy. The best source of information on the application of multiple objectives in decision making is contained in several books (e.g., Keeney and Raiffa, 1976) and related journal literature on the multiple objective planning techniques. Today, the U.S. Water Resources Council identifies just the national economic development objective but agencies are required to identify the beneficial and adverse effects under each of the four accounts.

The **national economic development** objective has been defined as maximizing the effect of alternatives on the net present value of the output of goods and services, no matter who receives them. Although economists may refer to this as the economic efficiency objective, you should keep in mind that what they mean is, maximizing the net benefits of all of the citizens as expressed by individual willingness to pay. As noted earlier, national economic development is not the same thing as financial or commercial development.

The **environmental quality** objective has been defined as maximizing the beneficial effects of alternatives on the ecological and aesthetic attributes of natural and cultural resources. Although environmental quality sustains and enriches human life, it is not usually measured in monetary terms. An ecosystem is a complete interacting system of organisms considered together with their environment. Ecology refers to the study of the dynamic and diverse interaction among all living and nonliving things, such as plants, animals, land, water, and atmosphere. Ecological effects include the quality of water, land, and air; the biology and geology of open and green space; wild and scenic rivers; lakes and shorelines; mountains and forests; prairie, wetlands, and estuaries; and other natural systems.

Cultural resources are the historical or archaeological remains of sites, structures, and objects used by people. This is the physical evidence of past and present habitation by humans. Archaeological and historic studies of artifacts, structures, and sites provide information to understand, reconstruct, and preserve physical evidence of the diversity of human cultures. Aesthetic effects are the human perceptions, enjoyment, and appreciation of pleasant surroundings. Included are the sensations of sight, sound, scent, and other human impressions of the natural and cultural resources.

All of these aspects of environmental quality may be described in terms of location, magnitude, duration, or frequency. Ecological and cultural effects are not measured in the same units. Where trade-offs between objectives are based on values that are not measured in the same units (economists say noncommensurable), choices must be made through the political system. Thus, Congress has passed legislation requiring the protection of the natural environment and mitigation of adverse effects must be included in each alternative plan. Mitigation usually refers to programs that rectify, repair, rehabilitate, or restore the damaged environment. Mitigation also may refer to the replacement in kind of damaged habitat for fish and wildlife. For example, when a city constructs a reservoir for use as a domestic and industrial water supply, it may have to provide public access to a stretch of river equivalent to that inundated by the reservoir.

The **regional economic development** objective is to consider changes in the distribution of regional economic activity, income, and employment resulting from each alternative plan. The federal guidelines recommend that regional economic development be treated as an income transfer and reported in a separate account to distinguish it from national economic development represented by the net benefits to individual consumers which contribute to general welfare. The region is usually defined as the two- to six-county area where the recreation project or program will have particularly significant income and employment effects. When these effects are outside of the region, they should be placed in a "rest of nation" category.

Regional income effects are equal to the sum of net economic benefits that remain in the region plus transfers of income to the region from the rest of the nation. Transfers of income include income from outlays to implement the plan and expenditures in the region by recreation users from outside the region, along with their indirect effects and induced effects, discussed in Chapter 14. Employment effects parallel those on regional income and can be derived from the same calculation. Changes in employment should be divided into relevant service, trade, agriculture, and industrial sectors of the regional economy. Also, employment effects should be classified as to level of skill required—unskilled, semiskilled, and highly skilled.

Finally, other social effects of alternative plans should be displayed for the information of decision makers. There may be effects on the quality of human life, health, and safety; on distribution of income and population; the fiscal condition of local government; energy conservation; long-term productivity of resources; and other significant effects of the alternative plans not measured in monetary terms. Effects are usually evaluated in terms of their impacts on community development in the region of the proposed recreation site.

## Concluding Advice

Information presented in all four accounts should provide decision makers with a reasonably complete picture of the social, environmental, regional and national economic effects of a particular project, policy or program. It is up to decision makers at the field, state and national level to balance the different effects of their projects against those of competing projects or programs. It is important to recognize that one's particular recreation project must compete with other equally deserving projects in the state and sometimes in the national arena. Thus the analysis must be carefully done and professionally presented.

While the focus of this book has been on the economic effects, the final decision on recreation projects and programs will necessarily reflect a balancing of the many competing demands society has on its scarce resources. Good analysis greatly improves the chances that officials will make the "best" decisions. However, the economist and the planner must always recognize the results of analysis are not a substitute for reasoned judgment and the democratic process of decision making. Take pride in the quality and thoroughness of your analysis and receive your satisfaction from knowing you provided decision makers with an objective assessment.

# References

Adams, Robert L., Robert C. Lewis, and Bruce H. Drake. (1973, December). *Outdoor recreation in America: An economic analysis.* Washington, DC: Bureau of Outdoor Recreation, U.S. Department of the Interior.

Aiken, Richard. (1985). *Public benefits of environmental protection in Colorado.* Unpublished master's thesis, Colorado State University, Fort Collins, CO.

American Automobile Association. (1995). *Your Driving Costs* (AAA Publication #2717). Heathrow, FL: Author.

Arrow, Kenneth, Robert Solow, Paul Portney, Edward Leamer, Roy Radner and Howard Schuman. (1993). Report of the NOAA panel on contingent valuation U.S. Department of Commerce. *Federal Register* 58:10:4602–14.

Bamford, Tara, Robert Manning, Lawrence Forcier and Edward Koenemann. (1988). Differential campsite pricing: An experiment. *Journal of Leisure Research* 20:4:324–342.

Barish, Norman. (1962). *Economic analysis for engineering and managerial decision making.* New York, NY: McGraw-Hill.

Baumol, William J., and Alan S. Blinder. (1982). *Economics: Principles and policy* (2nd ed.). New York, NY: Harcourt Brace Jovanovich.

Becker, Gary S. (1965, September). A theory of the allocation of time. *The Economic Journal* 75:493–57.

Becker, Gary S. (1976). *The economic approach to human behavior.* Chicago, IL: University of Chicago Press.

Bergstrom, John, Ken Cordell, Alan Watson and Gregory Ashely. (1990, December). Economic impacts of state parks on state economies in the south. *Southern Journal of Agricultural Economics* 22:2:69–77.

Bernoulli, D. (1954, January). Exposition of a new theory on the measurement of risk. *Econometrica* 22:25–36.

Bishop, Richard C., and Thomas A. Heberlein. (1979, December). Measuring values of extra-market goods: Are indirect measures biased? *American Journal of Agricultural Economics* 61:926–30.

Bockstael, Nancy, and Kenneth McConnell. (1981). Theory and estimation of the household production function for wildlife recreation. *Journal of Environmental Economics and Management* 8:3:199–214.

Bohm, Peter. (1972). Estimating the demand for public goods: An experiment. *European Economic Review* 3:111–130.

Bouwes, Nicolaas W., and Robert Schneider. (1979, August). Procedures in estimating benefits of water quality change. *American Journal of Agricultural Economics* 61:535–539.

Brookshire, David S., and Thomas D. Crocker. (1981). The advantages of contingent valuation methods for benefit-cost analysis. *Public Choice* 36:2:235–52.

Brookshire, David, Larry Eubanks and Alan Randall. (1983, February). Estimating option prices and existence values for wildlife. *Land Economics* 59:1–15.

Brookshire, David, Mark Thayer, William Schulze and Ralph d'Arge. (1982). Valuing public goods: A comparison of survey and hedonic approaches. *American Economic Review* 72:1:165–177.

Brown, Gardner, and Robert Mendelsohn. (1984, August). The hedonic travel cost method. *Review of Economics and Statistics* 66:427–433.

Brown, Perry, Glenn Haas and Michael Manfredo. (1977). *Identifying resource attributes providing opportunities for dispersed recreation.* Fort Collins, CO: Colorado State University, Department of Recreation Resources.

Brown, Perry, Jacob Hautalauoma and Mortaon McPhail. (1977). *Colorado deer hunting experiences.* Transaction of 42nd North American Wildlife and Natural Resources Conference, Wildlife Management Institute, Washington, DC.

Brown, Thomas. (1993). Measuring nonuse values: A comparison of recent contingent valuation studies. In J. Bergstrom (Compiler), *Benefits and costs transfer in natural resources planning, sixth interim report* (Western Regional Research Publication W-133). Athens, GA: University of Georgia, Department of Agricultural and Applied Economics.

Brown, William B., and Farid Nawas. (1973, May). Impact of aggregation on the estimation of outdoor recreation demand functions. *American Journal of Agricultural Economics* 55:246–49.

Bureau of the Census. (1980). *1980 Census of Population.* Washington, DC: U.S. Department of Commerce, U.S. Government Printing Office.

Bureau of Outdoor Recreation. (1973a). *Outdoor recreation in America: Appendix A, An economic analysis.* Washington, DC: U.S. Government Printing Office.

Bureau of Outdoor Recreation. (1973b). *The 1970 survey of outdoor recreation activities.* Washington, DC: U.S. Government Printing Office.

Burton, Diana, and Peter Berck. (1996, February). Statistical causation and national forest policy. *Forest Science* 42:86–92.

Callahan, John, and Douglas Knudson. (1966). *Economic aspects of commercial outdoor recreation enterprises in southern Indiana* (Research Bulletin 814). Lafayette, IN: Purdue University, Agricultural Experiment Station.

Carson, Richard, Nicholas Flores, Kerry Martin, and Jennifer Wright. (1996, February). Contingent valuation and revealed preference methodologies: Comparing the estimates for quasi-public goods. *Land Economics* 72:80–99.

Caulkins, Peter, Richard Bishop and Nicolass Bouwes. (1985, May). Omitted cross price variable biases in the linear travel cost model. *Land Economics* 61:182–187.

Cesario, Frank J. (1976, February). Value of time in recreation benefit studies. *Land Economics* 52:32–41.

Cheron, Emmanuel J., and J. R. Brent Ritchie. (1982). Leisure activities and perceived risk. *Journal of Leisure Research* 14:2:139–54.

Cheshire, P., and M. Stabler. (1976, March). Joint consumption benefits in recreational site surplus: An empirical estimate. *Regional Studies* 10:97–104.

Cicchetti, Charles J. (1973). *Forecasting recreation in the United States.* Lexington, MA: D.C. Heath and Co.

Clawson, Marion, and Jack L. Knetcsh. (1966). *Economics of outdoor recreation.* Baltimore, MD: Johns Hopkins University Press.

Coppedge, Robert. (1977). *Income multipliers in economic impact analysis* (Cooperative Extension Publication 400 X-5). Las Cruces, NM: New Mexico State University.

Cordell, Kenneth, John Bergstrom, Lawrence Hartmann and Donald English. (1990). *An analysis of the outdoor recreation and wilderness situation in the United States: 1989–2040* (General Technical Report RM-189). Fort Collins, CO: Rocky Mountain Forest and Range Experiment Station, USDA Forest Service.

Cropper, Maureen, and Paul Portney. (1992, Summer). Discounting human lives. *Resources No.* 108:1–4.

Daubert, John T., and Robert A. Young. (1981, November). Recreational demands for maintaining instream flows: A contingent valuation approach. *American Journal of Agricultural Economics* 63:667–76.

Davis, Robert K. (1963, October). Recreation planning as an economic problem. *Natural Resources Journal* 3:239–49.

Dillman, Donald. (1978). *Mail and telephone surveys: The total design method.* New York, NY: John Wiley & Sons.

Douglas, Aaron, and David Harpman. (1995). Estimating recreation employment effects with IMPLAN for the Glen Canyon Dam region. *Journal of Environmental Management* 44:233–247.

Downing, Kent. (1979). *Costs of providing dispersed recreation along forest roads: A pilot study* (Report to U.S. Forest Service). Logan, UT: Utah State University.

Downing, Mark, and Teofilo Ozuna, Jr. (1996). Testing the reliability of benefit function transfer approach. *Journal of Environmental Economics and Management* 30:316–322.

Driver, Beverly. (1977). Item pool for scales designed to quantify the *psychological outcomes desired and expected from recreation participation.* Fort Collins, CO: Rocky Mountain Forest and Range Experiment Station, USDA Forest Service.

Driver, Beverly L., and Perry J. Brown. (1975). A social-psychological definition of recreation demand, with implications for recreation resource planning. In *Assessing demand for outdoor recreation* (pp. 64–88). Washington, DC: National Academy of Science.

Dwyer, John, John Kelly and Michael Bowes. (1977). *Improved procedures for valuation of the contribution of recreation to national economic development* (Water Resources Center Report No. 128). Urbana, IL: University of Illinois, Urbana-Champaign.

Economic Research Associates. (1975). *Evaluation of public willingness to pay user charges.* Washington, DC: U.S. Department of the Interior.

Epperson, Arlin. (1977). *Private and commercial recreation.* New York, NY: John Wiley, Inc.

Federal Reserve Bank of St. Louis. (1995). *Annual U.S. economic data.* St. Louis, MO: Author.

Fisher, Anthony, and John Krutilla. (1972, May). Determination of optimal capacity of resource-based recreation facilities. *Natural Resources Journal* 12:417–444.

Fix, Peter. (1996). *The economic benefits of mountain biking: Applying the TCM and CVM at Moab, Utah.* Unpublished master's thesis, Department of Agricultural and Resource Economics, Colorado State University, Fort Collins, CO.

Fox, Irving, and O. C. Herfindahl. (1964, May). Attainment of efficiency in satisfying demands for water resources. *American Economic Review* 54:198–206.

Freeman, Myrick. (1993). *The measurement of environmental and resource values: Theory and practice.* Washington, DC: Resources for the Future.

Gamble, Hays. (1965). *Community income from outdoor recreation.* A paper presented at the Maryland Governor's Recreation Conference, Ocean City, MD.

Gibbs, K. C., and F. L. Reed. (1983). *Estimation and analysis of costs for developed recreation sites in U.S. Forest Service Region One* (Research Bulletin 42). Corvallis, OR: Oregon State University, Forest Research Lab.

Gibbs, K. C., and W. W. S. van Hees. (1981). Cost of operating public campgrounds. *Journal of Leisure Research* 3:3:243–53.

Gibson, Betty Blecha. (1980, December). Estimating demand elasticities for public goods from survey data. *American Economic Review* 70:1069–76.

Gittinger, J. Price. (1982). *Economic analysis of agricultural projects* (2nd ed.). Baltimore, MD: Economic Development Institute, Johns Hopkins University Press.

Goeldner, Charles, T. A. Buckman and K. P. Duea. (1984). *Economic analysis of North American ski areas.* Boulder, CO: University of Colorado, Business Research Division.

Goldbloom, Andrew. (1988). *The 1987 annual economic impact of Texas state park visitors on gross business receipts in Texas.* Austin, TX: Texas Parks and Wildlife Department.

Greenley, Douglas, Richard Walsh and Robert Young. (1982). Economic benefits of improved water quality: Public perceptions of option and preservation values. Boulder, CO: Westview Press.

Grubb, Herbet, and James Goodwin. (1968). *Economic evaluation of water oriented recreation in the preliminary Texas water plan.* Dallas, TX: Texas Water Development Board 84.

Guldin, Richard. (1980, September). Wilderness cost in New England. *Journal of Forestry* 78:548–552.

Haroldson, Ancel. (1975). *Economic impact of recreation development at Big Sky, Montana* (Research Report No. 75). Bozeman, MT: Montana State University, Agricultural Experiment Station.

Hellerstein, Daniel. (1995, August). Welfare estimation using aggregate and individual observation models. *American Journal of Agricultural Economics* 77:620–630.

Hendee, John C., Richard P. Gale, and William Catton, Jr. (1971, Fall). A typology of outdoor recreation activity preferences. *Journal of Environmental Education* 3:28–34.

Heritage Conservation and Recreation Service. (1980). *Third nationwide outdoor recreation plan* (Volumes 1–4 based on the 1977 National Recreation Survey). Washington, DC: U.S. Department of the Interior, Government Printing Office.

Hoehn, John, and Alan Randall. (1987, September). Satisfactory benefit-cost indicator. *Journal of Environmental Economics and Management* 14:226–247.

Hof, John G., and H. Fred Kaiser. (1983). Long-term outdoor recreation participation projections for public land management agencies. *Journal of Leisure Research* 15:1:1–14.

Hof, John, and John Loomis. (1983, July). A recreation optimization model based on the travel cost method. *Western Journal of Agricultural Economics* 8:76–85.

Horvath, Joseph. (1973). *Preliminary executive summary: Economic survey of wildlife recreation, southeastern states.* Atlanta, GA: Georgia State University.

Howe, Charles. (1971). *Benefit-cost analysis for water system planning* (Water Resources Monograph #2). Washington, DC: American Geophysical Union.

Hughes, Jay M. (1970). *Forestry in Itasca County's economy: An input-output analysis* (Agricultural Experiment Station Misc. Report 95, Forestry Series No. 4). St. Paul, MN: University of Minnesota.

Huszar, Paul C., and David W. Seckler. (1974, November). Effects of pricing a "free" good: A study of admission at the California Academy of Sciences. *Land Economics* 50:364–73.

Ise, John. (1961). *Our national park policy: A critical history.* Washington, DC: Resources for the Future.

Johnson, Rebecca, and Eric Moore. (1993). Tourism impact estimation. *Annuals of Tourism Research* 20:279–288.

Johnson, Rebecca, Fred Obermiller and Hans Radtke. (1988). *The economic impact of tourism sales.* Corvallis, OR: Oregon State University, Department of Forest Resources Management.

Kalter, Robert, and Lois Gosse. (1969). *Outdoor recreation in New York state: Projections of demand, economic value and pricing effects for the period 1970–1985* (Special Cornell Series No. 5). Ithaca, NY: Cornell University.

Kalter, Robert J., and William B. Lord. (1968, May). Measurement of the impact of recreation investments on a local economy. *American Journal of Agricultural Economics* 50:243–55.

Keeney, Ralph, and Howard Raiffa. (1976). *Decisions with multiple objectives.* New York, NY: John Wiley and Sons.

Kite, Rodney, and William Schulze. (1967). *Economic impact on southwestern Wyoming of recreationists visiting Flaming Gorge Reservoir* (Research Report #11). Laramie, WY: University of Wyoming, Agricultural Experiment Station.

Kling, Catherine, and Cynthia Thomson. (1996, February). The implications of model specification for welfare estimation in nested logit models. *American Journal of Agricultural Economics* 78:103–114.

Krutilla, John. (1967). Conservation reconsidered. *American Economic Review* 57:787–796.

Kurtz, William B., and David A. King. (1980). Evaluating substitution relationships between recreation areas. In D. Hawkins, E. L. Shafer and J. Rovelstad (Eds.), *Tourism marketing and management issues* (pp. 391–403). Washington, DC: George Washington University.

Lancaster, Kelvin J. (1966, April). A new approach to consumer theory. *Journal of Political Economy* 74:132–57.

LaPage, Wilbur, and Dale Ragain. (1974, Spring). Family camping trends: An eight-year panel study. *Journal of Leisure Research* 6:101–12.

Leibenstein, Harvey. (1950, May). Bandwagon, snob and Veblen effects in the theory of consumer demand. *Quarterly Journal of Economics* 64:183–207.

Leuschner, W. A., and R. L. Young. (1978, December). Estimating the southern pine beetle's impact on reservoir campsites. *Forest Science* 24:527–43.

Libeau, Clayton. (1969). *Cost-effectiveness analysis.* Washington, DC: Forest Service, U.S. Department of Agriculture.

Lichty, Richard W., and Donald N. Steinnes. (1982). Ely, Minnesota: Measuring the impact of tourism on a small community. *Growth and Change* 13:2:36–9.

Lind, Robert. (1990). Reassessing the government's discount rate policy in light of new theory and data in a world economy with a high degree of capital mobility. *Journal of Environmental Economics and Management* 18:2:S8–S28.

Lipsey, Richard, and Peter Steiner. (1981). *Economics* (6th ed.). New York, NY: Harper and Row Publishers.

Loomis, John B. (1982). Use of travel cost models for evaluating lottery rationed recreation: Application to big-game hunting. *Journal of Leisure Research* 14:2:117–124.

Loomis, John. (1989, February). Test-retest reliability of the contingent valuation method: A comparison of general population and visitor responses. *American Journal of Agricultural Economics* 71:76–84.

Loomis, J. (1990, January). Comparative reliability of dichotomous choice and open-ended contingent valuation techniques. *Journal of Environmental Economics and Management* 18:78–85.

Loomis, John. (1993). An investigation into the reliability of intended visitation behavior. Environmental and Resource *Economics* 3:183–191.

Loomis, John, Thomas Brown, Beatrice Lucero and George Peterson. (1996, November). Improving validity experiments of contingent valuation methods. *Land Economics* 72:450–461.

Loomis, John, and Joseph Cooper. (1990, July). Comparison of environmental quality induced demand shifts using time-series and cross-section data. *Western Journal of Agricultural Economics* 15:83–90.

Loomis, John, Brian Roach, Frank Ward and Richard Ready. (1995, March). Testing transferability of recreation demand models across regions: A study of Corps of Engineers reservoirs. *Water Resources Research* 31:721–730.

Lucas, Robert. (1963). Bias in estimating recreationists length of stay from sample interview. *Journal of Forestry* 61:912–914.

Lyon, Gale H., Dean F. Tuthill, and William B. Matthews, Jr. (1969). *Economic analysis of marinas in Maryland* (MP 673). College Park, MD: University of Maryland, Agricultural Experiment Station.

MacCleery, Douglas. (1981). *Adjusting federal outdoor recreation programs to a tight budget situation.* Presented at the National Energy and Tourism Conference II, Washington, DC.

Main, Alden. (1971). *Impact of forestry and forest-related industries on a local economy, Baldwin County, Alabama.* Unpublished doctoral dissertation, Auburn University, Auburn, AL.

Mansfield, Edwin. (1980). *Statistics for business and economics.* New York, NY: W.W. Norton.

Manthy, Robert, and Thomas Tucker. (1972). *Supply costs for public forest land recreation* (Research Report 158). East Lansing, MI: Michigan State University, Agricultural Experiment Station.

Martin, William E., Russell L. Gum, and Arthur H. Smith. (1974). *The demand for and value of hunting, fishing, and general rural outdoor recreation in Arizona* (Technical Bulletin 211). Tucson, AZ: University of Arizona, Agricultural Experiment Station.

Maslow, Abraham H. (1965). *Eupsychian management.* Homewood, IL: Richard D. Irwin, Inc.

McConnell, Kenneth E. (1975, May). Some problems in estimating the demand for outdoor recreation. *American Journal of Agricultural Economics* 57:330–34.

McConnell, Kenneth E. (May 1977). Congestion and willingness to pay: A study of beach use. *Land Economics* 53:187–95.

McConnell, Kenneth, and Ivar Strand. (1981). Measuring the cost of time in recreation demand analysis: Application to sport fishing. *American Journal of Agricultural Economics* 61:153–156.

McKean, John R. (1981). *An input-output analysis of sportsman expenditures in Colorado* (Technical Report 26). Fort Collins, CO: Colorado State University, Colorado Water Resources Institute.

McKean, John R., and Kenneth C. Nobe. (1984). *Direct and indirect economic effects of hunting and fishing in Colorado, 1981* (Technical Report No. 44). Fort Collins, CO: Colorado State University, Colorado Water Resources Research Institute.

McMillan, Melville L., Bradford G. Reid, and David W. Gillen. (1980, August). An extension of the hedonic approach for estimating the value of quiet. *Land Economics* 56:315–28.

Michaelson, Edgar. (1975, December). Economic impact of mountain pine beetle on outdoor recreation. *Southern Journal of Agricultural Economics* 7:42–50.

Millard, Frank W., and David W. Fischer. (1979). The local economic impact of outdoor recreation facilities. In Carlton S. Van Doren, George B. Priddle, and John E. Lewis (Eds.), *Land and leisure: Concepts and methods in outdoor recreation* (2nd ed.). Chicago, IL: Maaroufa Press.

Miller, Ronald, Anthony Prato and Robert Young. (1977, March). *Congestion, success and the value of Colorado deer hunting experience.* Transactions of 42nd North American Wildlife and Natural Resources Conference, Wildlife Management Institute, Washington, DC.

Mishan, E. J. (1976). Cost-benefit analysis (2nd ed.). New York, NY: Praeger Publishers.

Mitchell, Robert, and Richard Carson. (1989). *Using surveys to value public goods: The contingent valuation method.* Washington, DC: Resources for the Future.

Moeller, George H., and Herbert E. Echelberger. (1974). *Approaches to forecasting recreation consumption—Outdoor recreation research: Applying the results.* (Technical Report NC-9). St. Paul, MN: North Central Forest Experiment Station, Forest Service.

Morey, Edward. (1981). The demand for site-specific recreational activities: A characteristics approach. *Journal of Environmental Economics and Management* 8:4:345–371.

Munley, Vincent G., and V. Kerry Smith. (1976, November). Learning-by-doing and experience: The case of whitewater recreation. *Land Economics* 52:545–53.

National Park Service. Public Use of the National Parks: Statistical Report. U.S. Department of the Interior, Washington, DC "Various Years".

National Park Service. (1983). *1982–1983 national recreation survey.* Washington, DC: U.S. Department of Interior.

National Park Service. (1995). *The money generation model 1995–1996.* Denver, CO: Office of Social Science, Socioeconomic Studies Division, National Park Service.

Neave, David, and Richard Goulden. (1983). *Provincial wildlife revenue sources and commitments.* Transactions of the 48th North American Wildlife and Natural Resources Conference, Wildlife Management Institute, Washington, DC.

Neuzil, Dennis. (1968, January). Uses and abuses of highway benefit-cost analysis. *Sierra Club Bulletin* 53:16–21.

Nordhaus, William D., and James Tobin. (1973). Is growth obsolete? In Milton Moss (Ed.), *The measurement of economic and social performance,* (pp. 509–31). New York, NY: National Bureau of Economic Research.

Odell, Robert, Jr. (1972, February). Use of recreation service charges. *Government Finance* 1:19.

O'Toole, Randall. (1995). State lands and resources. *Different Drummer* (The Theorean Institute, Oak Grove, OR) *2*:3:34–35.

Owen, John D. (1971, January–February). The demand for leisure. *Journal of Political Economy* 79:56–76.

Owen, John D. (1969). *The price of leisure.* Rotterdam, the Netherlands: Rotterdam University Press.

Parsons, George, and Mary Jo Kealy. (1992, February). Randomly drawn opportunity sets in a random utility model of lake recreation. *Land Economics* 68:93–106.

Peterson, George, Dan Stynes and Ross Arnold. (1985, Spring). The stability of a recreation demand model over time. *Journal of Leisure Research* 17:121–132.

Power, Thomas. (1996). *Lost landscapes and failed economies: The search for a value of place.* Covello, CA: Island Press.

Radtke, Hans, Stan Detering and Ray Brokken. (1985, December). A comparison of economic impact estimates for changes in the federal grazing fee: Secondary versus primary data I/O models. *Western Journal of Agricultural Economics* 10:382–390.

Rajender, G., F. Harston, and D. Blood. (1967). *A study of the resources, people and economy of Teton County, Wyoming.* Laramie, WY: University of Wyoming, Division of Business and Economic Research.

Randall, Alan. (1987). *Resource economics: An economic approach to natural resources and environmental policy.* Columbus, OH: Gird Publishing.

Randall, Alan, Berry Ives and Clyde Eastman. (1974). Bidding games for valuation of aesthetic environmental improvements. *Journal of Environmental Economics and Management* 1:132–149.

Reiling, Stephen D., and Mark W. Anderson. (1983). *Estimation of the cost of providing publicly-supported outdoor recreation facilities in Maine* (Bulletin 793). Orono, ME: University of Maine, Maine Agricultural Experiment Station.

Reiling, Stephen D., Mark W. Anderson, and Kenneth C. Gibbs. (1983). Measuring the costs of publicly supplied outdoor recreation facilities: A methodological note. *Journal of Leisure Research* 15:3:203–18.

Reiling, Stephen, Kevin Boyle, Marcia Phillips and Mark Anderson. (1990, May). Temporal reliability of contingent values. *Land Economics* 66:128–134.

Rhody, Donald, and Robert Lovegrove. (1970). *Economic impacts of hunting and fishing expenditures in Grand County, Colorado, 1968.* Fort Collins, CO: Colorado State University.

Ribaudo, Marc, and Donald Epp. (1984, May). The importance of sample discrimination in using the travel cost method to estimate benefits of improved water quality. *Land Economics* 60:397–403.

Rowe, Robert, William Schulze and William Breffle. (1996). A test for payment card bias. *Journal of Environmental Economics and Management.*

Samuleson, Paul. (1954). The pure theory of public expenditure. *Review of Economics and Statistics* 36:387–389.

Sandrey, Ronald, Steven Buccola and William Brown. (1983, November). Pricing policies for anterless elk hunting permits. *Land Economics* 59:432–443.

Sassone, Peter G., and William A. Schaffer. (1978). *Cost-benefit analysis: A handbook.* New York, NY: Academic Press.

Schor, Juliet. (1991). *The overworked American.* New York, NY: Basic Books.

Schultze, Charles. (1977). *The public use of the private interest.* Washington, DC: The Brookings Institution.

Schulze, William, Ralph d'Arge and David Brookshire. (1981, May). Valuing environmental commodities. *Land Economics* 57:151–172.

Scitovsky, Tibor. (1976). *The joyless economy: An inquiry into human satisfaction and consumer dissatisfaction.* London, UK: Oxford University Press.

Shabman, L. A., and Robert J. Kalter. (1969). *The effects of New York state administered outdoor recreation expenditures on the distribution of personal income* (Agricultural Economic Research Report No. 298). Ithaca, NY: Cornell University.

Smith, V. Kerry, William Desvousges and Mathew McGivney. (1983). The opportunity cost of travel time in recreation demand models. *Land Economics* 59:259–278.

Smith, V. Kerry, and Yoshiaki Karou. (1990, May). Signals or noise? Explaining the variation in recreation benefit estimates. *American Journal of Agricultural Economics 72*:419–433.

Sorg, Cindy, and John Loomis. (1984). Empirical estimates of amenity forest values: A comparative review (General Technical Report RM-107). Fort Collins, CO: Rocky Mountain Forest and Range Experiment Station, USDA Forest Service.

Stewart, Fred, David Browder and Jerry Covault. (1992). Opportunity cost of wilderness designation for three roadless areas within the Lolo National Forest. In C. Payne, J. Bowker and P. Reed (Compilers), *The economic value of wilderness* (General Technical Report SE-78). Athens, GA: Southeastern Forest Experiment Station.

Stoevener, H. H., R. B. Retting, and S. D. Reiling. (1974). Economic impact of outdoor recreation: What have we learned? In Donald R. Field, J. C. Barron, and B. F. Long (Eds.), *Water and community development: Social and economic perspectives.* Ann Arbor, MI: Ann Arbor Science Publishers.

Stokey, Edith, and Richard Zeckhauser. (1978). *A primer for policy analysis.* New York, NY: W. W. Norton & Co.

Strauss, Charles. (1975, July–September). A financial management study for Pennsylvania parks. *Trends* 44–48.

Stynes, Daniel, George Peterson and Donald Rosenthal. (1986, February). Log transformation bias in estimating travel cost models. *Land Economics* 62:94–103.

Sutherland, Ronald J. (1982, September). A regional approach to estimating recreation benefits of improved water quality. *Journal of Environmental Economics and Management* 9:229–47.

Thayer, Mark A. (1981, March). Contingent valuation techniques for assessing environmental impacts: Further evidence. *Journal of Environmental Economics and Management* 8:27–44.

Tyre, Gary L. (1975). Average costs of recreation on national forests in the south. *Journal of Leisure Research* 7:2:114–20.

U.S. Bureau of Labor Statistics. (1977). *Consumer expenditure survey, 1972–73* (Report 455–4). Washington, DC: U.S. Department of Labor.

U.S. Bureau of Labor Statistics. (1996). *Consumer expenditures in 1994* (Report 902). Washington, DC: U.S. Department of Labor.

U.S. Department of the Interior. (1986). Natural resource damage assessments; Final rule. *Federal Register* 51:148:27614–27753.

U.S. Department of the Interior. (1994, March 25). Natural resource damage assessments; Final rule. *Federal Register* 59:58:14261–14288.

U.S. Department of the Interior, National Park Service. (1993). *Federal recreation fee report to Congress, 1993.* Washington, DC: U.S. Government Printing Office 0–357–870.

U.S. Fish and Wildlife Service. (1988). *National survey of hunting, fishing and wildlife associated recreation.* Washington, DC: U.S. Department of the Interior.

U.S. Fish and Wildlife Service. (1993). *1991 national survey of hunting, fishing and wildlife associated recreation.* Washington, DC: U.S. Department of the Interior.

U.S. Fish and Wildlife Service. (1994). *The reintroduction of gray wolves to Yellowstone National Park and central Idaho* (Final Environmental Impact Statement). Helena, MT: Author.

U.S. Forest Service. (1980). *The 1980 national outdoor recreation trends symposium* (Vols. 1 and 2, General Technical Report NE-57). Washington, DC: U.S. Department of Agriculture.

U.S. Forest Service. (1981). *ROS users guide.* Washington, DC: U.S. Department of Agriculture.

U.S. Forest Service. (1983). *Recreation information management (RIM) handbook.* Washington, DC: U.S. Department of Agriculture.

U.S. Forest Service. (1990, May). *The forest service program for forest and rangeland resources: A long-term strategic plan; Recommended 1990 RPA program.* Washington, DC: U.S. Department of Agriculture.

U.S. Forest Service. (1995, October). *The forest service program for forest and rangeland resources: A long-term strategic plan; Draft 1995 RPA program.* Washington, DC: U.S. Department of Agriculture.

U.S. Forest Service. (1996a). *The 1994–95 national survey on recreation and the environment.* Athens, GA: Southeastern Forest Experiment Station and University of Georgia.

U.S. Forest Service. (1996b, June 26). *Forest service tests recreation fees* [News Release]. Washington, DC: Author.

U.S. General Accounting Office. (1982). *Increasing entrance fees, national park service* (GAO/CED-82–84). Washington, DC: U.S. Government Printing Office.

U.S. National and Oceanic and Atmospheric Administration. (1996, January 5). Oil Pollution Act Damage Assessments; Final Rule. *Federal Register* 61:4:439–510.

U.S. Office of Management and Budget. (1992, October 29). *Guidelines and discount rates for benefit-cost analysis of federal programs* (Circular A-94). Washington, DC: U.S. Government Printing Office.

U.S. Water Resources Council. (1980, April 14). Principles, Standards and Procedures for Planning Water and Related Land Resources. *Federal Register* 45:73:25301–25348.

U.S. Water Resources Council. (1983, March 10). *Economic and environmental principles and guidelines for water and related land resources implementation studies.* Washington, DC: U.S. Government Printing Office.

Vaske, Jerry, Maureen Donnelly and Dan Tweed. (1983). Recreationist defined versus researcher defined similarity judgments in substitutability research. *Journal of Leisure Research* 15:3:251–262.

Verhoven, Peter, and Roger Lancaster. (1976). Municipal recreation and park services. *Municipal Year Book* 43:203–215.

Vickerman, R. W. (1975). *The economics of leisure and recreation.* London, UK: MacMillan Press.

Vickrey, William. (1972). Economic efficiency and pricing. In S. Mushkin (Ed.), *Public prices and public products.* Washington, DC: The Urban Institute.

Walsh, Richard. (1986). *Recreation economic decisions: Comparing benefits and costs.* State College, PA: Venture Publishing, Inc.

Walsh, Richard G., and Gordon J. Davitt. (1983, Spring). A demand function for length of stay on ski trips to Aspen. *Journal of Travel Research* 22:23–29.

Walsh, R., R. Ericson, D. Arosteguy and M. Hansen. (1980). *An empirical application of a model for estimating the recreation value of instream flow* (Colorado Water Resources Institute A-036). Fort Collins, CO: Colorado State University.

Walsh, Richard G., and Lynde O. Gilliam. (1982, July). Benefits of wilderness expansion with excess demand for Indian Peaks. *Western Journal of Agricultural Economics* 7:1–12.

Walsh, Richard, Donn Johnson and John McKean. (1992, March). Benefit transfer of outdoor recreation demand studies: 1968–1988. *Water Resources Research* 28:707–713.

Walsh, Richard G., John B. Loomis, and Richard S. Gillman. (1984, February). Valuing option, existence and bequest demand for wilderness. *Land Economics* 60:14–29.

Walsh, Richard G., Nicole P. Miller, and Lynde O. Gilliam. (1983, May). Congestion and willingness to pay for expansion of skiing capacity. *Land Economics* 59:195–210.

Walsh, Richard, and John Olienyk. (1981). *Recreation demand effects of mountain pine beetle damage to the quality of forest recreation resources in the Colorado front range.* Fort Collins, CO: Colorado State University, Department of Economics.

Welsh, Michael, Richard Bishop, Marcia Phillips, and Robert Baumgartner. (1995). *GCES non-use value study.* Madison, WI: Hagler Bailly Consulting, University Research Park.

Wilman, Elizabeth A. (1980, September). The value of time in recreation benefit studies. *Journal of Environmental Economics and Management* 7:272–86.

Ziemer, Rod F., Wesley N. Musser, and R. Carter Hill. (1980, February). Recreation demand equations: Functional form and consumer surplus. *American Journal of Agricultural Economics* 62:136–41.

# Index

## C

## D



## E

*M*



*N*



*O*

### P

*Y*



*Z*

# Other Books from Venture Publishing

*The A•B•Cs of Behavior Change: Skills for Working with Behavior Problems in Nursing Homes*
by Margaret D. Cohn, Michael A. Smyer and Ann L. Horgas
*Activity Experiences and Programming Within Long-Term Care*
by Ted Tedrick and Elaine R. Green
*The Activity Gourmet*
by Peggy Powers
*Advanced Concepts for Geriatric Nursing Assistants*
by Carolyn A. McDonald
*Adventure Education*
edited by John C. Miles and Simon Priest
*Aerobics of the Mind: Keeping the Mind Active in Aging—A New Perspective on Programming for Older Adults*
by Marge Engelman
*Assessment: The Cornerstone of Activity Programs*
by Ruth Perschbacher
*Behavior Modification in Therapeutic Recreation: An Introductory Manual*
by John Datillo and William D. Murphy
*Benefits of Leisure*
edited by B. L. Driver, Perry J. Brown and George L. Peterson
*Benefits of Recreation Research Update*
by Judy M. Sefton and W. Kerry Mummery
*Beyond Bingo: Innovative Programs for the New Senior*
by Sal Arrigo, Jr., Ann Lewis and Hank Mattimore
*Both Gains and Gaps: Feminist Perspectives on Women's Leisure*
by Karla Henderson, M. Deborah Bialeschki, Susan M. Shaw and Valeria J. Freysinger
*The Community Tourism Industry Imperative—The Necessity, The Opportunities, Its Potential*
by Uel Blank
*Dimensions of Choice: A Qualitative Approach to Recreation, Parks, and Leisure Research*
by Karla A. Henderson
*Effective Management in Therapeutic Recreation Service*
by Gerald S. O'Morrow and Marcia Jean Carter

*Evaluating Leisure Services: Making Enlightened Decisions*
by Karla A. Henderson with M. Deborah Bialeschki
*The Evolution of Leisure: Historical and Philosophical Perspectives (Second Printing)*
by Thomas Goodale and Geoffrey Godbey
*File o' Fun: A Recreation Planner for Games & Activities—Third Edition*
by Jane Harris Ericson and Diane Ruth Albright
*The Game Finder—A Leader's Guide to Great Activities*
by Annette C. Moore
*Getting People Involved in Life and Activities: Effective Motivating Techniques*
by Jeanne Adams
*Great Special Events and Activities*
by Annie Morton, Angie Prosser and Sue Spangler
*Inclusive Leisure Services: Responding to the Rights of People with Disabilities*
by John Dattilo
*Internships in Recreation and Leisure Services: A Practical Guide for Students (Second Edition)*
by Edward E. Seagle, Jr., Ralph W. Smith and Lola M. Dalton
*Interpretation of Cultural and Natural Resources*
by Douglas M. Knudson, Ted T. Cable and Larry Beck
*Introduction to Leisure Services—7th Edition*
by H. Douglas Sessoms and Karla A. Henderson
*Leadership and Administration of Outdoor Pursuits, Second Edition*
by Phyllis Ford and James Blanchard
*Leadership in Leisure Services: Making a Difference*
by Debra J. Jordan
*Leisure and Family Fun (LAFF)*
by Mary Atteberry-Rogers
*Leisure Diagnostic Battery Computer Software*
by Gary Ellis and Peter A. Witt
*The Leisure Diagnostic Battery: Users Manual and Sample Forms*
by Peter A. Witt and Gary Ellis
*Leisure Education: A Manual of Activities and Resources*
by Norma J. Stumbo and Steven R. Thompson
*Leisure Education II: More Activities and Resources*
by Norma J. Stumbo
*Leisure Education Program Planning: A Systematic Approach*
by John Dattilo and William D. Murphy
*Leisure in Your Life: An Exploration—Fourth Edition*
by Geoffrey Godbey
*Leisure Services in Canada: An Introduction*
by Mark S. Searle and Russell E. Brayley
*The Lifestory Re-Play Circle*
by Rosilyn Wilder

*Marketing for Parks, Recreation, and Leisure*
by Ellen L. O'Sullivan
*Models of Change in Municipal Parks and Recreation: A Book of Innovative Case Studies*
edited by Mark E. Havitz
*Nature and the Human Spirit: Toward an Expanded Land Management Ethic*
edited by B. L. Driver, Daniel Dustin, Tony Baltic, Gary Elsner, and George Peterson
*Outdoor Recreation Management: Theory and Application, Third Edition*
by Alan Jubenville and Ben Twight
*Planning Parks for People*
by John Hultsman, Richard L. Cottrell and Wendy Zales Hultsman
*Private and Commercial Recreation*
edited by Arlin Epperson
*The Process of Recreation Programming Theory and Technique, Third Edition*
by Patricia Farrell and Herberta M. Lundegren
*Protocols for Recreation Therapy Programs*
edited by Jill Kelland, along with the Recreation Therapy Staff at Alberta Hospital Edmonton
*Quality Management: Applications for Therapeutic Recreation*
edited by Bob Riley
*Recreation and Leisure: Issues in an Era of Change, Third Edition*
edited by Thomas Goodale and Peter A. Witt
*Recreation Programming and Activities for Older Adults*
by Jerold E. Elliott and Judith A. Sorg-Elliott
*Recreation Programs that Work for At-Risk Youth: The Challenge of Shaping the Future*
by Peter A. Witt and John L. Crompton
*Reference Manual for Writing Rehabilitation Therapy Treatment Plans*
by Penny Hogberg and Mary Johnson
*Research in Therapeutic Recreation: Concepts and Methods*
edited by Marjorie J. Malkin and Christine Z. Howe
*A Social History of Leisure Since 1600*
by Gary Cross
*A Social Psychology of Leisure*
by Roger C. Mannell and Douglas A. Kleiber
*The Sociology of Leisure*
by John R. Kelly and Geoffrey Godbey
*Therapeutic Activity Intervention with the Elderly: Foundations & Practices*
by Barbara A. Hawkins, Marti E. May and Nancy Brattain Rogers
*Therapeutic Recreation: Cases and Exercises*
by Barbara C. Wilhite and M. Jean Keller

*Therapeutic Recreation in the Nursing Home*
by Linda Buettner and Shelley L. Martin
*Therapeutic Recreation Protocol for Treatment of Substance Addictions*
by Rozanne W. Faulkner
*A Training Manual for Americans With Disabilities Act Compliance in Parks and Recreation Settings*
by Carol Stensrud

Venture Publishing, Inc.
1999 Cato Avenue
State College, PA 16801

Phone: (814) 234-4561; FAX: (814) 234-1651